THE JOHN PHII  RIES

Exploring
PROVERBS

VOLUME ONE

An Expository Commentary

JOHN PHILLIPS

kregel
PUBLICATIONS

Grand Rapids, MI 49501

Exploring Proverbs, Volume One: An Expository Commentary

© 1995 by John Phillips

Published in 2002 by Kregel Publications, a division of Kregel, Inc., P.O. Box 2607, Grand Rapids, MI 49501. For more information about Kregel Publications, visit our Web site: www.kregel.com.

Scripture quotations are from the King James Version of the Holy Bible.

ISBN 0-8254-3478-5

Printed in the United States of America

02 03 04 05 06 / 3 2 1

CONTENTS OF VOLUME ONE
Proverbs 1:1–19:5

Exploring
PROVERBS
VOLUME ONE

PREFACE

I thought this book would be impossible to write. How could anyone come up with a comprehensive, reasonably accurate, alliterated outline for the book of Proverbs? But in spite of all its eddies, bays, and backwaters, I found that the great river of Proverbs has a discernible flow. I explored its main streams and tributaries for nearly a year and discovered that they could be navigated and named.

The results of my study are the summary outline appearing at the front of both volumes and the expanded outlines interspersed throughout the commentary. These outlines will be an invaluable resource for preachers and Bible teachers and will help average readers see the book of Proverbs as a whole. Within the structure of these outlines is a detailed analysis of every chapter, every verse, and every line.

So many commentaries on Proverbs are boring. Often commentators resort to technicalities or state the obvious. I wanted my book to be interesting so I set the goal of illustrating each proverb. I have drawn illustrations from science, nature, fiction, history, personal experience, and above all the Bible. My publisher has been particularly understanding. Instead of cutting and deleting these illustrations, he has let them stand practically as submitted. As a result this book is almost a handbook of illustrations. (Nobody has to tell the average preacher the value of illustrations or how hard it is to find effective ones!)

Here then is the wisdom of Solomon—outlined, analyzed, illustrated, and available in an understandable and readable form. So come explore with me the proverbs of a king who in his day had the reputation of being the wisest man in the world. He lived a long time ago but his proverbs are remarkably up-to-date.

John Phillips

DIRECTORY OF OUTLINES

SUMMARY OUTLINE
OF THE BOOK OF PROVERBS

The outline is expanded throughout the body of the text.

Volume One

Introduction (1:1-9)

Observation (1:10–29:27)

Part One: Moral Issues (1:10–9:18)

Section 1: The Way of Wickedness (1:10-19)

Section 2: The Way of Wisdom (1:20–9:18)

    I. Wisdom's Plea (1:20-33)
    II. Wisdom's Protection (2:1-22)
    III. Wisdom's Path (3:1–5:23)
        A. It Is a Pleasant Path (3:1-22)
        B. It Is a Peaceful Path (3:23-26)
        C. It Is a Positive Path (3:27-35)
        D. It Is a Parental Path (4:1-9)
        E. It Is a Proper Path (4:10-19)
        F. It Is a Perfect Path (4:20–5:23)
            1. The Way of Virtue Pondered (4:20–5:2)
            2. The Way of Vice Pondered (5:3-23)
    IV. Wisdom's Precepts (6:1-35)
        A. How They Goad Us (6:1-11)
        B. How They Guide Us (6:12-19)
        C. How They Guard Us (6:20-35)
    V. Wisdom's Presence (7:1-27)
    VI. Wisdom's Patience (8:1–9:18)
        A. Her Plea Is Public (8:1-9)
        B. Her Riches Are Real (8:10-21)
        C. Her Influence Is Infinite (8:22-31)
        D. Her Friends Are Fortunate (8:32-36)
        E. Her Blessings Are Boundless (9:1-6)
        F. Her Foes Are Fools (9:7-12)
        G. Her Paths Are Pure (9:13-18)

Part Two: Miscellaneous Issues (10:1–19:5)

Section 1: The Lot of the Godly and the Ungodly Contrasted
(10:1–15:33)

I. Blessings Gained or Lost (10:1-32)
II. Behavior Good and Bad (11:1–15:33)
    A. Values to Be Considered (11:1-31)
    B. Vignettes to Be Considered (12:1-28)
    C. Verities to Be Considered (13:1-25)
    D. Viewpoints to Be Considered (14:1-35)
    E. Virtues to Be Considered (15:1-33)

Section 2: The Life of the Godly and the Ungodly Compared
(16:1–19:5)

I. The Right Focus in Life (16:1-33)
II. The Right Features in Life (17:1–19:5)
    A. How to Build Contentment (17:1-28)
    B. How to Build Character (18:1–19:5)

Volume Two

Part Three: Monarchial Issues (19:6–29:27)

Section 1: Proverbs of Solomon—Edited by Himself (19:6–24:34)

I. The Favor of the Throne (19:6-11)
II. The Fury of the Throne (19:12–20:7)
III. The Fear of the Throne (20:8-30)
IV. The Functions of the Throne (21:1–24:34)
    A. His Majesty's Intentions (21:1–22:10)
    B. His Majesty's Intimates (22:11-29)
    C. His Majesty's Interests (23:1–24:34)
        1. Words to His Subjects (23:1-14)
        2. Words to His Son (23:15–24:34)

Section 2: Proverbs of Solomon—Edited by Hezekiah (25:1–29:27)

I. The King and His Subjects (25:1–27:27)
    A. Those of Whom to Beware (25:1–26:28)
    B. Thoughts on How to Behave (27:1-27)
II. The King and His Sins (28:1–29:14)
III. The King and His Sons (29:15-27)

Conclusion (30:1–31:31)

INTRODUCTION
Proverbs 1:1-9

AUTHOR'S INTRODUCTION

We can imagine how the world learned of Solomon's wisdom: When ships from his merchant navy sailed down the Red Sea to trade for gold, silver, ivory, almug trees, peacocks, and apes, the Hebrew sailors put into ports and sang the Psalms of David as they filled their water pots. They praised the Lord for His goodness. In Sheba the queen—or some of her servants—heard these sailors sing. The words of the songs spoke of a living God and struck a chord in the queen's empty, hungry, thirsty heart. She made inquiries and was told of a king named Solomon reigning far to the north in a land called Israel. The more she heard about him, the more she longed to see him. Perhaps he could answer her questions.

She decided to go to Jerusalem. She would go armed with spices and gold and precious stones—and questions. So her camels were loaded and her escort prepared. She traveled all the way up the long reaches of the Nile, across the sands of Sinai, and up into the hill country of Judah.

When the queen of Sheba arrived in Israel, she was overwhelmed! She saw the temple. She saw Solomon's palace. She saw his servants. She sat at his table. She learned the songs of Zion. She listened to the wise man's proverbs. She discussed affairs of state, her anxieties about treaties of war and peace, her perplexities about royal family affairs, and her religious longings. Then she asked her questions. Question after question. "What mean ye by this service?" "What is the use of that implement?" "What lies behind the veil?" "Is there a deeper, richer meaning behind all these sacrifices?"

Solomon told the queen all that her heart wanted to know until at last even her fund of questions was exhausted and she thought about going home. There remained no more spirit in her. She wished she could stay and sit at Solomon's feet forever. But back she went, and we can be sure that she took the writings of Moses and Samuel and David and Solomon with her in her camel bags.

Sitting high and lifted up on her camel, the queen pored over Solomon's prayer at the dedication of the temple:

Moreover concerning a stranger, that is not of thy people Israel, but cometh out of a far country for thy name's sake; (For

15

> they shall hear of thy great name, and of thy strong hand, and of thy stretched out arm;) when he shall come and pray toward this house; Hear thou in heaven thy dwelling place, and do according to all that the stranger calleth to thee for: that all people of the earth may know thy name, to fear thee, as do thy people Israel; and that they may know that this house, which I have builded, is called by thy name (1 Kings 8:41-43).

The startled camel driver pricked up his ears as a loud *amen* sounded out across the desert sands.

The queen of Sheba was not the only one who came to Israel. People and princes came from near and far to hear the wisdom of Solomon and they went away to spread his fame.

Many of Solomon's astute sayings were distilled into proverbs. Generally each was completed in the form of a distich—a verse of two lines. His wise sayings were collected, other treasures of divinely inspired wisdom were added to the collection, and the whole was eventually published in the book we call Proverbs. Many of the sayings in the book were composed by Solomon himself. Others were drilled into him by David and Nathan when they were grooming the young prince for the throne (1:6–9:18; 19:20–24:34; 27:1–29:27).

The proverbs Solomon learned at school emphasized moral purity. They were accompanied with direst warnings against "the strange woman." Sadly, Solomon chose to ignore this advice. It did not take him long to make tragic shipwreck of his life by cultivating an appetite for women. Many of the women in his harem were foreign; he married some of them out of political expediency to cement peace pacts with neighboring kingdoms. This policy was foolish because in the end political compromise led to religious compromise. Solomon paid dearly for not heeding the warnings. In the end his inattention to these proverbs cost him his kingdom.

Solomon had a fool for a son. But then what could Solomon expect when in one of the most hallowed and important areas of life he himself played the fool? Poor Rehoboam! He had an Ammonitess for a mother (1 Kings 14:21,31—note how the significant statement is recorded twice) and a fool for a father. Many of the proverbs regarding fools and folly were doubtless coined or collected by Solomon in the hope of getting some sense into Rehoboam's head. Some hope! Solomon could instruct his son and heir in these wise maxims ad infinitum, but instruction would do no good. All Rehoboam could see was his father's example.

If we would avoid playing the fool, we must not only explore the book of Proverbs but also follow its advice.

CHAPTER 1
Proverbs 1:1-9

Introduction (1:1-9)
   I. The Purpose of the Book (1:1-6)
     A. Its Primary Author (1:1)
     B. Its Practical Authority (1:2-6)
       1. Recognizing Truth (1:2a)
       2. Receiving Truth (1:2b-3)
         a. Ability to Acknowledge Truth (1:2b)
         b. Aptness to Accommodate Truth (1:3)
       3. Relaying Truth (1:4-5)
         a. Words for Those Who Are Simple (1:4)
         b. Words for Those Who Are Sophisticated (1:5)
       4. Ratifying Truth (1:6)
  II. The Principles of the Book (1:7-9)
     A. Reverence for God (1:7)
     B. Respect for Authority (1:8-9)
       1. The Command (1:8)
       2. The Cause (1:9)

The book of Proverbs begins with an introduction in which Solomon stated his purposes for collecting these pithy sayings and his general observations on the basic principles of life. The introduction serves as a summary of the whole book.

I. THE PURPOSE OF THE BOOK (1:1-6)

A. Its Primary Author (1:1)

The introduction tells us that this book contains "the Proverbs of Solomon the son of David, king of Israel." However, not all of the proverbs were necessarily coined by Solomon. Many years after Solomon's death Hezekiah asked his scribes to compile Solomon's proverbs, and these compilers apparently added the sayings of other wise men to the collection. Still, by and large, the primary human author of the book of Proverbs was Solomon.

From his earliest days Solomon could observe the living example of Israel's greatest and godliest king. King David, Solomon's father, was a man after God's own heart (Acts 13:22) in spite of his sad fall into adultery, deceit, and murder. By the time Solomon was born, David had thoroughly repented of those terrible sins. He had turned the episode to good account by adding his penitential Psalms to the Hebrew hymnbook.

Solomon could also observe his mother Bathsheba. She was a wise woman who had learned life's bitter lessons the hard way. His tutor, benefactor, and friend was the wise prophet Nathan. No doubt he encouraged Solomon to memorize all the early books of the Bible. Thus Solomon was greatly blessed in both his parents and in his early education. God also blessed him with a keen intellect, a teachable spirit, an eager curiosity about life, a catholicity of interests, and a disposition toward spiritual things.

We can imagine the long hours Solomon spent with David. How the boy reveled in the heroic stories of David's youth! How eagerly he listened to his father's counsel. Solomon knew all we know about David—and more. We have to rely on the Hebrew histories and hymnbook for our knowledge, but Solomon could talk to people such as Joab and Abishai. Solomon could cross-question his father.

Solomon knew David in his mature years after he had recovered from the domestic and political disasters that had overtaken him earlier. Solomon knew David when he was holding in trust enormous stockpiles of money and materials for the temple project. Solomon was to fall heir to both the treasures and the trust.

If we are to appreciate all the moral, social, physical, political, religious, and spiritual advantages Solomon had, we must painstakingly read the books of Samuel and Chronicles and the Psalms of David—all with young Solomon in mind. Much history lies behind the words, "the Proverbs of Solomon the son of David."

The Hebrew word translated "Proverbs," *mishlai*, is derived from the root word *māshāl*, which means "to rule" as in Genesis 1:18 and 3:16. *Mishlai* therefore are words and sayings that are supposed to rule and govern life. The book of Proverbs then is not simply a collection of bits of human wisdom. It contains God's rules.

All countries have proverbs, the distilled wisdom of cultures and races. "Look before you leap," "A stitch in time saves nine," "A penny saved is a penny earned," "Early to bed, early to rise, makes a man healthy, wealthy, and wise" are examples of English proverbs. A Zulu proverb says, "He who walks into a thunderstorm must put up with the hailstones." Scandinavians say, "Mix gray locks and golden and spoil two heads" and "Love makes an old man blind." These are sage human sayings, but the proverbs of the Bible are far more than that. They embody the philosophy of Heaven for the benefit of people living on earth.

B. Its Practical Authority (1:2-6)

1. Recognizing Truth (1:2a)

When I first joined the staff of the Moody Bible Institute Correspondence School, I was put in charge of course development. Part of my job description was to write testing instruments for the courses published by the school. The task seemed easy enough. I thought I would simply have to read the course material and write exam questions, but I soon discovered that writing meaningful objective-type questions is a sophisticated and complex operation. Before I could start to write the questions, I had to state the goals and objectives the school wanted each student to achieve as a result of completing the course. I also had to state how these objectives could be achieved and how the exams would measure the achievement of these goals.

My objectives in writing an exam had to be clearly stated. For example, the goals of a test could be as follows:

- To ascertain if the student has mastered the facts taught
- To see if the student has mastered the principles involved
- To discover whether the student can recognize the principles in other settings
- To see if the student is applying the principles to his own life

This whole process of formulating objectives and stating them in a particular form was new to me, although of course it is a common technique in modern education and business management. Solomon apparently grasped the technique centuries ago, for he stated his objectives in writing the book of Proverbs with unmistakable clarity:

- "To know wisdom and instruction" (1:2)
- "To perceive the words of understanding" (1:2)
- "To receive the instruction of wisdom, justice, and judgment, and equity" (1:3)
- "To give subtilty to the simple" (1:4)
- "To give...the young man knowledge and discretion" (1:4)
- "To understand a proverb" (1:6)
- "To understand...the interpretation" (1:6)

Solomon's first objective was to make it possible for us "to know wisdom and instruction." The book of Proverbs contains six different Hebrew words for "wisdom." The word used here is *chokmah*, which occurs frequently in the Old Testament.[1] For example Exodus says that the people who were endowed with the necessary skill to make Aaron's high priestly garments and the craftsmanship to build the tabernacle possessed this kind of wisdom (Exodus 28:3; 35:31). *Chokmah* refers to a person's ability to make the right choices at the opportune times. In the Septuagint *chokmah's* Greek equivalents are *sophos* ("clever, skillful, experienced"), *phronimos* ("sensible, thoughtful, prudent, wise"), and *sunetos* ("intelligent, sagacious, wise").

The word translated "instruction" in Proverbs 1:2 means "admonition" or "discipline" and is sometimes translated "chastisement." There can be little recognition of truth without discipline. Only a disciplined mind can see the pros and cons of an issue and be willing to learn by correction.

2. Receiving Truth (1:2b-3)

In order to receive truth we need to be willing to *acknowledge* it when it is presented to us. Solomon wanted us to be able "to perceive the words of understanding" (1:2). The word translated "understanding" is *bīnah*, which is usually translated "discernment." Many people cannot see the truth when it is staring them in the face—often because the truth is unpalatable and they do not want to see it. Our English proverb reminds us, "There are none so blind as those who will not see." The soul-winner often encounters this kind of self-imposed blindness when he tries to encourage people to see their need for Christ.

Some people are blind to glaring and outrageous doctrinal errors. Even other unsaved people can see through their beliefs and ridicule them. Deluded victims of the cults are totally blind. They cannot "perceive the words of understanding" because Satan has blinded their minds (2 Corinthians 4:4). For instance those who have been deceived by Christian Science accept the outrageous teaching of Mary Baker Eddy that pain is an error of mortal mind. Mark Twain saw through that belief and told us so in one of his humorous essays.

This last summer, when I was on my way back to Vienna from the Appetite Cure in the mountains, I fell over a cliff in the twilight and broke some arms and legs and one thing or another, and by good luck was found by some peasants who had lost an ass, and they carried me to the nearest habitation, which was one of those large, low, thatch-roofed farmhouses, with apartments in the garret for the family, and a cunning little porch under the deep gable decorated with boxes of bright-colored flowers and cats; on the ground-floor a large and light sitting-room, separated from the milch-cattle apartment by a partition; and in the front yard rose stately and fine the wealth and pride of the house, the manure-pile. That sentence is Germanic, and shows that I am acquiring that sort of mastery of the art and spirit of the language which enables a man to travel all day in one sentence without changing cars.

There was a village a mile away, and a horse-doctor lived there, but there was no surgeon. It seemed a bad outlook; mine was distinctly a surgery case. Then it was remembered that a lady from Boston was summering in that village, and she was a Christian Science doctor and could cure anything. So she was sent for. It was night by this time, and she could not conveniently come, but sent word that it was no matter, there was no hurry, she would give me "absent treatment" now, and come in the morning; meantime she begged me to make myself tranquil and comfortable and remember that there was nothing the matter with me. I thought there must be some mistake.

"Did you tell her I walked off a cliff seventy-five feet high?"
"Yes."
"And struck a boulder at the bottom and bounced?"
"Yes."
"And struck another one and bounced again?"
"Yes."
"And struck another one and bounced yet again?"
"Yes."
"And broke the boulders?"
"Yes."

"That accounts for it; she is thinking of the boulders. Why didn't you tell her I got hurt, too?"

"I did. I told her what you told me to tell her: that you were now but an incoherent series of compound fractures extending from your scalp-lock to your heels, and that the comminuted projections caused you to look like a hat-rack."

"And it was after this that she wished me to remember that there was nothing the matter with me?"

"Those were her words."

"I do not understand it. I believe she has not diagnosed the case with sufficient care. Did she look like a person who was theorizing, or did she look like one who has fallen off precipices herself and brings to the aid of abstract science the confirmations of personal experience?"...

It was a night of anguish, of course—at least, I supposed it was, for it had all the symptoms of it—but it passed at last, and the Christian Scientist came, and I was glad. She was middle-aged, and large and bony, and erect, and had an austere face and a resolute jaw and a Roman beak and was a widow in the third degree, and her name was Fuller. I was eager to get to business and find relief, but she was distressingly deliberate. She unpinned and unhooked and uncoupled her upholsteries one by one, abolished the wrinkles with a flirt of her hand, and hung the articles up; peeled off her gloves and disposed of them, got a book out of her hand-bag, then drew a chair to the bedside, descended into it without hurry, and I hung out my tongue. She said, with pity but without passion:

"Return it to its receptacle. We deal with the mind only, not with its dumb servants."

I could not offer my pulse, because the connection was broken; but she detected the apology before I could word it, and indicated by a negative tilt of her head that the pulse was another dumb servant that she had no use for. Then I thought I would tell her my symptoms and how I felt, so that she would understand the case; but that was another inconsequence, she did not need to know those things; moreover, my remark about how I felt was an abuse of language, a misapplication of terms.

"One does not *feel*," she explained, "there is no such thing as feeling: therefore, to speak of a non-existent thing as existent is a contradiction. Matter has no existence; nothing exists but mind; the mind cannot feel pain, it can only imagine it."

"But if it hurts, just the same—"

"It doesn't. A thing which is unreal cannot exercise the functions of reality. Pain is unreal; hence, pain cannot hurt."

In making a sweeping gesture to indicate the act of shooting the illusion of pain out of the mind, she raked her hand on a pin in her dress, said "Ouch!" and went tranquilly on with her talk. "You should never allow yourself to speak of how you feel, nor permit others to ask you how you are feeling; you should never concede that you are ill, nor permit others to talk about disease or pain or death or similar non-existences in your presence. Such talk only encourages the mind to continue its empty imaginings." Just at that point the *Stubenmädchen* trod on the cat's tail, and the cat let fly a frenzy of cat profanity. I asked, with caution:

"Is a cat's opinion about pain valuable?"

"A cat has no opinion; opinions proceed from mind only; the lower animals, being eternally perishable, have not been granted mind; without mind, opinion is impossible."

"She merely *imagined* she felt a pain—the cat?"

"She cannot imagine a pain, for imagining is an effect of mind; without mind, there is no imagination. A cat has no imagination."

"Then she had a *real* pain?"

"I have already told you there is no such *thing* as real pain."...

She broke in with an irritated—

"Peace! The cat feels nothing, the Christian feels nothing. Your empty and foolish imaginings are profanation and blasphemy, and can do you an injury. It is wiser and better and holier to recognize and confess that there is no such thing as disease or pain or death."

"I am full of imaginary tortures," I said, "but I do not think I could be any more uncomfortable if they were real ones. What must I do to get rid of them?"

"There is no occasion to get rid of them, since they do not exist. They are illusions propagated by matter, and matter has no existence; there is no such thing as matter."

"It sounds right and clear, but yet it seems in a degree elusive; it seems to slip through, just when you think you are getting a grip on it."

"Explain."

"Well, for instance: if there is no such thing as matter, how can matter propagate things?"

In her compassion she almost smiled. She would have smiled if there were any such thing as a smile.

"It is quite simple," she said; "the fundamental propositions of Christian Science explain it, and they are summarized in the four following self-evident propositions. 1. God is All in all. 2. God is good. Good is Mind. 3. God, Spirit, being all, nothing is matter. 4. Life, God, omnipotent Good, deny death, evil, sin, disease. There—now you see."

It seemed nebulous; it did not seem to say anything about the difficulty in hand—how non-existent matter can propagate illusions. I said, with some hesitancy:

"Does—does it explain?"

"*Doesn't* it? Even if read backward it will do it."

With a budding hope, I asked her to do it backward.

"Very well. Disease sin evil death deny Good omnipotent God life matter is nothing all being Spirit God Mind is Good good is God all in All is God. There—do you understand now.?"[2]

Well of course the words of the Christian Science doctor explained nothing, but countless thousands of deluded people imagine Mary Baker Eddy's propositions are true. These "blind" people reject the truth of God and believe the words of a dead woman. They do not "perceive the words of understanding."

When we do perceive the truth, we must also be willing to *accommodate* it. Solomon told us we must be willing "to receive the instruction of wisdom" (Proverbs 1:3). People have a great capacity for blocking out unpalatable facts.

The man at the pool of Bethesda, for instance, faced a humanly hopeless situation: he had a long-term incapacitating illness. He had been abandoned at the pool and had suffered thirty-eight years. His only hope for healing was pinned on getting into the pool first when the waters were agitated. He could not get into the pool by himself and he had no friends to help him. He hoped against hope for a double miracle—the miracle of getting into the pool first and the miracle of being healed by the seething water. There he stayed, blocking out of his mind the utter hopelessness of his case, until Jesus worked a real miracle for him.

The sick man was eager indeed, we must note, to accommodate the truth of Christ—but not before he tried to block out Christ's glorious question with irrelevant comments about the pool and his own paralysis. The Lord did not ask whether he believed the stories about the pool. Jesus simply asked, "Wilt thou be made whole?" (John 5:6)

3.   Relaying Truth (1:4-5)

Solomon had *words for those who are simple.* He wanted "to give subtilty to the simple, to the young man knowledge and discretion" (Proverbs 1:4). The Hebrew word translated "subtilty" here and the Hebrew word *arum* come from the same root. *Arum* is the word used to describe the serpent in Genesis 3:1: "Now the serpent was more subtil than any beast of the field which the Lord God had made." (Ezekiel 28:12 tells us how "wise" Satan was before his fall and Ezekiel 28:17 tells us how that wisdom was corrupted.) *Arum* is translated "crafty" in Job 5:12; 15:5. God does not want to make us crafty, but He does want us to be equipped to deal with those who are.

The word translated "simple" means "artless, guileless, unsuspecting." Some people are so gullible that they believe everything they are told. They are easy prey for the con man. Solomon wanted us to be prepared to meet such deceivers. Eve in her guileless innocence was no match for the old serpent who appeared before her in disguise; he was persuasive but full of malice and malignity. His mind, created for the universe, was narrowed by sin to a diabolical cunning. However Eve had one weapon the devil feared. Eve had the Word of God, which would have rendered her invincible, had she relied on it. All she needed to say in response to each temptation was "Thus saith the Lord." Solomon wanted to put this same almighty Word into the hands of the simple. A mastery of the book of Proverbs will go far toward equipping even the most guileless for life's treacheries.

Solomon also had *words for those who are sophisticated:* "A wise man will hear, and will increase learning; and a man of understanding shall attain unto wise counsels" (Proverbs 1:5). Apollos is the classic New Testament example of such a man (Acts 18:24-28). Although he was well-versed in Scripture and a gifted orator, he was still teachable. When he first came to Corinth he only knew about John's baptism and was ignorant of the believer's baptism based on the Lord's ordinance, so he was quite willing to allow Priscilla and Aquila to explain truth to him in an area where he was deficient. Apollos allowed this godly couple to teach him the way of God more perfectly.

Often successful preachers are not very teachable. When challenged on a point, they sometimes dig in their heels and defend their beliefs, right or wrong. A wise man will never be too sophisticated to learn, even from someone who has not had all his educational, social, or natural advantages.

4. Ratifying Truth (1:6)

Solomon had one more objective for those who are willing to heed his advice: "To understand a proverb, and the interpretation; the words of the wise, and their dark sayings." The literature of the world contains much human wisdom and it is not all irrelevant. The wise man will seek out what others have learned. He will study it and put it to the test, discriminating between the good, the bad, and the mediocre.

The word translated "interpretation" in Proverbs 1:6 can also be rendered "satire." To interpret is to get the point of what is being said in an obscure saying. Solomon was well-versed in interpretation and the queen of Sheba came to Jerusalem with the express purpose of testing his skill. She arrived armed with "hard questions" (*hard* implies *abstruse* and *difficult*) and went away awed and amazed at Solomon's ability to elucidate all her perplexities (1 Kings 10:1-7).

In Solomon's day the oriental people loved riddles. There was for instance the famous riddle of the sphinx. When anyone passed by, the sphinx asked him, "What has one voice, and yet becomes four-footed and two-footed and three-footed?" According to mythology the sphinx ate any traveler who could not give the correct answer. In a Greek legend Oedipus passed that way and gave the correct answer: "Man crawls on all fours as a baby, walks upright in the prime of life, and uses a staff in old age." The sphinx was so enraged by his answer that she threw herself to her death from the rock on which she lived outside the city of Thebes. Hopefully the riddles propounded to Solomon were of a more serious nature.

II. THE PRINCIPLES OF THE BOOK (1:7-9)

A. Reverence for God (1:7)

Having shared his purposes for writing the book of Proverbs, Solomon stated the first and most fundamental principle for obtaining wisdom: "The fear of the Lord is the beginning of knowledge: but fools despise wisdom and instruction." The word translated "fear" simply means "reverence." It occurs fourteen times in Proverbs. Unless the Lord is enthroned in the human heart, there can be no real knowledge of His truth.

All the world's religions bear witness to the abysmal inability of the mind and heart of unregenerate man to arrive at a knowledge of divine truth. The militant violence of Islam, the crass idolatry and foul immoralities of Hinduism, and the endless quest of Buddhism are evidences of this inability.

According to Buddhism, how a person lives determines how he will return to earth in his reincarnation. If he has a good karma, he will enjoy an improved lot in the next life. If not, he may come back as a member of a lower caste or even as a cow, a cockroach, or a caterpillar. Everything depends on one's own good works. And the great ever-mastering hope is to have one's life merged and lost in "the Good Unspeakable, the eternal bliss that lies in the last Nothingness"! As one astute observer commented, "A cheerful faith, truly, to dwell through aeons in monotonous misery in order that consciousness may be swallowed up at last in some void and formless abstraction called 'the Utter Peace.'"[3]

All striving after true knowledge, wisdom, and instruction must begin with the Lord and the Book He has given. Herein lies "the beginning." Those who set aside God's Biblical revelation cannot hope to arrive at a knowledge of His truth. The Bible is His great signpost alongside the highway of life. "This is the way, walk ye in it," God says (Isaiah 30:21). Any atheist, religious philosopher, secular humanist, educator, politician, or scientist who disregards this signpost will never arrive at the desired haven. His logic is based on a wrong premise so he will ultimately arrive at a wrong or incomplete conclusion. The arguments of Job's friends illustrate this faulty logic.

"Fools despise wisdom and instruction." Three Hebrew words are translated "fools" in Proverbs. The one used in Proverbs 1:7 is ʾevîl. Occurring nineteen times in Proverbs, this word refers to the person who has a lax or careless habit of mind or body. It is the height of human folly to ignore the Bible and then to hope for wisdom.

After World War I, the war to end all wars, the League of Nations was founded as a forum for settling international disputes. As a symbol of their hope for a war-free world, the members built the Palace of Peace in the Hague. Each participating nation made a contribution to the palace. England gave the stained glass windows, Germany donated the iron gates, Italy gave the marble, and Japan sent the tapestries. The United States gave busts of the world's statesmen.

The palace housed a great library of approximately seventy-five thousand books in some sixty languages, all devoted to the themes of progress, prosperity, and peace. And what was the result? World War II swept away all the vain hopes of the nations. When I was in Amsterdam some years ago I could not even find the Palace of Peace listed on the itinerary of any tour.

Only one book really deals with peace and that book is the Bible.

A dozen pages from this Book are worth more than all the thousands of volumes in the Palace of Peace. There can be no peace for the world so long as it ignores the Prince of Peace. Apart from Him the world will remain adrift on a wild and stormy sea, without compass, chart, or rudder as it faces the rocks and shoals ahead.

"The fear of the Lord is the beginning of knowledge: but fools despise wisdom and instruction." Man seems incapable of learning from his mistakes. As one cynic said, "All we learn from history is that we learn nothing from history."

B. Respect for Authority (1:8-9)

In Proverbs 1:8 Solomon gave *the command:* "My son, hear the instruction of thy father, and forsake not the law of thy mother." Probably the father and mother mentioned here are David and Bathsheba. No young man ever had better instructors in the good and right way to live than young Solomon. But he was not alone in having godly parental models.

What an impact Abraham had on Isaac! God Himself bore testimony to Abraham's diligence and success as a father: "I know him, that he will command his children and his household after him, and they shall keep the way of the Lord" (Genesis 18:19). God made this statement before Isaac was even born. God had observed the firm hand Abraham kept on willful and headstrong Ishmael (Genesis 16:12; 17:25). For instance, although he was a natural-born rebel, thirteen-year-old Ishmael did not dare refuse the painful rite of circumcision even though by eastern standards he was already a young man.

What a hold Jochebed had over the young Moses! (See Exodus 2:7-10; 6:20.) We do not know how long the princess of Egypt left Moses in the care of his mother; we do know, however, that by the time Moses went to live with Pharaoh's daughter, his mother's instruction and influence were paramount. Not all the professors of Egypt nor all the famed "wisdom of the Egyptians" (Acts 7:22) could destroy the foundation Jochebed had laid in the youngster's heart.

God always upholds parental authority. It is the earliest authority a child knows. Happy is the child who submits to it. Doubly happy is the child who has a godly hand at the helm of his life.

Explaining the motivation behind the instructions given by parents, Solomon stated *the cause:* "For they shall be an ornament of grace unto thy head, and chains about thy neck" (Proverbs 1:9). An obedient child is a joy to behold. The one who learns early in life to bow to parental authority will learn to respect all authority.

Eventually the one who has been raised to respect authority will be entrusted with authority.

The reference in Proverbs 1:9 to the neck is interesting. The submissive neck, the neck that bows to authority, is set in contrast to the stiff neck, the symbol of pride and rebellion.

Solomon's own son Rehoboam did not learn to be submissive. He had scarcely seated himself on the throne when the northern tribes sent a delegation asking for an end to the tyrannies started during Solomon's reign. In return they promised loyalty to the throne of David. Believing his authority was being called into question, Rehoboam ignored the advice of elder statesmen who had served his father and who unanimously told him to accede to the demands of the people. Instead he listened to his young companions who urged upon him "the divine right of kings." So this foolish young man tried to browbeat the delegation and threatened their tribes with vengeance. As a result he lost half his kingdom (1 Kings 12:1-19).

Solomon would have turned over in his grave. Or would he? Doubtless in the bitterness of his heart he knew only too well what a fool Rehoboam was. Solomon probably could have foretold some such folly. The stiff-necked Rehoboam sported a royal diadem, but he won no garlands for his brow. The chain of high office was his, but he did not wear chains of honor around his neck.

OBSERVATION
Proverbs 1:10–29:27

PART ONE:
Moral Issues
Proverbs 1:10–9:18

OBSERVATION
(1:10–29:27)

———🌣———

PART ONE:
Moral Issues
(1:10–9:18)

The book of Proverbs can be divided into three main parts. The first part deals with *moral* issues (1:10–9:18), the second part deals with *miscellaneous* issues (10:1–19:5), and the third part deals with *monarchial* issues (19:6–29:27).

The proverbs in Part One appear to have been taught to Solomon by his instructors. They are couched in the second person (thou, thy, thee, thine). If Solomon had stored these proverbs in his heart instead of in his head, he would have gone down in history as the greatest of all kings.

We can divide Part One into two sections: *the way of wickedness* (1:10-19) and *the way of wisdom* (1:20–9:18). Wisdom is personified as a woman and wickedness is incarnated in the immoral woman.

CHAPTER 2

Proverbs 1:10-19

Section 1: The Way of Wickedness (1:10-19)

I. THE PROPOSALS OF THE SINFUL MAN (1:10-14)

A. The Invitation (1:10-11a)

"My son, if sinners entice thee, consent thou not. If they say, Come with us..." There it is, a bold and unblushing invitation to sin. Solomon was warned at the very outset to be wary of any invitation to wrongdoing.

The word translated "sinners" here is one of the mildest Hebrew words for "sin." Derived from *chātā'*, which means "to miss the mark, to stumble, to fall," it refers to coming short morally. The condition envisioned is not necessarily willful (though it certainly is in this context). The word refers to our thoughts, words, and deeds, not to our inbred condition of essential sinfulness.

34

The sinner and the world say, "Come"! They beckon us down the broad road that leads to destruction. They extend the invitation to everyone, for the ungodly like fellowship in their chosen path. And they do not beckon in vain. Thanks to our fallen human nature, we have a strong bent toward sin.

In contrast to the sinner and the world, the Spirit and the bride stand at life's crossroads with the invitation to follow a different route. They also say, "Come"! (Revelation 22:17)

Sooner or later each individual must choose which invitation to accept. Happy is the young person who has been taught to say a determined no to that first invitation to accept a drink of alcohol, to smoke a cigarette, to try some marijuana, or to indulge in illicit sex. The invitation may be sincere, generous, and enticing, but the answer must always be the same: "No thanks!" One thing leads to another. It's better to choose a lonely path through life than one that ends up in what Solomon's tutor called "all evil" (Proverbs 5:14).

The classic Biblical example of a young man who refused the invitation to sin is Joseph. He had been totally abandoned, sold into slavery by his callous and jealous brothers, and banished to a foreign land. By sheer force of personality and ability he had achieved some kind of status in Egypt in the house of his master Potiphar when the enticement came. How powerful it was! He was a lonely slave. His visions had not come true. His father was far away and doubtless thought him dead. The moral climate of Egypt was utterly worldly and carnal. Immorality was rampant. An offer of love and passion was his for the taking and the cost of refusal was high. Nevertheless Joseph said an emphatic no to the invitation and wisely couched his refusal in spiritual terms. The temptress had no reply to an argument based on the holiness of God. Joseph's decision was the watershed, the "great divide" of his life (Genesis 39:1–41:46).

B. The Incitement (1:11b-13)

Solomon swiftly unmasked the true nature of sin. The invitation to join the gang is followed by an incitement to violence. The sinners make no attempt to disguise the nature of their proposition. Those who respond to their invitation are quickly drawn in all the way.

First comes *the murder proposition:* "Come with us, let us lay wait for blood, let us lurk privily for the innocent without cause: Let us swallow them up alive as the grave; and whole, as those that go down into the pit" (Proverbs 1:11-12). Note the threefold "Let us." It is an echo from the past. We heard it in Genesis 11:3-4 where the policy and lifestyle of Nimrod led to the building of the tower of Babel.

Who would have thought when opening the book of Proverbs that full-grown sin would leap so aggressively and untameably from the first page? We would have expected Solomon to lead up gradually to this climax—to show sin manifesting itself in a child-hood lie or tantrum, then a theft perhaps, then some act of immorality, then an angry blow, and then and only then a coldblooded premeditated murder.

But sin does not need any incubation period. It needs no process of evolution. It leaps full-grown into our experience as it leaped full-grown into the world. The very first person ever born on this planet murdered his own younger brother and then threw his insolence into the face of God Himself. Thus Solomon, before he wrote a dozen verses, grappled with the problem of full-grown sin.

Sin knows nothing of moderation. Society imposes restraints but sin pays little heed. None of us can know where sin will end. From its first page Proverbs warns that those who cast in their lot with bad companions are striking a devil's bargain.

People in the law-abiding segment of society find it hard to believe that propositions to enter a life of violence and crime really abound, but they do. Millions have been drawn into syndicated crime, racketeering, the drug trade, pornography, loan sharking, and murder.

Others have become involved with gangs. Not infrequently initiation into a gang cannot take place until the candidate has offered convincing proof that he has committed an act of violence. Some gangs even demand that initiates commit murder before they can be accepted as members. The world's big cities are plagued with gangs. Some 350 gangs with a combined membership running into the tens of thousands are known to exist in Los Angeles alone. Offering a life of excitement and crime, gangs can be highly attractive to young people being reared in slums. Gangs offer a means to dissipate boredom, a "family" (something thousands have never had), status, money, sex, and power—at a price. Often youngsters become involved out of fear or peer pressure. Whatever the reason, they are drawn by gangs into a life of violence.

In addition to the invitation to a life of violence, sinners offer *the money proposition:* "We shall find all precious substance, we shall fill our houses with spoil" (Proverbs 1:13). People who enjoy relative security and affluence find it difficult to imagine the glittering allure of an offer of swift and easy wealth.

In our own day this proverb can readily focus our attention on the underworld of drugs. In a May 1988 cover story *Time* magazine highlighted the case of "Frog," who was arrested in Los Angeles for teaching the tricks of his trade. Frog boasted of his ability to make two hundred dollars a week selling crack; he made no secret of his membership in an ultraviolent street gang; he bragged about renting a souped-up sports car on weekends, though he had not yet mastered the trick of driving with a stick shift. At his height of four feet ten inches he had trouble seeing over the dashboard, for Frog was only thirteen years of age. His eager apprentices were aged ten and eleven. In Frog's world nine- and ten-year-olds could make one hundred dollars a day just tipping off drug dealers when police were in the area. In New York City an aggressive teenage drug pusher can make up to three thousand dollars a day. One dealer who started selling marijuana and cocaine when he was fourteen years old estimates he made two hundred thousand dollars a year— until he himself became an addict.[1]

Proverbs 1:13 does not point to a make-believe world. It points to a real, hard, cruel world—the only world some unfortunate people have ever known.

C. The Inadvisable (1:14)

Proverbs 1:14 highlights another feature of gangsterism: "Cast in thy lot among us; let us all have one purse." Today we would say, "Share and share alike." It is an invitation to exploitation.

In one of his stories Sir Henry Rider Haggard recounted how his fictional hero Allan Quatermain became entangled in a get-rich-quick scheme involving a gold mine. His partner was to provide the experience and Allan was to provide the capital. His partner turned out to be a scoundrel, and Allan lost his money and nearly lost his good name. Quatermain said, "Before it was all over he had the capital and I had the experience."

Proverbs warns against the common purse. Human nature being what it is, there will always be a victim. The early church experimented with the concept of the common purse. Their motives were the highest and their goals were the purest, but the experiment simply did not work (Acts 2:44-45; 4:34–5:10; 6:1-3; Romans 15:25-27). If the concept was subject to abuse even among the redeemed, how much less can we expect from a common purse in society at large! The philosophy of communism (now demonstrated to be the basic cause for the former Soviet Union's economic woes) is based on the idea of a common purse: "To each according to his need; from each according to his ability" is the essence of the communist creed. Or as a cynic summed up the way the theory worked out in practice, "What's yours is mine, and what's mine is mine."

II. THE PERILS OF THE SINFUL MAN (1:15-19)

A. A Word of Warning (1:15-16)

Notice the reference to *thy foot:* "My son, walk not thou in the way with them; refrain thy foot from their path" (Proverbs 1:15). Perhaps Solomon had been rereading the Hebrew hymnbook and the exhortation with which that collection of poems begins was fresh in his mind: "Blessed [happy, happy] is the man that walketh not in the counsel of the ungodly, nor standeth in the way of sinners, nor sitteth in the seat of the scornful" (Psalm 1:1).

The Lord Jesus vividly reminds us that two paths run through life: "Enter ye in at the strait [narrow] gate: for wide is the gate, and broad is the way, that leadeth to destruction, and many there be which go in thereat: Because strait [narrow] is the gate, and narrow is the way, which leadeth unto life, and few there be that find it" (Matthew 7:13-14).

Two "ways" run through history. The way of Cain runs via the judgment of the flood, past the tower of Babel and the confusion of tongues, by way of the murder of Christ, to the lake of fire. It is the way of the world, the flesh, and the devil. It has its roll call of colorful characters, consummate villains, and giant intellects. Its sidewalks are lined with establishments offering power, pleasure, prosperity, promotion, and even piety. Its grand capital is Babylon; its most popular resort is Vanity Fair; its final destination is Hell.

The other way is the way of Abel, Seth, Melchizedek, Abraham, Moses, David, and Christ. It runs by Gethsemane, Gabbatha, and Golgotha to glory. Those fleeing the City of Destruction look for the Celestial City and go home by the way of the cross. This way has a roll call of giants (Hebrews 11). Its steep slopes are not wanting in attractions: at the place of prayer, the table of the Lord, and the daily quiet time, the Lord of that way draws especially near to His own. Its grand capital is the new Jerusalem; its most popular resorts are the local church and the house of the "Interpreter";[2] its end is an eternity of bliss.

Note also the reference to *their feet:* "For their feet run to evil, and make haste to shed blood" (Proverbs 1:16). The Hebrew word translated "evil" here means "wicked, injurious." The Hebrew word comes from a root meaning "the breaking up of all that is good or desirable, the act of doing injury to others." The corresponding Greek words point to moral depravity, corruption, and lewdness. Truly the steep and slippery path of evil leads downward to all kinds of vice and violence. So depraved is unregenerate human nature that it much prefers this path to the path the Savior trod.

Twice in the book of Genesis God responded to sin with a holocaust. Once He answered human wickedness with a flood; once He answered it with fire.

In the days of Noah society became completely pornographic. "Every imagination of the thoughts of [man's] heart was only evil continually" (Genesis 6:5). The world was "filled with violence" (6:11). Men's feet ran to evil and made haste to shed blood. The world plunged into anarchy, war, crime, and all kinds of brutal behavior.

In the days of Lot society became completely perverted and accepted the vile lifestyle of Sodom without question. Lot, who ventured to protest a common display of Sodomite lust, was almost killed by the mob that resented his words. Again men's feet ran to evil and made haste to shed blood.

The days of Noah and Lot have returned. The earth is again filled with violence. Pornography is a multibillion-dollar business. Perversion is mildly regarded as an alternate lifestyle. Proverbs warns us to beware of the companionship of those who are involved in this violence, pornography, and perversion. God desires His people to raise their voices in protest against the sins of this age, which is ripening fast for judgment.

B. A Word of Wisdom (1:17-19)

Notice the *illustration* Solomon used: "Surely in vain the net is spread in the sight of any bird" (Proverbs 1:17). There are two ways of looking at this proverb. Some people understand it to mean that spreading the net is not a vain procedure because although birds see the net being spread, they will still fly into it. One translator rendered this verse, "It is in vain that birds behold the net spread for them." The Septuagint supports this rendering: "For not unreasonably is the net spread before birds." According to this interpretation, the proverb warns those tempted to follow others into a life of sin that the net has been spread for their destruction. In other words they are fools if, disregarding the warning, they continue on in that way.

Other people understand the proverb to mean that spreading

the net is useless because birds see the snare and fly away. According to this interpretation, the proverb warns those who are tempted that they will be all the more culpable if in spite of the warning they continue on their lawless way. Even birds have more sense; when they see the net spread, they flee.

Whichever way the illustration is interpreted, it is intended to warn the unwary of the peril of the path to which they are about to be lured.

Wild birds are notoriously wary. However they can often be conditioned to relax their caution. To shoot wild ducks, for instance, men build blinds and make realistic decoys and use craftily designed calls to lure the birds within range of hidden guns. The wild turkey is harder to shoot. Unlike its barnyard cousin, it is sage, canny, and elusive. It can run, fly, and swim if necessary. It is adroit on the wing and has been clocked traveling at fifty-five miles per hour for at least a mile. Some wildlife biologists think that hunting the wild turkey only increases the sharpness of the survivors.

Next Solomon made an *observation:* "They lay wait for their own blood; they lurk privily for their own lives" (Proverbs 1:18). Sin is self-destructive. Those who set traps for others often fall into traps themselves.

No worse monster ever lived than Herod the Great, whose favorite wife was the Hasmonean princess Mariamne. On the merest suspicion he had her put to death, only to be haunted ever after by her memory. Josephus wrote that Herod would wander around the palace calling for his wife and ordering his servants to bring her to him. Then he saw a harlot who looked very much like the beautiful Mariamne. He took the woman against all the warnings of common sense and contracted a foul venereal disease. It was just retribution. Ulcers, gangrene, and worms ate his living flesh. The stench of his decaying body was so great that it nauseated the unfortunates whose duty it was to attend him. His death was appropriate to his life of crime.

Men do not always reap the consequences of their deeds in this life, but history records enough cases to assure us that the proverb is true. Full reckoning sometimes has to await the judgment of the great white throne. We can be sure however that when the retribution comes, it will be fitting.

Finally Solomon provided an *application:* "So are the ways of every one that is greedy of gain; which taketh away the life of the owners thereof" (Proverbs 1:19). In the rush to become rich many people abandon moral principles, honesty, and integrity. They build fortunes on products such as alcohol, which enslaves millions and brings misery into countless homes. They push weak people against the wall. They engage in dishonest and unscrupulous business practices, yet they are lauded by their fellow men for being successful. They are given recognition by the state, rewarded with honorary doctorates, and presented with the keys to great cities. But God remains unimpressed.

One of the great financial fortunes in America was amassed by a man who was the son of a Bay State politician and grandson of an Irish immigrant. This man became a bank president at twenty-five and a millionaire at thirty. He was a shipbuilder, a movie czar, and the manager of an investment banking corporation. He mastered the technique of stock-exchange manipulation. His businesses made him rich enough to retire in his early forties with enough capital to fund a million-dollar trust for each of his children. He became the first chairman of the Securities and Exchange Commission, in which capacity he outlawed the speculative practices that had made him a multimillionaire. Nobody will ever know how many people were ruined as a result of this man's determination to be rich. Still he was honored by his country with appointments as chairman of the United States Maritime Commission and as ambassador to a major world power.

Yet a hand of retribution seems to have been at work behind the scenes. A series of misfortunes struck his family. Death after death, disaster after disaster, as well as scandal after scandal dogged the footsteps of his family. "So are the ways of every one that is greedy of gain; which taketh away the life of the owners thereof."

CHAPTER 3

Proverbs 1:20-33

Section 2: The Way of Wisdom (1:20–9:18)

I. Wisdom's Plea (1:20-33)
   A. Wisdom Is Offered to Men (1:20-23)
      1. Where Wisdom Pleads (1:20-21)
         a. Wisdom's Publicity (1:20a)
         b. Wisdom's Places (1:20b-21)
            (1) Where the Throngs Are (1:20b)
            (2) Where the Thoroughfares Are (1:21a)
            (3) Where the Throughways Are (1:21b)
      2. What Wisdom Pleads (1:22-23)
         a. A Specific Example (1:22)
         b. A Spiritual Experience (1:23)
   B. Wisdom Is Offended by Men (1:24-33)
      1. The Refusal (1:24-25)
         a. Wisdom's Call Disregarded (1:24)
         b. Wisdom's Call Despised (1:25)
      2. The Reaction (1:26-28)
         a. Derision (1:26)
         b. Desolation (1:27a)
         c. Destruction (1:27b)
         d. Distress (1:27c)
         e. Desperation (1:28)
      3. The Reason (1:29-30)
         a. Wisdom Detested (1:29)
         b. Wisdom Despised (1:30)
      4. The Result (1:31-33)
         a. The Law of Reaping (1:31)
         b. The Law of Retribution (1:32)
         c. The Law of Relaxation (1:33)

———— ❦ ————

This lengthy section of Proverbs extols the way of wisdom. Wisdom is personified as a beautiful woman and her call is contrasted with the seductions of a wanton woman.

I. WISDOM'S PLEA (1:20-33)

A. Wisdom Is Offered to Men (1:20-23)

1. Where Wisdom Pleads (1:20-21)

"Wisdom crieth without," says Proverbs 1:20, describing *wisdom's publicity*. There is nothing clandestine, secret, or underhanded about wisdom. It is not hidden. It is open and available to all. It is visible and audible to those who have eyes to see and ears to hear.

The secret societies, lodges, and mystery religions of the world offer esoteric knowledge—but only for the initiated. Only those who follow the tortuous mazes of a cult and participate in its secret rites along the way find the inner shrine, and usually some horror lurks there. Nearly all the religions of antiquity were mystery religions. They offered knowledge and power to the initiates. But only those who climbed the winding stairways from one degree of initiation to another found the ultimate secret. When unmasked, the secret was invariably one of the deep things of Satan.

Some years ago when I was changing planes at Gatwick airport in England, I was browsing in the airport bookstore. I came across a book entitled *The Brotherhood* by Stephen Knight. The subtitle is "The Explosive Exposé of the Secret World of the Masons." I read that the Masonic lodge, a secret society, is one of the most powerful organizations in the world. Candidates for initiation into the society are required to believe in some kind of supreme being. No distinction is made between Jehovah, Allah, and the trinity. The Masonic god is described as the "great architect." The true identity of this "great architect" is deliberately kept from the majority of Masons who rise no higher than the third degree. The true identity of the Masonic god, known by a loftier hierarchy, is shocking and terrible indeed. Suffice it to say that the god's name is a composite one linking Jehovah with one of the foulest gods of Canaan and one of the idol-gods of Egypt.[1] How can a genuine Christian continue to be a Mason once the secret is revealed to him?

Wisdom will have nothing to do with secret cults that operate in darkness. She offers her treasures in broad daylight and calls to everyone.

Illustrating where the call can be heard, Proverbs 1:20-21

describes *wisdom's places*. Where does Wisdom advertise her presence? "She uttereth her voice in the streets [where the throngs are]; She crieth in the chief place of concourse [where the thoroughfares are], in the openings of the gates [where the throughways are]: in the city she uttereth her words." Although wisdom seems to be a rare commodity, man's wisdom can be found wherever men are found, and God's wisdom can be found wherever His Word is found.

The "openings of the gates" were busy spots in Bible times. All the commerce of a city flowed through its gates. The markets were conveniently located at the gates. The city government held its meetings at the gates. By mentioning the gates, Solomon was telling us to seek wisdom where people are. He was urging us to look and listen. Wisdom can be found where the wise judge weighs the evidence, probes the testimony, and comes to a verdict. Wisdom can be found where the successful merchant closes an advantageous deal. Occasionally wisdom can even come from the mouth of a fool.

Wisdom is as available today as it was in Solomon's time. Flood tides of books, newspapers, and magazines pour daily from printing presses. Audio and video cassettes are easily obtainable. Schools, colleges, and universities beckon. Libraries bulge with resources. Pulpits, law courts, and the halls of government instruct and inform. Wisdom can be found everywhere, although we often need to separate it from a great deal of accompanying folly.

We are inundated with facts today; computers spew out information with lightning speed. Sifting mountains of data for wisdom is virtually a hopeless task, but we can simplify the search by remembering that "the fear of the Lord is the beginning of wisdom" (Psalm 111:10). We can find true wisdom when we acknowledge God. Since He is the source of true wisdom and He is the God of the Bible, wisdom is readily accessible to everyone who wants to find it.

2. What Wisdom Pleads (1:22-23)

Wisdom pleads for the thoughtless throng to stop, look, and listen. Proverbs 1:22 gives *a specific example* of her pleading: "How long, ye simple ones, will ye love simplicity? and the scorners delight in their scorning, and fools hate knowledge?" Wisdom looks askance at the simple, the scornful, and the foolish. These people cannot be bothered with wisdom. Give them money and they waste it. Employ them and they dissipate their opportunities. Offer them an education and they will not study. In the summer they idle away their time; in the winter they find themselves out of work, poorly clad, and inadequately housed. Nothing could be farther from their minds than wisdom.

John Bunyan wrote of the scorners. In my library I have an edition of his *Pilgrim's Progress* that is greatly enhanced by its illustrations depicting Bunyan's characters. There is a striking picture of Atheist volubly deriding Christian. Atheist is dressed like a dandy. His face is hard and a sneer twists his lips. One arm is outstretched in a scornful gesture and his other hand holds a walking stick on which he is about to lean. He is so concerned with making fun of Christian that he does not notice that the stick is poised over the edge of a precipice. Christian's horrified countenance conveys a warning but Atheist ignores it. Atheism and wisdom have been strangers for years.

Wisdom points the scorners, the simple, and the foolish to *a spiritual experience:* "Turn you at my reproof: behold, I will pour out my spirit unto you, I will make known my words unto you" (Proverbs 1:23). *Wisdom* is one of the New Testament names for the Holy Spirit. Paul called Him "the spirit of wisdom" in Ephesians 1:17. True wisdom has a spiritual quality to it. True wisdom turns away from the wisdom of this world (1 Corinthians 1:23-30), which knows little or nothing of God and is often sensual and devilish (James 3:15). The fear of the Lord is the beginning of true wisdom (Proverbs 9:10). When we are confronted with avowed atheistic, materialistic, and humanistic philosophies, we can discard the data they provide, for true wisdom does not keep company with such ungodly philosophies.

The life of Charles Darwin illustrates the fact that true wisdom is not compatible with worldly philosophies and values. Charles was a wastrel at school, both at Shrewsbury where he was supposed to study the classics and at Edinburgh where he was sent to study medicine. His father, thoroughly annoyed with his son's behavior, brought him home and demanded that he either make up his mind to accomplish something or be cut off from additional funds. So Charles opted to prepare for the Christian ministry and went off to Cambridge where he wasted more time than ever.

For a while he still subscribed to the thirty-nine articles of the Church of England. Once he even quoted a Bible text to settle a point of morality being discussed aboard the *Beagle* and was both surprised and intimidated by the laughter of the sailors.

Charles vacillated a long time before actually publishing his *Origin of Species*. He finally released his manuscript so that the credit for his theories would not go to a rival, A. R. Wallace. Professor Sedgwick, the Cambridge geologist, recognized Darwin's motive in writing the book and described it as "a dish of rank materialism cleverly cooked and served up merely to make us independent of a Creator."[2]

The reaction to Darwin's book was mild until T. H. Huxley jumped on what he considered to be a big enough stage to make his own reputation. Huxley had a brilliant mind. He went to school in the East End of London, taught himself German, and was reading advanced books on geology and logic at age twelve. He wanted to become an engineer, but studied medicine instead and joined the navy as an assistant surgeon. After being discharged for refusing to return to active service, he decided to devote his life to scientific research despite his lack of formal education. Huxley at once saw the possibilities of Darwin's fledgling theories. Darwin had to decide between the praise of men and the praise of God. We know what he decided. He accepted Huxley's offer to become Darwin's "bull-dog," to snarl and snap at those who rejected Darwin's theories.

Huxley (who invented the word *agnostic*) readily saw that the theory of evolution would afford him "an excellent means to vent his spite on the clergy." The theory would give men a working hypothesis for atheism and give him a platform on which he could make himself famous.

As for Darwin, he paid dearly for his apostasy. Having substituted natural selection for God, he worshiped at the shrine of his false god for the rest of his life. He became chronically ill although there was nothing organically wrong with him. One scholar wrote:

> Psychologically there can be little doubt he was suffering from a feeling of guilt. Not long before the death of Darwin the Duke of Argyle talked to him at his bedside. He tried to rekindle in Darwin's soul some of his lost knowledge of God. Darwin just shook his head and expressed his own spiritual hopelessness and confusion.[3]

We cannot have it both ways. We have to choose between the wisdom of God's Word and the foolishness of all such theories as Darwin's.

B. Wisdom Is Offended by Men (1:24-33)

1. The Refusal (1:24-25)

Wisdom reproves men because her call is *disregarded:* "Because I have called, and ye refused; I have stretched out my hand, and no man regarded" (Proverbs 1:24). We can picture a pause between this verse and the preceding one as Wisdom takes her stand with arms outstretched at the great intersection of life. As the heedless surge past, she raises her voice to offer them evidence of God's wisdom, love, and power, but they ignore her. Yet how urgently she is needed!

We are all on a brief and hurried journey from the womb to the tomb. Apart from divine wisdom we have no satisfying answers to all the important questions of life: Where did we come from? Why are we here? Where are we going? What is life all about? Why is evil so prevalent and triumphant? Is there life beyond death? Is there a God? How can God be known? Only the wisdom contained in the Bible can answer questions such as these. Foolish answers to these questions are plentiful, but they are all wrong to a greater or lesser degree. Wisdom stands, calls, and is disregarded, so she warns.

Her call is *despised* too: "But ye have set at nought all my counsel, and would none of my reproof" (Proverbs 1:25). When Wisdom came to Cain after God rejected his offering, he went away in a rage. "And the Lord said unto Cain, Why art thou wroth? and why is thy countenance fallen? If thou doest well, shalt thou not be accepted? and if thou doest not well, sin lieth at the door [a sin offering lieth at thy door]" (Genesis 4:6-7). Wisdom was urging Cain to acknowledge that his religious notions were unacceptable to God. She was also urging him to emulate his righteous brother's example. A sin offering was at hand; all Cain had to do was avail himself of the salvation God had provided for him. Cain however despised the way of wisdom. He murdered Abel, became a fugitive and a vagabond, and went out from the presence of God. Cain founded a brilliant but godless civilization, one that could have no final end but the flood. No one can defy wisdom with impunity, even though the consequences of such folly may sometimes be long delayed.

2. The Reaction (1:26-28)

Wisdom's first reaction to the deliberate choice of folly is one of *derision:* "I also will laugh at your calamity; I will mock when your fear cometh" (Proverbs 1:26).

The people who forged the Soviet Union, who so wholeheartedly embraced atheistic communism and promoted the Bolshevik revolution, hated God. Zinoviev, friend and colleague of Lenin, most blatantly expressed the attitude of the Soviet Union toward God: "We shall grapple with the Lord God in due season, we shall vanquish Him from His highest heaven, and wherever He seeks refuge, and we shall subdue Him forever."[4] God responded, "Is that so?" His derisive answer is found in Psalm 2:4: "He that sitteth in the heavens shall laugh: the Lord shall have them in derision." Seventy-five years later the mighty Soviet Union and its unhappy satellites stood before the world in economic, social, and ethnic disarray. Wisdom mocks at the abysmal folly of people who embrace such philosophies, while she weeps over the inconceivable misery, hardship, and suffering of their victims.

The result of despising wisdom is *desolation:* "When your fear cometh as desolation" (Proverbs 1:27). The word translated "desolation" here can also be translated "tempest," for when desolation comes, it comes suddenly and often violently. People can pursue folly for a long time, but in the end folly proves itself to be what it is and presents its own rewards.

Imagine the incredible folly of Lot. He returned to Sodom after the disastrous war described in Genesis 14. Although he was rescued by Abraham, Lot learned nothing. Did he seek to be restored to the fellowship of God's people? No. He returned to Sodom and took his family with him! Still worse, he accepted a promotion and became one of Sodom's magistrates sworn to uphold its filthy lifestyle. Like a tempest indeed, desolation came. In one night of holocaust and horror, Lot lost both his family and his fortune. He ended up drunk and dishonored in the wild hills beyond the cursed and stricken cities of the plain (Genesis 19:30-38).

Despising wisdom also results in *destruction:* "And your destruction cometh as a whirlwind" (Proverbs 1:27). The word translated "destruction" here means "calamity."

We are reminded of the calamities that befell Zedekiah, the last Old Testament king of the Jews. Put on the Judean throne by Nebuchadnezzar, Zedekiah had no use for Jeremiah or the Word of God. During Zedekiah's reign the temple was polluted with idolatry, and injustice was common. When a strong political party in Judea urged him to break his promises to the king of Babylon, he bowed to their pressure. Against all the pleas of Jeremiah, Zedekiah chose the path of folly. Before long the Babylonian army returned to hammer at the gates of Jerusalem. Momentarily encouraged by an Egyptian advance against the Babylonians, Zedekiah congratulated himself, but eventually his gamble failed and he fled. The Babylonians pursued him and brought him as a prisoner to Nebuchadnezzar. Thereafter the foolish and faithless Zedekiah experienced one calamity after another. He was tried and condemned and his sons were put to death before his eyes; then he was blinded and carried in chains to Babylon where he died in prison.

Another consequence of ignoring Wisdom's call is *distress:* "When distress and anguish cometh upon you" (Proverbs 1:27). What must Lot have thought when he came to himself up on the mountain? He could see the still waters of the Dead Sea, beneath which Sodom and Gomorrah were buried.[5] He could see his daughters whispering to each other and he nursed secret memories of his shame. He thought of his other children who had perished in the fire-and-brimstone doom of Sodom. He thought of his wife turned into a pillar of salt, and distress and anguish came upon him. Did Lot in his misery visit that terrible monument that had once been his wife and talk to it? Did he say, "Oh my beloved, forgive me! Forgive me for my folly. I should have stayed with Abraham. That was wisdom's path. Would God I had died for you! Would God I could turn the clock back and choose all over again"?

The end result of disregarding wisdom is *desperation:* "Then shall they call upon me, but I will not answer; they shall seek me early, but they shall not find me" (Proverbs 1:28). Marc Antony waited too long to seek wisdom. After the death of Julius Caesar the rule of the Roman world lay almost within Antony's grasp. Now a triumvir fresh from the victory of Philippi, he arrived in Asia Minor to wring gold from the subject kings to satisfy the greed of his legionnaires. From Cilicia, Antony peremptorily summoned Cleopatra of Egypt to appear before him to answer for the aid Egypt had given to the conspirators. She came and met the noble Roman—a man in the prime of life, great of form and royal of mien, attended by generals, master of a third of the world. She came and Antony lost his heart and all his common sense to Cleopatra. She came and conquered.

Infatuated, he bestowed royal gifts on his imperial paramour. He gave her the greater part of Cilicia, the ocean shore of Arabia Nabatea, the province of Coele-Syria, the rich island of Cyprus, and all the library of Pergamus. Antony named the children Cleopatra bore him "Kings, the Children of Kings." In addition to the son Ptolemy there were twins whom Antony called *Alexander Helios* ("the sun") and *Cleopatra Selene* ("the long-winged moon").

Then Antony warred against the Parthians, and Artavasdes, king of Armenia, was led in triumph through the streets of Alexandria. Cleopatra visited Samos and Athens and on her worthless advice the noble Octavia was driven, like some discarded concubine, from Antony's house at Rome. The cup of Antony's folly was full to the brim, for this master of the world no longer had the gift of reason; he was lost in Cleopatra.

When Octavius declared war against him, Antony at last called upon Wisdom but she would not answer. His attempt to seek her came too late. The stage was set for the battle of Actium. The combined fleets of Antony and Cleopatra came to grips with the navy of the caesar and the warships grappled near a rocky coast. The vessels of Antony and Cleopatra drove back the ships of the caesar and victory inclined to Antony. Then suddenly fear seized Cleopatra. She called to her sailors to hoist the sails and flee in haste from the battle. The besotted Antony, with victory within his grasp, chased after his Egyptian love. Wreck and ruin fell upon his fleet and great Antony was devastated. At Alexandria Antony tried once more to turn the tide of his fallen fortunes, but his sailors and soldiers deserted him and left him to his fate. Antony committed suicide. He was the victim of his own folly.

3. The Reason (1:29-30)

Wisdom gives two reasons why the time comes when she can no longer be found. The first is that she has been *detested:* "They hated knowledge, and did not choose the fear of the Lord" (Proverbs 1:29). The hate and the choice are linked together. People detest wisdom because wisdom cannot be separated from the fear of the Lord, and the fear of the Lord is the last thing to appeal to the unregenerate human heart. Many people want no part of any wisdom that directs their thoughts to God.

One such person was Julian Huxley, the grandson of T. H. Huxley who made Darwinism popular. Julian helped establish the United Nations Educational, Scientific, and Cultural Organization (UNESCO) and was its first director general. He hated God. "God," he once said, "has nothing left to do—all belief in His interventions having been debunked." He declared that God has been forced to abdicate, evacuating section after section of His kingdom. "Operationally," Julian said, "God is beginning to resemble, not a ruler, but the last, fading smile of a Cheshire cat." Such men hate knowledge, even though they have a reputation for cleverness and the world applauds them. Their abysmal folly will be fully revealed when they stand at last before the God whom they have blasphemed and denied.

The opposite attitude can be seen in the young man who received a packet of agnostic literature in the mail and returned the literature with this letter:

Dear Sir,

If you have anything better than the Sermon on the Mount, the parable of the Prodigal Son, and that of the Good Samaritan, or if you have any code of morals better than the Ten Commandments, or anything more consoling and beautiful than the Twenty-third Psalm, or anything that will throw more light on the future, and reveal to me a Father more merciful and kind than the One revealed in the New Testament—send it along.

The infidel removed the young man's name from the mailing list.

Which of the two was wise, Huxley or the anonymous young man? To which of the two would you go with a heartache, a terrible loss, the news that you have terminal cancer, or the discovery that your beloved son is on drugs? How terrible it is to detest wisdom simply because wisdom and God are inseparable.

The second reason Wisdom withdraws is that she has been *despised:* "They would none of my counsel: they despised all my reproof" (Proverbs 1:30). Wisdom's patience is great, but not endless. When Wisdom is despised once too often, she leaves us to ourselves.

Samson was one who despised counsel. The highest wisdom told Samson to let his hair grow long. To refrain from cutting his hair was part of the Nazarite vow, intended to set him apart from the rank and file of even the people of God (Judges 13:5). The special spiritual significance of the Nazarite vow had been drilled into him since infancy. His long hair made him immediately recognizable as a person uniquely consecrated to God. It was the outward confession of his inward commitment. Seeing his hair, everyone knew the special dimension of consecration that was his. They knew of his special anointing with Holy Spirit power. There was a direct relationship between Samson's hair and Samson's power, and Samson knew it. It was the highest wisdom to protect the seven locks of his long hair with his life.

But Samson despised all reproof. He played fast and loose with his great gifts, acted like an overgrown schoolboy, and played practical jokes. He was stronger than Hercules, but had a fatal fondness for women, which proved to be his Achilles heel. He played the fool and allowed Delilah to wheedle out of him the secret of his hair. Shorn of his locks, blinded and weak, he ground corn like a woman for the Philistines. By his folly he told Wisdom he would have none of her counsel, and Wisdom left him to his own ways.

4. The Result (1:31-33)

Wisdom's plea ends with a threefold exhortation in which she expounds the laws of reaping, retribution, and relaxation. Proverbs

1:31 states the *law of reaping:* "Therefore shall they eat of the fruit of their own way, and be filled with their own devices."

The Israelites reaped the consequences of not heeding the wisdom of the Mosaic law that decreed that their land should be allowed a sabbath rest. One year in every seven had to be set aside as "a sabbath of rest unto the land, a sabbath for the Lord" (Leviticus 25:4). The land was not to be plowed or planted, reaped or gleaned. Giving the land a rest was sound agricultural law as well. Today farmers achieve a similar objective by rotating crops and using fertilizers.

The Lord involved Himself in the provision for a sabbath rest and linked His name to the command. He promised that the bounty of preceding years would provide more than enough bread for the sabbatical year. Thus no one would need to plan and toil for a whole year. The people could give their full attention to spiritual truths during that time; the Lord could be predominant in their thoughts. For one whole year in every seven, the land could rest, the people could rest, and God could rest.

But the Israelites thought they knew better than God. They became greedy. They hated to think of the money they were losing by keeping what seemed to be a foolish law. As for devoting the year to the Lord, nothing could have been farther from their thoughts. From the start they ignored the commandment.

The command however came with a warning. If the decree was neglected, God would bring the land into desolation and its people would be scattered. His warning was crystal clear: "Then shall the land enjoy her sabbaths, as long as it lieth desolate, and ye shall be in your enemies' land; even then shall the land rest, and enjoy her sabbaths" (Leviticus 26:34).

The years passed and God watched the folly of His people as they disregarded the sabbatical year. He sent droughts and famines to remind the Israelites of His law, but they still ignored Him. Finally He sent the Assyrians and the Babylonians to fulfill His Word. Years later a scribe recorded not only the captivity but its purpose: "To fulfil the word of the Lord by the mouth of Jeremiah, until the land had enjoyed her sabbaths: for as long as she lay desolate she kept sabbath, to fulfil threescore and ten years" (2 Chronicles 36:21; also see Jeremiah 25:9-12; 29:10).

The law of reaping is inexorable. We cannot ignore wisdom with impunity. God's Word, the embodiment of the highest wisdom, cannot be set aside, although men in their folly always seem to think it can.

Proverbs 1:32 states the corresponding *law of retribution:* "The turning away of the simple shall slay them, and the prosperity of fools shall destroy them." The word translated "simple" here refers to the artless, the guileless, the unsuspecting—in short, to the gullible. The word translated "fools" refers to the dense or stupid, especially the impious. Those who ignore wisdom will eventually find themselves in trouble.

The gullible person goes on his merry way, even barging into situations that can kill him. Such people get hooked on drugs, play around with illicit sex, and stumble into danger zones in the inner city where predators await the unwary.

The stupid man sometimes acquires wealth, but it ruins him. When the prodigal son fell heir to a fortune it ran through his fingers like quicksilver. He "wasted his substance with riotous living" (Luke 15:13). When he spent his last penny, his fair-weather friends vanished and he faced starvation and utter destitution in a cold and callous land far from home. He is the classic example of the English proverb that says, "A fool and his money are soon parted."

Happily, the third law indicates that a different result is possible. Proverbs 1:33 states the *law of relaxation:* "Whoso hearkeneth unto me shall dwell safely, and shall be quiet from fear of evil." The Hebrew word translated "evil" here is *rā'a'*, which refers to the breaking up of all that is good and desirable. Corresponding Greek words refer to corruption and lewdness and could easily apply to the world of Noah's day. He lived in a vile pornographic society that was ripening fast for judgment. It was a world full of knowledge but utterly devoid of wisdom, a world that followed the way of Cain.

Noah proved the law of relaxation to be true. Not only did he "dwell safely" in that corrupt and violent culture; he also preached of righteousness to his generation. Moreover as he worked on the ark, he raised a memorial to coming judgment. He was "moved with fear" yet worked "by faith" (Hebrews 11:7). The fear of the Lord was truly the beginning of wisdom in his life.

To his contemporaries Noah must have seemed an arrant fool, but when the flood came only Noah and his family had a place of refuge. Within the ark they were able to "dwell safely" even when the fountains of the great deep were broken up, when the windows of heaven were opened, when the world was torn apart by the tempest and drowned in the flood. Those within the ark rested in perfect peace and safety. They even had rest from an accusing conscience; they had lived in accordance with God's Word and, like Paul, were "pure from the blood of all men" (Acts 20:26).

CHAPTER 4

Proverbs 2:1-22

II. Wisdom's Protection (2:1-22)
   A. The Conditions for Acquiring Wisdom (2:1-4)
      1. We Must Be Receptive (2:1)
      2. We Must Be Responsive (2:2-3)
      3. We Must Be Resolute (2:4)
   B. The Consequences of Acquiring Wisdom (2:5-22)
      1. Delight in the Lord (2:5-8)
         a. A Constructive Fear (2:5a)
         b. A Considerable Find (2:5b-8)
            (1) The Origin of Wisdom (2:5b-6)
            (2) The Object of Wisdom (2:7)
            (3) The Outcome of Wisdom (2:8)
      2. Deliverance by the Lord (2:9-22)
         a. Perception (2:9)
         b. Pleasure (2:10)
         c. Preservation (2:11-22)
            (1) From the Villainous Man (2:11-15)
               (a) The Need for Discretion (2:11)
               (b) The Nature of Discretion (2:12-15)
                  i. Protection from the Wicked Man's Way (2:12a)
                  ii. Protection from the Wicked Man's Words (2:12b)
                  iii. Protection from the Wicked Man's Walk (2:13)
                  iv. Protection from the Wicked Man's Wickedness (2:14-15)
                     a. His Companions (2:14)
                     b. His Crookedness (2:15)

(2) From the Vile Woman (2:16-22)
    (a) She Is Flattering (2:16)
    (b) She Is Forgetful (2:17)
    (c) She Is Fatal (2:18-22)
        i. The Need to Recognize Her (2:18-19)
            a. Death Lurks Where She Lives (2:18)
            b. Doom Lurks Where She Lives (2:19)
        ii. The Need to Repudiate Her (2:20-22)
            a. The Path of the Wise Man (2:20-21)
                1. Marked by Purity (2:20)
                2. Marked by Protection (2:21)
            b. The Path of the Wicked Man (2:22)

The theme of Proverbs 1 is Wisdom's plea; she offers wisdom to one and all. In Proverbs 2 the theme is Wisdom's protection from many of life's ills.

II. WISDOM'S PROTECTION (2:1-22)

A. The Conditions for Acquiring Wisdom (2:1-4)

If we want to be wise we need to be receptive, responsive, and resolute. First we must be *receptive:* "My son, if thou wilt receive my words, and hide my commandments with thee" (Proverbs 2:1). The word *if* underlines the element of choice in the process of acquiring wisdom. God created people, not puppets.

When God created the animals, He endowed each kind with its own instincts—its own code of signals to govern its behavior. An animal does what it does because it is what it is. No bee has to go to school to learn how to build a shelter, gather nectar, make honey, or defend its hive. A bee does everything by instinct.

God did not lock people into such specific behavioral patterns. He gave them bodies and souls. He gave them the ability to see, taste, feel, hear, and smell. He gave them the ability to think, to respond emotionally, and to make decisions. He also gave Adam—and all his descendants—a spirit. God's intention was for the human spirit to be indwelt by the Holy Spirit. By cooperating with the Holy Spirit Adam would be all that God intended a person to be. But when Adam sinned, the Holy Spirit left his human spirit and he was left without a governing principle. Adam became a fallen creature, and the human race inherited his lost condition. Fallen man's intellect is bent in the direction of folly; his emotions can run rampant; his will may be weak in one situation or stubborn in another.

The regenerated man is cleansed of his sin by the blood of Christ. The Holy Spirit again indwells his human spirit. The regenerated person can once more cooperate with God's Spirit and become all that God wants him to be. The possibility is there but the will is key; he still must choose to cooperate.

Wisdom is available to us and by virtue of our regeneration we have a predilection toward the Word of God—the ultimate depository of divine wisdom—but wisdom must be received. We must be receptive.

We must also be *responsive:* "Incline thine ear unto wisdom, and apply thine heart to understanding; Yea, if thou criest after knowledge, and liftest up thy voice for understanding" (Proverbs 2:2-3). In other words, we need to make an active and determined effort to become acquainted with wisdom. We need to make an active and determined effort to get to know the Word of God where the highest wisdom is stored.

One of the best-taught and wisest of the Bible teachers I have known became my friend when I joined the staff of the Moody Bible Institute. Robert Little, then the radio pastor of the MBI network, was a quiet, humble believer who was widely respected, much loved, and renowned for his Bible knowledge. Other staff members and I tried to stump him with hard Bible questions, but he always had answers. Many were the secret deeds of kindness he did and great was his patience. Although people were always telephoning him to solicit help, advice, and information, he was patient with them all.

On one occasion an elderly man approached Mr. Little at the close of a service. The man thanked him for his message and said, "Mr. Little, I wish I had your knowledge of the Bible." The aging Bible teacher replied, "My dear friend, you're too late. In fact I would judge you are about fifty years too late. If you wanted my knowledge of the Bible you should have started fifty years ago. That's how long it has taken me to acquire my knowledge of the Bible. I'm sorry, my friend, but you will never have my knowledge of the Bible. But it is never too late to make a serious start." Likewise, we must be responsive if we want to acquire wisdom.

We must also be *resolute:* "If thou seekest her as silver, and searchest for her as for hid treasures" (Proverbs 2:4). Mining for silver and finding hidden treasure both call for determined resolve.

When I was a boy some of my favorite stories were about looking for hidden treasure. I remember how young Jim Hawkins found the map of Treasure Island in a dead buccaneer's old sea chest. Squire Trelawney fitted out a ship and the *Hispaniola* set sail to find the treasure. Dr. Livesey was the ship's surgeon; Long John Silver was the cook. Smuggled aboard as crew was a ruthless band of cutthroats, the survivors of old Flint's pirate ship. One and all—the squire, Long John Silver, and the pirates—were motivated by one resolve: to find hidden treasure.

As soon as the ship dropped anchor near Treasure Island, the crew mutinied. War broke out between the pirates and the other treasure seekers. After various adventures, Jim was captured by the pirates. To his astonishment he discovered that the squire had given the all-important map to Long John. The climax to the story occurs in the treasure hunt. The one-legged Long John Silver urges his companions on to the site where they only find a hole in the ground. The treasure is gone. The sole reward for all their murders and villainies is one golden guinea! Poor Ben Gunn, a former pirate who had been marooned on the island years before, had found and concealed the treasure.

Our search for wisdom must be just as resolute as the search for gold in Robert Louis Stevenson's *Treasure Island*. People wear themselves out to unearth worldly treasure, which they often squander. We should give ourselves unstintingly to the quest for eternal treasure, the wisdom that can only be found in the Word of God.

B. The Consequences of Acquiring Wisdom (2:5-22)

1. Delight in the Lord (2:5-8)

The first result of acquiring wisdom from God will be a new delight in the Lord Himself, the ultimate fount of all wisdom. We will have *a constructive fear:* "Then shalt thou understand the fear of the Lord" (Proverb 2:5). The fear of the Lord is the beginning of wisdom—not the end. Fear of the Lord leads us to trust, and trust leads us to love.

When we hear and receive God's words, hide His commandments in our hearts, apply ourselves to understanding, and ask earnestly for divine wisdom, we will be on our way to understanding the fear of the Lord.

The fear of the Lord is not a slavish fear. It is a reverential awe that inspires all those who find themselves in the presence of an all-powerful, all-wise, all-loving God. People who lack such reverence are grossly ignorant of their own sinfulness and God's awesome holiness.

Isaiah began his prophetic ministry on a note of constructive fear. Being very much aware of the sins of his generation, he pronounced one woe after another upon his apostate nation (Isaiah 5:11,18,20-22). But then he saw the Lord! He saw the seraphim—the burning ones, the sinless sons of light—standing before the throne. Their minds had never been sullied by sinful thoughts. Their hearts had always poured out undiluted love for the living God. Their wills had never been seduced from unswerving loyalty to Him and swift obedience to His commands. Yet they hid their faces in their wings because they dared not look upon the awesome holiness of God. Suddenly Isaiah saw himself and added one more woe to his collection. "Woe," he said, "is me!" Isaiah's fear, his awe of God, was constructive, not destructive. The moment he confessed himself to be lost and undone, he was cleansed and commissioned (6:1-13).

When we acquire wisdom we will have such a constructive fear. We will also have *a considerable find*. We will find the origin, the object, and the outcome of wisdom.

The Lord is *the origin of wisdom:* "Then shalt thou...find the knowledge of God. For the Lord giveth wisdom: out of his mouth cometh knowledge and understanding" (Proverbs 2:5-6). Knowledge and understanding did not come from the mouths of Buddha and Muhammad. Knowledge and understanding do not come from the mouths of politicians, educators, philosophers, or scientists. Wisdom and knowledge do not come from the mouths of familiar spirits; the utterances of mediums have not contributed a single sentence to the golden sayings of mankind.

People considered to be wise by the world have made numerous quotable statements. Some have made astute observations about life, the world of nature, and other topics. Great thinkers have contributed to religious thought. Such men have attracted millions of followers, but true wisdom cannot be found in worldly ideologies. "The Lord giveth wisdom."

Years ago when I was in charge of course development for the Moody Correspondence School, we produced a course on the cults. One of the cults we reviewed was Bahai, which has a headquarters in the Chicago area. I wanted a photograph of the Bahai temple for a course illustration, so I wrote to the cult headquarters and requested one.

Instead of the photograph, I received a visit from a cult representative. A good-looking, immaculately groomed, polished, and cultivated woman came into my office. She produced my letter and politely asked why I wanted the photograph. I explained that we were producing a course on comparative religion and were including a chapter on Bahai. She requested permission to read the chapter and I watched her as she perused it. She betrayed no emotion. As she handed over the desired picture, she simply requested that we soften the expression "Bahai cult" to "Bahai faith."

Then she asked, "Have you ever seriously considered what the Bahai faith has to offer mankind?" I responded that the Bahai cult is a conglomerate of nine major world religions, including Christianity. Each of these religions is seen as offering a particular contribution to man's search for God. The religions are not seen as contradictory but as complementary. They all equally offer hope and peace to the world. Various great prophets have arisen, according to Bahai, and each has added to the total of man's religious knowledge.

Then I asked my visitor, "Have you ever read the Gospels?" She said she had.

Next I brought up Islam, which is a religion of hate. Militant Islam to this day engages in terrorism, holds hostages, and advocates violence. Originally Islam was spread by the sword and it still occasionally calls for a holy war against infidels. Islam upholds polygamy and is repressive of even the most basic rights of women.

I asked my visitor, "Would you please tell me in what way Muhammad contributed anything in advance of the teaching and example of Christ?" The woman gave me a dignified smile, stood up, bade me a polite "Good morning," and left. She had no answer, for God has not spoken through Confucius, Buddha, Zoroaster, or Muhammad. He spoke in the Old Testament through His servants and prophets, and now He has spoken through His Son. *Jesus* is God's last Word to man. "Out of his mouth cometh knowledge and understanding."

We will also find *the object of wisdom:* "He [the Lord] layeth up sound wisdom for the righteous: he is a buckler to them that walk uprightly" (Proverbs 2:7). The expression "He layeth up" comes from the same Hebrew word that is translated "hide" in 2:1. It means "to lay up, to hide as one hides a treasure." So the wicked may look for wisdom, but they cannot find it. Even the righteous must dig for it. The expression "sound wisdom" comes from the Hebrew word *tushīyah,* which refers to stability. Solomon was telling us that only those who find God's wisdom have stability in life. The object of wisdom is to protect us from instability and the onslaughts of life.

The Lord underscores the source of stability in His parable of the two builders (Matthew 7:24-27). The foolish man builds his house on the sand—on the philosophies, opinions, theories, and religions of men. But he discovers that human opinions will not stand the test of tide and tempest. The wise man builds his house on the rock—on God's Word. When wind and rain come, all is well. The wise man builds his life on the sayings of Him who says, "I am...the truth" (John 14:6).

T. H. Huxley—scientist, agnostic, and friend of Darwin—based his life on human opinions. For a while he lived in a small country town in England. One Sunday morning he said to a friend, "I suppose you are going to church." The man affirmed that he was. "Suppose you stay home with me instead," said Huxley, "and talk to me about your religion."

"No thanks," the friend replied. "You're too clever for me, Huxley. I couldn't hope to refute your arguments."

Huxley looked at him and said, "Suppose you simply told me what your religion has done for you."

The other man agreed to stay home on those terms. Throughout the morning he shared his faith in the risen Christ with the famous champion of unbelief.

With the suspicion of a tear in his eye, Huxley finally said, "I would give my right hand if I could believe that."

Huxley went through life encased in the armor of his own worldly cleverness. The celebrated and famous agnostic built his house on the sand. His Christian friend, on the other hand, was protected by wisdom from on high. Although not nearly so clever as the skeptical Huxley, the unknown humble believer was ten thousand times wiser. He built on the Rock.

Finally we will find *the outcome of wisdom:* "He [the Lord] keepeth the paths of judgment, and preserveth the way of his saints" (Proverbs 2:8). The Lord preserved young David from danger. During those perilous years after he killed Goliath of Gath, David was pursued by the relentless jealousy and malice of King Saul. The crown prince Jonathan put himself at David's feet, but that friendship only added to the sourness of Saul's soul. However "David went out whithersoever Saul sent him, and *behaved himself wisely*" (1 Samuel 18:5, italics added). As a result Saul made David commander over the men of war.

Still "Saul was afraid of David, because the Lord was with him" (1 Samuel 18:12). Twice the Lord saved David from Saul's attempts to murder him. Thinking some gesture of appeasement might be in order, Saul promoted David to the rank of captain over a thousand men. Again we read, "David *behaved himself wisely* in all his ways" (18:14, italics added). David's behavior only increased Saul's fears (18:15).

Saul's daughter Michal fell in love with David; the romance further inflamed Saul and he "became David's enemy continually" (1 Samuel 18:29).

There followed a brief brush with the Philistines, a sobering reminder to King Saul as to who the real enemy was. The historian noted that at this time too "*David behaved himself more wisely than all the servants of Saul;* so that his name was much set by" (1 Samuel 18:30, italics added).

Thus the Lord preserved the life of one of His saints. The story of David during his fugitive years illustrates the way of wisdom in the treacherous situations of life.

2. Deliverance by the Lord (2:9-22)

a. Perception (2:9)

When we acquire wisdom we will have light in darkness: "Then shalt thou understand righteousness, and judgment, and equity; yea, every good path." God is on the side of righteousness, justice, and fair play. Although His hand is not always visible in human affairs, it is always there. Wisdom discerns that hand, even as folly scoffs at it.

God's hand is not always clearly visible in history because of sin. Other wills besides God's will are at work in the universe. God created these wills and respects them. Ultimately He will control them, but He does not always curb them immediately when they are exerted in rebellion.

Dr. A. E. Wilder Smith, a respected scholar, told of an incident that took place during his student days. One of his professors, an avowed Marxist, convened a class to study natural science but devoted the entire session to ridiculing Christianity. His main line of attack was simple: "Did God create evil? If God is all-powerful, He cannot be all-loving; if He is all-loving, He cannot be all-powerful." The clever diatribe went on and on. "Did your God design the cat so it could play with the mouse and torment it before killing it? Did your God create rattlesnake venom? Did your loving God create the malarial parasite? It seems to me that that parasite was designed. It shows signs of careful, thoughtful planning. It seems to have been deliberately designed to plague and torture the host animal, or man."[1]

The answer to all such questions cannot be found with human reasoning. The answer lies in divine revelation—in the Bible—or nowhere. The solution to the problem of evil is related to what the Bible calls "the mystery of iniquity" (2 Thessalonians 2:7). This mystery began in eternity past, became a human problem in the garden of Eden, and reached its climax at Calvary. The ultimate issues of the mystery lie beyond the grave. The mystery of iniquity cannot be solved if it is divorced from the person of Christ and His great work at Calvary.

The atheistic professor and people like him have wrong ideas about the omnipotence of God. Indeed they have wrong ideas about God altogether. C. S. Lewis said that omnipotence does not mean power to do the intrinsically impossible. We can attribute miracles to God, but not nonsense. We cannot say that God can give free will to a creature and at the same time withhold free will from that creature.

Much of the evil in the universe comes from Satan, much comes from his fallen angels and demons, and much comes from man's own sin. Truth about the mystery of iniquity can be derived from the Bible alone—a source of information derided by atheists and agnostics. No wonder the clever professor could not understand the reality of evil in the universe. His mind was closed to truth. He was reasoning round and round within a closed philosophical system. He deliberately left the most potent factors out of his calculations. People who believe the Bible may not always be clever, but they are right. They understand God's righteousness, judgment, and equity. Atheists and agnostics don't.

b. Pleasure (2:10)

Wisdom brings its own rewards: "Wisdom entereth into thine heart, and knowledge is pleasant unto thy soul." Those who have acquired wisdom have had their eyes opened. They are unlike blind old Pew, one of the villains in *Treasure Island*. What terror he struck into the heart of young Jim Hawkins! What consternation Pew's visit to the Admiral Benbow Inn brought to the drunken old pirate who lodged there! Pew cursed his companions as they ransacked the inn looking in vain for the treasure map and he cursed his own blindness. Finally when his companions abandoned him to his fate, when the warning signal sounded and the drumming of hoofbeats was heard, Pew changed his tune. He staggered to and fro. Tap, tap, tap went his stick. He dashed here; he dashed there. Then utterly confused, he ran straight under the hooves of the leading horse and was trampled by the galloping revenue officer and his men. Pew's dying screams rang to the heaven above.

Those who are acquainted with the wisdom of God's Word no longer stumble in darkness. They are not like Pew, who was abandoned to his fate in his hour of need. On the contrary, truly wise people have the answers to the big questions about life and death, time and eternity, sin and salvation. They have inside information, so to speak. Wisdom resides in their hearts. The knowledge they possess is pleasant to their souls.

c. Preservation (2:11-22)

(1) From the Villainous Man (2:11-15)

(a) The Need for Discretion (2:11)

The remainder of Proverbs 2 shows how wisdom can save us from the villainous man and the vile woman. Proverbs 2:11 emphasizes our need for discretion: "Discretion shall preserve thee, understanding shall keep thee." To some people discretion is refraining from words or deeds that might lead to unpleasant consequences. Such avoidance, however, may not be discretion; it could be cowardice. These people may merely wish to avoid confrontation. Actually discretion is counting the cost. As the English proverb says, "Look before you leap."

When I was young I lived in one of Britain's big cities. The wall around my elementary school was high. The top of the wall was covered with a pile of cement in which jagged pieces of broken glass had been embedded. The idea of course was to discourage ambitious and energetic youngsters from climbing over the wall. One day I saw a cat walking on top of that wall with extreme discretion. Before taking a step the cat would carefully put out one paw and gingerly test the surface. If the paw touched glass, the cat withdrew his foot. If the paw found a small patch of cement free from glass, the cat tested it carefully to make sure he could safely put weight on that paw. His progress along the top of the wall was slow, but it was sure.

Proceeding with discretion does not mean never speaking out, never making a move. It means making decisions with care, with eyes open. If we have discretion, we weigh what we are doing and where we are going. Wisdom gives discretion; discretion gives direction. We live in a perilous world so we need discretion.

(b) The Nature of Discretion (2:12-15)

In this wicked world we need what discretion gives: protection from *the wicked man's way*. Discretion's role is "to deliver thee from the way of the evil man" (Proverbs 2:12). God does not promise to protect us from the evil man, but from the evil man's way.

With the exception of the Biblical writers and John Bunyan, no author has captured human nature in words as well as Charles Dickens. True to life, his characters encounter evil in their world. We follow the career of poor Oliver Twist, for instance, with deep feelings. Raised in an orphanage, bullied by the parochial beadle Mr. Bumble, ill-treated by the coffin maker to whom he was apprenticed at a tender age, Oliver Twist ran away to London. There he fell into the clutches of Fagin.

Of all Dickens' villains, few surpass Fagin. He fenced stolen property. He kept an assortment of street-wise boys in his den, and he trained them to pick pockets, spy, and recruit other boys. Little knowing or understanding the life of crime to which he would be introduced, Oliver Twist fell in with Fagin's gang of thieves. First Fagin left Oliver locked up, alone and with nothing to do for days. Then Fagin let him see how his young companions—the Artful Dodger, Charlie Bates, and the rest—"manufactured" silk handkerchiefs. How Oliver laughed to see Fagin posing as a prosperous citizen and the boys deftly relieving him of handkerchief, watch, and wallet! Then to his horror Oliver discovered the trick was not a game; Fagin planned to train him to be a thief.

But Fagin could not succeed with Oliver as he had with so many other boys and girls. Oliver, young and unhappy as he was, could not be seduced. He knew it was wrong to steal. "He is different from other boys," Fagin explained to Monks, a man who wanted Oliver corrupted and hopefully hanged or deported. Fagin could find nothing in Oliver's character to work on. Oliver's discretion and his horror of wickedness kept him from the evil man's ways. Oliver was encased in an impenetrable armor of childhood and childlike innocence.

Discretion will also keep us from *the wicked man's words*, "from the man that speaketh froward things" (Proverbs 2:12). The word translated "froward" means "perverse." The Hebrew word occurs nine times in Proverbs (2:12,14; 6:14; 8:13; 10:31-32; 16:28,30; 21:8). The only other place the word occurs in the Old Testament is Deuteronomy 32:20, where in his great song Moses described the perverseness of the children of Israel in the wilderness.

Many people speak perverse words today. What is worse, a

humanistic establishment and a sensation-loving media give many of them approval and credibility.

The tragic career of Absalom, David's handsome and charming son, received a tremendous boost when Ahithophel agreed with the young man's grievances and spoke perverse words. Absalom had nursed his private resentments until he saw his chance to subvert the loyalty of David's subjects. Having grievances of his own, Ahithophel threw in his lot with Absalom and gave a new and grave impetus to the rebellion.

Ahithophel was diabolically clever (2 Samuel 16:23). Upon learning that Ahithophel had openly espoused Absalom's cause, David prayed that God would turn Ahithophel's clever counsel to confusion (2 Samuel 15:31). Then David commissioned his friend Hushai to go to Jerusalem as a secret agent to try to confound Ahithophel's counsel (2 Samuel 15:32-37).

Absalom was rebellious, but he did not stoop to the abominable and public acts of wickedness described in the Bible until he fell under Ahithophel's spell. Ahithophel counseled Absalom to commit adultery publicly on the roof of the royal palace with ten of David's concubines (2 Samuel 15:16; 16:20-23). Ahithophel urged an immediate campaign designed to kill David (2 Samuel 17:1-4). Ahithophel's counsel was clever but wicked. If Absalom had possessed true wisdom, he would never have listened to the advice. And by listening to David's secret agent, Absalom showed that he lacked understanding too. Worst of all, he listened to his own corrupt heart, which taught him to rebel against David, the Lord's anointed.

Discretion will protect us from *the wicked man's walk* too. Wicked people "leave the paths of uprightness, to walk in the ways of darkness" (Proverbs 2:13). That verse describes what Ahithophel did. Once he walked with David, in friendship and fellowship, to the house of God (Psalm 55:12-14). He turned against David after the seduction of Bathsheba and the murder of her husband. Ahithophel never forgave David. Ahithophel was Bathsheba's grandfather (2 Samuel 23:34; 11:3) and he saw in Absalom's rebellion a golden opportunity to wreak his private revenge. We see how cunningly he worked when he counseled Absalom to defile David's concubines (to slake his rage against David for what he had done to Bathsheba) and encouraged the speedy assassination of David (to glut his anger at Uriah's murder). Ahithophel should have left vengeance in God's hands. Instead he left "the paths of uprightness, to walk in the ways of darkness" and ended up committing suicide (2 Samuel 17:23). He plunged at last into eternal darkness and earned for himself the opprobrium of being David's Judas.

Discretion will protect us from *the wicked man's wickedness.* Wicked men "rejoice to do evil, and delight in the frowardness of the wicked" (Proverbs 2:14).

It was a dark day for King Ahab when he married Jezebel (1 Kings 16:31). She was the daughter of Ethbaal, king of the Zidonians and former priest of Astarte, the vile nature goddess of Canaan. Ahab soon fell under the spell of his wicked wife and did whatever she told him to do.

Jezebel planned and executed the murder of Naboth. Naboth, who lived in Jezreel near Ahab's palace, owned a vineyard adjacent to the king's. He displeased Ahab by refusing to sell it to him. Naboth was on strong legal ground because his property belonged to his family and heirs as much as to himself.

Although Ahab was inclined to respect the strength of Naboth's legal position, Jezebel was contemptuous. Finding the king sulking in disappointment, she promptly took matters into her own murderous hands. The niceties of the law did not deter her. She told her husband, "Arise, and eat bread, and let thine heart be merry: I will give thee the vineyard of Naboth" (1 Kings 21:7). She arranged for Naboth's murder and as soon as the deed was accomplished, she told Ahab the coast was clear for him to take possession of the coveted property.

When he heard that Naboth had suddenly and conveniently died, Ahab did not bother to inquire into the circumstances of the death. He immediately looked over his new property and found delight in the fruit of his wife's wickedness. Thus he became an accomplice to her crime. He did not have long to rejoice in what he considered to be his good fortune, however, for even as he was surveying the vineyard, Elijah met him and pronounced his death sentence (1 Kings 21:17-22).

Proverbs 2:15 continues the description of wicked people: "Whose ways are crooked, and they froward in their paths." What a crooked man Ahab was! If we want to find out how crooked something is, all we need to do is place it alongside something straight. So we see Elijah and Ahab standing alongside each other—the man whose life was as straight as a plumbline and the man who was as crooked as a corkscrew.

The two confronted one another in Naboth's vineyard. There in his rich robes stood Ahab, rubbing his hands over his new acquisition. A shadow fell across his path. He spun around and saw the rugged prophet, a camelhair garment wrapped around his awesome righteousness. The last time Ahab had seen the fearless prophet was on mount Carmel. Ahab's guilty conscience smote him. "Hast thou found me, O mine enemy?" he said (1 Kings 21:20). Elijah delivered his message of doom and strode away. Ahab never saw him again. After the prophecy of Ahab's death the Holy Spirit added, "There was none like unto Ahab, which did sell himself to work wickedness in the sight of the Lord, whom Jezebel his wife stirred up" (1 Kings 21:25). Having lived a crooked life, Ahab died a violent death (1 Kings 22:30-38).

(2) From the Vile Woman (2:16-22)

(a) She Is Flattering (2:16)

The vile woman is as dangerous and deadly as the villainous man. Happy is the man who escapes her clutches. Wisdom is designed "to deliver thee from the strange woman, even from the stranger which flattereth with her words" (Proverbs 2:16). Flattery is insincere praise—praise that has an ulterior motive. The "strange woman" is an apostate, such as the priestesses of the notoriously immoral Canaanite cults. In these false religions the priestesses of the groves were prostitutes and worship culminated in sexual encounters. The "stranger" is literally a foreigner. In the present context the word points to a woman who is so far removed from her childhood training that she is virtually a foreigner.

The classic Biblical example of the flatterer is Delilah. She cared little for Samson, but she knew that he was susceptible to her physical charms. As far as she was concerned, he was a cash proposition. The Philistine lords promised her a fortune if she would extract from him the secret of his power. "Entice him," they said, "and see wherein his great strength lieth, and by what means we may prevail against him, that we may bind him to afflict him: and we will give thee every one of us eleven hundred pieces of silver" (Judges 16:5).

Delilah accepted their challenge. "And Delilah said to Samson, Tell me, I pray thee, wherein thy great strength lieth, and wherewith thou mightest be bound to afflict thee" (Judges 16:6). We can read between the lines. In effect she was saying: "Samson, you are so strong. And you are such a hero. Tell me about the time you demolished the gates of Gaza. You must be the strongest man in the world, the strongest man who ever lived. Have you always been this strong, Samson? Did you know that the five lords of the Philistines have a price on your head? They are all afraid of you. They have posted a fifty-five hundred silver shekel reward to any man who can take you prisoner. I heard about it in the market this morning. I just laughed. Capture you? What makes you so strong, Samson? Do you know what they want to do to you? They want to bind you and then blind you. Isn't that silly? As if anyone could bind you! They want to afflict you, but it's you who will afflict them. How do you do it, Samson? What makes you so strong? I suppose you must lift weights and work out every day. Or is it what you eat?"

And so with flattery and honeyed words she wheedled the secret out of him. Before the week was out she had the secret and the Philistines had him.

(b) She Is Forgetful (2:17)

The vile woman "forsaketh the guide of her youth, and forgetteth the covenant of her God." Some unfortunate women are born and bred to a life of sin. Sin is all they have ever known. The heart of God weeps over such women. But the woman described in this proverb knew better. She was a sinner by choice.

She was raised in a believer's home. The "guide of her youth" perhaps was a godly father or a spiritual mother. The "covenant of her God" was probably the Abrahamic covenant, which was temporarily modified by the Mosaic and Palestinian covenants. If she was a Hebrew, she knew that God's law was emphatic in its statements against all kinds of immorality. Death was the penalty for most forms of sexual misbehavior. But she did not care. She abandoned goodness. No more dangerous person exists than a woman who has abandoned all morality and decency.

(c) She Is Fatal (2:18-22)

i. The Need to Recognize Her (2:18-19)

The wise man warns that *death lurks where she lives:* "For her house inclineth unto death, and her paths unto the dead" (Proverbs 2:18). The prostitute is a wholesale purveyor of disease. Treachery and violence are frequent guests in her home. Foolish is the man who goes there. Death lurks inside and never far away is the pimp. A foul creature who lives off the earnings of each girl he has in his power, the pimp can often be as dangerous as a snake.

While I was in the British army I was stationed in several countries where prostitution was legal. All areas where sex was for sale were posted as out of bounds by the army. These areas were known as "red light districts" because in former times women of the streets advertised their services by putting red lights in the windows of their "houses of ill repute." Now we associate a red light with danger. God hangs the danger signal over the house of the harlot.

The wise man also warns that *doom lurks where she lives:* "None that go unto her return again, neither take they hold of the paths of life" (Proverbs 2:19). A preacher friend of mine explained the principle underlying this proverb by telling the story of a girl who kept herself pure while living in an impure environment at college. A single woman who had long since lost her virginity mocked the girl for being so old-fashioned. "Any time I want, I can be like you," the virgin replied. "But never again can you be like me. I'll be able to present myself to my husband pure. You will present yourself to yours soiled."

The man who traffics with a harlot loses something he can never regain. Something irreversible happens in the transaction. Something irreplaceable is lost. The man who has sexual relations with a profligate woman is forever soiled in body, memory, and conscience. His conscience awakens and will never be quieted until it is seared, or until it is silenced by the precious blood of Christ. A man who slakes his sexual thirst by joining his body to that of a streetwalker is as foolish as one who drinks water drawn from a sewer. Often he loses his bodily purity along with his moral purity. Moreover he irrevocably guarantees himself a date with judgment, either in this life or the next. God solemnly warns that all immorality earns His personal wrath (Hebrews 13:4).

ii. The Need to Repudiate Her (2:20-22)

a. The Path of the Wise Man (2:20-21)

The path of the wise man is *marked by purity:* "That thou mayest walk in the way of good men, and keep the paths of the righteous" (Proverbs 2:20). The path that leads to the harlot's house is deliberately contrasted with the path chosen by good men. The bad woman and the good man are placed opposite each other. The bad woman knows how to take advantage of fallen human nature—she knows how to allure. The good man's way through life may look drab by comparison, but he is not deceived by outward appearances. He is not fooled by the cheap philosophy that says, "It's only natural. It's fun! Everybody does it."

The way of the good man leads to honor and reward. The path taken by Lord Shaftesbury, one of England's great reformers, led to honor. One of his biographers said, "Like his Master, he went about going good." His great heart of compassion reached out to those who worked incredibly long hours under outrageous conditions for starvation wages in Britain's factories and mines. His heart went out to people who were incarcerated in barbarous prisons and asylums and were treated worse than animals. He was concerned about farm laborers who toiled endlessly and were little better than serfs. He looked with pity on the plight of the waifs and strays on the city streets. The record of his achievements fills a volume of some eight hundred pages.

Lord Shaftesbury's funeral was a national event. Groups carrying banners honoring the great parliamentarian lined the route of the procession. People came from the many segments of society that had benefited from his reforms of social ills. Lord Shaftesbury had revolutionized the industrial world. The duke of Argyll voted him an accolade in the House of Lords and affirmed that the social reforms of the past century could be attributed not to any political party, but to the tireless efforts of one man—Shaftesbury. "Walk in the way of good men," counsels the proverb. It leads to reward.

The path of the wise man is also *marked by protection:* "The upright shall dwell in the land, and the perfect shall remain in it" (Proverbs 2:21).

The nation of Israel received promises of protection. Israel is the only nation on earth with which God has made a treaty. God's original, basic, and unconditional treaty with Abraham was comprehensive. The Abrahamic covenant concerned a land and a Lord and contained clauses dealing with sovereignty and salvation. This original covenant, while irrevocable, was conditioned by the terms of both the Mosaic and Palestinian covenants. Eventually it was replaced by the new covenant.

The Palestinian covenant detailed the terms under which the Hebrew people would be allowed to occupy the promised land—a land that God repeatedly calls "my land" in the Old Testament. God promised peace and prosperity in the land as long as the people remained true to Him. If they walked in His ways and enthroned His love and His law in their hearts, they would be invincible and nations from the ends of the earth would court the favor of the Israelites and be instructed by them in the knowledge of God. Contrarily, God promised that apostasy, impiety, idolatry, immorality, and injustice would result in drought, disease, disaster, defeat, and deportation.

The Old Testament prophets preached the same truth that Proverbs 2:21 declares. They warned, but in vain! The Assyrians came and deported the northern tribes. A small remnant of godly Israelites escaped when they saw the disaster coming. They took refuge in Judah, but then the Babylonians came and deported the remaining two tribes.

Men like Ezekiel and Daniel and his friends did not escape the general deportation, but God had a higher good in mind for them. Daniel became the prime minister of Babylon. His three friends were promoted to high office. Ezekiel earned deathless fame as the author of one of the greatest and most far-reaching prophetic books of the Bible.

Proverbs 2:21 therefore has to be seen in the light of the larger context. The principle this proverb embodies was seen at work in the lives of the godly Israelites. Even though they suffered the common fate of their nation, God turned their exile into blessing. They enjoyed the benefits of their foreign homeland and knew the blessing of God upon them there. Thus although God suspended the substance of the proverb because of Israel's apostasy, the spirit of the proverb remained operative.

b. The Path of the Wicked Man (2:22)

"But the wicked shall be cut off from the earth, and the transgressors shall be rooted out of it." There was no refuge for the wicked man, even in the promised land. His plight was still worse when the time of deportation came.

The point this proverb makes is not so much that wicked people die, for good people die too. Nor is it that wicked people often die terrible deaths, for many good people have died under terrible circumstances. The point of this proverb goes much deeper. It refers less to the fact or form of the wicked man's death and more to its fitness. This proverb takes us behind the scenes where we see the Grim Reaper standing in the shadows. Scythe in hand, he is ready to cut the wicked man down. The reaper waits with pick and shovel to root someone up.

The proverb suggests a picture of a blighted tree cut down, rooted up, and carried away to a place where it can do no more harm. The tree is cut down first. Next the far-flung root system is dug up. It is much easier to cut down a tree than it is to get rid of all the roots. Likewise when evil men die, their evil influence remains. Muhammad, Hitler, and Lenin died many years ago, but no one has fully uprooted the movements they left behind.

The proverb is illustrated in the history of Israel. For centuries the Hebrews found themselves caught up in idolatry and its evils. Foul priests, false prophets, and foolish kings supported the root system of idolatry. The tree grew, flourished, and poisoned generation after generation. Then God cut the nation down. The savage Assyrian and Babylonian invasions resulted in countless deaths. Evil men who had supported religious apostasy were destroyed by the thousands. The rooting-out process, however, took longer. The Babylonian captivity ran through the lifetimes of two generations. There in Babylon—the ancestral home and heartland of idolatry—the scourge was burned out of the Hebrew soul. When the Jews finally returned home, they were completely cured of their idolatry. It had been rooted out.

CHAPTER 5

Proverbs 3:1-22

III. Wisdom's Path (3:1–5:23)
   A. It Is a Pleasant Path (3:1-22)
      1. The Law Is Endeared to Us (3:1-4)
         a. An Admonition (3:1)
         b. An Assurance (3:2)
         c. An Appeal (3:3)
         d. An Announcement (3:4)
      2. The Law Is Enthroned by Us (3:5-12)
         a. The Question of Our Trust (3:5-6)
            (1) Our Priorities Are Dictated (3:5)
            (2) Our Paths Are Directed (3:6)
         b. The Question of Our Treasure (3:7-10)
            (1) A Plea (3:7)
            (2) A Pledge (3:8-10)
               (a) The Way to Health (3:8)
               (b) The Way to Wealth (3:9-10)
                   i. Tithing Is Required by God (3:9)
                   ii. Tithing Is Rewarded by God (3:10)
         c. The Question of Our Trials (3:11-12)
            (1) What the Lord's Chastening Provokes (3:11)
            (2) What the Lord's Chastening Proves (3:12)
      3. The Law Is Enriched for Us (3:13-22)
         a. Happiness Guaranteed (3:13-15)
            (1) A Word of Assurance (3:13)
            (2) A Word of Assessment (3:14-15)
               (a) Wisdom's Wealth Is Beyond All Count (3:14-15a)
               (b) Wisdom's Wealth Is Beyond All Compare (3:15b)

    b. Health Guaranteed (3:16-17)
       (1) A Word about the Tenure of Life (3:16a)
       (2) A Word about the Tenor of Life (3:16b-17)
          (a) A Prosperous Life (3:16b)
          (b) A Pleasant Life (3:17a)
          (c) A Peaceful Life (3:17b)
    c. Heaven Guaranteed (3:18-22)
       (1) The Lost Tree (3:18)
          (a) Laying Hold of It (3:18a)
          (b) Living Happily by It (3:18b)
       (2) The Lord's Truth (3:19-20)
          (a) Wisdom and the Foundation of the
              Universe (3:19)
          (b) Wisdom and the Functioning of the
              Universe (3:20)
       (3) The Last Test (3:21-22)
          (a) Essential Truth Hedged Firmly (3:21a)
          (b) Essential Truth Held Fast (3:21b-22)
             i. The Divine Plea (3:21b)
             ii. The Divine Pledge (3:22)

We have looked at Wisdom's *plea* and Wisdom's *protection*. Now let us look at wisdom's *path*.

III. WISDOM'S PATH (3:1–5:23)

A. It Is a Pleasant Path (3:1-22)

1. The Law Is Endeared to Us (3:1-4)

This new segment of Proverbs begins with *an admonition:* "My son, forget not my law; but let thine heart keep my commandments" (3:1). The admonition brings the head and the heart together. It is not enough to have God's Word in our heads. We must be like the psalmist who declared that he had hidden God's Word in his heart (Psalm 119:11). The danger of simply storing God's Word in our heads is that our treacherous memories will fail to call it to mind when it is most needed. But if we hide God's Word in our hearts, it will remain there and it will control our response to the vicissitudes of life.

It was not easy for an Old Testament Jew to forget God's Word. He was required by law to write Bible texts on the doorposts of his house. When he went out, the texts on his doorposts called after him: "Where are you going? With whom will you be? What business are you transacting? Be mindful of your conduct. Guard your conversation. Watch out for your character. Listen to your conscience. God never sleeps." When he returned home, the texts on his doorposts cross-examined him: "Where have you been? What have you been doing? Examine yourself. You cannot get away from God."

We may remind ourselves of Bible verses we have memorized, but even so, God's Word can be pushed from our minds in the rush and bustle of life. Peer pressure, the demands of business, the hot lure of temptation, and other distractions can join forces to crowd God's Word out of our minds. But when God's Word is in our hearts, it will always hold center stage.

Most of Daniel's contemporaries in exile conveniently forgot God's law regarding eating ceremonially unclean food. We can hear their excuses as they told themselves: "We are virtual prisoners. We are exiles. It is good policy to bow to the king's will. It's not as though we are breaking a moral law." Daniel scorned such sophistry. He "purposed in his heart that he would not defile himself" by eating the king's meat (Daniel 1:8). His contemporaries vanished into the anonymity of history, but Daniel became one of the most famous men of all time.

Proverbs continues with *an assurance:* "For length of days, and long life, and peace, shall they add to thee" (3:2). The "first commandment with promise" (Ephesians 6:2) is the fifth commandment. It says, "Honour thy father and thy mother: that thy days may be long upon the land which the Lord thy God giveth thee" (Exodus 20:12). This promise was confirmed to Solomon at Gibeon on the condition that he would walk in God's ways.

The ten commandments—the Decalogue—can be divided into two sets of five. The first five, enjoining duty to God, are characterized by the expression "the Lord thy God." The remaining five, enjoining duty to man, are characterized by the expression "thou shalt not." All the commandments in the Decalogue contain a negative except the fifth commandment. Children are not told what *not* to do but what they *are* to do. So much parental correction errs in emphasizing the negative rather than the positive.

The fifth commandment is linked with the commandments

enjoining duty to God because parents are a child's first authority figures. A child's parents stand in the place of God to the child until he reaches the age of understanding and responsibility. Parental responsibility therefore should be held in awe by both parent and child. The promise of long life appended to this commandment states a general rule, not an absolute certainty. Many children die young, but happy are they for they are transplanted to a better world. Obviously not all those who have made it a lifelong practice to honor their parents live to a ripe old age. There are other factors in the equation of life. We can be sure that the Judge of all the earth, who is too wise to make any mistakes, takes this promise under the fifth commandment fully into account when weighing the issues of time and eternity for each life.

The world says, "The good die young." That statement is not necessarily true, but the fact that the saying exists indicates an observably high mortality rate among good young people. Still, all things being equal, people who honor their parents grow up to honor the law and those in authority. Moreover they are disposed to honor God and respond positively to divine truth when it is revealed. Thus they avoid many of life's snares, pitfalls, temptations, and dangers. They have a much greater likelihood of long life than those who grow up being disrespectful of parents, disdainful of authority, and ignorant of life's stern rules. For instance, those who are ignorant of God's demand for purity may expose themselves to disgusting and deadly diseases. On the pragmatic and negative level, those who do not smoke, drink, take drugs, or engage in promiscuous sex are far more likely to live longer than those who do. Even insurance companies make allowances for factors such as these.

Proverbs 3:3 adds *an appeal:* "Let not mercy and truth forsake thee: bind them about thy neck; write them upon the table of thine heart." It was the habit of devout Jews to wear phylacteries—small cases of parchment or black sealskin. These were worn on the arm or bound by a band to the forehead (Matthew 23:5). The phylactery worn on the forehead contained four pockets and in each pocket was placed a copy of a passage of Scripture. The passages commonly used were Exodus 13:1-10,11-16; Deuteronomy 6:4-9; 11:13-21. The Scripture portions chosen give some Biblical sanction to the custom, but the use of phylacteries arose from a wooden literalism that degenerated into an empty formalism.

The phylacteries of the Pharisees brought down the wrath of the incarnate Christ. Running all over town with texts plastered on one's forehead could not make one holy. That was not what Moses meant! "Lay up these my words in your heart," Moses said (Deuteronomy 11:18). "Write them upon the table of thine heart," echoes the proverb.

Better than wearing phylacteries is memorizing Bible verses. It is easy enough to get God's Word into our heads. Memorizing, simply a matter of rote and repetition, is the way we learn multiplication and the tables of weights and measures. To get God's Word into our heads only involves a learning process, but to get God's Word into our hearts—a much more difficult task indeed—involves a love process. God always goes after the heart. When the *mind* is engaged in an issue the motive is "I ought to"; when the *will* is engaged in an issue the motive is "I have to"; but when the *heart* is engaged in an issue the motive is "I want to." We must engage our hearts in the issue of our relationship to God's Word. Then we will not only hear it; we will also heed it.

In Proverbs 3:4 there is *an announcement* of the results of hiding God's Word in our hearts: "So shalt thou find favour and good understanding in the sight of God and man." When the Lord Jesus was twelve years of age His understanding astounded the doctors of the law, and after that incident in Jerusalem He "increased in wisdom and stature, and in favour with God and man" (Luke 2:52).

When Moses built the tabernacle, one of the most important furnishings was the ark. It was a chest made of acacia wood overlaid with gold (symbolic of the humanity and deity of Christ). Its lid was the mercyseat, sprinkled with blood and overshadowed with the golden wings of the cherubim. God Himself sat enthroned there in the holy of holies.

All the details of the ark and mercyseat spoke, in type and shadow, of Christ. Jesus was God's sacred ark. Within the ark of the covenant resided the unbroken copy of the law of God, and within the heart of Jesus, God's law found its resting place, unbroken and loved. No wonder He grew in favor with God and man. He was the living incarnation of the symbolic ark.

2. The Law Is Enthroned by Us (3:5-12)

a. The Question of Our Trust (3:5-6)

The book of Proverbs takes the Mosaic law and breaks it up into its glowing primeval colors, as a prism divides a ray of light. The 613 commandments in the law covered all aspects of life, including the simply prosaic and pragmatic matters of fact. In Proverbs those commandments are transformed into poetry, flashing and scintillating with color. The wise man wanted us to see in a spectrum of color what happens when we enthrone God's Law in our hearts.

First *our priorities are dictated:* "Trust in the Lord with all thine heart; and lean not unto thine own understanding" (Proverbs 3:5). *Trust* is the key word. Our God is utterly dependable. His character makes it impossible for Him to lie. His wisdom is so great He can never make a mistake. Our God can be trusted. He has high and holy purposes and no ulterior motives. His love is so limitless He can never be unkind. Yet perfect love is always balanced by absolute holiness. As Preston Moore, a preacher friend of mine, says, "He will never let us go, never let us down, and never let us off."

So we can trust Him. We must trust Him. We must trust Him with all our heart. Anything less is an insult. A divided heart and a double mind are almost as bad as no trust at all. However, God is patient; He will begin a relationship with us when we have only a flawed faith, but He demands complete commitment. He expects us to trust Him even in the darkest times, and He expects our trust to grow.

Poor old Job is the classic example of trust. He lost everything. Once he had been rich; now he was poor. Once he had been blessed with a lovely family of attractive boys and girls; now he was utterly bereaved. Once he had enjoyed good health; now he was afflicted by a horribly disfiguring and incurable disease. Once his wife had stood by him; now she advised him to curse God and die. Once he had been highly honored; now he was viewed with suspicion. Once his integrity had been unquestioned; now even his friends accused him of secret sin. Once he had walked in communion with God; now he appealed passionately to a silent Heaven.

Job must have listened with growing dismay to the accusations of his friend Eliphaz, who opened what was to be a prolonged and heated debate. Job had no explanation to offer for the dreadful disasters that had overtaken and overwhelmed him, but he knew God. He said, "Though he slay me, yet will I trust in him" (Job 13:15).

"Lean not unto thine own understanding," adds Proverbs 3:5. But even Job faltered here. He spoiled his magnificent, magnanimous vow of total trust by adding, "But I will maintain mine own ways before him" (Job 13:15). Job's statement has been paraphrased, "Though He slay me, I will wait for Him; and before Him my doings defend." Indeed most of the book of Job is the record of men defending their own doings. Read Job's last speech in chapters 29–31 and count the number of times Job used the personal pronouns "I," "me," and "my" in defending his doings; he talked about himself and his integrity no less than 195 times. He knew better, however, after God finished talking to him (Job 42:6).

Moses is a more perfect example of trust. One trial of his faith took place after the Israelites packed their bags and marched out of their grim Goshen ghetto, the scene of their sufferings and fears. Pharaoh halted between two opinions, torn between fear and fury. His son was dead, his realm laid waste, and now he was losing the services of a vast army of slaves. Then he made up his mind. He mobilized and marched. Soon the rear guard of the Hebrews saw the chariots of Egypt maneuvering behind them and poising to strike. The Hebrews were terror-stricken. Behind them was the crack corps of the Egyptian army; before them was the deep water of the Red Sea. The Israelites were trapped.

"Trust in the Lord with all thine heart; and lean not unto thine own understanding," says the proverb. Moses did just that. "Stand still, and see the salvation of the Lord," Moses told the people (Exodus 14:13). He did not know how they would escape, but he knew God.

"Speak unto the children of Israel, that they go forward," God said (Exodus 14:15). The situation seemed hopeless. If the Israelites stood still, the Egyptian soldiers would get them. If the Israelites went forward, the Red Sea would drown them. Moses looked at that vast host of anxious moms and dads, terrified boys and girls. It made less sense to go forward than it did to stand still. Yet Moses, who possessed a giant intellect and had been trained in the best universities of Egypt, decided not to lean on his own understanding. He did what he was told. He trusted God in the dark, so to speak. He moved to the front of the people, beckoned them to follow, and rod in hand marched boldly toward the sea. Moses had his priorities right. He chose to trust God at all costs.

When we enthrone God's law in our hearts, our priorities are dictated and *our paths are directed:* "In all thy ways acknowledge him, and he shall direct thy paths" (Proverbs 3:6). Little did I know years ago when I lived in northern British Columbia that God was about to change my life forever. One day I received a letter from a man I did not know. He was inviting me to come to a city I had never seen, to accept a position I didn't know existed, on terms I could not evaluate. The letter from the director of the Moody Correspondence School invited me to come to Chicago to become the school's business manager. To accept the invitation seemed impossible at the time. I was married, my wife Jean and I had three small children, and we had recently built a new house. We had started a church, were planning to erect a building, and were discipling a number of new converts. Jean did not want to go since her family all lived in British Columbia and her mother was an invalid. Chicago had a terrible reputation. We were happy and involved where we were. *Why go to Chicago?* we wondered. *Who will take care of our fledgling church?*

I knew the Bible says, "In all thy ways acknowledge him, and he shall direct thy paths," so I decided to seek counsel. But the man I wanted to consult was Stephen Olford and he lived in London, halfway across the world. Then God gave me an opportunity to go to London—via Chicago! The Lord was beginning to direct our paths. When I went to Chicago I was tremendously impressed with the Moody Bible Institute. I was even more impressed with Harold Shaw, the man who had invited me. He was one of the most spiritual men I have ever known and he became one of my dearest friends. I went to England and Stephen counseled me to go to Chicago. I was convinced that we should go.

When I returned home, I found that Jean was equally convinced that we should not go! She liked beautiful British Columbia. Her roots were there. She was afraid of Chicago. I told the Lord that I was convinced but Jean wasn't. I knew Jean was loyal and spiritual, so in consideration of her desires I decided to wait. Our lives were in the Lord's hands. Stephen Olford's wise counsel about leaving a fledgling church—"If the work is of God, it will stand; if it's not, it would be best for it to collapse"—applied equally well to my situation at home. If the invitation from Moody was of God, it would stand the test of a further delay. If the invitation was not of God, it would be best if it fell through. Jean had every right to her point of view and indeed many of her arguments made sense. I said to the Lord, "If You want us to go to Chicago, You tell Jean. You've convinced me; now convince her." I decided to say no more.

Several months passed. I continued working as an accountant for a lumber company owned by dear friends of mine. Our infant church flourished. Harold Shaw was willing to wait. No more was said. Most mornings I had coffee break with friends or with those we were cultivating for Christ, but one morning I decided to have coffee break with my wife instead. As I opened the door of our house, Jean met me in the hall. She was all smiles. "Guess what!" she said. "We're going to Chicago." Within six months we obtained our United States papers (in itself almost a miracle) and were on our way. A tremendous young couple took our place in the church and the man also took over my job. The work continued to grow.

The Lord continued to direct our path. Moody Bible Institute proved to be God's glorious will for our lives. Within six months I was put in charge of all course development. This assignment honed my writing gifts. I was given my own program on the Moody radio network. I began writing articles for *Moody Monthly* and teaching in the Moody Evening School. Moody Press published my first eight books. Churches opened their doors to me and I developed preaching skills. I was surrounded by talented people, had access to a fine library, and met countless people from all segments of the Lord's vast work in this world. The Lord had directed our path. My wife found fulfillment too in some wonderful new friendships and in becoming a partner in my work as an author. She proofreads all my manuscripts, corrects my mistakes, and steers me away from a mere masculine point of view!

The Lord is eminently worthy of our trust. When we enthrone God's law in our hearts, our paths are directed at moments of crisis and in ordinary decisions.

b. The Question of Our Treasure (3:7-10)

(1) A Plea (3:7)

When we trust Him, the Lord takes care of all aspects of our lives. This segment of Proverbs provides some sound advice concerning the material aspects, but first there is a plea, "Be not wise in thine own eyes: fear the Lord, and depart from evil" (Proverbs 3:7). A Biblical example of a man who was wise in his own eyes and therefore fell into evil is Jeroboam.

Ahijah the Shilonite secretly anointed Jeroboam to be king over ten of Israel's tribes. Jeroboam had been one of Solomon's bright young men, but when Solomon heard of the anointing, he tried to kill Jeroboam. So Jeroboam fled to Egypt where Pharaoh Shishak groomed him for a promised throne, doubtless hoping to cement future good relations with a possible king.

As soon as Jeroboam assumed leadership of the ten-tribe fledgling kingdom of Israel, he leaned on his own understanding. He decided to sever all relations with Jerusalem, for Jerusalem was the site of the glorious temple built by Solomon, and Jerusalem was in Judah where Rehoboam reigned. For centuries the tribes had gone to Jerusalem to celebrate annual feasts but Jeroboam decided that he could not afford to have his subjects engage in such sentimental and spiritual pilgrimages. He feared that the lure of Jerusalem, the temple, and the established religion might undermine his own authority. He thought, *The next thing will be that the tribes will want to make peace with the throne of David.*

Jeroboam made a radical decision. He would start his own religion. After telling his people that the annual pilgrimages were "too much," he made two golden calves. He set one up in Bethel, a place of sacred memories, and one in Dan, the remotest and most northern of the tribes. "Behold thy gods, O Israel," he said, "which brought thee up out of the land of Egypt" (1 Kings 12:28; cf. Exodus 32:1-8). This was outright apostasy. Jeroboam also built a temple of sorts on "the high places," which were notoriously linked with the licentious worship of the Canaanites (1 Kings 12:31). He changed the religious calendar and consecrated priests from the lower classes of society. He created a man-made religion with man-made gods, man-made sanctuaries, man-made priests, and man-made feasts. God immediately sent a prophet to denounce the new religion, but Jeroboam ignored the prophet. "And this thing became sin unto the house of Jeroboam, even to cut it off, and to destroy it from off the face of the earth" (1 Kings 13:34). Jeroboam should have heeded Solomon's proverb.

(2) A Pledge (3:8-10)

(a) The Way to Health (3:8)

If we learn to "fear the Lord, and depart from evil, It shall be health to thy navel, and marrow to thy bones." *Synecdoche,* a figure of speech in which the part is substituted for the whole, is used here. It is used in everyday life as commonly as it is in the Bible. For instance some years ago I was in a hospital waiting to be X-rayed for a suspected ulcer. While I was in the crowded waiting room, I heard the radiologist ask the nurse what kind of workload he had that morning. She replied, "Five stomachs and three gallbladders." I almost laughed aloud at her reply. The eight of us who were waiting were greatly flattered! The nurse was simply using synecdoche.

While working in the correspondence school of Moody Bible Institute, I always disliked the days when R. J. Little was out of town. He was Moody's wise and knowledgeable radio pastor and when he was away I had to take his calls. And what calls they were! People throughout the listening area would phone in and try to stump him with hard questions. I used to wonder how he ever had time to do his other work. The prize question put to me was posed by a woman: "I'm reading Proverbs. What does this here verse mean? 'It shall be health to thy navel.'" Quite unprepared for her question, I replied, "Ma'am, you have the wrong kind of doctor." (Today some surgical procedures are actually done through the navel!)

That evasive answer will not suffice here. There is a lesson we can learn from this verse. A navel bears a threefold testimony to life. It bears mute but potent testimony to *a past life*. It is a constant reminder of a life that we once lived *within the womb*. It was a dark, imprisoned kind of life—restrictive, narrow, circumscribed, and regulated by forces beyond our control. It was a life of utter dependence—without liberty, without scope. However, it was the only life we knew. We were quite unaware that there was much more for us to experience. Life in the womb illustrates the life of the natural man who does not know God.

A navel also bears mute testimony to *a present life*. Birth transformed our whole experience. We were ushered into life in an altogether new world. At first we were practically unaware that something quite revolutionary had happened. One thing we did know, even though we could not have verbalized it: we were no longer content with our old way of life. We wanted milk. Soon we would want meat. After birth we had a new appetite. Then we began to discover and explore the dimensions of our new way of life. Its potential proved to be enormous. Seeing vast new horizons, we grew and developed.

However, before any of the advantages of this new life could be realized, the umbilical cord had to be cut. It attached us to an old way of life for which we were no longer suited. It is incongruous and ridiculous, therefore, even to think of someone not wanting to make a clean break with the past life once he is born into the new. Once the cord was cut, we were free! All that remains to remind us of the break is a navel. The sudden, short, and sharp break was accomplished for us once and for all by the great physician's hand.

Furthermore a navel bears mute testimony to *a promised life:* As there was a life within the womb, so there is a life *beyond the tomb*. We are poised on the edge of eternity. While we were in the womb we could not begin to imagine what awaited us in this world after birth; likewise, while we are on earth we cannot begin to imagine what awaits us in the world to come after death. Beyond the womb lay a new life, a wondrous world, a new dimension, a potential we could not comprehend. It would have been pointless for someone to describe life in the world when we were in the womb because we did not have the capacity to understand. We had no frame of reference. The world was there, but we remained ignorant of it.

Beyond the tomb lies eternal life, a wondrous world, a new dimension, an incomprehensible potential. We read what has been revealed in the Word of God about Heaven and home, about "joy unspeakable and full of glory" (1 Peter 1:8), but we do not have the capacity to understand it. Paul did not even have the capacity to pass his knowledge on after experiencing the joy for himself. But it's there waiting for us when this phase of life is over. The navel bears silent witness that more, very much more, is ahead. One day the great physician will cut the cord that binds us to this present life. We will open our eyes in a world of wonder, beauty, and glory beyond anything we can now begin to imagine. As a newborn babe gazes on a face—so shall we. That will be our first taste of Heaven and home.

(b) The Way to Wealth (3:9-10)

The twin proverbs in verse 9-10 underline the importance of honoring God with our substance. Tithing is *required by God:* "Honour the Lord with thy substance, and with the firstfruits of all thine increase" (3:9). Abraham set an example early in the spiritual history of God's redeemed people. He had just returned from a tremendous triumph: he had overthrown the all-victorious kings of the East in a lightning attack and had rescued Lot. Now the king of Sodom was coming to offer his congratulations and to try to negotiate a deal. He was going to suggest that Abraham trade souls for spoils.

Abraham, however, was protected from accepting this nefarious trade-off by his prior meeting with Melchizedek—the king of Salem—a king-priest and one of the great Old Testament types of Christ. At that meeting Melchizedek placed the emblems of Christ's passion before Abraham. Abraham received a fresh revelation of God as "the most high God, possessor of heaven and earth"—a revelation calculated to stand him in good stead during his meeting with the king of Sodom. Overwhelmed by the superiority of Melchizedek and all the spiritual realities before him, Abraham responded the only way he could—he gave "tithes of all" to Melchizedek. The king of Sodom wanted to use money as a trap. The king of Salem, however, showed Abraham a more excellent way. Melchizedek taught Abraham to use money for a tithe. Thus the king of Sodom's snare was set in vain (Genesis 14:17-23).

God demands first place in everything. The first fruits belong to Him. The tithe belongs to Him. A set and predetermined percentage of all our income belongs to Him. We can never expect Him to bless our financial affairs if we leave Him to the last or leave Him out altogether.

Tithing is not only required by God; it is also *rewarded by God:* "So shall thy barns be filled with plenty, and thy presses shall burst with new wine" (Proverbs 3:10). My father taught me the grace of giving. He had a small automobile business in southern Wales. He bought, fixed, and sold cars. One of a handful of craftsmen in our hometown who were licensed to work on Rolls Royce cars, he was a generous and consistent giver to the Lord's work all his life. There wasn't a missionary or Christian worker in our part of the country who did not know that my father was always good for a free engine tuneup, a meal at our table, and a tank full of gas.

His small business survived the hard times of the great depression but when World War II broke out, my father faced ruin. Food was heavily rationed and gasoline even more so. The government commandeered all private cars; only individuals doing essential war business could own one. No new cars were made for the civilian market; factories were turned over to production of tanks and guns. My father laid off his employees and paced the floor of his workshop as he prayed. He faced certain bankruptcy.

Just then he heard a footstep behind him. He turned and recognized the manager of a large Austin car dealership that owned a fleet of several hundred rental cars. The man said, "How are you, Leonard?"

"I'm not sure, Mr. Brooks," responded my father. "I think I'm going to have to close." Little did my father realize that God had sent him an angel unawares.

The Austin dealer was in a similar squeeze. He could not buy any new cars either. Another problem was how to keep his fleet of rental cars running throughout the war years. He had no mechanics; all the men he had were in the armed services.

"Len," he said, "I'd like to bring you an engine to be rebored and rebuilt. We can get the parts. What do you say?" The next day an engine along with pistons, rings, valves, and spark plugs was delivered to my father's workshop. Two days later my father returned the rebored and rebuilt engine to the dealer.

A week passed. Then once more Mr. Brooks appeared in my father's empty shop. "Well, Leonard," he said, "I have some good news for you. That engine we sent to you was a test. We took it back to our shop, stripped it down, and checked it out. We know there is a big black market for new parts, so we wanted to check not only the quality of your workmanship but also your honesty. You passed the test. Every new part we gave you was in place. Now, how many engines can you rebore and rebuild in a week? We will keep you supplied until the war ends." Mr. Brooks was as good as his word, and God was as good as His Word. God honored my father for honoring Him.

c. The Question of Our Trials (3:11-12)

Tithing does not guarantee that we will never face testings and trials. We note *what the Lord's chastening provokes:* "My son, despise not the chastening of the Lord; neither be weary of his correction" (Proverbs 3:11). The truth embodied in this proverb was first propounded by Eliphaz in his initial debate with Job. While rubbing salt into Job's wounds, Eliphaz said, "Behold, happy is the man whom God correcteth: therefore despise not thou the chastening of the Almighty" (Job 5:17). It is doubtful that Job appreciated the truism. He was not convinced that the Lord was chastening him, and in point of fact He wasn't. (Incidentally, Proverbs 3:11-12 is quoted in the New Testament in Hebrews 12:5-6.)

David quickly recognized the chastening hand of the Lord in the disasters that overtook him at the time of Absalom's rebellion. During David's headlong flight from Jerusalem he was met by Shimei, whom Alexander Whyte picturesquely called "a reptile of the royal house of Saul."[1] Shimei disliked David. As David came to Bahurim on the east side of Olivet in Benjamite territory, this evil man threw stones and curses at David. David's nephew Abishai offered to take off Shimei's head, but David declined saying: "Let him curse; for the Lord hath bidden him. It may be that the Lord will look on mine affliction, and that the Lord will requite me good for his cursing this day" (2 Samuel 16:11-12).

In time Shimei came crawling to David, apologizing in abject fear (2 Samuel 19:18-20). Again Abishai demanded that the evil man be executed, and again he was rebuffed. David was far too conscious of his own sin and chastisement to want to wreak vengeance on another sinner. He did not despise the chastening of the Lord. He bowed to it and learned from it.

We note too *what the Lord's chastening proves:* "For whom the Lord loveth he correcteth; even as a father the son in whom he delighteth" (Proverbs 3:12). The Lord chastened Jehoshaphat, one of Judah's good kings. He was a contemporary of Ahab and Ahaziah, two of Israel's worst kings. Somehow these evil men created a fatal fascination for Jehoshaphat. He joined with Ahaziah to emulate the great Solomon and build a mercantile marine. Second Chronicles 20:35-36 tells us of Jehoshaphat's serious mistake: "And after this did Jehoshaphat king of Judah join himself with Ahaziah king of Israel, who did very wickedly: And he joined himself with him to make ships to go to Tarshish: and they made the ships in Ezion-gaber."

The words "after this" are significant. Jehoshaphat planned this enterprise after he had been on the throne of Judah for some twenty years, after God marvelously delivered Judah from the combined armies of Moab and Ammon (2 Chronicles 20:20-30), after God miraculously delivered Jehoshaphat from the Syrian troops who had him in their grasp (18:20-32), and after a prophet rebuked Jehoshaphat for helping Ahab (19:2-3). There was no excuse for this new compromise with the ungodly.

King Jehoshaphat needed to be chastened. "Then Eliezer the son of Dodavah of Mareshah prophesied against Jehoshaphat, saying, Because thou hast joined thyself with Ahaziah, the Lord hath broken thy works. And the ships were broken, that they were not able to go to Tarshish" (2 Chronicles 20:37).

3. The Law Is Enriched for Us (3:13-22)

a. Happiness Guaranteed (3:13-15)

This passage begins with *a word of assurance:* "Happy is the man that findeth wisdom, and the man that getteth understanding" (Proverbs 3:13). The word translated "happy" here can also be translated "Oh, the blessednesses." This verse is the first of eight beatitudes in Proverbs (3:13; 8:32,34; 14:21; 16:20; 20:7; 28:14; 29:18).

The Bible consistently teaches that there can be no happiness without holiness. Such a notion is quite contrary to the thoughts of unsaved people. Disregarding Scripture, they spend their lives in a quest for happiness. They look for it everywhere. They think they can find it in pleasure, in money, in marriage, or in religion. However, all these approaches are flawed if God and His Word are left out. We are living in a world that lies in the lap of the evil one and he certainly has no interest in making anyone happy; there is no way he could even if he wanted to.

We remember what Screwtape told Wormwood about pleasure. In *Screwtape Letters* by C. S. Lewis, Screwtape is a senior devil to whom Wormwood, a junior devil, reports. Wormwood's assignment is to conduct a particular human being safely through the mazes of life down to Hell. Unfortunately for Wormwood, he fails. His client becomes a Christian. Screwtape writes Wormwood a series of letters not only to castigate and threaten him but also to instruct him in ways of preventing his client from becoming a mature Christian.

One letter deals with the question of pleasure. Screwtape acknowledges that pleasure is a useful tool for evil spirits to use in ensnaring human beings. But it is a problematic tool at best because pleasure is really God's invention. "All we can do," Screwtape tells his understudy, "is distort pleasure." The formula of Hell, Screw-tape says, is simple—offer an ever-increasing craving for an ever-decreasing pleasure. The supreme goal is to get a man's soul—for nothing.

"Happy is the man that findeth wisdom." That is Heaven's recipe for happiness. And since Jesus "is made unto us wisdom" (1 Corinthians 1:30), happy are those who find Him.

After this word of assurance comes *a word of assessment:* "The merchandise of [Wisdom] is better than the merchandise of silver, and the gain thereof than fine gold. She is more precious than rubies: and all the things thou canst desire are not to be compared unto her" (Proverbs 3:14-15). Wisdom, in other words, is far better than wealth.

In the gripping story *King Solomon's Mines* Sir Henry Rider Hag-gard's fictional heroes—Allan Quatermain, Captain Good, and Sir Henry Curtis—found their way across the desert's burning sands and over the mountain's icy steeps to a forgotten land. There they helped lead a successful revolt against the country's tyrant king. As a reward a repulsive old witch named Gagool led them to the secret treasure chamber of Solomon.

Gagool led them into the heart of a mountain, opened a secret door, and pointed them into the chamber. There they gloated over wealth beyond the dreams of avarice. They found enough gold to launch a fleet of battleships and enough diamonds to pay off a national debt. They dug their fingers into the gold and gloated over their astounding good fortune.

Meanwhile Gagool crept away and slammed the secret door shut. The three adventurers were locked in a pitch-black vault, buried in the bowels of the earth. The hours crept by. The three sat there in growing desperation and despair. They had no light, no food, no water, and no hope of rescue. The witch's parting words still rang around the chamber: "Eat of them," she cackled. "Drink of them. ...Take your fill, white lords!"

They were surrounded by an immense fortune in diamonds and gold. "Yet," Quatermain recounted, "we would gladly have bartered them all for the faintest chance of escape. Soon doubtless we should be glad to exchange them for a bit of food or a cup of water, and, after that, even for the speedy close to our sufferings. Truly," he concluded, "wealth, which men spend all their lives in acquiring, is a valueless thing at the last."

Wealth cannot buy us health or happiness. It cannot buy us one more moment of time. It cannot buy love or avert hate. It cannot buy peace with God. Wisdom can. What is the use of wealth without wisdom? A man who inherits a fortune but who has no sense soon finds that his money grows wings and flies away. A wise man can acquire wealth, but he avoids the pitfalls that imperil those who make haste to be rich. A wise man knows what to do with wealth when he obtains it. He knows that happiness is not to be found in silver, gold, and rubies. Someone said, "There are two kinds of people: those who love things and use people, and those who love people and use things." Jesus said, "A man's life consisteth not in the abundance of the things which he possesseth" (Luke 12:15).

b. Health Guaranteed (3:16-17)

(1) A Word about the Tenure of Life (3:16a)

"Length of days is in [Wisdom's] right hand." Again our gaze is directed toward Wisdom, depicted as a beautiful and desirable woman. We are invited to look at her right hand in which she holds up the prescription for long life. Those who embrace Wisdom are far more likely to find length of days than those who hold hands with Folly.

Long life was included in God's Old Testament promise to His people. The provision was appropriate in a covenant emphasizing earthly conditions. Thus Abraham lived to the ripe old age of 175 and Isaac lived to be 180, but Jacob only lived until he was 147. The passions of Jacob's youth left their mark on him; thus he said to pharaoh: "The days of the years of my pilgrimage are an hundred and thirty years: few and evil have the days of the years of my life been, and [I] have not attained unto the days of the years of the life of my fathers in the days of their pilgrimage" (Genesis 47:9).

The Jews divided old age into three stages. From sixty to seventy was what they called "the commencement of old age"; from seventy to eighty was "hoary-headed age"; a man over eighty was said to be "well-stricken in years." Abraham, for example, was "well stricken in age" when he sent his servant to seek a bride for Isaac (Genesis 24:1).

When Abraham died, the Holy Spirit made this comment: "Then Abraham gave up the ghost, and died in a good old age, an old man, and full of years" (Genesis 25:8). Old age itself is not necessarily a blessing. What is desirable is "a good old age." A man can live a long time and end his days shriveled and warped, drained and empty, bereft of all that makes life worth living. What is desirable is to arrive at old age "full." Only wisdom can guarantee such a triumphant climax to life.

(2) A Word about the Tenor of Life (3:16b-17)

Wisdom calls us to *a prosperous life:* "In her left hand riches and honour" (3:16b); *a pleasant life:* "Her ways are ways of pleasantness" (3:17a); and *a peaceful life:* "All her paths are peace" (3:17b). Wisdom offers a quality of life that all of us would like to have.

Sin is the great spoiler. Sin bankrupts us; it turns loveliness into ugliness and harmony into discord. Before the serpent appeared in Eden, Adam and Eve enjoyed a rich, full, happy life. The world lay at their feet. The living God was their constant companion. Stretching before them was a future filled with "joy unspeakable and full of glory." All Eve needed to do when Satan made his insidious suggestion was to call upon wisdom. Eve simply had to say, "Thus saith the Lord." That response would have left the devil facing the drawn and naked Sword of the Spirit—the one weapon he feared. Foolishly Eve threw away her sole means of protection and relied on her own understanding.

Wisdom calls us back to the Word of God and offers—as much as is possible in a world saturated with evil and under a curse—the tenor of life that once reigned in Eden. Wisdom offers length of days, riches and honor, pleasantness and peace.

c. Heaven Guaranteed (3:18-22)

(1) The Lost Tree (3:18)

Proverbs 3:18 offers a further word of assurance: Wisdom "is a tree of life to them that lay hold upon her; and happy is every one that retaineth her."

There were two notable trees in that primeval paradise of Eden: the tree of the knowledge of good and evil (which was the tree violated by Adam and Eve) and the tree of life. No sooner did the gates of the garden clang shut behind the guilty pair than God posted cherubim and a flaming sword at the entrance to keep safe the way to the tree of life. God was acting as much in grace as in government. If Adam and Eve had eaten of the tree of life in their fallen condition, they would have lived forever in their sins. They would have become like the fallen angels—deathless, sinful, and beyond all redemption. Earth would have become an outpost of Hell. Imagine what it would be like if every evil person who ever lived was still alive, getting older and older in wickedness. The cherubim were posted to prevent such a consequence.

The tree of life was eventually transplanted to a fairer world than this, presumably at the time of the flood. That tree cannot now be violated by sinful men. When John was on his tour of the celestial city, he saw the tree there. It had flourished wondrously in its new environment. He wrote:

> And he shewed me a pure river of water of life, clear as crystal, proceeding out of the throne of God and of the Lamb. In the midst of the street of it, and on either side of the river, was there the tree of life, which bare twelve manner of fruits, and yielded her fruit every month: and the leaves of the tree were for the healing of the nations (Revelation 22:1-2).

Wisdom now offers us the virtues of the tree of life. If we are wise, we can have eternal life. Wisdom points the way. On page after page of the Word of God, wisdom points unwaveringly and unerringly to Christ. "For God so loved the world, that he gave his only begotten Son, that whosoever believeth in him should not perish, but have everlasting life" (John 3:16).

(2) The Lord's Truth (3:19-20)

We can trust the guarantee of the One who created the universe. Proverbs 3:19 states the truth about creation. This proverb points to *wisdom and the foundation of the universe:* "The Lord by wisdom hath founded the earth; by understanding hath he established the heavens."

According to popular belief the universe just happened. Having exploded out of nowhere and out of nothing, it proceeded to evolve. Through a "fortuitous concourse of atoms," people say, life emerged quite by accident and it too proceeded to evolve. Learned doctors, armed with scholastic degrees and lauded by secular humanists, assure us their assumptions are true. But out of nothing comes nothing.

When I was in high school I had a math teacher who was a great believer in mental arithmetic. He would pose problems we had to solve in our heads. He would call out the steps in the problem one by one, giving us time between steps to resolve each new factor mentally. He would say, for instance, "Begin with 150. Multiply by 3. Add 75. Divide by 5. Add 195." Then he would pounce on someone and ask for the answer. After a few warm-up exercises he would give us more difficult problems. Sometimes he would add complications and occasionally he would trick us. Those of us who had not given up on a complex problem might have arrived at an answer such as 73,192. Having watched our struggles sardonically, he would say, "Multiply your answer by zero." All of a sudden the problem seemed simple—the answer was zero! No matter how large the number, if you multiply it by nothing, you have nothing. Ten billion nothings are still nothing. So much for the scientist who assures us that the universe came from nowhere out of nothing.

Wisdom takes us back to the beginning and introduces us not to nothing, or even something, but to Someone—to God. "There!" says Wisdom. "Out of His wisdom all was created. He knows all the laws of physics, all the laws of chemistry and biology. He knows the mathematics of the universe, all its detailed and complex equations. He knows all the laws known to science and all the laws not known to science. He knows them not because He has investigated them, but because He has invented them." The more complex the universe is discovered to be, the greater tribute it is to His genius, wisdom, and omniscience. Folly says, "It just happened." Wisdom motivates us to bow at the feet of the Almighty.

Sir Isaac Newton reportedly had a friend who was an atheist. The friend did not believe in God, but preferred to take the position that the universe just happened. One day the friend was visiting his learned colleague and Newton showed him a model of the solar system. The sun, the planets, and the moons were all in place. The sizes of the spheres were in proportion and the planets and the satellites revolved around the sun at their relative speeds. The friend admired the model. "It's intriguing," he said. "Who made it?" "Nobody," said Newton. "It just happened!"

Having stated the role of wisdom in creation, Proverbs then links *wisdom and the functioning of the universe:* "By his knowledge the depths are broken up, and the clouds drop down the dew" (3:20). This proverb points to two extremes: the violence of an erupting volcano and the gentleness of the dew. Both involve enormous forces. Geologists are only now beginning to explore the forces that result in earthquakes and volcanic activity, both of which produce awesome phenomena.

John Milne invented the seismograph in 1880. R. D. Oldham discovered the earth's core in 1906. Andrija Mohorovicic discovered the boundary between the earth's crust and mantle in 1909. In 1912 Alfred Wegener proposed the theory of continental drift, a hypothesis confirmed by NASA in 1987. Bit by bit, building on each other's discoveries, scientists have put together a picture of the earth's crust and core. In the center is a massive core of iron and nickel. Actually the center comprises two cores: the inner core is solid and extends more than 3,000 miles below the earth's surface; the outer core is liquid and extends from about 1,800 miles down. Next comes the mantle, which makes up the bulk of the earth's mass. The mantle extends upward to approximately 55 miles below the higher mountains and to within approximately 3 miles below some parts of the oceans. Part of the upper mantle is somewhat fluid. Then comes the earth's crust, which is loaded with useful chemicals and is more accessible to investigation and measurement. The crust is composed of light rocks in the continents that are 15 to 55 miles thick, and heavy rocks in the ocean crusts that are 3 to 5 miles thick.

From time to time the massive forces at work beneath the earth's crust make their presence felt in the form of earthquakes, landslides, and erupting volcanoes. Earthquakes are notoriously destructive. The magnitude of an earthquake is described by means of the Richter scale (developed by Charles Richter in 1935) which measures the heights of waves recorded on a seismograph. The higher the number, the more destructive the earthquake. On October 17, 1989, for instance, the second most powerful earthquake in United States history devastated the San Francisco area. It measured 7.1 on the Richter scale. Shocks were felt as far away as Sacramento and Los Angeles. Highways buckled, houses and bridges collapsed. Fires broke out. Major damage occurred over a seven-county area.

About six hundred volcanoes are currently active around the world, and they can be equally destructive. A volcanic explosion tosses rock and clouds of hot gas and dust high in the air. Molten lava pours down the mountain. The heat can melt icecaps and glaciers, precipitating further destruction. Volcanoes do not occur in a random way. Most are located at plate boundaries, as the famous Ring of Fire around the Pacific ocean illustrates.

The occurrence of an earthquake or the eruption of a volcano bears testimony to Proverbs 3:20: "By his knowledge the depths are broken up." These terrible events are a sobering reminder of God's awesome power and knowledge, and of our feebleness and limitations. We cannot accurately predict a natural disaster. God, on the other hand, knows all the factors that control earthquakes and volcanoes.

The forces that cause dew to form are equally amazing. Suspended in the air above the earth are some 54,460 billion tons of water. The hydraulics involved in lifting such a mass of moisture from the sea to the sky stagger our imaginations. That water is transported and dropped in the form of precipitation. Some of that water is suspended invisibly in what we call humidity. On a still, cloudless night the humidity in the atmosphere silently condenses, forming dew. The drops drench grateful plants and cling like gleaming gems to spiders' webs. This mighty miracle is performed so softly that we do not see it being done. Such is God's wisdom, power, and gentleness. Wisdom sees God's hand in the dew as well as in the earthquake. Everything bears testimony to the Creator. Blind indeed are those who think these miracles just happen.

(3) The Last Test (3:21-22)

(a) Essential Truth Hedged Firmly (3:21a)

Since God by wisdom founded the earth, the test of men on earth is whether they will bow to that wisdom. Solomon taught those who desire to pass the test that truth is to be hedged firmly: "My son, let not them depart from thine eyes." The word "them" perhaps refers to the wisdom, understanding, and knowledge previously mentioned in connection with God's creation and control of the physical universe. The admonition is to hold "them" in view at all times. Our thoughts should be hedged in, so to speak, by these guardians.

We sometimes use the words *knowledge, understanding,* and *wisdom* as though they were synonyms. A simple illustration will help us discern the differences. A little girl watches her mother doing the ironing. The child is intrigued by the process as the iron eats up the wrinkles and creases in each garment. The phone rings. As the mother goes to answer it, she says to her little girl, "Don't touch that iron; it's hot." The child now has *knowledge*—the iron is hot. As soon as her mother disappears, the little girl decides to try her own hand at ironing. Unfortunately she touches the iron in the wrong place and is burned. She now has *understanding*—the iron is hot. The next day the mother continues with the ironing and again she is summoned by the phone. Again she issues a warning: "Don't touch the iron; it's hot." Again the temptation to do some ironing comes over the little girl. She puts out her hand to grab the iron. Then she remembers her burned finger and leaves the iron alone. She now has *wisdom*—the iron is hot.

Most of us learn life's stern lessons by bitter experience. Some of us never learn them at all and keep on getting our fingers burned. God wants to impart His wisdom to us. We must keep that wisdom well in view if we wish to profit from it.

(b) Essential Truth Held Fast (3:21b-22)

Truth is also to be held fast: "Keep sound wisdom and discretion: So shall they be life unto thy soul, and grace to thy neck." The word translated "keep" means "to watch or guard." Adam was told to "keep" the garden. He failed to keep sound wisdom and discretion and lost his paradise.

"Soul" and "neck" refer to our inner life and our outer life. In the Bible the neck is used symbolically to indicate whether we are rebelling against or responding to the circumstances of our outer life. To be stiff-necked is to be rebellious and stubborn (Deuteronomy 31:27; Psalm 75:5). Where the neck speaks of slavery (Deuteronomy 28:48) the imagery derives from the practice of putting a yoke on the neck of a beast of burden. Conversely when pharaoh wanted to honor Joseph, he put a gold chain around Joseph's neck (Genesis 41:42). When the father of the prodigal saw his wayward son coming home, he ran to meet him "and fell on his neck, and kissed him" (Luke 15:20).

God makes sound wisdom and discretion available to us so that we may have stability in our inner and outer lives. It is our responsibility to see that we don't forsake wisdom for some forbidden fruit.

CHAPTER 6

Proverbs 3:23–4:19

B. It Is a Peaceful Path (3:23-26)
  1. In Times of Stability (3:23-24)
    a. Protection for Our Steps (3:23)
    b. Protection in Our Sleep (3:24)
  2. In Times of Stress (3:25-26)
    a. When Fear Stalks (3:25)
    b. Where Faith Stands (3:26)
C. It Is a Positive Path (3:27-35)
  1. Its Inherent Goodness (3:27-34)
    a. As Stated Negatively (3:27-31)
      (1) Don't Delay (3:27-28)
        (a) Procrastinating Evilly (3:27)
        (b) Pretending Evilly (3:28)
      (2) Don't Devise (3:29)
      (3) Don't Dispute (3:30)
      (4) Don't Desire (3:31)
    b. As Stated Affirmatively (3:32-34)
      (1) The Lord's Secret (3:32)
      (2) The Lord's Smile (3:33)
      (3) The Lord's Scorn (3:34)
  2. Its Inherited Glory (3:35)
D. It Is a Parental Path (4:1-9)
  1. Solomon's Wisdom Relayed to His Posterity (4:1-2)
    a. A Call to Hear (4:1)
    b. A Call to Heed (4:2)
  2. Solomon's Wisdom Received from His Parents (4:3-9)
    a. What Solomon Acknowledged (4:3-4)
      (1) His Tribute (4:3)
      (2) His Teacher (4:4)

Proverbs continues to set before us wisdom's path. We must choose whether or not to follow the path. Wisdom points the way for us but does not drag us resisting, struggling, arguing, and protesting along that path.

B. It Is a Peaceful Path (3:23-26)

1. In Times of Stability (3:23-24)

When all goes well we are most prone to relax our watchfulness and most susceptible to a fall. Thus we are promised *protection for our steps:* "Then shalt thou walk in thy way safely, and thy foot shall not stumble" (Proverbs 3:23). A stumble can be serious at any stage and in any walk of life.

The apostle Paul experienced this protection during his voyage to Rome. The voyage went well until the ship arrived at the fair havens on the island of Crete. The harbor was not commodious, so the majority on board voted to try to make it to Phenice at the western end of the island, a much more favorable place to anchor for the winter. Paul knew better. He was a seasoned sailor and had already been shipwrecked three times. He did not stumble in his speaking. "Sirs," he said, "I perceive that this voyage will be with hurt and much damage, not only of the lading and ship, but also of our lives" (Acts 27:10). He spoke out of natural wisdom based on his experiences at sea, his knowledge of the Mediterranean, and his understanding of the meteorology of the region at that time of the year.

The centurion in charge of the prisoners had to make the decision. He consulted with the master (*kubernētēs*, "steersman") and the owner of the ship (*nauklēros*, "shipowner"), both of whom advised the centurion to take a chance. He took their advice because, after all, they were the experts. The centurion stumbled. He should have listened to God's man.

At first all went well, but then a storm came and the ship was caught in the grip of the tempest. Efforts to bring the ship under control failed. The tempest obscured the navigation aids and all hope was gone. Shipwreck was a certainty.

Again Paul, sure he was right, spoke up—this time with wisdom from above:

> Sirs, ye should have hearkened unto me, and not have loosed from Crete….be of good cheer: for there shall be no loss of any man's life among you, but of the ship. For there stood by me this night the angel of God, whose I am, and whom I serve, Saying, Fear not, Paul; thou must be brought before Caesar: and, lo, God hath given thee all them that sail with thee (Acts 27:21-24).

Then Paul shared another word of natural wisdom. He advised everyone to eat something.

Later when Paul discovered that the sailors were preparing to abandon ship and leave the passengers and prisoners to their fate, he spoke up and advised the centurion to intervene. Throughout the whole story Paul stands forth as a man in touch with wisdom. God kept his foot from stumbling. He did not make a single mistake.

In times of stability we are promised *protection in our sleep:* "When thou liest down, thou shalt not be afraid: yea, thou shalt lie down, and thy sleep shall be sweet" (Proverbs 3:24). This promise stands in contrast to the terrible curse built into the Palestinian covenant; apostasy would bring down the curse on the heads of the Hebrew people.

> And it shall come to pass, that as the Lord rejoiced over you to do you good, and to multiply you; so the Lord will rejoice over you to destroy you, and to bring you to nought; and ye shall be plucked from off the land whither thou goest to possess it. And the Lord shall scatter thee among all people, from the one end of the earth even unto the other; and there thou shalt serve other gods, which neither thou nor thy fathers have known, even wood and stone. And among these nations shalt thou find no ease, neither shall the sole of thy foot have rest: but the Lord shall give thee there a trembling heart, and failing of eyes, and sorrow of mind: And thy life shall hang in doubt before thee; and thou shalt fear day and night, and shalt have none assurance of thy life: In the morning thou shalt say, Would God it were even! and at even thou shalt say, Would God it were morning! for the fear of thine heart wherewith thou shalt fear, and for the sight of thine eyes which thou shalt see. And the Lord shall bring thee into Egypt again with ships, by the way whereof I spake unto thee (Deuteronomy 28:63-68).

The path of wisdom is to give the Lord our love and loyalty. If we follow this path we will have peace; we will be able to sleep because we know that, come what may, all will be well. For example, Abner found peace when he switched to the path of wisdom. After the death of King Saul, his general (Abner) defied the Lord's anointed (David) by setting up one of Saul's sons (Ishbosheth) as a puppet king. A desultory civil war broke out. Abner's cause was hopeless from the start and finally he came to his senses and surrendered to David. The Holy Spirit's comment is succinct: "And David sent Abner away; and he went in peace" (2 Samuel 3:21).

We can picture Abner going home that night with the peace of David in his heart. Peace means that the war is over! He went to bed that night, put his head on his pillow, and, as the proverb says, his sleep was sweet. There is no greater boon this side of Heaven than to be able to go to bed at night with the peace of God garrisoning our hearts (Philippians 4:7). His peace is what guarantees a good night's rest.

2. In Times of Stress (3:25-26)

But what about those times when storm clouds gather and circumstances threaten us? Proverbs 3:25 addresses the time *when fear stalks:* "Be not afraid of sudden fear, neither of the desolation of the wicked, when it cometh."

Elisha retained his peace when faced with threatening situations. In his day Israel was constantly under threat of invasion by Syria. Fortunately for the king of Israel, on several occasions Elisha was able to warn him of ambushes set to capture him. The frustrated Syrian king demanded that his counselors disclose who the spy was. One counselor astutely told the Syrian king that no spy was warning the enemy of his plans. Rather, Elisha the prophet was supernaturally enabled to discover the king's plots. "Elisha, the prophet that is in Israel, telleth the king of Israel the words that thou speakest in thy bedchamber" (2 Kings 6:12). "Go and spy where he is, that I may send and fetch him," said the king (6:13). We can assume that Elisha heard that too!

At that time Elisha was in Dothan, a town on a caravan route not far from Samaria, so the Syrian king sent soldiers to surround the town. Elisha was unperturbed, but his servant was greatly alarmed at the sight of the Syrian soldiers. He couldn't understand how Elisha could be so calm in the face of such imminent danger. "And Elisha prayed, and said, Lord, I pray thee, open his eyes, that he may see. And the Lord opened the eyes of the young man; and he saw: and, behold, the mountain was full of horses and chariots of fire round about Elisha" (2 Kings 6:17). What better security could one want?

We who love the Lord have the same security. Paul, whose life was full of hairbreadth escapes, told us that our life "is hid with Christ in God" (Colossians 3:3). No matter what happens, "we know that all things work together for good" (Romans 8:28). No foe can daunt us; no fear can haunt us. We're on the victory side. No harm can touch us without God's permission, and even then He draws a predetermined line, the book of Job assures us. So those who have responded to the highest wisdom and belong to the family of God need not be afraid, even when calamity comes.

We can have peace in times of stress because we know the place *where faith stands:* "For the Lord shall be thy confidence, and shall keep thy foot from being taken" (Proverbs 3:26). Faith takes its stand in the Lord. Thus we can put all the power of the enemy into proper perspective.

In the book of Revelation we see all the might of Satan massed and mobilized against the people of God. Satan appears unmarked as a great red dragon. He has at his command principalities and powers, the rulers of this world's darkness, and wicked spirits in high places, and he summons them to war. Demons surge up from the abyss. Fallen, godless men hail the beast as their sovereign lord. He is depicted as a monster possessing great ferocity and power. Countless millions of men march to his drumbeat. Terror and torture are his weapons. Such is the power of the enemy.

And what does God have to counter all this raw power? A Lamb! (Literally a little lamb in Revelation 5:6.) The Lamb has what the enemy does not have: omniscience and omnipotence. Wisdom points our faith to that all-victorious, nail-scarred Lamb. That is where faith stands.

C. It Is a Positive Path (3:27-35)

1. Its Inherent Goodness (3:27-34)

a. As Stated Negatively (3:27-31)

The series of proverbs now before us abound in good advice. The first word of wisdom here is *don't delay*. Proverbs 3:27 warns us against *procrastinating evilly:* "Withhold not good from them to whom it is due, when it is in the power of thine hand to do it." God takes note of such meanness and malice.

When the children of Israel at last approached the frontiers of the promised land, Moses tried to negotiate with the Edomites, the Moabites, and the nomadic Ammonites. All three nations could claim some kind of kinship to Israel. The Edomites were descended from Jacob's twin brother Esau, and the Moabites and Ammonites were descended from Abraham's nephew Lot. The response of Edom was to mobilize, threaten, and refuse free passage through their territory (Numbers 20:18-21). The response of Moab was far worse. Moab hired Balaam to come and curse the Hebrew people (Numbers 22:5-7). Evidently the Ammonites joined in this venture (Deuteronomy 23:3-4). The Moabites and Ammonites had it in their power to do good to Israel and not only refused to do so but also acted with malice. Moab and Ammon suffered terrible spiritual consequences. Moses, under inspiration of the Holy Spirit, decreed:

An Ammonite or Moabite shall not enter into the congregation of the Lord; even to their tenth generation shall they not enter into the congregation of the Lord for ever: Because they met you not with bread and water in the way, when ye came forth out of Egypt; and because they hired against thee Balaam the son of Beor of Pethor of Mesopotamia to curse thee....Thou shalt not seek their peace nor their prosperity all thy days for ever. Thou shalt not abhor an Edomite (Deuteronomy 23:3-7).

God cares about the smallest details of our lives. The man who owes you money and has the means to pay it back, yet keeps on putting you off is a fool, for God sees him and takes note of his behavior. Moral principles are rooted in God's laws, which are all fair and just. We cannot break them with impunity. God does not look kindly on people who procrastinate to the point of criminal inactivity.

We are also warned against *pretending evilly:* "Say not unto thy neighbour, Go, and come again, and to morrow I will give; when thou hast it by thee" (Proverbs 3:28). Such a miserly, miserable attitude incurs the displeasure of God. Some people take perverse delight in using the power money gives them to dominate other people. Anyone who has received such treatment knows the anxiety and bitterness it engenders.

Dorothy Sayers built one of her intriguing murder mysteries around just such a theme. Lord Peter Wimsey and his bride were to spend their honeymoon in a house that Lord Peter had purchased in the country. They arrived at night after the wedding and found that Mr. Noakes, who had sold Lord Peter the house for cash, had failed to make good on his promise to leave everything in good order. The house was in total darkness and securely locked. When the newlyweds did find a way to get in, they saw evidences of Mr. Noakes's occupancy everywhere, but he himself had vanished.

As the story unfolds we learn that Mr. Noakes was not as wealthy as other people imagined. Indeed he was deep in debt. Among his creditors was the gardener and odd-job man, Frank Crutchley. Crutchley, it seems, had been persuaded to put his life savings of forty pounds into one of Noakes's business ventures. When Crutchley needed the money for a venture of his own and demanded repayment, Noakes produced only promises, and the two exchanged hard words.

Then the missing Mr. Noakes was discovered lying in the basement. He was dead and one of the obvious suspects was Frank Crutchley. When the police superintendent interviewed him, he made no bones about his grudge against Noakes. "He promised to let me have [the forty pounds] when I came today," Crutchley told the policeman. The suspect was staggered to learn that when the police searched the body, they found a very large sum of money—the cash that Lord Peter had paid for the house. Evidently Noakes had had the money in his pocket all the while he was putting Crutchley off with promises. Noakes's meanness was the death of him in the end. *(Busman's Honeymoon)*

Solomon was indeed wise to write, "Say not unto thy neighbour, Go, and come again, and to morrow I will give; when thou hast it by thee."

His next piece of advice is *don't devise.* Proverbs 3:29 says, "Devise not evil against thy neighbour, seeing he dwelleth securely by thee."

Scheming the downfall of an unsuspecting neighbor is a nefarious business. This is what David did (2 Samuel 11–12). Once he cast his eyes on Bathsheba he couldn't wait to get his hands on her. Then, after their encounter, Bathsheba sent the alarming news that she was pregnant and her husband was away at the war. The Mosaic law called for the death penalty—for both her and David. David decided to cover his tracks. He ordered Uriah back from the front, treated him with flattering attention, and sent him home to spend the night with his wife. The reason of course is transparent.

However the scheme didn't work. Uriah's sense of loyalty to his comrades at the front was so strong that he refused to go home to be with his wife while they were roughing it in the trenches. David tried to inebriate Uriah to make the scheme work, but even a drunken Uriah was more honorable than a devising David.

David's last device was to write to Joab, commander-in-chief at the front. The letter outlined a plan to get Uriah killed in battle. Uriah was David's neighbor and one of David's most loyal soldiers. He dwelt securely in the knowledge that David was the Lord's anointed and a just man. Not for one moment did Uriah suspect what was going on. He headed back to the battlefront, confidently carrying David's letter to Joab. Few scenes in Scripture are more tragic.

David thought he had gotten away with his sins, but his wisdom had forsaken him. It was driven off by his lust and his fear that his sin would come home to roost. Before the episode was over, God saw to it that David's sin did indeed come home to roost.

Solomon's next word of advice is *don't dispute.* Proverbs 3:30 states, "Strive not with a man without cause, if he have done thee no harm." This verse warns against being quarrelsome.

Nabal was a quarrelsome man. The Holy Spirit described him as being churlish. Nabal belonged to a brighter age in David's history when David was still behaving himself wisely. At that time David was a fugitive from King Saul. Toward the end of David's fugitive years he and his band of outlaws, whom he later called his "mighty men," had an encounter with Nabal.

Nabal was a successful, wealthy farmer. David and his men were outlaws, but certainly not brigands. On the contrary they protected Nabal's shepherds. David must have had a considerable problem with his commissariat (he had at least six hundred men to provide for) so he sent some of his men to ask Nabal for a donation.

Nabal responded in a quarrelsome way. The fool (which is exactly what his name meant) actually tried to pick a fight with David. Nabal sneered: "Who is David? and who is the son of Jesse? there be many servants now a days that break away every man from his master. Shall I then take my bread, and my water, and my flesh that I have killed for my shearers, and give it unto men, whom I know not whence they be?" (1 Samuel 25:10-11) Nabal's own servants, who had been forced to live with his quarrelsome temper and tongue, summed him up: "He is such a son of Belial that a man cannot speak to him" (25:17). Added to Nabal's other charms was drunkenness.

When David's men returned with Nabal's insulting message, David prepared to teach the man a lesson. Had it not been for the intervention of Nabal's wife and David's willingness to listen to reason, Nabal's quarrelsomeness would have embroiled him in a fight that could have had only one end. No wonder the proverb warns us against being quarrelsome. Sooner or later a quarrelsome person invariably picks on someone well able to defend himself.

Solomon's next piece of advice is *don't desire:* "Envy thou not the oppressor, and choose none of his ways" (Proverbs 3:31). Often the oppressor seems to ride high, wide, and handsome. He swaggers through life. He always has his coterie of sycophants who toady to him. The proverb advises us to beware of seeing anything glamorous or desirable about the oppressor's lifestyle. The word translated "oppressor" means "the man of violence."

One of the greatest oppressors in history was the pharaoh who ground the Hebrew people beneath his heel. Moses, who grew up in the royal courts as the adopted son of this pharaoh's daughter, had every opportunity to enjoy the fruits of oppression. The finest education, treasures, and pleasures Egypt could offer were available to him, but none of these advantages tempted him. His birth mother had done her work too well during the early days of his life (Exodus 2:1-10). Consequently when he was grown, Moses turned his back on the ruling Egyptian elite who had done their best to initiate him into their fold. Moses was not interested in further oppression of the Hebrews. On the contrary he deliberately renounced all that his foster mother offered him and threw in his lot with the downtrodden nation of slaves. As a result Moses is highly honored to this day. As for the pharaoh of the oppression, scholars are still not unanimous as to his identity.

b. As Stated Affirmatively (3:32-34)

The good advice continues. We are introduced to *the Lord's secret:* "For the froward [those who turn aside] is abomination to the Lord: but his secret is with the righteous" (Proverbs 3:32). It is interesting to observe all the things labeled as "abomination" in this book: 6:16-19; 8:7; 11:1,20; 12:22; 15:8,9,26; 16:5; 17:15; 20:10,23; 21:27; and 28:9. The word "secret" here refers to "secret counsel," that which is sealed up from all except those to whom God reveals it.

It is a serious thing to turn aside, to be labeled an "abomination" by the living God. The froward deprive themselves of all but their own flawed thinking and their own inadequate resources. Other people may consider the froward to be very clever, but they will confess themselves to be arrant fools when the time comes to die.

Adoniram Judson's biography reads like a chapter out of the book of Acts. Yet when he was young he almost lost his soul on the quicksand of unbelief, thanks to the influence of an agnostic friend.

At Providence College Judson met a classmate named Jacob Eames, an avowed unbeliever who was brilliant, witty, and daringly outspoken. He fascinated Judson, who was flattered by the attention Eames paid to him. Spurred on by charismatic Eames, Judson abandoned the faith of his fathers, followed Eames along the slippery path of unbelief, and became an outspoken and aggressive unbeliever.

During a tour of the northern states, nineteen-year-old Judson stopped one night at a wayside inn. The landlord, full of apologies, explained that the only vacant room he had left was next to one in which a young man lay ill. The sick man, it was feared, might be dying. Judson didn't care and assured the landlord that death meant nothing to him.

The partition between the two rooms was thin. During the night the most terrible cries awakened Judson. The heart-rending sounds shook him, unbelieving though he was, but he tried to pull himself together. What would his companions say? What would Jacob Eames say if he knew of this weakness just because a fellow was dying next door? But it was no use. The awful sounds continued as the dying man screamed his way into eternity. He poured out the most frightful blasphemies and then the most pitiful wails. Judson hid his head beneath the blankets and stopped his ears. Finally all was quiet. The man next door had died.

Shattered, Judson rose with the dawn. He sought out the landlord and asked about the young man next door. "He's dead," the landlord said.

"Dead!" exclaimed Judson. "Who was he?"

"He was a student from Providence College," the landlord explained. "A very fine fellow. His name was Jacob Eames."

That night Judson learned the value of a soul. He learned what happens to a froward person who becomes an abomination to the Lord. He also learned the secret counsel of the Lord and dedicated his life to taking the gospel to a pagan land.

The next proverb introduces us to *the Lord's smile:* "The curse of the Lord is in the house of the wicked: but he blesseth the habitation of the just" (3:33).

Jacob and Esau were twins. They were raised in the same home and received the same spiritual education. They both grew up to establish dynasties.

Esau founded a house on infidelity, worldliness, and carnality. The people he fathered, the Edomites, became bitter enemies of God and His people. Herod the Great, who massacred the babes of Bethlehem, and who would have murdered the infant Christ if he could, was a descendant of Esau. So was Herod Antipas, who murdered John and mocked at Jesus. So was Herod Agrippa I, who murdered James and tried to murder Peter.

Jacob, on the other hand, founded a house on an ever-growing trust in God. Early in life he coveted the blessing of God. His sons became the founders of the twelve tribes of Israel. From his family came a long line of prophets, priests, and kings. Numerous illustrious names fill the honor roles of this family. Moses, the world's greatest lawgiver, was a member of this family, and Jesus, the incarnate Son of the living God, was a descendant of Jacob. In spite of all its faults and failures, the house that Jacob founded has known the blessing of God and will one day know it to the full.

At the end of the Old Testament God summed up the stories of Esau and Jacob: "Was not Esau Jacob's brother? saith the Lord: yet I loved Jacob, And I hated Esau" (Malachi 1:2-3).

Proverbs 3:34 advises us of *the Lord's scorn:* "Surely he scorneth the scorners: but he giveth grace unto the lowly." Atheists are great scorners until they meet the Lord, the great Scorner. The proverb reminds us of the French revolutionaries in the eighteenth century. They tore the cross from the cathedral of Notre Dame and promoted atheism, hatred, and violence. One of them said to a peasant,

"We are going to pull down all that reminds you of God." The peasant was not impressed. He replied, "Well, citizen, then pull down the stars."

Scorners evidence the very highest form of folly. They mock God but the day will come when God will mock them.

In contrast to His treatment of the scornful, He gives grace to the lowly. Often the lowly are the victims of the scornful—the butt of their sarcasm—but God identifies Himself with the lowly. When His Son, the Creator of all the suns and stars of space, stepped out of eternity into time, He chose to be born of a lowly peasant woman from a scorned town of despised Galilee. "Can there any good thing come out of Nazareth?" Nathanael scornfully replied when his friend Philip told him they had found the Messiah (John 1:46). The Lord did not come with pomp and circumstance, with a shout, with the voice of the archangel, and with the trump of God. He was born in a stable, with manure for carpeting, cobwebs for curtains, and bats to fly his honor guard. He was lowly, and He described Himself as such (Matthew 11:29). He knows how to give grace to the lowly.

2. Its Inherited Glory (3:35)

The path of wisdom is not only one of inherent goodness; it is also one of inherited glory: "The wise shall inherit glory: but shame shall be the promotion of fools" (Proverbs 3:35). The word translated "fool" here means "dense, stupid." In contrast to the shame that fools pile up, the wise fall heir to glory.

Think of the glory that the world gave to David Livingstone, the son of humble parents. He went to Africa to be a missionary—to evangelize what, in those days, was a savage continent. When he saw the horrors of the slave trade, he added another goal to his purpose: to emancipate the slaves. The stories he brought back from the missionfield awoke the conscience of England. When he penetrated deeper into Africa, he realized that someone needed to unravel the puzzle of the tangle of great rivers that drained the heart of the continent. Wanting to find the hidden sources of the Nile, he decided to add another goal: to explore.

This humble missionary was concerned only with the glory of God and the good of the benighted Africans. During his furloughs, however, he was lauded and lionized by his countrymen. When he disappeared, a major American newspaper funded Stanley's mission to find him.

When this lowly missionary, whose practical wisdom was renowned, died alone on his knees by his camp cot far from civilization, his heart was cut out and buried in the country he loved. His body was carried to the coast and sent home to England where he was given a state funeral and buried in Westminster Abbey. Perhaps the greatest of all tributes given in this world was bestowed by *Punch,* a magazine ordinarily devoted to humor:

> He needs no epitaph to guard his name,
> Which men shall prize while worthy work is known.
> He lived and died for God, be this his fame,
> LET MARBLE CRUMBLE, THIS IS LIVING STONE.

The words inscribed on the brass plate that marks his resting place in the Abbey would perhaps have pleased the missionary more: "Other sheep I have, which are not of this fold: them also I must bring" (John 10:16).

D. It Is a Parental Path (4:1-9)

1. Solomon's Wisdom Relayed to His Posterity (4:1-2)

The wise man began this section with an attempt to get the attention of the younger generation, a task that is not always easy. He wrote, "Hear, ye children, the instruction of a father, and attend to know understanding. For I give you good doctrine, forsake ye not my law." David used a similar form of address in the Psalm he wrote after escaping from Abimelech, king of Gath (Psalm 34:11).

When David became increasingly pessimistic about his chances of eluding Saul's unremitting campaign of persecution, he visited Nob, a bedroom community for the priests in the territory of Benjamin. The tabernacle was temporarily there. David talked Ahimelech the high priest into giving him the showbread and Goliath's sword. Then, foolishly enough, David sought political asylum in Gath. The people of Gath soon put two and two together. Here was a young Hebrew named David showing up in town with the sword of their champion Goliath, who had been slain by a lad called David. Suddenly David realized his predicament and extricated himself from it by pretending to be mad (1 Samuel 21).

Once safely hidden in a cave, David waited for his men to reassemble and composed Psalm 34 while he was waiting. The Psalm is an acrostic, specially designed to be committed to memory. The first part of the Psalm is a song in which David praised God for his deliverance. The second part is a sermon in which David instructed his men in some of the lessons he had learned.[1] He began the sermon in verse 11: "Come, ye children, hearken unto me: I will teach you the fear of the Lord."

Proverbs 4:1 employs the same appeal: "Hear, ye children, the instruction of a father." The proverb sounds like David. Possibly what follows is some of the instruction that Solomon received from his father, instruction he would like to pass on to his own son. But first Solomon had to get his son's attention. David had good material to work with, but Solomon was not as fortunate.

2. Solomon's Wisdom Received from His Parents (4:3-9)

a. What Solomon Acknowledged (4:3-4)

After calling for attention, Solomon first gave *his tribute:* "For I was my father's son, tender and only beloved in the sight of my mother" (Proverbs 4:3). The circumstances of Solomon's birth would certainly tend to make him especially precious to his parents. He was born after the tragedy resulting from David's sin with Bathsheba. As soon as Uriah was killed, David married Bathsheba to give some legitimacy to the child who was to be born, but the son born of their illicit union died shortly after birth. Yet God's judgment of David took into account his repentance. In grace He allowed David and Bathsheba to have other sons, one of whom was Solomon, the child destined to be the crown prince and heir to the throne.

David learned many lessons in his lifetime. His fugitive years were rich in experience and many of his great Psalms grew out of that period. The serious illness he suffered after his sin with Bathsheba (Psalm 32:3-4; 39:10; 41:8), the rebellion of Absalom, the other tragedies in his family, and the defection and subsequent suicide of Bathsheba's grandfather Ahithophel—once David's close friend and valued counselor—all taught him lessons and gave birth to more Psalms.

These lessons, David's love for the Lord, his trust in God, his desire to build a temple in Jerusalem, and his skill in war and statecraft formed a vast treasure from which David could draw to teach and train his son and heir. Bathsheba too, with her sad memories and grateful thanks, had much to contribute to her son's education. Solomon paid tribute to his parents, as many of us could pay tribute to ours.

After his tribute Solomon made mention of *his teacher:* "He taught me also, and said unto me, Let thine heart retain my words: keep my commandments, and live" (Proverbs 4:4). Solomon must have had an army of counselors. Like his illustrious descendant,

Jesus of Nazareth, Solomon probably astonished his instructors
with his questions and answers (Luke 2:46-47).

One of Solomon's instructors was Nathan, the wise, fearless, and
farsighted prophet who was prominent throughout David's reign
and in the early years of Solomon's reign. We can also be sure the
precocious prince dug deeply into the minds and memories of Joab
the general and Zadok and Abiathar the priests. We can picture
Solomon cross-questioning the clever Hushai—David's friend—
and drawing stories out of Benaiah and David's other mighty men.
Nathan particularly would have had long sessions with Solomon to
discuss the temple he was to build (2 Samuel 7; 1 Chronicles 17:1-15).

Solomon was grateful for all who had contributed to his sense of
history and his deep interest in people, nature, and religion. But he
remembered his father best: "He taught me also." More than
anything else, David taught his boy to understand the Scriptures
and appreciate diplomacy.

b. What Solomon Acclaimed (4:5-9)

The wise man wanted to review five topics with his own son. First,
Solomon wanted to say something about *the pursuit of wisdom:* "Get
wisdom, get understanding: forget it not; neither decline from the
words of my mouth" (Proverbs 4:5). But Rehoboam was not interested. We can picture him fidgeting and giving vague answers to
questions or staring out the schoolroom window, his thoughts far
away with his harebrained friends on a prankish enterprise. We can
imagine him asking irrelevant questions, hoping to get his father
sidetracked on a more interesting topic, or turning in ill-prepared
lessons. "Get wisdom! Get wisdom!" We can almost hear the edge in
Solomon's voice as Rehoboam's shallow mind sorely tested his
patience.

Second, Solomon wanted to say something about *the passion of
wisdom:* "Forsake her not, and she shall preserve thee: love her, and
she shall keep thee" (Proverbs 4:6). Solomon apparently was using
the marriage relationship here as an analogy.

When I was married, I received Jean Wilson in all her totality into
my life. True, when we exchanged vows I did not know all that I was
receiving! Marriage is the lifelong process of discovering all that was
involved in making that commitment to a new relationship. I
married a wise, loyal, and loving woman who has enriched my life.

Solomon was telling Rehoboam to take Wisdom as a man takes a
bride. "Love her," the wise man was saying. "Engage your passions
to Wisdom. Invite her into your life. Cultivate her strengths; court

her counsel. Listen to her; do what she suggests. You'll never be sorry. She'll never let you down."

Third, Solomon wanted to say something about *the priority of wisdom:* "Wisdom is the principal thing; therefore get wisdom; and with all thy getting get understanding" (Proverbs 4:7). How could Solomon get it through his son's thick head that nothing was more important in life than obtaining wisdom? Once he had wisdom he would have everything. Wisdom would guide and guard all his other choices and decisions.

Wisdom will decide what friends we make in life. It will determine our business choices. It will decide whom we marry and how we bring up our children. It will decide what we believe and how we behave.

"With all thy getting…" That phrase sums up the lifestyle of millions of people today. Life can degenerate into an endless round of getting. Such was the life of the rich fool. He was a competent businessman and an able farmer. He had had an outstanding year. He was sitting up in bed congratulating himself and making plans for business expansion and early retirement. His plans for the future included having a rip-roaring good time, but Jesus said he was a fool. The farmer had made every provision to get, but no provision to go. "God said unto him, Thou fool, this night thy soul shall be required of thee: then whose shall those things be, which thou hast provided?" (Luke 12:20) "With all thy getting get understanding," Solomon said.

Fourth, Solomon wanted to say something about *the promotion of wisdom:* "Exalt her, and she shall promote thee: she shall bring thee to honour, when thou dost embrace her" (Proverbs 4:8). We must put wisdom on a pedestal. We cannot think too highly of wisdom.

There are two kinds of wisdom: the wisdom of the Word and the wisdom of the world. "The wisdom of this world is foolishness with God," the Holy Spirit declares (1 Corinthians 3:19). Paul threw down the gauntlet: "Where is the wise? where is the scribe? where is the disputer of this world? hath not God made foolish the wisdom of this world?" He added, "The world by wisdom knew not God" (1 Corinthians 1:20-21).

Nowhere is the folly of this world's wisdom more evident than in people's religious beliefs. Nothing can be more foolish than idolatry: a man makes an image of stone or wood, calls it a god, and worships it.

The Mormons believe that a dissolute young man named Joseph Smith found some golden plates covered with Egyptian hieroglyphics. The angel Moroni gave him some magic glasses by means of which he was able to translate the plates into simulated

KingJames English. The result? *The Book of Mormon*. Millions believe it to be a divine revelation equal to the Word of God.

Christian Scientists believe that pain is not real—a theory they could easily disprove for themselves by jamming their fingers in a door. Mary Baker Eddy even declared that death is not real. After burying a succession of husbands, she finally died and proved herself wrong. Yet millions still believe that she was a true prophet.

Solomon urged us to exalt wisdom—not the wisdom of the world, but the wisdom of the Word. Great is the folly of those who defame, deny, or disregard the wisdom of God's Word. God's Word should occupy an exalted position in our hearts and minds. It will protect us from the wisdom of this world—its religious wisdom, its philosophical wisdom, and its scientific wisdom when it contradicts the Bible.

Fifth, Solomon wanted to say something about *the prize of wisdom:* "She shall give to thine head an ornament of grace: a crown of glory shall she deliver to thee" (Proverbs 4:9). A certain type of beauty and dignity is the ornament of every person who has acquired wisdom. A crown of glory adorns the brows of those who are in love with wisdom.

It is fashionable in some quarters these days to sneer at Harriet Beecher Stowe. Yet her hand rang the death knell of slavery in the United States. Many honor her. A crown of glory clings to her memory. Born in 1811 to a minister, she married a minister, and six of her brothers were ministers.

Harriet's book *Uncle Tom's Cabin* was founded on the higher wisdom of the Word of God. When her father was dying, he reminded his family of Hebrews 12:22: "Ye are come unto mount Sion, and unto the city of the living God, the heavenly Jerusalem." The text made a deep impression on Harriet's mind and formed the backbone of her book.

Harriet was appalled by the way black women were treated and the way black families were torn apart by the auctioneers. She had seen firsthand the callous cruelty of the merchants of misery in the slave markets and she wanted to expose them.

In her book Uncle Tom was a Christian. He spoke of the heavenly Jerusalem, of the vast company of angels, and of Jesus to little Eva on her deathbed. His confidence was real. The highest wisdom had entered Mrs. Stowe's soul and it revealed itself in her tale. If a slave can be saved; if a slave can find himself at home on mount Sion, in the city of the living God, in the heavenly Jerusalem; if a slave can take his place among countless angels; if a slave can belong to the general assembly and church of the Firstborn; if a slave can come to

God, the judge of all; if a slave's spirit can be numbered among the spirits of just men made perfect—in what way is a black man different from a white man? How can a white man sell a black man to another white man?

This logic lay behind Harriet's book. The world recognized her wisdom at once and crowned her with glory by translating the book into forty languages and buying millions of copies. Published almost 150 years ago, the book is still read. It was the spiritual force behind the American Civil War. Abraham Lincoln once called Mrs. Stowe "the little lady who made a big war."

Some American blacks now despise Uncle Tom. Nevertheless *Uncle Tom's Cabin* put in motion the forces that set the slaves free. Long live the memory of Harriet Beecher Stowe!

E. It Is a Proper Path (4:10-19)

1. Wisdom Is Life's Guarantee (4:10)

The general Old Testament rule was that evil people died young and godly people lived to a ripe old age. So Solomon said, "Hear, O my son, and receive my sayings; and the years of thy life shall be many." Rehoboam however did not listen to his father. Rehoboam's inglorious reign of only seventeen years began disastrously, thanks to his abysmal folly. Indeed his greatest prowess was dubious at best: he had eighteen wives and sixty concubines and produced twenty-eight sons and sixty daughters (2 Chronicles 11:21). He left the throne but little else to his son Abijam.

Abijam continued the senseless policies of his father, still trying to get back the departed tribes by means of war and showing only halfhearted interest in spiritual things. Abijam reigned for only three years, long enough to prove himself as big a fool as his father.

Sometimes of course God allows a wicked, foolish man to have a long life because God's larger plan can override the general rule. In the case of wicked King Manasseh, who reigned for fifty-five years, God's purpose was to speed the inevitable judgment of the nation of Judah as well as manifest His patience to Manasseh.

2. Wisdom Is Life's Guardian (4:11-19)

a. The Past (4:11)

In Proverbs 4:11 Solomon reviewed the education of his son: "I have taught thee in the way of wisdom; I have led thee in right paths." Possibly Solomon was repeating what his father had told him. When a child chooses a wrong path, it is a great comfort to the parent to know that his own conscience is clear—that he pointed the child to the right path.

A preacher I know had a son who chose wrong company and made bad choices when he was a teenager. The boy had been brought up in a home where the Lord was loved and honored and His Word was taught and applied, so the boy's behavior was particularly painful to the father. One time the boy and his friends were picked up in a raid on a rock concert. Another time the school called his mother to pick him up because he was intoxicated. Once he ran away from home. For a while the father felt it advisable to get out of the Lord's work until the situation was more in hand. In the end, the parents' prayer, patience, love, forgiveness, and firmness paid off. The boy was soundly saved and chose to attend a Christian university because of its reputation for discipline! He was a joy to his parents and he became his father's best friend.

Parents make mistakes of course. What parent hasn't? But at least let them be honest mistakes. At the time that preacher's boy was drinking with his worldly friends, the father said to his wife: "Well, he can never say he learned to drink in our house. He's never seen a bottle of wine or a can of beer in our refrigerator." Even when he was most rebellious, either of those parents could have said to him, "I have taught thee in the way of wisdom; I have led thee in right paths." The boy walks in those paths now, but what a comfort it was in the dark and depressing years for the parents to know that they had done all they could to teach their son the good and right way.

b. The Present (4:12)

Proverbs 4:12 continues the discussion of how wisdom guards our lives: "When thou goest, thy steps shall not be straitened; and when thou runnest, thou shalt not stumble." The word translated "straitened" means "to be hemmed in." Unsaved people complain that the Christian life is too narrow, too hemmed in. Of course it is narrow! It is hemmed in with prohibitions. Christian parents have to say no to a whole spectrum of activities their children would like to participate in because "everybody does it." The Hebrew hymnbook begins with the power of negative thinking—Psalm 1:1. Jesus Himself declared that the way was narrow: "I am the way, the truth, and the life: no man cometh unto the Father, but by me" (John 14:6). Ruling out cooperation and compromise with all other religions, the Christian faith teaches that all other religions are wrong. Jesus alone can bring people to God and Heaven.

Truth is always narrow; error is broad. Error says, "Twice one is three," or "Twice one is twelve," or "Twice one is a million." Truth says, "Twice one is two." Whether the truth in question is mathematical, medical, biological, or religious, truth is truth and by its very nature it is narrow and exclusive.

Truth is also dogmatic. We expect teachers in our schools to be narrow and dogmatic about truth. We would soon fire the teacher who told our children that it didn't make any difference whether or not they behaved, or whether or not they learned the multiplication tables. We would fire the teacher who said he was broad-minded about arithmetic.

"Your way is too narrow," says a hypocritical world. The narrow way, however, broadens out at the end when it takes on the infinite dimensions of eternity. The horizons of the narrow path are lost in the vastness of a boundless shore in a land of fadeless day, where time is not counted by years and where Christ sits on the right hand of the Majesty on high. There for endless ages we will explore the marvels and mysteries prepared for us by the God of omniscient genius and omnipotent power, the God who will never run out of ideas for making Heaven an exciting place to be.

The broad road does not lead there. Those who tread it find that their horizons are limited. Time and sense assert a growing tyranny. The path soon narrows.

The path narrowed for Barbara Hutton. Her obituary was in *Time* magazine on May 21, 1979. Not everyone makes the pages of *Time,* not even the obituary column, but Barbara, dying at the age of sixty-six, was a celebrity. The granddaughter of F. W. Woolworth, she had inherited a fortune of multiplied millions of dollars at the age of twelve. But her money did not make her happy. Neither did her seven husbands—not the Laotian prince, nor the Russian count, nor the Prussian count, nor the Hollywood movie star Cary Grant. Barbara was plagued with illnesses ranging from kidney disease to cataracts and in her last years she was a recluse, often bedridden, weighing only eighty pounds. She died of a heart attack. The newspapers called her "the poor little rich girl."

c. The Promise (4:13)

Solomon kept coming back to his theme: wisdom is life's guardian. He wrote, "Take fast hold of instruction; let her not go: keep her; for she is thy life." Wisdom protects the quality of life and the length of life. God promises that those who cleave to sound instruction and never let it go, will have the best of life. How Solomon wished he could get that lesson through scatterbrained Rehoboam's dull head.

Judas failed to take fast hold of instruction. We can picture him, rope in hand, heading for a steep place where he can commit suicide. He let Wisdom go and lost his life. Incarnate Wisdom wooed and warned him, but in vain.

Jesus knew Judas better than Judas knew himself. Jesus knew the reason why Judas joined the apostolic band. Jesus knew his desire for fame and fortune in what he fondly imagined would be an empire of pomp and power. Jesus knew his growing disillusionment as it dawned on him that the kingdom would be spiritual and that the man he had believed to be the Messiah was not interested in an earthly kingdom but seemed bent on an early death on a Roman cross. Jesus knew when the evil thought entered the soul of Judas— the thought that he should cash in and get out. Jesus warned Judas again and again about the dangers of covetousness. "One of you is a devil," He pointedly said (John 6:70). "One of you shall betray me" (Matthew 26:21). Jesus spoke with ever-increasing bluntness. "That thou doest, do quickly" was the parting shot as Judas left the upper room to perform his nefarious errand (John 13:27). Stolidly, stubbornly, Judas refused all instruction. The result was a rope, ruin, and an eternity of woe.

d. The Protection (4:14-19)

(1) The Path of the Godless (4:14-17)

(a) The Deterrence (4:14-15)

Solomon pointed his son, as David had pointed him, away from the path of the godless. *"Stay out!"* he said. "Enter not into the path of the wicked, and go not in the way of evil men" (Proverbs 4:14). *"Stay away!"* he said. "Avoid it, pass not by it, turn from it, and pass away" (4:15). All too often we ignore this excellent counsel. Thanks to our fallen nature, we often find evil to be much more attractive than good is. Sin is contagious; goodness isn't. Health is not contagious. Many diseases are either infectious, contagious, or both. We can all too easily catch a disease, but we cannot catch health. A person who has cancer cannot be cured by being around an athlete. Dirt is conveyed by contact; cleanliness is not.

Some time ago a friend of mine was hospitalized with infectious hepatitis. Before I went to see him, I asked my doctor to give me a protective inoculation. Because this particular disease is so virulent, he refused and advised me to stay away. "We doctors," he said, "have to expose ourselves to this infection because it is our duty to do so. I never advise anyone else to do the same. Stay out! Stay away!"

That doctor's medical advice was the same as Solomon's spiritual advice. The Lord Jesus emphasized the same principle when He taught us to pray, "Lead us not into temptation, but deliver us from evil" (Matthew 6:13). Generations of parents have tried to communicate the same message to their children.

(b) The Description (4:16-17)

In the description of the path of the godless we are told *what disturbs the wicked man:* "They sleep not, except they have done mischief; and their sleep is taken away, unless they cause some to fall" (Proverbs 4:16). One of the extraordinary features of sin is that it compels the sinner to involve someone else in his evil. Sin hates goodness.

When I was in the British army I was stationed for two years on Haifa docks in a small detachment of about twenty men. My lifestyle greatly irritated my superior officer. What seemed to irk him most was my refusal to drink even one glass of beer. All the other fellows drank and some of them, including the officer, were almost confirmed drunkards.

The officer had many fine qualities and when he was sober we were good friends. He was considerably older than I was. A hardened career soldier of wide experience, he was a native cockney with all the wit and shrewdness of a Londoner from the East End. But he did everything in his power to get me to drink. Once he even offered me his pay for three months if I would just get drunk once! Whatever made him think that I could be bought so cheaply, I don't know. Drink was abhorrent to me. If he had offered me his pay for ten years, it would not have tempted me. Not that I was perfect, of course. Like anyone else, I was vulnerable elsewhere.

The point is, my determined sobriety troubled this man's conscience. He lost sleep while he plotted to drag me down to his level. All the time I knew him, he never stopped probing for some weakness he could exploit. He would argue shrewdly along the lines of radical unbelief. He would bring up what he considered to be lewd passages in the Bible and parade them before me in search of an argument. He also had a vast fund of dirty stories, suggestive poems, and vile limericks he used to recite, trying to get me to laugh. Admittedly some of them were outrageously funny. He would watch me keenly as he told the stories and would be delighted if he detected so much as the barest involuntary twitch of my lips. I concluded after nearly two years of temptation that my fall would be a prize feather in his cap. The Lord protected me, however, and made me invulnerable. I have always been grateful for the horror of drink my father instilled in me. I have pondered too the officer's relentless attempts to undermine my resistance. Solomon certainly was drawing the officer's portrait in Proverbs 4:16.

Proverbs 4:17 tells us *what delights the wicked man:* "For they eat the bread of wickedness, and drink the wine of violence." Bread and wine were the staples of life in Bible times, a man's necessary food. So Solomon was saying that an evil person finds sin and wickedness as natural and necessary to his lifestyle as food and drink.

Bread and wine are the elements of communion, the emblems of the Lord's passion! They awaken in us a remembrance of His body broken, His blood outpoured. The bread and the wine remind us that the Lord Jesus loved lost and sinful men enough to die for them. He bore all our sins in His body on the tree. He shed His precious blood to wash away our stains. As the old hymn puts it, "His blood can make the foulest clean; His blood availed for me."[2] Even people who avidly pursue a life of sin and crime, who feast on their ungodly triumphs, are not beyond redemption.

The word translated "wickedness" in Proverbs 4:17 emphasizes the restless activity of the fallen nature. The original word refers to the activity of ungodly people, especially to their lawlessness. The same word is used in Job 3:17. When Job's accumulated disasters overtook him, he wept aloud. He wished he were already dead, lying peacefully in his tomb where "the *wicked* cease from troubling" (italics added).

The word is used again in Isaiah 53:9. In describing the death of Christ, the prophet foresaw the malice of His enemies extending beyond His death to His burial in a dishonorable grave. "He [the pronoun can be translated "one" or "they"] made his grave with the *wicked*" (italics added). In other words, the animosity of the Jewish leaders toward the incarnate Son of God would be so great that they would plot to desecrate His body by burying Him in a common grave reserved for criminals. His enemies probably would have dumped His body in the fires of Gehenna where the city's garbage was burned if their plans had not been foiled by Joseph of Arimathaea. Yet the Lord died even for these wicked men.

There has always been a criminal element in society—people who live for wickedness and by violence. We are well warned to steer clear of such people.

(2) The Path of the Godly (4:18-19)

Next Solomon compared the growth of wickedness to the growth of godliness. Proverbs 4:18 gives *a confirmation* of godliness: "But the path of the just is as the shining light, that shineth more and more unto the perfect day." People who love the Lord and walk with Him are like those who advance toward the dawn.

In my travels across the United States and Canada, I often begin driving before dawn. Starting out in complete darkness, presently I see a touch of dark gray tingeing the distant horizon. Then the black outlines of the hills loom darker than the sky. Soon the sky becomes lighter and the gray is touched with a dull red, the harbinger of the rising sun. The light strengthens and a broad band of red spreads across the horizon. Then the rim of the sun appears above the horizon and the remaining darkness flees. The red ball of the sun hanging in the sky rapidly rises until, from its throne on high, it floods the world with the bright light of day. What I see as I drive east is a picture of "the path of the just." We are heading toward the dawn and Heaven's eternal day.

Years ago I attended a church service in Vancouver, British Columbia. At the close of the service a letter was read to the congregation from Dr. Northcote Deck, a former medical missionary and godly man who was dying from leukemia. Knowing how far his disease had progressed and how much longer he had to live, the doctor had written the letter and sent it to the North American churches where he had found fellowship and support through the years. "Brethren," he wrote, "David speaks of the valley of the shadow of death. I have now entered the valley. But, brothers and sisters, I have found no shadows in the valley at all! On the contrary, I have found that the path of the just is as the shining light that shineth more and more unto the perfect day." What a way to die! Jesus Himself said, "I am the light of the world: he that followeth me shall not walk in darkness, but shall have the light of life" (John 8:12).

Proverbs 4:19 provides *a contrast:* "The way of the wicked is as darkness: they know not at what they stumble." The wicked Haman certainly did stumble. An Agagite, Haman was a descendant of Amalekite kings (Numbers 24:7; 1 Samuel 15:8,32; Esther 3:1) and had inherited Amalek's vengeful malice against the nation of Israel. Haman hated Jews in general and one Jew in particular—Mordecai. Mordecai refused to bow and scrape before Haman, even though Haman held high office in Persia and had the ear of the king. Mordecai's refusal infuriated Haman, who persuaded King

Ahasuerus to sign a decree commanding the extermination of all Jews in the empire. Haman himself planned to hang Mordecai on a special gallows erected for the purpose. Haman was riding high, wide, and handsome when he stumbled. Little did he know in the abysmal darkness of his soul that when he tangled with Mordecai and the Jews, he called down a curse on his own head. God had promised Abraham, "I will bless them that bless thee, and curse him that curseth thee" (Genesis 12:3).

Haman's wife and counselors warned: "If Mordecai be of the seed of the Jews...thou shalt not prevail against him, but shalt surely fall before him" (Esther 6:13). Haman's friends knew he was heading for disaster by persecuting Mordecai. Haman, however, ignored the warning. He did not know that Queen Esther was a Jewess and Mordecai's cousin. Truly Haman's way was dark. He continued to head toward certain doom, for as we know, Esther interceded for her people and Haman was hanged on the very gallows he had prepared for Mordecai. Haman knew not at what he stumbled until it was too late. Many stumbling blocks lie in the path of the ungodly, but the ungodly are too blind to see them.

CHAPTER 7
Proverbs 4:20–5:23

ii. Drudgery (5:9b)

iii. Debt (5:10)

iv. Disease (5:11)

(b) Counting the Moral Loss (5:12-13)

   i. Realizing One's Folly Too Late (5:12)

   ii. Regretting One's Failure to Hate (5:13)

(c) Counting the Spiritual Loss (5:14)

(3) By Being Contented (5:15-20)

(a) Legitimate Desires Are Recognized (5:15-17)

(b) Legitimate Desires Are Restricted (5:18-20)

   i. By the Laws of Marriage (5:18-19)

   ii. By the Laws of Morality (5:20)

(4) By Being Convicted (5:21-23)

(a) God Perceives Our Sin (5:21)

(b) God Punishes Our Sin (5:22-23)

   i. Eventually in This Life (5:22)

   ii. Everlastingly in That Life (5:23)

Continuing his efforts to drive some sense into young Rehoboam's head, Solomon asked him to ponder carefully the difference between the way of virtue and the way of vice. The way of virtue is wisdom's path.

F. It Is a Perfect Path (4:20–5:23)

1. The Way of Virtue Pondered (4:20–5:2)

a. How to Have a Healthy Life (4:20-22)

First Solomon gave his son *a call:* "My son, attend to my words; incline thine ear unto my sayings" (Proverbs 4:20). Solomon had learned some of his lessons from the hard experiences of life. He longed to be able to prevent his son from repeating some of his own mistakes. He called for attention, but the English proverb is apt here: You can take a horse to water, but you cannot make him drink. A wise man can seek to instruct his son, but he cannot force him to listen and heed instruction. We all have mental devices for blocking out unwelcome information.

Next Solomon gave *a command:* "Let them not depart from thine eyes; keep them in the midst of thine heart" (Proverbs 4:21). The wise man tried to impose his will on his son. Sometimes a weak personality will respond submissively to a strong personality. This approach works as long as the stronger personality is able to continue being dominant.

But what happens if the weaker person manages to break away from the restraints imposed on him? The story of the prodigal son gives us the answer. He grew up under the control of a godly father. We can well imagine the firm discipline as well as the generous love the prodigal experienced at home. The boy was obliged to attend the services in the local synagogue where he received a thorough indoctrination in the Word of God. He was obliged to attend family prayers and conform to his father's high standards of morality. Doubtless the boy loved his father, but he grew heartily sick of all the obligations. The far country assumed a glitter and glamour in his thinking. It represented freedom from the galling restraints of home. When he finally asserted his independence, he followed the swing of the pendulum into the wildest excesses. The lesson here is simple: parents can and must command obedience in their homes, but they cannot legislate holiness.

Then Solomon offered *a comment:* "For they are life unto those that find them, and health to all their flesh" (Proverbs 4:22). A constantly repeated theme of Proverbs is that both quality of life and length of life are enhanced by paying heed to the book's wisdom.

A new appliance usually comes with a book of instructions. The manufacturer knows best how his product should be handled and protected. Often the manufacturer's warranty requires compliance with the instructions. The wise person pays heed. He reads the instructions and follows them. A person who takes care of his purchase and heeds the instructions can expect long and efficient performance from the appliance. However, the person who ignores the instructions and operates the appliance incorrectly or neglects or abuses it cannot expect the same results. He cannot blame the manufacturer if the appliance breaks down early.

The human body is far more complex than any man-made machine. The Maker Himself has sent general instructions for a good, long life. These instructions are found in the Word of God. Happy is the person who heeds them; foolish is the one who doesn't.

b. How to Have a Holy Life (4:23–5:2)

Solomon listed some of the ingredients in a good life. The first is *a clean heart:* "Keep thy heart with all diligence; for out of it are the issues of life" (Proverbs 4:23). Above all we must guard the heart. The heart, the symbol of our hidden inner life, is the source of all our behavior.

Sir Walter Raleigh, one of Britain's great sea captains in the days of Queen Elizabeth I, was a fearless adventurer. He was a great favorite of the queen, but was disliked by her successor James I. In the end the king condemned Sir Walter to death. The executioner, whose sympathy evidently was with the prisoner, had no joy in his task. Hoping to ease the sailor's last moments, the executioner told Sir Walter how to place his head on the block to ensure swift decapitation. The prisoner thanked him. "It matters little, friend," Sir Walter said, "whether or not the head is right so long as the heart is right."

The heart must be right if the life is to be right. The heart can be right only if it is cleansed by the precious blood of Christ and indwelt by the Holy Spirit of God. Even then the heart must be kept with all diligence. It needs to be protected with the breastplate of righteousness (Ephesians 6:14).

In Psalm 24:3-4 clean hands and a pure heart are linked together because we do what we do because we are what we are. The heart determines what we are and therefore what we do. Jesus said, "Those things which proceed out of the mouth come forth from the heart; and they defile the man. For out of the heart proceed evil thoughts, murders, adulteries, fornications, thefts, false witness, blasphemies: These are the things which defile a man" (Matthew 15:18-20). No wonder we need a new heart! The natural human heart is "deceitful above all things, and desperately wicked" (Jeremiah 17:9). David asked the Lord to create a clean heart within him (Psalm 51:10). The new covenant involves having God's law written in our hearts (Jeremiah 31:33).

The second ingredient in a good life is *a cautious mouth:* "Put away from thee a froward [perverse] mouth, and perverse lips put far from thee" (Proverbs 4:24). The mouth can get a person into all kinds of trouble. Evil speech is a sure indication of an evil heart. Thus the wise man urged us to put away perverse speech. People can control their speech when they want to, when it is in their best interest to do so. A foulmouthed man will control his language in the presence of a boss who will not stand for foul talk.

Shimei is the classic Biblical example of a man with a foul mouth. A Benjamite and former partisan of King Saul, Shimei hated David. When Absalom rebelled, Shimei was delighted. When David had to flee Jerusalem, Shimei was overjoyed. When he discovered that David was coming his way, he took full advantage of the occasion. He cursed and threw stones. "Come out," he cried. The Hebrew can be translated, "Be gone," or "Get out." Shimei warmed to his theme: "Come out, thou bloody man, thou man of Belial: The Lord hath returned upon thee all the blood of the house of Saul, in whose stead thou hast reigned; and the Lord hath delivered the kingdom into the hand of Absalom thy son: and, behold, thou art taken in thy mischief, because thou art a bloody man" (2 Samuel 16:7-8). Little did Shimei know that all that stood between him and sudden death was the grace of David. Solomon, who of course knew all about Shimei and in the end ordered his execution, warned his son against a "froward mouth."

The third ingredient in a good life is *a controlled eye:* "Let thine eyes look right on, and let thine eyelids look straight before thee" (Proverbs 4:25). A great deal of temptation comes through the eyes. Not to look at something provocative and appealing to the flesh requires considerable discipline.

Satan's strategy in the garden of Eden was to persuade Eve to look. He succeeded in getting her to fix her gaze on the forbidden fruit. How desirable it appeared! The longer she looked the more her desire grew. The longer she looked the more difficult it was to tear her eyes away. Soon she lost all sense of proportion. She forgot all about her husband, all about God's warning of sure and certain judgment. That tree and its fruit was all she could see. At last the look became a lust. "When the woman saw that the tree was good for food, and that it was pleasant to the eyes, and a tree to be desired to make one wise, she took of the fruit thereof, and did eat" (Genesis 3:6). Her fall began with a look. We can understand the sad story because of our own bitter experiences.

The fourth ingredient in a good life is *a careful foot* (Proverbs 4:26-27). Solomon advised a *planned* walk: "Ponder the path of thy feet, and let all thy ways be established." He advised a *perfect* walk: "Turn not to the right hand nor to the left." And he advised a *protected* walk: "Remove thy foot from evil." There are some places to which we should not go, some doorways we should never darken.

Consider the steps of Abraham and Lot. On that eventful day when Abraham suggested to Lot that they part company because of the squabbling of their herdsmen over available pasture, both men made a choice. Genesis 13 records their decisions: "Lot…*pitched* his tent" (13:12, italics added); "Abram *removed* his tent" (13:18, italics added). There in a nutshell is the difference between Abraham (who became the friend of God and the father of all believers) and Lot (the great Old Testament prototype of the backslider).

Lot's feet took him pell-mell down to Sodom, where he lost family, faith, and fortune and almost lost his soul. Abraham's feet

took him over the hills and far away. He couldn't wait to put distance
between himself and the filthy city of the plains. No one could be in
that part of the world for any length of time and not know of
Sodom's reputation as the homosexual capital of the world. Abraham didn't want to be around when God poured out the red-hot
lava of His wrath against that vile lifestyle. We all need to be careful
where we place our feet.

The fifth ingredient in a good life is *a consecrated ear:* "My son,
attend unto my wisdom, and bow thine ear to my understanding:
That thou mayest regard discretion, and that thy lips may keep
knowledge" (Proverbs 5:1-2). With almost monotonous regularity
Solomon pleaded with his son to pay attention. Perhaps David had
pleaded with Solomon to pay attention. If David was the first to
make the plea, he failed to make his point with Solomon; the plea
is followed by a warning against falling into the clutches of the
wrong kind of woman, and Solomon made shipwreck of his life on
this perilous shore. If Solomon was talking to Rehoboam, that silly
young man should receive a measure of our sympathy. He could
have said to his father, "Physician, heal thyself." Or he could have
said, "What you are speaks so loudly I cannot hear a word you say."

Solomon's palace was a pandemonium of jealousy, intrigue, and
lust, thanks to his utter inability to control his insatiable desires.
Rehoboam grew up in that environment. His father had an enormous harem, so we can at least understand why Rehoboam turned
a deaf ear when Solomon preached about sexual restraint. Even
though Solomon did not follow his own instructions, what he had
to say was divinely inspired. We must heed it as the highest wisdom.

2. The Way of Vice Pondered (5:3-23)

Solomon, either writing out of his experience and observation or
repeating instruction he had received as he grew up, here concentrated on the wanton woman, providing the book's first major
portrait of the harlot. Part One of Proverbs includes five discourses
on immorality (2:16-22; 5:3-23; 6:24-35; 7:5-27; 9:13-18), 5:3-23
being one of the longest.

a. The Snare Evaluated (5:3-6)

(1) The Wanton Woman's Smiles Are Seductive (5:3-5)

Solomon warned against the wanton woman's smiles and *the
promise they reveal:* "The lips of a strange woman drop as an

honeycomb, and her mouth is smoother than oil" (Proverbs 5:3).
Two Hebrew words, *nākar* and *zūr*, are used in the Bible to depict
the "stranger." The word *nākar* refers to a temple prostitute. In the
foul Canaanite religion, idol worship was consummated by having
sexual relations with one of the priests or priestesses. *Zūr*, the word
used in Proverbs 5:3, refers to a Hebrew woman who has become an
apostate and has sold herself to the immoralities of one of the pagan
cults. She is a professional harlot.

The wanton woman baits her trap with honeyed words. She is well
versed in what to say to seduce careless men. She knows how to
inflame the passions of those who stop to listen to what she says. She
is an old hand at enticement. She knows which words to use in her
approach, how to respond to the reply, how to make the next
conversational move. She has no trouble sizing up each prospective
client. She knows how to choose the words that will lead him on.

Solomon continued to warn against the wanton woman's smiles
and *the peril they conceal.* Those inviting lips conceal the *danger* into
which she is luring the unwary: "Her end is bitter as wormwood,
sharp as a twoedged sword" (Proverbs 5:4). Her lips also conceal
the *death* that lurks in her shadow: "Her feet go down to death; her
steps take hold on hell" (5:5). The last thing a person thinks of
when listening to the siren voice of a wanton woman is the danger
and death that accompany her, so Solomon warned of the wormwood and bitterness that seize the soul and conscience of the
adulterer.

The Bible is blunt about sexual sins. There is nothing prudish or
Victorian about the Bible. But although the Bible is quite frank, it
contains nothing prurient in its pages. It does not pander. The so-
called adult novel, on the other hand, moves the reader slowly and
enticingly through one torrid scene after another. Such a book
titillates, excites, and stimulates, gloating over every detail and
constantly stirring the filth portrayed. The Bible, however, cuts
through sin like a surgeon's knife. The cut exposes to view the moral
ruin, the physical wreckage, and the shameful death that result
from sexual sin. The writer of pornography is a depraved sensualist;
the Holy Spirit is a surgeon.

(2) The Wanton Woman's Smiles Are Subtle (5:6)

Approaching a victim, the wanton woman turns on all her
charms. Solomon said, "Lest thou shouldest ponder the path of life,
her ways are moveable, that thou canst not know them." She is very
slippery and can swiftly change her ground. On no account does

she allow the man she is enticing to think of the consequences of what he is about to do.

Her swiftly changing moods and appeals are bewitching, but her manner of life may be more bitter to her than death. Behind her smiles and seductive charms may lurk an abysmal hopelessness. The wanton woman may abhor what she does. She may abhor the men who help accomplish her ruin. But she does not show her feelings. She smiles, displays her wares, whispers her enticements, and lures some poor dupe on. She employs all her arts to prevent him from pondering the path of life. Her road is the path of death.

b. The Snare Evaded (5:7-23)

(1) By Being Cautious (5:7-8)

The snare of the wanton woman can be evaded by being cautious, critical, contented, and convicted. Solomon began his discussion of the ways a man can avoid falling into the trap of sexual sin by urging the exercise of caution. He said, "Hear me now therefore, O ye children, and depart not from the words of my mouth" (Proverbs 5:7). He was saying, "*Stay awake to my demands.*" Listening to good common sense is essential to avoiding the pitfalls of immorality. Nobody can set aside the moral teaching of the Bible with impunity. The Bible categorically and unbendingly prohibits premarital and extramarital sex. Again and again the Holy Spirit says, "Listen to my demands."

The wise man added, "Remove thy way far from her, and come not nigh the door of her house" (Proverbs 5:8). He was saying, "To evade the snare of the wanton woman, be cautious and *stay away from her doors.* Following Solomon's advice would solve much of the problem she creates.

When Joseph was tempted by Potiphar's wife, he ran out of the room. He ended up in prison, but had he obliged her he might have ended up dead. And at least in prison he was safe from the woman's incessant appeals, for being her husband's slave, Joseph was unable to run away from the house. Envisioning the wider choices of a free man, Solomon said, "Stay away from the prostitute's house."

(2) By Being Critical (5:9-14)

(a) Counting the Personal Loss (5:9-11)

Being critical in order to evade the snare, one must count the losses that will result from having relations with a harlot. Four serious consequences, or personal losses, follow in the wake of such immorality. The first consequence is *dishonor:* "Lest thou give thine honour unto others" (Proverbs 5:9). Many a man has had his reputation ruined by being caught in a compromising liaison with a whore—especially if he holds a public office. The political consequences of course depend on the moral climate of the age and the accepted social practices of his culture. In lands where Judeo-Christian ethics have leavened society, dishonor is often a consequence of trafficking with a prostitute. One indicator of the increasing decadence of western culture is that such behavior is increasingly tolerated and increasingly common.

The second consequence of sexual immorality is *drudgery:* "Lest thou give...thy years unto the cruel" (Proverbs 5:9). Through his misbehavior, a man may fall into the clutches of an evil man or woman. Blackmail is a common aftermath of an encounter with a harlot, especially if the man involved has good reason to conceal what he has done. Some nations use harlots to decoy targeted men into compromising situations, then confront the victims with proofs of guilt and pressure them into becoming spies. Such men indeed give their years unto the cruel.

The third consequence is *debt:* "Lest strangers be filled with thy wealth; and thy labours be in the house of a stranger" (Proverbs 5:10). The word translated "stranger" here means "foreigner," the courtesan priestess of an immoral cultic religion. The harlot of course is in the profession for money. A high-priced prostitute can quickly transfer a man's wealth into her own coffers.

The fourth consequence is *disease:* "And thou mourn at the last, when thy flesh and thy body are consumed" (Proverbs 5:11). A whole battery of diseases awaits those who engage in sexual misbehavior. According to the United States Public Health Service's Center for Disease Control, venereal diseases have reached epidemic proportions in the United States. A new infection strikes every forty-five seconds and in its wake are pain, blindness, arthritis, infertility, brain damage, heart disease, and death. In spite of half a century of penicillin and wonder drugs, cases of venereal disease are increasing rapidly. Gonorrhea is the most prevalent, syphilis is the most dangerous, and both are horrible. Millions of people have contracted a new generation of venereal disease, including highly contagious strains of herpes. Herpes, which has no cure, produces blisters, fevers, and pounding headaches. It has been linked to cancer of the cervix and can be passed on to newborn babies. The most terrifying disease associated with promiscuous sexual behavior is AIDS, a killer for which there is no cure so far.

Often the house of the harlot is the vestibule to the funeral home. Harlots have few, if any, scruples about passing on their diseases. One investigator interviewed twenty prostitutes in a number of cities. They all had herpes. "Of course it wouldn't be good for business to mention it," one joked. Another boasted that she and her sister had probably given the disease to a thousand men. "We're not running a convent," she said.[1]

(b) Counting the Moral Loss (5:12-13)

The personal losses resulting from immorality are great; the moral loss is far greater. All too often a person realizes his folly too late and says, "How have I hated instruction. And my heart despised reproof" (Proverbs 5:12). All too often conscience lies dormant or is held down by desire when temptation is at its peak. But once the deed is done, conscience awakens. The bill is presented in terms of remorse, guilt, and shame; in terms of a gnawing conscience; in terms of a horrible disease contracted by the offender and passed on to a loved one. Too late the transgressor awakens to his folly. He should have listened when he was warned. He admits, "[I] have not obeyed the voice of my teachers, nor inclined mine ear to them that instructed me!" (5:13) If we refuse to learn the harsh facts of life from our parents, teachers, and godly guides, we learn them in the school of hard experience.

(c) Counting the Spiritual Loss (5:14)

"I was almost in all evil in the midst of the congregation and assembly." The worst loss of all is to bring disgrace and dishonor on the people of God and the circle of one's fellowship. Immorality is an excommunicating sin in the church (1 Corinthians 5:9); in Old Testament Israel immorality was a capital offense.

Today some people underrate the seriousness of formal excommunication. When it is deserved and delivered, all too often the culprit simply runs off to another church and fondly imagines that he has escaped the spiritual consequences of his sin. Not so! No one can run away from God, and God upholds the legitimate discipline of the congregation of His people. The purpose of excommunication is to separate the local church from evil and to preserve the integrity of the church's testimony in the community. Excommunication is also designed to lead the offender to repentance, confession, and restoration. The disgrace of a church member is shared by the church. If the disgrace comes from the pew, that is bad enough; if it comes from the pulpit, that is even worse. If immorality is found in a national Christian figure such as a television evangelist, the disgrace is the worst possible. It gives the enemies of the gospel great cause to blaspheme.

(3) By Being Contented (5:15-20)

(a) Legitimate Desires Are Recognized (5:15-17)

A man can evade the snare of a wanton woman by being contented with God's provision. "Drink waters out of thine own cistern, and running waters out of thine own well. Let thy fountains be dispersed abroad, and rivers of waters in the streets. Let them be only thine own, and not strangers' with thee."

There is no question that the sex drive is powerful in most people. It is especially strong during our youth and can easily get out of control in those vulnerable years between puberty and marriage. When a society's moral standards are high, some restraint is imposed. When a society's norms are low, great latitude is allowed, exposing young people to enormous temptation and pressure. But God's moral laws are absolute; they take no notice of the fluctuating standards of relative morality. Nobŏdy breaks God's moral laws with impunity.

God knows how we are made. His provision for satisfying sexual desire is marriage. In Genesis 2:18 we read, "The Lord God said, It is not good that the man should be alone; I will make him an help meet for him." God created Eve and brought her to Adam. "And Adam said, This is now bone of my bones, and flesh of my flesh: she shall be called Woman, because she was taken out of Man. Therefore shall a man leave his father and mother, and shall cleave unto his wife: and they shall be one flesh. And they were both naked, the man and his wife, and were not ashamed" (2:23-25). The sex urge can be allowed to function within the confines of marriage.

The verses in Proverbs are highly poetic. "Drink waters out of thine own cistern" simply tells us to satisfy our legitimate sexual thirst in the legitimate way. The expression translated "Let thy fountains be dispersed abroad" in the King James version, is translated "Let not thy fountain be dispersed abroad" in the Septuagint. The rendering in the Septuagint makes more sense. The expression is simply a command not to be sexually promiscuous. One paraphrase words the proverb as follows: "Drink from your own cistern, drink fresh water out of your own well. Are you to seek your pleasures here and there, and drink them in the streets? Have them at home, never share them abroad."

The word translated "fountains" in Proverbs 5:16 indicates the plural of emphasis. The original word means "your own wife." In the Song of Solomon the Shulamite is described similarly by her beloved. He calls her "a fountain sealed" and "a fountain of gardens, a well of living waters" (Song of Solomon 4:12,15).

(b) Legitimate Desires Are Restricted (5:18-20)

Legitimate desires are restricted *by the laws of marriage:* "Let thy fountain be blessed: and rejoice with the wife of thy youth. Let her be as the loving hind and pleasant roe; let her breasts satisfy thee at all times; and be thou ravished always with her love" (Proverbs 5:18-19). The words "thy fountain" refer to a man's own wife.

The living God, the Author of our being, freely acknowledges the physical side of our nature. Within the confines of the marriage relationship He permits much. After all, God designed the entire sexual side of life. He designed it to give pleasure and to ensure the propagation of the race. Given His omniscient genius and omnipotent power, God could have designed some other way to guarantee the continuation of the human race. He had an infinite number of options, yet He chose the one with which we are familiar. Ever since the fall, however, His design has been under pressure from sin.

Our legitimate sexual desires are also restricted *by the laws of morality:* "And why wilt thou, my son, be ravished with a strange woman, and embrace the bosom of a stranger?" (Proverbs 5:20) Solomon knew that the natural attraction of a woman for a man must not be allowed to get out of bounds.

God invented marriage and instituted it before sin entered the world. Since then sin has distorted everything, including sex. In our day the massive onslaught of permissiveness, pornography, and perversion has had devastating effects on society. Thus marriage is now a safeguard of special significance.

The hunger drive is almost as strong as (in some cases much stronger than) the sex drive, but we keep our appeals to the hunger drive in proportion. The idea of promoting gluttony the way people promote sex is ludicrous. Imagine a giant billboard featuring a well-padded man drooling over an apple pie. Or imagine a novel featuring a banquet and describing in detail an obese glutton in ecstasy over a calorie-laden, cholesterol-rich steak flanked by a baked Idaho potato laden with butter, sour cream, bacon bits, and cheese. Imagine whole books and movies promoting the sensual pleasure of eating! What people have done with sex is just as ludicrous.

The Bible keeps sex in proportion and forbids all deviant forms of sexual experience. We are to be satisfied with sex within marriage. All other sexual experimentation is forbidden. The Bible's laws of morality leave no room for the promiscuity and wide latitude permitted by the world.

(4) By Being Convicted (5:21-23)

Being convicted of sin can help us evade the snare of the wanton woman.

(a) God Perceives Our Sin (5:21)

"For the ways of man are before the eyes of the Lord, and he pondereth all his goings." When I was a boy my parents hung a text on my bedroom wall. I cannot say that I always appreciated the plaque. It read, "Thou God seest me." It was supposed to convey a message of comfort as in Genesis 16:13. But the text conveyed a threat to me. The thought of that all-seeing eye spying on my youthful transgressions troubled my conscience. The text would haunt me even more today—looking back over things I have done that I ought not to have done and things I have not done that I ought to have done—if it were not for the fact that those things, some of which I confessed with bitter tears, are now under the blood.

God's eye sees all. We do not get away with transgressions. Sometimes retribution is delayed. Sometimes it comes swiftly. We would do well indeed to take that text into all the situations of life that involve sex.

In my hometown there was a bold Christian commonly known as Banner Williams. Everywhere he went he carried a big banner displaying a couple of Bible texts. Old Banner Williams always marched ahead of our annual parade. We knew the parade was coming when we saw this intrepid warrior marching down the route, heedless of the comments of the crowd. With our treacherous memories and convenient consciences, we need to hire our own private Banner Williams to march before us in the parade of life and carry a big banner reading, "Thou God seest me."

(b) God Punishes Our Sin (5:22-23)

God sees our sin and He punishes it. He does so *eventually in this life:* "His own iniquities shall take [hold of] the wicked himself, and he shall be holden with the cords of his sins" (Proverbs 5:22). This consequence is true of all sins, but especially enslaving sins.

I remember visiting a hospital in Toronto where my brother was the head pathologist. He showed me half a human lung that had recently been cut out of the body of a heavy smoker who died of lung cancer. That pitiful lung was as black as a chimney. The patient had become a slave to the habit of smoking and in the end it killed him.

Those who take drugs or embark on a course of sexual sin suffer even more horrible consequences. In the end their iniquities take hold of them. They become prisoners of their own lusts. Eventually they cross a line to the other side where retribution waits.

God punishes our sin *everlastingly in that life:* "He shall die without instruction; and in the greatness of his folly he shall go astray" (Proverbs 5:23). The lost carry their lusts and guilt with them beyond the grave. Death does not alter character. Terrible are the words with which the Bible draws to a close, words that are surrounded by sights and sounds of eternity: "He that is unjust, let him be unjust still: and he which is filthy, let him be filthy still" (Revelation 22:11). The filthy man carries his vileness with him into a lost eternity. The lusts, passions, and cravings he cultivated and indulged on earth will remain with him forever. He will be consumed by a gnawing craving that he will be completely unable to satisfy.

CHAPTER 8

Proverbs 6:1-11

Solomon turned from the question of women to the question of wealth. His wise words are not so much about acquiring wealth as about protecting whatever assets we have.

IV. WISDOM'S PRECEPTS (6:1-35)

A. How They Goad Us (6:1-11)

1. If We Have Become Surety (6:1-5)

a. The Problem (6:1-2)

The problem stated in Proverbs 6:1 is simple but can be serious: becoming surety for *a friend* ("My son, if thou be surety for thy friend") or *a foreigner* ("If thou hast stricken thy hand with a stranger"). The wise man arrived on the scene too late. The foolish deed had already been done. Somebody gullible had been persuaded to follow his heart rather than his head. The gullible person could ill afford the luxury of guaranteeing someone else's indebtedness.

For a number of years I worked in the loan department of a large Canadian bank. From time to time the manager would assess the finances of someone applying for a loan and decide that the person was not a good risk. As a rule, a bank will loan money only to a person who has money. When forced to decline a loan to a customer, the manager would often say, "Do you know anyone who would cosign your note for you?" The manager wanted the best of both worlds. He wanted to make the loan and keep the customer happy, and he wanted some kind of security that would make the head office happy. The solution was for the customer to find a guarantor. Then if the customer defaulted, only the guarantor would be unhappy.

Usually the guarantor was a good friend of the customer. Out of the goodness of his heart, the guarantor was willing to give his friend a break. Sometimes the arrangement worked out all right, but I had to charge back many loans to guarantors because debtors were unable to meet their obligations. Usually the guarantors were wealthy and suffered no serious hardships. The bank manager was not likely to accept the guarantee of a man who did not have sufficient resources.

Solomon unerringly put his finger on the problem. By *becoming surety* the gullible person in Proverbs 6:1 stood in danger of *being snared:* "Thou art snared with the words of thy mouth, thou art taken with the words of thy mouth" (6:2). So far the agreement was in words only and the would-be guarantor had made a promise to the debtor, not the creditor. At this point the possibility still exists that the guarantor-to-be can extricate himself. But first he needs to evaluate the difficult situation into which his promise has put him. He may be mortgaging his own future. He can no more afford to guarantee his friend's debt than his friend can afford to incur the debt.

b. The Proposal (6:3-5)

(1) Help Yourself (6:3a)

"Do this now, my son, and deliver thyself, when thou art come into the hand of thy friend." So far the gullible person is still in the hands of his friend, not the friend's creditor. The guarantor-to-be must put his pride in his pocket, go back to his friend, confess that he has made a mistake, and seek to be released from his promise. Hopefully this request will not strain the friendship. If the friend to whom the promise was made is a real friend, he will release the would-be guarantor from his generous but rash promise and seek another solution to the financial problems.

(2) Humble Yourself (6:3b-5)

The urgency is indicated in Proverbs 6:3-4: "Go, humble thyself, and make sure thy friend. Give not sleep to thine eyes, nor slumber to thine eyelids." The longer the delay the more difficult it will be to undo the damage. Once the debtor passes on the guarantor's pledge to the creditor, it will be too late. Haste is needed so that the transaction will not proceed that far. Once the pledge gets into the hands of the creditor, the friend's release will carry no weight. History reveals that the moneylender invariably wants his pound of flesh.

The urgency is illustrated in Proverbs 6:5: "Deliver thyself as a roe from the hand of the hunter, and as a bird from the hand of the fowler." Both the roe and the bird rely on speed to escape danger.

This counsel contains a great deal of common sense. What good is a promise, however well-intentioned, when the guarantor simply does not have the means to keep it? The promise only gives a false sense of security. It is far better to face reality before both debtor and guarantor lose everything. It is far better to save a friendship by honesty and common sense than to see a friendship end in bitterness, hard feelings, and recrimination. It is far better to face awkward facts at the outset while it is still possible to make more realistic arrangements. Everything depends on honesty and speed.

2. If We Have Become Slothful (6:6-11)

a. A Call to Look (6:6-8)

(1) The Ant's Wisdom (6:6)

Wisdom in financial matters is many-faceted. We can become poor by something we do—by being surety for a friend, for instance. Or we can become poor by something we don't do—by being lazy and refusing to work. One is as bad as the other. Solomon had no use for slothfulness. He profitably invested every passing moment of his time (Ecclesiastes 3:1-8). He never wasted a minute. Perhaps nothing irritates an organized, energetic, dynamic individual more than the sight of a lazy person lying in bed, lolling around the house, wasting time, and dissipating opportunities.

Wisdom's precepts goad us if we have become slothful. Proverbs 6:6 contrasts the lazy man and the busy ant: "Go to the ant, thou sluggard; consider her ways, and be wise." The ant never seems to be still. The ant colony is built on the twin principles of discipline and work. If the colony is disturbed its activity accelerates to a fever pitch.

(2) The Ant's World (6:7-8)

The ant's world has always fascinated people. It is so much like our own world, yet so utterly alien. The ant works *without force:* "Which having no guide, overseer, or ruler" (Proverbs 6:7). The ant colony is centered around the queen. The queen is bigger than her subjects, but she is really simply an egg-laying machine. Her function is to provide millions of eggs that the workers take and cultivate as needed. The workers tell the queen what kind of ants are needed for the continuing well-being of the colony. Thus, keeping the colony in balance is a joint effort of the workers and the queen. The workers continually attend to the queen and she responds to the stimuli she receives. This joint enterprise ensures that there will always be the proper proportion of workers, soldiers, pupae, and future queens in the colony.

People admire the efficiency of the ant colony. It is highly structured, ruthlessly efficient, and tightly controlled. Communism is an effort by misguided men to produce a human society modeled on the ant heap. But people aren't ants. Ant society is organized by blind instinct, but people aren't puppets. They cannot be bred, regimented, sorted by caste, or manipulated like ants.

Solomon's interest in the ant centered on the colony's work ethic and on the fact that ants do not have to be forced to work. Ants are not slothful. They are an example of industry. They do not need slave drivers to make sure they get up in the morning and fulfill their appointed tasks. Let the slothful man consider that! The ant works without force.

The ant works *without fail.* Come wind or weather, the ant goes about its business undeterred by circumstances. The ant "provideth her meat in the summer, and gathereth her food in the harvest" (Proverbs 6:8). This statement is true of ants found in Israel. The ant species worldwide is numerous and specialized. Different kinds of ants have different customs. All ants, however, are remarkably provident. They instinctively look ahead and while the season is favorable prepare for hard days to come. What the ants do by blind instinct, people ought to do as a matter of simple common sense.

Solomon—the wise ruler with an ingrained habit of careful observation, a lively curiosity, and an ability to draw inferences and come to conclusions—had often watched the ants at work. How he admired their efficiency. He had seen the busy ant scouts ranging far and wide to look for sources of food. He had seen the ant soldiers quickly taking on intruders. He had seen the panic when an anthill was disturbed and the little creatures ran to and fro; the concern was to get the eggs away from the danger zone and the activity swiftly settled down to organized efficiency. Almost miraculously the damage was repaired and the ants resumed the ordinary business of life—seeking out and storing up food.

We can see Solomon pointing out this nature lesson to his son. "There! See that? Look at that one! And what about that one there? He seems to be carrying a load five times too big for him. See if you can find a lazy one, son."

b. A Call to Listen (6:9-11)

(1) Laziness Rebuked (6:9)

The lesson of the ant failed to impress the slothful son, so Solomon asked, "How long wilt thou sleep, O sluggard? when wilt thou arise out of thy sleep?" Now the frustrated father tried reason and barely-veiled demands.

In *Pilgrim's Progress* John Bunyan used a conversation between Christian and Hopeful to warn against laziness. Bunyan wrote:

> I saw then in my dream, that they went till they came into a certain country, whose air naturally tended to make one

drowsy, if he came a stranger into it. And here Hopeful began to be very dull and heavy of sleep; wherefore he said unto Christian, I do now begin to grow so drowsy that I can scarcely hold up mine eyes; let us lie down here and take one nap.

CHRISTIAN. By no means…lest sleeping, we never awake more.

HOPEFUL. Why, my brother? Sleep is sweet to the labouring man; we may be refreshed if we take a nap.

CHRISTIAN. Do you not remember that one of the Shepherds bid us beware of the Enchanted Ground? He meant by that, that we should beware of sleeping; "Therefore let us not sleep, as do others, but let us watch and be sober" (1 Thess. v. 6).

(2) Laziness Reviewed (6:10-11)

We note *the lazy man's rationale:* "Yet a little sleep, a little slumber, a little folding of the hands to sleep" (Proverbs 6:10). That is how the lazy man reasons. He yawns. He stretches. He finds a shady spot where he is protected from the full strength of the summer sun and settles down. "I'll just take a little nap," he says. And he yawns again, falls asleep, and wastes the entire afternoon. "Just a little nap!" That's the lazy man's excuse for idling away his time.

Of course there is such a thing as a healthy nap. The secret of my father's ability to work hard night and day was his nap. He bought, sold, and repaired cars in his own shop close to home, and he traveled away from home to preach on weekends and often during the week. He was an exceedingly good preacher and would stay up late studying, but he seemed tireless. He would rush in for his midday meal and eat it while telling my mother what he needed her to do for him. (My mother served as housewife, mother, accountant, secretary, purchasing agent, speaker at mothers' meetings, and I don't know what else! Truly a helpmate, she was always available, always cheerful, always patient, and always on top of things.) Then Dad would tell us kids to be quiet and he would stretch out on the couch. Regular as clockwork, before we could count to fifty, Dad was asleep. Half an hour later he would wake up and be on his way out of the house. That half-hour nap seemed to renew all his vital forces. He never wasted a minute and lived into his late seventies.

The lazy man is also a great believer in the nap, except that his idea is to take a nap to avoid doing work. Solomon, under the inspiration of the Holy Spirit, gave us God's mind on such a criminal waste of time. "How long?" he demanded. "How long?"

We note too *the lazy man's robber:* "So shall thy poverty come as one that travelleth, and thy want as an armed man" (Proverbs 6:11). Six Hebrew words convey the idea of poverty in the book of Proverbs: *rūsh*, which refers to being in want of the necessities of life;[1] *dal*, which refers to being impoverished or reduced in one's circumstances;[2] *heser*, which refers to being in want;[3] *'anī*, which refers to being wretched;[4] *'ebyōn*, which refers to being utterly destitute, absolutely helpless, and deprived of both wealth and will;[5] and *yārash*, which refers to being dispossessed.[6]

The lazy man can expect to be left without the necessities of life. His misfortunes are already coming toward him as he rolls over in his bed of idleness. His poverty is coming as "one that travelleth"— as a highwayman. It is coming like an armed man. The word picture is certainly vivid. The lazy man will be helpless when poverty comes—as helpless as a man looking into the barrel of the trigger-happy highwayman.

CHAPTER 9

Proverbs 6:12-19

The wise man continued extolling wisdom's precepts. As we have seen, they can prevent us from becoming surety and from becoming slothful. Wisdom's precepts can also guide us away from criminal behavior.

B. How They Guide Us (6:12-19)

1. The Criminal (6:12-15)

Proverbs 6:12-13 describes *the wicked man's deeds:* "A naughty person, a wicked man, walketh with a froward mouth. He winketh with his eyes, he speaketh with his feet, he teacheth with his fingers." The expression translated "a naughty person" literally means "a man of Belial" or "a worthless person." The word translated "wicked" means "injurious" and is derived from a word meaning "the breaking up of all that is good." Solomon had moral depravity, corruption, and lewdness in view.

Solomon painted a picture of the kind of man who uses nods, winks, and gestures to communicate his wishes or intentions to his confederates. Such a man uses what we would call "body language" to convey his thoughts. In eastern courts, where bribery and corruption were commonly part of legal proceedings, one could observe a great deal of this kind of communication between those who had come to a prior understanding and accomplished a complete rape of justice. The Lord, however, is not deceived by such people. He reads body language as well as any other language. In His estimation such people are worthless and wicked.

Charles Dickens knew how to describe the language of looks— in *Oliver Twist*, for example. The old Jew, Fagin, received word from one of his spies that Nancy, who had befriended the poor little orphan Oliver Twist, had entered into secret discussions with Oliver's friend Mr. Brownlow in order to protect the youngster from being kidnapped again by Fagin's gang of thieves. Fagin decided to break the news to Nancy's boyfriend, the violent burglar Bill Sikes. Dickens described how the wily Fagin worked on Bill's feelings until Sikes was beside himself with rage at what he considered to be Nancy's betrayal. Fagin was careful to avoid actually suggesting that Nancy be murdered, but he did not need to put the suggestion in words.

"You won't be—too—violent, Bill?" said the Jew. Dickens added: "The day was breaking, and there was light enough for the men to see each other's faces. They exchanged one brief glance; there was a fire in the eyes of both, which could not be mistaken." The agreement was all clinched with a look. Within an hour Sikes had brutally murdered Nancy.

The description of the wicked man's deeds is followed by a description in Proverbs 6:14 of *the wicked man's deceit:* "Frowardness is in his heart, he deviseth mischief continually; he soweth discord." The word translated "frowardness" can also be translated "deceitfulness." Deceitfulness, devilry, and discord are the wicked man's daily delight. He is little concerned that what he says and does messes up the lives of other people.

Of all the reprehensible frauds who prey upon the world, religious frauds are the worst. The old prophet introduced in

1 Kings 13:11 is an example. He lived in Bethel, and when Jeroboam set up his false altar at Bethel, the old prophet's sons went to the dedication while the old prophet stayed home. His sons came home agog with excitement. A young prophet from neighboring Judah had appeared out of nowhere. He had denounced the king, the false priests, and the altar. He had smitten the king, miraculously paralyzing his arm, and just as miraculously had healed him when the king pleaded for mercy. Then the king had invited the young prophet to the palace for a meal. The young prophet had categorically refused, saying that his mandate from Heaven forbade him to break bread with anyone at Bethel, now cursed with Jeroboam's golden calf.

This news took the old prophet by storm. Moved with envy and malice against the successful young prophet, the old prophet resorted to a policy of deception and mischief. He found the young prophet and invited him to come home for the night. The young man refused, citing the terms of his commission. Then the wicked old man pretended to have received a direct revelation from God. "Now that you have successfully discharged your mission," he said in effect, "it's all right for you to come home with me. We are on the same side; we are brothers in the faith. Besides, my boys are eager to meet you. They were tremendously impressed by your courage, conviction, and power." And so the deceiver laid siege to the young man's heart. "But he lied unto him," comments the Holy Spirit (1 Kings 13:18).

It was getting dark. The roar of a lion could be heard out on the hills. The young man was hungry and tired. At last he yielded. He became disobedient to the heavenly vision and the consequence was his death warrant (1 Kings 13:22).

Proverbs 6:15 describes *the wicked man's doom:* "Therefore shall his calamity come suddenly; suddenly shall he be broken without remedy." The Bible does not tell us what happened to the wicked old prophet who deceived the young prophet from Judah. Significantly the old prophet ended up burying the young prophet from Judah in his own grave in Bethel. At the end of the episode the old man was obsessed by thoughts of his own death which he realized could not be far away. He had sealed his own doom by his wickedness. He said to his sons, "When I am dead, then bury me in the sepulchre wherein the man of God is buried; lay my bones beside his bones" (1 Kings 13:31). Those who transgress the moral laws whereby God governs the universe never escape His judgment.

2. The Creator (6:16-19)

a. An Exclamation (6:16)

Solomon shifted the focus of his attention. He still had more to say about the criminal but he wanted to say it with special reference to the Creator. God's absolute morality places Him unswervingly on the side of right and against all wrong.

The fact that we do not always see God's hand visibly at work redressing wrongs on earth does not·mean for a moment that He does not care. He cares much more than we do. Nor does it mean that He does not act. He acts decisively, but other factors enter into the equation: His compassion, His patience, His infinite grace, His wisdom, and the prayers of His people.

A preacher friend of mine was once confronted by a distraught parent who was angry against God because his only son had been tragically killed. "Where was God when my son was killed?" the father demanded. My friend wisely replied, "Where He was when *His* Son was killed." The greatest demonstration of God's reaction to wrong, of course, is Calvary.

Proverbs 6:16 gives insight into the Creator's attitude toward wickedness: "These six things doth the Lord hate; yea, seven are an abomination unto him." "Six things...yea, seven" is an idiomatic Hebrew expression. The prophet Amos used it with great effect in his opening broadside against the sins of the nations in his line of fire (Amos 1:3,6,9,11,13; 2:1,4,6). The expression implies that the list is not exhaustive. The seven things listed in Proverbs 6:17-19 are all characteristics of fallen Lucifer, and all of them stand in stark contrast to the characteristics of the Lord Jesus.

b. An Explanation (6:17-19)

The Lord hates the *disdainful look*—the "proud look" in Proverbs 6:17. We use a similar expression when we speak of a person "looking down his nose" at someone else. Pride is the father of all sin. The proud look is scornful and contemptuous, the look of a person who imagines himself to be much better than others. Satan cast his evil gaze on the throne of God and planned an even higher seat of glory for himself. The Lord Jesus looked down from His lofty throne in compassion and grace upon poor, fallen man, made of the dust of the earth.

The Lord also hates the *deceitful tongue*—the "lying tongue" of Proverbs 6:17. Satan is the father of lies (John 8:44). He came into the garden of Eden to deceive. The idiom of his language is the lie. He is the author of all untruth, the ultimate source of all religious, philosophical, scientific, social, economic, and political error. The Lord Jesus is the Truth. It is impossible for Him to lie. He told the truth to Caiaphas knowing it would cost Him His life (Matthew 26:62-66). Pilate tried to fend off the growing feeling that he was the one who was really on trial by asking, "What is truth?" even while staring it in the face (John 18:38).

The Lord hates the *deadly hand,* the "hands that shed innocent blood" (Proverbs 6:17). Jesus said that Satan "was a murderer from the beginning" (John 8:44). Little did Eve realize, as she listened to the serpent's buttered lies, that her firstborn son would grow up to be a murderer. Since then, rivers of blood have flowed in crimson tides. We think of gruesome murders committed out of malice, spite, envy, and greed. We think of blood shed in atrocities, persecutions, repressions, rebellions, and holocausts. We think of blood shed in the name of war. And the end of bloodshed is not yet. John foretold that when the winepress of God's wrath is trodden without the city, blood will come out of the winepress, "even unto the horse bridles, by the space of a thousand and six hundred furlongs" (Revelation 14:20). This distance is roughly two hundred miles.

But turn your eyes from the murderer's hands and look at the hands of Jesus. They were placed in blessing on the heads of little children. Those hands gave sight to the blind. At their touch leprosy fled and the dead arose. His hands fed the hungry multitude, restored the severed ear of Malchus, and provided the precious blood that cancels all our sin. His hands still bear the imprint of the Roman nails.

According to Proverbs 6:18 the Lord also hates the *depraved heart,* the "heart that deviseth wicked imaginations." Adam lived long enough to see what sin had done to his ruined race, to realize that as far as man was concerned, "every imagination of the thoughts of his heart was only evil continually" (Genesis 6:5). Adam lived for 930 years, long enough to see wickedness take deep root on earth, long enough to see the sinful trend that would take hold of his posterity and end in the flood.

How Satan gloats over the depravity of man. The depraved heart is seen today, for example, in people who publish, peddle, and purchase pornography. They are an abomination in the sight of God. In contrast to the condition of their hearts, the heart of the Lord Jesus is pure, holy, and undefiled (Hebrews 7:26). He "knew no sin" (2 Corinthians 5:21).

Then too the Lord hates the *delinquent foot*. "Feet that be swift in running to mischief" are an abomination to Him (Proverbs 6:18). Satan ran swiftly to cause trouble for Job. When Satan appeared before the living God to give an account of himself, the Lord asked, "Whence comest thou?" Satan replied, "From going to and fro in the earth, and from walking up and down in it" (Job 1:7). Clearly he was up to no good. Asked if he had taken note of Job and his integrity and piety, Satan immediately slandered him. Given permission to destroy Job's wealth, Satan wasted no time.

A sequence of disasters befell Job with lightning speed. A messenger came with the news of the theft of Job's oxen and asses and the murder of his herdsmen. "While he was yet speaking" another messenger came with the news of the destruction of Job's sheep and servants (Job 1:16). "While he [the second messenger] was yet speaking" another came with the news of the loss of Job's camel caravans and the slaughter of their keepers (1:17). "While he was yet speaking" another came with news of the death of all Job's children (1:18-19). Each disaster followed hard on the heels of the previous one. Satan's feet were truly swift in running to mischief.

In contrast, the feet of the Lord Jesus always brought Him swiftly to where He could help and heal. Back and forth He went—north and south, east and west—always seeking out the diseased, the downtrodden, and the distressed. He was never in a hurry, yet He was never too late or too soon.

The Lord also hates the *dishonest witness*, the "false witness that speaketh lies" (Proverbs 6:19). In contrast to the dishonest witness, the Holy Spirit says of Jesus that He is "the faithful witness" (Revelation 1:5).

Satan tried to use false witnesses to secure the death of Christ. The wretched men who ran the religious affairs of Israel were his dupes. They knew they could get nothing on Jesus. Any honest witness would tell of His feeding the five thousand with a little lad's lunch, of His ridding the Gadarene demoniac of a legion of evil spirits, of His healing of people by the thousand, and of His raising of the dead—Jairus's daughter, the son of the widow of Nain, and Lazarus. Blind Bartimaeus would tell of receiving his sight, Zaccheus of being made good, the woman at the well of being made pure, and Malchus of being healed within that very hour. The religious leaders were not interested in honest witnesses. They wanted false witnesses who would distort Jesus' words, take them out of context, and give them a sinister twist. Matthew 26:60 says, "Many false witnesses came." Two were willing to twist Christ's teaching concerning the temple. But even that charge was inadequate, and the priests decided to force Him to confess His deity publicly so they could use that claim against Him.

Finally the Lord hates the *deliberate meddler,* the one who "soweth discord among brethren" (Proverbs 6:19). Satan the meddler stirred up Cain against Abel, Ishmael against Isaac, Esau against Jacob, and the sons of Jacob against Joseph. Jesus, on the other hand, is the healer of broken homes, the reconciler of estranged brethren, the Prince of Peace. He matched Peter the doer with John the dreamer; Simon the Zealot with Matthew the former traitor; down-to-earth Philip with guileless Nathanael.

How well I recall a little fellowship of believers with whom I met in a small building on the slopes of mount Carmel to remember the Lord during my army days in Haifa. In that peaceful circle were Jews and Arabs, British and Germans, Russians and Armenians—all one in Christ. Only Christ could have made them true brothers and sisters, loved of the Lord and beloved of each other. In the world outside, Satan—the great mischief-maker—set Germany and England at war, Arab and Jew in bitter hostility, and Russians and Armenians at odds.

In secular and sacred history we can find many people who were living incarnations of these seven things the Lord hates. The one who comes most forcibly to my mind is Jezebel. She had *a proud look.* Apparently she was a handsome woman, for she is famous for painting her face and adorning her hair. Indeed it seems she thought her looks would somehow influence the redoubtable Jehu (2 Kings 9:30). But she was sadly mistaken.

We can picture Jezebel's proud look when she asked Ahab if he was going to allow Naboth to keep his vineyard. We can see the flash in her eye as she said, "Dost thou now govern the kingdom of Israel?" (1 Kings 21:7) We can see the proud toss of her head as she said, "I will give thee the vineyard of Naboth." No stubborn citizen would stop this imperious daughter of a neighboring pagan king!

Jezebel also had *a lying tongue*—or what amounted to the same thing: she forged letters. "She wrote letters in Ahab's name," the historian said (1 Kings 21:8). Lies were a useful instrument of statecraft in Jezebel's reign.

Jezebel's *hands shed innocent blood.* They were dyed crimson. She "cut off the prophets of the Lord" (1 Kings 18:4) and would have murdered Elijah if she could have laid hands on him (19:1-2). Indeed her name is linked with the first recorded use of civil power in Israel against the true faith.

Jezebel's *heart devised wicked imaginations.* Her evil heart gave Israel over to an immoral idolatry far worse than the idolatry of

Jeroboam (1 Kings 16:30-33). She was a devotee of the Phoenician goddess Astarte. And Jezebel's evil heart planned the murder of Naboth.

Jezebel's *feet were swift in running to mischief.* The awful relentless plan and purpose of Jezebel is underlined in the polysyndeton that carries on the story of Naboth: "*And* she wrote in the letters, saying, Proclaim a fast, *and* set Naboth on high among the people: *And* set two men, sons of Belial, before him, to bear witness against him.... *And* then carry him out, *and* stone him, that he may die" (1 Kings 21:9-10, italics added).

Jezebel demanded that *false witnesses* be used to doom poor Naboth. They were to accuse him of blaspheming God and the king (21:10,13).

To complete the picture of Jezebel, we note that she *sowed discord* in the land. When her son Joram hoped to come to some kind of terms with Jehu, Joram said, "Is it peace, Jehu?" Jehu answered, "What peace, so long as the whoredoms of thy mother Jezebel and her witchcrafts are so many?" (2 Kings 9:22) It is no wonder that many centuries later when exposing the spiritual degeneracy of the church at Thyatira, the Lord referred to "that woman Jezebel" (Revelation 2:20). The behavior of that church was reminiscent of wicked Jezebel who embodied the things the Lord hates.

CHAPTER 10
Proverbs 6:20-35

C. How They Guard Us (6:20-35)
  1. From Adversity (6:20-23)
    a. The Call (6:20-21)
      (1) To Hear Parental Advice (6:20)
      (2) To Heed Parental Advice (6:21)
    b. The Consequence (6:22-23)
      (1) The Constant Presence of Heeded Advice (6:22)
        (a) What It Shows Us (6:22a)
        (b) When It Shields Us (6:22b)
        (c) How It Sharpens Us (6:22c)
      (2) The Constant Protection of Heeded Advice (6:23)
        (a) Imparting Light (6:23a)
        (b) Imparting Life (6:23b)
  2. From Adultery (6:24-35)
    a. Guile (6:24-26)
      (1) The Fatal Lure (6:24)
        (a) The Character of the Temptress (6:24a)
        (b) The Conversation of the Temptress (6:24b)
      (2) The Flaming Lust (6:25)
        (a) Beguiled by Her Loveliness (6:25a)
        (b) Beguiled by Her Look (6:25b)
      (3) The Fearful Loss (6:26)
        (a) Financial Loss (6:26a)
        (b) Final Loss (6:26b)
    b. Guilt (6:27-29)
      (1) The Question Asked (6:27-28)
      (2) The Question Answered (6:29)
        (a) The Forbidden Deed (6:29a)
        (b) The Foul Defilement (6:29b)

   c. Grief (6:30-35)
      (1) A Comparison: Pardonable Guilt (6:30-31)
         (a) Rationalization Can Be Made for Theft (6:30)
         (b) Restitution Can Be Made for Theft (6:31)
      (2) A Contrast: Persisting Guilt (6:32-35)
         (a) Adultery Is Destructive (6:32)
         (b) Adultery Is Dishonorable (6:33)
         (c) Adultery Is Distressing (6:34-35)
            i. The Desire for Revenge Is Unavoidable
              (6:34)
            ii. The Desire for Revenge Is Unappeasable
              (6:35)

Wisdom's precepts *goad* us. They instill in us at least a modicum of fiscal common sense. They *guide* us, setting clearly before us the behavior of the wicked man. We should avoid emulating him, if for no other reason, because the Lord hates his behavior. Wisdom's precepts also *guard* us from adversity and from adultery. Happy are those who are kept from both.

C. How They Guard Us (6:20-35)

1. From Adversity (6:20-23)

a. The Call (6:20-21)

Here is a call both to hear and to heed parental advice: "My son, keep thy father's commandment, and forsake not the law of thy mother: Bind them continually upon thine heart, and tie them about thy neck." Thank God for spiritual fathers and saintly mothers.

Few youngsters have had a more remarkable mother than John and Charles Wesley had. The twenty-fifth child of her father, she had nineteen children of her own! Deeply impressed by an account of Danish missionary activity in India, Susanna Wesley wanted to be a missionary. Instead she lived in Borley rectory as the wife of a struggling minister. So Susanna looked around for a missionfield closer to home and found one in that manse. Her own children became her missionfield.

She later wrote: "It came into my mind that I might do more than I do. I resolved to begin with my own children. I take such proportion of time as I can best spare to discourse every night with each child by himself." Each child in turn had his or her own time alone on an appointed day of the week with Susanna. When people began to comment on her remarkable influence on her children, she described her simple system. "There is no mystery about it," she wrote. "I just took Molly alone with me into my own room every Monday night, Betty every Tuesday night, Jacky every Thursday night, and so on. That was all!" But it was enough! Out of that home came John and Charles, who were destined to bring spiritual revival to England. Susanna made sure her children heard and paid heed to her advice.

b. The Consequence (6:22-23)

(1) The Constant Presence of Heeded Advice (6:22)

Parental advice *shows* us, *shields* us, and *sharpens* us: "When thou goest, it shall lead thee; when thou sleepest, it shall keep thee; and when thou awakest, it shall talk with thee." Asleep or awake, at home or abroad, at all times and in all places, the person who has listened to the godly counsel of wise and loving parents is hedged about with sound advice that will keep him from adversity.

I remember the sound advice my father gave me when I graduated from high school in England. At the ripe old age of fifteen I was prepared to plunge into the business world. World War II was at its height and even prestigious financial institutions such as Barclays Bank (two thousand branches in Britain and two thousand branches overseas) were prepared to consider my application because young men were at a premium. As soon as they reached eighteen they were swept into the armed forces. I was hired as a junior clerk and was told to report to the bank's local head office in Cardiff, the capital city of Wales. My father's advice was "Make yourself indispensable." How I lived with that sage counsel! It stayed with me night and day.

I was put in charge of what the bank called "the local exchange." Twice every day the junior clerks from all the downtown banks met in a room at our bank to exchange checks drawn on each other's banks and paid into accounts at various downtown banks by depositors. I made myself indispensable at those times. The junior clerks sorted, listed, totaled, and prepared huge piles of checks for exchange. Woe betide the clerk who failed to show up on time. If he was late, he had to run all over town, personally visiting every bank to exchange checks the hard way. Two or three goofs like that and the unfortunate clerk would find himself dispensable.

I not only had to run the local exchange; I had to tend to the manager's office, run errands for the lords of creation in the head office upstairs, answer the telephone (inconveniently placed at the far end of the office), tend to customers needing directions, and make sure all outgoing mail was properly enveloped, stamped, and ready for the late afternoon mail call. Nobody ran faster, worked harder, licked stamps better, and added columns of figures swifter than John Phillips. I was indispensable. That great financial institution, I was sure, would collapse without me. I would swagger down St. Mary Street on my lunch hour, carefully eyeing my watch to make sure I'd be back on the job ten minutes early.

I was indispensable to the manager when he wanted his blotting paper renewed. I was indispensable to customers who phoned in to ask about their bank balances. I was indispensable to all the other banks in town that eagerly waited to get their corporate hands on their checks at the local exchange before their account balances were depleted. I was indispensable to important people all over England who waited for mail from the bank. I was indispensable to the awesome and remote Mr. Meredith (who presided over the affairs of hundreds of Barclays Bank branches in South Wales) when he suddenly realized he had forgotten the kippers his wife had asked him to bring home for supper.

I was so indispensable that the British army claimed me to help handle its terrible mismanagement of Palestine. I was so indispensable that when I was discharged from the army, Barclays Bank refused to give me back my job. "Sorry, old fellow," said the man who now wore the mantle of Mr. Meredith, a new man whose domestic well-being I had never secured. "You see, we are overstaffed. All those other fellows came back from the war ahead of you. They filled all the positions we had available or will ever have available for the next dozen years. The trouble is, Phillips, they all made themselves indispensable too."

Oh well, I was in God's hands. I joined the Bank of Montreal, went to Canada, and made myself indispensable to them instead! All humor aside, all my father's advice has been invaluable. It has always stood me in good stead. It has always been there when I needed it to keep me up to the mark.

(2) The Constant Protection of Heeded Advice (6:23)

"For the commandment is a lamp; and the law is light; and reproofs of instruction are the way of life." Solomon particularly had in mind spiritual advice based on the Word of God. That advice, if heeded, guarantees light and life. "Law is light," said Solomon. *"Lex est lux,"* said the Romans.

Leviticus 17:11 says, "The life of the flesh is in the blood." Emphasizing the sanctity of the blood, God said, "Ye shall therefore keep my statutes, and my judgments: which if a man do, he shall live in them" (Leviticus 18:5).

Solomon's reference to the Word of God, which offers life, is all the more important because of what follows. The verses following Proverbs 6:23 present a lengthy warning against involvement with an immoral woman. Darkness and death lurk where she lives, while light and life are imparted by Solomon's advice. Wisdom's precepts guard us from adultery.

2. From Adultery (6:24-35)

a. Guile (6:24-26)

(1) The Fatal Lure (6:24)

Proverbs 6:24 is the beginning of Solomon's third warning against immorality. Solomon legalized his lust by adding the women he wanted to his ever-growing harem. Even so, he gained wisdom from his experience with women. In one of his more bitter moments (perhaps when he was grieving over the Shulamite who refused to be added to his collection and whose beauty of face, form, and faith haunted him ever afterward with a terrible sense of what he had lost through his lust[1]) Solomon wrote:

> I find more bitter than death the woman, whose heart is snares and nets, and her hands as bands: whoso pleaseth God shall escape from her; but the sinner shall be taken by her. Behold, this have I found, saith the preacher, counting one by one, to find out the account: Which yet my soul seeketh, but I find not: one man among a thousand have I found; but a woman among all those have I not found (Ecclesiastes 7:26-28).

Solomon had a thousand wives and concubines, but not one of them brought him lasting joy. The one woman with whom he could

have found his true heart's desire was repelled by his utter carnality
and turned him down stone cold.

In Proverbs 6:24 Solomon turned his attention to the harlot.
Guile, guilt, and grief are her stock-in-trade. She offers a fatal lure,
a flaming lust, and a fearful loss. Solomon noted her fatal lure and
warned of both the *character* and the *conversation* of the temptress:
"To keep thee from the evil woman, from the flattery of the tongue
of a strange woman."

The harlot's character is "evil." The Hebrew word translated
"evil" denotes the breaking up of all that is good. The Greek
equivalents of the Hebrew word point to moral depravity, corruption, and lewdness. The harlot is also described as "a strange
woman," a designation which points primarily to a foreigner, a
priestess of an immoral religious cult that specializes in prostitution.

The harlot's character is bad and her talk is beguiling. She is full
of flattery. She knows what to say to make her prospective client feel
that he is a most desirable and distinguished fellow. "Why, with my
good looks, I could get anyone," she infers, "yet I have chosen you."
"Hello, handsome," she may say. "What are you doing tonight?" She
plays with him as a fisherman plays with the fish he can see
swimming around his lure. The longer the poor fish of a fellow
lingers listening to the woman's banter, the more likely he is to get
hooked.

(2) The Flaming Lust (6:25)

Solomon, wise in the ways of women, warned against being
beguiled by her loveliness: "Lust not after her beauty in thine heart." He
also warned against being *beguiled by her look:* "Neither let her take
thee with her eyelids." This kind of woman can put a world of
meaning into what she says with her eyes, her eyelids, and her
eyebrows. She has mastered the sudden look downward in pretended modesty; the well-known wink; the raised eyebrows; the
slanting look; the sudden raising of both eyebrows in pretended
surprise or horror; the drawing together of the eyebrows in a scowl
of disapproval; the crafty look out of slits formed by eyelids half
drawn down. Oh yes, the harlot can speak volumes with her eyes.

Ah, those eyes! They light up her face. They beckon and bewitch.
Half her attraction is in her eyes and she knows how to use them.
"Come," they say, "look into our depths. Read our promise." They
gleam, glitter, dance, and delight. They swim with tears and sparkle
with mirth. They are merry and they mock.

"Don't be fooled by her eyes, boy," Solomon said. And who should know better than Solomon? He had been fooled many times already. There was one woman, however, whose eyes he had read correctly. "Turn away thine eyes from me, for they have overcome me," he wrote (Song of Solomon 6:5). He had read scorn in her eyes. All of a sudden, though still eminently desirable, she was "terrible as an army with banners" (Song of Solomon 6:4).

(3) The Fearful Loss (6:26)

Solomon knew the high price of the harlot. She offers *financial loss:* "For by means of a whorish woman a man is brought to a piece of bread." Mr. Quest, one of the characters in Sir Henry Rider Haggard's classic *Colonel Quaritch, V.C.,* knew the truth of this proverb.

Mr. Quest was the town lawyer and banker. What he coveted was to be the lord of the manor, to own the stately mansion and broad acres that had been in the de la Molle family for generations. To that end he schemed. His bank held extensive mortgages on the property, so he was able to arrange for Edward Cossey, son and heir of the owner of the bank, to acquire the mortgages. The wily lawyer was within sight of his goal, for he had a hold over young Cossey. Mr. Quest sprang the trap and the mortgages were his. He called in all the money owed, knowing full well that old Squire de la Molle could not meet the payments, and then sat back to wait for the coveted property to fall into his hands.

But Mr. Quest had a guilty secret too. He was a bigamist. In his youth he had fallen into the hands of an unscrupulous woman. He married her when he was drunk and lived to regret it. Over the years she drained him of all his wealth. Mr. Quest yearned for position, prosperity, power, and respectability, but the woman into whose clutches he had fallen had the whip hand. She blackmailed him. She squandered the money she forced him to give her and she demanded more and more. The higher he climbed the social ladder in the little English market town where he lived, the lower his nemesis sank in vice and squalor. Always she held over his respectable head the threat of exposure.

His other wife Belle, not knowing she was married to a bigamist and longing to be set free from a marriage grown hateful, complicated the lawyer's affairs. Belle had brought a small fortune to the marriage, but Mr. Quest had used it to buy the silence of the harpy who preyed upon him. His salary disappeared into the same insatiable maw.

In the end all Mr. Quest's schemes collapsed around his head when the evil woman showed up when court was in session and he was pleading a case. She was drunk, dissolute, and dreadful. Years of dissipation and foul, vicious living had written her awful character on her face. She was inflamed with anger, arrayed in soiled and gaudy finery, wild-eyed, abusive, and foulmouthed. Having already run through the wretched lawyer's fortune, she had come to claim her pound of flesh. She had come to reduce him to a piece of bread.

Woe betide the man who falls into the clutches of an evil woman! So said Sir Henry. So said Solomon. So says the Spirit of God.

The wayside harlot described by Solomon offers not only financial loss; she also offers *final loss:* "The adulteress will hunt for the precious life" (Proverbs 6:26). She is after the man's soul. Some scholars render the verse differently: "The harlot is only out to earn a meal, but the adulteress preys upon your very life." Either way, immorality has devastating consequences. It leaves an indelible mark on the soul, the mind, the memory, and the conscience of the one who commits it. Nobody escapes the consequences. Those consequences may seem to sleep for a while, but watch out when they awaken!

Ask Reuben. Just when Jacob's heart was breaking over the death of his beloved Rachel, his oldest son Reuben committed adultery with Bilhah, who was Rachel's maid and Jacob's third wife. Bilhah was the one Jacob would most likely have turned to for comfort. The deed was known to Jacob (Genesis 35:22) and it was one more terrible cross for him to bear.

We can see Reuben and Bilhah carrying their guilt around the camp. Their secret thoughts must have tormented them: *Does Jacob know? If not, how long can we keep the secret? If he does know, why doesn't he act? The penalty is death. Does Jacob want to bring the matter to court? Does he know or doesn't he?* The suspense must have been intolerable. We can see the guilty pair exchange looks. Those looks were intercepted and read by Jacob, but he said nothing.

The years passed. Most likely the guilty passion faded as guilty passions do. Dislike, or at least distaste, grew up between Reuben and Bilhah. In time even the memory of the deed was buried and almost forgotten. Reuben began to think he'd gotten away with his sin. Twenty-two years came and went in Canaan, followed by seventeen years in Egypt. Reuben breathed more freely.

But then came the summons to Jacob's deathbed. In his last will and testament the dying patriarch bequeathed the future to his boys—determining both their position and power in the Hebrew Old Testament kingdom. His eyes, kindled by the light of prophecy, swept around the bed and lighted in turn on each of his sons. He pulled himself up, leaned forward on his staff, cleared his throat, and began. He looked at Reuben: "Reuben, thou art my firstborn, my might, and the beginning of my strength, the excellency of dignity, and the excellency of power" (Genesis 49:3). We can almost see Reuben swell with pride. The haunted look left his face. He concluded that the deed which had preyed on his guilty conscience for the best part of forty years was never known to Jacob after all.

Reuben listened eagerly for word of his place in the kingdom. As firstborn, of course, he knew the double portion would be his. Rosy visions of future greatness for his tribe rose up in his mind's eye. But what was he hearing? "Unstable as water, thou shalt not excel; because thou wentest up to thy father's bed; then defiledst thou it" (Genesis 49:4). Jacob paused and again his eyes swept around the circle. His voice quivered. His old hands shook on his staff. The next words rang out. They could be heard across the courtyard and up and down the halls: "He went up to my couch."

The ax had fallen. It took nearly forty years, but Reuben's sin found him out. Adultery always catches up with the adulterer. The nature of that sin is to give itself away and demand payment in full. It hunts for the precious life. It goes after the soul.

b. Guilt (6:27-29)

(1) The Question Asked (6:27-28)

In giving us precepts to guard us from the guilt of adultery, Solomon asked: "Can a man take fire in his bosom, and his clothes not be burned? Can one go upon hot coals, and his feet not be burned?" Let us ponder the question well. When someone traffics with a harlot or tampers with another man's wife, he is playing with fire. The law of cause-and-effect works rigorously here as does the law of sowing and reaping. As surely as God is God, He sees to it that immorality is paid for in the end. David, Samson, and the prodigal son all found this out. The only reason Judah escaped the penalty for his bad behavior was that he repented. But even he did not escape. Two of his sons became vile and died under the anger of God.

(2) The Question Answered (6:29)

To ask the question is to answer it. Of course a man cannot play with fire and not get burned. "So he that goeth in to his neighbour's wife; whosoever toucheth her shall not be innocent." Woe to that man who breaks down the high and holy fence God has put around marriage, the first of all human institutions. God will not be mocked in this area of life.

Marriage is God's idea. He instituted it, set up its rules, decreed its boundaries, and declared its sanctity. A man's relationship with his wife is to be loving and loyal. It is to mirror God's relationship with His Old Testament people and Christ's relationship with His church.

The home is to be the cradle of society. Within its walls children are to be born and raised in an atmosphere of love, trust, and discipline. The home is the basic unit of national life. As the home goes, so goes the nation.

Unfortunately relativism in morals and humanism in philosophy are prominent in a decadent society like ours, and these philosophies have an adverse effect on the homes of our nation. Our society's permissiveness was graphically expressed by a cartoon that appeared years ago in *The New Yorker* magazine. The cartoon depicted two older women sitting together in a living room. One was saying to the other, "No, no, it's Frank and Gloria who are married but not living together. George and Judy are living together but not married." A society with permissive views of marriage and the home cannot remain strong. No matter how widely accepted these views are, they do not make wrong behavior right.

A *Time* magazine article some years ago gave statistics on common law marriage and said, "It used to be called 'living in sin.' Now it is simply 'living together.'" The article stated that divorce is now so common that according to a Census Bureau report nearly half of all children born today can expect to spend a meaningful portion of their lives before age eighteen in single-parent families. The journalist added, "The report did not speculate on what psychological effects that may have on the young."[2]

Adultery contributes heavily to the breakdown of many marriage relationships. This sin is hardly an indictable offense in human courts any more, but it is high on the list of human offenses visited by retribution from the supreme court in Heaven.

c. Grief (6:30-35)

Wisdom's precepts guard us from the grief and persisting guilt that result from adultery.

(1) A Comparison: Pardonable Guilt (6:30-31)

Solomon compared the consequences of breaking the seventh commandment, "Thou shalt not commit adultery," and the eighth commandment, "Thou shalt not steal" (Exodus 20:14-15). There is tolerance for the man who steals another man's wealth, but not for the man who steals another man's wife. Solomon pointed out that *rationalization* can be offered for ordinary theft: "Men do not despise a thief, if he steal to satisfy his soul when he is hungry" (Proverbs 6:30). Such thievery is wrong, but it is at least excusable.

In her book *The Good Earth* Pearl Buck traced the fortunes of Wang, a small-time farmer. In a time of drought he was forced to flee his beloved fields and journey south where, rumor had it, food was plentiful. So it was, at a price. Wang and his family huddled together in a makeshift shanty by the city wall near the house of a wealthy lord. Wang's wife and children begged but received little because so many others plied the same hopeless trade. Poor Wang pulled a rickshaw for fewer pennies than he needed to buy even the ghost of a meal for his family. He pulled heavy loads and still he starved. He felt his strength giving way.

Wang's wife had once been a slave in a house just like the one whose wall propped up the rags and tatters of their shanty. So when a revolution came and she joined a mob that invaded and pillaged the wealthy lord's house, she knew just where to go. She came away with a handful of gems. Stolen in a time of hunger and desperation, those gems assured Wang's fortune in the days ahead. Nobody saw anything wrong in a starving woman stealing from a rich lord. Solomon understood such flexible morality. Sometimes theft can be rationalized.

Also, *restitution* can be made for theft: "If he be found, he shall restore sevenfold; he shall give all the substance of his house" (Proverbs 6:31). A thief can make repayment. When he is caught he can be made to pay his debt to society. In Bible times a thief was required under the law of the trespass offering to repay the full amount stolen plus an additional twenty percent (Leviticus 5:16). Zacchaeus, convicted of his particular style of theft, promised the Lord he would restore fourfold all that he had robbed and give half of his estate to the poor (Luke 19:1-9). In an extreme case, Solomon said, a thief could be made to restore sevenfold and forfeit his entire estate.

Restitution can be made for stealing a man's wealth, but what restitution can be made for seducing a man's wife?

(2) A Contrast: Persisting Guilt (6:32-35)

In contrast to the pardonable guilt of the thief, the adulterer's guilt persists because his sin is destructive, dishonorable, and distressing.

Adultery is *destructive:* "But whoso committeth adultery with a woman lacketh understanding: he that doeth it destroyeth his own soul" (Proverbs 6:32). Adultery is a sin against the body. Paul warned: "Flee fornication. Every sin that a man doeth is without the body: but he that committeth fornication sinneth against his own body" (1 Corinthians 6:18). (Adultery of course is an aggravated form of fornication.) Adultery is also a sin against the soul. In Old Testament times the law of God mandated the death penalty for adultery for both guilty parties (Leviticus 20:10).

In the New Testament the Lord showed mercy to the unfortunate woman taken in adultery. "In the very act," gloated the Pharisees pressing their case for the prosecution. Their words immediately raise the question, Why pick on the woman? Why wasn't the man on trial too? The Pharisees' accusation is typical of the hypocrisy of society. All too often the man gets away with adultery, even boasting of his "conquest" to his friends. The Lord did not condemn the woman; neither did He condone her behavior. "Go, and sin no more," He said (John 8:1-11).

The word translated "understanding" in Proverbs 6:32 can be translated "heart." One version renders the phrase, "lacks heart and understanding." An adulterer "is devoid of common sense," says another translator. Adultery is a stupid crime because, driven by lust and passion, panting for a momentary satisfaction of desire, the guilty pair pay no heed to consequences.

Adultery has a physical consequence. The Bible regards adultery as a defilement. That was Jacob's assessment, we remember, of Reuben's sin with Bilhah. "Thou wentest up to thy father's bed; then defiledst thou it," the patriarch said (Genesis 49:4).

Adultery has a psychological consequence. Guilt always attaches to this sin, no matter how sophisticated the rationalization may be. Guilt does untold damage to a person's moral fiber and mental health.

Adultery also has a spiritual consequence. God sets aside as unclean any person who commits this sin. It is one of the excommunicating sins of the church (1 Corinthians 5:11). God certainly forgave David for committing adultery with Bathsheba, but the era of his great military conquests was over. In that regard God put him aside; he was no longer a chosen vessel. Man may fail to carry out discipline, but God never fails. Adultery usually disqualifies a person from any further public usefulness in the Lord's service. Yes, the price of adultery is enormously high. No wonder God says that the person who commits it lacks common sense.

Adultery is *dishonorable:* "A wound and dishonour shall he get; and his reproach shall not be wiped away" (Proverbs 6:33). Even in today's dissolute society, dishonor often results, especially when the adulterer is a prominent person.

In the United States two television evangelists came down with a crash because of adultery. Their downfall came within months of each other. One of the men ruled a considerable television empire and presided over other financially profitable business ventures, all of which were billed as a ministry requiring enormous donations from a gullible public. At the height of his career he was accused by a competing television evangelist of immorality. A scandal erupted. Then the authorities investigated the man's financial affairs. He was put on trial for fraud, found guilty, and sentenced to a long term in prison. The secular humanist media had a heyday.

This scandal had barely subsided before another one erupted. The accuser in the first scandal was himself accused of immorality— of having weird relations with a common prostitute. This man went before his vast television audience and confessed and wept before the cameras. However, he refused to bow to the discipline of his denomination and was excommunicated. Yet he continued his television "ministry" as if nothing had happened and countless admirers continued to send him the money needed to keep up the farce. Again the media exulted. It is impossible to assess the harm these two men did to the legitimate cause of Christ.

"A wound and dishonour shall he get; and his reproach shall not be wiped away," says the Holy Spirit of God. How true! All of us need to pray earnestly, "Lead us not into temptation, but deliver us from evil," lest we find ourselves disqualified, disgraced, and discarded by the Holy Spirit. He does not insist on a clever vessel, but He does insist on a clean one.

"I was almost in all evil," Solomon said (Proverbs 5:14). Nothing but the grace of God has preserved us when we've been in similar circumstances. "As for me," confessed Asaph, "my feet were almost gone; my steps had well nigh slipped....until I went into the sanctuary" (Psalm 73:2,17). There perspective, balance, and moral stability were restored to him. "It is good for me to draw near to God: I have put my trust in the Lord God, that I may declare all thy works," was Asaph's final word (73:28). He was telling us the way to avoid all moral snares.

Adultery is *distressing*. It provokes in the jealous husband a desire
for revenge that is *unavoidable:* "For jealousy is the rage of a man:
therefore will he not spare in the day of vengeance" (Proverbs 6:34).
There is no passion so strong, so unquenchable, so determined, and
so vindictive as jealousy. Elsewhere Solomon said, "Jealousy is cruel
as the grave" (Song of Solomon 8:6). Apparently he had experienced his share of the rage.

In the second book of his trilogy on the Zulu nation, Sir Henry
Rider Haggard wrote of jealousy and revenge in the story of
Mameena, the "Child of Storm." Mameena was an extraordinarily
beautiful, clever, and ambitious black woman who aspired to be the
chief woman in Zululand. Her path to power led her through
sundry marriages, each one raising her higher on the social ladder.
She cared nothing for the passions she evoked in men. She had only
one passion—power.

The turning point in the story came when she was married to a
Zulu chief named Saduko. Mameena set her eyes on Umbelazi, the
brother of the prince Cetewayo. The prince Umbelazi was handsome, powerful, and generous. Mameena decided that when the
Zulu king Panda died, Umbelazi would assuredly become the next
king. After all, she reasoned, he was his father's favorite. So Mameena
made her play for Umbelazi. She abandoned Saduko and ran away
with the prince Umbelazi. Soon she had him as firmly in her coils
as she had had all her previous mates.

In time it became evident in Zululand that Umbelazi and Cetewayo
were rivals for the throne. Their squabbles were incessant and
because both princes commanded the loyalty of large armies, it was
equally evident that there would be civil war. Saduko commanded
a tribe loyal to Umbelazi, the man who had stolen his wife. Saduko's
secret rage, resentment, and consuming jealousy were to tip the
scales.

Gnawed by a sense of guilt and a measure of shame, Umbelazi
tried to appease Saduko. Umbelazi sent Saduko gifts, promoted
him, and gave him command over great regiments. Meanwhile the
political pot boiled.

The day came when the divided nation demanded that King
Panda make his intentions public—when he died, who would
inherit the throne, Umbelazi or Cetewayo? The king, rendered
powerless by the powerful factions that sided with one or the other
of the two princes, wrung his hands. Finally he blurted out, "When
there are two bulls in the herd, they must fight."

Soon the two armies squared off for the fatal battle. Both sides
were strong and they expected a fearful fight. Umbelazi strode

down the ranks of his warriors to inspire them, cheer them on, and promise great rewards once victory was achieved. Then the battle began. Saduko's regiments thundered forward to meet the serried ranks of Cetewayo's forward regiments. But instead of a fight there was a surrender. Saduko's regiments inverted their spears and shields and were welcomed into the ranks of Cetewayo.

Saduko had his revenge. Jealousy, cruel as the grave, had no scruples in the day of vengeance. Saduko's soul was filled with such rage that even dishonor, treachery, and betrayal were useful tools for paying back Umbelazi for stealing Mameena. Within hours Umbelazi was dead and Cetewayo was assured the throne. Saduko's vengeance was complete.

Similar stories are common. The man whose wife has been stolen usually knows only one goal: vengeance fired by jealousy and rage. The desire for revenge is *unappeasable:* "He will not regard any ransom; neither will he rest content, though thou give him many gifts" (Proverbs 6:35).

CHAPTER 11

Proverbs 7:1-27

V. Wisdom's Presence (7:1-27)
  A. How Dear It Is (7:1-3)
    1. A Source of Life (7:1-2a)
    2. A Source of Love (7:2b-3)
  B. How Near It Is (7:4)
  C. How Clear It Is (7:5-27)
    1. Warning of the Harlot's Seductive Wiles (7:5-21)
      a. Her Corner: Like a Spider's (7:5-12)
        (1) The Trap Seen (7:5)
        (2) The Trap Set (7:6-9)
          (a) The Youth's Folly (7:6-7)
          (b) The Youth's Footsteps (7:8-9)
            i. Where He Wandered (7:8a)
            ii. Where He Went (7:8b-9)
        (3) The Trap Sprung (7:10-12)
          (a) The Harlot's Dress (7:10)
          (b) The Harlot's Deportment (7:11)
          (c) The Harlot's Domain (7:12)
      b. Her Coils: Like a Serpent's (7:13-21)
        (1) How She Caught Him (7:13)
        (2) What She Taught Him (7:14-21)
          (a) She Sounded So Pious (7:14)
          (b) She Sounded So Personable (7:15)
          (c) She Sounded So Provocative (7:16-18)
            i. Her Bed So Delectable (7:16-17)
            ii. Her Bribe So Desirable (7:18)
          (d) She Sounded So Persuasive (7:19-21)
            i. The Final Argument (7:19-20)
              a. I Am Quite Solitary (7:19)
              b. It Is Quite Safe (7:20)
            ii. The Final Agreement (7:21)

2. Warning of the Harlot's Secret Wares (7:22-27)
    a. She Deals in Death (7:22-23)
        (1) The Folly of Her Victim (7:22)
        (2) The Fate of Her Victim (7:23)
    b. She Deals in Doom (7:24-26)
        (1) Listen to the Voice of Holiness (7:24-25)
        (2) Listen to the Verdict of History (7:26)
    c. She Deals in Damnation (7:27)

Solomon dealt thoroughly with the issue of immorality. Three times in his first six chapters he turned to this theme. What Solomon told us about the perils and pitfalls of promiscuity is all perfectly true. He was inspired by the Holy Spirit to write his proverbs. We can only wish he had been a monogamist. However, as the book of Jonah so clearly reveals, God sometimes has to do His perfect work with imperfect instruments.

Technically Solomon was not an immoral man. He had a legal loophole. He had the power, influence, wealth, and position necessary to marry the women who inflamed his lust. He simply added them to his harem; in his opinion that procedure sanctified his sensuality.

In spite of Solomon's imperfections, he wrote under direct revelation and inspiration of the Holy Spirit as he extolled the way of wisdom.

V. WISDOM'S PRESENCE (7:1-27)

A. How Dear It Is (7:1-3)

Solomon's words in Proverbs are *a source of life:* "My son, keep my words, and lay up my commandments with thee. Keep my commandments, and live" (Proverbs 7:1-2). Notice that this exhortation is a command that goes far beyond cautioning or counseling. Whether Solomon knew it or not, he was writing Holy Writ. He had all the authority of the inspiring Spirit of God behind him. Because he was writing Scripture, his words were alive. They still throb with authority and life.

Peter had the same sense of writing words that were life-giving. He spoke of "the word of God, which liveth and abideth forever" (1 Peter 1:23). That Word regenerates; it imparts life, the very life of

God. It is "incorruptible seed." All else is transient, but "the word of the Lord endureth for ever" (1:25).

"Keep my commandments, and live," Solomon said to his son. Solomon was concerned for the life of his son because he had just seen a young man, a young man just like his son, going to his death (Proverbs 7:7-27). The word translated "live" here implies "live forever." The Word of God offers spiritual life, resurrection life, and eternal life.

Solomon pointed to the inspired wisdom of the Word as a source of life and *a source of love:* "Keep...my law as the apple of thine eye. Bind [my commandments] upon thy fingers, write them upon the table of thine heart" (Proverbs 7:2-3). If only that young man going to his death had cherished God's Word as carefully as he cherished the tender pupil of his eye! Instead he had fallen into the clutches of a prostitute.

How sensitive the eye is. Just one speck of dust in the eye can cause immediate, intense pain that demands instant attention. Nobody ignores a speck of dust in the eye. For years I wore contact lenses and in the windy city of Chicago it was all too easy to get dust in my eye. Immediately I had to stop, get that lens out, and cleanse my eye. The pain was insistent until I did. When the Holy Spirit says, "Keep... my law as the apple [the pupil] of thine eye," He is demanding that we be equally sensitive to His Word. Morally speaking, the slightest impurity presented to our eyes should cause intense awareness that something is wrong and that God's Word is demanding attention.

Solomon added, "Bind [my commandments] upon thy fingers" (Proverbs 7:3). If only that young man going to his death had bound God's Word upon his fingers! Then his fingers would have cried out, "Touch not!" So much immorality begins with touching. Modern psychology advocates a great deal of touching that God's Word forbids. "Touch not the unclean thing," God says in both Testaments (2 Corinthians 6:17; Isaiah 52:11).

Solomon, like a master surgeon, probed deeper. "Write [my commandments] upon the table of thine heart," he said (Proverbs 7:3). Once a person gets God's Word into his heart—not just into his head—God's Word will slay each temptation the moment it comes to mind. When we love God's Word, it monitors everything else. We cannot learn the importance of this truth soon enough.

All too often we have God's Word in our heads, but not in our hearts. God's Word in the head is not strong enough in itself to control the hot passions of youth. Although the irresistible logic of God's Word may be clearly understood and accepted in the head, the irrepressible love of God's Word in the heart is what holds the bulwarks of the soul against the full force of the foe. Hence Solomon's command to his son had a sense of urgency. Unfortunately, although we can command obedience in our homes, we cannot legislate holiness. The roots of holiness lie much deeper than the obedience of the mind. God's Word must be dear to our hearts and we must abide by its wisdom if we are to resist the temptations of Satan.

B. How Near It Is (7:4)

"Say unto wisdom, Thou art my sister; and call understanding thy kinswoman." There are some things a man would never do in the presence of a much loved and honored sister. Well, let wisdom be that sister. Let wisdom be always at your side to prevent you from speaking that lie, telling that lewd joke, perusing that filthy book, watching that pornographic movie, indulging in that vile lust, or yielding to that sensual urge.

The word translated "kinswoman" in Proverbs 7:4 means "close friend." The only other place the word occurs in Scripture is in connection with Boaz. The word is used the first time he is introduced into the story of Ruth; the Holy Spirit said, "Naomi had a *kinsman* of her husband's, a mighty man of wealth" (Ruth 2:1, italics added). When Naomi discovered that Boaz had shown his love for Ruth, she rejoiced. "The man is near of kin unto us, one of our next kinsmen," she said (Ruth 2:20). With a kinsman like Boaz, the redemption and royalty of Ruth were assured. If we call understanding our "kinswoman," it will do for us all that Boaz did for Ruth. It will lead us into honorable relationships and put us on the road to glory.

Every child of God can have wisdom as a sister and understanding as a kinswoman. We need to keep them close by, for they provide clear warning of danger.

C. How Clear It Is (7:5-27)

1. Warning of the Harlot's Seductive Wiles (7:5-21)

a. Her Corner: Like a Spider's (7:5-12)

(1) The Trap Seen (7:5)

Wisdom (the sister) and understanding (the kinswoman) are to be kept close by for a purpose: to keep young men from sin and shame—"that they may keep thee from the strange woman, from the stranger which flattereth with her words." Solomon saw the danger and he warned his son.

As usual, the words translated "strange" and "stranger" point to the Hebrew apostate and the foreign woman. Solomon had a lot of experience with foreign women. His first wife was an Egyptian princess, doubtless steeped in all the idolatry of her native land. Rehoboam's mother was Naamah, an Ammonitess. Her people worshiped the god Milcom in the same way the neighboring tribes worshiped Molech, to whom little children were offered in sacrifice. Indeed when Solomon himself grew old, "his wives turned away his heart after other gods . . . and after Milcom the abomination of the Ammonites." He built a high place "for Molech, the abomination of the children of Ammon" (1 Kings 11:1-9).

Solomon's heart was already wandering along these evil paths when he wrote his proverbs. His heathen wives worshiped pagan gods in temples that were little more than houses of prostitution where sexual immorality was elevated to the consummation of worship. In his younger days he steeled his heart against such practices, but in later years he allowed his wives to set up shrines to their pagan deities and surrendered to their lure himself. There was little Solomon did not know about foreign women. Yet when he wrote the book of Proverbs, he could still see those women as a trap and he still had enough sense to warn his son about them.

(2) The Trap Set (7:6-9)

(a) The Youth's Folly (7:6-7)

"At the window of my house I looked through my casement, And beheld among the simple ones, I discerned among the youths, a young man void of understanding." The youth Solomon observed may have been one of Rehoboam's friends. We know from the advice Rehoboam's friends gave him when he became king what a foolish group they were (1 Kings 12:1-14). Their advice cost him most of his kingdom.

In any case Solomon recognized that the group gathered outside his window were "simple ones." He contemptuously labeled them with a word meaning "artless, guileless, unsuspecting." A group of simpletons, these silly young men were filled with a sense of importance and brilliance; they were sure that wisdom and wit resided in them alone. We can imagine their idle chatter, their crude jokes, their silly nonsense, their shallowness, and their idea of fun. We can imagine their wolf calls and obscene whistles to any woman who caught their eye. Men like them can be seen on the street corners and in the back alleys of big cities to this day. To think that his son and heir enjoyed the company of such nincompoops galled Solomon to the depths of his being.

One among these "simpletons" caught Solomon's attention. He saw this young man detach himself from the others and drift away. Solomon followed him with his eye.

(b) The Youth's Footsteps (7:8-9)

Solomon noticed *where he wandered.* The wise man saw the youth "passing through the street near her corner" (Proverbs 7:8). The word translated "street" here means "back street." As a spider builds its web in a dark corner, so this woman plied her trade down one of the town's back streets.

From the way Solomon suddenly introduced the woman into his narrative, we gather that he knew where her house was and what went on there. Perhaps he had a somewhat prurient interest in her. Perhaps he had seen her at work before. Perhaps he had strolled past her house to take a closer look. Or perhaps he had sent one of his spies to check the woman out. In any case it seems that he was remarkably well informed.

The moment the silly young man strolled nonchalantly down that back street, Solomon knew what would happen next. The spider's web was there and so was Mrs. Spider.

The fact that King Solomon allowed prostitution to go on under his very nose says something about the decline in his personal morality. But then, Solomon took much too great an interest in human nature in general and in women in particular to interfere. We can imagine his train of thought. *This is a case to be pondered, not prosecuted. What? Prosecute the woman? Stone her? Why, she is far too interesting a case for that!* The harlot interested him. So did the young man. Apparently Solomon had no thought whatsoever of warning him or arresting both of them. Solomon's morality had already degenerated into a mere philosophy. The psychology of the case interested him. He was little concerned with the sin.

Solomon watched the young man and noted *where he went:* "He went the way to her house, In the twilight, in the evening, in the black and dark night" (Proverbs 7:8-9). The word translated "went" means "sauntered." He was in no hurry. He did not walk purposefully down that street on his way to somewhere else. He leisurely made his way down that street. Perhaps he did not know its evil reputation, although that hardly seems likely given the company he kept. Maybe he went on a dare. Many a young man has thrown away his virtue because of peer pressure. Perhaps he had been to her house before. Maybe he was just curious.

The time he chose to go—"in the twilight, in the evening"—suggests that his stroll was deliberate. He went about the time, in that day and age, when decent folk were home eating dinner. This woman plied her trade mostly at night. The best time to catch her alone and ready for a customer was in the twilight, in the evening. "In the black and dark night," Solomon added. He stayed at his window, a peeping Tom, until it was too dark to see any more.

It was twilight when the silly young man went strolling down that street. There is a moral here. There was still light enough for him to see where he was going, to think about what he was doing. He was putting himself in the way of temptation. Before long it was black and dark night in his soul. He reminds us of Judas, who toyed with the temptation to make money by betraying the Master until at last he went out "and it was night" (John 13:30). A few hours later Judas was dead and damned.

(3) The Trap Sprung (7:10-12)

Solomon saw the woman from his window. Apparently he recognized her. He knew all about her. He knew details that the swiftly fading light of a semitropical sunset would have obscured. Solomon described the woman well. He told us about her *dress:* "And, behold, there met him a woman with the attire of an harlot, and subtil of heart" (Proverbs 7:10). She was dressed to show off her wares. She was wily. She knew how to bait her trap, how to catch this sauntering stranger's eye, how to hold it, and how to turn the look into lust.

The temptation was as old as the human race. The same subtle serpent who seduced Eve taught this woman her wiles. The downward steps in that first temptation were swift—"[Eve] saw...she took...and did eat...and gave" (Genesis 3:6). All the steps are in the compass of one short verse with a polysyndeton beating out the time as the *ands* draw attention to the stages of Eve's seduction. She saw! The serpent kept Eve's gaze riveted on the forbidden fruit so that the look might become a lust. The tree was pleasant to the eyes and good for food—it was a tree to be desired. She took! The desire became a deed. She ate! The choice led to a chain reaction. She gave! Eve the sinner became a seducer. The deadly virus was passed on.[1] Likewise the woman Solomon saw designed her dress to catch and hold the young man's eye. She subtly kept his gaze riveted until he couldn't resist what she offered next.

Continuing his description of the harlot, Solomon told us about her *deportment:* "She is loud and stubborn; her feet abide not in her house" (Proverbs 7:11). This woman, as we learn later, was married. She plied her profession only when her husband was away, and then she was like someone released from prison. She doubtless found married life to be extremely dull and irksome. She had long since tired of her husband. She wanted excitement, a new conquest, someone young and fresh. As soon as her husband left and it was dark enough, she went looking for prey.

With the young man Solomon was watching, the harlot was loud and stubborn. Her subtlety told her that the right approach with him was to take him by storm and refuse to let him go. With someone else she might have tried a different approach. She might have pretended to be poor, or frightened, or lonely. But she had seen this young man coming and she knew his type was best taken by a bold frontal attack. How well Solomon knew the wiles of prostitutes.

Completing the description of this harlot, Solomon told us about her *domain:* "Now she is without, now in the streets, and lieth in wait at every corner" (Proverbs 7:12). She was a woman of the streets, a streetwalker. Solomon knew the streets she worked. He knew her favorite corners—places where two streets met, where there was twice the traffic and twice the chance of making a quick catch.

If the young man Solomon was watching thought he could lead her on, flirt a little, and then run on home for supper and boast to his friends the next day of his "little bit of fun," he had grossly miscalculated. He had underestimated her expertise and overcalculated his own powers of resistance. His miscalculations are typical mistakes of those who deliberately walk in temptation's path.

b. Her Coils: Like a Serpent's (7:13-21)

(1) How She Caught Him (7:13)

Of course the harlot would never have caught the young man if he had been somewhere else—pursuing his education, improving his skills, developing his business, worshiping his God, or shouldering family responsibilities. People should expect to be trapped if they hang around a singles' bar, move into an "adult" apartment complex, or stroll through the French Quarter of New Orleans.

The harlot wasted no time before throwing her serpent-like coils around this foolish young man. "She caught him, and kissed him, and with an impudent face said unto him..." The word rendered "impudent" here means "hardened, bold-faced." She used the bold approach.

Like any boy becoming a man, this foolish youth had strong drives and desires and found it hard to say no. Also he liked to be thought of as a man of the world. He wanted to be considered sophisticated and suave. He wanted to save face at all costs, so he was vulnerable. The experienced woman knew of his vulnerability and took all his defenses before he even knew they were down. If he had slapped her face when she clutched at him and kissed him, he might have escaped. If he had simply shoved her off and taken to his heels, ignoring her mocking laughter, he could have escaped. But he didn't. He rather liked that kiss. It held the tantalizing promise of something more. He dallied and was lost. Her coils tightened around him.

(2) What She Taught Him (7:14-21)

(a) She Sounded So Pious (7:14)

Having linked her arm in his, she began to talk: "I have peace offerings with me; this day have I payed my vows." She thought, *Maybe this youth is religious. I will talk religion.* The fact that her religion made no sense to her made no difference. About to propose a sin of the deepest dye, she sugarcoated the bitter pill with pious talk. She assumed the gullible youth knew little about what the Bible calls "pure religion and undefiled" (James 1:27). Her "pay now; sin later" philosophy reminds us of the sale of indulgences by the Roman Catholic Church.

Some years ago when I was in Rome I visited the famous *Sancta Scala* ("Pilate's Staircase") made famous by Martin Luther. There I saw devout people painfully climbing that steep stairway on their knees, pausing on each step to mutter a ritualistic prayer to the virgin Mary. These deluded people were trying to earn an indulgence for their sins, an indulgence promised to them by the pope.

From time to time the papacy proclaims a holy year when the faithful must make a pilgrimage to Rome if they want to earn a plenary indulgence—forgiveness for all their sins. They must visit the prescribed churches and shrines. They must pay their religious vows.

In the Middle Ages the rapacious popes, greedy for gold, sold indulgences wholesale. People could even pay up ahead of time and purchase pardon for sins they planned to commit at a later date. This practice, as much as anything else, gave impetus to the Reformation. Imagine buying an indulgence! "Pay now; sin later" has been the official dogma of a vast and powerful church.[2]

The harlot was saying, "I'm all paid up. I have credit in hand enough for both of us. So it's not wrong. How can it be wrong when I've already offered a peace offering ahead of time?"

(b) She Sounded So Personable (7:15)

The harlot's talk was not only pious; it was also personable. "Therefore came I forth to meet thee, diligently to seek thy face, and I have found thee," she said. In other words, "I saw you coming. This meeting is not by chance. I've been watching you. I want you. You're my kind of man." Her approach was all so intimate—the urgent use of personal pronouns, the deliberately created aura and atmosphere of personal interest—and it was all so hypocritical.

In *Treasure Island* Long John Silver used a similar tactic. When the wily old pirate first met Jim Hawkins, cabin boy on the treasure-bound *Hispaniola,* Long John made a friend of the boy by telling him he was "smart as paint." Then Long John slipped aboard as cook and went out of his way to cultivate Jim's good opinion. After all, young Hawkins was a friend of the squire who owned the ship and a friend of Dr. Livesey, the ship's surgeon. Long John—leader of a conspiracy to take the ship, murder all hands except those loyal to him, and sail away from Treasure Island loaded down with guilt and gold—needed the good will of the young cabin boy.

Then by a lucky coincidence Jim overheard Long John subverting one of the few members of the crew still true to the captain and the squire. Long John painted in rosy colors the life of "a gentleman of fortune," a common cutthroat pirate. He disclosed his own plans to turn respectable and ride high, wide, and handsome once the treasure was secured and those loyal to the captain were dead. His persuasive words won over the wavering crew member. Once he had him, Long John was lavish with flattery and praise. He told the sailor he was "smart as paint." Young Hawkins, hidden in the apple barrel, heard it all. He was horrified at the strength of the conspiracy and quite disillusioned when the one-legged cook used the same words to describe the new pirate as he had once used to describe him. "Smart as paint"!

And the poor sucker in Solomon's narrative believed the harlot when she told him he was the man she had been looking for! She had used those words before and she would use them again. Solomon could see through her, but her victim was deceived.

(c) She Sounded So Provocative (7:16-18)

Adroitly she began to speak of the promise she held. She made *her bed so delectable:* "I have decked my bed with coverings of tapestry, with carved works, with fine linen of Egypt. I have perfumed my bed with myrrh, aloes, and cinnamon" (Proverbs 7:16-17). "I want you to come and see my bedroom," she was saying. She described it as expensive, exotic, and exciting to the senses. She was no cheap whore, no common prostitute. She was exclusive, high priced, the desire of the rich and famous. Her words were all calculated to turn the young fool's head and fan the fires of his lust. *If I can get him into the house,* she thought, *to see all the glitter and glamour, I'll soon have him in my bed.*

She made *her bribe so desirable:* "Come, let us take our fill of love until the morning: let us solace ourselves with loves" (Proverbs 7:18). The word translated "loves" can be rendered "much love." She was saying, "You're so lonely. I'm so lonely. Come and comfort me and I'll comfort you." All pretense was thrown aside. He was powerless to resist. His arm crept around her waist. Deliberately she added fuel to the fire. She offered her bed and her body.

(d) She Sounded So Persuasive (7:19-21)

i. The Final Argument (7:19-20)

Her final argument was that she was *solitary* and they would be *safe.* "For the goodman is not at home, he is gone a long journey: He hath taken a bag of money with him, and will come home at the day appointed" (Proverbs 7:19-20). Her reasoning was like this: "We will have the house to ourselves. There's nobody at home but me. As for my husband, he thinks more of his money than me. He's always going off on these business trips and leaving me to fend for myself. I know him. He'll not be home for months. He told me when to expect him. Come on! There's nothing to worry about. He's gone, I tell you, on a long journey. Please don't leave me. I can't stand being alone. When I saw you my heart missed a beat. That's why I came running after you. Come on! What are you waiting for? The watchmen will be along in a minute. Nobody can see us. It's almost dark now. Here, hold my bag while I open the door."

ii. The Final Agreement (7:21)

"With her much fair speech she caused him to yield, with the flattering of her lips she forced him." So against his better judgment, fighting a losing battle with his conscience, the foolish young man gave in. He was conscious only of her nearness, her loveliness, her willingness, the calculated but seemingly careless pressure of her body against his, the heady fragrance of her perfume, and her honeyed words. His defenses suddenly collapsed.

"She caused him to yield," said Solomon, an old hand at this game. "She forced him." The simpleton never had a chance. The only chance he ever had was to take to his heels when she first approached him. Solomon saw him throw that chance away at the outset. Solomon already knew how the story would end. Yet he was content to watch, moralize, nod his head knowingly, and do nothing.

2. Warning of the Harlot's Secret Wares (7:22-27)

a. She Deals in Death (7:22-23)

The wise man continued with his clear warning to avoid the harlot who deals in death and doom. He pondered *the folly of her victim* and said, "He goeth after her straightway, as an ox goeth to the slaughter, or as a fool to the correction of the stocks" (Proverbs 7:22). Either way the victim is ruined. Death and disgrace await him.

The victim in our story was foolish because the woman was not to be trusted. Her own words testified to that. Her husband, a far greater fool than the young man, apparently trusted her. Otherwise he would not have gone away. But then, she might have been lying about having a husband too. In any case she was utterly unscrupulous and the young man was bereft of common sense when he put his life and reputation in her grasping little hands. A man in the heat of passion, however, never thinks of the consequences.

Many a man who has done what this dupe did has found himself not only in the hands of a harlot, but also in the hands of a blackmailer. This harlot had the young man at her mercy. A word from her could be his death sentence—he could face death at the hands of an outraged husband or death at the hands of the law. From now on he was going to pay in one way or another. He would pay with his health: a promiscuous person is a potential purveyor of disease. He would pay with his memory: he would never be able to forget losing his innocence to a common slut of the streets. He would pay with his money. The anonymous note would come demanding money—or else. He would pay for more gilded furniture for that accursed bedroom. He would pay for costly spices for that hateful bed.

And of course the courts might make the fool pay for his crime. He might be placed in the stocks, the public pillory in the center of town, if a merciful judge reduced his sentence from death to disgrace. Such a judge might take into consideration the character of the woman, the age and inexperience of the youth, and the fact that this was a first offense. However, the woman doubtless would accuse the youth of rape and produce a confederate, perhaps the chaperon her husband also trusted, to "prove" her charge.

There was always the chance that Solomon would review the case when it came to trial. Some twinges of the king's own conscience might prompt him to pronounce the lighter sentence. Who would know more about the case than Solomon? Who would know more about lust? Who but he could have saved the young man instead of watching him?

Even the lighter sentence was no laughing matter. In one of Jeffry Farnol's rollicking sea stories, an unjust judge seizes the hero, an escaped galley slave, and puts him in the public pillory. Then Farnol describes the horseplay that often attended such a victim. The position itself was galling. The prisoner's head and hands were secured between two pieces of wood so that he was helpless. Then he became the target for all the bullies in town. They would stand back and throw refuse, delighting when a rotten egg or overripe tomato made a direct hit, full in the face. A man with a personal grudge against the prisoner could come up and punch his helpless, bespattered face. (In Farnol's story, the village bully crowns the afternoon's entertainment by scoring a direct hit with a dead cat.) Added to all this persecution was the torment of heat, thirst, and flies. A well-known prisoner would also be tormented by the thought that he would never be able to live down the disgrace.

"As an ox goeth to the slaughter!" That was Solomon's final verdict as he watched the young man follow the harlot into her house and saw her shut the door. Behind that door no one could see the deeds of shame that ensued. But God could see. Even if the youth escaped all human retribution, which many seem to do, he would not escape God's. Solomon had doubtless visited the stockyards and seen oxen contentedly grazing on the fodder provided for them, ignorant of the doom that was only a heartbeat away. Once that door closed on the young man, he had no more chance of escape than an ox that has been bought, paid for, marked for death, and shut up in the slaughterhouse.

Thinking of the death the harlot deals in, Solomon pondered *the fate of her victim* and said, "He goeth after her...Till a dart strike through his liver; as a bird hasteth to the snare, and knoweth not that it is for his life" (Proverbs 7:22-23). Having discarded logic and enthroned lust, the youth was caught helpless in the harlot's hands. He would not come out from her house the way he went in. He would sneak away in the morning before sunrise, forever branded as an adulterer and marked for whatever punishment the future might hold.

The reference to the liver suggests perhaps that Solomon thought it likely the young man would contract a foul venereal disease.[3]

b. She Deals in Doom (7:24-26)

Knowing that a harlot deals in doom, Solomon again pleaded for a hearing. He urged his son to *listen to the voice of holiness:* "Hearken unto me now therefore, O ye children, and attend to the words of my mouth. Let not thine heart decline to her ways, go not astray in her paths" (Proverbs 7:24-25).

Solomon, despite his faults and failures, knew God. Moreover he was actually writing Scripture, even though he probably was not cognizant of that fact. His words therefore are much more than the call and counsel of a father to a son. His call is a call to holiness, a call to walk in the good and right way, a call to avoid the back alleys that lead to the harlot's door.

We cannot help being impressed with the repeated pleas of Solomon for his son to listen. But Solomon knew most of what he was saying was falling on deaf ears, so he said in effect, "If you will not listen to the Word of God, to the voice of holiness, at least *listen to the verdict of history.*" Proverbs 7:26 states the argument: "For [the harlot] hath cast down many wounded: yea, many strong men have been slain by her."

Our newspapers are full of scandals. The cheap tabloids that specialize in exposing scandals keep armies of reporters nosing around politicians and celebrities in search of some sensational secret. Many a politician has had his career blighted by the front-page exposure of some moral indiscretion he hoped had been buried and forgotten. Most people have a double standard. They expect a much higher moral profile in those they elect to public office than they expect from themselves, and woe betide the politician who lets them down. Many a promising career has suddenly been shipwrecked on the hidden shoal of a past immorality. As Sir Henry Rider Haggard once said:

For those who sell themselves into [such] dominion, paying down the price of their own honor, and throwing their soul into the balance to sink the scale to the level of their lusts, can hope for no deliverance here or hereafter. As they have sown, so shall they reap and reap, even when the poppy flowers of passion have withered in their hands, and their harvest is but bitter tares, garnered in satiety.

c. She Deals in Damnation (7:27)

Solomon wanted his son to listen because the harlot deals in damnation. "Her house is the way to hell, going down to the chambers of death." The harlot trades in desire, disease, and death. Her house is the temple of lust, the gateway to a lost eternity. Those who enter the doors of the harlot's house put their souls in peril. People laugh at Hell and make jokes about it, but the Bible takes it seriously. The Lord Jesus regarded both Heaven and Hell as real places.

The house of Shaws in Robert Louis Stevenson's *Kidnapped* is in one sense like the house of the harlot. When young David Balfour visited his Uncle Ebenezer at the old family house of Shaws, the old miser reluctantly let his orphaned nephew in and grudgingly gave him half of his miserly supper. Then Ebenezer asked his nephew if he would run an errand for him and David agreed. David continued telling the story:

> "Well," [my uncle] said, "let's begin." He pulled out of his pocket a rusty key. "There," says he, "there's the key of the stair-tower at the far end of the house. Ye can only win into it from the outside, for that part of the house is no finished. Gang ye in there, and up the stairs, and bring me down the chest that's at the top. There's papers in't," he added.
>
> "Can I have a light, sir?" said I.
>
> "Na," said he, very cunningly. "Nae lights in my house."
>
> "Very well, sir," said I. "Are the stairs good?"
>
> "They're grand," said he; and then as I was going, "Keep to the wall," he added; "there's nae banisters. But the stairs are grand under foot."
>
> Out I went into the night. The wind was still moaning in the distance, though never a breath of it came near the house of Shaws. It had fallen blacker than ever; and I was glad to feel along the wall, till I came the length of the stair-tower door at the far end of the unfinished wing. I had got the key into the

keyhole and had just turned it, when all upon a sudden, without a sound of wind or thunder, the whole sky lighted up with wild fire and went black again. I had to put my hand over my eyes to get back to the color of the darkness; and indeed I was already half blinded when I stepped into the tower.

It was so dark inside, it seemed a body could scarce breathe; but I pushed out with foot and hand, and presently struck the wall with the one, and the lowermost round of the stair with the other. The wall, by the touch, was of fine hewn stone; the steps too, though somewhat steep and narrow, were of polished mason work, and regular and solid under foot. Minding my uncle's word about the banisters, I kept close to the tower side, and felt my way in the pitch darkness with a beating heart.

The house of Shaws stood some five full stories high, not counting lofts. Well, as I advanced, it seemed to me the stair grew airier and a thought more lightsome; and I was wondering what might be the cause of this change, when a second blink of the summer lightning came and went. If I did not cry out, it was because fear had me by the throat; and if I did not fall, it was more by Heaven's mercy than my own strength. It was not only that the flash shone in on every side through breaches in the wall, so that I seemed to be clambering aloft upon an open scaffold, but the same passing brightness showed me the steps were of unequal length, and that one of my feet rested that moment within two inches of the well.

This was the grand stair! I thought; and with the thought a gust of a kind of angry courage came into my heart. My uncle had sent me here, certainly to run great risks, perhaps to die. I swore I would settle that "perhaps," if I should break my neck for it; got me down upon my hands and knees; and as slowly as a snail, feeling before me every inch, and testing the solidity of every stone, I continued to ascend the stair. The darkness, by contrast with the flash, appeared to have redoubled; nor was that all, for my ears were now troubled and my mind confounded by a great stir of bats in the top part of the tower, and the foul beasts, flying downwards, sometimes beat upon my face and body.

The tower, I should have said, was square; and in every corner the step was made of a great stone of a different shape, to join the flights. Well, I had come close to one of these turns, when, feeling forward as usual, my hand slipped upon an edge and found nothing but emptiness beyond it. The stair had been carried no higher: to set a stranger mounting it in the darkness was to send him straight to his death; and (although, thanks to the lightning and my own precautions, I was safe enough) the mere thought of the peril in which I might have stood, and the dreadful height I might have fallen from, brought out the sweat upon my body and relaxed my joints.

Such was the house of Shaws. Such is the harlot's house. Behind the painted wall of her chamber yawns the gaping mouth of Hell.

CHAPTER 12

Proverbs 8:1-31

b. The Time Described (8:24-26)
  (1) Before Earth's Deep Was Formed (8:24)
  (2) Before Earth's Domains Were Formed (8:25-26a)
  (3) Before Earth's Dust Was Formed (8:26b)
2. Wisdom and the Recent Past (8:27-31)
  a. Wisdom and the Divine Power (8:27-29)
    (1) The Creation of the Stars (8:27a)
    (2) The Creation of the Sky (8:27b-28a)
    (3) The Creation of the Sea (8:28b-29)
  b. Wisdom and the Divine Person (8:30-31)
    (1) His Peer (8:30a)
    (2) His Pleasure (8:30b)
    (3) His People (8:31)

Solomon moved away from his window and his thoughts turned once more from the wicked woman to Wisdom herself. The subject matter seesaws back and forth like that all through the first nine chapters of the book of Proverbs. The purpose of course is to throw the wicked woman and Wisdom into sharp relief through stark, deliberate contrast. We see a similar treatment in Genesis, where Joseph's immaculate goodness is contrasted, by association, with Judah's immoral behavior (Genesis 38). The story of Judah's unprincipled behavior is sandwiched almost arbitrarily between the story of Joseph's good behavior at home and the story of his good behavior abroad. As a jeweler displays the glories of a diamond by setting it against a dark background and shining a light on it, so the Holy Spirit draws our attention to the contrast between the sinful woman and sublime Wisdom.

VI. WISDOM'S PATIENCE (8:1–9:18)

A. Her Plea Is Public (8:1-9)

1. Where Wisdom Stands (8:1-3)

"Doth not wisdom cry? and understanding put forth her voice? She standeth in the top of high places, by the way in the places of the paths. She crieth at the gates, at the entry of the city, at the coming in at the doors."

The harlot's house was down a back street, but Wisdom's voice sounds from the mountaintops. The harlot prowled the streets and lurked at the intersections, but Wisdom stands on the great highways of life where the principal caravan routes cross. The harlot could not wait to close the door on her victims and her vice, but Wisdom takes her stand by the city gates where the multitudes come and go. Had the harlot's husband listened to Wisdom as he urged his camels out of the city, he would have turned around and gone home to put his house in order. His marriage surely was more important than his money. At least Wisdom would have told him so.

The fact that wisdom can be found everywhere is significant. It is not hard to find if we have ears to hear, eyes to see, ready minds, and receptive hearts.

2. Whom Wisdom Seeks (8:4-6)

"Unto you, O men, I call; and my voice is to the sons of man. O ye simple, understand wisdom: and ye fools, be ye of an understanding heart. Hear; for I will speak of excellent things; and the opening of my lips shall be right things." What a pity Adam and Eve did not listen to wisdom when the serpent spoke in the glens and glades of the garden! What a pity Cain did not listen to wisdom when he saw the fire fall indicating God's approval of Abel's offering. What a pity the antediluvians did not listen to wisdom when Enoch and then Noah raised their voices to warn of sin, unrighteousness, and judgment to come. What a pity Nimrod did not listen to wisdom and abandon his grandiose scheme to build a one-world sovereignty, a one-world society, and a one-world sanctuary from which God was to be excluded. What a pity Ishmael, Esau, Reuben, Achan, Samson, Eli, Saul, Absalom, Shimei, Joab, Solomon, Rehoboam, Jeroboam, Ahab, and thousands of others did not always listen to wisdom. What a pity when all too often we ourselves do not listen to wisdom—to excellent things, to right things. The voice of wisdom speaks to the sons of man and this voice is not far from any of us.

As I sit writing in a room in a small town in South Carolina, all about me is quiet. The room is in an old southern mansion that has been converted to a hotel. The town is off the beaten track, so there are not many guests. For most of the day I am alone and silence reigns. Yet the room itself is bursting with sound. The airwaves carry programs from a score or more of radio stations in this area. The great networks have client stations in the big city fifty miles away, and these stations relay programs even to this secluded corner. Day and night all kinds of programs are being aired. The airwaves are alive with movies and music, news and views, sermons and songs, truth and trivia, fact and fiction, perspectives and propaganda.

It's all available to me, but as I write I'm not even aware it's there. I have a radio and a television in the room and simply by reaching out my hand and turning a knob I can avail myself of all the information coming my way. I can turn the volume up or down, or I can change from channel to channel. I can be informed, insulted, educated, entertained, or edified just by turning the dial.

I also have a different kind of receiver in my room. The highest and holiest wisdom is as close as that radio and television, for right alongside them is my Bible. By reaching out my hand I can take up that Book of books, turn its pages, and open my heart and mind to the Holy Spirit. The wisdom of the Word—the revealed and inspired wisdom of the living God—is in my room. Wisdom is never farther away than that Book. "Unto you, O men, I call," Wisdom says, pointing to that Book.

3. Why Wisdom Summons (8:7-9)

Wisdom summons us so she can offer us sound, straight, and simple words. She gives *sound words:* "For my mouth shall speak truth; and wickedness is an abomination to my lips" (Proverbs 8:7). We are surrounded with lies, so much so that thoughtful people wonder where truth really is. We live in an age of propaganda. Propagandists keep on saying something over and over again until at last people accept it as truth even though it may be the most atrocious lie. The Communists, for example, spread their lying philosophy of God-hate, political oppression, and economic folly around the world by developing the technique of the Big Lie. The basic premise of the technique is that if we tell a lie big enough and often enough people will believe it.

Advertisers also often slant the truth to sell their products. Advertising is pervasive and persuasive, implying for instance that if we smoke Whiffy cigarettes we will be as beautiful as a movie star, as rugged as an athlete, and as successful as a business tycoon. It is all a colossal lie and fraud. What is being offered is cancer by the carton.

Nearly all religion is built on the technique of the Big Lie. The Mormons say that Joseph Smith was a prophet. The Roman Catholic Church claims that the pope is infallible when he speaks *ex-cathedra*. Hinduism builds up gurus as holy men. Muslims say the Koran is divinely inspired. Liberal theologians teach that salvation has to be earned. The lies go on and on; we are surrounded by them.

"My mouth shall speak truth," declares divine wisdom. That wisdom is forever enshrined and gloriously available to us in God's Word.

Wisdom also gives *straight words:* "All the words of my mouth are in righteousness; there is nothing froward or perverse in them" (Proverbs 8:8). The word translated "froward" here means "twisted, crafty." Solomon was saying that the Word of God, the Bible, is absolutely dependable—all of it. And so we speak of the plenary, verbal inspiration of the Scriptures. We may not understand all of the Bible, we may not always interpret it properly, and we may have to depend on translations not equally dependable. Nevertheless the original autographed documents are God-breathed, divinely inspired, inerrant, infallible, and wholly dependable. All God's words are righteous. All God's words are right. We may not like them and we may not want to obey them, but they are right.

God's words were conveyed by men and thus we discern different writing styles in the Bible. We trace the outline of human personalities there. The human authors of this extraordinary collection of documents were drawn from all walks of life. Moses and Daniel were statesmen, Amos was a cowboy, Ezekiel was a priest, Joshua was a soldier, Peter was a fisherman, Paul was a scholar, Jude was a peasant, and Jonah was a preacher. God's words were recorded by men over a period of some fifteen hundred years in places as far apart as Rome in the West and Babylon in the East. No wonder the poet Dryden could write:

> Whence but from heaven could men unskilled in arts
> In different ages born, from different parts
> Weave such agreeing truths?
> Or how, or why
> Should all conspire to cheat us with a lie?
> Endless their pains, unwanted their advice,
> Starving their gains, and martyrdom their price.

Behind these men was the Holy Spirit of God, the Spirit of wisdom Himself. In some mysterious way, while giving full play to the human thought process, the sovereign Spirit of God saw to it that men wrote down exactly what was in His omniscient mind. Thus the Bible contains the words of highest wisdom.

Furthermore Wisdom gives *simple words:* "They are all plain to him that understandeth and right to them that find knowledge" (Proverbs 8:9). Mystery is bound to surround the Book that contains a distillation of the wisdom of God concerning the children of men.

But the person who is indwelt by the Holy Spirit has the capacity to understand the Word of God. Jesus said, "When he, the Spirit of truth, is come, he will guide you into all truth" (John 16:13).

Since we are fallen creatures, our thought processes are greatly impaired by sin. "The natural man receiveth not the things of the Spirit of God: for they are foolishness unto him: neither can he know them, because they are spiritually discerned" (1 Corinthians 2:14). The unregenerate person is spiritually blind and deaf. It takes the Holy Spirit to open his blind eyes and unstop his deaf ears.

The Scriptures contain unfathomable depths. How could it be otherwise when the words are those of an infinite God? A man can study the Bible all his life and still feel he has but touched the fringe of Inspiration's garment. At the same time a little child can read and understand the Bible. It is that simple.

Consider Uncle Tom. Although he was only a poor uneducated slave, he had somehow acquired the basics of the alphabet. He could stumble through a simple piece of writing by moving slowly, syllable by syllable, mouthing each word. And what did he read? The Bible! "Let—not—your—heart—be—troubled. In—my—Father's—house—are—many—mansions. I—go—to—prepare—a—place—for—you." How simple! There are only five two-syllable words in those sentences. All the rest are monosyllables. How sublime! There is truth enough here to save a soul and truth enough to occupy the keenest mind for a lifetime.

B. Her Riches Are Real (8:10-21)

1. The Value of Wisdom (8:10-11)

As we revel in the value of wisdom's words, we see wisdom's wealth *being compared:* "Receive my instruction, and not silver; and knowledge rather than choice gold" (Proverbs 8:10). We also see wisdom's wealth *beyond compare:* "For wisdom is better than rubies; and all the things that may be desired are not to be compared to it" (8:11).

Silver, gold, and rubies—even in superabundance—are only "things." But things can dominate our lives. The poor man may spend his life worrying about the things he does not have. The rich man may spend his life worrying about the things he does have. Yet Jesus said, "A man's life consisteth not in the abundance of the things which he possesseth" (Luke 12:15). The world of thought is far more important than the world of things. Things are deceptive. They hold our thoughts down so that we become occupied with the material, the physical, the temporal, and the transient.

John Bunyan taught the value of wisdom through allegory. He introduced us in *Pilgrim's Progress* to a man holding a muck rake. My edition of this classic contains a full-color picture of this man. The picture shows him old and gray. His long, white, tangled beard hangs down. His broad shoulders are stooped. His back is bent over almost double. His clothes are poor, worn, and ragged. He has caught up a few dismal-looking weeds with his rake. Behind him is the figure of One arrayed in light who has a gleaming crown of glory in His hand. The shining One holds the crown over the old man's head as though He would be glad to place it there. But the old man pays no heed. He is ignorant of what he is missing. His staring eyes are fixed on the few straws and strands that his muck rake has gleaned.

In the allegory Interpreter said, "Thou seest him rather give heed to rake up straws and sticks, and the dust of the floor, than to what he says that calls to him from above with the celestial crown in his hand." The man, Bunyan wrote, could look no way but downward.

Wisdom would have us look up. A desire for wealth will rivet our gaze on this world. Wisdom would teach us to gaze at the world to come, to lay up treasure in Heaven, and to become "rich toward God" (Luke 12:21). Wisdom is better than wealth. Wealth can be lost but wisdom partakes of the infinite nature of God and endures forever.

2. The Virtue of Wisdom (8:12-13)

So that we can benefit from the virtue of wisdom, Solomon would have us note *where wisdom dwells:* "I wisdom dwell with prudence" (Proverbs 8:12). Wisdom and prudence are twin sisters. The word translated "prudence" means "good sense." A person can have wisdom without having good sense. Good sense brings wisdom down to earth, makes it practical, and relates it to the everyday concerns of life. A person can have a lot of wisdom in some areas but lack common sense in other areas.

Solomon, for instance, had a great deal of wisdom. He is famous for his wisdom in resolving the conflict between two harlots who were fighting over the same baby, each claiming the child as her own. There was no identification mark on the infant and the baby had no way of knowing his mother. There were no witnesses able to give evidence. How then could anyone discover whose baby he was? The women were equally vociferous in laying claim to the child. The problem seemed to defy solution. So Solomon called for a sword and a soldier. "Divide the living child in two," the king said, "and give half to the one, and half to the other." Then Solomon keenly watched the faces and reactions of the two women. Horrified, the real mother cried out to let the other woman have the child. Pointing to the woman who protested the slaying, the king said, "Give her the living child....She is the mother thereof." Solomon's reputation as a wise judge was thus established and fear of him fell over the whole kingdom (1 Kings 3:16-28).

Solomon had great wisdom when he had to resolve such conflicts. He had remarkable insights into human psychology, political science, and natural history. But he had no common sense, no prudence, when he had to decide whom to marry. What abysmal folly it was for him to marry an Egyptian woman and make her his queen. How foolish he was to marry an Ammonite woman, to trust the future of God's people to a son who was half pagan. What utter stupidity he demonstrated by marrying a thousand women. By the time Solomon was ready to write the book of Proverbs he had doubtless seen how imprudent he had been, but by then it was too late. The best he could do was to advise people to become both wise and prudent.

Solomon advised us to note *what wisdom does:* "I wisdom...find out knowledge of witty inventions" (Proverbs 8:12). This fragment of Scripture has been translated in various ways. "Knowledge and insight I command" is one rendering. "I find out knowledge and discretion" is another. "I find the knowledge [which cometh] of reflection" is yet another. Obviously there is no consensus among scholars. The Septuagint rendering is "I call upon understanding [that is, It is I who inspire all good and righteous thought]."

The Hebrew word translated "witty" in the King James version means "sagacious." It is akin to the Greek word *oida* ("to know intuitively") rather than the word *ginosko* ("to get to know by effort"). Wisdom gives men flashes of insight into the true nature of people and things. A flash of insight led to the invention of the alphabet and writing. A flash of insight led to the mechanical kindling of fire. A flash of insight led to the invention of the wheel. Every inventor has a dash of this kind of genius.

Consider the inventive genius of the human mind through the centuries. Some 4,000 years before the birth of Christ the Egyptians are said to have started mining and smelting copper. About 3500 B.C. the potter's wheel appeared in Mesopotamia, as did wheeled vehicles. About 2900 B.C. the Egyptians built the great pyramid of Giza, and about the same time the first massive stones were raised at Stonehenge. By that time man's understanding of engineering and astronomy was considerable. In 260 B.C. Archimedes expounded the principle of the lever. The Romans developed concrete about 200 B.C., and the Chinese invented paper about 140 B.C. The Chinese also invented the ship's rudder about the time of Christ's birth.

In A.D. 600 the first windmills were built in Persia. In A.D. 1040 the Chinese invented gunpowder and about the same time invented movable type. In 1070 they began to use the magnetic compass. In 1288 they invented a small cannon. In 1310 clocks driven by weights first appeared in Europe. In 1450 eyeglasses were invented. In 1590 Zacharias Janssen invented the compound microscope, and a few years later Hans Lippershey developed the telescope. The first navigable submarine was built in 1620. The first adding machine was invented in 1642 by Pascal. Torricelli made the first barometer in 1643. The pendulum clock was invented in 1654, and a few years later Robert Hooke invented the balance spring for watches. In 1698 the first practical steam engine appeared. In 1709 Daniel Fahrenheit developed the first accurate thermometer. In 1733 John Kay invented the flying-shuttle loom. In 1764 James Hargreaves invented the spinning jenny. The first hot-air balloon was launched by Montgolfier in 1783. The cotton gin was invented in 1793.

In 1800 Alessandro Volta invented the first battery. In 1804 canning food was introduced. In 1837 Samuel Morse patented the telegraph. In 1839 Charles Goodyear discovered how to vulcanize rubber. The sewing machine was invented in 1851 by Isaac Singer. The first oil well was drilled in 1859. In 1865 Joseph Lister discovered the use of antiseptics. In 1876 Alexander Graham Bell invented the telephone. In 1877 the internal combustion engine was introduced. In 1879 Edison discovered how to make electric lights. The phonograph was invented in 1888. The first moving picture was shown in 1895.

In 1903 the Wright brothers flew the first successful airplane. Plastics were introduced in 1909. In 1924 the first television was made. In 1928 penicillin was discovered. In 1929 Robert Goddard launched the first instrumented liquid-fuel rocket. The first electron microscope was built in 1931. Nylon was invented in 1934. The first radar was conceived in 1937. In 1942 Enrico Fermi built the first nuclear reactor. The transistor was invented in 1948. In 1957 the basic idea for the laser was developed.

This list of course is by no means complete. All these inventions were the result of hard work and genius. Every now and then someone got a flash of insight and displayed extraordinary wisdom in an invention.

Next Solomon pointed out *what wisdom detests:* "The fear of the Lord is to hate evil: pride, and arrogancy, and the evil way, and the froward [perverse] mouth, do I hate" (Proverbs 8:13). God draws a line through the human race and through all of history. On one side of the line are evil, pride, arrogance, evil ways, and evil words. On the other side of the line stands wisdom. Wisdom deliberately and categorically disassociates itself from all the things on the other side of the line. People who practice them are not wise; they are fools.

"To depart from evil" (Job 28:28) is a far cry from hating evil. A person can depart from evil and still hanker after it in his heart. Hatred of evil can come only from divine wisdom.

In contrast, human wisdom urges tolerance of evil and rationalization. Humanistic psychology, largely a vast excuse-making apparatus, attempts to come to terms with aberrations in human behavior.

Human laws based on human wisdom address the symptoms of evil, never the cause. The cause lies much deeper than the legislative, judiciary, and executive branches of government dare probe. Many of our laws are the result of compromise. All too often lawmakers actually legalize such evils as prostitution and sodomy. Some legislators would even like to legalize gambling and drugs. Because of the flaws in our legal system, few drug czars, Mafia dons, or international terrorists ever see the inside of a prison.

Even when laws are just and impartially applied, they do not get to the heart of human misbehavior and sin. Human laws do not deal with the lust behind the adultery or the hate behind the murder. Judges do not sentence people for their evil desires. Yet the heart is where the root of sin lies. We are not sinners because we sin; we sin because we are sinners. An apple tree is not an apple tree because it bears apples; it bears apples because it is an apple tree. We do what we do because we are what we are. Only divine wisdom deals with what we are inside and it begins by hating sin.

3. The Victory of Wisdom (8:14-16)

Solomon saw all-conquering divine wisdom reigning and noted its sagacity, strength, and supremacy. Proverbs 8:14a speaks of its *sagacity:* "Counsel is mine, and sound wisdom." Proverbs 8:14b speaks of its *strength:* "I am understanding; I have strength." Proverbs 8:15-16 speaks of its *supremacy:* "By me kings reign, and princes decree justice. By me princes rule, and nobles, even all the judges of the earth."

Solomon reviewed the entire judiciary, from the supreme court (as represented by the king) to the district courts (as represented by the princes and nobles) on down to the local courts (as represented by the judges). If there is one thing a man must have if he is to occupy a position of authority over other men, it is wisdom. A wise ruler will reign in the affections of his people. A man who makes foolish decisions and hands down unfair or unfounded sentences will soon earn his people's hatred.

David's sense of honesty and fair play made him a popular king. No doubt Solomon had often observed his father on the throne. Solomon had seen David weigh issues. Solomon had heard David ask penetrating questions. Solomon had observed that David consulted with his counselors and referred to the Book of the Law. Solomon had noticed the upward glancing of the eye when David was perplexed and felt special need of the wisdom from above. Solomon had often marveled at his father's impartiality and passion for truth and justice—justice often tempered with mercy. No wonder David was called "a man after [God's] own heart" (1 Samuel 13:14).

Of course Solomon knew of the classic occasion recorded in 2 Samuel 1 when a young Amalekite came to David to report the death of King Saul. The Amalekite told how Saul had attempted suicide and had asked him to finish him off. "So I stood upon him, and slew him, because I was sure that he could not live after that he was fallen: and I took the crown that was upon his head, and the bracelet that was on his arm, and have brought them hither unto my lord." The young man doubtless thought he was bringing good news and expected a great reward. He must have been astonished and then alarmed at David's reaction, for David did not rejoice over the news. Saul on some twenty-four occasions had tried to murder David, but when Saul died, David rent his clothes in a gesture of grief and commanded a period of mourning and fasting in memory of Saul and Jonathan.

Then David turned on the Amalekite. David's questions were to the point. "Whence art thou?" he demanded. "I am...an Amalekite," the man said. David read a world of significance into that answer (see 1 Samuel 15:1-28) and looked at him with growing distaste. "How wast thou not afraid...to destroy the Lord's anointed?" David asked at last. On at least two occasions David could have done what this Amalekite had done and rid himself of his enemy, but that was not David's way. He always left Saul for God to deal with.

Far from rewarding the young man for slaying Saul and bringing the news and the insignia of royalty, David was appalled. The man was not only a homicide; he was also a regicide. There could be only one punishment for that crime—death. "Thy blood be upon thy head," David said after he passed sentence, "for thy mouth hath testified against thee, saying, I have slain the Lord's anointed."

That was the kind of justice men respected. Every man there that day knew that if David had found King Saul in his death agonies, he would have cherished him. He would have bound up the king's wounds, as the good Samaritan bound up wounds on another occasion. David would have poured in oil and wine. He would have tenderly carried the king to a place where he could have received the best of care. David would have prayed for Saul's recovery. That was why people loved David. He was not only just; he was also good.

4. The Voice of Wisdom (8:17-21)

Having seen wisdom reigning, Solomon heard wisdom's voice saying, "I love them that love me; and those that seek me early shall find me" (Proverbs 8:17). Solomon was telling us *whom wisdom loves.* Love is reciprocal. It is a two-way street. Those of us who seek after wisdom will always find wisdom seeking after us.

We do not have to wait until we are old to seek wisdom. The older we get, the more set in our ways we may become. The sooner we start looking for wisdom the better. Joseph, Samuel, David, Solomon, Josiah, and Daniel all sought wisdom early in life.

Consider Samuel. Even before he was born he was the subject of importunate prayer. When he was born Hannah "called his name Samuel, saying, Because I have asked him of the Lord" (1 Samuel 1:20). When Hannah brought Samuel to Eli she said, "For this child I prayed" (1:27). For this child she never ceased to pray.

Hannah gave her little boy back to God just as soon as he was able to dress himself, comb his hair, and run around the house. When she handed him over to Eli, she redoubled her prayers. And little Samuel sought the Lord early. He loved the Lord and the Lord loved him. And little Samuel found the Lord—or rather the Lord found him. Samuel responded early to the spiritual education the old priest gave him. Soon he knew as much as Eli about the burnt offering, the meal offering, the peace offering, the sin and trespass offerings, the table and the showbread, the golden lampstands, the golden altar, and the veil. Soon he knew much more than Eli. Wearing the little coat his mother had made him, Samuel became a feature and an attraction at the tabernacle.

As his young heart opened like a flower to divine truth, and as his godly mother prayed to water the seed as it was sown, little Samuel heard something Eli never heard—or at least, to give him the benefit of the doubt, no longer heard. Samuel heard God call and speak to him by name.

Like his illustrious Lord when He was manifest in flesh, Samuel grew in favor with God and man and God was with him. Soon all Israel knew that God, who had been silent so long, was talking again. The dark days of the judges were about to end. A new day was dawning. People called Samuel "the seer" because he was able to see into the hearts of men and into the heart of God.

Solomon also heard wisdom's voice saying, "Riches and honour are with me; yea, durable riches and righteousness. My fruit is better than gold, yea, than fine gold; and my revenue than choice silver" (Proverbs 8:18-19). Solomon was telling us *what wisdom lavishes.* The riches offered by wisdom are durable. Other riches have a habit of disappearing, but wisdom once acquired cannot be squandered.

The difference between wisdom's riches and other riches is illustrated by James Michener in his book *Caribbean.* He brilliantly summarized a basic difference between British colonies in the Caribbean and the Spanish settlements. All Spain wanted was gold and silver—more and more wealth. The purpose of Spain was to obtain silver from eastern Peru and gold from Mexico. The bustling new cities of Panama, Porto Bello, Cartagena, and Havana all saw great treasure ships weigh anchor. Splendid galleons and escorting battleships left in vast convoys for Spain year after year. In spite of fever, pestilence, storm, and voracious buccaneers, pirates, and privateers, the treasure fleets sailed to Seville. This gold and silver tide was the envy of all the other nations. They thought, as the Spanish king thought, that all this treasure, wrung with callous cruelty from Spanish possessions in the New World, had made Spain rich and powerful.

"Not so!" said Michener. The control of vast treasures of silver and gold is not what makes a nation great. England's power and wealth were based on something more solid than bullion: the character, integrity, and industry of its citizens at home and abroad. A nation's true wealth lies in its people, especially in its workers, farmers, craftsmen, artisans, and builders. English settlers in the Caribbean and in other British colonies around the world rolled up their sleeves and went to work, and trade flourished between the mother country and her colonies. The character of British citizens, when all is said and done, was based on the Bible. The Bible was the book that Spain—in the grip of pope and priest, superstition and the Inquisition—so greatly despised and so foolishly burned.

Solomon heard the voice of wisdom saying, "I lead in the way of righteousness, in the midst of the paths of judgment: That I may cause those that love me to inherit substance; and I will fill their treasures" (Proverbs 8:20-21). Solomon was telling us *where wisdom leads.* There is a right way and a wrong way to obtain riches, if riches we must have. Riches that are not acquired "in the way of righteousness" cannot bring happiness.

Consider the way Mr. Bumble tried to improve his financial situation in Charles Dickens' classic *Oliver Twist.* Mr. Bumble, the village beadle, was the man who beat and bullied poor little orphaned Oliver. Mr. Bumble in the course of his parochial duties called on the Widow Corney to whom he made himself waggishly pleasant. The widow however was called away on an errand. Dickens wrote:

> Mr. Bumble's conduct on being left to himself, was rather inexplicable. He opened the closet, counted the teaspoons, weighed the sugar-tongs, closely inspected the silver milk-pot to ascertain that it was of the genuine metal, and, having satisfied his curiosity on these points, put on his cocked hat corner-wise, and danced with much gravity four distinct times around the table. Having gone through this very extraordinary performance, he took off his cocked hat again, and, spreading himself before the fire with his back towards it, seemed to be mentally engaged in taking an exact inventory of the furniture....
>
> ...As there were no sounds of Mrs. Corney's approach, it occurred to Mr. Bumble...to allay his curiosity by a cursory glance at the interior of Mrs. Corney's chest of drawers.
>
> ...Mr. Bumble, beginning at the bottom, proceeded to make himself acquainted with the contents of the three long drawers... arriving, in course of time, at the right-hand corner drawer.... Beholding therein a small padlocked box, which, being shaken, gave forth a pleasant sound, as of the chinking of coin, Mr. Bumble returned with a stately walk to the fireplace; and, resuming his old attitude, said, with a grave and determined air, "I'll do it!"

Well, so he did. He married the Widow Corney. It took the new Mrs. Bumble just two months to reduce the once haughty beadle to a state of abject servility. Dickens gave us another glimpse of that same living room. Mr. Bumble was once more alone, reminiscing gloomily over his fallen fortunes and eight short weeks of marriage.

"And to-morrow two months it was done!" said Mr. Bumble, with a sigh. "It seems a age....I sold myself ...for six teaspoons, a pair of sugar-tongs, and a milk-pot; with a small quantity of second-hand furniture, and twenty pound in money. I went very reasonable. Cheap, dirt cheap!"

Mr. Bumble's way of improving his financial fortunes was the way of folly. Wisdom's path never leads to regrets.

C. Her Influence Is Infinite (8:22-31)

1. Wisdom and the Remote Past (8:22-26)

a. The Time Declared (8:22-23)

Solomon's thoughts took wing and his words take us out beyond the confines of time and space as the Holy Spirit draws aside the veil to show us wisdom abiding with the godhead and actively participating in the creation of the universe. Then his words bring us back down to earth to admire wisdom's fingerprints on our own planet.

We are taken back for a moment to a place and time when God the Father, God the Son, and God the Holy Spirit, coequal and coeternal, dwelled together in all their wisdom, *before Their works began:* "The Lord possessed me in the beginning of his way, before his works of old" (Proverbs 8:22). Just as the Bible begins with the phrase, "In the beginning" (Genesis 1:1), the voice of wisdom repeats the phrase as the Holy Spirit takes us one step beyond the confines of time and space and the limitations of human knowledge. (The word translated "God" in Genesis 1 is *Elohim,* the God of creation. In Proverbs the word translated "the Lord" is *Jehovah,* the God of covenant.)

The Hebrew word translated "possessed" in Proverbs 8:22 is *kānāh,* which means "acquired." In the Septuagint the corresponding Greek word means "created." Here wisdom is seen as being brought forth. The Hebrew word occurs eighty-six times in the Old Testament and is rendered "possessed" only four of those times.

Wisdom, love, power, and holiness are all Divine attributes, as are omniscience, omnipotence, and omnipresence. All creation is the stage on which God displays His attribute of wisdom. His divine wisdom, in all its majesty, is exhibited to the universe. However, His wisdom existed before the rustle of an angel's wing disturbed the silence of eternity. The wisdom of God is seen in creation—and in redemption too. Before time began, Father, Son, and Holy Spirit planned both creation and redemption. In the wisdom of God, creation was to be the stage on which God would display His power (Romans 1:20); redemption was to be the stage on which God would display His love (Ephesians 2:1-7; 3:10). (Paul reminded the clever Corinthians of the awesome wisdom of God in 1 Corinthians 1:18-31.)

The whole passage now before us (Proverbs 8:22-31) is one of great majesty and mystery as wisdom and various members of the godhead are introduced in such a way that we cannot always be sure which is which. Obviously at times the passage is speaking of wisdom, but it is equally obvious that at times the passage is speaking of Christ. It is not easy, however, to draw a hard and fast line and say, "Here the passage is speaking of wisdom (Wisdom personified) and here the passage is speaking of the Son." Some have tried to solve the problem of this passage by suggesting that at some point in eternity past the Son took creature form in order to create, just as later He took human form in order to redeem. Thus He is worshiped as Creator and Redeemer in Heaven (Revelation 4:11; 5:9). This suggestion is interesting, but perhaps we should simply let the mystery stand.

Let us be satisfied with understanding that at times this passage speaks of wisdom, at times it speaks of Christ, and at times it speaks of both. We can no more draw the line in this mystery than we can draw a line between the absolute deity and perfect humanity of Christ. The best we can do when confronted with such mysteries as these is simply to stand back and worship.

In a sense wisdom is Christ. It certainly is incarnate in Him. The Holy Spirit affirms that in Christ "are hid all the treasures of wisdom and knowledge" (Colossians 2:3). Yet the Holy Spirit Himself is called "the spirit of wisdom" in Ephesians 1:17. So it may well be that at times the passage is speaking of the Spirit of God.

We do know that starting in Proverbs 8:22 the Spirit of God takes us not just back to the beginning of creation, but back "before his works of old." Indeed He takes us back before the beginning. And there we find God.

Astronomers long believed that the universe had no beginning and was eternal; their hypothesis was known as the "steady state" theory. Then came the "big bang" theory. Its proponents said the universe resembled a white-hot fireball in the first moments after a primeval explosion occurred. Various lines of reasoning confirmed this hypothesis. For instance, the residual radiation diffused throughout the universe has exactly the pattern of the wavelengths scientists postulate would have resulted from the light and heat produced by the original explosion.

In 1913 Vesto Melvin Slipher discovered that a dozen galaxies in the vicinity of the Milky Way are moving away from the earth at enormous speeds. This discovery is another indication that the universe is expanding. His slides clearly revealed the all-important "red shift," an indication of a rapid motion away from the earth.

Then Hubble, the great astronomer who probed the depths of space to a distance of one hundred million light-years, confirmed Slipher's assertions that all the galaxies are moving away from the earth at enormous speeds. Hubble's famous law states: "The further away a galaxy is, the faster it moves." Thus he formulated the law of the expanding universe.

About the same time the fact that the second law of thermodynamics applies to the universe led to the conclusion that the whole thing is slowly running down. This led Arthur Eddington, another renowned astronomer, to state that if it is running down, it must at one time have been wound up—that at the exact moment of the big bang, all the universe was packed into the space of an atomic nucleus.

The theory of the astronomers is that when the universe was just one second old, its density had dropped to that of water and its temperature had decreased by a billion degrees. Calculations show that about 30 percent of the hydrogen in the universe was transformed into helium in the first three seconds of the history of the cosmos. Scientists do not know when "the beginning" was, but astronomers estimate that it was at least fifteen billion years ago.

These discoveries have greatly annoyed scientists. Einstein, the first to show his irritation, seems to have been bothered by the notion that the universe had a beginning because of the theological implications.[1] The idea of God as the Creator annoyed him. Eddington was similarly put out. "The notion of a beginning is repugnant to me," he said even while admitting the reasonableness of the "big bang" theory. Allan Sandage of the Palomar Observatory, who documented the uniformity of the expansion of the universe, likewise recoiled from the idea of a beginning. "It cannot really be true," he complained.

Robert Jastrow, founder and director of NASA's Goddard Institute for Space Studies and professor of astronomy and geology at Columbia University, said that such conclusions (that the universe had a beginning) come from the heart, not the head. The story ends in a nightmare for the agnostic astronomers, he said, and for the man who has lived by his faith in the power of reason. He painfully pulls himself over the mountains of ignorance. He arrives at the summit, pulls himself over the last rock—and there he discovers the theologians waiting for him. They have been there for centuries![2]

Having arrived at "the beginning," we need to take that final quantum leap back to "before his works of old"—back to *before this world began*. There we meet God. Proverbs 8:23 states, "I was set up from everlasting, from the beginning, or ever the earth was." There we have the "steady state" with which some scientists feel more comfortable—though they still resolutely blind themselves to the fact that "God is there," as David would remind them in Psalm 139:7-12. God provides and *is* the "steady state."

Our human wisdom falters in our attempts to contemplate eternity, for we are creatures of time. We are born and we die. We have a beginning. Our world had a beginning, and the universe had a beginning too. Therefore we cannot fully comprehend eternity. We can feel somewhat comfortable with the concept of an eternity to come, for as Solomon mused elsewhere, God has set eternity in our hearts (Ecclesiastes 3:11). But we have trouble comprehending an eternity past and One who had no beginning.

Standing at the beginning of time we behold the vast ocean of eternity. We suddenly realize that time and space are finite concepts. Beyond time and space are eternity and the Infinite.

On one occasion David Livingstone, the famous missionary-explorer, took some natives with him on a journey from the heart of Africa to the coast. They had never seen the ocean and when they first glimpsed the vast sea stretching to the distant horizon where sea and sky merged, they were astonished. "We marched with our white father," they said, "believing what our ancestors had always told us, that the world has no end. But all at once the world said to us, 'I am finished; there is no more of me!'"

That is what astronomers find as they probe back into the past. All of a sudden the comfortable space-time-matter universe says, "I am finished; there is no more of me." Then God steps forward and says, "But here am I."

Our own little span of time is going to run out. Someday it will say, "I am finished; there is no more of me." And God will say, "But here am I." If God was there before time began, He will be there when time runs out. And so will eternity. That ought to be the most disconcerting thought of all to the secular humanist, the materialist, and the atheist.

In that vastness beyond time dwells wisdom. Wisdom comes to us as we scurry along our little trails in time and says, "Prepare to meet thy God" (Amos 4:12). Wisdom warns us to prepare for eternity.

b. The Time Described (8:24-26)

Wisdom speaks of the time before creation in words finite man can understand. Wisdom, having invaded time, is quite prepared to meet man on the ground of reason, though eventually man must meet Wisdom on the ground of revelation. Wisdom is prepared to meet men where they are as a good place to start. Since Wisdom is reasonable, she is quite willing to introduce herself to man where he exists—in a space-time-matter universe.

Wisdom therefore speaks of time *before earth's deep was formed:* "When there were no depths, I was brought forth; when there were no fountains abounding with water" (Proverbs 8:24). Wisdom begins by talking about the sea. Man has always been fascinated by the sea. When Ferdinand Magellan paused, at one point in his voyage around the world, to toss spliced lengths of rope over the side of the ship, the sailors kept on reporting back, "No bottom with this line." The explorer waited patiently for the end to hit the bottom, but it never did, so he concluded that the oceans were "immeasurably deep."

The ocean covers more than 70 percent of the earth's surface. In some areas the ocean's bottom lies more than six miles below the surface. The ocean is never still; there are always waves. Sometimes they lap quietly against the shore. Sometimes they march in endless angry ranks from far out in the sea and hurl themselves with devastating force against the land. The ocean is filled with life; it is home to an astonishing variety of species, many of which multiply with amazing abandon.

Of the 197 million square miles that comprise the earth's surface, 145 million square miles are buried beneath the sea. Wisdom decreed this ratio of land to water. If the oceans were reduced by 50 percent, the amount of evaporation would be reduced proportionately and similar changes would take place in rivers and lakes. The humidity and temperature of the atmosphere and the character of the seasons would be disastrously affected. Thus we can see God's wisdom even in the proportion of sea to land on this chosen planet.

The oceans are salty. Each cubic mile of sea water contains 166 million tons of dissolved salts. According to an old Norse fable, the sea is salty because a magic salt mill grinds away somewhere at the bottom of the ocean. We now know that this old wives' tale is more or less true. Geologists and oceanographers identify the mill as the "mid-ocean" rift that wends its way for some forty thousand miles through all the major ocean basins. The theory is that fresh basalt flows up into the rift from the earth's mantle in the places where the sea's floor is moving apart at the rate of several centimeters a year.

Modern oceanography was the brainchild of Robert Boyle, who in the 1670s showed that rivers carry small amounts of salt to the sea. In all, 73 elements apart from hydrogen and oxygen have already been detected in sea water. Also there is evidence that the salinity of the ocean has remained constant for long periods of time. In general, sea water contains from 3-4 percent salt. Inland seas such as the Mediterranean and the Caspian, where evaporation is high, contain a higher percentage of salt. Sea water contains 55.2 percent chlorine, 30.4 percent sodium, 7.7 percent sulfur, 3.7 percent magnesium, and 3.0 percent other elements including potassium, carbon, bromine, nitrogen, and phosphorous. Among the metallic elements dissolved in the ocean are millions of tons of silver, copper, nickel, and tin. Scientists have compared the composition of sea water with the fluids in man and animals and have found them to be much alike. Salt, an essential element in the composition of the sea, plays an important part in evaporation and currents and preserves the ocean from corruption.

Man has always been interested in oceanic waves and tides. Twice every day the gravitational pull of the moon causes the waters of the sea to rise higher and higher along the coast until they reach a given point. Having reached a high-water mark, the waters then recede and pile up on the shore on the opposite side of the earth. These tides act as a regular pulse beat in the great heart of the ocean and contribute to its general health and purity.

The process of evaporation and the flow of the currents keep the ocean water perpetually circulating from the equator to the poles and back again. Water in its natural state is 800 times heavier than the atmosphere, yet every day the sun draws enormous quantities of water to the sky by evaporation. The air in a room 60 feet square at a temperature of 68 degrees F., for example, can hold 252 pounds of water.

Waves begin when the frictional drag of a breeze on a calm sea creates ripples. The steep side of each ripple gives the wind its chance to act upon the water. Because winds are by nature turbulent and gusty, wavelets of all sizes are soon created. The process continues as smaller waves give way to bigger ones that store energy more efficiently. Waves are measured in terms of their height, period, and wavelength. A mariner's rule is that ordinarily a wave will be no higher than half the speed of the wind, although there are notable exceptions. More destructive than waves generated by the wind are those created by some sudden impulse such as an underwater earthquake, a landslide, a volcano, or the explosion of a nuclear bomb.

Oceanography has now become a complex science. Every new piece of information bears further witness to the genius of the Creator and His omniscient wisdom. When Jesus lived on earth—incarnate Wisdom indeed—He could actually walk on water, still storms, and hush waves with a word. There was nothing about the waves He did not know. Things that are over our heads were quite obviously under His feet! Not even the greatest scientific genius living today knows how Jesus did what He did or knows what He knew. Those who observed Him firsthand declared, "What manner of man is this, that even the wind and the sea obey him?" (Mark 4:41)

Wisdom speaks next of time *before earth's domains were formed:* "Before the mountains were settled, before the hills was I brought forth: while as yet he had not made the earth, nor the fields" (Proverbs 8:25-26).

There is nothing I love more than driving westward across the United States. As I leave the Great Lakes behind, I see vast prairies and rolling seas of grain stretch endlessly toward the sunset. Then the badlands appear, their twisted, tortured, barren shapes enlivened by the sight of an occasional cowboy or ghost town. Then on the distant western rim of the world appears a gray smudge that hour after hour hardens into the Rocky Mountains. Higher and higher they climb, their snow-capped peaks drawing attention to their great height. At last they stand stark and magnificent. No wonder they seemed to the early pioneers to be a barrier raised by nature itself to block their way to the Eldorado lands of the coastal plain.

I have flown over mountains. I have driven across them. I have been down in their deep valleys and up to their towering heights. They never fail to fill my soul with awe. Whenever I see them I feel like saying what Stan Ford, a preacher friend of mine, said when I took him for a drive through the mountains near Chattanooga. We pulled off the road by one of the scenic sites where the view was especially magnificent, we got out of the car, and Stan stood for a minute or two drinking in the glory of it all. Then he exclaimed, "Well done, God!"

The world's highest mountains are in the Himalayas. Mount Everest raises its proud head 29,028 feet into the sky. Annapurna stands 26,504 feet in Nepal, and Aconcagua in the Andes is 22,834 feet high. Mount McKinley, the highest mountain in the United States, is but a bit of a babe compared with scores of its rivals in the Himalayas and the Andes. It stands 20,320 feet.

"Let the dry land appear" was the divine decree (Genesis 1:9). And lo, the mountains appeared. Who can see them and not be reminded of the following words of Oliver Goldsmith?

Like some tall peak that rears its awesome form,
Swells from the vale and midway leaves the storm;
Though 'round its breast the rolling clouds are spread,
Eternal sunshine settles on its head.

Mountains cover a fifth of the land surface of the world, though some continents such as Africa have only a few. The enormous amount of energy it took to raise the mountains simply staggers the imagination.

Think of the energy of earthquakes. In October 1989 the San Francisco earthquake lasted only fifteen interminable seconds and measured 7.1 on the Richter scale. Scientists warn that this earthquake was a mere dress rehearsal and predict that far worse ones will come. People felt the 1989 quake across a million square kilometers from Los Angeles to southern Oregon to western Nevada. There were some six thousand lesser aftershocks. Damage was spectacular and widespread. Even so, this earthquake was not as bad as the 1906 quake. It came in two stages, each of which lasted one minute and five seconds and "shook the city like a terrier shaking a rat."

Yet the most devastating earthquakes are but fleabites compared to the lion-roaring energy that heaved up the Himalayas, the Andes, the Rockies, the Alps, and the other mountain ranges of the earth. And additional forces were strong enough to smooth out the foothills and the plains.

The Holy Spirit says of the Lord Jesus, whose wisdom planned this planet, that He "hath measured the waters in the hollow of his hand, and meted out heaven with the span, and comprehended the dust of the earth in a measure, and weighed the mountains in scales, and the hills in a balance" (Isaiah 40:12). How perfectly balanced our world is! Planet Earth spins through space as smoothly as a well-balanced top. There is no tremor; we are not even conscious of movement. Such is His vision and skill.

Then too wisdom speaks of time *before earth's dust was formed:* "While as yet he had not made...the highest part of the dust of the world" (Proverbs 8:26). How did Solomon know about "the highest part of the dust"? We have all seen dancing particles of dust caught in a sunbeam, whirling and swirling like stars in a galaxy. One estimate is that 43 million tons of dust settle on the United States in one year—the equivalent of some 360 pounds of dust per capita. The average house accumulates some 40 pounds of dust a year!

Some of this dust is manmade. Industries involved in making steel, cement, and flour contribute their quota. Coal-burning power plants belch nearly half a million tons of ash into the sky every day.

Natural dust comes from various sources such as the soil. In the 1930s the huge dust storms that plagued the prairies lifted huge amounts of soil from the Great Plains and dumped it on New England and even on ships three hundred miles out to sea. Volcanic ash is another source of natural dust. The explosion of the island of Krakatoa in the Pacific on August 27, 1883, flung ash and debris fifty miles into the stratosphere. The sea adds its quota of particles too. The wind picks up salt and hauls three hundred million tons of it skyward each year. Some dust comes from outer space—from the moon, for instance, and even from Halley's comet and the planet Mars.

Dust in earth's atmosphere paints much of our world with color—the beautiful blue of a summer sky, the orange and red glory of a sunset. Solomon was quite right when he referred to "the highest part of the dust of the world," probably much more right than he knew.

Dust, scientists now know, plays an important part in making rain. In 1938 researchers learned that for ice crystals to appear in super-cooled clouds, a nucleating or seeding agent might be required. Findeison suggested that dust starts the process of the nucleation of snow crystals. Today we know that much of the world's precipitation is triggered by natural dusts in the atmosphere. These act as nuclei in causing water droplets in clouds to freeze. Some artificial nuclei (dry ice and silver iodide, for instance) work more effectively than natural ones. The nature and origin of the nuclei necessary to initiate the formation of ice crystals, and hence precipitation, has been the subject of considerable debate among meteorologists. Some think these nuclei originate mainly from the earth's surface as dust particles carried aloft by the wind. Some think the debris of meteorites may be an important source. Soil particles have been found to be associated with high cirrus clouds. The use of the electron microscope and electron-diffraction techniques tends to confirm that in a large majority of cases, soil particles are at the center of natural snow crystals.

How astonishing then it is to hear Solomon, who lived nearly a thousand years before Christ and who had no telescopes or microscopes to help him in his observations, mention "the highest part of the dust of the world." He did not know what we know about dust, but the Holy Spirit of God—the Spirit of wisdom—knows more about creation than the most brilliant scientist will ever know. Only the highest wisdom could have caused Solomon to write of the dust in this way.

2. Wisdom and the Recent Past (8:27-31)

a. Wisdom and the Divine Power (8:27-29)

Our attention is now drawn to the evidence of wisdom here, there, and everywhere in God's creation. In Proverbs 8:27 Solomon called attention to *the stars:* "When he prepared the heavens, I was there." The starry heavens are "God's Oldest Testament," a source of ceaseless wonder and awe. The nursery rhyme captures our reaction to the stars best:

> Twinkle, twinkle, little star,
> How I wonder what you are;
> Up above the world so high
> Like a diamond in the sky.

With the naked eye a person can see about seven thousand stars, just a few of the one hundred billion stars in the local galaxy, the Milky Way. Modern telescopes have taught us facts about the stars that would have boggled even Solomon's mind. For example, we have learned that light travels in waves. The shifting wavelength of a star's light as it moves toward or away from the earth is called the Doppler effect. When a star moves rapidly away from the earth, the waves appear to be stretched out. Since the wavelength of red light is longer than that of other visible wavelengths, there is always a shift toward the red end of the spectrum of a receding star. When a star travels toward the earth, its wavelengths appear shortened and shift toward the blue end of the spectrum. The rate of shift in either direction indicates the speed of the star.

Everything is in motion—suns and planets, solar systems and galaxies, worlds without end. They are constantly revolving in orbit, hurrying on journeys toward destinations unknown. The moon revolves around the earth. The earth makes its annual pilgrimage around the sun. The sun, some thirty thousand light-years from the center of the galaxy, pursues its way around the galactic center in a giant revolution that takes some two hundred thousand light-years to complete. Each galaxy is on a voyage of discovery. All this speed and motion is timed with mathematical precision down to minute parts of a second. All the starry heavens are a tribute to Wisdom, who grasps all the laws of mathematics, chemistry, physics, thermodynamics, and biology and plays with them as a child plays with a ball.

What endless mysteries and wonders we keep on discovering in outer space. A neutron star, for instance, cannot be seen because it is too small. It rotates once a second or even faster. Some neutron stars have intense magnetic fields, though there are strict limits. Degenerate neutron pressure cannot support more than two and a half solar masses of burned-out stellar debris. When massive stars die they become mysterious black holes in space. Although a typical neutron star measures only twenty miles in diameter, its density is so enormous that a single teaspoon of its material would weigh forty billion tons! As David said in another connection, "Such knowledge is too wonderful for me" (Psalm 139:6). It is not too wonderful for Him. Everywhere in space, astronomers see the fingerprints of God. The wonder is that so many of them remain atheists. Abraham Lincoln once said, "I can see how man can look at the earth and be an atheist, but I cannot understand how he can look at the sky and say, 'There is no God.'"

In Proverbs 8:27-28 Solomon called our attention to *the sky:* "When he set a compass upon the face of the depth: When he established the clouds above."

The tremendous variety of clouds in the sky never fails to fascinate man. About a century and a half ago Luke Howard, an English pharmacist, first attempted to classify clouds according to shape and height. Although more complex systems have been proposed based on a sounder knowledge of atmospheric processes, Howard's system remains popular because it is simple. He suggested three height categories—high (20,000 feet and above), medium (6,500 to 20,000 feet), and low (below 6,500 feet). Using these three divisions he identified ten basic cloud types, eight of which fall into the three height categories and two of which occur in more than one height range.[3]

Nowadays meteorologists have the most sophisticated instruments and weather satellites to help them, but even so they cannot unerringly predict the weather. There are air masses to be considered, huge volumes of atmosphere that form over large surfaces of the earth. Beneath these air masses are a variety of surfaces—ice in Greenland, tundra and forest in Canada, vast oceans and burning deserts, and so on. There are also weather fronts, the lines of cloud and rain familiar to us now because of weather maps on television and newspaper weather reports.

Once weather of a certain character has developed, the wind carries it to other areas. The study of wind patterns is in itself a big subject. The coming and going of the seasons is a factor too. Weather is also affected by hurricanes and cyclones, which form in giant circles around a center. Solomon was right when he spoke of God in His wisdom setting a compass.

In Proverbs 8:28-29 Solomon called our attention to *the sea:* "When he strengthened the fountains of the deep: When he gave to the sea his decree, that the waters should not pass his commandment: when he appointed the foundations of the earth." Solomon began here with "the deep," yet it is only within the past generation that large-scale maps of the ocean floors have been developed. Interest in accurate information was first generated in the 1800s when plans were made for laying the transatlantic telegraph cable. After World War I, Harvey Hayes of the United States Naval Experimental Station in Annapolis, Maryland, invented the sonic depth finder, which made possible an explosion of knowledge of the sea floor. Scientists discovered that the sea floor is as varied as the land. Beneath the sea are mountains, volcanic cones, vast canyons, and abysmal plains.

More inventions and discoveries followed. These made mapping the ocean floor an exact science: multi-beam echo technology, long-range side-scan sonar imaging systems, NASA's Seasat, and the Geosat altimeter. Marine technology has developed to the extent that scientists now send people and instruments down to the deepest parts of the oceans. Computers also provide fast, accurate, three-dimensional, acoustical mapping of any underwater site. Even so, more than 98 percent of the world's ocean bottom is still waiting to be explored. Robot technology promises to fill in the gaps in our knowledge.

We may not know what is yet to be discovered in what Solomon calls "the fountains of the deep," but God does. His wisdom, which plowed the underwater canyons and raised up their crags, now opens new crevices and stirs up the waters of the seven seas.

"He gave to the sea his decree," said Solomon, noting the law of the tides and the line beyond which the inrushing waters may not pass.

There was once a king of England, Norway, and Denmark known to history as King Canute. He was a wise king, so beloved of his subjects that they wished to render to him the homage due only to God. To prove his mortality he had them carry his throne to the seashore and set it up below the high-tide mark. Presently the tide came in. The waters lapped at the footstool of his throne. King

Canute arose and swayed his scepter over the sea. "Stand back, ye ocean tides!" he cried. But the proud waves rolled on. Only God can draw that line controlling the tides.

After the battle of Marengo, Napoleon struck a medal for his veterans. It bore the simple legend, "I was there." That is what Wisdom says when she hears us refer to the laws of *nature*. Wisdom knows better. Wisdom has a better name for the One who invented all these laws.

Wisdom was there too "when he appointed the foundations of the earth." And what massive foundations they are! Down, down we must go to reach the first foundation stones of this planet, the *Laurentian* rocks. These rocks of enormous hardness and thickness contain immense deposits of iron ore. Above the Laurentian rocks are the *Cambrian* rocks, a deposit of some five thousand feet of solid strata. The *Silurian* rocks follow; a great thickness more than a mile and a half deep, these rocks are mostly formed from corals and shells. Rocks of the *Devonian* period follow. If geologists are to be believed, this rock chronicles a time of upheaval and volcanic activity. Next come rocks of the *Carboniferous* period, when the world's enormous coal deposits were formed. Rocks of the *Permian* period follow; this period was marked by the crumbling and folding of the earth's crust and the building of some of our great mountain chains. The *Triassic* period and the *Jurassic* period were marked by the gradual raising of the continents. Then we come to the *Cretaceous* period when according to geologists the continents again sank beneath the sea, to be followed by the *Tertiary* period as the continents emerged again from the sea in much the shape and form they are today. Finally we arrive at the *Glacial* period, when the world was given its final cleansing before the coming of man. If this geological reconstruction of events is true, how vast were God's works and over what vast periods of time they took place![4]

At the point where time merges into eternity, back when God spun the world into space and laid down its great undergirding bedrocks, wisdom was there.

b. Wisdom and the Divine Person (8:30-31)

Out of the misty past emerges a distinct personality. He comes from back beyond all beginnings, back beyond the foundation of the world. His voice—distinct, different, definite—is recorded in Solomon's writings. We hear that voice and we recognize it at once. It is the voice of Jesus.

Now we note *His peer:* "Then I was by him, as one brought up with him" (Proverbs 8:30). The One who here describes Himself in terms of time ("Then I was") is the One who elsewhere describes Himself in terms that transcend all time ("Before Abraham was, I am" [John 8:58]). There never was a time when the Father and the Son did not exist. They were and are coexistent, coequal and coeternal, as is the Holy Spirit.

The expression "one brought up with him" signifies One who was constantly with God. The expression is a translation of the Hebrew word 'āmōn, which is derived from the root 'āman, meaning "to be constant or steady." This word is used to describe Moses when Joshua fought with Amalek in the valley. Moses, the mediator on high, raised his arms in intercession. As long as Moses' arms were raised, Joshua prevailed. But Moses after all was mortal. His hands grew heavy and when he let down his hands, Amalek prevailed. So Aaron and Hur came alongside to help. They seated Moses on a stone and, one on each side, they helped him hold up his hands. "And his hands were *steady* until the going down of the sun," the Holy Spirit says. "And Joshua discomfited Amalek and his people with the edge of the sword" (Exodus 17:12-13, italics added).

Solomon also used the word when, seeking a weak point in her armor of innocence, he flattered the Shulamite: "How beautiful are thy feet with shoes, O prince's daughter! the joints of thy thighs are like jewels, the work of the hands of a cunning workman" (Song of Solomon 7:1). The phrase translated "the hands of a cunning workman" can also be rendered "*steady* hands." The phrase refers to work done painstakingly, patiently, and properly. Father, Son, and Holy Spirit all cooperated in the wondrous work of creation. Wisdom was their constant companion.

Having noted the peer of the divine person, we also note *His pleasure:* "I was daily his delight, rejoicing always before him" (Proverbs 8:30). What did Father, Son, and Holy Spirit do before time began, before even the angels were brought into being? What did they do from everlasting to everlasting? They found pleasure in each other. All three have existed from all eternity in mutual wisdom, love, and power. Each delights at all times in the others. Each is infinite so each finds inexhaustible satisfaction in the others. Each is omniscient, omnipotent, and omnipresent. Each is full of holiness, full of love, possessed of a wisdom beyond any imaginable to a mere creature of time. We can be sure that the endless ages of eternity past were full of awesome mysteries, majestic harmony, and "joy unspeakable and full of glory" (1 Peter 1:8).

What God has chosen to reveal of Himself in the realms of creation and redemption fills our souls with awe. In these two realms alone He gives us glimpses, bright and brilliant beyond all thought, of His eternal purposes. One such purpose concerns the children of men, and so we note *His people:* "Rejoicing in the habitable part of his earth; and my delights were with the sons of men" (Proverbs 8:31). Surely that is why God made man in His image. That is why God did not write man off when Adam sinned, but initiated instead a wondrous, infinite, and costly plan of salvation.

According to Screwtape, it is a source of astonishment and outrage to the demon world that God actually likes "disgusting little human vermin."[5] Whether or not that is true, God's love for people is a source of wonder and praise in Heaven.

The only explanation for God's infinite love, compassion, and grace for the poor lost sinners of Adam's ruined race lies in His character. He loves us because He loves us. Moses explained to Israel, "For thou art an holy people unto the Lord thy God: the Lord thy God hath chosen thee to be a special people unto himself, above all people that are upon the face of the earth." Then, knowing how unlovely, complaining, and rebellious the Israelites were, Moses added, "The Lord did not set his love upon you, nor choose you, because ye were more in number than any people; for ye were the fewest of all people: But because the Lord loved you" (Deuteronomy 7:6-8). He loved them because He loved them. Thus the Holy Spirit explained the inexplicable in the character and purposes of God.

God's purposes as expressed in the church are more awesome. We are not only redeemed by the precious blood of Christ, but we have also been made joint heirs with Christ and are actually seated with Him in the heavenlies, above principalities and powers and every name that is named, not only in this world but also in the world to come (1 Peter 1:19; Romans 8:17; Ephesians 1:18-21; 2:6). Moreover we are to be like Him for all eternity (1 John 3:2). No wonder John Nelson Darby wrote:

> And is it so—I shall be like Thy Son?
> Is this the grace which He for me has won?
> Father of glory, (thought beyond all thought!)
> In glory, to His own blest likeness brought!

CHAPTER 13

Proverbs 8:32–9:18

D. Her Friends Are Fortunate (8:32-36)
   1. Wisdom's Blessing Described (8:32-34)
      a. Those Who Hearken and Hear (8:32-33)
      b. Those Who Watch and Wait (8:34)
   2. Wisdom's Blessing Discovered (8:35)
   3. Wisdom's Blessing Despised (8:36)
E. Her Blessings Are Boundless (9:1-6)
   1. Her House (9:1)
   2. Her Hospitality (9:2-3)
      a. The Supper (9:2)
      b. The Summons (9:3)
   3. Her Help (9:4-6)
      a. Her Priority (9:4-5)
      b. Her Principle (9:6)
F. Her Foes Are Fools (9:7-12)
   1. Reproof (9:7-8)
      a. Reproving the Wicked Man (9:7-8a)
      b. Rebuking the Wise Man (9:8b)
   2. Reasoning (9:9)
   3. Revelation (9:10-11)
      a. Knowing the Lord (9:10)
      b. Knowing the Word (9:11)
   4. Responsibility (9:12)
G. Her Paths Are Pure (9:13-18)
   1. The Foolish Woman's Clamor (9:13)
   2. The Foolish Woman's Call (9:14-15)
      a. Her Place (9:14)
      b. Her Ploy (9:15)

3. The Foolish Woman's Clients (9:16)
4. The Foolish Woman's Claim (9:17)
5. The Foolish Woman's Curse (9:18)

Wisdom has been pictured and personified as a wise woman. She has been deliberately contrasted with the harlot, the wicked woman. We have seen that Wisdom's plea is public, her riches are real, and her influence is infinite. Now we will see that her friends are fortunate, her blessings are boundless, her foes are fools, and her path is pure.

D. Her Friends Are Fortunate (8:32-36)

1. Wisdom's Blessing Described (8:32-34)

This passage begins with a call to those who will *hearken and hear:* "Now therefore hearken unto me, O ye children: for blessed are they that keep my ways. Hear instruction, and be wise, and refuse it not" (Proverbs 8:32-33). Whenever we see the word *therefore* in the Bible, we should stop and see what it's there for. *Therefore* always draws our attention to the immediately preceding context. In this case the preceding context introduced us to wisdom incarnate in Christ. No wonder we are told to hearken and hear.

I was a boy in Britain when the Battle of Britain was fought. The English countryside was subjected to massive air raids as Hitler threw the whole weight of the Luftwaffe against the one foe that stood between him and world conquest. German bombers and their supporting fighters came over in waves, many hundreds of planes at a time. All Britain had to defend herself with was a handful of Spitfires and Hawker Hurricanes and a small coterie of fighter pilots.

If we had visited one of those R.A.F. bases we would have seen men who were unshaven, bleary-eyed, and unkempt and who had not taken their uniforms off for days. In the officers' mess these men waited wearily between battles for Fighter Command to order them back into the air. Then suddenly the intercom would blare, "Bandits! Bandits!" and give a coordinate indicating where the enemy was. Immediately these pilots would spring to their feet and run for their planes. One of them would pause for a moment to respond over the intercom: "Message received and understood."

"Now therefore hearken...hear...and be wise," the Holy Spirit says. The proper response is simply "Message received and understood."

Wisdom's call is to those who *watch and wait:* "Blessed is the man that heareth me, watching daily at my gates, waiting at the posts of my doors" (Proverbs 8:34). Solomon wanted us to picture a household expecting the arrival of the master or an important guest. Inside all has been done to ensure that the master or guest will be comfortable. At the gate all has been done to ensure a royal welcome. The gatekeeper in the lodge at the end of the driveway is at his post ready to open the gates. He watches for the first sight or sound of the carriage. At the house the porter and footmen are ready so that the moment the carriage arrives, its door can be opened, the luggage taken out, and the passenger helped down from the coach and welcomed. At the top of the stairs the family gathers to escort the traveler inside the house.

That is the kind of welcome incarnate wisdom desires and deserves. No guest more important than He ever arrived at the portals of a human heart. Blessed (happy) are those who thus welcome Him home (Revelation 3:20).

2. Wisdom's Blessing Discovered (8:35)

"For whoso findeth me findeth life, and shall obtain favour of the Lord." The word translated "whoso" comes into its own in the New Testament where we read in the text of texts, "For God so loved the world, that he gave his only begotten Son, that *whosoever* believeth in him should not perish, but have everlasting life" (John 3:16, italics added). Indeed the Bible ends with that wondrous word still sounding out from the great heart of God: "*Whosoever* will, let him take the water of life freely" (Revelation 22:17, italics added).

"Whoso findeth me findeth life." The search is rewarded at last. "Ye shall seek me, and find me, when ye shall search for me with all your heart," announced the Lord to Old Testament Israel just as the final deportation of the Jews to Babylon for their seventy-year captivity was about to begin (Jeremiah 29:13). At the end of the captivity the prophet Daniel did just what Wisdom urges. On behalf of Israel he sought her (Daniel 9:1-3,21-27) and the nation was reborn. However, the quest for divine wisdom went on. Then Jesus came.

What a meteor shower of "finds" we have at the beginning of the gospel story as told by John! No sooner did Andrew find Jesus than he found his brother Simon. "We have found the Messias," Andrew said (John 1:41). Then Jesus found Philip, and Philip found his friend Nathanael. "We have found him," Philip said (1:45). "Whoso findeth me findeth life, and shall obtain favour of the Lord," Wisdom says. Andrew, Peter, Philip, and Nathanael found that to be true. All who find Him agree.

Sir James Simpson discovered chloroform. Because of this find, a greater-than-life photo of the man adorns the wall of the entrance to the medical research section of the Chicago Natural History Museum. The museum accorded Simpson this honor because his discovery of chloroform revolutionized medicine. Before his day, surgery was a nightmare.

One day a newspaper reporter interviewed the famous researcher. The journalist asked his first question: "Sir James, would you please tell me what you consider to be your most important discovery?"

The scientist promptly replied, "My most important discovery was when I found out that I was a sinner in the sight of a holy God."

The startled newsman did not think that answer would get his article on the front page, so he tried again. "Thank you, Sir James," he said. "Now would you tell me what you consider to be your second most important discovery?"

The famous scientist replied, "Young man, my second most important discovery was when I found that Jesus died for a sinner like me." Sir James had found wisdom, he had found life, and he had obtained favor of the Lord.

3. Wisdom's Blessing Despised (8:36)

"But he that sinneth against me wrongeth his own soul: all they that hate me love death." Judas was such a man. Judging by his character, we conclude that this man (the only Judean among the Lord's twelve apostles) followed Jesus because he expected to derive earthly advantage from the establishment of the Messianic kingdom. It does not seem that he loved the Lord at first and turned against Him later (John 6:70). John bluntly labeled Judas a thief. Again and again Jesus warned Judas that He knew what he was up to. Soured by the Lord's refusal to accept the crown the Galileans would have pressed upon Him, and conscious that the Jewish establishment was plotting Christ's death, Judas sold Jesus for the price of a female slave. Thus Judas wronged his own soul, stubbornly resisted every effort of Jesus to save him, and ended up a ghastly suicide (Acts 1:18; Matthew 27:3-5).

E. Her Blessings Are Boundless (9:1-6)

1. Her House (9:1)

"Wisdom hath builded her house, she hath hewn out her seven pillars." The harlot had a house to which she lured her victims; Wisdom has a house to which she invites her pupils. Some scholars think the "seven pillars" refer to the pillars of the inner court of the temple. Others think the reference is to the church. Certainly the early church was built on seven pillars of wisdom.

The church was built on salvation; only saved people were given access to the church. It was built on baptism; believers were baptized by immersion, publicly confessing their faith in Christ. It was built on doctrine; the teaching of the apostles, as inspired by the Holy Spirit, was an essential part of the structure of the early church. It was built on fellowship; believers loved each other. It was built on the breaking of bread; on the first day of each week this feast of remembrance was observed in obedience to the Lord's command. It was built on prayer; the early Christians realized that God's people have an access into the holy of holies that was denied to all but the high priest in Old Testament times. It was built on giving; the early church had compassion for the poor.

Truly salvation, baptism, doctrine, fellowship, breaking of bread, prayer, and giving are seven pillars of wisdom. Any church built on these pillars will grow (Acts 2:41-47). The early church certainly did. Paul told us it is in the church that the principalities and powers in the heavenlies can see the manifold wisdom of God displayed (Ephesians 3:10).

2. Her Hospitality (9:2-3)

Wisdom's blessings include her house and her hospitality. Solomon spoke of her *supper:* "She hath killed her beasts; she hath mingled her wine; she hath also furnished her table" (Proverbs 9:2). He also spoke of her *summons:* "She hath sent forth her maidens: she crieth upon the highest places of the city" (9:3). These verses give us a picture of a bountiful banquet to which all are invited. There is nothing secretive or selective about Wisdom's invitation. The feast is spread. Those hungry for the insights she gives can come and eat and be filled.

Some years ago when I succumbed to the temptation to buy a complete *Encyclopedia Britannica,* I thought I was purchasing a feast.

The table was spread indeed. The volumes were full of facts and figures. Much of the information, however, was written in highly technical language and was over my head. The section on light, for instance, contained pages of mathematical formulas and equations, none of which meant anything to me. Much of the rest of the encyclopedia was also quite irrelevant to my needs. The section on eagles, for example, told me all the things I didn't need to know and was stolidly silent on the things I did need to know. There were endless pages of information on topics and people I wasn't interested in. What difference did it make to me that Rip Van Winkle fell asleep in the reign of George III, woke up in the administration of George Washington, and nearly lost his head hollering for the wrong George? Doubtless the *Encyclopedia Britannica* met the needs of some people, but its amassed wisdom proved to be of little use to me.

My experience with the Bible has been quite different. The Bible is the bountiful table Wisdom spreads. I find more help, insight, and instruction, and more practical, reliable, down-to-earth counsel in half a dozen verses of the Word of God than in all the volumes of my encyclopedia put together. I never sit down to Wisdom's table and come away feeling empty.

3. Her Help (9:4-6)

Wisdom's blessings also include her help that is available particularly to simple people. Proverbs 9:4-5 states her *priority:* "Whoso is simple, let him turn in hither: as for him that wanteth understanding, she saith to him, Come, eat of my bread, and drink of the wine which I have mingled." Wisdom's doors are open primarily to the simple, artless, guileless, and unsuspecting.

Where is the great educational institution today that opens its doors to the simple, that advertises especially to attract the simple? I have friends who graduated from Harvard and Princeton, and they are among the brightest people in the land. They did not gain acceptance to these Ivy League institutions by being simple. What great university combs its lists of applicants to weed out the simple so that they can be given priority in enrollment? Not one! The world's great schools send their recruiting officers out to comb the campuses for the bright students, not for the simple.

We all know what the world thinks of the simple. Even its nursery rhymes reflect its attitude:

Simple Simon went a-fishing
For to catch a whale;
But all the water he had got
Was in his mother's pail.

Poor Simple Simon accosted the pie man on his way to the fair; Simon hoped he could get a taste of one of those pies. The pie man said, "Show me first your penny." Simon was a simpleton, we would say. The world laughs at simpletons, or if it is too polite or too charitable to laugh, it quickly decides it has bigger fish to fry. The Simple Simons are left to the philanthropists or the sociologists.

But God loves the simple. That is why He uses so many uneducated and unsophisticated people to get His work done in the world (1 Corinthians 1:26). D. L. Moody, for instance, was a simple man. He was uneducated, unsophisticated, not much bothered by what people thought of him, and not unduly impressed by cultured people. Furthermore he had a disconcerting honesty and directness that often ruffled his more polished neighbors' feathers. This direct manner contributed in no small degree to his success as an evangelist.

The religious establishment shuddered at Moody and cold-shouldered him. He had no ecclesiastical standing and was not ordained. People were appalled at his grammar and the newspapers made fun of him. But as was said of his Master, "the common people heard him gladly" (Mark 12:37). He spoke their language. He spoke with authority and not as the clergy. His tremendous sincerity and complete simplicity attracted crowds.

In spite of his simplicity, some of his greatest triumphs were with agnostics in the great universities. One afternoon in 1874 two of the cleverest men in England went to hear Moody: Gladstone, four times the prime minister of Britain, and Matthew Arnold, the famous educator. "I thank God I have lived to see the day," said Gladstone, "when He should bless His church on earth by the gift of a man able to preach the Gospel of Christ as we have heard it today." Arnold replied, "And I would give all I possess if I could only believe it."

D. L. Moody, essentially a simple man, heard Wisdom's call. He ate at her table and drank her wine. He was so wise that even the great ones of this world wondered at him. They said of him what had been said of Jesus: "Whence hath this man this wisdom...?" (Matthew 13:54)

Still talking to the unwise man, Wisdom states her *principle:* "Forsake the foolish, and live; and go in the way of understanding" (Proverbs 9:6). Doubtless Solomon had his son Rehoboam in mind as he wrote that verse. How his son's addlebrained companions must have irked Solomon. What a different course the kingdom of Israel would have taken if Rehoboam had listened to this one proverb. Instead of forsaking the counsel of the old men, he would have forsaken the counsel of the foolish young hooligans who crowded around him (2 Chronicles 10).

"Forsake the foolish, and live." Never was this advice more appropriate than during the time of the Korah rebellion. Korah, Moses' cousin, joined forces with Dathan and Abiram, princes of Reuben, to oust Moses and Aaron. The three rebels resented the leadership of Moses and Aaron, envied them, and coveted their positions of authority in both the secular and sacred realms.

Then God stepped in. The stage was set for a showdown. Moses, aware that God was about to act in fearful judgment upon these foolish men and their followers, appealed to the whole congregation: "Depart, I pray you, from the tents of these wicked men, and touch nothing of theirs, lest ye be consumed in all their sins" (Numbers 16:26). Then the earth opened its mouth and swallowed up all the conspirators. "And all Israel that were round about them fled at the cry of them: for they said, Lest the earth swallow us up also" (16:34). They were not a moment too soon. The supernatural earthquake was followed by "fire from the Lord" that consumed 250 Korah sympathizers (16:35). The results of following Solomon's advice may not always be this spectacular, but they are always just as sure.

F. Her Foes Are Fools (9:7-12)

1. Reproof (9:7-8)

Wisdom's friends are fortunate and her foes are fools. The scorner and the wicked man are foes of Wisdom because they are not susceptible to correction. Proverbs 9:7-8 states the results of *reproving a wicked man:* "He that reproveth a scorner getteth to himself shame: and he that rebuketh a wicked man getteth himself a blot. Reprove not a scorner, lest he hate thee." Far from accepting reproof, even when it is meant kindly, wicked people resent criticism of their behavior. They cannot rest until they take revenge. If they can do their critic harm, they will.

King Zedekiah and his princes hated the prophet Jeremiah for telling them the truth. The sins and iniquities of Judah were so blatant that judgment was inevitable. God used the nation of Babylon as His instrument of judgment. Jeremiah counseled the people of Judah to submit to the chastening hand of God and surrender unconditionally to Nebuchadnezzar. The princes accused Jeremiah of high treason. They were scornful of his advice, resented deeply his exposure of their sins, and wasted no time in venting their dislike. They took the prophet and threw him into a dungeon in the prison court. The prophet sank in the mire, but as far as the princes were concerned, he could stay there and starve (Jeremiah 38:1-6). Their foolish behavior did not change the facts for a single moment. All it did was aggravate their guilt.

The results of *rebuking a wise man* are quite different: "Rebuke a wise man, and he will love thee" (Proverbs 9:8). We see an illustration of this proverb in Peter's acceptance of Paul's rebuke. After endorsing the principle that Gentiles did not have to become Jews in order to become Christians—that is, Christians are free from the law as a system—Peter went back on his publicly-stated position. He had had happy fellowship with Gentile Christians in Antioch, but when representatives of James' faction in the Jerusalem church showed up in Antioch, Peter reverted to the Jewishness of his earlier years and refused to have any further fellowship with Gentiles. This reversal of his position caused considerable consternation and concern in the Antioch church and Paul took Peter to task for his hypocrisy, inconsistency, and betrayal of principle (Galatians 2:11-14). Peter, being a wise man, accepted the rebuke humbly, loved Paul for it, and later spoke of him in terms of genuine affection (2 Peter 3:15).

2. Reasoning (9:9)

"Give instruction to a wise man, and he will be yet wiser: teach a just man, and he will increase in learning." Wisdom and knowledge are by nature cumulative. We learn by adding to what we already know. We begin by learning the alphabet. Then we learn to recognize and pronounce simple words. After that we use complex words. We add words to our vocabulary. We put sentences together and learn laws of grammar. We learn to write and compose paragraphs.

In mathematics we learn to count, to add up simple sums, and then to figure more complex sums. We learn how to subtract, how to multiply, and how to divide. We learn how to handle fractions, decimals, and square roots. We go on to geometry, algebra, trigonometry, and calculus. Moreover, we learn from our mistakes. When a teacher marks answers as being wrong, we do not just shrug our shoulders; we rework the problems until we get them right.

People who refuse to learn from their mistakes not only continue to make the same mistakes; they compound them. People who are wise accept instruction and increase in learning. They find out where they went wrong, what they did wrong, and why. The same principles that enable us to add to our skills in the arts and sciences enable us to add to our ability to handle life's sterner equations.

3. Revelation (9:10-11)

The teachable man learns that he who would really live must *know the Lord:* "The fear of the Lord is the beginning of wisdom: and the knowledge of the holy is understanding" (Proverbs 9:10). Wisdom begins with the fear of the Lord and ends with the knowledge of the holy. Wisdom begins with conversion, which leads to happiness. Wisdom continues with consecration, which leads to holiness.

Some years ago a popular phrase appeared on bumper stickers, billboards, and greeting cards. The phrase was "HAPPINESS IS..." and it was followed by an often unexpected definition. The car in front of you might declare: "HAPPINESS IS...never having to say you're sorry"; or "HAPPINESS IS...ice cream on your apple pie." A Christian musician picked up on the idea and used it in a catchy little song with a lilting tune:

> Happiness is to know the Savior,
> Living a life within His favor,
> Having a change in my behavior—
> Happiness is the Lord.[1]

The knowledge of the Lord described in this little ditty is the result of conversion, which leads to happiness. "The fear of the Lord is the beginning of wisdom." But beyond that initial experience comes consecration, which leads to holiness—what Solomon called here "the knowledge of the holy."

Moses knew true happiness at his conversion. He chose "rather to suffer affliction with the people of God, than to enjoy the pleasures of sin for a season" (Hebrews 11:25). To say he knew happiness when he chose to suffer sounds like a paradox, but the statement reflects the highest wisdom. Many a martyr has sung at the stake in the grip of "joy unspeakable and full of glory" (1 Peter 1:8).

Moses knew holiness at his consecration. At the burning bush God's awesome voice commanded: "Draw not nigh hither: put off thy shoes from off thy feet, for the place whereon thou standest is holy ground" (Exodus 3:5). That encounter forty years after his conversion marked a great advance in his spiritual life. To know the Lord as the source of all happiness is great indeed; to know Him as the source of all holiness is far greater. Moses' ministry dated from that experience.

The teachable man also learns that he who would really live must *know the Word.* "For by me thy days shall be multiplied, and the years of thy life shall be increased" (Proverbs 9:11). So says divine wisdom, which was incarnated in the Savior, the living Word, and which is inherent in the Scriptures, the written Word.

The promise of long life is also included in God's commandment that children obey their parents (Exodus 20:12). This commandment is repeated in the New Testament (Ephesians 6:1-3). However, we must always remember that the promise of wealth, health, and a long life was part of the Old Testament covenant with Israel (Deuteronomy 28:1-14). In the New Testament, which views everything from the resurrection side of the cross, death is robbed of its terror, so length of days in terms of a long natural life is no longer as important. The promise of a long life on earth is replaced by the certainty of eternal life. Although the Jews had a hope of Heaven (Hebrews 11:10), they really looked for their blessings in this life. They were, and are, God's earthly people. The blessings that dominated their thoughts were material, physical, temporal, and conditional.

As Spirit-baptized, Spirit-indwelt believers living in the church age, we are God's heavenly people. Our center is not in the *land* but in the *Lord.* Our blessings are spiritual, heavenly, eternal, and unconditional. The Old Testament related everything to a *place;* the New Testament relates everything to a *person.* Under the Old Testament covenant the Jew had to be in *Canaan;* under the new covenant the believer is to be in *Christ.* All our blessings are in Him.

It was right and proper that God should promise long life to an earthly people who were obedient and faithful. But because of Calvary we are seated with Christ in the heavenlies and we can look beyond this life to the life to come. Before Calvary a Hebrew was entitled to expect long life on earth if he lived according to the divine wisdom made clear to him in the Old Testament Scriptures. Our perspective—our wisdom—is higher, holier, and happier than his.

4. Responsibility (9:12)

"If thou be wise, thou shalt be wise for thyself: but if thou scornest, thou alone shall bear it." No one can live my life for me; I cannot live your life for you. We make our own decisions, for better or for worse, and we live with the consequences, good or bad. You cannot be wise for me; I cannot be wise for you. A wise man can give us sound advice and share the benefit of his knowledge, experience, and accumulated wisdom, but he cannot make us take his advice.

Sometimes in Scripture the word translated "nevertheless" indicates that good advice has been given but not taken. For example, the word is used in the story of the twelve spies in Numbers 13. When Moses sent the spies into Canaan to assess the strength of the enemy and bring back a report on the land, ten brought back an evil report. They saw cities walled up to heaven, they saw the sons of the Anakim there (a hybrid race of giants), and they saw themselves as grasshoppers. "We came unto the land whither thou sentest us," they said, "and surely it floweth with milk and honey; and this is the fruit of it [displaying the enormous bunch of grapes they had gleaned at Eshcol]. *Nevertheless* the people be strong that dwell in the land, and the cities are walled, and very great: and moreover we saw the children of Anak there" (Numbers 13:27-28, italics added).

Then Caleb and Joshua spoke up. The people had heard the majority report. Now it was time for them to hear the minority report, which is often far better. They said:

> The land, which we passed through to search it, is an exceeding good land. If the Lord delight in us, then he will bring us into this land, and give it us; a land which floweth with milk and honey. Only rebel not ye against the Lord, neither fear ye the people of the land; for they are bread for us: their defence is departed from them, and the Lord is with us: fear them not (Numbers 14:7-9).

Their advice was sound. Joshua and Caleb put the Lord back into the picture and that made their outlook different. Caleb and Joshua saw the balance of power swinging decisively over to Israel.

But their advice was spurned. "*Nevertheless*," said Caleb some forty years later, "my brethren that went up with me made the heart of the people melt: but I wholly followed the Lord my God" (Joshua 14:8, italics added). Caleb was wise, but he was wise for himself. The people were scornful and they alone bore the consequences. "Would God that we had died in the land of Egypt!" they said, "or

would God we had died in this wilderness!" (Numbers 14:2) And the
people took up stones to kill Joshua and Caleb. The scornful words
were hardly out of the mouths of the people before God broke in.
"Your carcases shall fall in this wilderness," He said (Numbers
14:29). Their prayer was answered! Of all the Israelites aged twenty
years and upward, only Joshua and Caleb lived to enter the promised land. It would be hard to find a more graphic illustration of
Proverbs 9:12.

G. Her Paths Are Pure (9:13-18)

1. The Foolish Woman's Clamor (9:13)

Part One of the book of Proverbs closes with Solomon's fifth and
final portrait of the evil woman. Having extolled the virtues of
Wisdom, he said, "A foolish woman is clamorous: she is simple, and
knoweth nothing." She may have a pretty face, but she has an empty
head. She may have physical appeal, but that is all she has. Any man
forced to live with her would soon become bored with her. Her
interests run to clothes and cosmetics, to fashion magazines and
gossip columns, to trash and trivia.

Doubtless Solomon had scores of such women in his harem. We
can well believe they kept the palace in a perpetual pandemonium
of jealousy, malice, gossip, and intrigue. In the growing cynicism of
his advancing years so evident in the book of Ecclesiastes, Solomon
must have wondered at his folly in marrying such women.

Mr. Stand-fast met such a woman toward the end of the second
part of John Bunyan's *Pilgrim's Progress*. Soon after, Christiana and
her boys, in the company of Mr. Valiant-for-Truth and Mr. Great-
heart, found Mr. Stand-fast on his knees in fervent prayer. They
joined this worthy pilgrim and asked him why he was so earnestly
engaged in prayer. Mr. Stand-fast told them he had just met Madam
Bubble:

> STAND-FAST....As I was thus musing, as I said, there was one
> in very pleasant attire, but old, who presented herself unto me,
> and offered me three things; to wit, her body, her purse, and
> her bed. Now, the truth is, I was both a-weary and sleepy; I am
> also as poor as an owlet, and that, perhaps, the witch knew.
> Well, I repulsed her once or twice, but she put by my repulses,
> and smiled. Then I began to be angry; but she mattered that
> nothing at all. Then she made offers again, and said, If I would
> be ruled by her, she would make me great and happy; for, said

she, I am the mistress of the world, and men are made happy by me. Then I asked her name, and she told me it was Madam Bubble. This set me further from her: but she still followed me with enticements....

GREAT-HEART. This woman is a witch, and it is by virtue of her sorceries that this ground is enchanted. Whoever doth lay their head down in her lap, had as good lay it down upon that block over which the axe doth hang.... She is a great gossiper! she is always, both she and her daughters, at one pilgrim's heels or another.... She is a bold and impudent slut; she will talk with any man. She always laugheth poor pilgrims to scorn; but highly commends the rich.... She loves to be sought after, spoken well of, and to lie in the bosoms of men. She is never weary of commending her commodities, and she loves them most that think best of her. She will promise to some crowns and kingdoms, if they will but take her advice; yet many hath she brought to the halter, and ten thousand times more to hell....She would have drawn thee into "many foolish hurtful lusts, which drown men in destruction and perdition." (1 Tim. vi. 9.)

2. The Foolish Woman's Call (9:14-15)

We note *her place:* "For she sitteth at the door of her house, on a seat in the high places of the city" (Proverbs 9:14). Here Solomon was adding some observations of his own about "Madam Bubble," the great whore. She is a public woman whose favors anyone can court. Solomon pictured her advertising her wares. She is like a spider waiting on her web. She sits at the door of her house to snare the unwary passerby. She is like a python, gliding forth to look for a victim around whom to throw her coils. She is certainly no "keeper at home," the role Titus 2:5 casts for the godly woman. "Madame Bubble" is a woman of the streets.

We note also *her ploy:* "To call passengers who go right on their ways" (Proverbs 9:15). Not content with showing off her fleshly wares, she uses other powers of persuasion. She is shameless. She calls out to those who pass by. The majority avert their eyes and stolidly keep on their way, quickening their steps as she approaches, shaking off her clutching hand, ignoring her only-too-evident invitation. She is not bothered by them. She is used to rejection. She has long since become hardened to the look of repulsion. She knows only too well that sooner or later a young fellow or old fellow will give her a second look and not shake off her hand. That is the fish she is angling for. *Let the rest go on their way with turned-up noses and disdainful glances,* she thinks. *I'm an experienced hand at this game.*

3. The Foolish Woman's Clients (9:16)

"Whoso is simple, let him turn in hither: and as for him that wanteth understanding, she saith to him..."

This chapter of Proverbs provides a clearly discernible, planned, and deliberate contrast between Wisdom and the foolish woman. Both are out on the streets. Both can be seen in the high places soliciting those who pass by to come to their respective houses. "Whoso is simple," Wisdom says, throwing her arms wide to embrace even the gullible travelers along the highway of life (Proverbs 9:4). "Whoso is simple," said Solomon, eyeing those most likely to hearken to the harlot on the street (Proverbs 9:16). If the simple will not respond to Wisdom's call, then likely enough he will fall afoul of the harpy. Only a simpleton thinks he can buy love. He can buy sex but not love. He can buy a body and lose a soul.

4. The Foolish Woman's Claim (9:17)

The whore knows just what to say to the simpleton who gives her a second look. That second look speaks volumes to her. It tells her that this fellow is not motivated by the high morals of religious conviction. He is not ruled by the Word of God. He is vulnerable.

"Flee...youthful lusts," the Holy Spirit counsels (2 Timothy 2:22). The man who fails to heed that wise advice opens himself to temptation. The evil woman sidles up to him and boldly assaults his shaky morals. "Stolen waters are sweet," she says, "and bread eaten in secret is pleasant" (Proverbs 9:17).

She is lying of course. Stolen water is no sweeter than any other kind of water. Bread eaten in secret, furtively, with constant looks over the shoulder, is not nearly as good as bread broken in hearty fellowship with good friends around the family supper table. The harlot's sophistry, however, appeals to the simple. It hints at excitement and intrigue. It suggests that sin is sophisticated and that those who embrace Biblical morality are somehow naive.

To this day an immoral lifestyle, pornography, perversion, and the like are billed as "adult." Activities that are illegitimate, depraved, and decadent are somehow supposed to be for grown-up people. The implication of course is that those who refrain from such activities are not mature enough to participate. So the foolish woman whispers in the prospective client's ear: "Be a man. Act grown up. Let's have fun." She suggests that there is nothing wrong with what she offers. "After all," she says, "everyone has appetites that need to be indulged. What I offer is not only right, but risqué and therefore spicier and more desirable than the humdrum pleasures of home."

5. The Foolish Woman's Curse (9:18)

So off goes Mr. Simpleton with Madam Bubble to her lair. "But he knoweth not that the dead are there; and that her guests are in the depths of hell."

What happens to Mr. Simpleton is like a dream. He takes the woman at her word. He follows her home, shrugging off the stares of those passing by. They go inside her house, she closes the door, and they get down to business. But once her arms are around him and the lights are turned out, the dream turns into a nightmare. The woman turns into a livid corpse. The man is gripped by horror as the corpse becomes a grinning skeleton with empty eye sockets, long bony arms, and dreadful fingers that clutch and hold. The horrible skull to which clings a hank or two of mousy hair has sharp, gnashing teeth. He struggles against the dreadful being who clasps him to her horrid chest. The harlot has become a horror.

He awakens in a cold sweat and gropes for the light. The woman is still there, but she has suddenly become hateful. The glamour has gone. In the broad light of day the woman of the shades and shadows with her lies and lures is seen for what she is, a disheveled and dreadful harlot whose hand is outstretched for her fee. He looks at himself in the mirror and is disgusted at what he sees.

Worse still, the nightmare haunts him. He has entered the house of death. The woman has sealed his doom. Her disease has become his disease. His soul and spirit have been defiled. Conscience, conveniently asleep when he was listening to the woman's words, has escaped from its kennel and is baying and barking of judgment to come.

OBSERVATION
Proverbs 1:10–29:27

PART TWO:
Miscellaneous Issues
Proverbs 10:1–19:5

OBSERVATION
(1:10–29:27)

———❦———

PART TWO:
Miscellaneous Issues
(10:1–19:5)

In general the book of Proverbs is grouped around three key points of interest. We have already explored the first point, *moral* issues, in Part One (1–9). Now in Part Two comes a series of chapters that cover *miscellaneous* issues (10:1–19:5); the wise man roams here, there, and everywhere commenting on all phases of human life and activity. In Part Three the point of interest will be *monarchial* issues—proverbs more or less of special interest to those in authority (19:6–29:27).

The first section of Part Two deals mostly with *contrasts* (10:1–15:33) and the second section deals mostly with *comparisons* (16:1–19:5).

CHAPTER 14
Proverbs 10:1-32

Section 1: The Lot of the Godly and the Ungodly Contrasted
  (10:1–15:33)

  I. Blessings Gained or Lost (10:1-32)
      A. Family Things (10:1)
      B. Financial Things (10:2-5)
         1. Profits and Loss (10:2)
         2. Assets and Liabilities (10:3-4)
            a. The Guarantor (10:3)
            b. The Guarantee (10:4)
         3. Work and Laziness (10:5)
      C. Final Things (10:6-7)
         1. Here (10:6)
         2. Hereafter (10:7)
      D. Foolish Things (10:8-14)
         1. The Prating Fool (10:8)
         2. The Perverted Fool (10:9)
         3. The Provoking Fool (10:10-12)
            a. A Winking Eye (10:10)
            b. A Wicked Mouth (10:11)
            c. A Warring Heart (10:12)
         4. The Punished Fool (10:13-14)
            a. Punished by the Rod of the Law (10:13)
            b. Punished by the Rules of Life (10:14)
      E. Familiar Things (10:15)
      F. Futile Things (10:16-17)
         1. The Futility of Rejecting Righteousness (10:16)
         2. The Futility of Rejecting Reproof (10:17)
      G. Fundamental Things (10:18-28)
         1. A Man's Words (10:18-21)

I. BLESSINGS GAINED OR LOST (10:1-32)

A. Family Things (10:1)

"A wise son maketh a glad father: but a foolish son is the heaviness of his mother." Many parents have understood the truth of this proverb. It describes the experience of a couple we knew. When their son was a teenager he went through a rebellious phase and seriously misbehaved. He ran away from home, experimented with drink and drugs, and had a brush with the law. His parents were sure he would end up in jail. He rebelled against parental discipline, chose his friends from a worldly crowd, and had no use for preachers or church.

The mother went into a depression. Doom and gloom reigned in the home and the devil had a heyday. The father even left the Lord's work for a year and took a job with a trucking company. Then the Lord dealt with the mother. He said to her: "What have I ever done to you that you should be so depressed? Have I stopped loving you? Have I turned against you? Don't you think I know all about your boy? Is my arm shortened that it cannot save? What do you mean by being depressed when you still have Me?"

She was convicted and asked the Lord and her family for forgiveness. She tuned up her soul to sing and when the son would come home, he would find his mother singing hymns in the kitchen or playing the piano. His little tricks for making life miserable no longer worked. Now he was the one out in the cold.

It was not long before that rebellious son was saved. He who had been a foolish son and the heaviness of his mother became a wise son making a glad father. The boy went back to high school and earned his diploma. He witnessed to his former friends. He went on to college, majored in Bible, and is now active in his church. He loves the Lord and he loves his parents. He studies his Bible and plans to raise his own children in the knowledge of God. Now he and his father are friends!

As we have seen, Solomon had a wayward son too. Solomon wanted to direct the affections of Rehoboam toward the Lord. The history books of the Bible record the extent to which Solomon succeeded and the extent to which he failed. However belatedly, at least he tried. At least he wrote the book of Proverbs, much of it with Rehoboam in mind. Whether or not Solomon's empty-headed son paid any attention to the proverbs, we would do well to heed them, for behind Solomon's keen mind and productive pen was the Holy Spirit of God.

B. Financial Things (10:2-5)

1. Profits and Loss (10:2)

"Treasures of wickedness profit nothing: but righteousness delivereth from death." Note carefully the phrase "treasures of wickedness." Judas sought such worthless trash. Peter told us that "this man purchased a field with the reward of iniquity" (Acts 1:18). The money Judas used was evidently not the ill-fated thirty pieces of silver that he received for his betrayal of Christ. Judas did not spend a penny of that money. He flung those accursed coins on the temple floor at the feet of the priests and they used the money to purchase a field to be used as a cemetery. This field was not the one Judas bought. Evidently Judas had other money, so he must have been dipping his hand in the bag for some time.

No wonder Judas was so indignant when Mary of Bethany poured her spikenard over Jesus' feet. "Why was not this ointment sold for three hundred pence, and given to the poor?" Judas demanded

(John 12:5). But he did not care about the poor. John, who saw through Judas, bluntly said, "He was a thief" (12:6). What really upset Judas was that the percentage he normally skimmed off the top of donations and appropriated to his own ends was being poured out and "wasted." That was his evaluation of Mary's worship. Doubtless he had in mind another field or two he wanted to buy. In the end his ill-gotten gains did him little good. The treasures of wickedness profited him nothing. The wickedness of Judas hastened his death. Overwhelmed by guilt and remorse, he hanged himself.

In contrast, "righteousness delivereth from death," as in the case of Peter. Peter betrayed the Lord too, once with oaths and curses. However Peter was guilty of weakness, not wickedness. Peter was a righteous man and, his faults and failings notwithstanding, he was delivered from death. Jesus called him "blessed," warned him of fierce temptation ahead, and prayed that his faith would not fail (Matthew 16:17; Luke 22:31-34). After denying Christ, Peter went out and wept bitterly. Doubtless in his misery and shame he considered the option of suicide, but the Lord's prayers prevailed. Peter's righteousness delivered him from death. After Pentecost he became the chief spokesman of the infant church.

2. Assets and Liabilities (10:3-4)

Proverbs 10:3 draws our attention to *the guarantor:* "The Lord will not suffer the soul of the righteous to famish: but he casteth away the substance of the wicked." Note the contrasts between "soul" and "substance" and between "the righteous" and "the wicked." The spiritual man is more concerned with his soul than with his substance. The wicked man is more concerned with his substance than with his soul.

"The Lord will not suffer the soul of the righteous to famish." Think for example of Abraham. He had been battered and bruised in his soul. He had been disappointed in Lot, who had walked out of the fellowship of believers to a life of ease, promotion, and prosperity in Sodom. Then news came that Lot and his family had been carried away as prisoners of war. Without a moment's hesitation Abraham mobilized the scanty force at his disposal, marched after the victorious invading army, executed a brilliant surprise attack at night, and rescued Lot.

We can well imagine that Abraham was physically, emotionally, and spiritually drained after these events. Consequently he was especially vulnerable to Satanic attack. Indeed Satan was already on the prowl in the person of the king of Sodom. However, God did not suffer the soul of His righteous servant to perish. Through the ministry of the king of Salem, God met Abraham, spread a table for him, and provided for both his physical and spiritual needs. (See Genesis 14.)

"He casteth away the substance of the wicked." In contrast to Abraham's acceptance of the replenishment of his depleted spiritual resources, we see Abraham's refusal to accept any of the spoils of Sodom. We see the king of Sodom heading back to his vile city, rubbing his hands over the inexplicable refusal. But the spoils would do him little good. Already the heavenly cauldrons of fire and brimstone destined for Sodom's utter overthrow were being heated to the boiling point. In one night of horror God would cast away the substance of the wicked people of Sodom. (See Genesis 19.)

Proverbs 10:4 draws our attention to *the guarantee:* "He becometh poor that dealeth with a slack hand: but the hand of the diligent maketh rich." This verse is a simple statement of the basic principles of good and bad management. We speak of a good business manager running "a tight ship." He keeps tight control over all aspects of his business. He watches his production schedules, demands constant quality control, and keeps overruns to a minimum. He sets realistic sales targets. He pays attention to costs and pricing, establishes proper purchasing procedures, and is persistent in the collection of accounts receivable. He is diligent and he makes money. The man who runs his business with a slack hand often goes bankrupt.

3. Work and Laziness (10:5)

"He that gathereth in summer is a wise son: but he that sleepeth in harvest is a son that causeth shame." In other words, "Make hay while the sun shines," or "Don't put off until tomorrow what you can do today." Shakespeare said, "There is a tide in the affairs of men which, taken at the flood, leads on to fortune." All these sayings are variations on the same theme.

In her book *The Good Earth* Pearl Buck told of the diligence and industry of her hero Wang Lung. Wang Lung, a farmer, was poor, but he loved the land and was addicted to hard work. He rose with the sun to plow and plant, sow and till, water and fertilize, weed and reap. His wife worked as hard as he did. He sold his grain carefully at a profit. He scrimped and saved. He invested his earnings in more land and chose his land well. Even when famine brought want and woe, grinding poverty and gnawing hunger, Wang Lung held onto his land. He sold his furniture. He even ate his poor faithful ox that had been reduced to skin and bones. He fended off his neighbors who wrongfully accused him of hiding and hoarding grain. When his uncle came with rich speculators and jingled coins, Wang Lung stubbornly refused to sell his land. In the end he became rich.

Wang Lung's uncle also owned land. But whereas Wang Lung's land was tended with care, the uncle's land was overgrown with weeds. While Wang Lung worked his fingers to the bone, his uncle lazed in the sun, ate sweetmeats, and smoked. While Wang Lung's wife and children toiled up and down the long furrows, his uncle's wife gossiped, complained, and demanded luxuries. When Wang Lung's land produced abundant harvests, his uncle's produced meager, inferior crops. His uncle was always being forced to sell his grain before it was fully ripe. He even sold it at giveaway prices while it was still standing in the field to save himself the trouble of harvesting and to get some ready cash. When hard times came, Wang Lung's uncle lost his land and then demanded that his nephew support him and his idle brood.

Stories like this one are told often and in all lands. As we say today, "Money does not grow on trees."

C. Final Things (10:6-7)

Having observed the preoccupation people have with making money, Solomon raised a caution concerning the here and the hereafter. Proverbs 10:6 warns about the *here:* "Blessings are upon the head of the just: but violence covereth the mouth of the wicked." The word "blessings" here points not only to good things, but to good things bestowed by another, particularly to good things bestowed by God.

Material things can be accumulated in legitimate ways or by lawless means, by virtuous methods or by violence. Many of the Old Testament saints were rich. The patriarchs were rich, Job was rich, and David and Solomon were rich. There is nothing wrong with being rich. However, the morality of the Bible lays social and spiritual responsibilities on the rich to care for the poor and further the work of God in this world. The morality of the Bible, furthermore, forbids getting rich by fraud, violence, or oppression.

Proverbs 10:6 applies to more than merely the making of money. The contrast between blessings and violence is well illustrated in the story of Joab and David. Joab was David's nephew and commander-in-chief of his uncle's armed forces. He had great ability, but was thoroughly ambitious, ruthless, and vindictive. After the death of Saul, Joab played a prominent role in the ensuing civil war. When Abner, who commanded the forces arrayed against David, surrendered, Joab murdered him. Joab's pretext was to avenge his younger brother Asahel, who had died at the hands of Abner in the course of the war. Joab's real reason was to remove a potential rival. He murdered Amasa, another of David's generals, for the same reason (2 Samuel 20:9-13). Joab held a whip hand over David. David had used him in the murder of Uriah and thereafter Joab became the classic example of "tool turned tyrant." David never did feel strong enough to deal decisively with this formidable man.

However, when handing over the reins of government to Solomon, David told him to be sure to get rid of Joab. The grounds for Joab's execution were the murders of Abner and Amasa. When Solomon attempted to carry out the sentence, Joab fled to the temple and laid hold of the horns of the altar, hoping to find sanctuary and safety in the sacred precincts. It was a vain hope however. He was dragged away and executed for his crimes by Benaiah, chief of the king's bodyguard. (See 1 Kings 2:5-6,28-34.)

While Joab's end was marked by violence, David's end was blessed. Noting this contrast and justifying the execution of Joab, who after all had been a national hero, Solomon said:

> The Lord shall return his blood upon his own head, who fell upon two men more righteous and better than he, and slew them with the sword, my father David not knowing thereof, to wit, Abner the son of Ner, captain of the host of Israel, and Amasa the son of Jether, captain of the host of Judah. Their blood shall therefore return upon the head of Joab, and upon the head of his seed for ever: but upon David, and upon his seed, and upon his house, and upon his throne, shall there be peace for ever from the Lord (1 Kings 2:32-33).

In spite of his terrible sin with Bathsheba, David was basically a good and godly man. His Psalms reflect his essential spirituality.

Having warned about the here, Solomon warned about the *hereafter:* "The memory of the just is blessed: but the name of the wicked shall rot" (Proverbs 10:7). Many examples of this contrast can be found in both sacred and secular history. We think of Noah and Nimrod, Samuel and Saul, Jonathan and Joab, Hezekiah and Haman, Paul and Pilate. In each case one man's name is blessed and the other's is covered with shame.

The whole world knows the name of Abraham, but how many

have heard of Abimelech who ruled the Philistines and continually wronged Abraham (Genesis 21:22-34)? Abimelech's name has long since been forgotten. Indeed we would never have heard of him at all had he not for a brief moment of time come into contact with Abraham.

Everyone knows the name of Moses, but who knows which pharaoh reigned at the time of the exodus? To this day we cannot say for sure. Was it Amenhotep III or Ramses II?

We all know about godly king Hezekiah, but what do we know or care about Rabshakeh (Isaiah 36)?

The classic Biblical illustration of Proverbs 10:7 comes from the Lord's story of the rich man and Lazarus. We all know the name of the poor beggar covered with sores who sat at the gate of the rich man, but was treated with more kindness by the scavenger dogs of the streets. Lazarus was well known in Heaven too. The angel sent to conduct his soul to Abraham's bosom had no trouble finding him. But nobody knows who the rich man was. He died a nameless nonentity and is now in a lost eternity—an unknown, abandoned man.

In this life one of two things happens to us. Either our sins get blotted out (Acts 3:19; Colossians 2:14) or our names get blotted out (Revelation 3:5). There can be no greater horror for a man than to wake up in a lost eternity to the terrible realization that his name has been blotted out. If he had been redeemed, his name would have been written in the Lamb's book of life (Revelation 20:11-15) to be remembered for Christ's sake forever.

D. Foolish Things (10:8-14)

Once again the fool is paraded before us. First we see *the prating fool:* "The wise in heart will receive commandments: but a prating fool shall fall" (Proverbs 10:8). The wise man recognizes good advice and accepts it. The fool is impervious to any advice. He is too busy running off at the mouth, too full of silly chatter. His talk is his own undoing.

Like all good soldiers, Naaman was as good at taking orders as he was at giving them. He was a man under authority. Naaman was a soldier, and a very successful one at that. He had climbed to the top of the professional ladder, but he was a leper.

His wife's little Hebrew slave girl (doubtless captured by Naaman in one of the many Syro-Ephraimitic wars of the period) told her mistress about a man of God in her native land who could heal leprosy. In due course Naaman went to Israel. Full of his own importance and full of his own ideas about how he would be healed, Naaman arrived at the house of Elisha. Elisha knew that Naaman's pride must be humbled and his own ideas annulled if ever he was to experience God's great salvation. So the prophet did not even go to the door. He sent his servant Gehazi with an unwelcome message: "Go and wash in Jordan seven times."

Furious, Naaman went away in a rage. But he was blessed with wise servants. "If the prophet had asked you to do some great thing," they said in effect, "would you not have done it? Why not do as he says? What do you have to lose?" Naaman was wise in heart. He bowed to the counsel of his servants, submitted to the commandment of God, and was healed.

In contrast to Naaman, Elisha's servant Gehazi was a prating fool. He watched in astonishment as Elisha refused to receive any reward from Naaman. *A king's ransom was his for the taking!* Gehazi thought. As soon as the prophet's back was turned, Gehazi ran after the Syrian general and palmed off a lie to this effect: "My master has just received some unexpected visitors. He needs some of your gifts after all. Could you spare him a talent of silver and two changes of raiment?" The grateful Naaman gave the servant more than he asked for. However, the wretched servant got more than he bargained for. Elisha was not deceived and he called down Naaman's leprosy upon Gehazi. (See 2 Kings 5.)

Gehazi had a certain amount of acumen when it came to human relations (2 Kings 4:12-17), but a knowledge of psychology does not qualify one for the Lord's work (2 Kings 4:18-37). Gehazi had no spiritual power. He was Elisha's Judas. The widow who came to see Elisha because her son was dead saw through Gehazi. She was not impressed by his words or his desire to bask in the reflected glory of his master's greatness. Gehazi was all talk (2 Kings 8:1-6). His talk was his undoing. Every time he looked with loathing at himself and saw what Naaman's leprosy was doing to his body, Gehazi must have cursed his prating tongue.

Besides the prating fool there is *the perverted fool:* "He that walketh uprightly walketh surely: but he that perverteth his ways shall be known" (Proverbs 10:9).

Perverted fools tried to hinder the upright Father Charles Chiniquy, one of the most remarkable converts to genuine Christianity in the nineteenth century. For twenty-five years he was a priest in the Roman Catholic Church. And Father Chiniquy was no nonentity. He pioneered the American Midwest for the Roman church. Moreover he was a personal friend of Abraham Lincoln. But for years Father Chiniquy struggled with a growing conviction that he was serving not the true bride of Christ, but the scarlet woman herself.

When after months of soul-searching Father Chiniquy broke with the Roman church, he brought thousands of converts with him. His defection aroused the ire of the Catholic hierarchy, as he revealed in his book *Fifty Years in the Church of Rome*. The book quickly became a classic on the corruptions and doctrinal errors of Rome, and the last chapter showed Rome unmasked.

Chiniquy wrote of no less than thirty public attempts on his life. He was assaulted by a mob of fifty men in Quebec, attacked with stones in a town near Sydney, Australia, and beaten with whips and sticks in New South Wales. He said, "When the bishops and priests saw that it was so difficult to put me out of the way with stones, sticks and daggers, they determined to destroy my character by calumnies, spread everywhere and sworn before civil tribunals as gospel truths."[1] He was haled before court after court in Illinois and Montreal.

In his book Chiniquy told how even before his conversion he incurred the wrath of the bishop of Montreal. The bishop sent a woman of the most depraved character to Chiniquy's confessional with the sole purpose of trapping him and ruining him. She made false accusations and then the bishop defrocked Chiniquy, refused to discuss the case with him, and summarily dismissed him. But Chiniquy was determined to fight. Investigators proved that the woman was one of the most depraved in Montreal, that she was possessed of a dangerous tongue, and that she was a frequent visitor to the bishop's palace. Chiniquy and his colleagues were able to get a written confession from the girl and a retraction from the bishop.

Reading this exposé, I was struck by the remarkable way in which Father Chiniquy was able to walk surefootedly in the most slippery and dangerous places and the remarkable way in which the perversity of his evil enemies was made known. The whole account is a commentary on Proverbs 10:9.

Next in the parade is *the provoking fool.* Solomon wrote of this fool's eye, mouth, and heart. He has *a winking eye:* "He that winketh with the eye causeth sorrow: but a prating fool shall fall" (Proverbs 10:10). The eye has appropriately been called the mirror of the soul. The eye has a language all its own. It can flash with anger or express mirth and surprise. The eye can be roving, shifty, or hostile. It can express grief; tears can speak volumes.

Thinking of the eye, I am reminded again of Mr. Bumble. He is no longer the beadle. Gone are his cocked hat and his former glory. Gone are his gold-laced coat and his staff of office. Having married

Mrs. Corney, he is master of the workhouse, but he and his wife have
not been compatible. When his wife overhears him lamenting his
fallen fortunes and confronts him, Mr. Bumble decides that the
crisis hour has come: they must decide once and for all exactly who
is going to rule the house and the workhouse. Charles Dickens
described what happens next:

> "Have the goodness to look at me," said Mr. Bumble, fixing
> his eyes upon her. ("If she stands such a eye as that," said Mr.
> Bumble to himself, "she can stand anything. It is a eye I never
> knew to fail with paupers. If it fails with her, my power is gone.")
> Whether an exceedingly small expansion of eye be sufficient
> to quell paupers, who, being lightly fed, are in no very high
> condition; or whether the late Mrs. Corney was particularly
> proof against eagle glances; are matters of opinion. The
> matter of fact is that the matron was in no way overpowered by
> Mr. Bumble's scowl, but, on the contrary, treated it with great
> disdain, and even raised a laugh thereat, which sounded as
> though it were genuine.

It was all a matter of the eye. In the end the widow reduces Mr.
Bumble to servitude.

The eye can communicate without words by winking. A wink can
convey a message as surely as words—and more swiftly. A wink can
be used to express interest in another person. A wink can convey a
secret understanding, an agreement already reached. A wink can be
used between two or more people to signal the gullibility of another
person. When someone is being teased or misled, a wink is often
used to enhance the amusement of those who know the secret. In
Bible times a briber would use a wink to let a corrupt judge know
what was expected of him. The Holy Spirit takes His stand against
all such winking with the eye.

The provoking fool has *a wicked mouth:* "The mouth of a righteous
man is a well of life: but violence covereth the mouth of the wicked"
(Proverbs 10:11). This contrast is seen in the words of Mordecai and
Haman, the great protagonists in the book of Esther. Haman—a
descendant of Agag the Amalekite, an ancient enemy of Israel—
hated Jews in general and Mordecai in particular. He plotted the
extermination of all the Jews in the Persian empire. Haman said to
the king:

> There is a certain people scattered abroad and dispersed
> among the people in all the provinces of thy kingdom; and

their laws are diverse from all people; neither keep they the king's laws: therefore it is not for the king's profit to suffer them. If it please the king, let it be written that they may be destroyed: and I will pay ten thousand talents of silver to the hands of those that have the charge of the business, to bring it into the king's treasury (Esther 3:8-9).

Mordecai the Jew realized that his cousin, Queen Esther, was the answer to the whole problem. He sought to overcome Esther's natural reluctance to speak to her formidable, quick-tempered husband on behalf of her people. Esther argued that speaking to the king was not so easy as Mordecai made it sound because anyone who came unbidden into the king's presence risked her life. Mordecai, however, cut through Esther's excuses. Thousands of lives hung in the balance.

"Think not with thyself that thou shalt escape in the king's house, more than all the Jews," Mordecai said to Esther. "For if thou altogether holdest thy peace at this time, then shall there enlargement and deliverance arise to the Jews from another place; but thou and thy father's house shall be destroyed: and who knoweth whether thou art come to the kingdom for such a time as this?" (Esther 4:13-14) His words were a well of life. Esther said, "So will I go in unto the king, which is not according to law: and if I perish, I perish." As it turned out, nobody perished except Haman and his sons.

Haman was a destroyer; Mordecai was a deliverer. Haman was a violent man; Mordecai was a virtuous man. Mordecai spoke with the mouth of the righteous and his words were a well of life. As for Haman, violence covered the mouth of this wicked man.

The provoking fool has *a warring heart:* "Hatred stirreth up strifes: but love covereth all sins" (Proverbs 10:12). The first part of this proverb is illustrated by the missionary journeys of the apostle Paul. The Jews hated him, dogged his footsteps, and stirred up strife.

At Antioch in Pisidia, as soon as Paul's missionary activities began to show significant success among both Jews and Gentiles, the Jewish unbelievers "were filled with envy, and spake against those things which were spoken by Paul, contradicting and blaspheming" (Acts 13:45). This opposition was only the beginning.

At Iconium "the multitude of the city was divided: and part held with the Jews, and part with the apostles. And when there was an assault made both of the Gentiles, and also of the Jews with their rulers, to use them despitefully, and to stone them, They were ware of it, and fled into Lystra and Derbe" (Acts 14:4-6).

At Lystra hatred and hostility increased: "There came thither certain Jews from Antioch and Iconium, who persuaded the people, and, having stoned Paul, drew him out of the city, supposing he had been dead" (Acts 14:19).

During Paul's second missionary journey, this time into Europe, the same pattern emerged. At Thessalonica "the Jews which believed not, moved with envy, took unto them certain lewd fellows of the baser sort, and gathered a company, and set all the city on an uproar, and assaulted the house of Jason" (Acts 17:5). Then "when the Jews of Thessalonica had knowledge that the word of God was preached of Paul at Berea, they came thither also, and stirred up the people" (17:13). At Corinth "the Jews made insurrection with one accord against Paul, and brought him to the judgment seat" (18:12).

The hostilities continued until at last a furious riot in the temple court in Jerusalem led to Paul's arrest by the Romans (Acts 21:30-34). Even then the Jews were not satisfied. A band of forty men took an oath not to eat or drink until Paul was dead; they were involved in a plot to launch an assault on the apostle when he was brought again before the Sanhedrin (23:20-21).

"Hatred stirreth up strifes: but love covereth all sins." The second statement in this proverb sums up the whole philosophy of atonement in the Old Testament. The Hebrew word for "atonement" is *kāphar*, which literally means "to cover." God covered the sins of the people.

On the annual day of atonement a goat was slain and its blood was taken inside the veil by the high priest, who sprinkled it on the mercyseat in the holy of holies. The sins of the people were symbolically laid on the head of another goat known as the scapegoat. The scapegoat was then taken away deep into the desert, into "a land not inhabited," and released in that "waste howling wilderness" (Leviticus 16:22; Deuteronomy 32:10). The scapegoat was left there to perish miserably, far from any pitying eye or saving hand. In this ritualistic way those sins were removed from sight. The love of God covered all those sins by taking them away.

That was the best that could be done with sin in Old Testament times. Sin was, so to speak, swept under the rug. It was not until Calvary that God could deal adequately with sin. At Calvary Old Testament symbolism was replaced by New Testament reality. Once and for all the Lord Jesus shed His blood as the full atonement for sin. Jesus then carried that blood into the holy of holies in Heaven, where he pleaded the merits of His finished work before God's mercyseat. The Lord Jesus took our sins away forever. They were not only covered; they were canceled. The New Testament believer is not simply forgiven; he is also justified. It is just as if he'd never sinned.

There is a striking difference between the love that covers sins and the hatred of a fool who is provoking. Following the provoking fool, *the punished fool* comes into view. He is punished for his folly by *the rod of the law:* "In the lips of him that hath understanding wisdom is found: but a rod is for the back of him that is void of understanding" (Proverbs 10:13).

Society has little patience with fools, especially when their folly leads them into antisocial or illegal behavior. The rod was laid on with a will in the old days, especially in the armed services. The navy especially was known for its harsh discipline and intolerance of any kind of misbehavior, even when the infraction was a case of sheer folly. Discipline was discipline. The law was the law.

Mutiny on the Bounty, a novel that conforms closely to fact, reveals how punishment was administered aboard the *Bounty.* Captain Bligh's clerk, Samuel, was mean, toadying, and spiteful. His petty persecution of the sailors was particularly resented. He hid behind the fact that the captain favored and protected him.

One continuous source of complaint in the lower decks was the inadequate and wretched food. Bligh ignored the complaints. The sailors suspected the captain and the clerk lined their pockets at the expense of the crew, who consequently had to live on short and even tainted rations. In response to a formal complaint forwarded to the captain by way of John Fryer, the master, Bligh snarled: "I'll make you eat grass before I've done with you....The first man to complain from now on will be seized up and flogged."

Soon afterward John Mills, the gunner's mate, acted like a fool. He was a surly individual, often drunk, and unable to control his temper. While off-duty John had the good fortune of catching a large fish that would supplement his and his messmates' meager rations. Then Samuel came along and demanded a slice of the fish. Mills demanded a glass of grog in payment. Samuel brushed the suggestion aside and renewed his demand, adding that the fish slice was for the captain's table. Mills snapped back and Samuel issued a veiled threat. Finally Mills flung ten or twelve pounds of raw fish in Samuel's face, knocking him to the deck. It was a foolish act.

The rod was prepared for John's back. Mills spent the night in irons and then he was trussed up to the gratings. "Three dozen," barked the captain. The brawny boatswain's mate laid on the lashes with his full strength while the crew stood at attention and watched.

Although the example of John Mills illustrates unjust and severe punishment, Solomon did not dismiss corporal punishment. For some kinds of crimes it would be a healthy deterrent today.

The fool is also punished for his folly by *the rules of life:* "Wise men lay up knowledge: but the mouth of the foolish is near destruction" (Proverbs 10:14). A fool's mouth gets him into trouble. So does his silly behavior. Consider the foolish behavior of Asa, king of Judah. Early in his administration he was responsible for religious reforms, but later his behavior deteriorated drastically.

During the reigns of Solomon, Rehoboam, and Abijah there was a progressive decline in the spiritual life of the kingdom of Judah. Maachah (Abijah's mother and Asa's grandmother) even went so far as to set up a vile Asherah as an object of worship (an obnoxious sex symbol of the fertility cults then growing in power in the land). When Asa came to the throne he was a mere boy of ten, so this evil-minded woman was still able to exert a demoralizing influence as Queen Mother.

Later Asa did away with the disgusting Asherah and inaugurated a great religious revival, but Asa's faith was soon tested. An enormous Egyptian army, under the command of Zerah the Ethiopian, invaded Judah. Asa had but a small army compared with the well-disciplined, veteran Egyptian battalions, so Asa appealed to God (2 Chronicles 14:11). God answered his prayer and gave him such a resounding victory over the Egyptians that Egypt ceased to be a threat to Judah for a full 330 years! In response to a prophetic word from Azariah, Asa threw himself even more wholeheartedly into religious reform.

In the meantime Baasha murdered Nadab (the son of and successor to Jeroboam) and ascended the throne of Israel. Baasha made a clean sweep of the royal family and commenced hostilities against Asa and the rival kingdom of Judah. Baasha saw an opportunity to increase his power at Judah's expense and sent his army south.

When Baasha's army penetrated as far as Ramah, midway between Bethel and Jerusalem, Asa panicked. He seemed to have forgotten how his victory over the Egyptians had been obtained. He talked and acted like a fool. Instead of praying, as he had done before, he hastily tried to repair his fences with Syria. Asa's father, Abijah, had made an alliance with Syria, but Asa had discontinued the treaty. So he now appealed to Ben-hadad, the Syrian king, for a new alliance.

"[Let there be] a league between me and thee," Asa said, "as there was between my father and thy father" (2 Chronicles 16:3). He then tried to cement the new alliance with gold and silver taken from the temple and the palace. Ben-hadad was ready to sign a new treaty. It was not to his advantage to have a strong Israel on his southern border any more than it was to Judah's advantage to have a strong Israel on its northern border.

The subsequent Syrian invasion of northern Israel caused Baasha to abandon Ramah. Asa was doubtless congratulating himself on the success of his foreign policy when he was confronted by the prophet Hanani with a message of reproof and judgment. There would be no more peace. Asa would live to rue the day he made an alliance with Syria. He had snubbed the living God who had given him such a notable victory over Egypt. Now he was on his own.

Enraged, Asa locked up the prophet in a prison called "the house of stocks." (The Hebrew word used in 2 Chronicles 16:10 indicates there would have been a pillory for Hanani's body and stocks for his legs. The "stocks" were in fact instruments of torture, confining the neck and arms and bending the body in an unnatural position.) Not long afterward Asa was attacked by a disease of the feet (gout perhaps) and again revealed his folly and spiritual decline by appealing to the physicians instead of to the Lord (16:12). The Lord left him to his doctors, who could not help him, and to his death. Asa suffered for his folly. The rules of life cannot be ignored.

E. Familiar Things (10:15)

"The rich man's wealth is his strong city: the destruction of the poor is their poverty." This proverb states the obvious. The rich man puts his faith in his money, but the poor man has no such defense in times of trouble. He is destroyed by his very insolvency.

We have all observed the deference generally shown to the wealthy. Rich people have influence, power, and resources that command respect and service, which is often rendered with servility. Of course it is not wise to trust in riches. Money can buy influence, but it cannot buy happiness, health, holiness, or Heaven. Money cannot buy love, respect, honor, or character. And wealth can be lost, often overnight. Nevertheless wealth can be a hedge against adversity. The rich man can use resources a poor man doesn't have to fend off at least some of life's everyday discomforts and ills.

Yet the rich man's strong castle is very vulnerable. Vance Havner used to tell a story about a pastor who taught his congregation that none of their possessions belonged to them. A wealthy parishioner invited the pastor home for Sunday dinner and after dinner they took a little walk. The rich man began to point out his assets. "That house is mine," he said. "All these fields, as far as you can see, are mine. Those three cars in the driveway are mine. All the equipment in that barn is mine. I have stocks, bonds, and securities in the bank—all mine. Yet you said this morning that they do not belong to me." The pastor replied, "Tell me all that again—a hundred years from now." Vance Havner's story was a modern version of the story of the rich fool (Luke 12:15-21).

F. Futile Things (10:16-17)

Solomon pointed out *the futility of rejecting righteousness:* "The labour of the righteous tendeth to life: the fruit of the wicked to sin" (Proverbs 10:16). A good man's earnings lead to prosperity while a bad man's gains lead to his downfall. Honest labor brings its own rewards. In the Old Testament the reward tended to be a long and peaceful life. Conversely the wicked use their profits in the service of sin, which always leads to death.

"The fruit of the wicked [tendeth] to sin." This truth can be illustrated by the lives of some of the most successful and influential men in the history of American finance. In 1923 these men met at the Edgewater Beach Hotel in Chicago: the president of the country's largest independent steel company, the president of National City Bank, the president of the country's largest utility company, the president of the country's largest gas company, the country's greatest wheat baron, the president of the New York Stock Exchange, a member of the President's cabinet, a man reputed to be the greatest "bear" on Wall Street, the head of the world's greatest monopoly, and the president of the Bank of International Settlements.

Consider the status of these men twenty-six years later. Charles Schwab had died bankrupt. Samuel Insull had died a fugitive from justice. Howard Hopson had gone insane. Arthur Cotton died abroad insolvent. Richard Whitney had just been released from Sing Sing Prison. Albert Fall had received a pardon so he could go home from prison to die. Jesse Livermore had committed suicide. Ivar Kreuger, whose suicide shook the financial world, was discovered to be a forger and was labeled "the biggest swindler in the annals of crime." Leon Fraser had also committed suicide. These men experienced the futility of rejecting righteousness.

Solomon next referred to *the futility of rejecting reproof:* "He is in the way of life that keepeth instruction: but he that refuseth reproof erreth" (Proverbs 10:17). One man who refused reproof was Ahaz, king of Judah. Although he had a godly father (Jotham) and grandfather (Uzziah), Ahaz was impervious to instruction and reproof. He became king at age twenty and, rejecting the example of his immediate forebears, became an idolater. He even forced his son to "pass through the fire" and sacrificed and burned incense in the high places (2 Kings 16:3-4).

The crisis in Ahaz's godless life came when war broke out between Judah and a strong alliance of Syria and Israel, his two northern neighbors. The Syro-Ephraimitic alliance seemed formidable but before they actually invaded Judah, God sent the prophet Isaiah to Ahaz to urge him to put his trust in the true and living God. Ahaz paid no attention to the prophet. Instead, being a born fool, Ahaz appealed to Tiglath-pileser, king of Assyria, for aid, and paid for this superpower's intervention with treasure from both the palace and the temple.

This appeal was like inviting the cat to come and keep peace between the canaries. The Assyrians were delighted to have an excuse to overrun the whole area. The Assyrian army attacked Philistia, overran Samaria, conquered Damascus, slew King Rezin of Syria, and connived to murder Pekah, the Israelite king. Ahaz was reduced to being a vassal of Assyria because, as a boy and as a king, he refused reproof and despised correction. This pattern of bad behavior leading to evil consequences is all too familiar.

G. Fundamental Things (10:18-28)

1. A Man's Words (10:18-21)

Solomon turned his attention to *the provocative tongue:* "He that hideth hatred with lying lips, and he that uttereth a slander, is a fool" (Proverbs 10:18).

Sigmund Freud was such a man. He called himself "a completely godless Jew."[2] Freud nursed a hatred of Christianity because some so-called Christians pushed his father around and splashed mud on his clothes. Angry at the bullies and ashamed of his father for not fighting back, Freud vowed to get even. He took revenge by labeling religion a sign of neurosis, a mark of infancy that people should discard to prove they had grown up.

The fundamental propositions of the so-called new morality are greatly indebted to the Freudian ethic. Its basic assumption is that it is quite natural, for instance, for a criminal to behave as he does. Furthermore it is quite unreasonable for society to put him on trial for being his antisocial self. Thus it was not Oswald who was to blame for President Kennedy's death; society was at fault.

Freudian psychoanalysis digs back into a person's past to find someone else on whom to fix the blame for his criminal behavior. Home and school discipline are thus undermined because parents are intimidated. They are made to fear that the application of conventional discipline might cause traumatic shocks and future psychological difficulties for their children. Thanks to Freud, people sanction all kinds of irresponsible behavior and make it respectable. Freud's teaching provides a philosophical and "scientific" basis that irresponsible people can use to justify their behavior. Mental sickness, not sin, is considered to be the root cause of bad behavior.

Freud hid hatred with lying lips and the Bible calls him and his kind fools. Those who embrace Freudian philosophy are in the same boat as this vindictive man. In theory and in practice his ideologies are contrary to everyday common sense.

After referring to the provocative tongue, Solomon mentioned *the prolific tongue:* "In the multitude of words there wanteth not sin: but he that refraineth his lips is wise" (Proverbs 10:19).

When God called Moses to be Israel's kinsman-redeemer, he complained:

> O my Lord, I am not eloquent, neither heretofore, nor since thou hast spoken unto thy servant: but I am slow of speech, and of a slow tongue. And the Lord said unto him, Who made man's mouth? or who maketh the dumb, or deaf, or the seeing, or the blind? have not I the Lord? Now therefore go, and I will be with thy mouth, and teach thee what thou shalt say" (Exodus 4:10-12).

When Moses persisted with his objections, God simply overruled him. The Lord said: "Is not Aaron the Levite thy brother? I know that he can speak well....thou shalt speak unto him, and put words in his mouth: and I will be with thy mouth, and with his mouth, and will teach you what ye shall do" (Exodus 4:14-15).

After the exodus was accomplished and the children of Israel were on their way to the promised land, the continuous complaining of the people finally got on Moses' nerves. Toward the end of the wilderness wanderings, the multitude came to Kadesh for the second time. There was no water there for the Israelites to drink and at once they blamed Moses and Aaron. After telling Moses to take his rod and gather the people together, God said: "*Speak* ye unto the rock before their eyes; and it shall give forth his water, and thou shalt bring forth to them water out of the rock: so thou shalt give the congregation and their beasts drink" (Numbers 20:8, italics added).

When a similar situation had developed on a previous occasion God had told Moses to *smite* the rock (Exodus 17:1-6). That incident pictured the smiting of Christ at Calvary (1 Corinthians 10:1-4). Christ was to be smitten only once. This time Moses was to speak to the rock. Now all God's blessings are available solely for the asking.

By this time Moses' temper had gotten the better of him—a remarkable fact in itself, since Moses was famous for his meekness (Numbers 12:3). We read:

> And Moses and Aaron gathered the congregation together before the rock, and he said unto them, Hear now, ye rebels; must we fetch you water out of this rock? And Moses lifted up his hand, and with his rod he smote the rock twice: and the water came out abundantly (Numbers 20:10-11).

Moses paid for his disobedience. At once God spoke again: "Because ye believed me not, to sanctify me in the eyes of the children of Israel, therefore ye shall not bring this congregation into the land which I have given them" (Numbers 20:12). Years later the Holy Spirit summed up the incident: "They angered him also at the waters of strife, so that it went ill with Moses for their sakes: Because they provoked his spirit, so that he spake unadvisedly with his lips" (Psalm 106:32-33).

"I cannot speak," Moses said when God first called him. Yet he was kept out of Canaan for speaking far too much. How we need to heed the words of Proverbs 10:19 and the sobering example of Moses. If one of God's choicest saints could forfeit future reward for speaking hastily, how serious this sin must be in the sight of God! If thirteen words could bring such immediate judgment, what might God say about the countless thousands of foolish words we habitually speak?

In contrast to the prolific tongue is *the productive tongue:* "The tongue of the just is as choice silver: the heart of the wicked is little worth. The lips of the righteous feed many: but fools die for want of wisdom" (Proverbs 10:20-21). In Scripture choice silver symbolizes redemption. Only redeemed lips can speak with authority on the truly important issues of life. The lips of the righteous do feed many indeed. The Bible contains the concentrated wisdom of such men.

Think for instance of the great laws enacted by Moses. No nation in history has ever reduced its legal code to ten sweeping, just, and comprehensive edicts such as those found in the Decalogue. All the jurisprudence of the West is founded on those simple but sublime commandments.

Think of the Psalms of David and Hezekiah in the Hebrew hymnbook. How our hearts are lifted, how our thoughts expand,

and how our spirits soar as we meditate on these magnificent poems. They suit our every mood and need.

Remember the prophets too. Think of the global vision of Isaiah, the sad certainties of Jeremiah, the mystical majesty of Ezekiel, and the unerring vision of Daniel.

Don't forget the world view of the apostle Paul, who had one of the greatest minds in the universe. His genius, quickened by the Holy Spirit, took the great insights of the Old Testament and passed them through the prism of Calvary, thus breaking them up into rainbow colors of truth.

The teachings of Christ stand in a class of their own. Think of the sermon on the mount; the parables of the good Samaritan, the prodigal son, and the great supper; the Olivet discourse; and the talks in the upper room. Who but Jesus ever fed the multitudes with words like His? Even His enemies confessed, "Never man spake like this man" (John 7:46).

"The heart of the wicked is [of] little worth," said Solomon succinctly. Who, having once been enlightened by the Holy Spirit, would want to exchange Moses for Charles Darwin, Solomon for Freud, Isaiah for Karl Marx, or Jesus for Muhammad? The speculations of the world's greatest philosophers pale into insignificance when placed alongside the glorious certainties of Scripture. The founders of the world's major religions are exposed as a poor lot at best when placed alongside Jesus. The world's great educators, statesmen, jurists, poets, and orators cannot be compared with the divinely inspired men who gave us the Word of God. After all, what this world's philosophers have to say, for the most part, comes from unregenerate, unenlightened, and sinful hearts. Their words at best are of little worth.

2. A Man's Wealth (10:22)

"The blessing of the Lord, it maketh rich, and he addeth no sorrow with it." This Old Testament blessing is in stark and studied contrast to the New Testament blessing of the Lord found in the eight beatitudes that open the famous sermon on the mount (Matthew 5:1-12).

The classic example of a man who enjoyed the Old Testament blessing of the Lord is Job. He was surrounded with material blessings. He had a loving wife and ten beloved children. He had vast flocks and herds. His three thousand camels alone marked him as a man of fabulous wealth. Above all, he enjoyed fellowship with God.

All this blessing stirred Satan's malice, envy, and hate and he used it as an excuse to slander Job before God. "Of course he serves You," Satan said in effect. "You have put a hedge around him. He enjoys health and wealth, home and happiness. He is invulnerable. You have blessed the work of his hands. He serves You only for what he can get out of You. Take the hedge away. Let me get at him. Let me strip him of his money, his children, his health, and the sympathy of his wife, and he'll curse You to Your face" (Job 1:1–2:13).

We know what happened. God gave Satan permission to try the experiment, and Job triumphed gloriously. But then Job's friends accused him of being an outrageous secret sinner. And what was the criterion by which they judged him? The Old Testament blessing of the Lord—"The blessing of the Lord, it maketh rich, and he addeth no sorrow with it." Job, they believed, had been rich because he had been good; now he was in dire straits because he was bad.

Job vehemently denied their explanation and accusation. He knew he was not wicked but even so he could not explain the calamities that had come upon him. In the end God gave Job back double because he still qualified for material prosperity under the Old Testament blessing of the Lord.

3. A Man's Wickedness (10:23-28)

a. His Folly (10:23)

"It is as sport to a fool to do mischief: but a man of understanding hath wisdom." Some people think it is funny to play practical jokes on people. No such joke is really funny, however, and some are harmful. The fool thinks a joke is good sport and cannot understand why the victim of the mischief is put out and why thoughtful people are not amused. Solomon had in mind not mere horseplay, but malicious mischievous behavior. Often practical joking gets out of hand. Sometimes it backfires. Not infrequently the victim cannot wait to get even.

Similar to a practical joke is the hoax. Adolf Eichmann, chief executor of the Nazi pogrom to exterminate European Jews, perpetrated one of the cruelest hoaxes of history on the Jews of Hungary. To Eichmann, his mission was as important as winning the war. He was particularly bitter because the Hungarian government, although allied to Nazi Germany, did its best to protect its 800,000 Jews. Indeed, Hungary kept them out of Eichmann's hands for almost five years. Finally Himmler acted and sent his henchman to Hungary to supervise the deportation of Hungarian Jews to the death camps.

The war by then had turned against Germany. Time was running out and many in the Nazi regime thought the government should strike deals and barter Jewish lives for badly needed trucks or clothing. Eichmann, a single-minded fanatic, would not compromise, so his colleagues were shocked to discover that he had agreed to a deal. Under the terms of one agreement the Nazi butcher agreed to let 1700 Hungarian Jews emigrate to Spain. We can imagine the delight and relief with which these fortunate Jews boarded the train. They were going to Spain! They were going to be free! The train pulled out of the station and they settled down to enjoy their ride to freedom, but it was all a cruel hoax. The true destination of that train was Bergen-Belsen, a Nazi death camp.[3]

Eichmann was not only evil; he was a fool. The hoax was his idea of a joke. But before the repercussions were all over, he was tried before a Jewish court in Jerusalem, and now he is awaiting his trial before the great white throne of God.

b. His Fear (10:24)

"The fear of the wicked, it shall come upon him: but the desire of the righteous shall be granted." This proverb reminds me of Fagin's last night in prison. He was to be executed the next morning for his many crimes. The judge's sentence, "to be hanged by the neck, till he was dead," burned into the wicked old man's soul. Dickens wrote:

> As it came on very dark, he began to think of all the men he had known who had died upon the scaffold; some of them through his means. They rose up, in such quick succession, that he could hardly count them. He had seen some of them die,— and had joked too, because they died with prayers upon their lips. With what a rattling noise the drop went down; and how suddenly they changed, from strong and vigorous men to dangling heaps of clothes!...
>
> It was not until the night of this last awful day, that a withering sense of his helpless, desperate state came in its full intensity upon his blighted soul; not that he had ever held any defined or positive hope of mercy, but that he had never been able to consider more than the dim probability of dying so soon....Now, he started up, every minute, and with gasping mouth and burning skin, hurried to and fro, in such a paroxysm of fear and wrath that even they [the guards]—used to such sights—recoiled from him with horror. He grew so terrible, at

last, in all the tortures of his evil conscience, that one man could not bear to sit there, eyeing him alone; and so the two kept watch together.

Oliver Twist and his benefactor Mr. Brownlow came to see Fagin in the hope of getting him to right at least one wrong. A terrible scene followed. Thinking he could escape the condemned cell if he had a hostage, the old Jew seized Oliver. The jailers however disengaged Oliver from Fagin's grasp. "He struggled with the power of desperation, for an instant," Dickens said, "and, then sent up cry upon cry that penetrated even those massive walls, and rang in their ears until they reached the open yard." Thus Dickens left the evil old man. Truly, "the fear of the wicked, it shall come upon him."

Throughout the novel there is a contrast between Fagin, who is wicked, and poor little Oliver Twist, who is righteous. Oliver desired to be free from the thieves among whom he had unwittingly been cast and free from the evil clutches of Fagin, who was determined to make a thief out of him. Oliver's desire was granted. His longing for love, peace, quietness, and goodness was granted too. "The desire of the righteous shall be granted." Throughout the story Dickens—a keen student of human nature—remained true, consciously or unconsciously, to the Biblical script.

c. His Foundation (10:25)

"As the whirlwind passeth, so is the wicked no more: but the righteous is an everlasting foundation." A whirlwind causes a great stir for a little while. It can even do a good deal of damage and leave behind considerable havoc and chaos. But then it is gone. The same is true of the wicked. But the righteous has an age-abiding foundation. He outlasts the storm.

The classic Biblical illustration of this proverb is Hezekiah's confrontation with Sennacherib, the terrible Assyrian king. Sennacherib's armies descended upon Philistia and Phoenicia to quell revolt. City after city either fell or hastened to come to terms with the invader. Word of the fearful atrocities the Assyrians committed and the wholesale deportations they practiced kept filtering into Jerusalem. The Assyrians were the terror of the ancient world. Many Judean towns were taken; even strongly defended Lachish fell. Hoping to buy off the enemy, Hezekiah, the godly Judean king, paid onerous tribute to Sennacherib.

Meanwhile news reached Sennacherib at Lachish of an alliance formed against him by Egypt, Ethiopia, and Philistia. Before marching off to meet this threat, the Assyrian king dispatched part of his army to force the immediate and unconditional surrender of Jerusalem, for he could not afford to have such a powerful enemy in his rear, sitting astride his supply lines. The whirlwind that had devastated the surrounding countryside now threatened King Hezekiah, who was in danger of being carried away by the storm.

After defeating the Egyptian coalition, Sennacherib turned his full attention to Jerusalem. Before long the city was under total siege. However, godly Hezekiah's foundation was strong; he loved the Lord. Moreover he had a dear faithful friend and counselor in the prophet Isaiah. Even so, defeat appeared certain for Hezekiah. No other city had successfully held out against the military might of Assyria. The psychological effect of the Assyrian campaign was as powerful as its army. The Assyrians wreaked fearful vengeance on cities they had to take by siege and storm.

But when the tempest howled around the walls of Jerusalem and Hezekiah's case seemed desperate, God acted. A sudden plague swept through the Assyrian army and in one night no less than 185,000 soldiers perished. The Assyrians withdrew, never to return. Sennacherib was murdered by two of his sons. (See 2 Kings 18:13–19:37.) "As the whirlwind passeth, so is the wicked no more: but the righteous is an everlasting foundation."

d. His Faithfulness (10:26)

"As vinegar to the teeth, and as smoke to the eyes, so is the sluggard to them that send him." A lazy man is an employer's bane. Malingering on the job, feather bedding, dragging one's feet, and all such devices for wasting an employer's time are contrary to morality, ethics, and spirituality.

Both of Solomon's illustrations underline the extreme irritation caused by the sluggard. Vinegar sets teeth on edge. Smoke makes eyes hurt. In eastern tents and houses, heat was provided by wood or charcoal fires. There were no chimneys. Smarting eyes must have been common. Just as smoke in the eyes can be harmful, so a sluggard's lackadaisical ways can cause harm.

An illustration of this proverb is found in the aftermath of Absalom's rebellion against David. The rebellion was crushed thanks to the efficiency, energy, and ruthlessness of Joab. He made sure that Absalom would cause no more trouble by assassinating him. That assassination was the last straw as far as David was concerned. Powerful as Joab was, David made up his mind to remove him from the army's high command. David soon had his opportunity.

Taking advantage of the unsettled conditions still existing in the country, another malcontent tried to capitalize on the old rivalry between Judah and the rest of the nation. The historian recorded: "There happened to be there a man of Belial, whose name was Sheba, the son of Bichri, a Benjamite: and he blew a trumpet, and said, We have no part in David, neither have we inheritance in the son of Jesse: every man to his tents, O Israel" (2 Samuel 20:1). So hard on the heels of the Absalom rebellion, a second rebellion was brewing. This one threatened to tear eleven of the twelve tribes away from David.

Ignoring Joab, David looked to Amasa to put down this rebellion and nip it in the bud. Like Joab, Amasa was David's nephew, the son of David's half sister Abigail. Amasa had actually joined Absalom's rebellion and had been appointed commander of Absalom's army. David not only forgave him but evidently saw in Amasa an opportunity to kill two birds with one stone. David could use Amasa to neutralize Joab and to offer an olive branch to all the former rebels.

David ordered Amasa to have the army ready in three days. Speed was of the essence, but Amasa dillydallied. "He tarried longer than the set time which he had appointed him" (2 Samuel 20:5). By this time David regretted his hasty promotion of Amasa and turned to Abishai, Joab's brother, and put him in charge. "David said to Abishai, Now shall Sheba the son of Bichri do us more harm than did Absalom: take thou thy lord's servants, and pursue after him, lest he get him fenced cities, and escape us" (20:6). Joab, ever an opportunist, ordered the men under his command to join forces with Abishai. Before long Amasa was dead, murdered by Joab. Sheba was dead thanks to Joab's drive and diplomacy. And Joab was back in the saddle.

Amasa certainly was vinegar to David's teeth and smoke to his eyes. We can certainly hear the irritation and alarm in David's voice as he spoke with Abishai. Doubtless Solomon was familiar with the incident and perhaps had it in mind when he wrote Proverbs 10:26.

e. His Future (10:27-28)

Raising a side issue, Solomon dealt with the question, *How long will a man live?* Proverbs 10:27 gives the answer: "The fear of the Lord prolongeth days: but the years of the wicked shall be shortened." This proverb states a general rule that is not without exceptions. In this sinful world godly people may die young. Certainly, though, those who fear the Lord have a better quality of life and often a longer span of life than those who are wicked.

The obvious Biblical illustration of this proverb is the longevity of the antediluvians. We do not know of course what special climatic or other conditions prevailed in the age before the flood. There is however an almost studied contrast between the godless line of Cain (Genesis 4) and the godly line of Seth (Genesis 5).

The godless line of Cain was marked by its preoccupation with this world. The Cainites built great cities and filled them with the fruits of art, science, and industry. They generated an industrial revolution that changed the face of society. They developed a feminist, pleasure-loving, materialistic, godless, and humanistic society dedicated to "the good life." They were interested in the occult and in exploring the deep things of Satan. How long did each of the Cainites live? Nobody knows. God ignores the issue. The Holy Spirit simply records their occupations. Whether the lives of the Cainites were short or long, their horizons were dominated by the things of time and sense.

In contrast to the Cainites, the godly line of Seth lived for the world to come. The Sethites simply lived for God and died. The death of each one is lovingly and tenderly recorded.

Genesis 5 reads like Heaven's register of births and deaths. We are told when each of the godly was born, how long he lived, and when he died. From one generation to the next we are told the name of the son who carried on the testimony for God in this world. And that is about all. The Sethites contributed little or nothing to the materialistic culture of the Cainites' world. While evil men and seducers were waxing worse and worse in Cainite society, the Sethites were renowned for their devotion to God.

And the godly all lived to a ripe old age! Indeed the ages of these patriarchs astonish us. Adam lived until he was 930, Seth until he was 912, Enos until he was 905, Cainan until he was 910, and Mahalaleel until he was 895. Jared lived until he was 962 and Methuselah lived to be 969. Lamech, the father of Noah, was 777 when he died. Enoch escaped death altogether.

The two people who lived longest were Jared and Methuselah. One was Enoch's father; the other was Enoch's son. This fact suggests the influence an especially godly man can have on his own immediate family. There can be no doubt that in those days godliness and longevity went hand in hand.

Solomon also dealt with the question, *How long will a man laugh?* The ungodly man often thinks he has the last laugh. However, Solomon wrote, "The hope of the righteous shall be gladness: but the expectation of the wicked shall perish" (Proverbs 10:28).

What hope does the godless person have? He can hope for the

best, as the world says. But what is "the best"? Is it health and strength, peace and prosperity, honor and respect, a rewarding occupation, promotion and applause, a loving family, congenial friends? These are the ingredients in what the world calls "the good life." The worldly man can hope for these things. But even if he attains them, death still lurks in the shadows. Death will not be denied. The godless man may laugh himself into Hell but he'll never laugh himself out of it. "The expectation of the wicked shall perish," Solomon said. How right he was. Even the wicked acknowledge that "you can't take it with you."

The contrasting truth is that "the hope of the righteous shall be gladness." Only those who love the Lord have what the New Testament calls a "blessed hope" (Titus 2:13). Whether or not we receive our "good things" (Luke 16:25) in this life, we certainly have something to look forward to. Jesus is coming again! Heaven and home are ahead. We have "an inheritance incorruptible, and undefiled, and that fadeth not away, reserved in heaven" (1 Peter 1:4). "At the appearing of Jesus Christ: Whom having not seen, [we] love; [we will] rejoice with joy unspeakable and full of glory" (1 Peter 1:7-8). Obviously it is the righteous person, not the wicked person, who has hope—and that hope is far beyond anything envisioned by Solomon.

H. Fatal Things (10:29-30)

Continuing his observations about various things, Solomon looked at the forces of *destruction* in the world: "The way of the Lord is strength to the upright: but destruction shall be to the workers of iniquity" (Proverbs 10:29). Those who are in "the way of the Lord" march forward surrounded by His strength. Jacob discovered the truth of this proverb and so did his Uncle Laban.

During all the years of his backsliding, Jacob found himself under the thumb of this wily, unscrupulous uncle. Laban cheated Jacob again and again. Finally God told Jacob to return home. But Laban did not want to lose the services of Jacob, who was extraordinarily successful at multiplying and raising sheep. Nor did Laban want to see his two daughters and all his grandchildren leave Padan-aram for distant Canaan.

Jacob knew the cunning, cruelty, and ruthlessness of his uncle. Jacob knew that Laban could exert considerable force to prevent his leaving. Laban was quite capable of confiscating Jacob's wealth, wives, and children and sending him home empty-handed. So Jacob decided to steal away when Laban was gone shearing his sheep.

Three days later Laban heard that Jacob, his wives, and his children had fled, taking their possessions with them. Laban summoned his servants and pursued Jacob until they caught up with him a week later at mount Gilead in the promised land. During the showdown between the two men, Jacob learned a truth he never forgot. God had put Himself between Laban and Jacob.

"And God came to Laban the Syrian in a dream by night, and said unto him, Take heed that thou speak not to Jacob either good or bad" (Genesis 31:24). When Laban arrived at mount Gilead, he said to Jacob: "It is in the power of my hand to do you hurt: but the God of your father spake unto me yesternight, saying, Take thou heed that thou speak not to Jacob either good or bad" (31:29).

There was a heated discussion, but Laban finally left. A shaken Jacob watched him go, glad to see the last of him. The Holy Spirit added: "And Jacob went on his way, and the angels of God met him. And when Jacob saw them he said, This is God's host: and he called the name of that place Mahanaim" (Genesis 32:1-2).

If we had a different kind of eyes, we too would see angels as we go on our way (Hebrews 1:14). Jacob discovered that indeed "the way of the Lord is strength to the upright," and Laban learned that "destruction shall be to the workers of iniquity."

Solomon also commented on the forces of *death:* "The righteous shall never be removed: but the wicked shall not inhabit the earth" (Proverbs 10:30). The word translated "the earth" here can also be rendered "the land"—that is, the promised land. This proverb reaffirms the terms of the Palestinian covenant and can be broadened to embrace the millennial age.

When the Lord returns to fight the battle of Armageddon, the world will be in a state of utter chaos. It is almost impossible for us to imagine what the world will be like. After the rapture of the church and the removal of the Holy Spirit in His role as restrainer, wholesale calamities will descend on this planet. There will be war, famine, pestilence, earthquakes, ecological disasters, and persecutions dwarfing all others.

The antichrist will come. Apocalyptic weapons will be used in war after war. Unprecedented persecution of Jews and others will produce a holocaust far worse than that unleashed by the Gestapo during World War II. Horrendous judgments will add to the horrors. Finally the armies of the West under the antichrist will confront the armies of the Orient under "the kings of the East" at Megiddo. The coming of the Lord from Heaven, in power and with His people, will change the focus of battle. The ultimate disaster will take place as the Lord's massed enemies are swept away in one final outpouring of God's wrath.[4]

The war will be over, but the world will be in ruins. The Lord will reign and the world will be renewed. The scattered survivors of seven or more years of horror will be summoned to the valley of Jehoshaphat. The surviving remnant of the Jews, instantly converted at the Lord's return, will be declared by the Lord to be His brethren. As for the surviving Gentiles, they will be sorted into two groups, "sheep" and "goats," according to their treatment of the beleaguered and persecuted Jewish people during the great tribulation. Those designated "goats" because of their mistreatment of Jews under the antichrist's regime, will be banished from the earth. The surviving remnant of both Jews and Gentiles will enter the millennial kingdom. Thus "the righteous shall never be removed: but the wicked shall not inhabit the earth."

I. Froward Things (10:31-32)

This chapter of Proverbs closes with a warning. *Its reality* is stated in 10:31: "The mouth of the just bringeth forth wisdom: but the froward tongue shall be cut out." *Its reason* is stated in 10:32: "The lips of the righteous know what is acceptable: but the mouth of the wicked speaketh frowardness." The word translated "frowardness" here is in the plural and can be rendered "great perverseness."

These two verses contrast once more the conversation of the righteous and the wicked. The talk of a good man, likened to buds of wisdom, is controlled by uncompromising righteousness and is always full of godly wisdom. A good man always speaks what is pleasing. The talk of a wicked man, on the other hand, is false; he breathes out malice. His tongue is like a rotten tree that will be cut down. He speaks what is willful and contrary.

God has given man no greater gift than the gift of speech. It sets man poles apart from the beasts. The difference is not that man can articulate sounds, but that he can clothe his thoughts in words. His words can express the most complex concepts and can soar on wings of poetry and oratory. His words can give shape to a sonnet or a sermon. They can give form and substance to a scientific principle or a nursery rhyme. Words can send armies to war and they can give shape and substance to just laws. Words can inflame passions, invoke laughter, or reduce an audience to tears. No wonder God holds us responsible for the words we utter. No wonder Solomon came back to this theme again and again.

CHAPTER 15

Proverbs 11:1-31

5. Comparative Values (11:16)
   a. The Sweet Woman (11:16a)
   b. The Strong Man (11:16b)
6. Contrasted Values (11:17-21)
   a. Compassion versus Cruelty (11:17)
   b. Deceitfulness versus Dependability (11:18)
   c. Life Found versus Life Forfeited (11:19)
   d. Abomination versus Acclamation (11:20)
   e. Guileful Plotters versus Godly People (11:21)
7. Confused Values (11:22-23)
   a. A Deceptive Appearance (11:22)
   b. A Divine Appraisal (11:23)
8. Complimentary Values (11:24-26)
   a. How to Make More Money (11:24-25)
   b. How to Make Men Mad (11:26)
9. Critical Values (11:27-29)
   a. Beware of Fantastic Folly (11:27)
   b. Beware of Financial Folly (11:28)
   c. Beware of Family Folly (11:29)
10. Character Values (11:30-31)
    a. Eternal Bliss (11:30)
    b. Earthly Blessing (11:31)

Solomon turned his attention to the values of life and explored a variety of issues of everyday interest. He kept his eyes open as he journeyed through life. We will benefit from paying attention to his astute observations.

II. BEHAVIOR GOOD AND BAD (11:1–15:33)

A. Values to Be Considered (11:1-31)

1. Commercial Values (11:1)

"A false balance is abomination to the Lord: but a just weight is his delight." God views dishonest business practices as an abomination. He takes a personal delight in honest business dealings.

A housewife went into the local food store and asked the butcher for a chicken weighing four pounds. The butcher had only one chicken left and it weighed three pounds. "I'm sorry," the woman said. "It isn't quite big enough. I'll have to go to another store."

The butcher, who was not scrupulously honest and didn't want to lose a customer, stopped her. "Madam," he said, "I just remembered that I may have one more chicken in the freezer. Please wait one moment." He carried the three-pound chicken to the freezer in the back of the store, waited a minute, then came back still holding the same chicken. "You're in luck, Madam," he said. "I found another chicken." He placed it on the scale and, unseen by the customer, slightly depressed the scale with his finger so that it indicated four pounds. "There you are, Madam. Will you take this one?"

The customer thought for a moment. "Tell you what," she said. "Since you were so helpful, I'll take *both*."

The story makes us smile because we do not like to be cheated and we like to think that the fraudulent merchant gets caught at his own game. We agree that "a false balance is abomination." In the book of Proverbs Solomon kept coming back to this theme of business integrity.

2. Conceited Values (11:2)

"When pride cometh, then cometh shame: but with the lowly is wisdom." Taken together, Moses and Miriam illustrate this proverb. They were the first two lepers in the Bible (Exodus 4:6-7; Numbers 12). Alexander Whyte said in his matchless book on Bible characters:

> But for her brother's marriage, Miriam would have been the sovereign woman in all Israel for all her days. But Moses' marriage was more than Miriam could bear....What Moses and Aaron were to the one half of the people, Miriam the sister of Moses was to the other half. Miriam was the first woman in Israel who had borne the honorable and universal name of a mother in Israel. And, but for Moses' marriage, Miriam would have shone beside Moses till her eye also was not dim, nor her natural strength abated.
>
> But Moses' marriage made Miriam as weak and as evil and as wicked as any weak and evil and wicked woman in all the camp. Miriam cried...in a storm of tears when she saw the Ethiopian woman coming to take her place....Her heart was full of hell-fire at Moses' innocent wife and innocent children, and even at her meek and innocent brother himself, until her

wild jealousy kindled her wild pride, and her wild pride her wild, insane and impious envy, and then her insane and impious envy soon led her into fatal trespass against Moses and against God.

Miriam's venomous tongue soon infected Aaron. Before long his heart also burned in resentment against Moses and the woman he had married. Suddenly, unexpectedly, the situation came to a head. God summoned Moses, Aaron, and Miriam to the door of the tabernacle. God spoke to them and Miriam became a leper, white as snow. Truly, "when pride cometh, then cometh shame."

There was no greater horror or shame for a person in Bible times than to be smitten with leprosy. The law was adamant. The leper was to be expelled from the camp to dwell in lonely isolation. Moses' heart was broken. Moses and Aaron mourned Miriam and looked in horror at her loathsome flesh. "But with the lowly is wisdom," so Moses knew what to do: "Moses cried unto the Lord, saying, Heal her now, O God, I beseech thee" (Numbers 12:13). Moses soon learned God's will. She was to be excommunicated for a week and then healed and restored.

3. Concrete Values (11:3-9)

a. The Righteous Man's Guidance (11:3)

"The integrity of the upright shall guide them: but the perverseness of transgressors shall destroy them."

Joseph's integrity guided him. As a young lad he settled all the important issues of life. He gave his heart to the Lord and opened himself to God's revealed Word. He established the principle of always seeking to do the things that please the Father. That decision was a solid foundation on which his developing character could be built. All Joseph had to do was remain true to his convictions.

His integrity guided Joseph when he was tempted and taunted by his brothers. His integrity guided him when he was sold into slavery; when he was entrusted with the management of Potiphar's affairs; when he was tempted by Potiphar's wife; when he was unjustly committed to prison; when he was forgotten by the butler; when he stood before the pharaoh; when all Egypt lay at his feet; when he married and began to raise a family; when his treacherous brothers were at his mercy; and when the time came for him to die. The whole extraordinary character and career of Joseph is summed up in this proverb: "The integrity of the upright shall guide them."

Conversely, "the perverseness of transgressors shall destroy them." The word translated "transgressors" means "traitors," those who are unfaithful to the covenant.

The classic example of unfaithfulness is Ahithophel, a citizen of Giloh in southwest Judah. He was the most brilliant of David's counselors, the father of one of David's mighty men (2 Samuel 23:34), and the grandfather of Bathsheba (2 Samuel 11:3). His insight was so remarkable that it was likened to the divine oracle (2 Samuel 16:23).

But Ahithophel was "a slippery customer," as we would say, for his cleverness was matched by his craftiness. He was David's Judas. Ahithophel sided with Absalom and was the brains behind the rebellion. The advice Ahithophel gave to Absalom was diabolically clever, but it was motivated largely by a desire for revenge. Ahithophel wanted to do David as much personal and public harm as possible. Unfortunately for Ahithophel, he had backed a young fool. Ahithophel was smart enough, however, to know when he was outwitted. When Absalom set aside his astute suggestions in favor of the counsel of Hushai, who was secretly on David's side, Ahithophel committed suicide (2 Samuel 17:23). Truly the slipperiness of this traitor destroyed him.

b. The Righteous Man's Goodness (11:4-7)

Solomon contrasted the righteous man with other elements in society. He placed him in contrast to *the wealthy man:* "Riches profit not in the day of wrath: but righteousness delivereth from death" (Proverbs 11:4). The Bible has a great deal to say about "the day of wrath."

God's wrath against sin of course is constant. Paul began his Epistle to the Romans by emphasizing this fact. "The wrath of God," he wrote, "is revealed from heaven against all ungodliness and unrighteousness of men, who hold the truth in unrighteousness" (Romans 1:18). For all who trust Christ and who are thereby clothed in His impeccable righteousness, the sting has been removed from that general wrath.

The "*day* of wrath" is something different. All Bible prophecy points forward to a day when God will step into the arena of human affairs and pour out His wrath upon the ungodly. However, in our reading we do not arrive at "that great and terrible day of the Lord" foreseen by so many Old Testament prophets until we get to the last book of the Bible.

The whole postrapture period is characterized by wrath and

judgment (Revelation 6:16-17), but only when the vials are outpoured will the full scope of God's wrath be felt. Then it will be too late to try to come to terms with God. The Holy Spirit repeatedly describes the vials as "having the seven last plagues; for in them is filled up the wrath of God" (Revelation 15:1). John wrote, "I heard a great voice out of the temple saying to the seven angels, Go your ways, and pour out the vials of the wrath of God upon the earth" (Revelation 16:1).

In that day of wrath one's only hope of escape will be righteousness. Those who still hold onto the faith will find safety in the hills, holes, and hide-outs (Matthew 24:15-18) until the storm is passed. Those who trust in their riches will find no safe retreat.

Solomon also contrasted the righteous man with *the wicked man:* "The righteousness of the perfect shall direct his way: but the wicked shall fall by his own wickedness" (Proverbs 11:5). The word translated "perfect" here means "without blemish." The word was used in descriptions of Old Testament animal sacrifices and suggests being without blame. The word translated "wickedness" and "the wicked" refers to lawlessness and to the lawless individual.

A good man makes good decisions and he does what is right. His journey through life is smoothed by the fact that he is moral, decent, and law-abiding. The wicked man, on the other hand, is governed by his lusts, passions, and ambitions.

The contrast between the two can be illustrated by a river. The life of a righteous person is like a river flowing between its banks in an orderly way toward the sea. Its power and progress are channeled and contained. The course of a lawless person is like a river overflowing its banks. When it floods, it spreads death and destruction to the surrounding countryside.

Throughout the book of Proverbs the way of the righteous man is extolled as the way of wisdom. In Proverbs 11 the righteous man is placed in contrast to *the worthless man.* There is *no help* for him: "The righteousness of the upright shall deliver them: but transgressors shall be taken in their naughtiness" (11:6). There is *no hope* for him: "When a wicked man dieth, his expectation shall perish: and the hope of unjust men perisheth" (11:7).

The word translated "naughtiness" in Proverbs 11:6 refers to "a man of Belial," as in 6:12. The word can also be rendered "worthless." In 11:6-7 the heavy emphasis is on transgressors, the worthless, the wicked, and the unjust. These kinds of people often see themselves as clever and wise, but God sees them as helpless and hopeless, for He sees their latter end.

Balaam is an outstanding Biblical example of the worthless man.

He was a Babylonian soothsayer (what we would call a psychic) who had a considerable reputation as a prophet. When the children of Israel arrived on the borders of Moab on their way to the promised land, Balak, the Moabite king, hired Balaam to come and curse the Hebrew people. Balak promised Balaam a generous reward for his services. That reward was his "expectation," to use Solomon's descriptive word. Balaam's determination to curse the people of God was the measure of his worthlessness. He was motivated by hope of financial gain.

All Balaam's cursing came to nothing. Each time he tried to curse God's people, God turned the curse into a blessing. Faced with the growing wrath of the Moabite king, and seeing his fat honorarium disappearing, Balaam changed his approach. His advice boiled down to this: "My lord king," he said, "you cannot win this war using the men of Moab. No army can stand against this people. So long as they walk in fellowship with their God they are invincible. So try the women of Moab. If you cannot curse the Israelites or conquer them, then corrupt them. Let your women entice them into sin. Then their God, the holy One of Israel, will judge them" (see Revelation 2:14). The plan worked. Balaam collected what the Bible calls "the wages of unrighteousness" (2 Peter 2:15), but his reward did him little good. He was slain by an avenging expedition of Hebrew soldiers (Numbers 31:8). Balaam was beyond help and hope. He was taken in his own worthlessness. His hope and his expectation perished.

c. The Righteous Man's Gain (11:8-9)

Solomon gave us *a vision of poetic justice:* "The righteous is delivered out of trouble, and the wicked cometh in his stead" (Proverbs 11:8). The word translated "delivered" is derived from a Hebrew word that means "to be drawn out" or "to be liberated with gentle effort."

Poetic justice is illustrated in the story of Daniel. His jealous enemies knew it would be impossible to catch Daniel doing anything wrong. His integrity was beyond reproach. So they laid a trap for him. They knew his habit of praying daily without concealment or embarrassment and that, they thought, was his Achilles heel. They persuaded King Darius to sign a decree that for a whole month anyone who offered a petition to God or man, except to the king, would be cast into the den of lions.

The conspirators were confident that Daniel would ignore such a preposterous decree. Sure enough, he did. They rushed to his house, caught him in the act of praying, and reported him to Darius. Darius, who could not reverse his decree, ordered the punishment to be carried out but spent a sleepless night regretting his folly in signing such an absurd and infamous document.

First thing next morning Darius hurried to the lion's den. "And when he came to the den, he cried with a lamentable voice unto Daniel: and the king spake and said to Daniel, O Daniel, servant of the living God, is thy God, whom thou servest continually, able to deliver thee from the lions?" (Daniel 6:20) Daniel could well have replied in Solomon's words, "The righteous is delivered out of trouble."

Darius could well have responded, "The wicked cometh in his stead," for that is what happened. Enraged at having been so manipulated, Darius wasted no time. He had Daniel drawn up out of the den and the conspirators put there in his place. "The king commanded, and they brought those men which had accused Daniel, and they cast them into the den of lions, them, their children, and their wives; and the lions had the mastery of them, and brake all their bones in pieces or ever they came at the bottom of the den" (Daniel 6:24).

During that rough-and-ready age poetic justice was often more highly visible than it is today. God's moral judgment of the world may be more concealed now, but it is the same.

After giving us a vision of poetic justice, Solomon gave us *the value of private judgment*: "An hypocrite with his mouth destroyeth his neighbour: but through knowledge shall the just be delivered" (Proverbs 11:9).

Charles Dickens gave us the best full-length portrait of the consummate hypocrite—his vile mouth, his nefarious schemes, and his eventual downfall. His name is Uriah Heep. Here is how David Copperfield described his first encounters with the detestable Uriah:

> As I came back, I saw Uriah Heep shutting up the office; and, feeling friendly towards everybody, went in and spoke to him, and at parting, gave him my hand. But oh, what a clammy hand his was! as ghostly to the touch as to the sight! I rubbed mine afterwards, to warm it, *and to rub his off....*
>
> [Later] "I suppose you are quite a great lawyer?" I said, after looking at him for some time.
>
> "Me, Master Copperfield?" said Uriah. "Oh, no! I'm a very umble person."
>
> It was no fancy of mine about his hands, I observed; for he

frequently ground the palms against each other as if to squeeze them dry and warm, besides often wiping them, in a stealthy way, on his pocket-handkerchief.

"I am well aware that I am the umblest person going," said Uriah Heep, modestly; "let the other be where he may. My mother is likewise a very umble person. We live in a umble abode, Master Copperfield, but have much to be thankful for. My father's former calling was umble. He was a sexton."...

He had a way of writhing when he wanted to express enthusiasm, which was very ugly; and which diverted my attention from the compliment he had paid my relation, to the snaky twistings of his throat and body.

As the story unfolded, Uriah Heep got his employer more and more under his thumb and exulted in the power he had over him. Still loudly proclaiming his humility, Uriah aspired to marry Mr. Wickfield's daughter Agnes. David Copperfield was horrified. He learned that Uriah not only controlled Mr. Wickfield's business but had some other hold over him—a hold so strong it could force Agnes into the hated marriage in order to save her father's good name. With his mouth Uriah had destroyed his neighbor.

Meanwhile Mr. Micawber, the perennially penniless friend of David Copperfield, was always hoping that something would turn up. Something did turn up. He was hired by Uriah as his confidential clerk. In the end the irrepressible Mr. Micawber uncovered and exposed Uriah's forgeries and other criminal activities. Thus Mr. Wickfield was saved from the clutches of the hateful Uriah and Agnes was saved from her dreaded suitor. "Through knowledge," the knowledge gained by Mr. Micawber, Agnes and her father were delivered out of trouble.

Of course *David Copperfield* is only a story. But like so many of Dickens' stories, it is based on a keen study of human character and the dynamics of human behavior.

4. Community Values (11:10-15)

a. The Character of a Community's Citizens (11:10-13)

(1) Those Who Help a Community (11:10-11)

Solomon, wise in statecraft, stated two principles for strengthening the forces of righteousness in a community. First, *extol the righteous and you extol society.* "When it goeth well with the righteous, the city rejoiceth: and when the wicked perish, there is shouting" (Proverbs 11:10). Second, *exalt the righteous and you exalt society.* "By the blessing of the upright the city is exalted: but it is overthrown by the mouth of the wicked" (11:11). History is full of examples of the truth of these principles.

The health of a community is linked inevitably to the way in which those in power treat upright, law-abiding, God-fearing citizens and the way in which those in power treat the lewd, immoral, and criminal element. A wise government extols and exalts the righteous and vigorously suppresses and punishes criminals, immoral persons, and subversives. Such a government makes laws that protect the righteous and define and punish unacceptable behavior.

The United States was founded by men who understood these principles. The pilgrim fathers came across the sea determined to build a nation on Biblical principles. They wrote their faith in God into the constitution of their country. They stamped their faith in God on their coins. They built their educational institutions on the Bible. They exalted righteousness and put curbs on wickedness. And they built a great country on freedom, equity, and justice. The society they built was essentially religious. The righteous fared well and the nation partook of the blessings of God. The wicked were punished.

While there is still a remarkably vital and vocal Christian minority in the United States, much has changed. Secular humanism has penetrated all levels of society. Schools and universities, the media, the courts, and the halls of Congress have all been deeply affected by this godless philosophy. The Bible and prayer have been banned from American classrooms. Considered old fashioned, Bible-based standards of morality, decency, and behavior have been severely eroded. Many parents have lost control of their children. The home has been attacked by immorality, sexual promiscuity, and easy divorce. Drugs have become epidemic. Pornography and sodomy have been given the protection of the courts. The work ethic has been eroded by socialism. The evangelical church, while still strong, finds itself under attack.

The United States, in other words, is in crisis. Its economy is threatened by an enormous national and private debt. Abortion-on-demand slaughters millions of unborn babes annually. Many cities are in the grip of crime. The courts tend to be lenient with criminals, and punishment is often cut short by a parole system that swiftly returns criminals to the streets.

It is time for America to return to the faith of its founding fathers and to the principles that made it great. Those principles are embodied in Proverbs 11:10-11. Happy is the nation whose God is the Lord and whose legislators believe the Bible, reward goodness, and punish evil. Woe to the nation that turns its back on the Word of God.

(2) Those Who Harm a Community (11:12-13)

Solomon shifted his attention to the *tactless bungler:* "He that is void of wisdom despiseth his neighbour: but a man of understanding holdeth his peace" (Proverbs 11:12). "A man who mocks his neighbor has no sense" is the way one translator rendered the verse. Another scholar suggested this wording: "The prudent man will hold his tongue." The phrase translated "despiseth his neighbour" is rendered "sneers at his fellow citizens" in the Septuagint. All translations indicate that Solomon was addressing contemptuous language.

The tactless bungler judges by appearances. Because a man wears odd-looking clothes and a funny hat, has shoes that squeak, goes to church, or pays his taxes without trying to hide part of his income, the foolish man sneers at him. Often the bungler is sneering at someone far bigger and far better than he is. Truly great men are sometimes eccentric. We all know about the absent-minded professor.

The tactless bungler will make fun of a true genius if the great man is also a humble and devoted believer in the Lord Jesus. Consider for instance the remarkable story of Michael Faraday. The son of a blacksmith, he was apprenticed to a bookbinder, but he rose to be the greatest scientist of his day. He loved chemistry. He discovered stainless steel, invented the electric motor and the dynamo, and discovered how a beam of light could be bent in a strong magnetic field. He pioneered work in ionization and coined a whole new vocabulary of scientific words. Someone said, "Prometheus is supposed to have brought fire for the service of mankind; electricity we owe to Faraday." For fifty years Faraday had no peer in the scientific realm. But some people sneered at him because he was a humble and devoted Christian and because he was perennially poor.

Faraday was an elder in a little church with a congregation that never exceeded twenty people. Few of his colleagues understood that and some despised him for it. *How can such a brilliant man,* they wondered, *believe the Bible, take it literally, and be content to find his friends among a handful of believers?* His associates saw him leave a meeting of the prestigious Royal Society, to which only the truly great scientists belonged, in order to sit at the feet of a certain local preacher who was notoriously illiterate. Filled with bewilderment, some of his contemporaries made contemptuous and sarcastic remarks. The wise held their peace.

On one occasion Faraday lectured to a distinguished panel of scientists. The Prince of Wales (afterward Edward VII) was among those present. For an hour Faraday held his audience spellbound as he demonstrated the nature and properties of the magnet. His lecture closed with a demonstration that brought the house down. The Prince of Wales rose to propose a motion of congratulation. The resolution was seconded and carried amid another thunderous burst of applause. The assembly waited for Faraday's reply, but he had vanished. He had slipped away to his little church for the weekly prayer meeting. We can imagine what people said about him behind his back, but those who sneered at him were the foolish ones. Michael Faraday had slipped away from the presence of an earthly prince to seek audience with the King of kings.

The tactless bungler can sometimes do harm with his untamed tongue, but the *talebearer* is even worse. "A talebearer revealeth secrets: but he that is of a faithful spirit concealeth the matter" (Proverbs 11:13). The talebearer is a malicious gossip who can do untold harm. The greatest scandalmonger in the universe is Satan. The greatest concealer of secrets in the universe is the Savior.

The Holy Spirit tells us that Satan is "the accuser of our brethren" and that he accuses them before God day and night (Revelation 12:10). Satan delights in parading our sins before God. Although he is a liar and the "father" of lies (John 8:44) he does not go into the presence of God to tell lies about us. That would never do, not in the presence of absolute Truth and before the throne where Omniscience sits. Besides, Satan does not need to tell lies about us. Sadly, he only needs to tell the truth about us. He is a talebearer who reveals secrets.

What happens when Satan accuses us? Paul answered this question in Romans 8:33. "Who shall lay any thing to the charge of God's elect?" he demanded. "It is God that justifieth." Justification is one of the greatest truths in the New Testament. When we are justified, it is just as if we had never sinned. Our sins are blotted forever from God's memory.

Yes, the adversary comes with tales to tell. He spitefully spills out the sad story of our sins. Then the Lord Jesus, our advocate—He who is "of a faithful spirit," as Solomon put it—steps forward. All He has to do is show His nail-pierced hands, for God is just.

> He will not payment twice demand,
> First at my Savior's pierced hand,
> And then again at mine.

"What about those sins?" Satan demands. "What sins?" God says. "There are no such sins. They have been put under the blood. They are behind My back. They have been buried in the depths of the sea. They have been blotted out. I remember them no more." The Lord Jesus "concealeth the matter."

b. The Competence of a Community's Counselors (11:14-15)

In Proverbs 11:14 Solomon stated *an underlying principle:* "Where no counsel is, the people fall: but in the multitude of counsellors there is safety." The word translated "counsel" here means "helmsman." A ruler who does not have a wise counselor to guide him in his decisions is like a ship at sea with no one at the helm.

Prince Otto Eduard Leopold von Bismarck-Schönhausen welded a group of jealous kingdoms and feudal states into a united nation. Modern Germany, his legacy to Europe, was a country that put fear into all the other nations of the continent. Known as Germany's "man of blood and iron," Bismarck was a Prussian, an aristocrat, and a Junker. He was kindly toward his own people and arrogant toward all others. A military and political genius, he defeated Denmark and Austria. He humiliated France by detaching Alsace and Lorraine from France and adding them to Germany.

On January 18, 1871, King William I of Prussia was crowned German emperor in the Hall of Mirrors in the palace of Versailles. However, the real power in Germany still lay in the hands of Bismarck, the Iron Chancellor.

When Kaiser William II was crowned in 1888, he fretted at the power and influence of his chancellor. Having made up his mind that he was going to take charge, William II clashed with Bismarck and dismissed him from office. At once the truth of Proverbs 11:14 was evident, for the young and inexperienced kaiser launched Germany on a headlong course to disaster.

When Bismarck was dismissed, the London weekly *Punch* published one of its greatest cartoons. The cartoon showed the kaiser leaning over the rail of the German ship of state as Bismarck descended the ladder. The title of the cartoon said it all: "Dropping the Pilot." Bismarck retired to an old ancestral estate near Hamburg to nurse his unrelenting resentment of William II. Meanwhile the headstrong and inexperienced kaiser steered the German ship of state at full speed toward World War I.

Turning his attention from national well-being to personal well-being, Solomon mentioned *an undesirable practice:* "He that is surety for a stranger shall smart for it: and he that hateth suretiship is sure" (Proverbs 11:15). We have already considered this principle in our study of 6:1-11, but here we will look at suretyship from quite a different point of view.

There never was a greater stranger in this poor old bankrupt world than Jesus (Matthew 25:35; Luke 24:18). He was far from home, a "root out of a dry ground," a "tender plant" indeed (Isaiah 53:2). He came to this lost and lonely planet to be surety for Adam's ruined race.

Throughout the Old Testament period the animal sacrifices were valid for only one reason: they were backed by a guarantee from Heaven that in time the entire indebtedness would be paid. There was a Guarantor, One who stood surety for all human sin.

When Jesus came to earth to be surety for us, He had to "smart for it." How terribly He smarted we will never fully know. When we see Him face to face and see the prints of the nails in His hands, we will understand better, but we will never know fully, even in eternity, the enormity of the debt He paid nor the greatness of the cost to Him. We will only be able to echo Paul's great words: "Ye know the grace of our Lord Jesus Christ, that, though he was rich, yet for your sakes he became poor, that ye through his poverty might be rich" (2 Corinthians 8:9). We will ponder Peter's words: "Who did no sin, neither was guile found in his mouth: Who, when he was reviled, reviled not again; when he suffered, he threatened not...Who his own self bare our sins in his own body on the tree, that we, being dead to sins, should live unto righteousness: by whose stripes ye were healed" (1 Peter 2:22-24).

Thus what Solomon saw as an undesirable practice and the height of human folly—to be surety for a stranger—was the very thing Jesus did to make possible our redemption from sin. No wonder Paul wrote:

> For the preaching of the cross is to them that perish foolishness; but unto us which are saved it is the power of God. For it is written, I will destroy the wisdom of the wise, and will bring to nothing the understanding of the prudent. Where is the wise? where is the scribe? where is the disputer of this world? hath not God made foolish the wisdom of this world? (1 Corinthians 1:18-20)

5. Comparative Values (11:16)

Solomon looked briefly at *the sweet woman* and *the strong man:* "A gracious woman retaineth honor: and strong men retain riches." Some people think the verse means that beauty is more powerful than strength and that honor is better than wealth. Truly, a beautiful, charming, and high-principled woman wields a power of her own. In her own right she exerts considerable moral influence. In many ways she is a greater force in the world than a strong, wealthy, and determined woman. Queen Victoria is perhaps the best illustration of the woman with moral influence.

Little more than a child when she became queen at age seventeen, Victoria soon revealed what stuff she was made of. When the Whig prime minister, Lord Melbourne, was defeated by his Tory rival, Sir Robert Peel, the new prime minister told the young queen she must replace the Whig-appointed ladies of her household with his appointees. She indignantly refused to do any such thing, rendered Peel's position as head of the government impossible, and persuaded Lord Melbourne to stay on as her prime minister— something almost unprecedented in British politics. During her long reign of more than sixty years, Victoria quarreled with several other leaders of the House of Commons.

A well-known incident concerned Lord Palmerstone, who was typical of the brash, cocksure, pugnacious, empire-building Englishmen of the age. He once had the temerity to tell Queen Victoria a dirty joke. Fixing a frosty eye on her prime minister, she replied, "We are not amused." That honorable woman had no trouble putting that strong man in his place.

The queen was the epitome of respectability and although not a radiant beauty, she was handsome enough. Her moral influence was enormous. The British people went *Victorian,* with all the virtues and vices the word implies.

Although the plight of the working classes was as described by Dickens, there was no popular uprising because respect for the queen and constituted authority was too great. Victorians did not rebel; they resolved their social problems by parliamentary reforms.

The Victorian era was one of extraordinary glory. The British empire expanded to embrace a quarter of the world. Victoria was crowned empress of India, Britain controlled the Suez canal, Singapore was founded in Malaya, and the Sudan and much of Africa took orders from London.

In 1897 the queen celebrated her diamond jubilee. She had been on the throne for sixty years and many British subjects could not remember a time when Victoria had not been queen. The jubilee crowned "the widow of Windsor," as Kipling called her, with glory and honor. Many strong and wealthy men lived in Victoria's dynamic empire, but the influence of that one gracious and honorable woman was greater than all of theirs.

6. Contrasted Values (11:17-21)

Next Solomon contrasted a variety of moral values in order to highlight their differences. First he contrasted *compassion* with *cruelty:* "The merciful man doeth good to his own soul: but he that is cruel troubleth his own flesh" (Proverbs 11:17). The Bible puts a great premium on mercy.

Shakespeare gave us the best commentary on this text in his romantic comedy, *The Merchant of Venice.* The whole play revolves around the issue of compassion versus cruelty. The story begins in Venice. The merchant of Venice is Antonio, whose mercantile fleet is at sea but is expected back in port laden with goods. Antonio's friend Bassanio applies to Antonio for a loan. Bassanio wants to court the wealthy heiress Portia but cannot do so as a penniless adventurer. Antonio, who does not have the three thousand ducats Bassanio desires, agrees to guarantee repayment of the money to the Jewish moneylender Shylock. Shylock agrees to advance the money to Bassanio but demands a very unusual bond: if the money is not repaid in time, Shylock may cut a pound of flesh from Antonio's body. Antonio, confident that his ships will return to Venice within the month, agrees to the strange demand.

Shylock, who nurses a deep hatred of all things Christian, has a special hatred for Antonio, the successful Gentile shipowner who has always treated him with contempt. In the provisions of the loan agreement, Shylock sees a chance to get even and fervently hopes he can one day get his pound of flesh.

When Antonio's ships are all wrecked, Shylock takes him to court. The duke of Venice and his court try in vain to persuade Shylock to forgo his revenge, but the Jew insists on his pound of flesh. He revels in the impotence of the Gentiles to extricate Antonio from his dilemma. Gleefully he whets his knife. Hatred has made him cruel.

At this point Portia, disguised as a lawyer, appears in court as counsel for the defense. The play rises to its climax as the two robed figures face each other—Portia in dark, flowing, legal robes and Shylock in his gabardine. Portia begins her defense by putting the problem on a higher plane than the duke had been able to do. She appeals not to justice, but to mercy. Her words have become some of the most beautiful and familiar in the English language:

> The quality of mercy is not strain'd;
> It droppeth as the gentle rain from heaven
> Upon the place beneath: it is twice blest;
> It blesseth him that gives, and him that takes:
> 'Tis mightiest in the mightiest: it becomes
> The throned monarch better than his crown.
>
> . . . .
>
> It is enthroned in the hearts of kings,
> It is an attribute to God himself.

Shylock however is unmoved, and he demands immediate application of the law. He wants his pound of flesh.

Then Portia springs her trap. Shylock, she says, has a case that cannot be denied. He is entitled to his pound of flesh and no one can prevent him from taking it. However, he can have nothing but his pound of flesh. The bond said nothing of blood. He can have his pound of flesh. Let him come forward with his knife, but if he sheds one drop of blood, he will be prosecuted to the full extent of the law. As Solomon put it, "A merciful man doeth good to his own soul: but he that is cruel troubleth his own flesh."

Next Solomon contrasted *deceitfulness* with *dependability:* "The wicked worketh a deceitful work: but to him that soweth righteousness shall be a sure reward" (Proverbs 11:18). This proverb is illustrated in the Bible in numerous ways, one example being the contest between Moses and the pharaoh.

Throughout his life, Moses sowed righteousness and reaped a sure reward. The pharaoh, however, worked a deceitful work and lied continually. After the plague of frogs the pharaoh promised, "Intreat the Lord, that he may take away the frogs from me, and from my people; and I will let the people go" (Exodus 8:8). He broke his promise.

After the plague of flies the pharaoh said, "I will let you go, that ye may sacrifice to the Lord your God in the wilderness....intreat for me" (Exodus 8:28). Moses replied, "I will intreat the Lord that the swarms of flies may depart...but let not Pharaoh deal deceitfully any more in not letting the people go to sacrifice to the Lord" (8:29).

After the terrible plague of hail the pharaoh again promised to let the people go (Exodus 9:27-28). Moses was skeptical (9:30) and rightly so because again the pharaoh broke his promise (9:35).

After the plague of locusts the pharaoh again promised to let the Hebrews go (Exodus 10:16-17) and once more broke his word (10:20). And so it went on. All this time the pharaoh was proving himself a liar and Moses was sowing righteousness and a sure reward. Moses went on doing so until his name became famous throughout the world for all the rest of time.

Solomon also contrasted *life found* with *life forfeited:* "As righteousness tendeth to life: so he that pursueth evil pursueth it to his own death" (Proverbs 11:19). This proverb states the inevitable law of sowing and reaping. All things being equal, we reap what we sow. This law is as true of the soil as it is of the soul.

Consider the case of Nancy, the one person who really cared for poor little Oliver Twist when he was in the den of thieves. Dickens writes about the pathos of her life: "The girl's life had been squandered in the streets, and among the most noisome of the stews and dens of London, but there was something of the woman's original nature left in her still."

The time came when Nancy, who had been ruined by Fagin, was able to help Oliver. Having knowledge of something that vitally affected the young orphan's future, she passed the information on to Rose Maylie, who was employed in the home where Oliver had found refuge.

Rose, whose circumstances were so different from Nancy's, looked with compassion on the poor woman of the streets and offered to help her change her life. Nancy responded: "I wish to go back....I must go back, because—how can I tell such things to an innocent lady like you?—because among the men I have told you of, there is one: the most desperate among them all: that I can't leave; no, not even to be saved from the life I am leading now."

Nothing Rose could say could change the young woman's mind. Nancy went back to her wretched life, back to the villainous Bill Sikes, back to a life of squalor and betrayal. In the end the man to whom she was so unhappily tied brutally murdered her.

Throughout his novel Dickens skillfully engages our emotions and directs our affections toward two victims of the evil Fagin: Oliver Twist and Nancy. Oliver won through to life; the unfortunate Nancy lost her life. All things being equal, we live with our decisions and reap what we sow.

In the next proverb Solomon contrasted *abomination* with *acclamation:* "They that are of a froward heart are abomination to the Lord: but such as are upright in their way are his delight" (Proverbs 11:20). It is sobering to realize that our lives are constantly under God's eye. How terrible it would be to hear Him sum up one's life as an abomination. How blessed it would be to earn His word of acclamation.

The lives of the Cainites were an abomination to the Lord. He says that "the wickedness of man was great in the earth, and that every imagination of the thoughts of his heart was only evil continually" (Genesis 6:5). The lifestyle of the antediluvians was detestable to the living God. The Holy Spirit says that "it repented the Lord that he had made man on the earth" (6:6). Such abominable behavior called for judgment.

In contrast to the descendants of Cain, Enoch earned God's acclamation. The Holy Spirit says that "he had this testimony, that he pleased God" (Hebrews 11:5). No higher approval could have been given. Jesus also pleased God (Matthew 3:17; 12:18; 17:5). Since Jesus pleased God, and Enoch pleased God, we can only conclude that in his day and age, in the midst of a perverted and pornographic society, Enoch lived as Jesus lived. God showed His approval of Enoch by taking him home to Heaven by way of the rapture before judgment fell on that evil civilization (Genesis 5:21-24). God's all-seeing eye is on us as well. How does He sum up our lives?

In Proverbs 11:21 Solomon contrasted *guileful plotters* with *godly people:* "Though hand join in hand, the wicked shall not be unpunished: but the seed of the righteous shall be delivered."

When we think of infamy and perfidy, two of the names that come to mind are Pope Alexander VI and his son Cesare Borgia. The two joined hand in hand with wickedness. As a cardinal, Alexander used bribery to ensure his election to the papacy. His life was one of unblushing scandal. Before becoming pope, Alexander fathered three sons and a daughter. Becoming pontiff made no difference to Alexander; he continued his profligate ways. Poisoning was his specialty and he used it frequently to eliminate his enemies and those whose fortunes he coveted.

Cesare Borgia was sixteen when his father became pope. In no time his father made him a bishop and then a cardinal. One of Cesare's first acts as a cardinal was to murder his older brother so that he would be next in line to the papacy. Instead of punishing Cesare, Alexander sent him to the court of Louis XII of France as a papal emissary.

After being appointed duke of Valentinois by the French king, Cesare returned to Rome and set out to unite the city-states of Italy. His methods were war, intrigue, murder, and intimidation. As a diversion he murdered his sister Lucrezia's husband. Terror was an ever-ready weapon in Cesare's arsenal. The purse of the papacy was at his disposal as he and his evil father joined hand in hand in wickedness. Some cities against which Cesare launched his mercenaries simply capitulated in their fear without a fight. He inspired Machiavelli to formulate his political philosophy of ruthless realism and guile.

There was one foe, however, that Cesare could not overcome by guile and violence. This enemy was the plague. It ravaged Rome and carried off Alexander VI. It almost carried off Cesare too, and it did cripple him politically by taking away his powerful patron on the throne of St. Peter. Indeed, Cesare soon faced Julius II, an implacable foe as ambitious as himself. Cesare was arrested, handed over to the Spaniards, bundled out of Italy, and locked up in prison. Truly the wicked did not go unpunished in this case.

"But the seed of the righteous shall be delivered." At the same time that the Borgias were joining hands in evil, Jerome Savonarola was raising his voice in Italy. He desired to see a great reformation in both church and state. He also had a passion for souls and rejoiced in the doctrine of justification by faith. Unrivaled as a preacher, Savonarola filled the vast cathedral of Florence with great crowds who eagerly hung on his words. He did not hesitate to denounce the powerful Medici family, the despotism of the aristocracy, or the sins of the prelates and clergy.

Savonarola's career was watched by the evil eye of the Borgias. They soon decided that he was dangerous and not fit to live. The deceitful Alexander VI extended a courteous invitation to Savonarola to visit him in Rome. Savonarola knew only too well the pope's reputation for treachery and refused to fall into the trap. In the hope of getting him under his power, Alexander VI next offered to make Savonarola a cardinal, but the popular preacher declined the offer. Threats and excommunication followed. Savonarola was denounced as a heretic and in 1498 he and two of his friends were seized, imprisoned, and tortured unmercifully. When his tormentors were finished with him, he was taken from prison, publicly degraded, hanged, and then burned.

If the Borgias thought they had put an end to Savonarola, they were very much mistaken. His ashes were thrown in the river Arno, but his followers venerated his memory and his spiritual seed continued. The very year Savonarola was martyred, Desiderius Erasmus made his first visit to England. Erasmus spurred Bible translation, produced a revolutionary Greek New Testament, challenged the Latin Vulgate championed by Rome, gave the Bible to the world, and threw open the door for the Reformation.

The Dark Ages were ending and the power of the papacy would

soon be challenged on all fronts. At Cambridge, Erasmus made a profound impression on Thomas Bilney, who in turn led Hugh Latimer to Christ. Latimer and Bishop Ridley lit a candle that would not go out, as for centuries England was in the forefront of the battle for the faith; she was Rome's most zealous foe.

7. Confused Values (11:22-23)

In Proverbs 11:22 our attention is drawn to *a deceptive appearance:* "As a jewel of gold in a swine's snout, so is a fair woman which is without discretion." Nothing could look more foolish than a costly jewel in the snout of a pig. No one could be more dismaying than a pretty woman without common sense.

Such a woman was Marie Antoinette, the Austrian child bride of Louis XVI, who was still the dauphin of France at the time of the marriage. Marie was a charming and beautiful girl with blond hair, dancing blue eyes, and an oval face. Well educated, she spoke perfect French. She was, however, very fond of amusement and gained a reputation for frivolity. She talked her husband into having a most extravagant coronation, and her passion for luxury and her careless prodigality knew no bounds.

Little did Marie Antoinette know or care that the people of France were starving, burdened with taxes, and ripe for revolution. When told that the common people had no bread, she is reputed to have said, "Then let them eat cake." She began playing cards for high stakes and developed an obsession for new fashions in clothes. The nation was bankrupt, yet she spent more and more money. They called her "Madam Deficit."

The last straw came when Lafayette tried to help the royal pair. He arranged for a Flemish regiment to serve as palace guards because French soldiers could no longer be trusted, but Marie Antoinette treated it all as a joke. She arranged an elaborate banquet to celebrate the arrival of the new guard. This final act of frivolity ignited the powder keg. The infuriated populace stormed Versailles, seized the king and queen, and incarcerated them. The French Revolution was under way. First Louis, then Marie Antoinette ended their days on the guillotine. She was a fair woman, but without discretion.

Proverbs 11:23 draws our attention to *a divine appraisal:* "The desire of the righteous is only good: but the expectation of the wicked is wrath." The contrast here is between what the good man desires and what the evil man deserves. God puts both men in the scales, just where He put Belshazzar and Daniel.

All Daniel wanted in life was goodness. Right from the start he determined never to compromise his convictions, never to water down God's Word, never to barter the truth, never to bow to expediency. When God put him on the scale, he weighed in as solid gold. God called him "a man greatly beloved" (Daniel 10:11).

On the other hand, Belshazzar's only expectation was wrath. When that drunken and profane king summoned Daniel to read the writing on the wall, his eye swept the banquet chamber and took it all in. There were dissolute guests in various degrees of intoxication. There were tables in disarray as a result of the revelry. There were sacred vessels from the burned-out temple in Jerusalem; these had been brought from the royal vaults at the whim of the decadent king and were still filled with wine with which to toast the graven images of Babylon. There was the king, sober now, white as a sheet, and shaking in his shoes. And there on the wall was the writing of a well-known hand; to Daniel the writing on the wall was just like a letter from home.

Daniel dismissed the promised gifts with contempt. Then after lecturing the king on his wicked life, Daniel read the blunt words announcing the king's doom: *"Mene, Mene, Tekel Upharsin."* The essence of the message was "Thou art weighed in the balances, and art found wanting." Nor did the doom dawdle. "That night," we read, "was Belshazzar the king of the Chaldeans slain." (See Daniel 5:24-31.)

8. Complimentary Values (11:24-26)

Proverbs 11:24-25 tells us *how to make more money:* "There is that scattereth, and yet increaseth; and there is that withholdeth more than is meet, but it tendeth to poverty. The liberal soul shall be made fat: and he that watereth shall be watered also himself."

Every farmer understands the principle stated here. The farmer who is stingy at the time of sowing will have a meager harvest in the time of reaping. The farmer who fails to water his crops will receive a poor return. Every businessman knows you have to spend money to make money. Every well-taught believer knows that while we do not give in order to get, "God is no man's debtor." Nobody can out-give God. As a general rule, the more we give the more we receive. The stingy person lacks common sense and spiritual understanding. We have both a social and a spiritual responsibility to be generous. The person who is mean with his money soon shrivels up inside.

One of the world's greatest givers was George Muller of Bristol,

England. When he first launched out into the orphanage work God had laid on his heart, all he had was some small change. He also had three dishes, twenty-eight plates, three basins, one jug, four mugs, three salt shakers, one grater, four knives, and five forks. By the time he finished his work, some ten thousand boys and girls had been housed, fed, clothed, educated, and settled in gainful employment. He had given away vast sums of money to help Sunday schools and day schools at home and abroad. He had given away nearly two million Bibles and New Testaments. He had circulated three million books and tracts.

How much money passed through his hands? Nobody knows but God. Figures are given, but they are in pounds sterling and in pre-inflation terms. If we were to take those figures, multiply them by the generous rate of exchange prevailing in those days to convert the sum into dollars, and then multiply the answer by an enormous inflation factor to reflect the changes in the purchasing power of the dollar, the resulting sum would be astronomical. Yet George Muller died as he lived—poor by the world's standards. However, he was one of Heaven's billionaires. Like Abraham, Muller died "full" (Genesis 25:8).

Solomon would have approved of George Muller, although the king did not set much of an example to anyone. He was too fond of spending money on himself and he did not have any scruples about squeezing more and more out of his tax-burdened people (1 Kings 12:1-4). God smiles on the generous person and places His stamp of disapproval on the stingy person.

Proverbs 11:26 tells us *how to make men mad:* "He that withholdeth corn, the people shall curse him: but blessing shall be upon the head of him that selleth it."

Today it is considered good business to hold goods until they are in short supply and then boost their price to multiply profits. It is considered good business to impose embargoes on imported goods in order to boost the prices of domestic products. It is considered good business to form cartels to control the market and inflate prices. Most businessmen seem unconcerned that poor people suffer as a result of such practices. The important thing, they believe, is to make money. Is it? God doesn't think so. The important thing is to be compassionate.

In the nineteenth century England was brought to the verge of revolution by the infamous Corn Laws, which were designed to keep the price of bread high and cut out foreign competition. However, a sullen and savage proletariat was growing in numbers. They were listening to Marx and Engels and turning against the rest of the country. Carlyle wrote, "This world is for them no home but a dingy prison-house." Revolution was in the air. Workers began to talk openly of burning down the mills to enforce a nationwide strike.

Had Solomon been alive then, he would have read Proverbs 11:26 to the members of the British Parliament and the smug House of Lords when they were debating the withholding of corn. Many of those men had Solomon's proverbs in their libraries. They must have forgotten to read this one. Fortunately England had enough common sense to repeal the offensive Corn Laws, but not before an outbreak of rebellion shook the landowners, mill owners, and aristocracy out of their complacency.

9. Critical Values (11:27-29)

Solomon warned us to beware of fantastic folly, financial folly, and family folly. First we are to beware of *fantastic folly:* "He that diligently seeketh good procureth favour: but he that seeketh mischief, it shall come unto him" (Proverbs 11:27). The Hebrew word translated "mischief" here comes from a root that indicates the nature of mischief: the breaking up of all that is good. The corresponding Greek words speak of moral depravity, corruption, and lewdness.

There can be no greater folly than to embark deliberately on a life of mischief. The person who seeks that kind of life will not have to seek trouble. His life will be a slippery, downward path. A person who seeks good has to exercise diligence; no such effort is required when a person seeks a life of lust and lawlessness.

King Manasseh was lawless, although his father, great King Hezekiah, had been one of the godliest of all Judah's monarchs. Manasseh was only twelve when he came to the throne and he reigned for fifty-five years, longer than any other Judean king. He undid all the good his father had done, plunged the nation into deeper apostasy than it had known before, and guaranteed its judgment. He re-established the high places for idol worship and re-erected the vile Asherahs. He made altars for the worship of the host of heaven within the temple courts. He reactivated the cruel worship of Moloch. He encouraged sodomy and all kinds of vice. And he paid no attention to the warnings of godly prophets. In fact he shed the blood of those who remained true to God. (See 2 Kings 21:1-16.)

Manasseh sought "mischief" and it came looking for him. God sold him into the hands of the Assyrians. Not only was he forced to pay tribute to Esarhaddon and Ashurbanipal, but this latter Assyrian king carried him captive to Babylon where belatedly he came to his senses. Restored to his kingdom, Manasseh made efforts to undo at least some of the damage he had done (2 Chronicles 33:12-19), but he still stands in contrast to his father Hezekiah, who diligently sought good and procured the favor of God.

We are also to beware of *financial folly:* "He that trusteth in his riches shall fall: but the righteous shall flourish as a branch" (Proverbs 11:28). The word translated "trusteth" here means "to confide in so as to be secure and without fear." The ultimate deception of riches is that they give people a false sense of security.

Lot seems to have been infatuated with money. Both he and Abraham were rich, but their differing attitudes toward riches became apparent as soon as a difficulty arose over sharing the land. The available pasture lands proved insufficient to sustain the large flocks and herds the two men possessed. As a result heated squabbles broke out between the herdsmen of the two believers.

Abraham took the initiative. Although the whole land had been deeded to him, the patriarch offered to divide the land with Lot and allow him to have first choice. The suggestion was that the two men part company to put an end to unseemly striving in front of the ungodly. "We be brethren," Abraham said (Genesis 13:8). He was saying that the things which united them were more important than the things which divided them. Such was Abraham's caliber. He did not trust in riches and land values; he trusted in God.

Lot, on the other hand, coveted the well-watered plains of Jordan that lay before him like an emerald, promising wealth and well-being. There in the plain nestled the vile cities of Sodom and Gomorrah, notorious for their acceptance of sodomy as an approved lifestyle. In those cities Lot saw great business opportunities for himself, great social opportunities for his wife, and great educational opportunities for his children. He trusted in his money. It was the height of folly even to consider bartering fellowship with Abraham, one of the greatest of all God's saints, for a chance to make more money. But Lot chose to go his separate way.

Then war broke out and all Lot had was swept away. As the proverb says, "He that trusteth in his riches shall fall." Lot and his family found themselves heading back to Babylonia in chains. They were destined for the slave market.

The proverb also says, "The righteous shall flourish as a branch." Abraham proved this truth. As soon as Lot packed his bags and headed off toward the Jordan valley, God told Abraham he had lost nothing. All the land was still his, even the area now claimed by Lot (Genesis 13:14-18). Even the battle that took Lot into captivity passed by Abraham. Indeed Abraham actually involved himself in the situation. He armed his servants, pursued the retreating invaders, and rescued Lot. Truly Abraham flourished as a branch.

When another crisis arose over money, this temptation also failed to leave any mark on Abraham. But Lot, having placed his confidence in the power of money to buy fame and position, fell a second time to the lure of riches. (See Genesis 14:21-24; 19:1.)

Finally we are to beware of *family folly:* "He that troubleth his own house shall inherit the wind: and the fool shall be servant to the wise of heart" (Proverbs 11:29). Isaac and Rebekah troubled their own house with favoritism and they inherited the wind. Isaac favored Esau. The father admired his son's manliness, physique, and prowess as a hunter. Isaac was fond of the venison Esau was so skilled at providing. Rebekah loved Jacob, whose skills were more domestic. Years of secret alienation are summed up in one brief but pregnant statement: "And Isaac loved Esau, because he did eat of his venison; but Rebekah loved Jacob" (Genesis 25:28).

We can picture two boys growing up in an atmosphere of favoritism, partiality, indulgence, and injustice. The trouble came to a head when Rebekah helped Jacob deceive Isaac so that Isaac would give him the patriarchal blessing. As a result Esau hated Jacob and Jacob was obliged to leave home to live out the best years of his life with his unscrupulous Uncle Laban. Rebekah promised herself that Jacob would be gone for but "a few days" (Genesis 27:44), but Jacob stayed with Laban for twenty years and Rebekah never saw her favorite son again.

Esau married two heathen women and sealed his future as a pagan. We can imagine what Isaac and Rebekah felt about that. The Holy Spirit says these pagan women brought grief to Isaac and Rebekah. Alexander Whyte said, "That great grief would seem to have been almost the only thing the two old people were at one about by that time." Esau grew up to found the Edomite nation, a people noted throughout the entire Old Testament for their bitter enmity toward the children of Israel. Truly, those who trouble their own house will inherit the whirlwind.

10. Character Values (11:30-31)

Solomon here pointed the way to *eternal bliss:* "The fruit of the righteous is a tree of life; and he that winneth souls is wise" (Proverbs 11:30). There is no joy in all the world like the joy of leading someone to Christ and knowing that an eternity of bliss will be that person's portion.

Consider for example the delightful story of Thomas Bilney. People called him "Little Bilney" because he was a nobody. However, reading the Erasmus translation of the New Testament opened Little Bilney's eyes. He turned away from the priests and their penances and pilgrimages and found Christ. He longed to make Christ known to the priest-ridden world of his day, but he was only Little Bilney. Who would pay attention to him?

Then he went to hear the popular preacher Bishop Hugh Latimer, known as the "honestest" man in England. Bilney was enthralled and he coveted Hugh Latimer's soul for Christ. If he could win Latimer to Christ, Latimer could win the masses.

One day as Latimer was descending from the pulpit, he felt an insistent tug on his robe and heard Thomas Bilney say, "Father Latimer, can I confess my soul to you?" The two retired to the confessional. Bilney fell on his knees and poured out a story unlike any Latimer had heard before. Bilney confessed his long search for peace and his disillusionment with the priests. He confessed to hearing Erasmus and obtaining a copy of the New Testament. He confessed to reading that New Testament and finding something no priest or pope could ever give him: peace with God through our Lord Jesus Christ.

Latimer's soul was taken by storm. Only too well did he know his own soul's emptiness. To Little Bilney's astonishment and delight, Hugh Latimer came around and knelt by his side. The "honestest" man in England knelt by the "faithfulest" man in England and opened his heart to Christ.

Little Bilney had chosen his man well. Soon Hugh Latimer's preaching was swaying the masses. He became the idol of the common people. Londoners cheered him on his way. He was their prophet and he took England by storm.

Then the political climate changed and Rome demanded its pound of flesh. Hugh Latimer was imprisoned, but that was not enough. His enemies wanted him burned at the stake. He and Bishop Ridley were taken to Oxford, to the open space before Balliol College. Latimer was eighty-four and Ridley was also old. They were to be burned to satisfy the religious bigotry and malice of Bloody Mary, who had recently ascended the English throne. As the fagots were piled around the two men, Latimer addressed his colleague with words that still ring down the centuries: "Be of good comfort, Master Ridley, and play the man: we shall this day light such a candle, by God's grace, in England, as I trust shall never be put out." Both leaned forward as if to embrace the flames, and a chariot of fire carried them to Heaven.

Hugh Latimer was right. A poet has caught the spirit of his last words:

> Latimer's light shall never go out
> However the winds may blow it about.
> Latimer's light has come to stay
> Till the trump of a coming judgment day.

Solomon said, "He that winneth souls is wise." Thomas Bilney has won the soul-winner's crown. So has Hugh Latimer. So have many other noble warriors, great and small, in the army of faith.

Solomon also pointed the way to *earthly blessing:* "Behold, the righteous shall be recompensed in the earth: much more the wicked and the sinner" (Proverbs 11:31). This proverb underlines the Old Testament state of affairs. As we have seen, God's moral government of human affairs was much more visible in that day and age when He was dealing with an earthly people with largely earthly promises than it is today when he is dealing with a heavenly people with largely heavenly promises. God's moral government was much more evident when people lived in a dispensation of law than it is in a dispensation of grace.

Proverbs 11:31 has a prophetic flavor. It anticipates the second coming of Christ, the setting up of the Lord's judgment throne in the valley of Jehoshaphat, and the dawn of the millennial age.

CHAPTER 16

Proverbs 12:1-28

B. Vignettes to Be Considered (12:1-28)
1. The Wise Man (12:1)
2. The Wayward Man (12:2-9)
   a. A Bad Man (12:2-3)
      (1) A Man without Favor (12:2)
      (2) A Man without Foundation (12:3)
   b. A Glad Man (12:4)
   c. A Mad Man (12:5-9)
      The insanity of thinking that:
      (1) Villainy Is Better Than Virtue (12:5)
      (2) Violence Is Better Than Virtue (12:6-7)
      (3) Vindictiveness Is Better Than Virtue (12:8)
      (4) Vanity Is Better Than Virtue (12:9)
3. The Working Man (12:10-12)
   a. A Word about Inhumanity (12:10)
   b. A Word about Industry (12:11)
   c. A Word about Integrity (12:12)
4. The Watchful Man (12:13-16)
   a. A Saved Man (12:13)
   b. A Satisfied Man (12:14)
   c. A Sensible Man (12:15-16)
      (1) He Hears Counsel (12:15)
      (2) He Has Compassion (12:16)
5. The Wordy Man (12:17-23)
   The man who speaks:
   a. Perverted Words (12:17)
   b. Piercing Words (12:18)
   c. Permanent Words (12:19)
   d. Profound Words (12:20-21)

Mark the use of the amazing word *but* in Scripture. *But* is the small hinge upon which great matters swing. Nobody made more frequent use of it than Solomon in the book of Proverbs. Here *but* is like a recurring note in a musical masterpiece. *But* is the beating of the drum to which Solomon's momentous musings march. In proverb after proverb, precept after precept, picture after picture, contrasts are passed before us in rapidly changing flashes of light and shade.

B. Vignettes to Be Considered (12:1-28)

1. The Wise Man (12:1)

"Whoso loveth instruction loveth knowledge: but he that hateth reproof is brutish." The word translated "instruction" here refers to discipline or correction.

Many people bridle at the whip, but David didn't. He was a wise man with a heart for God. He loved instruction and therefore loved knowledge. David was a king and throughout history kings have not been noted for taking correction kindly or meekly, especially when they have just transgressed a moral law.

David sinned as badly as anyone. After he seduced Bathsheba and murdered her husband, he continued to sit on the throne and dispense justice and judgment as if nothing had happened, as if there were no God in Heaven, and as if there were no gossiping subjects in the court or countryside.

Yet all that time his conscience gnawed at his soul. In one of his penitential Psalms he revealed what was going on deep down in his heart: "When I kept silence, my bones waxed old through my roarings all the day long. For day and night thy hand was heavy upon me: my moisture is turned into the drought of summer" (32:3-4). In another Psalm referring to that same period he said, "Behold, thou desirest truth in the inward parts: and in the hidden part thou shalt make me to know wisdom" (51:6). So by the time the Lord sent Nathan the prophet to him, David was more than ready to receive instruction.

David knew his sin was great. Its enormity pressed upon his soul. He had committed two capital offenses. He had been guilty of presumptuous sin. He also knew his Bible well enough to know that no provision was made under the Mosaic law for removing the guilt of that kind of sin. There could be only a "fearful looking for of judgment" (Hebrews 10:27).

When Nathan arrived, David was still going through the motions of dispensing judgment and justice. He could still get indignant at injustice wrought by others. Thus Nathan told his now-famous story: A rich man who possessed flocks and herds in plenty received an unexpected visitor and wanted to prepare a feast for his guest. The rich man had a poor neighbor who owned nothing but one little lamb. The rich man stole that lamb and cooked it for his guest.

David was furious. His beard bristled; his eyes flashed. "The man that hath done this thing shall surely die," he said, "and he shall restore the lamb fourfold." Out came Nathan's sword. It was at David's throat before he even knew Nathan had a sword. "Thou art the man," he said.

Nathan ranks among the peers of the prophetic order. It was an act of high courage thus to beard the royal lion in his den. David's response is noteworthy too. A lesser man would have summoned the executioner to punish someone who was daring enough to publicly denounce the king. Instead David was relieved. The confrontation was like the lancing of a boil. "I have sinned," he said.

Meekly David bowed his head to hear the divine sentence. Bleakly he looked at Nathan. David longed for a fresh word from God. "Instruct me, Nathan," we can almost hear him say. "Can my sin be removed? Or must I bear it into eternity?" The answer came swiftly. "The Lord also hath put away thy sin; thou shalt not die," Nathan said. (See 2 Samuel 12.)

David, who loved correction and instruction, pondered the words of Nathan. How could God bypass his sin? Doubly he deserved to die! Yet God said, "Thou shalt not die." No sin offering or trespass offering could cover his sin and give him life in the place of death. David later wrote, "Sacrifice and offering thou didst not desire...burnt offering and sin offering hast thou not required" (Psalm 40:6). "Thou desirest not sacrifice; else would I give it," he said. "Thou delightest not in burnt offering. The sacrifices of God are a broken spirit: a broken and a contrite heart, O God, thou wilt not despise" (51:16-17). Being a wise man, David thus pondered God's ways with his sin and his soul.

David pondered much over the full and free salvation so magnanimously bestowed upon him by God. At last, having received correction, David received knowledge. He could write: "Blessed is he whose transgression is forgiven, whose sin is covered. Blessed is the man unto whom the Lord imputeth not iniquity" (Psalm 32:1-2). About a thousand years later the apostle Paul entered into that great truth. He wrote, "David...describeth the blessedness of the man, unto whom God imputeth righteousness without works" (Romans 4:6-8).

David attained the full measure of his stature in Christ. He took a quantum leap in understanding. He suddenly saw that salvation was by faith, not works. The Old Testament sacrifices could no more take away sin than they could restore lost innocence. All he needed was God's naked word: "God hath removed your sin." Calvary would take care of the rest.

There was all the difference in the world between brokenhearted David and unrepentant Joab. Although Joab was David's general and David's nephew, and although he lived for years alongside "a man after God's own heart" and sang David's Psalms, he learned nothing. Joab hated reproof. He was spiritually "brutish," no better than a beast of the field. David found forgiveness and life, but Joab found shame and death. At the last Joab, thinking he could be saved by making some kind of religious gesture, seized the horns of the altar, but it did him no good. He was dragged away to execution.

2. The Wayward Man (12:2-9)

a. A Bad Man (12:2-3)

Next in a series of pictures of different kinds of men is a portrait of a bad man. He is a man *without favor:* "A good man obtaineth favour of the Lord: but a man of wicked devices will he condemn" (Proverbs 12:2).

Before Solomon described a bad man, he made a statement about a good man, and so we are reminded of Barnabas. The Bible says Barnabas was a good man (Acts 11:24) and it says that of remarkably few people. He was the kind of man people would die for (Romans 5:7). He had a great heart of compassion, so much so that the apostles nicknamed him "son of consolation" (Acts 4:36). He held onto his earthly possessions lightly. Indeed he sold them and gave the proceeds to further the Lord's work in Jerusalem.

Barnabas obtained favor of the Lord. And this good man was praised in all the churches. Never did he serve the church better than when he befriended the boycotted Saul of Tarsus and introduced him to the Jerusalem church (unless it was when he went to Tarsus to bring Saul to Antioch). Until then Barnabas had been the chief man among the brethren; thereafter he took a back seat to Saul. Barnabas gladly allowed himself to be eclipsed by his Spirit-filled, clear-thinking, gospel-preaching, missionary-minded, Bible-teaching, soul-winning colleague. Barnabas joined Paul on his first missionary journey, but even when their paths no longer ran side by side, Paul thought tenderly of his "beloved brother Barnabas." That was Paul's name for this good man who obtained favor of the Lord.

Having introduced us to Barnabas and his initial act of generosity that put him in the spotlight, the Bible introduces us to Ananias. "But," says the Holy Spirit, "a certain man named Ananias, with Sapphira his wife, sold a possession..." (Acts 5:1). Ananias did what Barnabas did. Probably he sold his land because he was inspired by Barnabas's example and coveted the applause Barnabas received. But Ananias, as Solomon would have put it, was "a man of wicked devices" and his wife was as devious as her husband.

The pair had a family conference. They decided to sell their land and give money to the Lord's work, but they agreed to keep back part of the price. They wanted to give the impression, however, that they were donating all the proceeds. So they lied to the omniscient, omnipresent Holy Spirit of God.

Their condemnation was not long delayed. Just as Ananias had whispered in Sapphira's ear, so the Holy Spirit whispered in Peter's. Before the day was over, the deceitful pair were denounced. The Holy Spirit struck them down, first one and then the other. Then they were buried, their names tarnished for the rest of time.

A bad man is not only without favor; he is also *without foundation:* "A man shall not be established by wickedness: but the root of the righteous shall not be moved" (Proverbs 12:3).

Jeroboam II was the last king to sit on the throne of the northern kingdom of Israel with even a semblance of divine authority. Those who followed him were a sorry lot indeed. Although godless and wicked, Jeroboam II was able enough and powerful. But ability and resolution alone cannot establish a kingdom, a business, or anything else. Only God can do that. Those who ignore God may seem to prosper, but nothing can really be permanently established by wickedness.

Jeroboam II ignored the warnings of a number of prophets. When he died his kingdom fell on hard times. Murder was never far from the throne. His son Zachariah, an evil king, reigned only six months (2 Kings 15:8). He had his father's weaknesses and none of his strengths. Zachariah was murdered by Shallum.

Shallum, who lasted only a month, was assassinated by Menahem, who managed to hang onto the throne for ten inglorious years. During Menahem's reign the dark shadow of Assyria, the superpower to the north, lay over the land. The imperious Tiglath-pileser demanded more and more tribute.

Menahem was able to secure the throne for his son Pekahiah, who hung onto it for a scant two years—long enough to prove himself to be another wicked king in a long succession of wicked kings. He was murdered by Pekah, the captain of the guard who then seized the throne for himself.

Pekah was as bad as Pekahiah. Pekah also did evil in the sight of the Lord. During his reign the armies of Tiglath-pileser overran the land. The Assyrians depopulated much of Gilead and Galilee. Then Pekah was murdered by Hoshea.

Hoshea, the last king of Israel, managed to hang on in Samaria for nine unhappy years. The armies of Shalmaneser, king of Assyria, forced him to pay onerous tribute. When he tried to extricate himself from this arrangement by entering into a protective alliance with Egypt, the Assyrians imprisoned him. Finally Samaria succumbed to siege. The Assyrians deported what was left of the population and thus brought the northern kingdom of Israel to an inglorious end (2 Kings 15:31).

In contrast to the kings of Israel, godly King Hezekiah, who was on the throne of Judah, survived the Assyrian holocaust. Hezekiah illustrates Solomon's principle: "The root of the righteous shall not be moved." Hezekiah's roots were in God. His foundation was sure. Although the tempest raged and the flood tides came, he triumphed because he rested in the everlasting arms.

b. A Glad Man (12:4)

"A virtuous woman is a crown to her husband: but she that maketh ashamed is as rottenness in his bones." Happy is the man who has a good wife; unhappy is the man who has a bad one. The proverb is illustrated by the story of Elkanah. He had two wives, one a saint and the other a scold.

Peninnah was the kind of woman who makes a husband ashamed. She had a mean spirit and a spiteful tongue. Elkanah must often have wondered why he ever married her. Perhaps she had a pretty face. (The cynic has said that beauty is more important in a woman than brains because men can see better than they can think!)

Peninnah had much for which to be thankful. Her husband was a good and godly man who did not neglect her. Above all, she had children, the mark of approval and acceptance in her day. But Peninnah was jealous. She was bitterly envious of Hannah, Elkanah's other wife.

Since Hannah had no children (a reproach in Bible times) Peninnah crowed over her continually. Peninnah made Hannah's life miserable, which was exactly what Peninnah wanted to do. With Peninnah expressing her meanness and malice, there was little or no peace and quiet in Elkanah's home—for him or Hannah or anyone else. Peninnah's temper and Hannah's tears kept the house in perpetual turmoil. Peninnah was rottenness in Elkanah's bones.

In contrast to Peninnah, Hannah was a virtuous woman. She was a crown to her husband. She was desperately unhappy because she was barren and because she was badgered and baited by her bitter rival, whose acid tongue and biting sarcasm left her totally demoralized. But Hannah knew what to do. She prayed. And she prevailed. God gave her a baby boy, whom she called Samuel.

Hannah gave Samuel back to God, and from his earliest childhood days the lad loved the Lord and responded to spiritual things. Behind his growth and development lay the prayer ministry of Hannah. "For this child I prayed," she told Eli (1 Samuel 1:27). We can be sure that she never stopped praying. How many times Hannah thanked God for Samuel! How many times Elkanah thanked God for Hannah!

Year after year Hannah and Elkanah went to Shiloh, where Eli the priest was raising their son. Year after year they went home praising God for the way this little boy was shaping up to be a prophet of the Most High. There never was a day when Elkanah did not bless God for Hannah, who had given him such a son! Moreover she gave her husband three other sons and a daughter, so Elkanah walked before his fellow men as a man crowned with glory and honor. When it became evident to all Israel that God had broken His long silence and was speaking again through Samuel, all Israel blessed Elkanah. In turn Elkanah blessed Hannah, and Hannah blessed God.

The difference between Hannah and Peninnah was a matter of the temper and the tongue. Peninnah used her tongue to provoke; Hannah used hers to pray. Peninnah's temper turned their home into a suburb of Hell; Hannah's holy temperament turned their home into a suburb of Heaven.

c. A Mad Man (12:5-9)

Here we see a fourfold picture of a man who acts as if he is insane. Bereft of all common sense, he thinks that villainy, violence, vindictiveness, and vanity are better than virtue. First Solomon dealt with the insanity of thinking that *villainy is better than virtue:* "The thoughts of the righteous are right: but the counsels of the wicked [lawless] are deceit" (Proverbs 12:5).

This verse reminds us of the contrast between wicked Herod and the wise men who came from the East to worship at the feet of the infant Christ. We do not know who the wise men were, but we do know that what they did was right and we can conclude that they were righteous. They worshiped the Son of God. Their hearts were open to the Lord's leading in their lives. They were willing to give up fame, fortune, home, and family to follow that beckoning star. The "Light, which lighteth every man that cometh into the world" (John 1:9) had burned brightly in their souls. They thought deeply about this newborn King whose advent was so momentous that God celebrated it by putting a new star in the sky. They pondered what they should bring to express their hopes and homage, and they came to Jesus.

Someone once said, "We sow our thoughts, and we reap our actions, we sow our actions, and we reap our habits, we sow our habits, and we reap our characters; we sow our characters, and we reap our destiny."[1] The thoughts of the wise men were translated into action. The action of committing their lives to follow that "kindly light" became a daily habit. By the time the wise men were pouring out their treasures at the feet of Jesus, their character was evident: they were righteous men. They believed God and it was counted to them for righteousness. They stood in the direct spiritual line of Abraham, who had also come from the East to worship God. Doubtless we shall meet them in Heaven, where they will still be putting their all at His feet.

In contrast to these wise men, Herod the Great (misnamed by a world that has all its values warped) was a wicked man. He intended to find the rival king whose ambassadors were such influential men and nip this threat in the bud. For Herod, there was no king but Herod. Having ascertained that Bethlehem was the most likely place to find the newborn Hebrew Messiah, he summoned the wise men. "And he sent them to Bethlehem, and said, Go and search diligently for the young child; and when ye have found him, bring me word again, that I may come and worship him also" (Matthew 2:8). Truly, "the counsels of the wicked are deceit."

We read of the wise men that having presented their gifts, and "being warned of God in a dream that they should not return to Herod, they departed into their own country another way" (Matthew 2:12). Truly, "the thoughts of the righteous are right." And as David said, "The steps of a good man are ordered by the Lord" (Psalm 37:23).

Meanwhile Herod waited anxiously for the return of the wise men. He took counsel with his wicked heart and sharpened his hate and resolve. When the wise men failed to show up, he acted with savage dispatch to kill all the babies of Bethlehem in the murderous hope that by so doing he would put an end to this rival king.

Next Solomon dealt with the insanity of thinking that *violence is better than virtue:* "The words of the wicked are to lie in wait for blood: but the mouth of the upright shall deliver them. The wicked are overthrown, and are not: but the house of the righteous shall stand" (Proverbs 12:6-7).

The personal histories of King Saul and David illustrate this proverb. Time and time again Saul lay in wait for David. Saul was insanely jealous of David and on at least twenty-four occasions tried to murder him. Toward the end Saul's whole life became one mad crusade to get David killed. At the last Saul was overthrown, not by David but by the Philistines. Saul died a suicide, afraid he would fall into the hands of his enemies. The Philistines found his corpse and contemptuously nailed it to the wall of Bethshan, a Canaanite city in Israel (1 Samuel 31:4,9-10).

In contrast to the overthrow of the wicked, "the mouth of the upright shall deliver them." We do not read that David ever said an ill word against King Saul, not even on the two occasions when David had Saul in his power.

On the first occasion David was in the wilderness of Engedi on the west shore of the Dead Sea, near the place where a difficult caravan route ran between the mountain and the sea. Saul came with three thousand soldiers and thought he had David trapped. Unaware that David had taken refuge in a particular cave, Saul entered that cave and lay down to sleep. As soon as Saul was asleep, David's men urged him to kill his enemy. Instead David contented himself with cutting off part of Saul's robe. He is "the Lord's anointed," said David, explaining to his men why he refused to harm Saul.

David and his men then escaped from the cave and called to Saul. David held up the piece he had cut from Saul's robe as proof that he had no evil designs on the king. "Thou art more righteous than I," Saul said after listening to David's righteous and reasonable words. Ashamed of himself, Saul went home. (See 1 Samuel 24.) Truly, "the mouth of the upright shall deliver them."

On the other occasion David was again being hunted by Saul, a thoroughly wicked man. This time David had hidden in the neighborhood of Ziph, a town in the hill country of Judah near a wilderness and a forest. Hoping to curry favor with Saul, the Ziphites told him David was in the vicinity. Again Saul took an army of three thousand men to kill David. However, David's spies told him where Saul was and how his camp was arranged. They also told David that Abner, Saul's general, was second in command.

With Abishai, David stole into the camp at night and once more Saul was in his power. Everyone seemed to be asleep. Saul slept with his spear stuck in the ground by his head. Abishai whispered to David, "Let me smite him, I pray thee, with the spear even to the earth at once, and I will not smite him a second time." Again David refused to harm his enemy because Saul was the Lord's anointed. Instead he took Saul's spear and water flask and retreated to a nearby hill. Then he hailed Saul and showed him the captured spear and flask to prove that he meant no ill to the king.

Again David pleaded with Saul to believe that he meant no harm. Saul replied, "I have sinned....behold, I have played the fool, and have erred exceedingly." Again Saul called off the hunt and went home. Once more "the mouth of the upright" had delivered David. (See 1 Samuel 26.)

The house of Saul eventually fell in ruins. David's house was established forever. "The house of the righteous shall stand." When David was king, he decided to build a house for God in Jerusalem. The Lord postponed the plan but gave David full credit for his intention. "Thine house and thy kingdom shall be established for ever before thee: thy throne shall be established for ever," God said (2 Samuel 7:16). David in his noble response remarked in wonder, "Thou hast also spoken of thy servant's house for a great while to come" (1 Chronicles 17:17).

God has His own inimitable way of working His wonders in securing the well-being of the homes and children of those who love and trust Him. The promises to David found their fulfillment in Christ, and so do God's promises to us.

Solomon next dealt with the insanity of thinking that *vindictiveness is better than virtue:* "A man shall be commended according to his wisdom: but he that is of a perverse heart shall be despised" (Proverbs 12:8). This proverb is illustrated in the contrasting attitudes of Solomon and his son Rehoboam when each in turn came to the throne. Solomon, at the beginning of his reign, said to the Lord:

> I am but a little child: I know not how to go out or come in. And thy servant is in the midst of thy people which thou hast chosen, a great people, that cannot be numbered or counted for multitude. Give therefore thy servant an understanding heart to judge thy people, that I may discern between good and bad: for who is able to judge this thy so great a people? (1 Kings 3:7-9).

Solomon's prayer was answered. Almost immediately Solomon was called upon to adjudicate the case of the two prostitutes. Each claimed that the child they brought with them was hers, and we all know by heart the clever method Solomon used to discover which woman was the mother. The historian told us that "all Israel heard of the judgment which the king had judged; and they feared the king: for they saw that the wisdom of God was in him, to do judgment" (1 Kings 3:28).

When Rehoboam came to the throne, he also had an immediate crisis on his hands. Ten of the tribes, resentful of the heavy taxation to which the country had been subjected, found a spokesman in Jeroboam, one of Solomon's former managers. They demanded redress: an immediate reduction in taxes.

At first it seemed that Rehoboam was going to show some common sense. He "consulted with the old men, that stood before Solomon his father." They counseled him to listen to Jeroboam and give immediate tax relief to the burdened tribes. After all, Solomon had raised much of the money for self-aggrandizement.

Then Rehoboam "consulted with the young men that were grown up with him." Their advice was much more to his liking. "You show them who's boss," they said in effect. "Increase the taxes. Let them know you're the king." Their advice was the most foolish counsel Rehoboam could possibly have received. And being a fool, he took it. That decision cost him ten of the twelve tribes, for "when all Israel saw that the king hearkened not unto them, the people answered the king, saying, What portion have we in David? neither have we inheritance in the son of Jesse: to your tents, O Israel: now see to thine own house, David." (See 1 Kings 12:1-16.) The foolish king was "of a perverse heart" and he was despised.

Finally Solomon dealt with the insanity of thinking that *vanity is better than virtue:* "He that is despised, and hath a servant, is better than he that honoureth himself, and lacketh bread" (Proverbs 12:9). The man who has a servant is better in terms of material well-being. The expression translated "he that is despised" can be rendered "he that is little noticed." The man who is little noticed by others, but has a servant, is better off than the man who boasts of his pedigree and titles, but is on the verge of starvation.

The novel *Kidnapped* by Robert Louis Stevenson provides an illustration of this proverb. The swaggering Alan Breck appeals to our imaginations right away. "My name is Stewart," he said when David Balfour first met him. "Alan Breck, they call me. A king's name is good enough for me." He was not bashful about heralding his own prowess. After the fight in the roundhouse, he said to Balfour, "O, man, am I no a bonny fighter?" There is something captivating about Alan Breck in spite of his boasting. Just once he appeared in false colors—in "Cluny's Cage."

Balfour tells us about Cluny Macpherson, chief of the clan Vourich. He had been one of the leaders of the great Scottish rebellion and there was a price on his head. His country conquered, Cluny was stripped of legal powers by act of Parliament. He was a fugitive, driven to living in holes and hide-outs. The "Cage" was one of Cluny's hide-outs. "He had caves, besides, and underground chambers in several parts of his country; and following the reports of his scouts, he moved from one to another as the soldiers drew near, or moved away." Thus he managed to survive. His weird-looking "Cage" was perched on a hillside in the heart of a labyrinth of dreary glens and hollows of the dismal mountain of Ben Alder.

The world thought little of Cluny though the court would have liked to see him hanged. But Cluny had a servant. He had many servants. "The least of the ragged fellows whom he rated and threatened could have made a fortune by betraying him," Balfour says. They would sooner have died for him.

Cluny made David Balfour and Alan Breck welcome, fed them like kings, and "brought out an old, thumbed, greasy pack of cards." David excused himself from the game. This irked the imperious Cluny. "What kind of Whiggish, canting talk is this, for the house of Cluny Macpherson?" he demanded. Alan came to Balfour's defense. "I will put my hand in the fire for Mr. Balfour," he said. "He is an honest and a mettle gentleman, and I would have ye bear in mind who says it. I bear a king's name, and I and any that I call friend are company for the best."

Balfour, overcome with weariness, found a corner and went to sleep while Alan and Cluny played cards. At the beginning Alan was winning and soon a glittering pile of golden guineas lay before him on the table. Then his luck changed. Presently Alan woke Balfour up and asked him for a loan. "Hut, David," he said when Balfour demurred, "ye wouldnae grudge me a loan?" The long and the short of it was that Alan lost his winnings, lost his own meager purse, and lost all of Balfour's money.

The pair, in flight from the king's soldiers, were reduced to facing the wilds of Scotland with an empty purse. Balfour had to beg Cluny to restore his money, and Alan was reduced to an embarrassed silence that turned belligerent. At that moment Cluny, the man who was despised but had servants, was better off than Alan Breck, who honored himself ("I bear a king's name") but lacked the means to buy so much as a loaf of bread. And Alan's pride would not allow him to humble himself before Cluny or apologize to Balfour.

3. The Working Man (12:10-12)

Thinking about *inhumanity,* Solomon wrote, "A righteous man regardeth the life of his beast: but the tender mercies of the wicked are cruel" (Proverbs 12:10).

When Jonah preached to Nineveh, the people of that bloodthirsty and cruel city not only repented in sackcloth and ashes; they also made sure their animals were included in the fast. The people had no guarantee that God's judgment would be averted, but they hoped and prayed. Jonah, in spite of his disgruntled mood, was impressed enough to tell us what happened:

> So the people of Nineveh believed God, and proclaimed a fast, and put on sackcloth, from the greatest of them even to the least of them. For word came unto the king of Nineveh, and he arose from his throne, and he laid his robe from him, and covered him with sackcloth, and sat in ashes. And he caused it to be proclaimed and published through Nineveh by the decree of the king and his nobles, saying, Let neither man nor beast, herd nor flock, taste anything: let them not feed, nor drink water: But let man and beast be covered with sackcloth, and cry mightily unto God: yea, let them turn every one from his evil way, and from the violence that is in their hands (Jonah 3:5-8).

There is something astonishing in the fact that the Ninevites extended their repentance to their cattle. When they believed God, it was counted unto them for righteousness (Romans 4:3), for "a righteous man regardeth the life of his beast." These people, who had committed horrible atrocities against their captured enemies, were so greatly changed that they wanted even the cattle in their barns and fields to share in their hoped-for salvation.

When revival broke out in Wales, the transformed miners reported a similar remarkable incident. When they went back to the mines to dig coal, they were astonished at the hapless pit ponies' reaction to kind treatment. The ponies, who were supposed to pull the drams of coal from the seams to the mine shaft, refused to work! They were not used to kindness. All they had known before were kicks and curses, so when the saved miners spoke to them kindly and in language purged of blasphemy and obscenity, the poor animals did not know how to respond. They did not know what was being said to them. The miners who before had abused the ponies now cared for them. The working men were righteous indeed.

In contrast to the Welsh converts, "the tender mercies of the wicked are cruel." Consider the treatment of widows in James Michener's *Centennial*. One of the heroes is the Arapaho Indian, Lame Beaver. He and his wife, Blue Leaf, were respected and loved members of their tribe for many years. Indeed the tribe owed much to Lame Beaver. When Lame Beaver died bravely in battle, he was given a chieftain's burial. But Blue Leaf was no longer the wife of a warrior and therefore had no right to a tepee of her own. The women of the tribe gathered around her tepee like a flock of vultures. The poles were seized. The bison skin vanished. The bed and bison rug were hauled away.

The law of the plains made no provision for old worn-out widows. The tribe could not allow its movements to be hampered by such "useless baggage." Blue Leaf had no son to offer her a home and no one else would dream of taking on such a burden as an old widow, so Blue Leaf was abandoned. Her daughter, Clay Basket, was still useful, so she found refuge with an uncle, but Blue Leaf was homeless and friendless.

When the snows came, Blue Leaf survived the first bitter night by huddling with the horses who showed her more compassion than people did. Her daughter found her, still alive but in pitiful condition, and pleaded in vain with her uncle to take her mother in. Then a blizzard struck the camp and in the morning Blue Leaf was found frozen to death.

Such were the "tender mercies" of the Arapahos. They freed themselves from the encumbrance of those who outlived their usefulness by granting them death from exposure and starvation. They let nature take its course. The survival of the fittest was their creed. Doubtless Darwin and his disciples would approve of this custom.

Solomon next wrote about *industry:* "He that tilleth his land shall be satisfied with bread: but he that followeth vain persons is void of understanding" (Proverbs 12:11). This proverb suggests pictures of two men. One is a driver; the other is a drifter.

The first man gets up in the morning, eats his breakfast, puts on his boots, picks up his hoe, and heads for the fields. From sunrise until sunset he toils and tills. Solomon's emphasis was on the result of the labor: "He...shall be satisfied with bread."

The second man rolls over in bed and lazes the morning away. He yawns, gets up, and eats a leisurely meal. A friend stops in—one of those "vain persons" who irked Solomon but pleased his son. They laugh over a stupid joke and make plans that do not include any work. In writing of the drifter, Solomon's emphasis was on the reason for his irresponsible behavior: the man is "void of understanding" and all too ready to follow "vain persons." The drifter uses no more sense in choosing his friends than he uses in employing his time. Woe betide him when hard times come. Without money or skills, he will find his days few and full of grief.

Solomon went on to write about *integrity:* "The wicked desireth the net of evil men: but the root of the righteous yieldeth fruit" (Proverbs 12:12). The word "net" illustrates the use of *metonymy,* the figure of speech in which one noun is used in place of another. Here the cause is substituted for the effect. We can read the verse, "The wicked desires what is caught in the net of the evil man." Evil men set their snares, victimize the unwary, and gloat over their ill-gotten gains. The wicked man looks on and covets what the evil man has obtained as a result of his criminal behavior.

Consider for instance the situation that arose in a small impoverished town in Arkansas where work for black teenagers was practically nonexistent. Even when work could be found, it required backbreaking labor in the rice paddies and soybean fields. Into this town came four brothers, each driving a fancy sports car. They had flashy clothes and plenty of money, and they offered up to two thousand dollars a month to any young man who would return with them to Detroit, where they made their money selling "crack." They had takers, plenty of them, from this and scores of similar dead-end towns. The youths whom the brothers approached lusted after "the net of evil men."

Time magazine said that this particular gang at one time controlled about half of Detroit's crack trade. They ran two hundred drug houses and sold to five hundred more, taking in three million dollars a week. The drug trade looked attractive. It offered cars, women, money, and power—at a price. The price was fear, intimidation, enslavement of thousands of drug users, and their very souls. The price was a life of crime from which few escape. Those who do escape live in fear of being caught and killed by the mob.[2] The story can be repeated around the world as the drug epidemic grows. The lure of money is potent. "The love of money is the root of all evil," Paul said (1 Timothy 6:10).

In contrast to the desire of those who lack integrity, "the root of the righteous yieldeth fruit." Take the case of Ondie Brum, whom I met some time ago at a conference near Atlanta. Ondie had been a drug addict and a habitual criminal. He had spent time in prison in three states. One judge, when sentencing him, told him that he was absolutely hopeless. Ondie took what cures the system offered for heroin addicts, but neither methadone, group therapy, nor shock treatments worked.

Ondie went from bad to worse, little heeding the tears of his blind wife or the accusing looks of his bewildered sons. Then a friend took him to a revival meeting and Ondie met Christ. He was set free! "When God set me free, He did not parole me," he says. "He pardoned me."

Now Ondie travels across the United States to preach Christ to everyone, although he has a special burden for prisoners and drug addicts. One pastor testified: "Ondie has helped me personally with my brother-in-law, who has been addicted to drugs for almost twenty years. Ondie's positive influence over many months has resulted in his conversion." One of Ondie's prize possessions is a letter signed by President George Bush:

> I would like to commend you on your program against drug abuse. Your film *Dead Wrong,* along with your personal testimony, are a powerful tool in the battle....I would like to give my name as one of your endorsements to school administrators. I hope they will listen to your program and give you an opportunity to speak to the students. Keep up the good work.

An even more impressive testimony is the quiet, godly life of this once-violent and vicious man. "The root of the righteous yieldeth fruit," Solomon said. In Ondie's life, where once wickedness reigned, godliness now reigns. As he and I drove back and forth day after day between the motel and the church where we were speaking, I saw the evidence of a transformed life and I knew I was in the presence of one who knew the cleansing power of the blood of Christ and the transforming miracle of regeneration by the Holy Spirit.

4. The Watchful Man (12:13-16)

a. A Saved Man (12:13)

"The wicked is snared by the transgression of his lips: but the just shall come out of trouble."

The point of this proverb reminds me of Hercule Poirot, one of Agatha Christie's favorite sleuths. Hercule did not run around with magnifying glass and dusting powder looking for hidden fingerprints. He did not identify the unusual brand of cigar smoked by the murderer from ash carelessly left at the scene of the crime or search the shrubbery for telltale footprints, like a Sherlock Holmes. Hercule Poirot used "the little gray cells." His favorite method of looking for a murderer was to make the most of his foreign appearance and his deceptively low-key approach. He would get people to talk and sooner or later the murderer always said too much, "snared by the transgression of his lips." The murderer would tell a lie, let slip a scrap of information only the murderer could have known, or be too eager to create a good impression, and Hercule Poirot would have the mystery solved.

The same technique is used in court. The prosecuting attorney tries to get the accused to say something incriminating. The defending attorney tries to trip up the witness and get him to say something that will completely discredit his testimony. It is a war of words based on the principle that "the wicked is snared by the transgression of his lips: but the just shall come out of trouble."

Solomon, in his official capacity as supreme judge of Israel, must have seen this principle at work in a thousand cases. All he had to do was get a person to talk and sooner or later he would say something incriminating or exonerating. "The truth will out," as we say. The just man has nothing to hide and that gives him an enormous advantage because he has no need to tell lies. Lies always lead to more lies. The liar ends up juggling complex and sometimes contradictory statements until at last he can juggle them no longer. The just man's words ring true.

b. A Satisfied Man (12:14)

"A man shall be satisfied with good by the fruit of his mouth: and the recompense of a man's hands shall be rendered unto him." Here Solomon applied the law of sowing and reaping to our words and works. Sooner or later, for richer or for poorer, for better or for worse, our words and works come home to roost. Nehemiah saw the results of his words and works, and he was well satisfied.

Nehemiah, the Persian emperor's cupbearer, was what came to be called in later times a "court Jew"—a gifted and influential Jew who rose to a position of power in the Gentile land where he lived. Nehemiah was like Joseph in Egypt, Daniel in Babylon, and Benjamin Disraeli in Britain.

Nehemiah received news that the repatriated Jews in the promised land were in desperate straits. The walls of Jerusalem were still in ruins and so were the gates of the city. So Nehemiah prayed and fasted. His concern showed on his face. (In those days a servant imperiled his life if he appeared sad before the king.) The king noticed that something was wrong and demanded an explanation. Nehemiah recorded his reaction: "I prayed to the God of heaven. And I said unto the king..." (Nehemiah 2:4-5). We can be quite sure that that prayer was little more than the upward glancing of the eye, for he had already done his extended praying. Nehemiah then explained to the king his deep desire to go to Jerusalem to rebuild the city. The king not only gave him permission; he armed him with letters commanding governors along the way to give him their aid. So Nehemiah was "satisfied with good by the fruit of his mouth."

When Julius Caesar returned from one of his wars, he summed up his campaign in the famous sentence, *Veni, vidi, vici* ("I came, I saw, I conquered"). Nehemiah might have used similar words when he reported back to the Persian emperor. The task of rebuilding the walls of Jerusalem was monumental and formidable. Yet it was accomplished in fifty-two days in the face of all kinds of opposition (Nehemiah 6:15). This accomplishment was a magnificent triumph for the energetic and practical Nehemiah.

As in Proverbs 12:14 mouth and hands are linked together, Nehemiah knew how to speak and he was not afraid to use his hands, even to lay them forcibly on the enemy. He tossed "all the household stuff" of his old enemy Tobiah out of one of the chambers of the temple (Nehemiah 13:8). When he discovered that the Jews had married pagan wives and their children could not even speak Hebrew, he took immediate action. He said, "I contended with them, and cursed them, and smote certain of them, and plucked off their hair" (Nehemiah 13:25). When he found out that one of the grandsons of Eliashib the high priest had actually married a daughter of the old villain Sanballat the Horonite, Nehemiah exploded. "I chased him from me," he said (Nehemiah 13:28). When the task of rebuilding was completed, he was satisfied with the work of his hands. "Remember me, O my God, for good," he wrote as he put down his pen (Nehemiah 13:31).

c. A Sensible Man (12:15-16)

A sensible man *hears counsel:* "The way of a fool is right in his own eyes: but he that hearkeneth unto counsel is wise" (Proverbs 12:15). A fool is cocksure of himself; a wise man never is. A wise man learns from his mistakes and listens to advice, but a fool never does.

Nobody has ever illustrated this principle better than Jack London in his classic *The Call of the Wild.* The sled-dog Buck and his teammates finally arrived at Skagway. Utterly worn out by the trail, they expected to get some rest, but it was not to be. Klondike fever was everywhere. Gold was to be found, so who cared that the dogs were bone-weary? Buck was sold to a couple of Americans, Hal and Charles. They were accompanied by Mercedes, sister of one and wife of the other. Callow tenderfeet, they were impatient to get to the gold fields. Hal and Charles loaded the sled with the tent, other necessities, and all the luxuries the pampered Mercedes insisted on taking along. The sled would not budge. London described the scene:

> Kind-hearted citizens...gave advice. Half the load and twice the dogs, if they ever expected to reach Dawson, was what was said. Hal and his sister and brother-in-law listened unwillingly, pitched tent, and overhauled the outfit....
>
> This accomplished, the outfit, though cut in half, was still a formidable bulk. Charles and Hal went out in the evening and bought six Outside dogs.

The dogs they bought were of little worth, but the greenhorns were not looking for any more advice. Mercedes insisted on riding on the over-burdened sled. London continued:

> The outlook was anything but bright. The two men, however, were quite cheerful. And they were proud, too. They were doing the thing in style, with fourteen dogs. They had seen other sleds depart over the Pass for Dawson, or come in from Dawson, but never had they seen a sled with so many as fourteen dogs. In the nature of Arctic travel there was a reason why fourteen dogs should not drag one sled, and that was that one sled could not carry the food for fourteen dogs. But Charles and Hal did not know this. They had worked the trip out with a pencil, so much to a dog, so many dogs, so many days....It was all so very simple.

After a disastrous trip during which the dogs suffered merciless whippings and some died of starvation, the ill-fated prospectors "staggered into John Thornton's camp at the mouth of White River." London continued:

> Hal did the talking. John Thornton was whittling the last touches on an axe-handle he had made from a stick of birch. He whittled and listened, gave monosyllabic replies, and when it was asked, terse advice. He knew the breed, and he gave his advice in the certainty that it would not be followed.
>
> "They told us up above that the bottom was dropping out of the trail and that the best thing for us to do was to lay over," Hal said in response to Thornton's warning to take no more chances on the rotten ice. "They told us we couldn't make White River, and here we are." This last with a sneering ring of triumph in it.
>
> "And they told you true," John Thornton answered. "The bottom's likely to drop out at any moment. Only fools, with the blind luck of fools, could have made it. I tell you straight, I wouldn't risk my carcass on that ice for all the gold in Alaska."
>
> "That's because you're not a fool, I suppose," said Hal. "All the same, we'll go on to Dawson." He uncoiled his whip. "Get up there, Buck! Hi! Get up there! Mush on!"
>
> Thornton went on whittling. It was idle, he knew, to get between a fool and his folly.

Thornton rescued Buck from his persecutors and the sled pulled away.

> Dog and man watched it crawling along over the ice. Suddenly, they saw its back drop down, as into a rut, and the gee-pole, with Hal clinging to it, jerk into the air. Mercedes' scream came to their ears. They saw Charles turn and make one step to run back, and then a whole section of ice give way and dogs and humans disappear. A yawning hole was all that was to be seen. The bottom had dropped out of the trail.[3]

Solomon was right. "The way of a fool is right in his own eyes: but he that hearkeneth to counsel is wise."

The sensible man also *has compassion:* "A fool's wrath is presently known: but a prudent man covereth shame" (Proverbs 12:16). The word translated "covereth" here means "concealeth." The prudent man's compassion throws into sharp relief the fool's public rage. Shimei was just such a fool.

David, who had granted the rich Shimei a stay of execution, was by no means deceived by him. When David handed the kingdom over to Solomon, he advised his son to execute Shimei. Solomon in turn summoned Shimei and said, "Build thee an house in Jerusalem, and dwell there, and go not forth thence any whither. For it shall be, that on the day thou goest out, and passest over the brook Kidron, thou shalt know for certain that thou shalt surely die: thy blood shall be upon thine own head" (1 Kings 2:36-37).

For a while it seemed that Shimei had learned his lesson and had become a loyal, law-abiding subject of David's throne. However Shimei chafed at his house arrest. At the end of three years two of his servants ran away. They preferred to seek asylum with a pagan king, Achish of Gath, than to endure the misery of servitude to Shimei one more day. Shimei was furious when he discovered that his servants had gone. When he learned where they were, he determined to get them back.

"And Shimei arose, and saddled his ass, and went to Gath to Achish to seek his servants: and Shimei went, and brought his servants from Gath" (1 Kings 2:40). His triumph was short-lived, however. He was summoned before Solomon, who read his sentence, which was based on Shimei's evil nature: "Thou knowest all the wickedness which thine heart is privy to, that thou didst to David my father: therefore the Lord shall return thy wickedness upon thine own head" (2:44). A few minutes later Shimei was executed.

Had Shimei been a prudent man, he would have swallowed his pride, resentment, and outrage at the defection of his servants. He would have submitted to the disgrace of being under house arrest and accepted the shame as something he had brought on himself. He was fortunate to be alive after the terrible words he had once said to David.

Had Shimei been a prudent man, he would have covered his shame by being grateful to David and Solomon for their grace. If Shimei had allowed the miracle of grace to change his nature, in time his shame might have been forgotten and his servants might have marveled at his new-found compassion. Instead Shimei deeply resented David, Solomon, grace, goodness, and glory. He fumed away until he stood exposed at last for what he was—a born rebel with a foul temper and an even fouler tongue. He was utterly devoid of even the most elementary common sense.

Shimei could not cover his lack of compassion toward his servants. This vile man could not cover his own shame. Still less could he, or would he, cover the shame of anyone else. Indeed he took pleasure in taunts and curses. (See 2 Samuel 16:5-8.)

5. The Wordy Man (12:17-23)

a. Perverted Words (12:17)

Solomon had much to say about the tongue—its abusive and abrasive power as well as its power to explain, exonerate, and exalt. Special perils lie in wait for the wordy man. Many sins are sins of the tongue. Thinking of the man who speaks perverted words, Solomon wrote, "He that speaketh truth sheweth forth righteousness: but a false witness deceit."

Imagine we are in court. The judge is on the bench and the prisoner is at the bar. Witnesses are summoned to testify. Attorneys probe for the truth because even in a court of law—surrounded by solemnity, sworn to tell the truth, the whole truth, and nothing but the truth—people still lie. All too often Truth lies stabbed and bleeding on the courtroom floor when the last witness has been called and the final verdict has been reached. The great illustration of lying in a courtroom is of course the trial of Jesus before the Sanhedrin.

Simon Greenleaf published a volume in which he re-examined the trial of Jesus. Greenleaf was dean of the Harvard Law School, and it was largely through his efforts that this school rose to eminence. He wrote a textbook, *A Treatise on the Law of Evidence*, which immediately became famous and ran through twelve editions, one following another almost every two years. Dean Wigmore of the Northwestern Law School declared that "in the opinions of every court for the last fifty years occur references to this work of Greenleaf's."[4]

The volume on the trial of Jesus came out when Greenleaf was a mature lawyer, sixty-three years old. This great work is entitled *The Testimony of the Evangelists, Examined by the Rules of Evidence Administered in Courts of Justice.*[5] In the preface, addressed "To The Members of The Legal Profession," he wrote:

> If a close examination of the evidences of Christianity may be expected of one class of men more than another, it would seem incumbent on us, who make the law of evidence one of our peculiar studies. Our profession leads us to explore the mazes of falsehood, to detect its artifices, to pierce its thickest veils, to follow and expose its sophistries, to compare the

statements of different witnesses with severity, to discover truth and separate it from error.

"The death of Jesus," Greenleaf said, "is universally regarded among Christians as a cruel murder, perpetrated under the pretense of a legal sentence after a trial in which the forms of law were essentially and grossly violated." The evaluation of the trial hinges on the credibility of the witnesses—those who testified against Him at the trial and were accused by the four evangelists as being false witnesses—and on the credibility of the evangelists themselves.

Among the many interesting points Greenleaf made about the laws of evidence is this:

> It is not possible for the wit of man to invent a story, which, if closely compared with the actual occurrences of the same time and place, may not be shown to be false. Hence it is that a false witness will not willingly detail any circumstances in which his testimony will be open to contradiction, nor multiply them where there is danger of his being detected, by a comparison of them with other accounts, equally circumstantial. He will rather deal in general statements and broad assertions; and if he finds it necessary for his purpose to employ names and particular circumstances in his story, he will endeavor to invent such as shall be out of reach of all opposing proof, and he will be most forward and minute in details, where he knows that any danger of contradiction is at least apprehended. Therefore it is that variety and minuteness of detail are usually regarded as certain tests of sincerity, if the story, in the circumstances related, is of a nature capable of easy refutation if it were false.

Greenleaf demonstrated the absolute credibility of Matthew, Mark, Luke, and John as witnesses to the extraordinary life and astonishing claims of Jesus. Their testimony would stand the most severe cross-examination in a court of law. Paul put it this way, years after his own spectacular conversion: "This is a faithful saying, and worthy of all acceptation, that Christ Jesus came into the world to save sinners" (1 Timothy 1:15). J. B. Phillips's translation reads, "This statement is completely reliable and should be universally accepted:—'Christ Jesus entered the world to rescue sinners.'"

To this day the Jews, in their resolute rejection of Christ, maintain that there was nothing illegal or irregular about the trial of Jesus and that the sentence was just. They maintain that he was accused of blasphemy and convicted by the evidence. The four evangelists put the lie to that claim and Simon Greenleaf proved them to be reliable, honest, and accurate witnesses. Truly, "he that speaketh truth sheweth forth righteousness: but a false witness deceit."

b. Piercing Words (12:18)

"There is that speaketh like the piercings of a sword: but the tongue of the wise is health." This verse reminds me of words that hurt a friend of mine who some time ago found himself in deep waters. His wife was dying of a particularly painful form of cancer in a hospital far away from where my wife and I were living. I discovered by talking to his daughter that he was taking his wife's impending death very hard indeed. His natural suffering was compounded by false teachers who were telling him that if he had enough faith his wife would get better. Their sophistries added to his anguish. Not only was his beloved dying an agonizing death; he believed her condition was his fault because his lack of faith was preventing her from being healed. Of all the devilish doctrines I have heard, I would find it hard to think of a crueler one than that. My friend's daughter told me her dad was distracted and tormented by those piercing words.

I decided to visit my friend. It was a two-day drive to the city where this tragedy was taking place, but I needed every mile to think about what to say to him. I found him walking up and down the corridor of the hospital ward, wringing his hands in despair, and bursting into tears afresh at the thought of his beloved one's agony and his inability to generate enough faith to secure her healing.

We found a secluded spot and I came straight to the point. "Mary is going to die," I said. "The doctors have done all that doctors can do, and you have worn yourself out praying. But she is going to die. Let me read what God says about this." I turned with him to 1 Corinthians 3:21-24. "All things are yours," I read. Then I said, "Notice what things the Bible says are yours: 'Whether Paul, or Apollos, or Cephas [no matter *who*], or the world [no matter *where*], or life, or death [no matter *what*], or things present, or things to come [no matter *when*]; all are yours; And ye are Christ's; and Christ is God's.'"

"Did you notice," I continued, "that one of the things God has given you at this time is *death*? It is yours! God says so. And why has He given you this extraordinary gift? Because He loves you. It is no fault of yours that Mary is dying, no matter what people say. She is dying because God wants her to die. Right now death is the kindest gift He could possibly give you. Death will release her from her sufferings and it will lift her into the immediate presence of the Lord she has loved and served so well these many years. For her it will be instant glory. Death is God's gift to her, and it is God's gift to you. You will no longer have to haunt the corridors of this hospital. You will be able to go home and get on with your life and prove for yourself that you are Christ's and Christ is God's and that He is too loving to be unkind, too wise to make any mistakes, and too powerful to be thwarted in His perfect will."

My friend smiled suddenly, for the first time since I arrived at the hospital. "Thank you," he said. "I needed that." I do not consider myself to be wise. I have made my quota of stupid mistakes. But on that occasion at least, "the tongue of the wise" was health. My friend was able to shake off the false teachings and with God's help take fresh charge of his life.

c. Permanent Words (12:19)

"The lip of truth shall be established for ever: but a lying tongue is but for a moment." Even the most elaborate fabrication will fail in the end. Lies carry the seeds of their own dissolution. They seem to be a convenient refuge for the moment, but they are made of sorry stuff. Because we are living in enemy territory, lies sometimes seem to prosper and serve their purpose. We live in a world presided over by the father of lies, the very idiom of whose language is the lie.

In contrast to lies, truth is hewn out of the bedrock of eternity. Truth is at one with the character of God. We can do nothing to thwart the truth. Since the highest court (much higher than fallen Lucifer's) is presided over by Him who is the truth, in the end all lies must fail.

Ultimate truth is found in the Bible. "Thy word is truth," Jesus said (John 17:17). He Himself is the truth (John 14:6). That is why the theory of evolution for instance is so palpably false. It flies in the face of revealed truth (Genesis 1; John 1:1-3; Colossians 1:15-16; Hebrews 1:1-2).

Consider the celebrated case of the Piltdown Man. The "scientific" name given to this supposed "missing link" is *Eoanthropus Dawsoni*, the Dawn-Man-of-Dawson; it was named after the man who had the doubtful honor of discovering it.

About the year 1908, Dawson received a small skull fragment from workmen who were digging in a shallow gravel pit at Piltdown, England, and had been requested to watch for fossils. Some years later, Dawson reported, he picked up two more small parts of a skull while visiting the same spot. A year after that, according to Dawson, part of a jawbone of some man or animal was discovered in the same spot. On that same occasion one of Dawson's friends found another tiny skull fragment. A year later a priest named Teilhard found a tooth. In the same gravel, assorted animal bones were also found. All the bones mentioned above were put together to create the Piltdown Man. The bones were said to be evidence of man's evolution from the apes.

Before the discovery was quite complete (the single tooth had not yet been found) Dawson and Woodward made a plaster-of-Paris reconstruction of the skull of the "missing link," as they presumed it to be. Hoping that they had a transition form, they made a plaster model of a head, half man and half ape. They gave the head the size they thought such an intermediate creature should have, with about 1,070 cubic centimeters of brain capacity. Into this plaster head-cast they pressed the skull fragments as they supposed them to relate to one another. Into the jaw, which they molded into what was considered the proper chinless shape, they forced the half-jaw fossil. They later gave the tooth a place next to the lower jaw.

Sir Arthur Keith, the head of the English Royal College of Surgeons, himself an evolutionist, took issue with Dawson and Woodward as to the manner in which their reconstruction of the skull had been accomplished. Keith figured the skull should be larger than they had made it. He thought the brain capacity should be about 1,500 cubic centimeters instead of 1,070. The argument was carried on for months in *Nature* magazine. The fragments themselves were arranged and rearranged. In 1925 Keith wrote a new book on human evolution in which he contended, "In its general conformation it [the skull] does not differ materially from human skulls of modern type."[6]

Nor were all evolutionists agreed on where in the jaw the tooth belonged. As to the half-jaw, scientists of the highest standing emphatically declared that it did not belong with the skull fragments at all. Indeed, some said it belonged to a chimpanzee.[7]

Evolutionists refuse to discuss the Piltdown Man anymore. Oxford University anthropologist I. S. Weiner, with the aid of Kenneth Oakley, a British Museum geologist, proved him to be an elaborate forgery.

Sooner or later, despite the propaganda of the National Geographic Society, *Time-Life* books, the media, and the academic community, "the lip of truth shall be established for ever: but a lying tongue is but for a moment." Any theory that contradicts the plain statements of Scripture concerning the origin of life and the creation of man cannot prevail. In time all lies, however elaborately crafted and cleverly propagated, must fail.

d. Profound Words (12:20-21)

Profound words give *peace* in the face of evil. "Deceit is in the heart of them that imagine evil: but to the counsellors of peace is joy" (Proverbs 12:20).

Think for instance of the contrast between Abner (King Saul's general) and Joab (David's general). Although Abner promoted the wrong cause, he was essentially a decent individual. Joab, who promoted the right cause, was essentially a wicked man. Joab accused Abner of deceit, but Joab was the one who was deceitful.

When Abner decided to end the civil war by taking his faction over to David, Joab reacted at once. He said to David: "Thou knowest Abner the son of Ner, that he came to deceive thee, and to know thy going out and thy coming in, and to know all that thou doest" (2 Samuel 3:25). Joab hurried after Abner, gave him a cheery greeting, and suggested they have a quiet talk together. Doubtless Abner thought Joab had been sent by David to work out the details of the surrender. In any case, Abner was completely disarmed by Joab's friendly manner. But we read that "Joab took him aside in the gate to speak with him quietly, and smote him there under the fifth rib, that he died" (3:27).

Joab used a similar, deceitful tactic to get rid of Amasa, another potential rival. "And Joab said to Amasa, Art thou in health, my brother? And Joab took Amasa by the beard with the right hand to kiss him. But Amasa took no heed to the sword that was in Joab's hand: so he smote him therewith in the fifth rib...and he died" (2 Samuel 20:9-10). The deception was all the more treacherous in this case because Amasa was blood kin to Joab. Joab was an evil man so he imagined that both Abner and Amasa were evil. Deceit was in Joab's heart. No wonder David eventually handed him over to judgment.

Abner was quite different from Joab. When Abner came to David to lay down the arms of rebellion, "David sent Abner away; and he went in peace" (2 Samuel 3:21). Peace means that the war is over. Abner went home that night with the peace of David reigning in his heart. Joy filled Abner's soul. For the first time in many years he knew that all was well. The Lord's anointed had sent him away in peace! Abner could not wait to tell others. He was foully murdered by Joab shortly afterward, but for the days he had left, this counselor of peace knew joy. Likewise when people come to great David's greater Son, the Lord Jesus, He sends them away in peace and His Spirit brings the fruit of love, joy, and peace into their hearts (Galatians 5:22).

Profound words also give *protection* in the face of evil: "There shall no evil happen to the just: but the wicked shall be filled with mischief" (Proverbs 12:21). The first part of the verse can be paraphrased, "Nothing happens in vain to the just." God always takes the long-range view. Since we tend to be preoccupied with the short-range view, this proverb seems overly optimistic to us. Some even say the statement simply isn't true. God, however, plans for the long haul and speaks from His omniscient perspective out of the vastness of eternity.

C. S. Lewis, in his fascinating book *The Great Divorce*, captures the idea of differing perspectives. The great divorce of which he writes is the divorce between Heaven and Hell, between the tragically narrow and bitter outlook of the lost and the glorious broad outlook of the redeemed. As the story begins, some of the people living in the drab gray city of the underworld get a chance to take a bus ride to the outskirts of Heaven. C. S. Lewis pictures the dismal world of the lost—its mean streets, endless drizzling rain, dingy lodgings, billboards from which posters hang in rags. Everything is old, run-down, and depressing. The little crowd at the bus stop is quarrelsome and mean-spirited. The more exciting inhabitants have long since moved away. Eternal twilight hangs over the city. The rumor is fearfully whispered about that eventually the sky will become totally and eternally dark.

The bus arrives at last, then makes its way up out of a vast abyss and comes up over the top of the cliff, leaving an enormous gaping canyon behind. The bus stops and its passengers, mere ghosts, alight into a bright, solid, real world. They are met by solid, bright people who have made the journey from Deep Heaven in the hope of being able to help some of the ghost people see reality from Heaven's point of view.

The narrator describes some of his own experiences in this outpost of Heaven. Like the other ghosts, he doesn't like the brightness and hard reality. His conversation with one of the bright people gets around to whether or not the redeemed feel eternal loss and unhappiness because some of their loved ones end up in Hell. The shining one to whom he is speaking simply labels that question as "the demand of the loveless and self-imprisoned that they should be allowed to blackmail the universe." In short, "Hell should be able to *veto* Heaven."[8]

C. S. Lewis's answer is profound. From the standpoint of Heaven, even Hell itself ceases to have any significance for the redeemed. "There shall no evil happen to the just," Solomon said, even though the wicked be "filled with mischief." To us nothing could be worse than the thought of a loved one banished forever in a lost eternity. That is because we are still in time, not yet in eternity. We are still bound (even though we have been redeemed and have the Spirit of God and the Word of God to guide us) by the limitations of our mortality.

For the ghost in *The Great Divorce,* Hell seems very real—a big place full of loneliness, anger, hatred, and envy. He describes to a bright one from Deep Heaven the vast abyss from which the bus ascended. His teacher points to a crack in the soil, so tiny that the ghost could not have identified it if it had not been pointed out to him. "I cannot be certain that this *is* the crack ye came up through," the bright one says. "But through a crack no bigger than that ye certainly came."[9] In other words, from the glorious standpoint of Heaven, all Hell is smaller than an atom. From the glorious standpoint of eternity, no evil happens to the just. All that happens to us here on earth will take on new and glorious significance in Heaven. We will see that everything that happened on earth was for our eternal good and His eternal glory. As hymnist Charles A. Tindley put it, "We'll understand it better by and by."

e. Perverse Words (12:22)

"Lying lips are abomination to the Lord: but they that deal truly are his delight." This proverb reminds me of the woman whose husband was caught lying to the judge. She said, "I told him he should only lie when it is beneficial. Now, I tell lies," she continued, "but I only tell lies when they're going to do me some good." Many people have a similar philosophy. But God hates all lies, even those we think are going to do us some good.

Machiavelli had lying lips. He was the first avowed proponent of the dogma that force and fraud are proper instruments of state-craft, that politics should be divorced from ethics, and that public and private virtue are two different things. His writings, *The Prince* and *Discourses,* contain numerous examples of successful violence and treachery. He drew models from the writings of the Roman historian Livy and from the careers of Cesare Borgia and Pope Alexander VI, whose infamous treacheries he greatly admired. "It is necessary for a prince that will achieve great matters to learn to be a cunning deceiver," Machiavelli wrote. "That man who will profess honesty in all his actions must needs go to ruin amongst so many that are dishonest."[10]

The Prince was never intended for publication. Written in 1513 for Lorenzo de Medici, the tyrant who had just overthrown the Florentine republic, the volume was meant to be a personal handbook of instructions on how to retain the power he had just seized. When the book was let loose upon the world in 1532, five years after Machiavelli's death, it took Europe by storm. It was translated into every European language and became the statesman's bible. Speaking of *The Prince*, someone said:

> It guided Thomas Cromwell in his unscrupulous service of Henry VIII. It inspired Catherine de Medici in the intrigues that culminated in the massacre of St. Bartholomew. It fortified Philip II in his efforts to entrap and assassinate Elizabeth. It strengthened Elizabeth in the great game she played, with crown and life at stake, against Mary, Queen of Scots.

It also inspired Napoleon, Hitler, and Stalin in their duplicities and atrocities.

"Lying lips are abomination to the Lord," wrote Solomon, who was wiser and shrewder than the crafty Italian writer and statesman. Machiavelli died in exile and dishonor after a life of disappointment. He was distrusted by everyone. Cesare Borgia, the incarnation of Machiavellian cunning and cruelty, was finally hounded out of Italy to perish in the Pyrenees. He was covered with loathing and dread. Thomas Cromwell's life ended on the gallows. Philip II failed in his machinations against Queen Elizabeth and saw his "invincible armada" torn to shreds by English sea dogs, fierce plunderers, stormy winds, and rocky coasts of the British Isles. The sanguinary and treacherous Catherine de Medici lived to see her sons die and the house of Valois, on behalf of which she sinned so deeply, reduced to extinction. Napoleon ended his days an exile on St. Helena. Hitler committed suicide. Stalin's memory is forever accursed.[11] "Though the mills of God grind slowly," says the English proverb, "yet they grind exceeding small."

f. Prudent Words (12:23)

"A prudent man concealeth knowledge: but the heart of fools proclaimeth foolishness." Sometimes it is best not to tell everything you know. Some things should not be told to everyone you know.

The prophet Samuel knew when and to whom to speak. He spoke prudently when he told Saul he would be Israel's first king, and when he later told Saul he had lost the kingdom forever.

Samuel did not take kindly at first to the idea of a monarchy, at least not until he met David. The Old Testament characters, even the greatest and godliest of them, were "men of like passions" as we are. Samuel seemed put out when the people demanded a king. He did not believe that a monarchy would be an improvement on the theocracy. Both systems of government had weak points because both ultimately had to involve people, and people are notoriously frail. Still, on the whole, a monarchy was more perilous than a theocracy, especially a monarchy related to a dynasty. A monarchy could easily become oppressive. A dynasty could alternate strong and weak kings, wise and foolish kings, good and bad kings, and godly and wicked kings.

In any case, the people's reason for demanding a monarchy couldn't have been worse. "Make us a king to judge us," they said, "like all the nations" (1 Samuel 8:5). Conformity to the world was the poorest of all reasons for wanting a king. The added reason, "Behold, thou art old, and thy sons walk not in thy ways," only rubbed salt into Samuel's wound. Under a theocracy his sons would not inherit his mantle anyway; God would raise up His own man.

Still the voice of God broke through Samuel's tumultuous thoughts: "Hearken unto the voice of the people" (1 Samuel 8:7). Their rebellion in this situation, God explained to Samuel, was no different from previous instances of rebellion. "They have not rejected thee," God said, "but they have rejected me, that I should not reign over them."

In the process of time it was revealed to Samuel that Saul, a Benjamite and a physical giant, was just the kind of man the people wanted (and deserved) as their king. Saul stumbled over Samuel when hunting for some lost asses, and although "all Israel from Dan even to Beer-sheba knew that Samuel was established to be a prophet of the Lord," Saul didn't (1 Samuel 3:20; 9:18). This lack of knowledge was an indication of Saul's spiritual ignorance.

When the time came for Samuel to reveal to Saul that he was to be the king, "as they were going down to the end of the city, Samuel said to Saul, Bid the servant pass on before us...but stand thou still a while, that I may show thee the word of God" (1 Samuel 9:27). The time for a public announcement had not yet come. Although it was important that Saul be apprised of what was in the wind, it was equally important that the news be kept private for the time being. "A prudent man concealeth knowledge."

Saul proved to be an erratic king, swinging from one extreme to another. Then he disobeyed by not completely destroying Amalek, and God rejected Saul. Samuel denounced Saul privately to his face

(1 Samuel 15:16ff.). A thoroughly humbled Saul pleaded with the prophet to forgive him. "Turn again with me," Saul said, "that I may worship the Lord" (15:25). Samuel refused because Saul's disobedience had gone too far.

Then Saul said, "I have sinned: yet honour me now, I pray thee, before the elders of my people, and before Israel, and turn again with me, that I may worship the Lord thy God" (1 Samuel 15:30). This time Samuel did as Saul requested. Being a prudent man, Samuel knew how to conceal a matter. The time was not appropriate to undermine Saul's reputation. Some semblance of authority had to be left to Saul if law and order were to be maintained in the country. Besides, Saul's successor had not yet been revealed. In any case, Samuel knew that the Spirit of the Lord had departed from Saul and it would soon be evident that he was only a shadow king. Only a fool proclaims foolishness, wrote Solomon. Even though Saul had all the makings and markings of a prize fool, Samuel was no fool.

6. The Willing Man (12:24)

"The hand of the diligent shall bear rule: but the slothful shall be under tribute." Solomon did not need to look far for an illustration of this proverb. He had in his employ a diligent young man named Jeroboam.

Jeroboam's father, a man named Nebat from the village of Zeredah in the Jordan valley, had been one of Solomon's officials. Jeroboam's mother Zeruah had already been widowed at the time of his birth (1 Kings 11:26). Solomon kept his eyes open for eager, diligent young men to help in the administration of his kingdom, and Jeroboam came to his attention. While Solomon was engaged in extensive building projects in Jerusalem, he noticed that young Jeroboam was obviously a man of industry and ability who was not afraid of hard work. Solomon asked Jeroboam to oversee the heavy work assigned to the tribes of Ephraim and Manasseh (11:27-28).

"The hand of the diligent shall bear rule," said Solomon ruefully, knowing only too well who would sit on the schismatic throne of ten of the tribes once he was dead—not his son, but that diligent young man Jeroboam. Rehoboam, Solomon's son and heir, illustrates the second part of the proverb: "The slothful shall be under tribute."

Rehoboam reigned over what was left of David's empire, the two tribes of Judah and Benjamin. He started energetically enough, fortifying a number of cities in his little kingdom. His motivation seemed to be fear that the virile Jeroboam might try to seize the rest of the kingdom (2 Chronicles 11:5-12). But Rehoboam's zeal did not last long, if his spiritual lethargy is a good indicator, for he soon lapsed into idolatry (1 Kings 14:21-24; 2 Chronicles 11:13-15; 12:1).

Rehoboam is an example of a slothful man. Surely he should have had sense enough to know that Jeroboam had his hands full consolidating his power and had no ambition to conquer Judah. The real threat to Judah came from another quarter: Egypt, under the powerful and expansionist Pharaoh Shishak, was the country Rehoboam should have watched. A David would have been out with his troops, hardening them against the day of battle, marching them, exercising them, teaching them tactics, and building a long line of fortifications along his southern borders. A diligent king would have been making sure that his first line of defense—his treaty relationship with the living God—was in good repair. But Rehoboam was far too fond of ease.

The sacred historian almost sarcastically commented that Rehoboam had eighteen wives, sixty concubines, twenty-eight sons, and sixty daughters (2 Chronicles 11:21). Rehoboam was much too fond of his pleasures. As a result, when the Egyptian army did come, the pharaoh quickly defeated Rehoboam and exacted a hefty tribute (1 Kings 14:25-28; 2 Chronicles 12:2-12). Both diligence and neglect of duty bring their own rewards.

7. The Woeful Man (12:25)

"Heaviness in the heart of man maketh it stoop: but a good word maketh it glad." Paul experienced both during his second missionary journey. James Stalker said:

> This journey was not only the greatest he achieved but perhaps the most momentous recorded in the annals of the human race. In its issues it far rivaled the expedition of Alexander the Great, when he carried the arms and civilization of Greece into the heart of Asia, or that of Caesar when he landed on the shores of Britain, or even the voyage of Columbus, when he discovered a New World. Yet, when he set out on it, he had no idea of the magnitude which it was to assume or even the direction it was to take.[12]

The man God used to accomplish this mission, though the chief of all the apostles, was very frail and human, "touched with the feeling of our infirmities" like the Master he served (Hebrews 4:15). Paul was savagely beaten at Philippi, bitterly persecuted at Thessalonica, and driven out of Berea. Sore in body, perplexed in mind, and anxious for the babes in Christ he had left behind, Paul continued on his way.

Driven out of Macedonia, Paul continued south into Achaia— the real Greece and the home of genius. His eyes took in the sights all about him, sights that reminded him of many boyhood history lessons. As he left Berea he looked back and saw the snowy peaks of mount Olympus, where the Greek gods supposedly lived. If, as some think, he went by sea, he sailed past Thermopylae, where the immortal Three Hundred stood against all the Persian hordes. As his voyage drew to an end, he saw the island of Salamis where Greece was again saved from enslavement by the valor of her sailor sons. But Paul cared little for sightseeing. He was full of that heaviness of heart of which Solomon wrote. Paul was bowed beneath a burden—his concern for the new converts at Thessalonica.

Paul arrived in Athens alone. Silas was gone and Timothy was gone. He hoped they were in Macedonia encouraging the infant church and gathering news for him. We can picture Paul wandering the streets of Athens. For the moment his anxieties were superseded by his indignation. *How could these clever Greeks be so stupid?* he must have wondered. *Look at all these idols and images! Why, there is even one to "the unknown god."* Before long he had an opportunity to preach to the intellectuals on famous Mars Hill. However, he was stung to the quick by the Athenians' reaction to the gospel and he left Athens never to return. The Athenians did not persecute him. Paul was used to persecution and would even have welcomed it. No, they just laughed at him.

Paul's former ache returned, more gnawing than ever. He felt renewed concern for the babes in Christ at Berea, Thessalonica, and Philippi. Truly, "heaviness in the heart of man maketh it stoop." Bowed and burdened, he came to the bustling Greek seaport of Corinth. He dreaded receiving the same kind of reception here that he had received in the snobbish university city of Athens, but he subordinated his fears and heartache and plunged into the work of evangelism. Then his colleagues came from Thessalonica with the best of news. All was well. The churches were flourishing and growing. Hallelujah! Paul seized his pen to write 1 Thessalonians. "A good word maketh [the heart] glad," wrote Solomon, and Paul certainly said, "Amen!"

8. The Worthy Man (12:26)

"The righteous is more excellent than his neighbour: but the way of the wicked seduceth them." The phrase translated "more excellent than his neighbour" can be rendered "guideth his neigh-bor." The word translated "seduceth" can be rendered "leads them astray."

This proverb is illustrated in the story of Naomi. In the days of her bereavement and backsliding she gave terrible advice. When her two widowed daughters-in-law, Orpah and Ruth, expressed an interest in her new resolution to return to Bethlehem, the place where God had put His name and where He visited His people, she reacted at once. She knew the deep hostility the Hebrews felt toward Moabites. "No, girls," she said in effect. "If I were you, I'd stay in Moab. You'll have a much better chance of getting remarried in Moab than in Bethlehem. I can't think of a single self-respecting Jew who would marry a Moabitess." This was dreadful, wicked advice—the advice of a woman who had been out of fellowship with God and His people for ten years (Ruth 1:10-15).

In Orpah's case "the way of the wicked" led her astray. She started out with Naomi but went back to Moab, back to the demon gods of her people, back into the dark. God blotted her name, so to speak, out of His Book, and we never read of her again. Naomi had Orpah's lost soul on her conscience for as long as she lived.

Ruth was made of sterner stuff. She went all the way with Naomi to Bethlehem. There she met Boaz, the kinsman-redeemer who was able and willing to do for Ruth, in an Old Testament picture-book kind of way, all that the Lord Jesus does for us in a real, spiritual, and eternal way. And Naomi—restored now to the Lord, back in fellow-ship with His people—was able to give the good, godly, spiritual counsel Ruth needed. Indeed, "the righteous guideth his neighbor."

Naomi told Ruth to go to Boaz, put herself at his feet, and ask to be redeemed. She was to ask that great prince of the house of Judah to make her his very own and put her into his family (Ruth 3:1-9). Ruth hastened to take this advice. As a result her soul was saved and her name will be honored for the rest of time. We need to remain in fellowship with God so that our words and actions may be a blessing to those around us, not a curse.

9. The Wasteful Man (12:27)

"The slothful man roasteth not that which he took in hunting: but the substance of a diligent man is precious."

The slothful man goes to a great deal of trouble to get something he thinks he wants. However as soon as he gets it, he loses all interest in it. He is like a child with a new toy. Soon he yawns over it. He's bored with it as soon as it is within his grasp. If the man is a hunter, he never uses the meat of his prey. By the time he gets around to roasting the meat, it is spoiled or stolen. It's too late, but he doesn't really care. His interest in the chase was only superficial at best.

The diligent man knows the value of what he has. He knows its substance and its worth. He remembers the time before it ever was his, how long he yearned for it, his joy when he obtained it, and how much he has come to prize it.

The shadows of the two men pictured in Proverbs 12:27 lie across the Epistle to the Hebrews. One Jew comes right up to the point of salvation. He has long hunted after the truth. He has paid a price in toil and persistence to pursue his quest. The establishment has eyed him with disfavor. Other obstacles have been in his way. But the truth as it is in Christ Jesus has been revealed to him at last. There is only one more step. He must accept Christ—he must roast that which he hath taken in hunting. He must appropriate all that there is in Christ for himself. The feast is within his grasp. At this point, however, for one reason or another, he gives it all up. The book of Hebrews has many dire warnings for him.

Another Jew goes all the way. The frowns and threats of organized religion, the disapproval of the establishment, the loss of status in the community, and the pressure of family and friends cannot deter him. He has long desired to have and to hold the glorious prize available in Christ and in Christ alone. Now, having made Christ his very own, he knows the worth and value of what he has. Having Him, he has all. He was diligent in his search for this great possession and now he is equally diligent in safeguarding it against all who would rob him of it if they could. He appreciates the substance of the gospel, the eternal verities that are now his.

Christ has become exceedingly precious to the second man. He has found the one thing truly worth possessing in this world and the world to come, and it is precious. He has found that precious cornerstone of which the apostle speaks in 1 Peter 2:6. He has been redeemed "with the precious blood of Christ" (1 Peter 1:19). He has found "precious faith" (2 Peter 1:1). He has staked his claim to "exceeding great and precious promises" (2 Peter 1:4). "Jesus is precious" is his testimony. Solomon would have approved of the second man.

10. The Worshiping Man (12:28)

"In the way of righteousness is life; and in the pathway thereof there is no death." Can it be that there is no death? It all depends on who is speaking.

Spiritists maintain there is no death. They claim to be in touch with those who have passed from this life to the next. Spiritists claim that they receive comforting messages from the other side and at the same time deny the cardinal doctrines of the Word of God. Spiritists are wrong; they are dupes of demons. Their mediums are deceived by familiar spirits who impersonate the dead and tell lies. All such communication with spirits is devilish and dangerous and is expressly forbidden by the Word of God (Leviticus 20:27).

Mary Baker Eddy, the founder of the Christian Science cult, taught that there is no death. Death, she said, is an error of mortal mind.[13] She should have known better. Her first husband, George Washington Glover, died in June 1844 at Wilmington, North Carolina. Her third husband, Asa Gilbert Eddy, died on June 3, 1882. The doctor said he died of a heart ailment, but Mary Baker Eddy knew better than the doctor. She said he died of "mental arsenic." (Husband number two made good his escape by eloping with one of his patients.) She seemed desperately eager to convince herself that there is no death. It was a profitable farce until she herself died of old age on December 3, 1910, and was buried in Mount Auburn Cemetery in Cambridge, Massachusetts.

If her claim was foolish, how could Solomon write, "There is no death"? When death comes to the child of God the transition from death to life is instantaneous.

When Jesus talked to Martha on the way to Lazarus's tomb, He could have said, as He did elsewhere, "A greater than Solomon is here" (Matthew 12:42). He could have said, as He did elsewhere, "I am come that [ye] might have life and that [ye] might have it more abundantly" (John 10:10). Instead Jesus spoke the last word on death. "Thy brother shall rise again," He said to Martha (John 11:23). When Martha affirmed her belief in the resurrection at the last day, He said: "I am the resurrection, and the life [the source of *resurrection* life]: he that believeth in me, though he were dead, yet shall he live [the source of *spiritual* life]: And whosoever liveth and believeth in me shall never die [the source of *eternal* life]" (John 11:25-26). In Christ death is swallowed up indeed (2 Corinthians 5:4).

There is no death for the believer. "Absent from the body... present with the Lord" was Paul's memorable way of stating his belief (2 Corinthians 5:6-8). So confident was he of entering into life at death, he could say that he had "a desire to depart, and to be with Christ; which is far better" (Philippians 1:23).

But it must also be said that death is very real indeed for the unbeliever. A lost eternity awaits him at the end of life's journey. He will not only be absent from the body but also absent from the Lord.

CHAPTER 17

Proverbs 13:1-25

C. Verities to Be Considered (13:1-25)
   1. Truth about Listening (13:1)
   2. Truth about Living (13:2-3)
     a. Having a Clean Mouth (13:2)
     b. Having a Closed Mouth (13:3)
   3. Truth about Laziness (13:4)
   4. Truth about Lying (13:5)
   5. Truth about Limits (13:6)
   6. Truth about Liberality (13:7)
   7. Truth about Life (13:8-11)
     a. A Perilous Life Depicted (13:8)
     b. A Prolonged Life Depicted (13:9)
     c. A Provocative Life Depicted (13:10)
     d. A Prosperous Life Depicted (13:11)
   8. Truth about Languishing (13:12)
   9. Truth about Law (13:13-14)
     a. A Godly Fear (13:13)
     b. A Good Foundation (13:14)
  10. Truth about Learning (13:15-16)
     a. How to Achieve Favor (13:15)
     b. How to Avoid Folly (13:16)
  11. Truth about Laxity (13:17)
  12. Truth about Lowliness (13:18)
  13. Truth about Longings (13:19)
  14. Truth about Liaisons (13:20)
  15. Truth about Lawlessness (13:21)
  16. Truth about Legacies (13:22)
  17. Truth about Labor (13:23)
  18. Truth about Love (13:24)
  19. Truth about Leanness (13:25)

In Proverbs 13 Solomon continues to roam through the fields of wisdom, understanding, knowledge, and experience and through the realms of reason and revelation. As he roams he picks up pearls of instruction and holds them up for us to examine and treasure. We follow hard at his heels. We wish he would pause, at least occasionally, to amplify and illustrate, but his eyes dart here, there, and everywhere. The best we can do is pick up his pearls one by one and try to see their beauty for ourselves.

C. Verities to Be Considered (13:1-25)

1. Truth about Listening (13:1)

"A wise son heareth his father's instruction: but a scorner heareth not rebuke." This is one of Solomon's favorite themes, one to which he returned repeatedly. Perhaps he was driven back to it by his own son's stolid stupidity.

It does not require much imagination to picture young Rehoboam daydreaming or doodling in the classroom or not paying attention to an intricate case in the courtroom. He would sit in court with a sullen face and a closed mind. He wanted to be out with the boys, not inside listening to arguments that seemed dry as dust to him.

Rehoboam's attitude surprised Solomon because he could remember his own keen interest in court cases. He was a wise son, eager to hear his father's instruction. He had a hundred questions at the end of each case. "Father, how did you know he was lying?" "If he was guilty, why did you not give him the maximum penalty prescribed by the law?" "Why were you so rough on that fellow? What he did didn't seem so bad to me."

Solomon rebuked his son for his inattention. "Don't you realize, my boy, that one day *you* will have to make these decisions for yourself? I'm not always going to be here, you know." Rehoboam's face became more sullen than ever because "a scorner heareth not rebuke." For people like Rehoboam, rebuke only produces resentment.

Of course Solomon had a touch of resentment in his own heart. When David was rebuked, he wrote his penitential Psalms. When Solomon was rebuked, he dug in his heels. There is no repentance, no tears of sorrow over sin, in the book of Proverbs.

For example consider Solomon's reaction to the reproof he received in 1 Kings 11. God told Solomon that after his death the kingdom would be divided and that ten of the tribes would set up an independent monarchy. Soon afterward the prophet Ahijah accosted young Jeroboam and told him he was to inherit the ten tribes. God's promise to Jeroboam was clear enough:

> It shall be, if thou wilt hearken unto all that I command thee, and wilt walk in my ways, and do that is right in my sight, to keep my statutes and my commandments, as David my servant did; that I will be with thee, and build thee a sure house, as I built for David, and will give Israel unto thee (1 Kings 11:38).

When Solomon heard about that promise, instead of bowing under the chastening hand of God as David would have done, he reacted violently. We read that "Solomon sought therefore to kill Jeroboam" (1 Kings 11:40). Solomon put Jeroboam's name at the top of his list of ten most wanted men. Doubtless Solomon also put a price on Jeroboam's head and offered a reward for proof of his death. Jeroboam however was too wily a fox to be caught easily. He sought political asylum in Egypt with Pharaoh Shishak.

It is very likely that Rehoboam knew all about this situation but simply did not care. He figured that if Jeroboam showed up, he'd arrest him and show him who was king. Perhaps Rehoboam might have *listened* better if his father had *lived* better. The problem was that Rehoboam knew his father too well and could have said, "With all due respect, Father, what you *are* speaks so loudly I cannot hear a word you *say*."

2. Truth about Living (13:2-3)

There can be no doubt that what we say plays a significant role in determining our quality of life. Solomon wrote about the advantage of having a *clean mouth:* "A man shall eat good by the fruit of his mouth: but the soul of the transgressors shall eat violence" (Proverbs 13:2). The word translated "good" here refers to what is pleasant to both taste and smell. The word translated "violence" refers to what is crude and unripe.

Most nations have proverbs about the tongue. The Turks say, "The tongue destroys a greater horde than the sword." The Persians used to say, "A lengthy tongue means an unhappy death; don't let your tongue cut off your head."

Lady Astor's words boomeranged when she said to Winston Churchill, "If you were my husband I should put arsenic in your tea." He replied, "Madam, if I were your husband I should drink it." On another occasion Bessie Braddock, a fellow member of Parliament, said to Churchill, "Sir, you are drunk." He replied, "Madam, you are ugly. However, in the morning I shall be sober!"

We can use our words to build or destroy, to make or to break. The man who swears at his boss is likely to find himself without a job in a hurry. A man who knows how to express himself well will usually move up through the ranks of his profession. A man who stumbles and stutters is handicapped from the start. A good command of the English language has opened doors in my life. Nothing so labels a person as the words he uses at home, at work, in general conversation, in everyday situations, and in emergencies. Solomon urged us to pay strict attention to the way we speak.

Solomon also wrote about the advantage of having a *closed mouth:* "He that keepeth his mouth keepeth his life: but he that openeth wide his lips shall have destruction" (Proverbs 13:3). This verse speaks of the contrast between the man with a closed mouth and the man with a big mouth.

Unfortunately most of us speak when it would be best to remain silent. Often we speak in anger and say things that should never be said. In a moment the damage is done and not a single word can be recalled.

The principle of the closed mouth is violated in the book of Job, one of the wordiest books in the Bible. Everybody is talking in the book of Job—the devil, Job himself, his wife, his three friends, and young Elihu. For the most part, in spite of all their wordiness, they have nothing to say. Their arguments are based on incomplete data. Satan knows nothing about Job's heart. Job, his wife, and his friends are ignorant of the reason for his calamities. Job's self-knowledge is imperfect and he protests his innocence both to his friends and to God in Job 10:7.

In Job 29–31 Job gives his last speech before young Elihu butts in and before God Himself speaks. If you read these chapters and put circles around the personal pronouns *I, me,* and *my,* you will see that Job refers to himself an astonishing number of times. Job's speech is a tremendous exposure of his own self-righteousness. In chapter 29 he talks about his prosperity; in chapter 30 he talks about his adversity; in chapter 31 he talks about his innocence. On and on he goes until we feel like handing back to him his own sarcastic words to Zophar (13:5). Yes, sometimes "silence is golden," as our own English proverb says.

3. Truth about Laziness (13:4)

"The soul of the sluggard desireth, and hath nothing: but the soul of the diligent shall be made fat." Nobody ever made his fortune by wishful thinking.

This proverb reminds us of Mr. Micawber, whose favorite expression was that sooner or later something would turn up. Mr. Micawber provided lodging for David Copperfield, who as a wholly unwanted boy was shipped off to London to do soul-destroying work at Murdstone and Grinby's warehouse. When David was introduced to Mr. Micawber, the boy was given a fair picture of the man. "Mr. Micawber," said Mr. Quinion, "is known to Mr. Murdstone. He takes orders for us on commission—when he can get any." When David was introduced to Mrs. Micawber, he was given more details. "I never thought," said Mrs. Micawber, "before I was married, when I lived with papa and mama, that I should ever find it necessary to take a lodger. But Mr. Micawber being in difficulties, all considerations of private feeling must give way."

The creditors provided further evidence of financial difficulties. David said, "The only visitors I ever saw or heard of, were creditors. *They* used to come at all hours....At these times, Mr. Micawber would be transported with grief and mortification, even to the length (as I was once made aware by a scream from his wife) of making motions at himself with a razor." Mr. Micawber however, though eternally insolvent, was irrepressibly optimistic. "Within half-an-hour," said David, "he would polish up his shoes with extraordinary pains, and go out, humming a tune with a greater air of gentility than ever. Mrs. Micawber was quite as elastic."

Mr. Micawber was always hoping something would turn up, but nothing much ever did—except his creditors, who turned up all the time. Eventually Mr. Micawber landed in debtor's prison. When David went to visit his landlord, Mr. Micawber expounded his philosophy.

> He solemnly conjured me, I remember, to take warning by his fate; and to observe that if a man had twenty pounds a year for his income, and spent nineteen pounds nineteen shillings and sixpence, he would be happy, but if he spent twenty pounds one he would be miserable. After which he borrowed a shilling of me for porter, gave me a written order on Mrs. Micawber for the amount, and put away his pocket-handkerchief, and cheered up.[1]

Nothing worthwhile ever turned up for the optimistic Mr. Micawber—not, that is, until the end of the story. Mr. Micawber fell into the clutches of the scoundrel Uriah Heep, but was able to turn his misfortune to good account. He was able to bear witness against Uriah Heep, who had stolen money belonging to Aunt Betsy,

David's benefactor. A grateful Aunt Betsy settled the Micawbers in Australia, where to his immense satisfaction Mr. Micawber became a magistrate. Dickens liked to reward his heroes and punish his villains! After all, Mr. Micawber was not really a sluggard, just an inveterate wishful thinker.

4. Truth about Lying (13:5)

"A righteous man hateth lying: but a wicked man is loathsome, and cometh to shame."

Abraham Lincoln is still known for his honesty. He began life in the Kentucky backwoods. His father was a shiftless farmer and his mother died when he was barely nine. Young Abe had less than a year of formal schooling, but he read all the books he could lay his hands on—*Aesop's Fables, Robinson Crusoe, Pilgrim's Progress,* the Bible. He first saw slavery on a large scale when he took a cargo of hogs and corn down the Mississippi to New Orleans. "If I ever get a chance to hit that thing," he said, "I'll hit it hard."

Later Lincoln read Blackstone and was admitted to the bar. Then he entered politics. He abandoned rough sarcasm and frontier coarseness of speech and taught himself to think clearly and speak with polish and power. Although he made it to the White House as leader of the newly formed Republican Party, the southern states refused to accept his election and seceded from the Union. On September 22, 1862, after the victory of the Union troops at Antietam, he issued his famous Emancipation Proclamation declaring that after January 1, 1863, all slaves would be free.

Solomon would have approved of Abraham Lincoln. People called him "honest Abe." He earned the title when he was working for Offutt's store, A man overpaid him four cents and was gone before Lincoln noticed the error. Before he went to bed that night, young Lincoln walked several miles to repay the pennies. Another time he did the same thing to make up a shortage after having accidentally used too small a weight in measuring out a pound of tea. Someone said Lincoln was "the most honest lawyer west of China." He would even remind opposing counsel if they overlooked points against his own case!

Surely the man who murdered Lincoln fits this description: "A wicked man is loathsome and cometh to shame." John Wilkes Booth entered Lincoln's private box in Washington's Ford's Theater shortly after 10:00 p.m. and shot the president through the head. Then the assassin leaped to the stage below and shouted, "*Sic semper tyrannis,*" which means, "Thus always to tyrants." Booth broke his leg in the leap but managed to escape through the back door, mount a horse, and flee to Virginia. There he was hunted down and shot for his dreadful crime. The kindest thing history records about him is that he was mentally unstable. The assassin came to shame, but his victim was revered. When Lincoln was assassinated, Secretary of War Edwin M. Stanton said, "Now he belongs to the ages."

5. Truth about Limits (13:6)

"Righteousness keepeth him that is upright in the way: but wickedness overthroweth the sinner." Righteousness, the determination to do what is right, stems from a right relationship to God and acts like the banks of a river. Righteousness keeps one's life on course and leads one in the right direction. The person who has already determined to do what is right is not easily swayed by temptation.

The supreme example of righteousness is the Lord Jesus. At the end of a forty-day fast in the wilderness—when He was at the limit of His physical endurance—Satan came to tempt Him. Satan presented Him with the same three primeval temptations that he had used with such success in the garden of Eden. Satan tempted Him with the lust of the flesh, the lust of the eyes, and the pride of life. Because of His righteousness the Lord Jesus did not yield to the temptations; in fact He was *unable* to yield.

The Lord stepped out of eternity into time with the predetermined resolve that He would always do the will of His Father in Heaven—"Lo, I come (in the volume of the book it is written of me,) to do thy will, O God" (Hebrews 10:7; Psalm 40:7-8). Or as He Himself said, "I do always those things that please [the Father]" (John 8:29). The parameters of His life were marked by God's Word and God's will. Since the Lord Jesus purposed in His heart that He would be governed by the Word of God and the will of God, nothing in Him could or would respond to Satan's suggestions. Any suggestion that He should transgress the will of His beloved Father in Heaven was repulsive to the Lord Jesus. Sin was not attractive to Him.

What was there for Jesus in Satan's suggestion that He perform a miracle to provide Himself with bread—that He satisfy a natural craving in a way contrary to the Word of God? Nothing! The Lord Jesus reacted instantly against any such suggestion because "righteousness keepeth him that is upright in the way."

The Lord immediately saw the nonsense in the suggestion that He do something daring—that He throw Himself down from the pinnacle of the temple. Satan could not push Him down and He had not the slightest intention of throwing Himself down. From the Lord's standpoint that temptation was downright silly.

There was no attraction in the temptation that He accept from Satan the war-torn, ravaged, and divided kingdoms of this world. Satan said, "Just fall down and worship me," but Jesus had no intention of falling down. The suggestion was nonsense to One determined to live in accordance with God's Word.

In response to each temptation the Lord Jesus simply quoted God's Word back to the evil one (Matthew 4:1-11). Satan never had the ghost of a chance against One who was determined that righteousness should keep Him in the way. Satan's suggestions were puerile compared to God's Word. Moreover they were offensive to the absolutely holy One who possessed the divine nature. We too will be kept safe in the hour of temptation if we have the same resolve, purpose, and determination as our Lord.

People fall prey to Satan's wiles because they do not keep the waters of their lives well within the banks set by the Word of God. As Solomon said, "Wickedness overthroweth the sinner." Eve sinned because she handled the Word of God deceitfully. She quoted God incorrectly three times, twice subtracting from His words and once adding to them (Genesis 2:16-17; 3:2-3). She left out the word "surely"; God had said, "Thou shalt surely die." She left out the word "freely"; God had said, "Thou mayest freely eat." Thus she minimized both the generosity of God and the certainty of punishment. She added the words "neither shall ye touch it," thus exaggerating the divine prohibition. Eve did not have the commitment necessary to keep within the banks of the Word of God at all times, in all places, under all circumstances, and at all costs.

6. Truth about Liberality (13:7).

"There is that maketh himself rich, yet hath nothing: there is that maketh himself poor, yet hath great riches."

In 1977 two of the world's richest men died: Howard Hughes, who was worth $2.5 billion, and J. Paul Getty, who was worth nearly $4 billion. Howard Hughes is an example of the first part of Proverbs 13:7.

Hughes inherited his father's tool company and used the profits from this business to launch a career in Hollywood. He went on to build the planes he designed at the Hughes Aircraft Company. He turned a small airline into the giant Trans World Airlines.

At the peak of his success, Hughes began to retire from the world, although he still ruled his empire with an iron hand. He became increasingly suspicious of other people and paranoid about catching infections. Relying on his staff for contact with the outside world, he lived mostly in hotels, where he closed off entire floors and sealed and darkened all the windows. In spite of his eccentricities, he prospered. Wealth rolled in from defense contracts, airlines, gambling casinos, and other ventures. In his final years, however, Hughes lived in his pajamas and ate a diet of fudge. When he died he was suffering from malnutrition and weighed about ninety pounds.

No less than thirty wills showed up after his death, some of them obvious forgeries. One man who claimed to be his son said he was born in a flying saucer in 1946! The Mormons laid claim to a sizable portion of his estate. At his funeral service the officiating priest, quoting 1 Timothy 6:7, said, "We brought nothing into this world, and it is certain we can carry nothing out." To paraphrase Solomon, Howard Hughes made himself rich, but he had nothing.

In contrast to Howard Hughes, Charles T. Studd is an example of the second part of Proverbs 13:7. While attending Cambridge University he was converted under the ministry of D. L. Moody. Studd was born to affluence, but he gave away his considerable fortune and went to China as a missionary. There he shocked the British civil service by donning Chinese garb, eating with the Chinese, substituting Chinese ways for western ways, and trying to identify himself with the nationals. When his health broke down so severely that he was unable to return to China, he went to India! Later in an effort to open up Africa from the Nile to the Niger, he led an intrepid band of Christian workers into the Congo forests. His motto was very simple:

> Some wish to live within the sound
> Of Church or Chapel bell,
> I want to run a Rescue Shop
> Within a yard of hell.

Some eighteen years later, when the mission he had founded was beset with financial problems because of the great depression, C. T. Studd declared to the mission board:

> I would lay before you the absolute necessity of nobody, man or woman, coming out here who does not recognize the absolute necessity of super-sacrifice of self, and demand it. If people want pretty houses and elegant furnishings, for God's sake and ours, let them stay at home in the nursery...no soldier

is worth a rap unless he does not care whether he lives or dies, so long as he dies fighting for the glory of God.[2]

"There is that maketh himself rich, yet hath nothing: there is that maketh himself poor, yet hath great riches." It does not take much discernment to know who has more now—Howard Hughes or C. T. Studd! As previously mentioned, the priest who officiated at Howard Hughes' funeral service quoted 1 Timothy 6:7: "We brought nothing into this world, and it is certain we can carry nothing out." While those words are true, in one sense it *is* possible to carry something out of this world. At least it is possible to send our riches on ahead. That is what C. T. Studd did with his.

7. Truth about Life (13:8-11)

In stating the truths about life, Solomon depicted a perilous life, a prolonged life, a provocative life, and a prosperous life.

Proverbs 13:8 talks about *a perilous life:* "The ransom of a man's life are his riches: but the poor heareth not rebuke." The rich man has the advantage of being able to buy his way out of many difficult and dangerous situations. The poor man has the advantage of not having to worry about threats from the envious. Why would anyone hold him for ransom?

Usually a ransom is defined in terms of money. The greater the value of the life, the greater the ransom sum demanded. Take the case of Richard the Lion-hearted, who ruled England from 1189-1199. Richard is known chiefly for his leadership of the crusade that aimed to free Jerusalem from Saladin. Richard, a born leader of men, twice led his victorious army to within a few miles of Jerusalem. However, the fierce quarrels among the French, German, and English contingents of his army proved too much for him. He himself insulted Leopold, duke of Austria, by tearing down his banner, and quarreled just as violently with Philip Augustus of France. In 1192 Richard patched up his differences with Saladin and sailed for home.

Unfortunately for Richard, a storm drove his ship ashore near Venice. He was captured by his old enemy Leopold, imprisoned at Dürenstein on the Danube, and handed over to Emperor Henry VI, who kept him in various castles. Under the threat of being delivered to his bitter foe, Philip of France, Richard agreed to harsh terms. He was to be ransomed for the colossal sum of 150,000 marks. Moreover he was to surrender his kingdom to the emperor and receive it back as a fief.

The *Encyclopedia Britannica* says that the raising of the ransom money was "one of the most remarkable fiscal measures of the Twelfth Century" and that it gave "striking proof of the prosperity of England." Although Richard spent little more than six months in England during his entire reign, he captured the imagination of his people. He reigned securely in their affections and long held his place in English history books as a great king. It is doubtful the people of England would have raised so much as a dime for Richard's young brother John, his successor on the throne. "The ransom of a man's life are his riches," wrote Solomon, and Richard's true riches lay in his ability to inspire the love and loyalty of his subjects. They ransomed him because they loved him. No cost, no personal sacrifice, was too great.

Proverbs 13:9 talks about *a prolonged life:* "The light of the righteous rejoiceth: but the lamp of the wicked shall be put out." "The light of the righteous" is Jesus! "In him was life; and the life was the light of men" (John 1:4). Jesus said, "He that followeth me shall not walk in darkness, but shall have the light of life" (John 8:12).

A friend of mine told me about an incident that happened during his boyhood in Africa. He and his missionary parents were on a journey across Angola. They stopped for a mid-day meal and rest, and while the others were asleep he borrowed a rifle and moved away from where the vehicle was parked to shoot something for the pot. Chasing an elusive gazelle, he strayed ever deeper into the bush. Absorbed in the chase, he did not notice the swift and silent approach of night. When he finally did notice the gathering shadows, he also realized that he was lost. Worse still, as the darkness swept in he could hear a lion roaring.

Back at the camp his parents and their native attendants awoke and noticed that my friend and a rifle were missing. Leaving his mother by the car to watch and pray, the others fanned out in search of him. Calling his name and hoping against hope, they hurried down the trails. Away in the forest my friend heard the calls. He dared not call back because of the lion, but he tried to make his way toward the sound, although it was difficult to decide from which direction the calls were coming.

Then the danger from the lion suddenly intensified as the beast stalked within sight. All seemed lost. Then an idea flashed into my friend's mind: the car was his one last hope. Desperately he cupped his hands and shouted, "Put on the lights! Put on the car lights!" His words traveled into the camp. His father and the natives were still beating the bush, but his mother heard and acted. Suddenly two bright beams of light stabbed the darkness. The startled lion growled and leaped back into the forest, and the would-be hunter gratefully followed the light back to the safety of the camp.

The light of the righteous! What is our glorious Light doing now? He is rejoicing in glory because the roaring lion has been vanquished. His people are within sight of their heavenly home and all is well.

As the Lord Jesus drew the parable of the lost sheep to a close He said, "Joy shall be in heaven over one sinner that repenteth" (Luke 15:7). At the end of the companion parable of the lost coin He said, "There is joy in the presence of the angels of God over one sinner that repenteth" (15:10). He did not say that the angels rejoice, although surely they do. He said that there is rejoicing in their *presence.* In other words, Jesus is rejoicing! The Father is rejoicing! The Holy Spirit is rejoicing! The "spirits of just men made perfect" (Hebrews 12:23) are rejoicing! Solomon said, "The light of the righteous rejoiceth." Jesus fills all Heaven with His hosannas and the everlasting hills echo with His hallelujahs.

"But the lamp of the wicked shall be put out." What is "the lamp" mentioned here? The Bible! The psalmist said, "Thy word is a lamp unto my feet, and a light unto my path" (Psalm 119:105). The Word of God is the only lamp we poor sinners have in this dark world of sin. It is our only guide to God. How great is the folly of those who abuse, neglect, and ignore the Word of God. In the end its light goes out for them. Their only light turns to darkness and how great, dreadful, and eternal that darkness is.

King Saul discovered how dreadful that darkness is. Acting out of his fierce jealousy of David, Saul committed crime after crime. He relentlessly persecuted David. He ordered the massacre of the priests who resided at Nob because one of them had given assistance to David (1 Samuel 22). An evil spirit also troubled Saul (1 Samuel 16:14-23). The demise of Samuel sounded like a death knell in Saul's guilty soul and deepened his darkness.

Then on the night before the battle of Gilboa, Saul became desperate. He "enquired of the Lord," but "the Lord answered him not, neither by dreams, nor by Urim, nor by prophets" (1 Samuel 28:6). The lamp had gone out and now he was wholly in the dark. So he resorted to witchcraft. As far as God was concerned, that was the last straw. Unexpectedly Samuel's ghost showed up at the seance, but only to rebuke the evil king. Saul wailed, "I am sore distressed; for the Philistines make war against me, and God is departed from me, and answereth me no more, neither by prophets, nor by dreams" (28:15). Samuel replied, "The Lord is departed from thee, and is become thine enemy" (28:16).

How great is the folly of those who neglect the Bible and seek counsel from psychics, spiritists, astrologers, and palm readers! When Saul discovered that the door of Heaven was barred and bolted against him, he knocked on the door of Hell. God simply opened that door and pushed him through. The next day he was dead (1 Samuel 28:19).

Proverbs 13:10 talks about *a provocative life:* "Only by pride cometh contention: but with the well advised is wisdom." Nothing provokes God like pride. Pride was the sin of Satan. Pride provoked war in Heaven and led to the ouster of a third of the heavenly host. "The pride of life" is one of the most potent weapons in Satan's arsenal.

Pride filled the heart of Cain when he murdered Abel. Pride led Korah, Dathan, and Abiram to rebel against Moses. Pride spurred Saul on in his relentless campaign against David. Pride drove Haman. Pride persuaded Darius to sign the foolish decree that consigned Daniel to the den of lions.

Pride ruled the heart of Monsieur the Marquis in Dickens' *Tale of Two Cities.* Trouble followed when Monsieur the Marquis did not receive his due at court.

> Monseigneur, one of the great lords in power at the Court, held his fortnightly reception in his grand hotel in Paris....
> Monseigneur having...taken his chocolate, caused the doors of the Holiest of Holiests to be thrown open, and issued forth. Then, what submission, what cringing and fawning, what servility, what abject humiliation! As to bowing down in body and spirit, nothing in that way was left for Heaven.

Among the cringing crowd was Monsieur the Marquis. "He was a man of about sixty, handsomely dressed, haughty in manner, and with a face like a fine mask." Snubbed by Monseigneur, Monsieur the Marquis

> went down-stairs into the court-yard, got into his carriage, and drove away. Not many people had talked with him at the reception; he had stood in a little space apart, and Monseigneur might have been warmer in his manner. It appeared, under the circumstances, rather agreeable to him to see the common people dispersed before his horses, and often barely escaping from being run down. His man drove as if he were charging an enemy.

The Marquis enjoyed the feeling of speed and reckless power. Then the inevitable happened. The carriage ran over a child and killed it. The Marquis had no feeling for the child and was most annoyed at the howl of despair of the father.

> The people closed round, and looked at Monsieur the Marquis....Monsieur the Marquis ran his eyes over them all, as if they had been mere rats come out of their holes.
> He took out his purse.
> "It is extraordinary to me," said he, "that you people cannot take care of yourselves and your children. One or the other of you is for ever in the way. How do I know what injury you have done my horses? See! Give him that."
> He threw out a gold coin.

It was this kind of pride that sparked the French Revolution and the excesses of the subsequent Reign of Terror. But the humblest cottager can have pride as fierce and unbending as that of the haughtiest aristocrat. Dickens continued:

> Without deigning to look at the assemblage a second time, Monsieur the Marquis leaned back in his seat, and was just being driven away with the air of a gentlemen who had accidentally broke some common thing, and had paid for it, and could afford to pay for it; when his ease was suddenly disturbed by a coin flying into his carriage, and ringing on its floor.

He stopped and railed at the cowed people and paid no heed to the indomitable Madam Defarge, who looked him straight in the eye as she knit his name and the crime into her woollen register—against the day of reckoning.

The next scene is set in Monsieur's mansion in the country. There Charles Darney, the nobleman's nephew and heir, bluntly told his aristocratic uncle that if he ever inherited the property, he would dispose of it to relieve the wretched people whose blood, sweat, and tears had rendered it accursed.

> "And you?" said the uncle. "Forgive my curiosity; do you, under your new philosophy, graciously intend to live?"
> "I must do, to live, what others of my countrymen, even with nobility at their backs, may have to do some day—work."

With the well-advised was wisdom. For work Darney did, and he attained his heart's desire—which is more than his haughty uncle did. Monsieur the Marquis was burned in his bed by the man whose child he had killed.

Proverbs 13:11 talks also about *a prosperous life:* "Wealth gotten by vanity shall be diminished: but he that gathereth by labour shall increase." In other words, there is a right way and a wrong way to acquire wealth. We should beware of schemes that promise short-cuts to wealth. Crime is a poor foundation for lasting wealth and gambling is a vain way to get rich. The gambling table, the casino, the deck of cards, and the racetrack all have their allure. But Lady Luck is a fickle courtesan. Her favors are here today and gone tomorrow. The stock market is a more sophisticated roulette wheel, but a sudden crash on Wall Street has been the undoing of many who were trying to get rich. Even mild runs on the market have swept many into sudden bankruptcy.

Plain old-fashioned gambling is once again in vogue. More than 80 percent of Americans regard gambling as an acceptable activity and compulsive gambling is on the rise. *USA Today* reported that Americans spent an estimated $394 billion on gambling in 1993. Worse still, the casino business is deliberately targeting families. It is building mega-resorts to attract whole families to the casinos. Howard Kline, publisher of *The Gaming Marketer* newsletter, said bluntly, "Families are 'the future.'" According to *USA Today* already some seven million children are gambling for money, and over a million of them have serious gambling-related problems. The newspaper warned that children are getting the message: Pull a lever or buy a lottery ticket and you can win big money and never have to work.[3]

Gambling is exciting, but gambling is immoral. The gambler takes an artificial risk to gain by chance—and always at someone else's expense. Gambling gives money and material gain the place of priority. The gambler turns his back on a good and loving heavenly Father to embrace capricious Lady Luck. Gambling offers something for nothing, undermines the work ethic, and can become as addictive as drugs. Moreover much of gambling is controlled by organized crime. Many a man has lost home, character, family, career, fortune, and even life itself on the roll of the dice.

The American sporting world received a shock when Pete Rose, one of its baseball heroes, showed up as an all-time loser. He was a real winner in baseball. Sports writers say that he was born to swing a bat and his career record of 4,256 hits is proof. He was every Little

Leaguer's idol, the kind of man every boy in baseball wanted to be—
until he was exposed as a gambler.

It is said that Pete Rose bet on ten to twenty college basketball
games at a time. He also bet on horses and professional basketball
games. He was even accused of betting on baseball games, including
those played by his own team. He is said to have lost four hundred
thousand dollars to just one bookie in one spring and he had to
borrow feverishly to pay his gambling debts. Not content with a
salary of ten thousand dollars a game, he wanted more and more.
In the end this winner lost, and lost big.

"Wealth gotten by vanity shall be diminished: but he that gathereth
by labour shall increase," Solomon said. The Bible backs the work
ethic. Hard work, careful spending, diligent saving, wise investing,
and prudent management not only steadily increase a man's wealth;
they also develop his character, and that is much more important
than money.

We are all familiar with the story of the race between the hare and
the tortoise. The hare bounded off at full speed, then stopped here
and there along the way. He stopped for a snack in a nearby
farmer's field. He stopped for a nap because the sun was hot. He
stopped for a chat with some friends. Even when the steadily
plodding tortoise passed him, the hare was unconcerned. *So what!*
he thought. *A few swift bounds and I'll soon pass that lumbering old fool
of a tortoise. Fancy anyone thinking that a tortoise could outstrip a hare!*
But the hare dallied too long. Suddenly alerted to the fact that he
had been left far behind, he tried a desperate spurt, but he was too
late. The tortoise had won.

The man who plods steadily on toward his goal is far better off in
the long-run than the man who hopes to reach his goal with "a
break" or chance and a wild bound or two.

8. Truth about Languishing (13:12)

"Hope deferred maketh the heart sick, but when the desire
cometh, it is a tree of life."

Two people had started the seven-and-a-half-mile walk from
Jerusalem to Emmaus. The two, Cleopas and possibly his wife, had
started for home, dismayed and discouraged by the events of the
past few days. It was all over. Their beloved Master had been
crucified and buried. They had heard wild rumors that there had
been a resurrection, and some of the women claimed they had seen
Him, but their stories were too incredible to be taken seriously. So

Cleopas and his companion were going home. Their fond hopes that they had found the Messiah had been dashed and they were sick at heart. Hope had been deferred once too often.

Walking twenty-five minutes from the western gate of Jerusalem brought them to the edge of a plateau from which they could look back and see the blood-stained city. Twenty minutes later they could see Bethlehem, where it had all begun. After another fifteen minutes the travelers left the well-paved Roman road and headed up a lovely valley. They went alongside a stream, over a bridge, past citrus groves and fruit orchards, and on to the height where Emmaus stood.

It was a long walk during the best of times but crucified hopes had made it seem interminable—until the Stranger joined them. He hailed them, joined them, and commented on their downcast, dejected air. He drew them out and listened earnestly, and they poured out all their disappointment. "But we had trusted that it had been he which should have redeemed Israel," they said (Luke 24:21). We can almost hear them saying, "It's all over! Three days have passed. And He was such a good man—holy, compassionate, and a worker of mighty miracles. Why did they have to kill Him? Why did they have to crucify Him?"

Then the Stranger began to speak. He expounded the Scriptures and their hearts burned within them (Luke 24:27,32). The last few miles simply melted away as they listened spellbound to His exposition of the Old Testament. When they reached Emmaus He bade them good night, but they wanted to hear more. It was inconceivable that they should just let Him go like that! When they invited Him into their home, He came in—He always does. They spread a simple meal and Cleopas sat Him at the head of the table. The Stranger took the bread, blessed it, and broke it. Suddenly they knew who He was and He vanished.

Back the two went to Jerusalem. My, how those miles sped by! We can well imagine that they laughed and sang and whooped and hollered like a couple of children let out of school on an unexpected holiday. What a story they had for the disciples huddled in that upper room!

"When the desire cometh," Solomon said, "it is a tree of life." Cleopas and his companion had eaten of that tree all right! No earthly paradise could compare with the taste of Heaven they had enjoyed that night! Doom and gloom had been forever banished by light and life. Jesus was alive! He had come back. He had taken away sin and sadness and left them joy and gladness!

9. Truth about Law (13:13-14)

"Whoso despiseth the word shall be destroyed: but he that feareth the commandment shall be rewarded" (Proverbs 13:13). Solomon was speaking about *a godly fear*. Joash and Jehoiada illustrate this proverb (see 2 Kings 11–12; 2 Chronicles 24).

King Joash of Judah owed his life and throne to Jehoiada the priest. Joash was born into an ill-fated family. His father Ahaziah was the son of the evil Athaliah, the vile daughter of Jezebel. When Athaliah heard that Ahaziah had been killed, she seized the Judean throne and made a clean sweep of all likely claimants. The only one to escape was Joash. Jehosheba, sister of Ahaziah and wife of Jehoiada, managed to smuggle the child and his nurse into the temple. There Jehoiada secretly raised him. It was a safe place because Athaliah had little use for the worship of Jehovah.

When Joash (also known as Jehoash) was seven, Jehoiada deemed the time ripe for a palace coup. He armed three companies of the guard and two companies of the Levites, swore them in, and suddenly produced the rightful king and publicly crowned him. By the time Athaliah discovered what was going on, it was too late. She hurried to the temple, was thrown out, and was executed.

Jehoiada made two covenants: the young king and his people would serve God; and both king and subjects would do their duty to each other. Revival broke out. The house of Baal was destroyed along with the images and the false priest. The long-neglected temple was repaired. As long as Jehoiada was the king's adviser, all went well. Jehoiada's name was revered and his reward was complete. He died full of honor. As the proverb says, "He that feareth the commandment shall be rewarded." This godly man had seen his advice followed and his principles and policies heeded. He could have received no greater reward than the knowledge that he had been instrumental in bringing revival to his people.

As soon as Jehoiada was in his tomb, King Joash reverted to the ways of his ancestors. He was a true descendant of Ahaziah, Athaliah, and Jezebel. The vile asherim, cult symbols of the greatest impurity, were set up everywhere, along with other idols. Zechariah, the son of Jehoiada, spoke up and denounced the king and the evildoers. Enraged, the king called for his murder; the multitude rioted and stoned Zechariah to death (Matthew 23:35).

The vile and ungrateful Joash soon saw the evidence of God's wrath. Hazael, the king of Syria, sent his army to threaten Jerusalem, and Joash had to buy him off by raiding the temple treasury.

Then Joash fell sick and the administration of the kingdom was conducted by his son. Joash's own servants conspired against him and slew him in his bed. They had never forgiven this wretched man for Zechariah's murder. Joash was buried in Jerusalem, but not in the royal sepulcher. As Solomon said, "Whoso despiseth the word shall be destroyed." Joash lacked godly fear.

Solomon was speaking the truth about law and in the same connection he referred to *a good foundation:* "The law of the wise is a fountain of life, to depart from the snares of death" (Proverbs 13:14). The "law of the wise" is the Word of God. Obedience to good teaching—to God's Word—saves us from many of life's snares and pitfalls.

Martin Luther experienced the protection of the Word of God. Having broken the chains that bound him to Rome, Luther prepared to go to the German city of Worms on the Rhine to appear before the Diet to defend his beliefs. Years before, he had enraged the papacy by nailing his theses to the church door at Wittenberg. In ninety-five propositions he had challenged the entire Catholic Church. Now he had to appear before Emperor Charles V of Germany, who was a devoted Catholic and the most powerful monarch to reign in Christendom since the days of Charlemagne. Charles V was a willing tool of Pope Leo X, the son of Lorenzo the Magnificent.

Proceedings against Martin Luther began on January 28, 1521, the date of the festival of Charlemagne. Never before had there been such an assembly. Kings, princes, prelates, and nobles were there. Electors, dukes, archbishops, landgraves, margraves, counts, bishops, barons, and lords of the realm were there. Deputies of the towns and ambassadors of the kings of Christendom were there. And Martin Luther, the son of a poor miner, was there—dressed in his monk's frock and hood, pale-faced and fatigued.

Aleandro, the Pope's nuncio—a man famous for his eloquence—was there with Luther's books piled up before him. "There are enough errors here," he cried, "to burn a hundred thousand heretics."

The chancellor of Treves addressed the lone champion, first in Latin then in German. "Do you admit that these books were written by you?" he thundered. "Are you prepared to retract these books?" The world held its breath. "I cannot and I will not retract," Luther said. Looking around the assembly, Luther continued: "Here I stand. I cannot do otherwise. So help me God! Amen."

Charles V took the floor. He boasted of his descent from the

Christian emperors of Germany, from the Catholic kings of Spain, from the archdukes of Austria, from the dukes of Burgundy, from a long line of defenders of the Roman faith. Then he declared:

> I am resolved to imitate the example of my ancestors. A single monk, misled by his own folly, has risen against the faith of Christendom. To stay such impiety, I will sacrifice my kingdom, my treasures, my friends, my body, my blood, my soul and my life. I am about to dismiss the Augustinian Luther, forbidding him to cause the least disorder among the people. I shall then proceed against him and his adherents, as contumacious heretics, by excommunication, by interdict, and by every means calculated to destroy them. I call on the members of the states to behave like Christians.

In other words, Luther was condemned to death. The fagot and the fire were what Rome had in mind for him—once it could lay its hands on him. However, Luther had been given safe conduct both to come to Worms and to return home, and his friend and protector, Frederick the Elector of Saxony, and other German princes had enough power to shield Luther from the perfidy of Rome. His enemies were quite ready to violate Luther's safe conduct, but his friends forestalled the schemes of Rome by kidnapping him, taking him to Wartburg Castle, and defying the emperor's orders that Luther be handed over to the authorities.

Martin Luther took his stand on the Word of God. God, in turn, protected him from his enemies. In debate, in dangers, and when beset by deceit and venomous dislike, Luther found the law of the wise to be a fountain of life enabling him to avoid the snares of death.

10. Truth about Learning (13:15-16)

We need to learn *how to achieve favor:* "Good understanding giveth favour: but the way of transgressors is hard" (Proverbs 13:15). David learned through his mistakes.

In all the vicissitudes of his life, David was never so greatly imperiled as during the Absalom rebellion, so David should have welcomed the news that the rebellion had been crushed. The king, however, could only think of Absalom. "Is the young man Absalom safe?" was David's first question. The diplomatic messenger said, "The enemies of my lord the king, and all that rise against thee to do thee hurt, be as that young man is" (2 Samuel 18:32). David broke down. "And the king was much moved, and went up to the chamber over the gate, and wept: and as he went, thus he said, O my son Absalom, my son, my son Absalom! would God I had died for thee, O Absalom, my son, my son!" (18:33)

We see in David's sorrow the meaning of this proverb: "The way of transgressors is hard." David was suffering for his own sin. When pronouncing judgment on David for the murder of Uriah, Nathan had prophesied, "The sword shall never depart from thine house" (2 Samuel 12:10). And just as David had pronounced judgment on the man in Nathan's parable—"He shall restore the lamb fourfold" (12:6)—four of David's sons were struck down. The first to die was the infant born to Bathsheba (12:15-18). Then Absalom murdered Amnon because David was unwilling to punish Amnon for raping Tamar (13:1-39). Then Joab murdered Absalom, although doubtless Joab viewed the act as an execution (18:14). Finally Solomon executed Adonijah because he raised the standard of rebellion (1 Kings 2:13,24-25).

Alexander Whyte described David's heartbroken wail over Absalom:

> Yes, that is love, no doubt. That is the love of a broken father, no doubt. But the pang of the cry, the innermost agony of the cry, the poisoned point of the dagger in that cry is remorse. I have slain my son! I have murdered my son with my own hands! I neglected my son Absalom from a child! With my own lusts I laid his very worst temptation right in his way. It had been better Absalom had never been born! If he rebelled, who shall blame him? I, David, drove Absalom to rebellion. It was his father's hand that stabbed Absalom through the heart. O Absalom, my murdered son!

Yet "good understanding giveth favour." David weathered the terrible Absalom storm. Because David had a good understanding of the grace and greatness of God, he bowed under God's chastening hand and poured out his sorrows in his Psalms. Thus he remained a man after God's own heart (Acts 13:22), the greatest and best of all Israel's kings and the one against whom all the later Judean kings would be measured. God's favor remained with him to the end.

We need to learn how to achieve favor and *how to avoid folly:* "Every prudent man dealeth with knowledge: but a fool layeth open his folly" (Proverbs 13:16). The prudent man thinks carefully about his decisions and considers all the factors in the equation. He thinks of all the *ifs, ands,* and *buts* of the issues involved. A fool does no such thing and soon his rashness is an open book for everyone to read.

The greatest of all human follies is to worship graven images. No one is more foolish than the man who makes an idol out of wood or iron or stone, then sets his creation on a pedestal and falls down and worships it. Christianity fought its fiercest battles against the raw paganism and crass idolatry of the Greek and Roman world. On Mars Hill, Paul ridiculed the Athenians for their idolatry. He opened his Roman Epistle with an even more pointed denunciation of image worship (Acts 17:16-34; Romans 1:22-23).

How great then was the folly of the church to lapse into idolatry! Three women took the lead in fastening image worship on the church. The first, *Helena* the mother of Constantine (324-337), introduced sacred relics and memorials into the church and thus changed Christianity from a purely spiritual worship to that pagan-ized form of religion which took such deep root in the following centuries.

The Emperor Leo III purged the church of idols, but after his death in 741 the crafty *Irene,* mother of Constantine VI, reimposed idolatry on the church. The Second Council of Nicaea (787), convened by her connivance, reaffirmed almost hysterically and certainly ecstatically that image worship was an essential part of the Christian faith.

At the Council of St. Sophia in 815 the church reverted to iconoclasm, but then *Theodora,* regent for the young Michael III, clamped idolatry back onto the Roman Church in 843. That church has never recovered, as anyone who visits a Roman Catholic church can see.

"A fool layeth open his folly," said Solomon. Nowhere was this truth more evident than at the Second Council of Nice, attended by approximately 350 bishops under the presidency of Tarasius. An-drew Miller wrote:

> Among the preliminary acts of the council, it was debated to what class heretics the Iconoclasts were to be ascribed. Tarasius, president of the Assembly, asserted that it was "worse than the worst heresy, being an absolute denial of Christ." After assenting to the decrees of the first six councils, and to the anathemas against the heretics denounced therein, they passed—acting, as they declared, under the guidance of the Holy Spirit—the following canon: "With the venerable and life-giving Cross

shall be set up the venerable and holy images, whether in colours, in mosaic work, or any other material, within the consecrated Churches of God, on the sacred vessels and vestments, on the walls and on tablets, in houses and in highways. The images, that is to say, of our God and Saviour Jesus Christ; of the immaculate mother of God; of the honoured angels; of all saints and holy men—these images shall be treated as holy, memorials worshipped, kissed, only without that peculiar adoration which is reserved for the Invisible, Incomprehensible God. All who shall violate this, as is asserted, immemorial tradition of the Church, and endeavor, forcibly or by craft, to remove any image, if ecclesiastics, are to be deposed and excommunicated; if monks or laymen, to be excommunicated."

The council was not content with this formal and solemn subscription. With one voice they broke out into a long acclamation. "We all believe, we all assert, we all subscribe. This is the faith of the Church, this is the faith of the orthodox, this is the faith of all the world. We who adore the Trinity worship images. Whoever does not the like, anathema upon them! Anathema on all who call images idols! Anathema on all who communicate with them who do not worship images. . . . Everlasting glory to the orthodox Romans, to John of Damascus! To Gregory of Rome, everlasting glory! Everlasting glory to all the preachers of truth."[4]

By the year 787 the church had already lost vast areas to militant Islam, a religion that, however false and fanatical, at least had the merit of being monotheistic and militantly iconoclastic. Muhammad began his prophetic career in 612. He took Mecca in 630 and Damascus in 635. By 637 Iraq had fallen, and by 642 Egypt and Babylon were fiefs of Islam. Cyprus was captured in 649 and much of Spain by 715. Ancient strongholds of Christianity in the Middle East, Asia Minor, and North Africa were irretrievably lost to Islam. Thus God made known His displeasure with the church's acceptance of idolatry.

Yet the Catholic Church continued on its idolatrous way. In time the eastern churches broke away. Then came the Reformation and an even more radical break with Rome. The prudent still deal with knowledge and take their stand with the great apostle Paul, who in his Epistle to the Romans roundly denounced idolatry (Romans 1:18-23).

11. Truth about Laxity (13:17)

"A wicked messenger falleth into mischief: but a faithful ambassador is health." So much rides on the intelligence and integrity of a messenger. A foolish ambassador can aggravate a situation whereas a wise one can do much to heal wounds.

This proverb is well illustrated by the story of the earl of Essex, Queen Elizabeth's favorite. One day the queen gave him a ring as the pledge of her affection and told him that if he were ever accused of a crime, he should send her the ring. She promised she would at once grant him audience so that he could plead his case before her. In the rough-and-tumble politics of the times, the earl was eventually accused of conspiracy and high treason. The queen waited for the ring but it never came, so the earl was executed.

Years later the countess of Nottingham, a relative but certainly no friend of the long-dead earl of Essex, lay dying. She sent a message to the queen, asking her majesty to come and hear a confession so that she could die in peace.

Elizabeth arrived at the bed of the dying woman and the countess produced the ring the queen had given to the earl of Essex. He had given the ring to the countess with the urgent request that she take it straight to Elizabeth. ("A wicked messenger falleth into mischief," said Solomon.) The countess had betrayed her trust and she implored Elizabeth's forgiveness. The queen, enraged by the perfidy of this ambassador, seized the dying woman in her bed and shook her until her teeth rattled. "God may forgive you," Elizabeth screamed. "God may forgive you, but I never shall!"

12. Truth about Lowliness (13:18)

"Poverty and shame shall be to him that refuseth instruction: but he that regardeth reproof shall be honoured." There are times when we all need good advice. It may not always be palatable, but the wise person pays heed anyway; the fool ignores good advice.

Jonah was a man who refused instruction. Called of God to go to Nineveh to proclaim its impending destruction, Jonah rebelled. As far as he was concerned the overthrow of that great Assyrian city was the best thing that could happen. He was enough of a prophet to know that the sins of Israel cried to high Heaven for judgment. He was enough of a politician to know that Assyria was by far the most likely superpower to be used of God to visit judgment upon Israel. He was enough of a patriot to believe that the overthrow of Nineveh would be better than the overthrow of Israel. No doubt he thought there wasn't a nation in the Middle East that would not rejoice at the overthrow of Nineveh.

Refusing instruction and thinking he knew better than God, Jonah decided to put as much distance as possible between himself and Nineveh. He boarded a boat and set sail into the sunset for far-off Tarshish. But poverty and shame came riding in on a storm (Jonah 1:6-10). The petrified sailors, calling on their gods, thought suddenly of their wild-eyed passenger sleeping in the bottom of the boat. "What meanest thou, O sleeper?" the shipmaster demanded. "Arise, call upon thy God...that we perish not." Then the sailors asked a series of soul-searching questions, the answers to which must have filled Jonah with shame: "What is thine occupation? and whence comest thou? what is thy country? and of what people art thou?" Then came the most embarrassing question of all: "Why hast thou done this? For the men knew that he fled from the presence of the Lord, because he had told them."

Jonah chose a downward path. He went down to Joppa (Jonah 1:3). He went down into the ship, down below the decks (1:5). He went down to the bottom of the mountains (2:6). All was lost. He was reduced to utter lowliness. Down in "the belly of hell" he began to pray (2:2).

In the end Jonah went to Nineveh and preached grudgingly enough. Then he became resentful because the Gentiles did what Israel refused to do—they repented. Like the elder brother in the Lord's parable, Jonah was full of mean-spiritedness because God showed compassion on the repentant prodigal city. So God came and reasoned with the petulant prophet. Indeed the last time we *see* Jonah he is standing sullen and silent as God speaks to him of divine mercy and grace.

But we *hear* more of him. He went back home to Gath-hepher (2 Kings 14:25), three miles north of Nazareth, and wrote his book. The book of Jonah is evidence he had regarded reproof. And he was honored, for his book was canonized by the Holy Spirit and added to the divine library. Moreover he is the only Old Testament prophet to whom the Lord directly likened Himself (Matthew 12:40-41). What greater honor could be bestowed on a child of Adam's ruined race?

13. Truth about Longings (13:19)

"The desire accomplished is sweet to the soul: but it is abomination to fools to depart from evil." A good person feels satisfaction when he obtains the desire of his heart. A wicked man detests giving up the evil to which he clings so tenaciously.

The second part of Proverbs 13:19 reminds us of the way African natives sometimes trap monkeys. The trapper puts nuts in a jar with a narrow neck and ties the jar securely in place. A monkey comes, sees the nuts, and plunges his hand into the jar to seize the prize. However with the nuts in his hand the monkey has doubled his fist, and his doubled fist will not pass through the neck of the jar. Now he has a problem. If he releases the coveted nuts, he can withdraw his hand. If he hangs onto the nuts, he is trapped. He prefers to hang onto the nuts. When the trapper shows up with a big stick, the monkey will chatter with rage, fear, and frustration, but he will not let go of the nuts, not even to save his life. Likewise a fool hangs onto his sins. He is mastered by his lusts, held fast by his evil desires.

In contrast, when the desires of a good man reach fruition, he enjoys the rewards of work well done—just as Solomon stated in Proverbs 13:19. The first part of this verse reminds us of David Brainerd. His perpetual desire was the conversion of the American Indians. According to F. W. Boreham, Brainerd's life text was John 7:37: "If any man thirst, let him come unto me, and drink." Brainerd wrote that text into his journal again and again: "I preached to the Indians from the text, Jesus stood and cried, If any man thirst let him come unto Me and drink."[5]

With this text David Brainerd quenched the thirst of his own soul. Had he known words written by Horatius Bonar a century later, Brainerd might have used them in his testimony:

> I heard the voice of Jesus say,
> "Behold, I freely give
> The living water; thirsty one,
> Stoop down, and drink, and live."
> I came to Jesus, and I drank
> Of that life-giving stream;
> My thirst was quenched, my soul revived,
> And now I live in Him.

Brainerd thirsted to lead Indians to Christ. During his first visit to the forks of the Delaware, a miracle happened that not only saved his life but also opened the coveted door to the savage Indian tribes. Indian scouts had passed the word that a white man was coming their way and a party of braves concealed themselves in ambush to kill him. They saw him pitch his tent and as they crept nearer, they saw him on his knees. Then they saw a rattlesnake raise itself to strike. Brainerd was oblivious to danger as he talked to his God. The snake's forked tongue flickered near the white man's face. Then for no apparent reason the snake turned away and glided into the bush. "The Great Spirit is with him," the Indians said. So instead of greeting Brainerd with hostility, the whole tribe came out to meet him and treated him as an honored guest.

Brainerd journeyed far and wide among the Indians for five brief but strenuous years. His days were spent in the saddle, his nights beneath the stars. A frail consumptive continually wracked with his cough, he was never free from pain. He exposed his emaciated frame to perils and privations until it was worn out and then he returned to New England to die. He was not yet thirty years old, but like Abraham, Brainerd died "full" (Genesis 25:8), his desire accomplished. In fact he accomplished more than he knew. His diary, published by Jonathan Edwards as *Brainerd's Journal*, did as much as any other single factor to turn the church toward missions.

14. Truth about Liaisons (13:20)

"He that walketh with wise men shall be wise: but a companion of fools shall be destroyed." As the English proverb says, "We become like the company we keep."

Ham, a companion of fools, was the subject of one of Alexander Whyte's sermons. Few have preached on sin like Alexander Whyte did. His messages were directed straight to the heart and conscience. He also used his imagination effectively, and never more so than when he spoke about Ham:

> There was an old vagabond, to vice industrious, among the builders of the ark. He had for long been far too withered for anything to be called work; and he got his weekly wages just for sitting over the pots of pitch and keeping the fires burning beneath them....It was of him that God had said that it grieved and humbled Him at His heart that He had ever made man. The black asphalt itself was whiteness itself beside that old reprobate's heart and life. Now Ham, Noah's second son, was never away from that deep hollow out of which the preparing pitch boiled and smoked. All day down among the slime-pits, and all night out among the sultry woods—wherever you heard Ham's loud laugh, be sure that lewd old man was either singing a song there or telling a story. All the time the ark was a-building, and for long before that, Ham had been making himself vile under the old pitch-boiler's instructions and

examples. Ham's old instructor and exemplar had gone down quick to hell as soon as the ark was finished and shut in. But, by that time, Ham could walk alone. Dante came upon his old schoolmaster in hell when he was being led through hell on his way to heaven; and so did Ham when he went to his own place. But that was not yet. Ham was not vile enough yet. His day of grace had not come to an end yet. His bed in hell was not all made yet. He had more grey heads to bring down to the grave first. He had to break his old father's heart first. As he will soon now do, if you will wait a moment. Ham had been born out of due time. Ham had not been born and brought up in his true and proper place. Ham should have been born and bred in Sodom and Gomorrah. Not the ark, lifted up above the waters of the flood, but the midnight streets of the cities of the plain were Ham's proper place.[6]

Said Solomon, "A companion of fools shall be destroyed." We are not told in Scripture what happened to Ham, but we do know what kind of seed he planted. From Ham came the accursed Canaanites, destined from the beginning to be destroyed.

Noah, on the other hand, walked with wise men. He was a descendant of Seth and a long line of godly men. Just before the flood the torch of testimony was handed on to him. Noah in turn handed it on to Shem. Eventually it was handed on to Abraham and to David and finally to Christ.

Enoch "walked with God" (Genesis 5:22,24) and was raptured to Heaven barely seventy years before Noah was born. Seth, the founder of the godly line, had been dead a scant fourteen years. Memories of creation, the garden of Eden, and the fall were still alive in Noah's day. Noah, we can be sure, would visit Jared and say, "Tell me about your son Enoch." Noah would visit his grandfather Methuselah and say, "Tell me about your father Enoch." The universal response would be, "Enoch walked with God." Enoch's example rubbed off on Noah, for we read that "Noah walked with God" too (Genesis 6:9). "He that walketh with wise men shall be wise," said Solomon.

15. Truth about Lawlessness (13:21)

"Evil pursueth sinners: but to the righteous good shall be repaid."

A strange nut-brown creature haunts the fields and hedgerows of my native land. That creature is the weasel and rabbits flee in terror from it. A weasel always picks out one rabbit and follows it with a slow, snakelike walk. A rabbit can run much faster than a weasel, so how can a weasel capture a rabbit?

The weasel knows what it's doing. It persistently follows the trail of the chosen rabbit down winding burrows and along galleries with cross passages, blind holes, and escape holes. Never once does the weasel lose the scent of its victim. The chase is often long. The rabbit may dash ahead, double back on its trail, and halt for a moment at the mouth of a hole. Still the weasel steadily follows. The field may be home to scores of other rabbits, but the weasel goes on past their hiding places and they seem to take no notice. They seem to know it's not their turn this time.

The chase continues as the weasel's insatiable thirst for blood drives it on. It never allows itself to be distracted. The chosen victim rushes from field to field, from hedge to hedge, but still its nemesis follows. Nothing ever turns the weasel aside. Its nose is close to the ground, its little eyes twinkle, and its blood lust grows as slowly but surely the chase nears its end. Finally the exhausted rabbit hides in the long grass, and across the meadow or stealing along the furrow, following the growing scent, the weasel comes and pounces.

"Evil pursueth sinners," wrote Solomon, drawing on a lifetime of experience as judge of the supreme court. In the end sin must be paid for. There is no escape. David laid with his own hands the paving stones along which retribution followed. So do we.

"But to the righteous," Solomon added, "good shall be repaid." We reap what we sow. That law is as true of the soul as it is of the soil. Repayment may not always come in this life, although often enough sooner or later it does. What we have earned is always paid in full on the other side. At His judgment seat Christ will ensure that good is repaid to the righteous.

16. Truth about Legacies (13:22)

"A good man leaveth an inheritance to his children's children: and the wealth of the sinner is laid up for the just." The inheritance may or may not be worldly wealth. It may be a good name.

The lack of an inheritance is part of the dilemma of black people in America. No greater curse has ever come home to roost on a society than the curse of slavery in America. Arab slave traders, black chieftains, and white slave dealers tore apart African tribal family life. For two centuries men and women were bought and sold like cattle. The black slaves had no secure family life. At the whim of a white master, an enslaved family could be torn apart and auctioned off. Black women were ravished; the spirit of black men was violated.

As often as not, black children grew up never knowing their fathers. The slaves had no surnames. Often they were arbitrarily given the surnames of their owners.

America sowed the wind and reaps the whirlwind. Today a large number of blacks have learned to create, cultivate, and cherish family life. Many have become educated, developed leadership skills, and taken their places in society. Some have become rich and powerful. Many are honored in the professions. But in some inner cities blacks bear eight times as many babies out of wedlock as do whites. According to one statistic given some time ago, one-fifth of all black children born in the United States are illegitimate, and in the big cities the figure doubles. In central Harlem more than half of all black children come from single-parent homes. Many of these children have no concept of what the word *father* is supposed to mean.

The consequences are inevitable. Deprived of a stable family life, deprived of a good and honored name, and strangers to mercy and kindness, often these ghetto children learn at an early age to prey on society. One unofficial statistic is that 80 percent of all crime in New York City is committed by nonwhites, mostly teenagers.

Of course slavery is not the only cause of the black man's problem in America. There are other contributing factors—the intrusive welfare system, for example, that subsidizes the no-win/no-work situation in which many underprivileged black people live.

Children growing up in stable homes—children who have loving parents and are heirs to honorable names—cannot begin to imagine what life is like for those deprived of these blessings. "Denied love, or dignity, or patrimony or tradition or any culture but television," they menace their neighbors and everyone else. Theodore White referred to such deprived children in his book *The Making of the President.* He graphically described them as having their bread given to them by welfare workers, as having no hope. "Their mothers despised, their hearth the gutter," they are a lost subculture full of rage and revolt.[7]

Society owes much to a good father who loves, protects, provides for, disciplines, and trains his children. He passes on to his children an example, an honored name, a tradition of achievement, and a legacy of values and stability. "A good man leaveth an inheritance to his children's children." A child who has not only a good father but also an honored grandfather has a legacy of stability and continuity. Those who have such a legacy ought to be filled with compassion for those who, having been deprived, find their role models in gang leaders.

Solomon said, "The wealth of the sinner is laid up for the just."
The cynical world says, "Crime pays." But does crime really pay?
Bosses of syndicated crime, drug lords, and those who exploit the
follies, lusts, and weaknesses of fallen mankind make big profits, but
God's curse rests on their money. Although they may be rich, many
criminals live in fear. We may not always see the swing of the scales,
but God's moral rule over this world is both ultimate and absolute.
We should not judge by appearances.

God taught Job not to judge by appearances. After all the fuss and
argument; after Eliphaz, Bildad, and Zophar had had their say; after
Job had given them his spirited tit for tat; after Elihu had pompously
lectured his betters—then God spoke. He asked Job a series of
questions regarding His ways in the world of nature. He asked him
about the stars, about life's origins, about the way of an eagle, about
the multitudinous events of a single day. God posed question after
question. And Job stood there, silent and rebuked like a small boy
at school with a dunce cap on his head.

The inference was obvious. "Job," God was saying, "you don't
know how I manage the material universe, so how can you possibly
know how I manage the moral universe? You do not know all the
factors in the simpler equation. What makes you think you know all
the factors in the more complex equation?" Job acknowledged his
folly.

We do not have all the answers either. God's ways in the moral
universe are mysterious. We can however be sure of this: "The
wealth of the sinner is laid up for the just." God will see to it.

God's people inherited the wealth of the sinner when Israel
conquered Canaan. Fulfilling His four-century-old promise to Abraham, God gave the Israelites houses they had not built, wells they
had not dug, and vineyards and olive groves they had not planted
(Deuteronomy 6:10-11). The wealth of sinners was stored up for
centuries for the just. When God's time came to make the transfer,
He did as He had promised.

17. Truth about Labor (13:23)

"Much food is in the tillage of the poor: but there is that is
destroyed for want of judgment."

The wealth of a nation lies in its work force. No nation can afford
to neglect the well-being, education, and steady gainful employment of its working class. It is not the wealthy landowner or the stock
market speculator who contributes to a nation's wealth. It is the
hard work of the poor that produces good harvests and increases a

nation's gross national product. The steady plodding, diligence, and skill of the work force produce national wealth.

Boaz was a mighty man of wealth. At the time of harvest he went to his fields to see how the work was progressing. He mingled with the workers and offered cheery, encouraging words to all. "The Lord be with you," he said. "The Lord bless thee," the reapers replied (Ruth 2:4). To one worker he offered a greeting, to another a word of appreciation. We can picture him glancing at Ruth and then giving a word of command. He was a great lord, a prince of the house of Judah. But Boaz did not produce those bumper harvests. He simply owned the fields. Had it not been for the hard-working laborers, the harvest would have been left rotting in the field. Indeed no furrows would have been tilled and no seeds would have been sown, so there would have been no crop to harvest. It was the farmhand who created the wealth. Although Solomon was an imperious and autocratic ruler, he never underestimated the value of the toil and sweat of the laboring man.

Solomon himself is an illustration of the second part of Proverbs 13:23: "There is that is destroyed for want of judgment." He spent millions on the aggrandizement of Jerusalem. The palace complex cost a fortune. He never tired of building palaces, public buildings, and parks, and all his projects were planned and carried out at enormous cost in terms of men, money, and materials. The aliens living in the country were reduced to serfdom and put to work. To build the temple Solomon drafted 30,000 men and sent them to Lebanon one month out of every three. He had 70,000 "that bare burdens" and 80,000 "hewers in the mountains." In addition 3,300 men were employed to supervise this vast body of laborers (1 Kings 5:13-16). Doubtless the people took pride in the work until the temple was completed. When the exactions continued just to gratify Solomon's soaring pride, resentment set in. In spite of his celebrated wisdom, Solomon became the living embodiment of his own proverb. He drove his people too hard, conscripted too many men, and overtaxed his subjects. He sowed those fertile but deadly seeds of revolt that Jeroboam so clearly exploited when Solomon died.

18. Truth about Love (13:24)

"He that spareth his rod hateth his son: but he that loveth him chasteneth him betimes." The old English proverb says, "Spare the rod and spoil the child." In our day corporal punishment has gone out of favor. What too many humanistic behavioral psychologists teach about child-rearing is nonsense. Still, no one can deny there were abuses in the old days when parents and teachers alike were far too free with the cane.

Huw Morgan in Richard Llewellyn's *How Green Was My Valley* was the victim of abusive corporal punishment. Huw was a miner's son in one of the Welsh valleys. The moment he set eyes on his first schoolteacher, Mr. Elijah Jonas-Sessions, young Huw knew he was in for trouble. Mr. Jonas was "small and pale in the eyes, with that look in them to warn you he had the tongue of a mountain adder, to be careful in what you said, or he would twist every word of it for you."[8]

Huw's apprehension was well-founded. The bullying teacher thrashed him cruelly and mercilessly for fighting, even though he had been picked on. As Huw waited for the first blow, "the stick swished twice as though Mr. Jonas were getting his length." Then again and again and again the cruel stick fell upon Huw until his back, cut to ribbons, was "one long hurt." Finally the stick broke and the teacher talked. "'Now then,' said Mr. Jonas, in falsetto, and breathless, 'fight again. Was just a taste. Back to your place. No more nonsense. Teach you manners.'"[9]

When poor Huw reached home his brother Ianto noticed that something was wrong. He made Huw lift his shirt. Then Dai Brando saw poor Huw's back. He and his friend Cyfartha Lewis were prizefighters and they decided to pay an informal call on Mr. Elijah Jonas-Sessions. We take grim satisfaction in what followed. The two prizefighters roughed the schoolmaster up playfully for starters. Then Dai bent the bully over his knee and gave him the thrashing of his life. The scene "could not have been bettered beyond the bounds of purgatory." When Dai was finished, he and Cyfartha gripped the sniveling teacher by the shoulders and feet and "swung him right through the open trap of the coal locker and shut the lid."[10]

When I was a youngster, I also had a bullying schoolmaster. I lived in fear of him, as did most of the other little boys in his class. He caned us coldly and efficiently at the least provocation. Thinking back, I'm sure the man was a sadist and never should have been entrusted with a roomful of boys and a stick. He would sometimes leave the room and go down the hall. Boys being boys, the classroom soon hummed with talk and often with horseplay. When the noise crescendoed, that schoolmaster would bounce back into the room. With an anticipatory gleam in his eye he would swish his cane. Then systematically, desk by desk and row by row, he would thrash every boy, guilty or innocent.

Obviously that kind of bully should be deprived of the right to inflict physical punishment. But as a society we have gone to the other extreme and tend to view all corporal punishment as wrong. The modern idea is to try to reason with young delinquents. Solomon, under the inspiration of the Holy Spirit, supported the discriminating use of the rod. We would do well to heed the Spirit of God. Properly administered, the rod can express as much love for one's child as a kiss.

19. Truth about Leanness (13:25)

"The righteous eateth to the satisfying of his soul: but the belly of the wicked shall want." The good man always has enough to take care of his needs. His prudence, temperance, and industry contribute to his well-being, and God blesses what he has. The wicked can expect to come to want. His desires are never satisfied. God's providence orders these different results.

This proverb reminds us of God's terrible indictment of old Eli, who was Israel's high priest toward the end of the days of the judges. How he became high priest we do not know. The office rightfully belonged to the priestly line of Eleazar, and Eli was a descendant of Aaron's youngest son Ithamar. That kind of irregularity was typical of the general disorder that marked this period in Israel's history. Eli also served as a judge.

Eli was a dismal failure, both as a priest and as a parent. He was so lax in dealing with his sons Hophni and Phinehas that their behavior in both spiritual and sexual matters became a public scandal (1 Samuel 2:23-25; 3:13). A man of God came to denounce Eli and pronounce judgment:

> Behold, the days come, that I will cut off thine arm, and the arm of thy father's house, that there shall not be an old man in thine house. And thou shalt see an enemy in my habitation...and there shall not be an old man in thine house forever....And it shall come to pass, that every one that is left in thine house shall come and crouch to him [the faithful priest] for a piece of silver and a morsel of bread, and shall say, Put me, I pray thee, into one of the priests' offices, that I may eat a piece of bread (1 Samuel 2:31-36).

Though Eli's place was taken by Samuel, the prophecy concerning the priesthood seemed to slumber on unfulfilled. True enough, Hophni and Phinehas died, and the word *Ichabod* came into the

Hebrew vocabulary when the sacred ark of the covenant was stolen by the Philistines. But for a time, the rest of the house of Eli prospered.

Then the grandson of Phinehas, the high priest Ahimelech, was murdered by King Saul. Later the high priest Abiathar—the son of Ahimelech and the friend of David—made the fatal blunder of backing Joab and Adonijah in their fight against Solomon's succession to the throne (1 Kings 1:7; 2:12-22). For this alliance Abiathar was deposed and Zadok, from the approved line of Eleazar, was installed firmly in the office of high priest. Only Solomon's sense of propriety and fair play saved Abiathar from execution.

The Holy Spirit notes that Abiathar's demotion was a fulfillment of the old prophecy (1 Kings 2:26-27). Doubtless the rest of the prophecy came true and Abiathar's descendants were reduced to beggary. The fruit of Eli's weakness and his sons' wickedness took a long time to ripen. God is never in a hurry, especially when it comes to judgment.

CHAPTER 18
Proverbs 14:1-35

D. Viewpoints to Be Considered (14:1-35)
  1. The Portals of the Home (14:1-3)
     a. The Housewife Seen (14:1)
     b. The Husband Seen (14:2-3)
        (1) His Walk (14:2)
        (2) His Words (14:3)
  2. The Pastures of the Farm (14:4)
  3. The Precincts of the Court (14:5)
     a. The Faithful Witness (14:5a)
     b. The False Witness (14:5b)
  4. The Presence of the Fool (14:6-9)
     a. The Scorning Fool (14:6)
     b. The Silly Fool (14:7-8)
        (1) He Does Not Treasure the Truth (14:7)
        (2) He Does Not Tell the Truth (14:8)
     c. The Scoffing Fool (14:9)
  5. The Passions of the Heart (14:10)
     a. In Times of Bitterness (14:10a)
     b. In Times of Bliss (14:10b)
  6. The Pathways of the World (14:11-13)
     a. The Haunted House (14:11)
     b. The Hellbent Highway (14:12)
     c. The Heavy Heart (14:13)
  7. The People on the Road (14:14-27)
     a. The Gullible Man (14:14-15)
        (1) The Man Who Backslides Anyway (14:14)
        (2) The Man Who Believes Anything (14:15)

Solomon continued his observations on various aspects of life. His keen mind moved here, there, and everywhere, his eager eye took in every passing scene, and his open ear listened to what people said. All was grist for his mill. He wanted to know about everybody and everything, and he wanted us to know as well.

D. Viewpoints to Be Considered (14:1-35)

1. The Portals of the Home (14:1-3)

a. The Housewife Seen (14:1)

"Every wise woman buildeth her house: but the foolish plucketh it down with her hands." The word translated "wise" here is *chokmoth*. It is plural but has a singular verb for emphasis. The grammatical structure here draws attention to the true wisdom of the wise woman. The verb "buildeth" is in the preterit tense, implying the outcome of past wisdom. The foolish woman's behavior is expressed in the future tense because the course she has adopted is continuous—its consequences continue to their logical end.

An English proverb says, "The hand which rocks the cradle rules the world." This saying, laid alongside Proverbs 14:1, sheds light on the history of Judah's kings. Little is said about the women in the lives of the kings of the northern kingdom of Israel. We do know, however, that Jeroboam's mother was a widow (1 Kings 11:26) and that Ahab was under the thumb of Jezebel, the evil woman he married (1 Kings 16:31-33). From the start the kings of the schismatic kingdom were a bad lot.

It is really in connection with the Davidic dynasty of Judah that the Holy Spirit emphasizes the mothers of the kings. There seems to be no discernible pattern of behavior when we look at Judah's kings themselves. A good king (Uzziah) was followed by a good king (Jotham); a good king (Jotham) was followed by a bad king (Ahaz); a bad king (Ahaz) was followed by a good king (Hezekiah); a good king (Hezekiah) was followed by a bad king (Manasseh); a bad king (Manasseh) was followed by a bad king (Amon). A pattern can be seen, however, when we look at the mothers of the kings.

1. Rehoboam - "His mother's name was Naamah an Ammonitess. And he did evil, because he prepared not his heart to seek the Lord" (2 Chronicles 12:13-14; also see 1 Kings 14:21). These verses explain a great deal about this weak, incompetent king.

2. Abijah (Abijam) - "His mother's name also was Michaiah the daughter of Uriel of Gibeah" (2 Chronicles 13:2). She is also called Maachah the (grand?) daughter of Absalom (Abishalom) (2 Chronicles 11:20; 1 Kings 15:2). According to Josephus, Uriel of Gibeah was the husband of Tamar, the daughter of Absalom. We can perhaps set this confusing genealogy out thus:

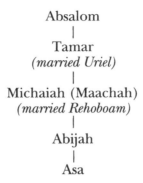

Absalom
|
Tamar
(married Uriel)
|
Michaiah (Maachah)
(married Rehoboam)
|
Abijah
|
Asa

The names of Abijah's mother are significant. The name *Michaiah* ("Who is like Jehovah?") is used when she is mentioned as the queen mother. The name *Maachah* ("Oppression") is used when she is mentioned as an idolater (2 Chronicles 15:16). The historian said of Abijah that "he walked in all the sins of his father, which he had done before him: and his heart was not perfect with the Lord his God, as the heart of David his father" (1 Kings 15:3).

3. Asa - His (grand?) mother's name was Maachah the (grand?) daughter of Absalom (Abishalom) (1 Kings 15:8-11). The chronicler added, "And Asa did that which was good and right in the eyes of the Lord his God" (2 Chronicles 14:2).

4. Jehoshaphat - "His mother's name was Azubah the daughter of Shilhi. And he walked in all the ways of Asa his father; he turned not aside from it, doing that which was right in the eyes of the Lord" (1 Kings 22:42-43).

5. Jehoram (Joram) - "He walked in the way of the kings of Israel, as did the house of Ahab: for the daughter of Ahab was his wife: and he did evil in the sight of the Lord" (2 Kings 8:18; also see 2 Chronicles 21:6).

6. Ahaziah - "His mother's name was Athaliah, the daughter of Omri king of Israel" (2 Kings 8:26). (Here Omri is named as the founder of this evil dynasty. Ahab and Jezebel were Athaliah's immediate parents.) Ahaziah "walked in the way of the house of Ahab, and did evil in the sight of the Lord, as did the house of Ahab: for he was the son in law of the house of Ahab" (2 Kings 8:27). The chronicler added: "His mother's name also was Athaliah the daughter of

Omri [Ahab]. He also walked in the ways of the house of Ahab: for his mother was his counsellor to do wickedly. Wherefore he did evil in the sight of the Lord like the house of Ahab: for they were his counsellors after the death of his father to his destruction" (2 Chronicles 22:2-4).

7. Jehoash (Joash) - "His mother's name was Zibiah of Beer-sheba. And Jehoash did that which was right in the sight of the Lord all his days wherein Jehoiada the priest instructed him" (2 Kings 12:1-2; also see 2 Chronicles 24:1-2).

8. Amaziah - "His mother's name was Jehoaddan of Jerusalem. And he did that which was right in the sight of the Lord, but not with a perfect heart" (2 Chronicles 25:1-2).

9. Azariah (Uzziah) - "His mother's name was Jecholiah of Jerusalem. And he did that which was right in the sight of the Lord, according to all that his father Amaziah had done" (2 Kings 15:2-3; also see 2 Chronicles 26:3-4).

10. Jotham - "His mother's name was Jerusha, the daughter of Zadok" (2 Kings 15:33). Zadok was the high priest (1 Chronicles 6:12). This may explain why Jotham's father Uzziah invaded the temple and tried to unite the mutually exclusive offices of king and priest in his own person (2 Chronicles 26:16). Jotham "did that which was right in the sight of the Lord: he did according to all that his father Uzziah had done" (2 Kings 15:34; also see 2 Chronicles 26:3-4).

11. Ahaz - He "did not that which was right in the sight of the Lord his God" (2 Kings 16:2; also see 2 Chronicles 28:1). No mention is made of this weak and wicked king's mother. Perhaps she died when he was very young. Proclaimed king at the age of twenty, Ahaz was a committed pagan.

12. Hezekiah - "His mother's name...was Abi, the daughter of Zachariah. And he did that which was right in the sight of the Lord" (2 Kings 18:2-3).

13. Manasseh - "His mother's name was Hephzi-bah. And he did that which was evil in the sight of the Lord" (2 Kings 21:1-2). According to Rotherham, Jewish tradition says that Hephzi-bah was the daughter of the prophet Isaiah—Hezekiah's dear friend,

counselor, and fellow believer. If this is so, Manasseh's pigheaded willfulness and diabolical wickedness are all the more astonishing. He ascended the throne when he was only twelve years old, having been born to godly King Hezekiah after his life was miraculously extended (2 Kings 20:1-11). The young man seems to have been a throwback to his paternal grandfather.

14. Amon - "His mother's name was Meshullemeth, the daughter of Haruz of Jotbah. And he did that which was evil in the sight of the Lord, as his father Manasseh did" (2 Kings 21:19-20; also see 2 Chronicles 33:21-22).

15. Josiah - "His mother's name was Jedidah, the daughter of Adaiah of Boscath. And he did that which was right in the sight of the Lord, and walked in all the way of David" (2 Kings 22:1-2; also see 2 Chronicles 34:2).

16. Jehoahaz - "His mother's name was Hamutal, the daughter of Jeremiah of Libnah. And he did that which was evil in the sight of the Lord, according to all that his fathers had done" (2 Kings 23:31-32).

17. Eliakim (changed to Jehoiakim) - "His mother's name was Zebudah, the daughter of Pedaiah of Rumah. And he did that which was evil in the sight of the Lord, according to all that his fathers had done" (2 Kings 23:36-37).

18. Jehoiachin - "His mother's name was Nehushta, the daughter of Elnathan of Jerusalem. And he did that which was evil in the sight of the Lord, according to all that his father had done" (2 Kings 24:8-9).

19. Mattaniah (changed to Zedekiah) - "His mother's name was Hamutal, the daughter of Jeremiah of Libnah. And he did that which was evil in the sight of the Lord, according to all that Jehoiakim had done" (2 Kings 24:18-19).

Three of King Josiah's sons sat on the throne: Jehoahaz, Jehoiakim, and Zedekiah. All were bad, yet Josiah was one of Judah's godliest kings. The finger points to the mothers.

The oft-repeated emphasis on the mothers and the wives of Judah's kings reveals what an influence these women must have been. The bad ones seem to have had a stronger influence than the good ones. Truly the moral, social, and spiritual welfare of a nation depends on the mothers of its children.

b. The Husband Seen (14:2-3)

Having shown the effect of the wife's influence, Solomon next drew attention to the husband and *his walk:* "He that walketh in his uprightness feareth the Lord: but he that is perverse in his ways despiseth him" (Proverbs 14:2). We see this proverb brought into focus when we think of the contrast between godly Hezekiah and his wicked father Ahaz.

Ahaz was at first intimidated by the neighboring Syrians and then infatuated with the even more formidable Assyrians. When Israel and Syria patched up their differences and formed an alliance against Judah, Ahaz decided to seek foreign aid from powerful Assyria. The prophet Isaiah warned him against any such move, promised the destruction of the Syro-Ephraimitic alliance, and gave the famous prophecy about the virgin birth of Christ (Isaiah 7:1-16).

But as Solomon said, he that is perverse in his ways despises the Lord, so Ahaz brushed aside the prophet and listened to his political advisers. He appealed to Tiglath-pileser, the Assyrian king, for aid and purchased an alliance with treasures looted from the temple and the palace (2 Kings 16:7-8). We can well imagine the Assyrians were delighted to have an excuse to move south. Their army made short work of Judah's enemies, but now Ahaz had the imperial, invincible, ruthless, and expansionist Assyria as a next-door neighbor. Their proximity did not seem to bother the spiritually insensitive Ahaz, even though Isaiah clearly foresaw that Assyria threatened everything Judah stood for as the people of God in this world.

Isaiah may as well have talked to a brick wall. Before long, Ahaz traveled to Damascus to pay homage to his terrible ally and returned like a dog with a new bone, wagging its tail. At Damascus he had seen a most attractive altar dedicated to a pagan god. Once back in Jerusalem, Ahaz ordered a facsimile to be made and installed in the temple court. He unceremoniously shoved aside the altar that had been made to divine specifications (2 Kings 16:10-14). No greater insult could have been offered to the living God. No wonder Hosea and Micah raised their voices in chorus with Isaiah to denounce the spiritual, social, and secular wickedness of the times.

How young Hezekiah could have turned out so well is somewhat of a mystery. Certainly his father can be given no credit. All we know of his mother is her name, *Abi,* a contraction of *Abijah,* which means

"Jehovah is a father." Perhaps Abi pointed her young son to the heavenly Father. Perhaps she encouraged Hezekiah (whose name means "Jehovah is strong") to cultivate the friendship of the prophet Isaiah. Certainly the two became firm friends. In any case, young Hezekiah saw through his father's follies.

Many years later when King Hezekiah became deathly ill, he consoled himself by remembering an incident that had befallen him when as a young man he had been visiting the upper Jordan. A storm came and the waters rushing down the mountainside turned the Jordan into a boiling flood. The young prince was swept off his feet by the angry waters and almost drowned. Desperately he called on the living God, and the rolling billows, instead of overwhelming him, cast him up on a cliff. His feet found a firm foothold on the rock. He was saved! The waters abated and he was able to go home (Psalm 42:6-9).[1] He never forgot that experience. It strengthened his growing faith in God.

All his days thereafter Hezekiah walked uprightly in the fear of God. Invading armies, subversive politicians, fickle citizens, childlessness, and even terminal illness could not shake his faith in God. Without wavering he walked hand in hand with God through perils that would have overwhelmed a lesser man. He had proved God and walked uprightly in His fear.

Solomon drew attention to the husband and *his words* in the next proverb: "In the mouth of the foolish is a rod of pride: but the lips of the wise shall preserve them" (Proverbs 14:3). Our words betray us. Out of the mouth of a fool come haughty, insolent words that are frequently his undoing. The wise man's words are often his best defense.

Hezekiah certainly was known by his words. He led a tremendous renaissance of learning and piety. There was a fresh outburst of interest in poetry (2 Chronicles 29:30) and his scribes were kept busy (Proverbs 25:1). In his personal testimony Hezekiah spoke of his songs (Isaiah 38:20), most likely the anonymous songs of degrees (Psalms 120–134). In addition to these songs written to give glory to God for his miraculous recovery from a terminal illness, Hezekiah wrote other Psalms that found their way into the Hebrew hymnbook. Psalm 45 may have been written by him to celebrate his marriage to Hephzi-bah. Some scholars believe that Psalms 111–118 are Hezekiah's. Psalms 46–48 seem to be his also; they may reflect the circumstances at the time of the Assyrian invasion and the miraculous deliverance of Jerusalem.

Although he stands second only to David among the Judean kings, Hezekiah was human. He had his share of the terrible pride that rules every human heart. After his sickness and recovery he welcomed ambassadors from Babylon to his court. Hezekiah was impressed by the fact that the Babylonians were seeking his friendship. Actually the Babylonians were eager to befriend anyone who would stand up to the Assyrians. Hezekiah foolishly showed off all his treasures. His friend, the prophet Isaiah, rebuked him for his pride. Although Babylon did not invade Judah until about a century later, Isaiah knew that Judah's peril lay not in nearby Assyria but in distant Babylon (Isaiah 39:1-8).

Hezekiah also manifested pride in another form—that particular form of pride, so common to all of us, that makes us think that in matters of sickness and death we know better than God. Isaiah told the king to put his house in order, for he was about to die. "Then Hezekiah turned his face toward the wall, and prayed unto the Lord, And said, Remember now, O Lord, I beseech thee, how I have walked before thee in truth and with a perfect heart, and have done that which is good in thy sight. And Hezekiah wept sore" (Isaiah 38:2-3).

Behind the self-righteousness evident in Hezekiah's words was the belief that the nation needed him and he needed a son. Apparently Hezekiah became ill either just before the Assyrian invasion of Judah or during the actual siege of Jerusalem, and he believed himself to be indispensable to his people during this crisis. But no one is indispensable. And Hezekiah thought that if he died without an heir, the royal line of David would die out. He forgot that God is able to raise up seed to David or Abraham or anyone else, even from stones (Matthew 3:9).

Sometimes God gives us what we in our pride and self-will demand of Him. He gave Hezekiah fifteen more years of life. Three years after his recovery he was given the son and heir for which he craved, but it would have been better if Manasseh had never been born. Hezekiah's prayer was a foolish prayer.

2. The Pastures of the Farm (14:4)

"Where no oxen are, the crib is clean: but much increase is by the strength of the ox." We can easily apply this proverb to our century. The battle lines in our day are drawn between the environmentalists and the industrialists, and the consumers are caught in between. It is as impossible in our age to operate a factory without generating waste products as it was in Solomon's day to keep oxen for plowing without having animal wastes in their stalls. A farmer could have a clean crib all right—if he had no oxen. But if he had no oxen, he could not farm wide fields.

Every year the United States alone produces 1.3 billion tons of agricultural manure and refuse. It produces 1 billion tons of mining wastes, 350 million tons of residential and industrial garbage and sewage, and 15 million tons of scrapped automobiles. Cars, power plants, factories, and residential heating units belch more than 142 million tons of toxic matter into the air every year. Most of these toxins are in the form of carbon monoxide, sulfur dioxide, nitrous oxide, hydrocarbons, solid particles, and radiation from atomic power plants and the industrial use of lasers and microwave technology. The air breathed by each person in Chicago in a single day is said to contain as much pollution as that derived by a smoker from two packs of cigarettes.

The awesome problem of nuclear wastes is horrendous.[2] When the spent fuel of nuclear reactors is recycled in order to salvage the reusable uranium and platinum, a rust-colored liquid is left behind. For years the practice was to put the liquid in million-gallon tanks and bury them underground. The liquid is so saturated with toxins, however, that it boils from the heat generated by the decaying radioactive substances it contains. The liquid is 250 times more lethal than the bomb dropped on Hiroshima. Some of the radioisotopes in the waste soon decay, but strontium 90 and cesium 137 both have approximate 30-year half-lives, which means they will have to be kept out of the environment for up to 1,000 years. Plutonium 239 has a half-life of 24,000 years, which means it must be kept out of the environment for approximately 250,000 years. Because of the danger of the underground tanks leaking their lethal contents into the ground, techniques are now used to solidify nuclear waste products into highly radioactive "salt cake." But what is to be done with the accumulating hundreds of thousands of tons of this waste?

The problem keeps growing. A dramatic example is the case of the freighter *Pelicano,* which sailed around the world looking for a port that would accept its cargo. Fourteen thousand tons of highly toxic incinerator ash had been loaded on the ship in Philadelphia and nobody wanted to unload the vessel. It plowed the seas for over two years. Then it began to dump its cargo clandestinely wherever an unguarded spot could be found.

Every industrialized country in the world has the problem of waste disposal. Rivers and lakes and underground streams are becoming contaminated. Vast amounts of lethal waste are dumped into the sea or spewed into the atmosphere. Acid rain kills vegetation.

The ozone layer, a blanket of oxygen molecules that protects the earth's surface from the sun's harmful ultraviolet radiation, is being thinned by manmade chlorofluorocarbons (CFS)—chemicals used as spray-can propellants, refrigerants, and industrial solvents.

The environmentalists are up in arms. The easy targets are nuclear energy plants, factories, oil companies, and big business. The industrial complex in the United States no doubt needs to do more, but it has already spent billions trying to curb pollution. Much pollution comes from other sources including municipalities, agriculture, and the general public. The problem is highly complex.

We could of course shut down industry altogether. If we banished cars from our streets and highways, there would be no automobile pollution. If we closed down power plants, we would have no pollution from utilities. If we washed no clothes, we would have no laundry detergents in our water supply. As Solomon said, "Where no oxen are, the crib is clean: but much increase is by the strength of the ox." It seems we can't have it both ways.

3. The Precincts of the Court (14:5)

Solomon wrote about two kinds of witnesses: *the faithful witness*— "A faithful witness will not lie"; and *the false witness*—"but a false witness will utter lies."

In glory the Lord Jesus is called "the faithful witness" (Revelation 1:5). Paul reminded his young friend Timothy that Christ is a faithful witness. Paul wrote:

> Fight the good fight of faith, lay hold on eternal life, whereunto thou art also called, and hast professed a good profession before many witnesses. I give thee charge in the sight of God, who quickeneth all things, and before Christ Jesus, who before Pontius Pilate witnessed a good confession (1 Timothy 6:12-13).

The trial before Pilate, as recorded in considerable detail by John, revolved around two issues: the Lord's sovereignty and the Lord's sonship. Most of the time Jesus said nothing.

Pilate raised the vexing question of the Lord's *domains:* "Art thou the King of the Jews?" (John 18:33) A great deal hinged on the answer to that question, for the caesar did not tolerate rival kings. Conviction for high treason swung in the balance, and death by crucifixion. The Jews eventually pressured Pilate to convict Jesus. "If thou let this man go," they said, "thou art not Caesar's friend"

(19:12). Pilate turned pale at the thought of influential Jews in Rome reporting to suspicious Tiberius that he had released someone who claimed to be a king—especially a king of the volatile and passionately nationalistic Jews.

Jesus was a king, but His kingdom was not of this world. He said, "If my kingdom were of this world, then would my servants fight" (John 18:36). He would have mobilized His armies long ago. But His kingdom was the kingdom of Heaven.

An even more vexing question concerned the Lord's *deity*. Pilate allowed his soldiers to rough up his prisoner, mock His claim to be a king, crown Him with thorns, and clothe Him in purple. Then he presented Him to the Jews, who in turn demanded His death. "He made himself the Son of God," they said (John 19:7). That statement struck terror into Pilate's hard heart. He asked Jesus, "Whence art thou?" (19:9) When Jesus did not answer, Pilate threatened Him with his power to sentence Him to death or set Him free. Jesus responded to the threat by telling Pilate he had no power over Him at all. Any power he had was given him from above. Again there was that reference to that other world.

Christ was the epitome of the faithful witness. He longed for Pilate's conversion. Through blunt statements of fact, dignified silence, and perfect peace and poise, He witnessed a good confession, even though He knew that death by crucifixion would be the outcome of the trial.

Before Pilate we see the faithful witness. Around Caiaphas we see the false witnesses. "A false witness will utter lies," Solomon said. "The chief priests, and elders, and all the council, sought false witness against Jesus, to put him to death" (Matthew 26:59). False witnesses must have come in droves, for Matthew added that "many" came (26:60). The word he used to refer to false witnesses is *pseudomarturia*. It occurs in only one other place in the New Testament—in Matthew 15:19. There Jesus said, "Out of the heart proceed evil thoughts, murders, adulteries, fornications, thefts, false witness, blasphemies." Lying testimony is native to the unregenerate heart. In his fallen state man is capable even of lying about the incarnate Son of God.

Men lie about Him still. For instance John Spong, a bishop of America's Episcopal Church, stated in his book *Rescuing the Bible* that the virgin birth of Christ is "an unthinkable notion." Spong declared that there is not much value in the doctrine of the trinity or in the belief that Jesus was sent to save fallen humanity from sin. The bishop is a false witness. *Time* magazine likened his statements to "excerpts from a tract by a staunch atheist."[3]

4. The Presence of the Fool (14:6-9)

a. The Scorning Fool (14:6)

"A scorner seeketh wisdom, and findeth it not: but knowledge is easy unto him that understandeth."

Greece gave the world a galaxy of giants: Archimedes, Aristotle, Aeschylus, Homer, Hesiod, Herodotus, Plato, Pythagoras, Pericles, Euripedes, Eratosthenes, Sophocles, and Socrates. As Wilbur M. Smith put it, "The only *thinking* civilization in the world before our own is that of Greece."[4] He commented that Plato and Aristotle have dominated the thought patterns of Western European civilization. The Greeks, he said, have "given us the staple of our vocabulary in every domain of thought and knowledge." Yet the apostle Paul, a greater thinker than any of the Greeks, wrote of them: "The world by wisdom knew not God" (1 Corinthians 1:21).

The French agnostic, Ernest Renan, was infatuated with the brilliant ancient pagan world. He said, "The ancient Greeks had no well-determined rule of faith and their religion, charming when taken as poetry, is, when viewed according to our theological ideas, a mere mass of contradictory fables."[5]

The Greek had a god for everything. If he wanted to get drunk he had Bacchus, if he wanted sex he turned to Aphrodite Pandemos, if he wanted to steal he could look to Hermes, or if he wanted to search for purity he could consider the worship of Artemis.

The gods of Greece were shameful, lustful, vengeful, gross, and evil. The cult of Dionysos was savage, brutal, bestial, and grossly immoral.[6] Euripedes said, "No more can men justly be called wicked, if we only imitate what the gods call good."[7] The Greek gods were guilty of almost every conceivable crime. E. G. Sihler wrote, "Neither purity nor humanity nor mercy has a seat at the Olympian board."[8]

Someone said, "Philosophy has found out many truths but not the truth." Cicero asked, "What is truth?" As Wilbur M. Smith put it, "After eight hundred years of the development of philosophy, and five hundred years of philosophical speculation, Greek civilization led to an altar on which was the inscription: 'To the Unknown God.'"[9] When Paul preached that Unknown God to the Athenians, they mocked. They were scorning fools. They failed to understand that Jesus is the truth (John 14:6).

"But knowledge is easy unto him that understandeth." A little child can grasp this great truth:

> Jesus loves me! this I know,
> For the Bible tells me so.
> (Anna B. Warner)

Anyone who will come to Jesus as a child can understand (Matthew 18:1-5). Those who come to Jesus find they have tapped the source of all wisdom and knowledge (Colossians 2:3).

b. The Silly Fool (14:7-8)

The silly fool does not *treasure the truth:* "Go from the presence of a foolish man, when thou perceiveth not in him the lips of knowledge" (Proverbs 14:7). It is a good idea to put some distance between ourselves and those who believe and talk nonsense.

In *Pilgrim's Progress* Christian and Hopeful were "going down the mountains along the highway toward the city." Bunyan continued:

> Now, a little below these mountains, on the left hand, lieth the country of Conceit; from which country there comes into the way in which the pilgrims walked, a little crooked lane. Here, therefore, they met with a very brisk lad, that came out of that country; and his name was Ignorance. So Christian asked him from what parts he came, and whither he was going.

Ignorance acknowledged that he was born in the country of Conceit. He told Christian and Hopeful he was going to the Celestial City. Asked how he hoped to get in at the gate, he said, "I pray, fast, pay tithes, and give alms." Christian pointed out to him that he had not started the right way; he had come by way of the crooked lane. Ignorance had a ready answer. "Gentlemen," he said, "ye be utter strangers to me, I know you not; be content to follow the religion of your country, and I will follow the religion of mine." He could see no need to go all the way back to get on the path the way they had. He couldn't think of anyone in his country who even knew the way to the place they had started from. Besides, the "fine, pleasant green lane" that came from the country of Conceit seemed to him to be as good a way as any to get on the road to Heaven.

Christian and Hopeful journeyed on past the town of Apostasy. They remembered a man called Little-faith who had been robbed and beaten thereabouts by three brothers—Faint-heart, Mistrust, and Guilt—the kind who molest all pilgrims whose faith is small. Christian and Hopeful recalled that because such robberies occurred even on the King's highway, it was prudent to wear the whole armor of God and to go in convoy.

Next they met a man called Flatterer, a false prophet who almost snared them, and a man called Atheist, who scoffed at them. Then they safely negotiated the Enchanted Ground where many pilgrims had been lulled to sleep.

Ignorance still followed them. They waited for him, still hoping to help him. But Ignorance was so full of religious conceit, so sure he was as good as they were, so blind to his need for repentance, so confident of his own goodness, and so unteachable that at last they had to leave him behind. They said:

> Well, Ignorance, wilt thou yet foolish be,
> To slight good counsel, ten times given thee?
> And if thou yet refuse it, thou shalt know,
> Ere long, the evil of thy doing so.

Thus Bunyan captured the spirit of the silly fool who does not treasure the truth.

The silly fool does not *tell the truth* either: "The wisdom of the prudent is to understand his way: but the folly of fools is deceit" (Proverbs 14:8). The fool tells lies. God considers lying to be the height of folly. Lying destroys character and trust, and is the antithesis of all that God is. In the end lying is always counterproductive.

Some business advertisements are frank, open, and direct, based on the adage that honesty is the best policy. But much modern advertisement is based on exploitation of gullible people.

One of my secondary tasks at the Moody Correspondence School was to write copy to promote the sale of the courses we produced, so to improve my advertising skills I attended numerous seminars in which successful advertising techniques were shared. Attending those seminars was an eye-opening experience.

I learned that "good" copy always promotes the customer's self-interest and appeals to his wants and desires. The successful advertiser does not spend much time describing his product. He tells you what his product will do for you. The copywriter must find words that will penetrate the reader's subconsciousness and cause him to experience vicariously the joy and pleasure of using the product. In other words, the advertiser does not try to sell the sausage; he tries to sell the sizzle. Many of the principles I learned are harmless enough on the secular level, although the Moody Correspondence School chose to use them sparingly because of the spiritual nature of its product.

Advertising techniques have become much more sophisticated since I attended those seminars. You and I now have to contend with massive subliminal seduction. This approach involves deception and deliberate sexual and sensual exploitation. Subliminal seduction in advertising is based on the fact that the mind reacts much more quickly than the eye. The mind can go from here to the sun and back in an instant, whereas light takes more than sixteen minutes to make the same trip. The modern advertiser operates in the twilight zone between the senses and the imagination.

The advertiser massages and manipulates his prospects without their being consciously aware of what he is doing. He plants suggestions in the subconscious mind to stimulate the memory, the emotions, and basic human drives. The advertiser exploits the fact that the subconscious mind can operate quite independently of the conscious mind. The brain has the capacity to store an estimated twenty billion bits of information in the subconscious, though we consciously use only a small part of the total in the course of a lifetime.

Using deceptive techniques in advertising seems clever to the worldling. All it proves, however, is that man is a fallen creature, manipulated by the god of this world—the father of lies—and his agents. We have a predisposition toward deceiving and being deceived. In a simpler age the wise man said, "The folly of fools is deceit."

What man calls clever, God calls folly. Modern merchandisers, propagandists, and manipulators who seek to exploit the gullibility of their fellow men are categorized by God as fools. A wise man, once he is aware of what is being done to him by these fools, puts himself on guard. He fortifies his mind and memory with the Word of God and draws on the indwelling Spirit of God to deliver him from all the wiles of the evil one.

c. The Scoffing Fool (14:9)

"Fools make a mock at sin: but among the righteous there is favour." In the original language the word translated "fools" is followed by a singular verb, suggesting to some another rendering: "A great fool makes a mock at sin." The word translated "sin" here is 'āshām, meaning a "trespass that requires the trespass offering."

Most of us are introduced to the mockery of sin when we are very young (a school playground is a fruitful place to learn to mock at sin) and throughout adulthood we are aware of such mockery. Dirty jokes are circulated with great zest. Most people find ethnic jokes funny, although politicians who have told such jokes have discovered them to be very expensive when the ridiculed group has screamed in protest. The screen and stage, and especially television, have deluged us with sitcoms that invite us to laugh at people's predicaments. (Most humor is at the expense of somebody else.) Many sitcoms have become raw and risqué. Making an unblushing mockery of sin, they prompt us to laugh at all kinds of sexual entanglements, dishonesty, drunkenness, and public figures who have fallen into sin.

However, God is not amused. Man in his fallen state may think this mockery of sin is funny, but God labels it folly. Paul warned against foolish jesting, which is not "convenient" (Ephesians 5:4). The word translated "convenient" is *aneko*, which means "fitting." Some jokes are quite out of place.

God sees nothing in sin to laugh at. The Holy Spirit indicates the seriousness of sin by using the word *'āshām* in this proverb. Sin is not funny; it is fatal—it requires a trespass offering. The cost of removing sin from our hearts and consciences and God's records is incalculable. God takes us directly to Calvary to show us how He views sin. Perhaps that is why there is so little humor in the Bible.

Sin sends people to Hell and there is nothing funny about that. It has been well said that our friends may be able to laugh us into Hell, but they will never laugh us out. Mockery is a potent weapon in Satan's hands. Those who reap the due reward of their sinful deeds will be in a place where misery reigns, where there is weeping and wailing and gnashing of teeth. When we imagine ourselves standing at Calvary in the darkness that shrouded the scene for three long hours, and hearing Emmanuel's orphan cry ring out in all its anguish and horror, we can better understand why God says that only a great fool mocks at sin.

5. The Passions of the Heart (14:10)

Proverbs 14:10 shows us the human heart *in times of bitterness* and *in times of bliss:* "The heart knoweth his own bitterness; and a stranger doth not intermeddle with his joy."

Charles Dickens experienced both bitterness and bliss. He was ten when his family moved to London. There his father, who was chronically in debt, was arrested for insolvency and put in a debtor's prison. Circumstances terminated young Charles' hope of an education and required that he be sent to work.

Just two days after his twelfth birthday Charles began his business life. His path to work took him through depressing streets to a tumbledown old house abutting the Thames. The house was overrun with rats and its general air of neglect, dirt, and decay was to haunt him the rest of his life. The scene of his misery and degradation was Warren's Blacking Shop. He later wrote of its rottenness and ruin, its dampness and offensiveness.

Charles was assigned to work with several boys from the ranks of London's lower class. His job was to cap the bottles of blacking with paper and string and then paste a printed label on each bottle. At this soul-destroying task he toiled ten hours a day. His childhood had come to an abrupt end.

David Copperfield was the fictional representation of Dickens himself. David Copperfield's parents were dead and his stepfather, Mr. Murdstone, coldly detested him. Mr. Murdstone allowed him to fall into a state of total neglect and then decided to rid the house of David altogether. He was packed off to London to work as a lackey in the wine house of Murdstone and Grinby. In telling his story David Copperfield says, "I now approach a period of my life, which I can never lose the remembrance of, while I remember anything; and the recollection of which has often, without my invocation, come before me like a ghost, and haunted happier times."

"The heart knoweth his own bitterness," said Solomon. Dickens, like his fictional hero, spoke of his own bitter days: "My whole nature," he said, "was so penetrated with the grief and humiliation of such considerations, that even now, famous and caressed and happy, I often forget in my dreams that I have a dear wife and children; even that I am a man; and wander desolately back to that time of my life."

Dickens, however, was equally capable of joy. For instance he was exuberant when his first story was published. With trepidation he had delivered it to the *Monthly Magazine,* an ordinary and unprepossessing publication. He said that he dropped his envelope stealthily one evening at twilight, "with fear and trembling," into "a dark letter-box in a dark office." He could hardly wait to buy the next issue of the magazine. Then with joy and delight he saw his story was there. It didn't matter that he was never paid for it. It was published! He was in print! He said, "I walked down to Westminster Hall, and turned into it for half an hour, because my eyes were so dimmed with pride and joy that they could not bear the street, and were not fit to be seen there." A stranger did not intermeddle with his joy. Some experiences are too bitter and others are too blissful to be shared.

6. The Pathways of the World (14:11-13)

Proverbs 14:11 takes us to *the haunted house:* "The house of the wicked shall be overthrown: but the tabernacle of the upright shall flourish." Both houses have resident spirits.

The upright man's house is likened to a tabernacle. The word translated "tabernacle" literally means "tent." The word was invested with special significance in Old Testament times. The tabernacle was God's chosen dwelling place among His people in this world from the days of Moses until the time of David. The most significant feature of the tabernacle was the holy of holies where the sacred ark, the figures of the cherubim, the mercyseat, and the presence of God were. The shekinah glory cloud, which overshadowed the camp and went before the people in all their journeying, rested there on the mercyseat. The cloud was the visible token that the holy One of Israel was in residence.

The home of the righteous is to be a place where God is in residence, where He feels at home, where He is acknowledged and made welcome. A plaque on the wall of the home of many a choice saint of God reads: "God is the Head of this house, the unseen Guest at every meal, the silent Listener to every conversation." Such a home is haunted—the Holy Spirit lives there.

Conversely, "the house of the wicked shall be overthrown." Some houses have seen so much wickedness and unhappiness that they deserve to be pulled down. Demons sometimes seem to attach themselves to a house connected with evil in the past. Cases of poltergeist activity may be attributable to the mischief of such demons.

Some houses do seem to be haunted. How else can we explain the strange happenings in the rectory at Epworth where John and Charles Wesley grew up? The ghost's appearings were far too frequent and well known to be denied. Indeed, until it was destroyed by fire, the rectory was called "the most haunted house in England." One of the Wesley children named the ghost "Old Jeffrey."

Old Jeffrey first appeared in the rectory in the year 1716 when the housemaid heard groans coming from the empty dining room. The Wesleys themselves heard strange knockings in different parts of the house. The ghost was seen twice: once by Mrs. Wesley and once by Robin Brown, a manservant. Between the two manifestations there were a variety of noises. The Wesleys heard the noise of bottles being dashed to pieces, of footsteps going up and down stairs, and of dancing in an empty room. On three occasions Mr. Wesley was pushed by invisible hands. The family dog, a mastiff purchased expressly to repel the intruder, was afraid of Old Jeffrey and crawled under a bed and howled when the ghost manifested its presence. Robert Southey, probably one of the most critical of Wesley's biographers, said that the ghost was that of a former Jacobite because it frequently interrupted family worship, especially when Mr. Wesley attempted to pray for the king of England or the Prince of Wales.[10]

Glamis Castle, whose history dates back to the eleventh century when the Scottish monarch Macbeth was ruler of Glamis, is also said to be haunted. Stories of hauntings at the castle seem to be well authenticated. The hauntings are supposed to have some connection with a terrible secret. The castle became the seat of the earls of Strathmore and the fifteenth earl, great-grandfather of Queen Elizabeth II, knew the secret. He told his friends that they should be thankful they didn't.[11]

Even when a house is not actually haunted, it can still harbor memories. We sometimes say, "If the walls could speak..." Maybe they can. Who is to say that God does not write on other walls as He wrote on the walls of Belshazzar's palace? If as Jesus said the stones can cry out (Luke 19:40) who is to say that the wood, stone, and plaster of a wall cannot hold memories?

The house of the wicked is a dreadful place whether it is haunted or not. Even if the walls do not hear, see, and record what takes place, God does. The house of the wicked is a terrible place to be born, to live, and to die because such a house will be overthrown.

Proverbs 14:11 may of course refer to the dynasty of the wicked. Sooner or later a fortune or a family founded on wickedness must fall.

Proverbs 14:12 looks at *the hellbent highway:* "There is a way which seemeth right unto a man, but the end thereof are the ways of death." This text needs to be written over the entrance to every temple and shrine of all the false religions in the world. The text needs to be placed over the door of every meeting place of all the false cults in Christendom and over the door of every liberal church.

This "way" is described in Jude 11 as "the way of Cain." This road runs by way of the murder of Abel to the flood, by way of the flood to Babel, by way of Babel to the murder of Christ, and by way of that crime of crimes to the lake of fire.

The word *religion* describes the way of Cain. Traveling on the highway of religion, man does not express his spirituality but his godlessness. Choosing the way of religion is the sin of sins. It is the sin against the first commandment. This sin dethrones the true God and enthrones Lucifer. The name *Lucifer* originates in Isaiah 14:12 and means "morning star" or "day star" or "light-bearer." Lucifer is described in the New Testament as "the god of this world" (2 Corinthians 4:4) and as "an angel of light" (2 Corinthians 11:14). Satan invented religion and in his religion fallen man expresses his opposition to God.

This "way of Cain" was instantly rejected by God (Genesis 4:1-16). Far from repenting, Cain turned his back on God and founded the vile civilization that ended in the flood. A quick look at "the way of Cain" reveals five major features of all false religion.

First, Cain substituted *reason for revelation.* He rejected the divinely revealed truth that God was not to be approached by fallen man apart from the sacrifice of an innocent victim (Genesis 3:15,21; Hebrews 11:4). Cain had his own ideas about the way God could be approached and he simply ignored what God had said about the matter. He thought his way was best.

Second, he substituted *beauty for blood.* No doubt Cain's altar was much more aesthetically pleasing—more pleasing to the senses of fallen human nature—than Abel's. Fruits and flowers, spices and herbs, color and fragrance, artistry and science were blended to produce the maximum effect. Cain's altar was the forerunner of the temples, cathedrals, choirs, organs, robes, and rituals that have been designed to make religion appealing to the senses. Cain must have shuddered as he looked at Abel's reeking altar with its blood and fire, and its slain lamb.

Third, Cain substituted *trying for trusting.* Cain's religion was based on one simple but false principle: works! His religion enshrined the idea that man can earn his salvation, that he can acquire and accumulate merit. Cain was not an atheist. On the contrary, he was religious and he worked hard at his religion. He sweated and toiled to produce the fruits and flowers that graced his altar.

All false religions have the same message. Read the *Vedas* of the Brahmins, the *Pinanas* of Sivna and Vishnu, the *Koran* of the Muslims, the *Zend-Auesta* of the Parsees, the *Tripitaka* of the Buddhists. Read the writings of Rome, of the Mormons, of the Jehovah's Witnesses, of Christian Science, and of the liberals. The message is always the same: salvation has to be earned. It has to be purchased with good works. Buddhists follow the eight fundamentals of right conduct, Muslims try fasts and pilgrimages, Hindus wash in the Ganges, Mormons work to become gods, and Jehovah's Witnesses put in time to satisfy the insatiable ambitions of the Watchtower organization. Liberals preach a so-called social gospel, and Rome demands penances and pilgrimages. They all follow "the way of Cain."

Fourth, Cain substituted *feelings for facts.* He felt good about his religious efforts and became enraged when God rejected them, root and branch. His good feelings soon evaporated, but as long as they lasted they satisfied this deluded founder of false religion. In contrast to Cain, Abel "obtained witness that he was righteous" (Hebrews 11:4). He came by way of Calvary and was justified by faith alone; his justification was based on the merits of Christ imputed by God to the believer.

Fifth, Cain substituted *persecution for persuasion.* He was enraged that Abel's offering was accepted and his was not. He hated his brother and all that Abel stood for in terms of divine revelation and blood atonement. Cain was too refined to slay a lamb but quite capable of shedding a martyr's blood. His religion allowed him to murder his brother.

Solomon turned from the hellbent highway and looked at *the heavy heart:* "Even in laughter the heart is sorrowful; and the end of that mirth is heaviness" (Proverbs 14:13). We are living in a sad world. All around us people are suffering from painful illnesses, poverty, neglect, famine, oppression, persecution, bereavement, and loneliness. In the affluent lands of the West we are shielded from some problems, but we still are aware of a pervading sadness.

The world has no cure for our melancholy. The world can amuse us and entertain us, but it cannot cure our sadness. We laugh uproariously at the antics of a clown, at slapstick comedy, or at some humorous but contrived situation and we forget ourselves for a few minutes. We applaud thunderously after a brilliant performance of a musical masterpiece. We express appreciation for the production of some well-plotted play. But when the curtain comes down and the clapping dies away, the sadness returns. People push for the aisles, crowds vanish into the night, and the emptiness remains.

When Lord Byron, the darling of society, was approaching his thirty-seventh birthday, he declared:

> My days are in the yellow leaf;
> The flowers and fruits of love are gone;
> The worm, the canker, and the grief
> Are mine alone.

Robert Burns wrote in "Tam O'Shanter":

> Pleasures are like poppies spread,
> You seize the flow'r, its bloom is shed;
> Or like the snow falls in the river,

> A moment white—then melts for ever;
> Or like the Borealis race,
> That flit ere you can point their place.

Benjamin Disraeli, an architect of the British empire and one of its foremost prime ministers, once declared: "Youth is a blunder; manhood a struggle; old age a regret."

These quotations are but echoes of Augustine's famous words: "Oh, God, Thou hast made us for Thyself, and our souls are restless until they find their rest in Thee."

The world does not have what it takes to make us happy. The truth of the matter is, this world is haunted. The ghost of our guilt lurks everywhere. Satan, who holds this world in his grasp, loathes us. His chief desire is to trap us into sin, assail us with guilt, make us as miserable as possible, and fasten our sorrows upon us eternally in Hell.

Thank God for Jesus! He does not simply offer us happiness, which all too often depends on what happens. He offers us joy. David knew about His joy and wrote, "Thou wilt show me the path of life: in thy presence is fulness of joy; at thy right hand there are pleasures for evermore" (Psalm 16:11). At the birth of Jesus the herald angels announced "good tidings of great joy" (Luke 2:10). Facing Calvary, Jesus spoke of His own joy (John 17:13) and He bequeathed it to us (John 16:24). Peter, facing Nero's persecutions, wrote of "joy unspeakable and full of glory" (1 Peter 1:8). So Solomon had hold of only one end of the stick when he wrote Proverbs 14:13.

7. The People on the Road (14:14-27)

a. The Gullible Man (14:14-15)

Proverbs 14:14 describes *the man who backslides anyway:* "The backslider in heart shall be filled with his own ways: and a good man shall be satisfied from himself."

As we consider the backslider, our thoughts go to Elimelech, who lived "in the days when the judges ruled" (Ruth 1:1-5). Although the days of the judges were marked by general disorder, there were still men in positions of influence who lived for God—Elimelech's relative Boaz, for example. Elimelech lived in *Bethlehem-judah* ("the house of bread and praise") so he would have known that if famine ever came, it would be temporary. Moreover his name meant "My

God is King," so every time he heard his name he would have been reminded of the sovereignty of God. Elimelech had much for which to be thankful.

Yet when famine came Elimelech denied the sovereignty of God in his life and prepared to go to Moab. The fact that the land of Moab was under God's curse (Deuteronomy 23:3) seems to have had little or no weight in Elimelech's decision. Being "filled with his own ways," he moved to Moab with his wife and two sons.

Doubtless Elimelech had plenty of "reasons" for moving to Moab. The backslider can always come up with logical reasons for his decisions. "Well," we can almost hear Elimelech say, "you can see what it's like around here. There's a famine in the land. There's no work and I have a family to support. I've heard that there are good job opportunities in Moab. Besides I don't intend to stay there long, just until things improve around this part of the country. We'll have to raise our boys in a pagan atmosphere, but I can be a testimony in Moab."

So off to Moab he went. When Elimelech moved to Moab, he walked out of the fellowship of God's people, away from the place where God had put His name, and away from the place where He visited with His people (Ruth 1:6). Moving to Moab was followed by marriage in Moab and by misery in Moab. Instead of being testimonies, Elimelech and his sons died as backsliders in Moab. If someone had warned Elimelech of the consequences of moving to Moab, he wouldn't have listened, for a backslider is full of his own ways. He will backslide anyway.

In contrast to Elimelech, Boaz remained in Bethlehem-judah. He rode out the storm, waited while God worked out His purpose in the famine (one of thirteen famines recorded in the Bible), and lived to see a revival when God once again visited His people. "A good man shall be satisfied from himself," Solomon said. We see Boaz reaping the harvest of his deeds when he is first introduced to us as a "mighty man of wealth" (Ruth 2:1). Whereas Elimelech died a backslider in the far country, Boaz lived, reigned in the affections of God's people, and became a direct ancestor of the Lord Jesus.

Proverbs 14:15 describes *the man who believes anything:* "The simple believeth every word: but the prudent man looketh well to his going." There is a great deal of deceit in this world. There is also a great deal of misinformation, not all of it deliberate. Therefore common sense ought to tell us not to believe everything we are told. At best wrong information can inconvenience us. At worst it can damn us.

Harry Ironside used to tell a story about a woman who, with her child, was traveling by train across the American Midwest. Snow was falling and the temperature was well below freezing. From time to time gusts of icy wind hit the train. The woman was evidently anxious. She asked the conductor to make sure she got off the train at the right place, a small whistle-stop on the prairie. He assured her that he would not forget but she was obviously worried and ill at ease.

A fellow traveler tried to reassure her. "I am a salesman," he said. "I travel this line two or three times a week. I know it like the back of my hand. If the conductor forgets, you can count on me. I'll let you know when we arrive at your stop." Presently the train stopped at a station and there was a brief bustle of activity. Then the whistle sounded and the train pulled away again into the night. "Your stop is the next one," the helpful salesman said.

After a while the train stopped again, but there was no sign of the conductor. "He must have forgotten," said the salesman. "I'll help you off the train." The woman and the child got off, the salesman handed down her baggage, and the train pulled away. It was dark and cold outside and visibility was down to zero because of the storm.

A few minutes later the conductor came through the coach and looked at the empty seat. "Where's the woman who was sitting there?" he demanded.

The salesman said, "I helped her off at the last stop. That was her stop."

"It was nothing of the kind," snapped the conductor. "That was just an emergency stop. You fool! What have you done? Her stop is the next one. We'll have to back up the train."

The train slowly backed up to the last stop and there the mother and the child were. They were frozen to death by the side of the track—victims of wrong information.

b. The Grave Man (14:16)

"A wise man feareth, and departeth from evil: but the fool rageth, and is confident." The word translated "rageth" can also be rendered "rushes on." The word translated "confident," *batah,* means "to be secure and without fear."

When I was in the British Army in Palestine just before Israel became a state, I was reminded how wise the Jews were who fled Nazi Germany. Cohen, a Jew who worked in my office, told me that he was the sole surviving member of his family. His mother, father, brothers, sisters, uncles, aunts, cousins, neighbors, and friends had all perished in the concentration camps of the Third Reich.

Many European Jews of his generation had wanted to be assimilated into the Gentile world around them. Most of them were secular Jews, agnostic if not outright atheistic. Rabbinic Judaism was as foreign to them as the tribal customs of the Aztecs. When Hitler came to power, most of the Jews of Germany remained confident of their future.

Hitler, however, made his intentions perfectly clear in *Mein Kampf*, the book that made him a millionaire. Except for the Bible, no other book sold as well in Germany during the Nazi regime. Few households felt safe without a copy of *Mein Kampf* prominently displayed. Its main thesis was simple: Since man is a fighting animal and the fighting capacity of a race depends on its purity, foreign elements must be purged out.

Jews throughout the world were pacifists and internationalists. Since Hitler considered pacifism to be the deadliest of sins, he sought to purge Germany and the world of Jews. Education, he wrote, must produce Germans who could be converted quickly into soldiers. Foreign policy must be unscrupulous because Germany needed more territory in Russia and the Baltic states.

In 1933 the Nazis gained a majority in the Reichstag and a couple of weeks later ordered a nationwide boycott of Jewish doctors, lawyers, and businesses. Before the year's end Himmler was given sweeping police powers.

In 1934 Hitler declared himself head of the German state. In 1935 the "Nuremberg laws" were passed to disenfranchise all those of "Jewish blood." In 1938 pogroms were staged all over Germany. Mobs burned synagogues, destroyed Jewish property, beat up some Jews, and killed many others. New anti-Jewish laws were enacted and the Jews were fined a billion marks. Soon the Jews would be confined to the ghettos and deported to concentration camps. Mass murder, torture, and genocide would become commonplace.

During this worsening situation most Jews simply hoped for the best, forgetting that a wise man feareth and departeth. I can still see my Jewish friend standing in my office and telling me how he had coveted assimilation, but finally realized that Germany was no place for him. "I was born in Germany," he said. "I spoke the German language. I attended German schools. I graduated from a German university. I worked for a German corporation. I was a German until *Hitler taught me I was a Jew.*" The moment he learned that lesson, he packed his bags and fled to Palestine. He was a wise man.

c. The Guilty Man (14:17)

"He that is soon angry dealeth foolishly: and a man of wicked devices is hated." One man whose life illustrates this proverb is England's powerful Plantagenet king, Henry II. Sixteen words he uttered in a fit of temper undid a lifetime of striving and planning for the good of England and the power of the throne.

In their youth Henry and Thomas Becket became firm friends. The son of a commoner, Becket was trained by Theobald, the archbishop of Canterbury, and became a polished man of the world. He was a brilliant talker and thinker and possessed great charm and diplomacy. Henry made his friend chancellor of England and Becket turned the position into one of far-reaching influence. Soon Becket was the power behind the throne and everyone knew it. His loyalty to the king was absolute.

Meanwhile the papacy under Alexander III was asserting itself throughout Europe. The church in England (Roman Catholic to the core) was at the height of its influence and power. Rome ruled with an iron hand. People worshiped God, His Son, and the virgin and bowed to pope, cardinal, bishop, and priest with simple unquestioning faith. The church was immensely rich and powerful because when rich men died they often left their lands and money to the church to pay for prayers to be said for the good of their souls. Churchmen were as arrogant as barons. Henry was determined to curb the power of the papacy in England and his closest ally was his chancellor.

Then Theobald died leaving vacant the post of archbishop of Canterbury, which was second in power only to the throne itself. Henry had a brilliant idea: *Why not make Becket archbishop of Canterbury? If I put such a loyal subject as Thomas in this all-powerful ecclesiastical post, I will have a leader in the church who has never failed to support me in my secular desires and designs.* From the standpoint of the throne the idea seemed perfect—a marriage of church and state designed to strengthen the throne.

"If you do as you say," Becket declared, "you will soon hate me, my lord king, as much as you love me now." But Henry was not to be denied.

However, Henry's hopes of combining the offices of archbishop and chancellor were soon dashed. The new archbishop at once resigned his post as chancellor and a remarkable change took place. The ostentatious, flamboyant, and worldly Becket disappeared. In his place appeared an austere ascetic, a zealot determined to uphold all the privileges and power of the Roman church in

England. Henry was stunned. War was declared between these two resolute and powerful men.

The fierce battle went on for years. Becket threatened to excommunicate Henry. (People thrust out of the church were believed to be damned and were boycotted, ostracized, and treated as lepers.) Henry retaliated by having his son Henry crowned as coregent by the archbishop of York, Becket's rival. And so it went on.

The fateful words were spoken when Henry was in France. Aggravated by the archbishop's latest move, Henry raised his fist above his head and cried in a towering rage, "What cowards have I about me that no one will deliver me from this lowborn priest!" He regretted the words at once, but it was too late. Four knights had already gone on their way to rid the king of his enemy. They arrived at Canterbury and followed Becket into the sanctuary. They exchanged bitter words with the archbishop and killed him.

Becket was considered a martyr and the pope made him a saint. Then the pope brought out his big guns and threatened to excommunicate Henry and put England under interdict. No bells would be rung, no masses would be said, no marriages would be performed, no confessions would be heard, and nobody would be shriven before dying. The threat was all an elaborate Roman farce but almost everyone believed it.

Henry capitulated. Rome's power and authority, against which Henry had been struggling for years, was fully reimposed in England. Other costly exactions were required. The king had to walk barefoot through Canterbury and humble himself before Becket's tomb. He had to make confession and beg forgiveness. Meekly this powerful king bared his back to receive stripes laid on him by the officers and monks of Canterbury. His back was cut open to the bone. He sat in silence and pain the whole night in front of the tomb of his baseborn priest.

The king had played dice with Rome and lost. He had lost his temper and dealt foolishly. A few words spoken in anger had given crafty Rome its opportunity, and Rome played as usual with loaded dice.

d. The Great Man (14:18-19)

A great man always wears a crown. Proverbs 14:18 tells us *why he is crowned:* "The simple inherit folly: but the prudent are crowned with knowledge." Nowhere is this principle more evident than in matters of money.

Years ago I lived in a small town in northwest Canada. A man came to town representing, so he said, a team of investors. The man, a former missionary, was known to some of the townspeople, so his integrity was not questioned. In fact his reputation for honesty and his former testimony gave him easy access to the Christian community. His story was simple. Not far from our town, on the banks of a river (which he named), there was a stretch of black sand. The investors he represented were forming a mining company to extract gold from that sand. The story was plausible and the man had brochures, surveys, feasibility studies, and technical details. We were invited to get in on a good thing, "now or never."

A number of people I knew took the plunge. Some invested moderately, some invested more than they could afford, and one woman invested her life savings. They lost everything. The scheme was an elaborate fraud. The simple inherited folly.

One friend of mine had been more prudent. He advised people not to be too hasty and went to see for himself if the salesman was telling the truth. He found the place on the river but no black sand. An old dilapidated tractor was on the site but that was all. "The prudent are crowned with knowledge."

People would not believe that the former missionary was lying (if he wasn't lying, he had certainly been duped) and they lost a considerable amount of money. If they had used a little common sense and listened to a wise man's advice, they would not have lost anything. All get-rich-quick schemes need to be treated with healthy skepticism.

Still thinking of the wisdom of the great man, Solomon told us *where he is crowned:* "The evil bow before the good; and the wicked at the gates of the righteous" (Proverbs 14:19).

Joseph was "taken from prison and from judgment" (Isaiah 53:8) and exalted to the right hand of the majesty of the pharaoh. Joseph was given a name that was above every name—*Zaphnath-paaneah* (Genesis 41:45), which means "savior of the world," or "revealer of secrets," or "abundance of life." The message was passed throughout Egypt that everyone should "bow the knee" to Joseph (41:43). This command would require complete prostration. The expression "bow the knee" is a translation of *abrek*, which according to one authority is a Sumerian title meaning "the seer." In Egypt the command *abrok* is still used to make camels kneel.

We can imagine what followed the crowning. "Now then, Joseph," the pharaoh said, "I have made you grand vizier of Egypt. The land is at your feet. You are in charge of all that concerns the throne. The Nile, the annual inundation, the planting, the harvest—all these things are yours to oversee. You will receive the briefings of the

reporters and the district inspectors. Provincial boundaries, alloca-
tions of land, orders for second crops, tax arrears, and law and order
in the provinces all come under your control.

"Joseph, you must understand that Egypt has a system of government dating back a millennium to the days of the great Menes,
founder of the first dynasty. The system is based on strong, authori-
tarian, and absolute power centered in the throne. We have a
tradition of rigid bureaucratic control. Some positions are appointed; some are inherited.

"But enough of all that for now. Come. That second chariot is
yours. I'll show you around. Is there anywhere you'd like to go first?"

Joseph responded, "Yes, there are two or three places I'd like to
visit. I would like to go first to the slave market where as a young lad
I was put up for sale." When they arrived, he saw the platform where
he had been poked and prodded and inspected like a horse or
young bull.

Every time the glittering entourage stopped, there was a flourish
of trumpets. The herald called, "Bend the knee." And before the
pharaoh and his new grand vizier every knee bowed.

"Now take me to Potiphar's house," Joseph said. "He's the man
who bought me. He was decent enough—but his wife! She's the one
who falsely accused me and made me waste twelve precious years in
prison." The chariots stopped and the fanfare sounded, summon-
ing the whole busy household. With terror in her eyes, the wretched
woman herself bent the knee. "Who is he?" she whispered to her
husband. "Zaphnath-paaneah, my dear," her husband replied.
"You used to know him as Joseph. The gods grant that your
accusation was true. I have to report to him tomorrow morning."

Then Joseph and the pharaoh visited the prison. Warders and
prisoners alike were summoned to bend the knee. How great was
the heart-searching! The chief of the prison wondered why he had
not taken Joseph's claims of innocence more seriously. Sure, he had
let Joseph run the prison, but only because he was too lazy to do it
himself. The prisoners remembered the toadying, spiting, and
backbiting that had gone on at Joseph's expense.

Throughout all Egypt people bowed the knee. The evil bowed
before the good, indeed.

e. The Glamorous Man (14:20)

"The poor is hated even of his own neighbour: but the rich hath
many friends." Few things speak as loudly in this world as wealth. It
casts an aura of glamour over those who possess it in abundance.

Even if a man is a scoundrel who made his money by deception and fraud, his riches cast a spell.

Because people so easily fall under the spell of riches, James taught the infant church to make sure they did not give the rich preferential treatment:

> If there come unto your assembly a man with a gold ring, in goodly apparel, and there come in also a poor man in vile raiment; And ye have respect to him that weareth the gay clothing, and say unto him, Sit thou here in a good place; and say to the poor, Stand thou there, or sit here under my footstool: Are ye not then partial in yourselves, and are become judges of evil thoughts? Hearken, my beloved brethren, Hath not God chosen the poor of this world rich in faith, and heirs of the kingdom which he hath promised to them that love him? But ye have despised the poor. Do not rich men oppress you, and draw you before the judgment seats? Do not they blaspheme that worthy name by the which ye are called? (James 2:2-7)

Some years ago I met an extraordinary woman who put this passage of Scripture to the test. She claimed to have been a mother superior in the Roman Catholic Church at one time—a friend of bishops and cardinals, and an inspector of convents. She had a fund of stories, but I never knew how much of a story could be believed. However, one of them sticks in my mind.

One Sunday morning she attended a fashionable church. She was a stranger and deliberately went in old clothes. She wore no makeup, left her hair straggly, and conveyed the impression of poverty. On the way out she greeted the pastor, who glanced at her without much interest, gave her a perfunctory handshake, and turned at once to a more interesting visitor.

The next Sunday she went back to the same church. This time she dressed to kill. Her hair had been elaborately styled and her face had been given a full treatment of powder and paint. With a mink stole draping her shoulders she breathed an air of importance and affluence.

On her way out this time, the pastor was most effusive. "Welcome to our church," he said. "We're so glad to have you with us. I hope you enjoyed the service. Did you sign our guest register? I'm sorry, but I didn't catch your name. This is your first visit? I do trust you will come back." The syrup oozed.

The woman looked the pastor up and down. "Oh, no," she said. "This is not my first visit to your church. As a matter of fact I was here last Sunday and you shook hands with me. But I was shabbily dressed and dowdily groomed and you practically ignored me. Oh no, this is not my first visit to your church, but it will certainly be my last. Good day to you." And she left.

f. The Gracious Man (14:21)

"He that despiseth his neighbour sinneth: but he that hath mercy on the poor, happy is he." This proverb is closely related to the preceding one.

A considerable body of legislation in the Mosaic law was designed to protect the poor. Money loaned to the poor, for instance, was not to be subject to interest. If to secure the loan a man's mantle was taken, it had to be returned to him by nightfall if that mantle was all he had to keep himself warm. (See Exodus 22:25-27.) Nobody was to be stingy to the poor. On the contrary, the poor were to be dealt with generously (Deuteronomy 15:7-8). At harvest time the gleanings of field and orchard had to be left for the poor (Leviticus 19:9-10). Wages were to be paid daily (Leviticus 19:13). A court case was not to be prejudiced against the poor litigant (Exodus 23:6). On the other hand, the scales of justice were not to be tilted in favor of an impoverished person just because he was poor (Exodus 23:3). Many of the denunciations of the prophets were against the ill-treatment of the poor by those in power.

Only one person born on this planet was able to choose beforehand the time, place, and circumstances of His birth. That person was Jesus, the Son of the living God. He chose to be born into a poor family. His mother, at her purification, brought the offering of the very poor (Luke 2:22-24; Leviticus 12:2,6,8). He could say, "The Son of man hath not where to lay his head" (Luke 9:58). John wrote: "Every man went unto his own house. Jesus went unto the mount of Olives" (John 7:53; 8:1).

In the valley of Jehoshaphat at the great assize that will determine which survivors of end-time events will be allowed to enter the kingdom, much will hinge on their treatment of the poor with whom the Lord Jesus identifies Himself (Matthew 25:35-40). Those selected for immediate banishment to the lake of fire will be condemned for despising the poor (Matthew 25:41-46). Our treatment of the poor is carefully noted in Heaven.

g. The Guileful Man (14:22)

"Do they not err that devise evil? but mercy and truth shall be to them that devise good."

The closing days of the Hebrew monarchy were evil. The kings were little more than puppets, the priests were corrupt, and the people were oppressed. All kinds of moral and spiritual wickedness were rampant. Josiah's noble attempt to call the apostate nation back to God had not survived his sudden death. Jeremiah and his colleagues preached in vain. Both Egypt and Babylon were bidding for world supremacy and the little land of Judah was nothing more than a pawn in the game of international chess.

After the captivity foretold by Jeremiah had come and gone, a small remnant of Jews returned to the promised land to reclaim it for God and to stake a claim for the coming of Christ. There were many problems, however. The land was desolate. Petty neighboring states resented the return of the Jews and organized opposition. Attempts were even made to misrepresent the Jews before the Persian superpower in order to stop further immigration and rebuilding.

Still some unknown singer found much about which to sing and he wrote Psalm 85. He thought over the terrible sins that had mandated the captivity and he thanked God for forgiving so *royally* (85:1-3). He thought of the many Jews who were content to stay in Babylon and of the many repatriated Jews who were more concerned with building their own homes than building the house of God. Indeed a brace of prophets would soon be needed to prod the national conscience. The psalmist thanked God for forgiving so *repeatedly* (85:4-7). Then he thought about the principles that lay beneath God's forgiveness and he thanked God for forgiving so *righteously* (85:8-13).

In Psalm 85:10 we catch the echo of Proverbs 14:22: "Mercy and truth shall be to them that devise good." For while many were falling by the wayside after the captivity, there were still Jews whose lives pleased God. There was indeed a galaxy of good men: Zerubbabel of the house of David; Joshua, the high priest of the house of Aaron; Ezra the scribe; Nehemiah the statesman; and Haggai and Zechariah, who knew God. So the psalmist sang, "Mercy and truth are met together; righteousness and peace have kissed each other."

The phrase "met together" is a translation of one Hebrew word. It occurs fifteen times in the Bible and in every instance has a hostile meaning. The word is appropriate here, for mercy and truth *are* at odds. When God's mercy would say, "Pardon the sinner," God's truth would say, "No, punish the sinner!" God's mercy says, "God is love." God's truth says, "God is light." God cannot administer mercy at the expense of truth and He cannot uphold truth at the expense of mercy.

But at Calvary righteousness and peace kissed each other. God can now uphold both His mercy and His truth. By sending His Son to die on Calvary, He found a way to give us both His peace and His righteousness. Mercy and truth are no longer at odds. Hallelujah, what a Savior![12]

h. The Garrulous Man (14:23)

"In all labour there is profit: but the talk of the lips tendeth only to penury." Today's parallel saying is "He's all talk" or "Talk is cheap." Sooner or later circumstances overtake the man who is all talk. Talk is no substitute for hard work.

In Nicholas Monsarrat's book *The Cruel Sea*, First Lieutenant James Bennett of HMS *Compass Rose* was a talker who was loud-mouthed, foulmouthed, and abusive toward those he considered his inferiors. Back home in Australia, Bennett had been a mere clerk in a shipping office in Sydney, but thanks to some fast talking and a selection board preoccupied with more important things than sifting boastful claims about past exploits, he had landed this appointment as an officer aboard a warship.

HMS *Compass Rose* was a little corvette designed for fighting submarines and not what Bennett had in mind when he volunteered for active service in World War II. He was already regretting his glib talk. He was a bully and routinely pushed the two new sub-lieutenants around. His conversation was crude, his manner offensive, and his decisions negative and mean. The captain soon realized that Bennett had less experience than his manner would lead one to believe. In short, he was all talk.

Life on a corvette in an Atlantic storm was extremely uncomfortable. The ship rolled and pitched, everything was always cold and wet, bruises were common, and sleeping was difficult. Furthermore the wardroom was a nightmare for the lower ranks when Bennett was present. Adding to the misery of the crew, Bennett was a malingerer, always delegating his duties to subordinates. The other sailors were thankful that after one nightmarish tour of duty Bennett decided he'd had enough of corvettes. He faked a case of stomach ulcers and was drafted ashore.

Later in the war the crew found out what had happened to Bennett. He had gone back to Australia on a lecture tour and concocted quite a story: The captain of the *Compass Rose* became ill, so Bennett took her out on convoy duty. After a four-day battle he sank two submarines. However as a result of lack of sleep and battle fatigue, he cracked up and was sent home. The newspapers raised a fuss because the hero had not been given a medal.

An Australian told the story to one of the officers who had served with Bennett aboard the *Compass Rose.* Incredulously the officer asked, "He goes round lecturing about all that?" "Sure," the Australian declared. "They had him on a recruiting drive. And talking in the factories....They say it stimulates production." The officer who listened to this tall tale soon set the record straight and added, "I loathed him and everything he stood for."

Sooner or later, one way or another, the person who is all talk is exposed. The fictitious image he builds is punctured. After all his talk of achievement and success, the bubble bursts.

i. The Good Man (14:24-25)

Notice *his wisdom:* "The crown of the wise is their riches: but the foolishness of fools is folly" (Proverbs 14:24). A wise man makes wise decisions. Because he makes wise decisions he prospers. His prosperity becomes the crown, the evidence, of his wisdom. In contrast to a wise man, a fool makes foolish decisions. He may decorate his folly but it is still folly and sooner or later is discerned to be such.

The story of the unjust steward in Luke 16:1-12 illustrates this proverb. Commenting on the parable Jesus said, "The children of this world are in their generation wiser [shrewder] than the children of light" (16:8).

The steward had been caught red-handed in dishonesty and had been fired. He was alarmed because he had too much pride to beg and was not cut out for manual labor. The prospect of unemployment frightened him and he knew it would be difficult to get another position after having been dismissed for dishonesty.

But he was a clever rogue. Before his termination date he summoned his master's creditors. We can paraphrase the negotiations: "How much is on your account?" he said to one. "Let me tell you what I'll do. I'm leaving my job and I'd like to do something for you before I go just to show how much I have appreciated doing business with you. If you'll settle your account now, I'll give you a 50 percent discount." He said to another, "You have been a good customer. As a token of my regard for you and your integrity I'd like to do something special for you. Settle your account before I leave and I'll give you a 20 percent discount."

Even the man's employer was impressed by his steward's shrewdness and wisdom. Although he was not honest, he was clever! Indeed his cleverness was his crowning achievement. He had built up a fund of goodwill with his master's customers. Certainly one of them would give him a job. The steward was far more shrewd in his worldliness than many believers are in their faith. He guaranteed his future employment, whereas all too often we neglect laying up treasure in Heaven.

However there is another lesson in this parable: "The foolishness of fools is folly." This unjust steward was a fool of fools. He was a fool in the first place for being dishonest and putting his livelihood in jeopardy. But he was an even bigger fool for not repenting when his dishonesty was discovered. Thinking only of his immediate future in this world, he failed to think of the world to come and those "everlasting habitations" mentioned by Jesus in Luke 16:9.

Even his master commended the unjust steward for his shrewdness. But like the cleverness of all worldlings, his shrewdness could only help him in his generation—in his lifetime. He was like the rich fool of the parable in Luke 12:15-21. The unjust steward foolishly forgot about eternity. He added one folly to another and became the biggest fool of all. The simplest believer is wiser than he was.

Having considered the good man's wisdom, let us notice *his witness:* "A true witness delivereth souls: but a deceitful witness speaketh lies" (Proverbs 14:25).

In Nordhoff and Hall's famous story based on the mutiny on the *Bounty,* Roger Byam was going to hang for mutiny because of Captain William Bligh's biased and bitter witness at the court-martial. Midshipman Robert Tinkler could witness to Byam's innocence, but Tinkler could not be found.

The mutiny itself had been unplanned and unrehearsed, although it had been fueled for months by the captain's tyranny and pettiness. Just hours before the mutiny Byam and Tinkler had been on deck together. When Fletcher Christian—master's mate, second in command, and leader of the mutiny—appeared, Tinkler drifted off to one side to loiter in the shadow of one of the guns.

Christian talked in a desultory fashion for a few minutes with Byam. Christian said the captain had invited him to supper, but he had refused the invitation. Christian also asked Byam do him a favor: "If, for any reason, I should fail to reach home, I'd like you to see my people in Cumberland....It would be a comfort to [them] to talk with one of my friends." Byam readily agreed to do that little service for his friend. "You can count on me," Byam said, shaking Christian's hand.

Meanwhile the captain came on deck though neither Byam nor Christian heard him approach. The captain overheard the last five words, but not the previous conversation, and he saw the handshake. When mutiny broke out a few hours later, the captain concluded that Byam was in it up to his neck. Once Tinkler tried to speak in defense of Byam but was harshly silenced by Bligh.

So at the time of the court-martial it was Byam's word against Bligh's, and Bligh was the captain. His witness was false, a downright lie based on fewer than half a dozen words taken out of context. The captain had nursed his resentment at losing his ship and his malice against Byam for months. Byam's only hope lay in Tinkler, but Tinkler had reportedly been lost at sea. So Byam was condemned as a mutineer and sentenced to hang at the yardarm.

Then Tinkler was found—alive and willing to testify. Yes, he had overheard the conversation between Byam and Christian. The commissioners appointed by the Lord High Admiral of Great Britain heard Tinkler's sworn testimony, concluded Byam was innocent, and annulled the verdict of the court-martial. Byam was acquitted, thanks to a true witness.

j. The Godly Man (14:26-27)

The godly man *knows how to be safe:* "In the fear of the Lord is strong confidence: and his children shall have a place of refuge" (Proverbs 14:26). Being brought up in a godly home is more beneficial than being brought up in an affluent or influential home. Godly parents pass on to their children something no money can buy: the example of implicit trust and confidence in the Lord.

It might appear that Amram and Jochebed, slaves in a ghetto in Goshen, had little to offer Aaron, Miriam, and Moses. Yet these parents were able to bequeath the fear of the Lord to their children— they were able to teach them that God is a strong and sure refuge.

"By faith," says the Holy Spirit, "Moses, when he was born, was hid three months of his parents, because they saw he was a proper child; and they were not afraid of the king's commandment" (Hebrews 11:23). According to the king's commandment, the infant should have been cast into the Nile. Amram and Jochebed put him in the

Nile, but they put him in a little ark of bulrushes first. They feared God far more than they feared the king.

They may have said to themselves, "How does God save someone who is condemned to death?" Then they probably thought of Noah, the judgment of the flood, and God's provision of an ark of safety. Noah and his family went through the storm, but they were quite safe. The ark (a perfect Old Testament picture of Christ) came between them and the fury of the storm. Encouraged by God's faithfulness to Noah, Amram and Jochebed put an ark between their little boy and the waters of death, and God honored their faith.

Faith was what Amram and Jochebed bequeathed to their children. No wonder that out of that slave hut came Moses, the great legislator, emancipator, and prophet; Aaron, Israel's first high priest; and Miriam, a prophetess! No wonder that Moses grew up to choose God and His people over all the treasures and pleasures of Egypt. No wonder he could boldly stand before all the pomp and power of a pharaoh and humble Egypt in the dust.

The godly man also *knows how to be sure:* "The fear of the Lord is a fountain of life, to depart from the snares of death" (Proverbs 14:27).

In this world we are like wild goats on steep mountain slopes. The one thing a wild goat needs is sure footing. The steep slopes where a goat lives are precipitous. One wrong step and the goat will fall to its death in a dark canyon below. The goat has to be surefooted in perilous heights. It also has to be able to leap from one rocky ledge to another. It has to learn very quickly how to keep itself from the snares of death. We too have to learn how to live in a perilous world.

We are also like tourists in the maze at Hampton Court in London. This famous palace was built by Cardinal Wolsey, an ambitious man who loved display and wealth and wanted to become pope. When Henry VIII saw Hampton Court he was so impressed he demanded that it be deeded over to him. On the grounds of this palace is a maze made of hedges.

When I was a little boy my aunt and uncle took me to see this palace and for the magnificent sum of one English penny we were allowed to enter the maze and wander at will. After only a few turns we were lost. All paths looked the same and seemed to lead to nowhere. We wandered around in that maze for an hour and when we arrived back in the middle for the third or fourth time, we decided to sit down. In the middle of the maze the authorities had thoughtfully provided a couple of benches where people could sit down and think about their lost condition.

My uncle, who had been to Hampton Court before, pointed to a bell button. "Press that," he said. I did so and soon an attendant appeared. "You fellows lost?" he asked. That seemed to me to be the understatement of the year! "Follow me," he said and we did. He took a turn to the left, a turn to the right, a turn here, a turn there, and we were soon back outside. We did not know the way, but he did.

This world is far more perplexing than that maze and far more perilous too. There are confusing crossroads in life and many of them are booby-trapped. Moreover we cannot retrace our steps. Thankfully, though we do not know the way, He does! If we love Him, trust Him, and obey Him, we will avoid the snares of death. He will lead us to the fountain of life and help us to avoid the pitfalls along the way.

8. The Palace of the King (14:28-35)

a. His People (14:28)

"In the multitude of people is the king's honour: but in the want of people is the destruction of the prince." A small country with a sparse population is always at risk when it has a powerful, populous neighbor. Solomon ruled over a small country that had a relatively small population and was surrounded by powerful neighbors. In his day Egypt was the threat. Later it would be Assyria, then Babylon, Persia, Greece, and Rome.

David's solution was to wage war. He thrashed Syria, Philistia, Moab, Ammon, and Amalek. He built a small but thoroughly efficient army and the word got around: leave Israel alone. Solomon's solution was to pursue peace. He was not a warrior-king like his father so his foreign policy was to make friends and influence people. He decided, "If you cannot fight them, join them." Instead of confronting the neighboring princes, he courted the neighboring princesses. That is why his harem grew so large. He began by marrying one of the pharaoh's daughters. Solomon may have thought his policy to be very clever, but it was disastrous.

Actually the size of the population was irrelevant in Israel's case. Moses declared, "The Lord did not set his love upon you, nor choose you, because ye were more in number than any people; for ye were the fewest of all people: But because the Lord loved you" (Deuteronomy 7:7-8). If Israel kept the commandments and the terms of the covenant, Moses promised, "The Lord thy God . . . will love thee, and bless thee, and multiply thee" (7:12-13). Israel's best defense against her powerful neighbors was not in trying to match them, man for man, chariot for chariot, but in resting in the covenant. Israel had something no other nation had: a treaty relationship with the living God (Genesis 12:1-3).

b. His Patience (14:29)

"He that is slow to wrath is of great understanding; but he that is hasty of spirit exalteth folly." Nine times out of ten, "a short fuse" is no asset. Quick-tempered people lose many friends and frequently land in hot water. Often only the kindness and patience of others saves them from even worse predicaments than the immediate, short-range results of their folly.

Consider the example of Israel's King Jehoram. He was a son of the wicked King Ahab and had succeeded his older brother Ahaziah on the throne. Jehoram destroyed the image of Baal his father had made but continued the calf worship instituted years before by Jeroboam. The prophet Elisha was active during Jehoram's reign. His feelings toward this great prophet ranged from ambivalence to dislike.

Jehoram's real enemy was Ben-hadad, king of Syria, whose commanding general, Naaman, had recently won a resounding victory over Israel. Some think it was Naaman who drew his bow "at a venture" and killed Ahab (1 Kings 22:34). Having learned from a little Hebrew slave girl in his household that he might be healed of his leprosy in Israel, Naaman applied to his king for a leave of absence. The Syrian king wrote a letter to Jehoram commanding him to heal Naaman of his leprosy (2 Kings 5:6). Notice how quickly God's message became mixed up. "Would God my lord were with the prophet that is in Samaria" is what the little maid had said (2 Kings 5:3).

When Jehoram received his important visitor and read the contents of the Syrian king's letter, he flew into a rage. He tore his clothes and screamed, "Am I God, to kill and to make alive, that this man doth send unto me to recover a man of his leprosy? wherefore consider, I pray you, and see how he seeketh a quarrel against me" (2 Kings 5:7).

Probably nothing but Elisha's timely message averted an explosion, angry words, and a declaration of war, for Naaman also had a short fuse. When two hotheads get together there's sure to be trouble. Solomon knew that patience is a great virtue in rulers.

c. His Purity (14:30)

"A sound heart is the life of the flesh: but envy the rottenness of the bones." A tranquil heart or mind affects the whole body. A mind at ease lengthens life and promotes health. Anger, malice, and envy keep the mind in turmoil and produce ulcers and other physical ills. Nothing hinders productivity more than envy. Nothing is harder to handle. Envy drives people to perform all kinds of evil deeds.

Shakespeare's great play, *Julius Caesar,* deals with envy. The story begins with a conspiracy against Julius Caesar. He was more of a politician than a soldier, although he did become a great soldier too. His campaigns in Gaul proved him to be a military genius. He conquered Britain, picked up the gauntlet flung in his face by the jealous Pompey, crossed the Rubicon with five thousand men, and made himself master of Italy. Julius Caesar made Egypt a Roman province, became the undisputed master of the world, and was offered a crown. He was politician enough to read the temper of Rome correctly, so he refused the crown. The aristocrats, however, strongly suspected that sooner or later he would make himself king.

Then Brutus, Caesar's close friend, joined with Cassius, Cinna, Casca, and other conspirators in a plot to murder Caesar. Shakespeare made it clear in the dialogue that their motive was envy. Seeking to enlist Brutus in the cause, Cassius said:

> I was born free as Caesar: so were you:
> We have both fed as well, and we can both
> Endure a winter's cold as well as he.

Cassius told Brutus of a time when Caesar was swimming in the Tiber and finding himself in trouble, cried to Cassius for aid.

> And this man
> Is now become a god; and Cassius is
> A wretched creature, and must bend his body
> If Caesar carelessly but nod on him.

After uttering these envious words, Cassius told Brutus of a time when Caesar was sick in Spain. "How he did shake," Cassius said. "'Tis true, this god did shake." He warmed to his theme:

> Ye gods, it doth amaze me,
> A man of such a feeble temper should
> So get the start of the majestic world,
> And bear the palm alone.

At that moment a shout from the crowd outside interrupted
Cassius. Brutus expressed the fear that new honors were being
heaped on Caesar. Cassius replied:

> Why, man, he doth bestride the narrow world;
> Like a colossus; and we petty men
> Walk under his huge legs, and peep about
> To find ourselves dishonorable graves.
> Men at some time are masters of their fates:
> The fault, dear Brutus, is not in our stars,
> But in ourselves, that we are underlings.
>
> . . . .
> Upon what meat doth this our Caesar feed,
> That he is grown so great?

Brutus, motivated by what he considered to be the highest good
of Rome, joined the conspirators who were motivated by their envy
of Caesar. On March 15 (the ides of March), 44 B.C., they stabbed
Caesar to death as he entered a meeting of the Roman senate. He
received more than twenty wounds from men who had accepted his
favors and whom he had believed to be his friends.

Civil war followed, the armies of Antony and Octavius defeated
the conspirators, and Brutus committed suicide. Antony's eulogy of
Brutus summed up the whole story:

> This was the noblest Roman of them all:
> All the conspirators, save only he,
> Did that they did in envy of great Caesar;
> He only, in a general honest thought
> And common good to all, made one of them.
>
> . . . .
>   "This was a man!"

Mark Antony, Caesar's friend, had almost the last word. With his
typical touch of genius, Shakespeare left the very last word to
Octavius, the future ruler of the world.

Envy brought about the murder of Julius Caesar, one of the
greatest men in the history of the Roman world. "Envy [is] the
rottenness of the bones," said Solomon. It would be better to have
bone cancer than an envious spirit. There is no end to the malice
of an envious spirit. How much better it is to have a sound heart.
Rulers particularly need to take Proverbs 14:30 to heart.

d. His Policies (14:31-33)

In this passage Solomon reviewed the policies of a king. Solomon's policies reflected his attitude toward *want:* "He that oppresseth the poor reproacheth his Maker: but he that honoureth him hath mercy on the poor" (Proverbs 14:31). There is no greater test of a government than the way it treats its poor citizens.

The United States is a land of plenty where there is "bread enough and to spare" (Luke 15:17).Yet in this great and affluent land with the highest standard of living in history, millions of people are homeless. They shamble through bus depots, sleep on steam grates, and occasionally die in public parks. At least a third of the homeless are said to be mentally ill. The nation spends millions of dollars on its poor but their number increases all the time. Our welfare programs are woefully inadequate and are subject to bureaucratic absurdities and red tape.

The problem of poverty is far worse in other parts of the world. Throughout the Caribbean and Latin America poverty is endemic. Burgeoning populations, city crowding, economic ills, unemployment, disease, and famine are rampant. Hospitals, schools, and social services for the chronically poor are virtually nonexistent in many countries. Anyone who has seen a Latin American shantytown can never forget it.

Behind the glitter and glamour of Brazil's famous Rio de Janeiro, with its fabulous beaches and spectacular scenery, lie the slums. A missionary friend of mine took me to visit a believer who lived in those slums. I saw a city made of mud and sticks—a city where a tin can is as precious as gold because it can be flattened and cut and used as roofing and siding to keep the rain out.

In Bolivia black lung disease afflicts the nation's miners. Many have a life expectancy of twenty-seven years. As a result there are many widows and multitudes of fatherless children.

In Ecuador the per capita income is less than nine hundred dollars. In Guatemala 2 percent of the population owns 70 percent of the land. In Haiti, the poorest country in the western hemisphere, one-third of the children do not live to be five years of age. In Mexico a quarter of a million people flock into the capital every year; they flee rural poverty only to be overwhelmed by urban poverty.

Africa is a continent in the grip of almost unending drought. The Sahara desert is expanding. Overgrazing, deforestation, and lack of rain have increased the desertification of lands bordering the Sahara. Approximately twenty African countries have been beset by famine. More than thirty million people—nearly a third of the continent's entire population—have been affected. The plight of millions is aggravated by war.

The Orient has its share of poverty. In India millions of boys and girls live on what Ghandi once called "an eternal, compulsory fast." The living conditions for millions in the Philippines are indescribable, especially in the big-city slums where more than six thousand people crowd into each square mile. In Sri Lanka half the people in Colombo, the capital, live in shanties made of tar paper; most of the children suffer from malnutrition and half the population drink polluted water. In Bangkok, Thailand, the slums are among the worst in Asia.

All over the world urbanization is increasing, compounding the problem of poverty. Studies reveal a sharp rise in child abandonment and child abuse. In some countries armies of children live in the streets. Their parents can no longer even pretend to support them. In Mexico alone the number of abandoned children is estimated at seven hundred thousand. Solitary toddlers have been seen trying to sell a few sticks of gum. In Latin America abandoned children are callously called "brown dust." Just reading about them is enough to make one weep.

Solomon reminded us that "he that oppresseth the poor reproacheth his Maker." God is equally the God of a homeless orphaned waif on a Manila street and a pampered darling of a well-to-do American family. God is equally concerned about a desperate parent in Mexico City who is forced to abandon a little one to the streets and an affluent parent in America who is able to feed and educate his child. "Ye have the poor always with you," Jesus said (Matthew 26:11). He bequeathed them to us, His church. We are to be concerned about the poor. How can we say that we love and honor Christ if we have no compassion for His poor? We must remember the strong words of James 2:14-17:

> What doth it profit, my brethren, though a man say he hath faith, and have not works? can faith save him? If a brother or sister be naked, and destitute of daily food, And one of you say unto them, Depart in peace, be ye warmed and filled; notwithstanding ye give them not those things which are needful to the body; what doth it profit? Even so faith, if it hath not works, is dead, being alone.

Solomon's policies also reflected his attitude toward *wickedness:* "The wicked is driven away in his wickedness: but the righteous hath hope in his death" (Proverbs 14:32). The lawless one is thrust down in his evildoing. The classic Biblical example of this proverb is the story of the Babylonian king Belshazzar in Daniel 5.

We can picture Belshazzar on the morning of the feast as he drove his chariot on the top of the high wall around Babylon. That wall was one of the wonders of the world. Chariots could be driven four abreast on the top of that wall. Perhaps Belshazzar stopped here and there to wave to the Medo-Persians far below. They looked like toy soldiers and their cordon around his city seemed a mere cobweb. Little did Belshazzar know that the last laugh would be theirs that very night. Cyrus's engineers were putting the finishing touches on great sluices and a new channel for the Euphrates river. That mighty river ran right through the heart of the city, but in a few hours its waters would be diverted and Cyrus's soldiers would walk dry-shod into Babylon on the river's rocky bed.

The banqueting hall that night was a sight to behold. All the grandeur, pomp, and ceremony of Babylon was on display. Some historians think the feast was held to honor Bel, the god of Babylon. But how could Bel, Marduk, or any other gods of gold, silver, iron, wood, or stone be properly honored if Jehovah of the Jews was not suitably dishonored? Belshazzar ordered that golden vessels once used in the temple in Jerusalem be brought from Nebuchadnezzar's treasure house to the banquet chamber and filled with wine. Then along with his nobles, generals, wives, and women he toasted the gods of Babylon with the golden vessels of the living God.

Centuries before, the Philistines had tried to dishonor the sacred ark of the covenant in front of their idol Dagon. God knew how to protect His interests *then;* He simply dismembered Dagon and pushed him flat on his face (1 Samuel 5:1-5). God knew how to protect His interests *now;* suddenly, silently, a sinister finger appeared out of the sleeve of the night and wrote on the wall the letters *MNMNTKLPRS*.

No one could read the writing, but the evil king's conscience began to trouble him. He stood there as white as a sheet and shook in his shoes. Then someone thought of Daniel—long since out of office, out of favor, and out of mind. He could read the writing. All he needed to do was add the letter *E*. Then the message was clear: "MENE MENE TEKEL PERES." Belshazzar had been weighed and found wanting. He had not been weighed on Solomon's scales or those of Moses. Belshazzar had been weighed on his own scales— against his own riches, power, privileges, knowledge, opportunities, and responsibilities. He was found to be wicked and he was driven away. "That night was Belshazzar the king of the Chaldeans slain. And Darius the Median took the kingdom" (Daniel 5:30-31).

Wicked Belshazzar had no hope in his death, but righteous Daniel had hope in his. The lions could not eat him, death could not harm him, and he was "greatly beloved" in Heaven (Daniel 9:23). Just before Daniel put down his pen for the last time, God let him into yet another secret:

> Thy people shall be delivered, every one that shall be found written in the book. And many of them that sleep in the dust of the earth shall awake, some to everlasting life, and some to shame and everlasting contempt. And they that be wise shall shine as the brightness of the firmament; and they that turn many to righteousness as the stars for ever and ever (Daniel 12:1-3).

This prophecy robbed death of all its terror for Daniel and for us.

Finally, Solomon's policies reflected his attitude toward *wisdom:* "Wisdom resteth in the heart of him that hath understanding: but that which is in the midst of fools is made known" (Proverbs 14:33). The second part of the proverb could be rendered, "And [even] in the midst of fools it [wisdom] will make itself known."

The men who surrounded Rehoboam were wise men. Solomon saw to it that his cabinet, which included the best brains and the sharpest intellects in the country, was handed over intact to Rehoboam when he ascended the throne. Even though Solomon did not have much hope for Rehoboam, at least he did what he could to save his son from his own foolishness and from the abysmal folly of his friends.

But if ever there was a cocksure individual, it was Rehoboam. When the delegation headed by the tough-minded Jeroboam came from the northern tribes to ask for redress for their grievances, the wise old men in the cabinet said that the delegation had justice and reason on their side. If Rehoboam would give the tribes their rights, the people would throw their love and loyalty wholeheartedly behind the Davidic throne. But if Rehoboam refused, rebellion would erupt. The tribe of Ephraim, descended from Joseph, had always envied the tribe of Judah. The Ephraimites would be only too glad to have an opportunity to set up a rival kingdom.

These old men knew that Jeroboam was ruthless and godless and Rehoboam would have little chance of ever winning back the northern tribes once they revolted. Solomon's cabinet warned

Rehoboam to give in to the delegation at once. Wisdom rested in the understanding hearts of these old men, but Rehoboam preferred the advice of fools.

Before the week was over Rehoboam knew all too well that wisdom did not rest in the hearts of his silly friends. When Rehoboam mobilized his army to try to force the ten tribes to accept his rule, he was peremptorily told by the prophet Shemaiah to disband his army at once (1 Kings 12:22-24). This time Rehoboam had enough sense to listen to sound advice.

e. His Power (14:34-35)

Solomon, who was well-versed in the principles of government, stated *the essential of power:* "Righteousness exalteth a nation: but sin is a reproach to any people" (Proverbs 14:34).

The men and women who came across the western seas to found a great new nation on the shores of America were driven by a quenchless thirst for God. When the *Mayflower* dropped anchor off Cape Cod in November 1620, the Pilgrim leaders persuaded forty-one adult male passengers to sign what is called "The Mayflower Compact," which stated the terms under which the Plymouth colony would be administered. This agreement of self-government, the first ever put in force in America, read:

> In the name of God, Amen. We whose names are underwritten, the loyal subjects of our dread Sovereign Lord King James, by the grace of God, of Great Britain, France, and Ireland, King, defender of the faith, etc. Having undertaken for the glory of God, and advancement of the Christian faith and honor of our king and country, a voyage to plant the first colony in the Northern parts of Virginia, do by these presents solemnly and mutually in the presence of God, and one another, covenant, and combine ourselves together into a Civil body politic; for our better ordering and preservation and furtherance of the ends aforesaid; and by virtue hereof to enact, constitute, and frame such just and equal laws, ordinances, acts, constitutions, and offices, from time to time, as shall be thought most meet and convenient for the general good of the colony; unto which we promise all due submission and obedience. In witness whereof we have hereunder subscribed our names at Cape Cod the 11th of November, in the year of the reign of our sovereign Lord King James of

England, France, and Ireland, the eighteenth, and of Scotland, the fifty-fourth. Anno Domini, 1620.

This compact was a notable beginning. The founding fathers of the United States of America went on to write their faith in God into the Constitution, to stamp the words "In God We Trust" onto the coin of the realm, and to found great educational institutions on the Word of God.

"Righteousness exalteth a nation," said Solomon, and the history of the United States reflects this truth. From time to time in this nation's relatively short history, God has visited the land with Holy Spirit revivals to bring it back to its roots. The United States has been richly endowed, greatly blessed, and exalted to the status of a global superpower. Its citizens have built many great and influential churches, sent missionaries by the thousands to earth's remotest bounds, and established countless Christian schools, institutions, and ministries. American generosity, humanity, and goodwill have been known all around the world.

The United States is still a bastion of the faith, but it is also the home of Hollywood. The land is riddled with pornography and perversion. Sodomy is countenanced. Thanks to a handful of godless men who served on the supreme court some years ago, abortion-on-demand slaughters countless babies every year. Scandals in high places rock the country. Organized crime flourishes. Our nation is inundated with drugs. Humanism in its worst and most subversive forms has taken over the schools, courts, media, political parties, and government. A large segment of the American church is apostate. Sin, which is a shame to any people, threatens the foundations of our country. Prayer and Bible reading have been banished from the classrooms of the public schools on the pretense of separating church and state.

The handwriting is on the wall. What the United States of America needs is another Holy Spirit revival that will put conviction back into the pulpits and pews; conscience back into government; common sense, decency, and discipline back into the schools; integrity back into business; commitment back into marriage; shame back into sin; courage back into the courts; character back into our leaders; safety back into the streets; purpose back into our youth; and God back into our national consciousness. Such a revival is the answer to our shame.

Solomon went on to refer to *the exercise of power:* "The king's favour is toward a wise servant: but his wrath is against him that causeth shame" (Proverbs 14:35). Rulers must reward worthy citizens and repress those who promote shameful things.

Consider how David and Solomon exercised power in dealing with Israel's two high priests, Abiathar and Zadok. The situation was extraordinary, for Jewish religious law contemplated only one high priest. Zadok was the rightful high priest because he was a direct descendant of Eleazar, the son of Aaron. Abiathar was also a descendant of Aaron, but from the line of Ithamar.

Abiathar's father was functioning as priest at the city of Nob when he and all the other priests at Nob were murdered because King Saul suspected them of disloyalty. Abiathar alone escaped and fled to David for protection. David, an outlaw at that time and the head of a band of tough guerrillas, allowed Abiathar to act as his priest. David always blamed himself for the murder of Abiathar's family, so he was reluctant to depose Abiathar when Zadok came with a delegation from the tribes to turn the whole kingdom over to David after the death of Saul. Consequently for much of David's reign there were two high priests.

At the time of the Absalom rebellion the two priests worked together in cordial harmony. They brought the sacred ark from Jerusalem to David and when the rebellion collapsed, they acted together again in suggesting to the people that they invite David back (2 Samuel 15:24-29; 19:11). So this unusual situation continued and David patiently waited for God to resolve the unnatural duplication.

In time a flaw in Abiathar's character was revealed. Contrary to David's clear will that Solomon should be heir and successor to the throne, Abiathar backed Adonijah, who hoped to forestall Solomon. Perhaps Adonijah promised that if the coup were successful, Abiathar would be confirmed as the one true high priest. The coup failed.

Meanwhile Nathan and Bathsheba had apprised David of what was going on behind his back. Acting promptly he ordered Zadok to crown Solomon king (1 Kings 1:32-45).

After David's death Abiathar again sided with Adonijah in a situation that Solomon considered to be treasonable. The king promptly deposed Abiathar and his two sons, Ahimelech and Jonathan, and installed Zadok as the one true high priest.

Zadok was a wise servant and the wise king's favor was toward him. The king's wrath was displayed toward the disloyal Abiathar. "Get thee to Anathoth," Solomon said, "unto thine own fields; for thou art worthy of death" (1 Kings 2:26). Thus Abiathar was disgraced, defrocked, and dismissed. He was lucky to escape with his life. Covered with shame, he was banished from Jerusalem and from all the activity connected with the building of the temple. He eyed from afar Zadok's sole occupancy of the high priestly office.

CHAPTER 19

Proverbs 15:1-33

E. Virtues to Be Considered (15:1-33)
   1. The Question of Tongues (15:1-4)
      a. Those Able to Give a Soft Answer (15:1)
      b. Those Able to Give a Sage Answer (15:2-3)
         (1) We Must Be Accurate (15:2)
         (2) We Will Be Accountable (15:3)
      c. Those Able to Give a Sweet Answer (15:4)
   2. The Question of Teaching (15:5-7)
      a. True Wisdom (15:5)
      b. True Wealth (15:6)
      c. True Words (15:7)
   3. The Question of Transgressors (15:8-12)
      a. The Lord Refuses Their Sacrifices (15:8)
      b. The Lord Repudiates Their Steps (15:9)
      c. The Lord Rebukes Their Stubbornness (15:10)
      d. The Lord Rejects Their Souls (15:11)
      e. The Lord Records Their Scorn (15:12)
   4. The Question of Temperaments (15:13-15)
      a. The Sorrowful Man (15:13)
      b. The Seeking Man (15:14)
      c. The Singing Man (15:15)
   5. The Question of Trouble (15:16-23)
      a. Trouble Caused by Ambition (15:16-17)
         (1) Better to Have Little Than to Have Trouble (15:16)
         (2) Better to Have Love Than to Have Trouble (15:17)
      b. Trouble Caused by Animosity (15:18)
      c. Trouble Caused by Apathy (15:19)
      d. Trouble Caused by Antipathy (15:20)
      e. Trouble Caused by Absurdity (15:21)

Solomon continued to move to and fro throughout his realm observing human behavior. Like a bee going from flower to flower, Solomon gathered the nectar from which he distilled the rich, sweet honey of his wisdom.

Most of the following proverbs set forth truth by presenting contrasts. A good man is placed alongside a bad one. A worthy act is enhanced by being placed alongside a base one. Solomon knew that a flashing diamond seems more lustrous when it is displayed on a black velvet background.

E. Virtues to Be Considered (15:1-33)

1. The Question of Tongues (15:1-4)

a. Those Able to Give a Soft Answer (15:1)

"A soft answer turneth away wrath: but grievous words stir up anger."

Eli probably never forgave himself for the grievous words he spoke to poor, unoffending Hannah, who had already heard enough harsh words at home. Alexander Whyte wrote:

Away back at the beginning of his life, Eli had taken far too much in hand. Eli was not a great man like Moses or Aaron, but he took both the office of Moses and the office of Aaron upon himself. Eli was both the chief judge and the high priest in himself for the whole house of Israel. The ablest, the most laborious, the most devoted, the most tireless and sleepless of men could not have done what Eli undertook to do.

Eli was altogether too busy and the result was that he did nothing well. Ministering at the altar, administering at the gate, minding his own house, minding the house of God—all went to wrack and ruin. Eli's worst failure was in minding his own house. There the ruin was beyond human remedy and divine forgiveness (1 Samuel 2:22-36; 3:12-14).

We can picture a worn-out Eli propped up against a post of the temple the day Hannah came along. She was barren, bitter, and broken. She had only one place to go—the house of God. She had only one person to implore—God. Hannah prayed silently. (God can hear us whether or not we speak out loud when we pray.) Her lips moved but made no sound. She wept and wrung her hands. She staggered under the load of her wretched plight. She had no son! She thought, *If God would give me a son, I would give him right back to God.*

Eli woke up with a yawn. He rubbed his eyes and stared. *The woman must be drunk,* he thought. She was no more drunk than Peter, James, and John were on the day of Pentecost, but Eli thought she was and he lashed out at her with his tongue. "How long wilt thou be drunken?" he snapped. "Put away thy wine from thee" (1 Samuel 1:14). His words were grievous indeed.

If the woman had been Peninnah, she would have pinned his ears back, priest or no priest. People would have come running to enjoy the spectacle of an angry woman giving the old priest a piece of her mind. She would have aired his family history and the antics of his no-good sons. "Drunk indeed!" Peninnah would have exclaimed. "Who are you to talk about people being drunk when you have sons who make themselves vile?"

Knowing that "a soft answer turneth away wrath," Hannah said to the angry priest:

No, my lord, I am a woman of a sorrowful spirit: I have drunk neither wine nor strong drink, but have poured out my soul before the Lord. Count not thine handmaid for a daughter of Belial: for out of the abundance of my complaint and grief have I spoken hitherto (1 Samuel 1:15-16).

Eli's wrath was disarmed. He was ashamed and could have bitten his tongue out. "Go in peace," he said, "and the God of Israel grant thee thy petition that thou hast asked of him" (1 Samuel 1:17).

b. Those Able to Give a Sage Answer (15:2-3)

"The tongue of the wise useth knowledge aright: but the mouth of fools poureth out foolishness" (Proverbs 15:2). *We must be accurate* in what we say. We should be sure we have all the facts and consider them carefully before we speak. It is foolish to jump to conclusions. It is even more foolish to blurt them out without respect to time, place, or circumstances.

The book of Job provides us with the classic Biblical examples of people who spoke, made accusations, argued, and hotly defended themselves without knowing all the facts.

The sons of Gilead are another example of those who speak foolishness. The legitimate sons of Gilead looked with scorn on young Jephthah, their illegitimate brother. He was born when there was no priest, no king, and no judge in Israel, and everyone did what was right in his own eyes (Judges 21:25). The moral and spiritual condition of Israel in those days shows that what is *right* in our eyes is often *wrong* in the eyes of the Lord.

When the legitimate sons of Gilead grew up, they turned on Jephthah with spite. "Thou shalt not inherit in our father's house," they said, "for thou art the son of a strange [foreign] woman" (Judges 11:2). They disinherited him and pushed him out of the family. Doubtless they congratulated each other for ridding themselves of a potential rival.

Jephthah however was hewn from rock. He fled to the land of Tob, east of Syria. In Tob he made a name for himself and, as David would do in later years, Jephthah gathered around himself a band of tough outlaws. Moreover he was a man of courage and conviction. He knew God and he brought up his daughter to love both him and God, even to the point of making the ultimate sacrifice (Judges 11:30-40).

Meanwhile the Ammonites descended on Israel east of the Jordan and held it in subjection for eighteen years. Then someone thought of Jephthah. In desperation the elders of Gilead, who years ago had treated Jephthah unjustly, swallowed their pride and appealed to the outlaw chief to help them.

"The tongue of the wise useth knowledge aright," Solomon said. Jephthah knew these people. Therefore when he spoke, his words were pointed and purposeful. Having been ill-treated by them once, he was not about to be used and then discarded again. He replied: "Did not ye hate me, and expel me out of my father's house? and why are ye come unto me now when ye are in distress?" The elders made a promise: "Go with us, and fight against the children of Ammon, and be our head over all the inhabitants of Gilead."

Jephthah wanted his brothers to repeat their promise so that there would be no misunderstanding afterward. He said, "If ye bring me home again to fight against the children of Ammon, and the Lord deliver them before me, shall I be your head?" Desperate enough to agree to anything, "the elders of Gilead said unto Jephthah, The Lord witness between us, if we do not so according to thy words." Now he had the promise under oath.

Still not quite satisfied, Jephthah "went with the elders of Gilead, and the people made him head and captain over them: and Jephthah uttered all his words before the Lord in Mizpeh." (See Judges 11:7-11.) Now the deal was "signed, sealed, and delivered" and he "had it in writing," as we say today. Jephthah was a wise man. The pledge of the Gileadites was both sworn and witnessed—before the supreme court of Heaven.

Our words must be accurate because *we will be accountable* for what we say: "The eyes of the Lord are in every place, beholding the evil and the good" (Proverbs 15:3). We had better mean what we say and do what we promise, for God is omniscient. His all-seeing eye misses nothing. He saw, for instance, what happened to Hagar.

Born and raised in Egypt, Hagar became Sarah's maid. Then she became "the other woman" in Sarah's wretched little scheme. *Since Abraham is childless and I am barren, Sarah reasoned, and since God has promised that Abraham will have a son, wouldn't it be a good idea for Abraham to marry Hagar? Then Hagar could bear Abraham a son and I could adopt him. According to the Code of Hammurabi, that son could legally be regarded as my son.* The plan was all very carnal and complicated.

Abraham went along with Sarah's scheme. However when Hagar became pregnant, she looked down her nose at Sarah. That was more than flesh and blood could stand. Sarah blamed Abraham, who in turn shrugged his shoulders and said, "Behold, thy maid is in thy hand; do to her as it pleaseth thee" (Genesis 16:6). That was all Sarah wanted to hear. She made Hagar's life miserable. That, too, was more than flesh and blood could stand. Hagar ran away and headed straight for Egypt. She had known more kindness and consideration there, in the world, than she had ever known among these "believers."

Hagar had been raised in a land where they worshiped cats, cows, and crocodiles, but she had been brought into the home of believers. What an opportunity Abraham and Sarah had to win this poor pagan to faith in Jehovah! Instead they treated her worse than a piece of furniture. They used her and abused her. She likely said to herself, "If that's how people who say they are saved and who worship Jehovah behave, I'd be better off as a pagan."

But the eyes of the Lord run to and fro in the earth, beholding the evil and the good. He saw the whole wretched business and heard every bitter word. He had not been an impartial observer. His name and His character had been misrepresented by the behavior of Abraham and Sarah, so He ran after Hagar. He loved that poor unhappy Egyptian woman as much as He loved Abraham and Sarah. They had failed to reveal Him to her, so He would reveal Himself to her.

God caught up with Hagar in the wilderness of Shur. She had arrived at the Egyptian frontier. The next day she would be back in Egypt and find herself in a bondage far worse than the one from which she had fled. If the eyes of the Lord had not been running to and fro throughout the earth, she would have been swallowed up by the eternal spiritual darkness of Egypt. She might well have said to her grandchildren, "Oh yes, I did hear about another God once. But I was not impressed by the lives of those who believed in Him."

So God intervened. Before it was forever too late—before Hagar could make the fateful decision to choose Egypt's darkness in preference to Abraham's light—God spoke. "The angel of the Lord found her," Moses wrote (Genesis 16:7). God always takes the initiative in salvation. "Hagar, Sarai's maid, whence camest thou? and whither wilt thou go?" He asked (16:8). These are searching questions that everyone who is running away from God should ask himself. Notice that God called Hagar "Sarai's maid," not "Abraham's wife." Hagar's "marriage" to Abraham had never been part of God's plan, nor could it ever be sanctioned by Him.

Before Hagar was the wide gate and the broad Egyptian way to eternal night. Behind her was the strait gate and the narrow way. God who had revealed Himself directly to Abraham and called him to Himself out of Babylon now revealed Himself directly to Hagar and called her to Himself out of Egypt. And Hagar believed! God was the God of all grace. He loved her just as much as He loved Abraham.

Then God told Hagar to put her faith to work at once. "Return...and submit," He said (Genesis 16:9). Surely these were the two hardest demands He could have made.

God also promised Hagar a son. "He will be a wild man," He told her (Genesis 16:12). He would be a born rebel, but he must never be able to say that he had learned his rebellion from his mother. That boy would be governed by pride and bitterness; he would be capable of mocking ribaldly at the things of God; and his descendants would embrace one of the most tenacious false religions in the world. That boy needed, more than anything else, to see a daily example of submission.

God won Hagar's heart. She packed her few things, turned around, and retraced her steps. Then she deliberately put herself in the place of subjection and did her best to raise her son within the sound of the gospel—the glorious gospel according to Abraham.

c. Those Able to Give a Sweet Answer (15:4)

"A wholesome tongue is a tree of life: but perverseness therein is a breach in the spirit." A wholesome tongue speaks gentle words that help and heal, build up and encourage.

Surely no sweeter words ever fell on the ears of Saul of Tarsus than the two spoken by Ananias: "Brother Saul" (Acts 9:17). The first time we see Saul he was only holding the coats of those who had rolled up their sleeves to murder Stephen. But Saul went on to plan and execute the most dreadful deeds of his own.

He became the chief inquisitor of the Sanhedrin and made havoc of the church. Entering house after house, he hauled Christians before the tribunal and committed them to prison. He pursued them from synagogue to synagogue and compelled them to blaspheme. First Timothy 1:13 tells us he was "a blasphemer, and a persecutor, and injurious." Acts 9:1 tells us he breathed out threatenings and slaughter. He obtained signed documents from the high priest in Jerusalem authorizing him to extend his activities to Damascus and elsewhere. Saul had blood on his hands. He had made many a woman a widow and many a child an orphan. Women as well as men were his targets.

Then Saul met Christ! Still blinded by the heavenly vision, he groped his way into Damascus and sat for three days—totally blind and prey to his thoughts. Now he was alone. The Sanhedrin would not want him. He was the greatest of all threats to them. He knew Caiaphas and his crowd. They would have a contract out on his life before the week was out. The Christians would not want him either. They would consider him a spy and an informer, and they would be afraid of him. None of them would trust him. After all, why should they? And his family would not want him now that he had become a Christian.

He had persecuted the Son of the living God. His religion had made him a murderer and his zeal had made him the chief of sinners. He had mobbed and maligned the people of God. The Judaism he had served was obsolete. The Jews had become the enemies of God. They had killed the Prince of glory. Saul's past was a lie, his present was darkness, and his future was a blank.

Then Saul heard the door open. He looked up but could see no one, for he was blind. A voice said, "Brother Saul," and heaven came down and glory filled his soul! The wholesome words of Ananias brought new life to Saul.

"A wholesome tongue is a tree of life: but perverseness therein is a breach in the spirit." A wound from a tongue can be deeper, sorer, and harder to heal than a wound from a sword. Harsh and bitter words, mean and untrue words, words spoken sarcastically or maliciously can hurt a person deep in his soul. Yet they often hurt those who speak more than those who are spoken to. Think for example of Peter (John 18:15-27; Matthew 26:69-75; Luke 22:54-62).

"I am not." The words rang out loud and clear, edged with annoyance, tinged with fear. The damsel in charge of the door had let Peter in. Now he stood in the inner courtyard of Caiaphas' house, not quite knowing why he was there. "Art not thou also one of this man's disciples?" the young woman had asked. Peter's ready lie was brought full-grown into the world: "I am not."

It was cold. The high priest's servants and some of his guard made a fire at which to warm their hands. Irresolutely and nonchalantly Peter drifted over to warm his. One of the men nudged a colleague. They whispered among themselves. They had been in Gethsemane. They said, "Art not thou also one of his disciples?" Peter was even more alarmed. Maybe they had seen him slashing around with his sword. What a fool he had been. "I am not," he said, and again the words were spoken with some heat.

But the high priest's servants noticed Peter's accent. The man was a Galilean. "Surely," they said, "thou also art one of them; for thy speech bewrayeth thee." Peter began to curse and to swear. The foul language of his unregenerate fishing days came pouring from his lips. "I know not the man," he said. The group around the fire were satisfied. No man who knew Jesus would talk like that.

The cock crowed, the Lord looked, and Peter burst into tears. He shouldered his way through the crowd, shoved his way out of the gate, and went (we suppose) to Gethsemane with a broken heart. What those lies and curses did to the unregenerate men standing by the fire and the young woman standing by the door, we shall never know. But we know what those words did to Peter. They pierced his very soul.

2. The Question of Teaching (15:5-7)

In Proverbs 15:5 Solomon spoke of *true wisdom:* "A fool despiseth his father's instruction: but he that regardeth reproof is prudent."

In Daniel Defoe's novel, Robinson Crusoe spoke of his father's instruction:

> My father, who was [wise], had given me a competent share of learning…and designed me for the law; but I would be satisfied with nothing but going to sea.
> …he pressed me earnestly, and in the most affectionate manner, not to play the young man, or to precipitate myself into miseries, which nature, and the station of life I was born in, seemed to have provided against.

Tearful reminders of his older brother—who, scorning parental advice, ran away to be a soldier and was killed—did no good. Robinson Crusoe continued:

> Though [my father] said he would not cease to pray for me, yet he could venture to say to me, that if I did take this foolish step, God would not bless me—I would have leisure hereafter to reflect upon having neglected his counsel, when there might be none to assist in my recovery.

So Robinson Crusoe ran away to sea and all the world knows how he was shipwrecked on a lonely island. Nine months passed and Robinson Crusoe was overtaken with a violent fever. He was filled with alarm, for he had no physician to advise him and no friend to help him. His father's prophetic words had come true. No one cared whether he lived or died. The prospect of death terrified him. Knowing he was in no condition to die, he was glad to find a Bible.

> It occurred to my thought, that the Brazilians take no physic but their tobacco for almost all distempers; and I had a piece of a roll of tobacco in one of the chests….
> I went, directed by Heaven, no doubt; for in this chest I found a cure both for soul and body. I opened the chest, and found what I looked for, namely, the tobacco; and as the few

books I had saved lay there too, I took out one of the
Bibles...which, to this time, I had not found leisure, or so
much as inclination, to look into.

Robinson Crusoe was now ready to listen to God:

I took up the Bible, and began to read....Having opened the
book casually, the first words that occurred to me were these:—
"Call on me in the day of trouble, and I will deliver; and thou
shalt glorify me."
The words were very apt to my case, and made some
impression upon my thoughts.

Nothing could be simpler. All the text told him to do was to call.
He did not need a priest or a preacher. He did not need to be
baptized or do penance. There was no need for someone to explain
a procedure. All he had to do was call. A little child can call. A
drowning man can call. A lost soul can call. Robinson Crusoe called.
"Before I lay down," he said, "I did what I never had done in all my
life—I kneeled down, and prayed to God to fulfil the promise to
me." Robinson Crusoe recovered from his illness and twenty-seven
years later was rescued.

In Proverbs 15:6 Solomon spoke of *true wealth:* "In the house of
the righteous is much treasure: but in the revenues of the wicked is
trouble."

I used to visit the home of a rich Christian, a business friend of
mine. He lived in a million-dollar house on a manicured estate. The
treasures in his house were evidence of his wealth. He had to take
the most elaborate precautions to protect his expensive and luxurious possessions from thieves. When we drove up to his home in his
top-of-the-line Cadillac, he had to activate a gate security device
before he could even get into his own yard. Then three belligerent
dogs would rush up, barking and snarling. To enter his house he
had to decode an electronic alarm system, and once inside he had
to reactivate the system. In effect he was behind bars in his own
home. His estate was under regular police surveillance and a
groundsman kept an eye on all property within the wired fence. I
wondered if much treasure in the house of the righteous was really
worth it. My friend lived in constant fear of theft.

"In the revenues of the wicked is trouble." Al Capone, the most
famous gangster in American history, illustrates this truth. He was
introduced to organized crime by Johnny Torrio, the boss of the
Chicago underworld who first realized the potential of prohibition.

Small-time bootleggers were springing up everywhere and Torrio set out to control and monopolize this lucrative trade. The venture was to be a mammoth task so Torrio needed an assistant—someone who could combine organizing genius with utter ruthlessness. When he spotted Alphonse "Scarface" Capone, Torrio made him his partner. Within ten years Capone would earn the label "Public Enemy Number One." He would become known as the most wicked and one of the richest men of his time.

Capone left the slums of Brooklyn, New York, where he had been raised. He was still loudmouthed but now he was impeccably groomed. Money poured in from the sale of beer and liquor, from gambling saloons and dog tracks, from dance halls and roadhouses, from prostitution and an assortment of other rackets. He climbed to the top of the heap by engineering five hundred callous murders and he stayed on top through murder and through corruption of politicians, judges, and policemen. His crime empire was backed by the Thompson submachine gun, the revolver, and the sawed-off shotgun. Rival gangs offered enormous sums of money to anyone who would kill Capone, but he had seven hundred of the toughest gangsters in America at his command. At the height of his career he was raking in 6.5 million dollars a week.

Capone was rich, but not without trouble. On one occasion three gunmen sprayed his car with gunfire. Their intended victim escaped because minutes earlier he had stepped into a restaurant. Thereafter Capone rode in a steel-lined car that weighed more than seven tons and was equipped with bulletproof glass and special locks. A scout car always went ahead of this armored car and a gang of marksmen rode after it. On another occasion in broad daylight eight carloads of gangland storm troopers assaulted Capone's headquarters. In seconds they pumped a thousand shots into it, but again they missed their target.

In the end Capone was punished for his wickedness. He was sent to a federal penitentiary—for tax evasion! Even in prison he lived in style but his past caught up with him. The syphilis he had contracted early in life destroyed his brain. During his final madness, friends who gathered to play cards with him always let him win; if anyone won by mistake, Capone would cry, "Get the boys and rub this guy out!" Strange to say, he died in bed, but he made his bed in Hell and from that bed there is no rising up.

In Proverbs 15:7 Solomon spoke of *true words:* "The lips of the wise disperse knowledge: but the heart of the foolish doeth not so." Jesus said, "A good man out of the good treasure of his heart bringeth forth that which is good; and an evil man out of the evil treasure of his heart bringeth forth that which is evil: for of the abundance of the heart his mouth speaketh" (Luke 6:45).

In the old days when a person went to see the doctor, his first order usually was "Put out your tongue." The condition of the patient's tongue revealed the condition of his health. When Dr. Livesey visited the pirates in the compound on Treasure Island, he examined several of the wounded buccaneers. One of them said, "Dick don't feel well, sir." The doctor replied, "Well, step up here, Dick, and let me see your tongue. No, I should be surprised if he did! the man's tongue is fit to frighten the French. Another fever." The pirate's tongue betrayed him.

One day Harold St. John was standing in the private chapel of Keble College, Oxford, admiring Holman Hunt's masterpiece *The Light of The World.* A party of tourists approached and stood chattering before the famous painting. The guide announced in a loud voice, "The original of this picture was sold for fifteen thousand dollars." Mr. St. John stepped forward and said, "Ladies and gentlemen, may I add that the true Original of this picture was sold for thirty pieces of silver." A hush fell on the tourists and they left in silence. The words of the mouth express the condition of the heart.

3. The Question of Transgressors (15:8-12)

Observing transgressors, Solomon noted that the Lord refuses their sacrifices, repudiates their steps, rebukes their stubbornness, rejects their souls, and records their scorn. His first statement regarding transgressors was that the Lord *refuses their sacrifices:* "The sacrifice of the wicked is an abomination to the Lord: but the prayer of the upright is his delight" (Proverbs 15:8).

Consider the case of Oral Roberts, the maverick television evangelist and self-styled faith healer who even claims to have raised the dead.[1] On January 4, 1987, he went before the students at Oral Roberts University and his television audience to beg for $4,500,000. Roberts climaxed the appeal by sharing the latest of several extraordinary revelations.

His first revelation had been a divine command to build the lavish complex in Tulsa, Oklahoma. In his next astounding revelation, Roberts said, Jesus had appeared, standing some nine hundred feet tall and ordering him to persevere. Then God (according to Roberts) had told him to ease his continuing need for money by demanding $240 from each supporter and promising spectacular breakthroughs in cancer cures as a reward. The "visions" produced $10,000,000 from his constituency.

But now came the most spectacular revelation of all: if the goal of $4,500,000 was not reached by March 1987, God would strike him down. "I'm asking you to help extend my life," Roberts said. The countdown was on. At stake was the 4,500-student Oral Roberts University and the City of Faith medical complex as well as the healer's life. He retired to his prayer tower—a two-hundred-feet-tall, glass-and-steel spire—to fast and pray and wait for his supporters to cough up the money. Many recognized a spiritual blackmailer at work.

Then Roberts received a reprieve[2]—"a stay of execution." Jerry Collins, a dog-track owner from Sarasota, Florida, bailed him out with a $3,100,000 donation. "I very seldom go to church," confessed the donor. The fact that the donation was given by a racetrack owner did not matter to Roberts. God, however, does not want the money of those who prefer the dog-track to His house.

Whatever the motive behind a donation, the principle of God's Word is clear: God wants *me* before He wants my *money* (2 Corinthians 8:1-5). Far from pleasing God, "the sacrifice of the wicked is an abomination to the Lord."

Contrasting the transgressor with the righteous, Solomon added, "The prayer of the upright is his delight." Think of all the things that bring delight to God's heart and imagine our prayers being included! He is pleased when millions of galaxies rush to do His bidding. The songs of the sinless seraphim rejoice His heart. His plans for all the countless ages yet to come delight Him. His Son delights Him. His Spirit delights Him. When we enter the courts of bliss we will be amazed at the reveling.

But hush. Here come His upright ones who have been redeemed by the blood of the Lamb and whose names have been written down in glory. There is an Abraham praying for Sodom, a Moses interceding for Israel, a Daniel on his knees reminding God of a prophecy needing to be fulfilled. There is Paul with his prayer list. But above all there is the Lord Jesus—our great high priest, our advocate with the Father—praying for His own. Those prayers, above and beyond all else in the universe, delight the heart of the Most High. When was the last time you brought delight to the heart of God?

Solomon's second observation regarding transgressors was that the Lord *repudiates their steps:* "The way of the wicked is an abomination unto the Lord: but he loveth him that followeth after righteousness" (Proverbs 15:9). The prayer of the wicked is refused because his way is displeasing to God.

Was there ever such a wicked man as King Manasseh of Judah? One would have thought that given the semi-miraculous circumstances of his birth—he was born three years after his father's spectacular healing—he would have been a prodigy of holiness. Manasseh's father was godly King Hezekiah (to this day some Jews actually believe he was the messiah). Hezekiah wrote Psalms, edited the book of Proverbs, and spearheaded a national revival. Manasseh's mother was godly Hephzi-bah (celebrated, some think, in the second part of Psalm 45). If, as some believe, Hephzi-bah was the daughter of the prophet Isaiah, what a grandfather Manasseh had! One would have thought that with such a heritage young Manasseh could have become the forerunner of the Christ Himself.

At least Manasseh had no excuse for his actions. He had hardly become accustomed to the throne, however, when he chose to follow the way of his dead and damned paternal grandfather Ahaz. Manasseh reversed all his father's reforms and plunged Judah into an apostasy from which it never recovered until after the Babylonian captivity. Isaiah protested and some believe Manasseh had him put inside a hollow oak tree and sawed in half. Perhaps Hebrews 11:37 does indeed refer to Isaiah when it says, "They were sawn asunder."

We can only measure the extent of the apostasies and abominations Manasseh introduced into Judah by looking at the kingdom when Josiah, Manasseh's grandson, ascended the throne a scant two years after Manasseh's death. An asherah—one of the vile sex pillars associated with the foul worship of Baal—stood in the temple. The land was overrun with idolatrous priests. Altars were dedicated to Baal, the sun, the moon, the planets, and all the host of heaven. In the valley of Hinnom (called Topheth in 2 Kings 23:10 for the first time in Scripture) people made their small, innocent children sit on the red-hot lap of Molech. The ancient groves, popularized centuries earlier by Solomon and for many years a curse and a source of stumbling to Judah, were used every day for the sex worship of the Canaanite gods. The altar at Bethel, consecrated to the worship of the golden calf, was fully operational, although the ten tribes that had been ensnared by that altar for centuries had long since been marched into oblivion for their folly in worshiping there. Josiah had to cleanse the land of all these abominations.

The depth of Manasseh's depravity was marked by the fact that Josiah had to break down "the houses of the sodomites, that were by the house of the Lord, where the women wove hangings for the grove" (2 Kings 23:7). Imagine, the road to the temple of the living God ran past a section of Jerusalem devoted to sodomy! No wonder God says that the way of the wicked is an abomination to Him. No wonder God says that the prayer of the wicked is an abomination.

The lesson for today is obvious. God has not changed His mind about the alternate lifestyle of Sodom (Genesis 19). Today sodomites not only live by the temple; people in our apostate society consecrate them to the ministry. Any society that tolerates that kind of evil has gone a long way down the road to judgment.

Solomon's third observation regarding transgressors was that the Lord *rebukes their stubbornness:* "Correction is grievous unto him that forsaketh the way: and he that hateth reproof shall die" (Proverbs 15:10). If there is anything a headstrong sinner dislikes, it is to be told the truth about himself and where his path is leading. He usually ends up hating the person who tries to correct him.

Jeroboam, the first sovereign of the northern kingdom of Israel, hated reproof. He was described in the Old Testament as "Jeroboam the son of Nebat, who made Israel to sin" (2 Kings 23:15). After successfully wresting the ten northern tribes away from Rehoboam, Jeroboam was not sure how secure he was on his throne. So he decided to keep his people away from Jerusalem and the temple— and the truths, traditions, and fond memories associated with those places. He was quite sure that the annual pilgrimages to Jerusalem must cease; new centers, new loyalties, and new convictions needed to replace the old. Accordingly he made two golden calves, deliberately distorting an event in Israel's history (Exodus 32). He set one up at Dan in the northern part of his kingdom and the other at Bethel, sacred to the memory of Abraham and Jacob. Jeroboam consecrated commoners as priests, changed the religious calendar, and set a date for dedicating the new high altar at Bethel.

But the dedication attracted an unwelcome visitor, an unknown young prophet from Judah. Unafraid of the king and his new college of cardinals, this Old Testament Martin Luther stepped boldly forward and with a ringing voice declared: "O altar, altar, thus saith the Lord: Behold, a child shall be born unto the house of David, Josiah by name; and upon thee shall he offer the priests of the high places that burn incense upon thee, and men's bones shall be burnt upon thee." Before the astonished king could recover, the man of God from Judah gave a sign: "This is the sign which the Lord hath spoken: Behold, the altar shall be rent, and the ashes that are upon it shall be poured out" (1 Kings 13:2-3).

Thus God's prophet corrected King Jeroboam. The words, however, were grievous to this opportunist king, who had so flagrantly forsaken God's way. He flung out his arm and gave orders for the prophet to be arrested. Immediately two extraordinary things happened. First the king's arm was paralyzed—we can picture how ridiculous he looked as he stood there with his outstretched arm frozen into immobility. Then with a roar the new altar cracked open and the ashes of the newly burned sacrifice poured out on the ground.

These phenomena brought the king down off his high horse in a hurry. After all, he couldn't go through life with his arm stuck out like that. "Intreat now the face of the Lord thy God," he said, still stubbornly refusing to accept the prophet's God as his God (1 Kings 13:6). Graciously the prophet did as he was asked and the king's arm was healed. The Holy Spirit added:

> After this thing Jeroboam returned not from his evil way, but made again of the lowest of the people priests of the high places: whosoever would, he consecrated him, and he became one of the priests of the high places. And this thing became sin unto the house of Jeroboam, even to cut it off, and to destroy it from off the face of the earth" (1 Kings 13:33-34).

"At that time," continued the sacred historian, "Abijah the son of Jeroboam fell sick" (1 Kings 14:1). The king thought of Ahijah, the prophet who had told him years before that he would one day be king of Israel; he told his wife to disguise herself and visit the aged prophet at Shiloh where he lived. Although he was now blind, the prophet was still in close touch with God. Ahijah saw through the woman's disguise at once and sent her back with a message of doom for Jeroboam and death for the young child. Sure enough, the child died the moment the queen's feet crossed the boundary of Tirzah, temporary capital of the new northern kingdom. About that same time Jeroboam was struck with a lingering disease that eventually brought about his death (2 Chronicles 13:20). He who hated reproof died.

Solomon's fourth observation regarding transgressors was that the Lord *rejects their souls:* "Hell and destruction are before the Lord: how much more then the hearts of the children of men?" (Proverbs 15:11) When the Lord looks into Hell He sees what Jesus described when He drew aside the veil for an instant to show us a soul in torment.

Jesus saw a rich man who had lived without regard for God or man. The poor beggar Lazarus, who had haunted the gates of the rich man's home, had received more kindness from scavenger dogs than from him. The rich man had lived as an unbeliever but he awoke in a lost eternity as a believer. All of a sudden he believed in prayer, but he was too late. He should have prayed while he was still on earth. His prayer was not only late; it was also misdirected. The rich man cried out to Abraham for mercy. Abraham was the greatest of Old Testament saints, but saints have no power to answer prayer.

The rich man was consumed by his woes. He could see, feel, hear, and remember. He was aware of an awful thirst that, he learned, could never be quenched. When he asked for Lazarus to bring him just one drop of water—just to bring the most fleeting, minimal alleviation of his torment—he was pointed to "a great gulf fixed." There was no road from Hell to Heaven.

All of a sudden the rich man also believed in preaching. We can imagine his urgent words. "I have five brothers. Send Lazarus to them so they do not come to this place of torment."

Abraham responded, "It would do no good." The rich man's brothers were doubtless wrapped up in the same Sadducean denial of an afterlife that he had once embraced. "They have the Bible," Abraham said. "They have Moses and the prophets."

The lost man was disposed to argue. "Ah," he said, "if one were to rise from the dead they would believe."

Abraham was adamant. "Oh no they wouldn't," he said. "If they will not believe the Bible, not even such a notable miracle as a resurrection would convince them."

Then silence descended and the lost man was confined with his woes for eternity. A poet caught the horror of Luke 16:19-31 and put these words in the lips of the lost man:

> Woe is me, I am benighted,
> Will this gloom no more be lighted,
> By one day of blessed sunlight
> Which we cheered in days of yore?
> ECHO ANSWERS, NEVERMORE.

> Memory like an adder stingeth
> All the wasted past upbringeth,
> If I could the viper strangle
> Half my misery would be o'er;
> But around my heart it coileth,
> All my frantic efforts foileth,
> Tis the worm that never dieth
> Gnawing at my bosom's door.
> Will it grant me no deliverance?
> Will it quit me nevermore?
> ECHO ANSWERS, NEVERMORE.

To my mouth my tongue is cleaving,
Not one drop my thirst relieving
Of the copious cooling water
I so freely drank of yore.
Even death is from me flying,
Mocking all my groaning, crying,
Tauntingly he doth remind me
How I fled from him before.
Now I call him, he evades me,
Will he strike me nevermore?
ECHO ANSWERS, NEVERMORE.

The Lord not only looks into Hell; He also looks into hearts. He sees what is there too. What He sees in the unregenerate human heart makes what He sees in Hell inevitable. He says, "The heart is deceitful above all things, and desperately wicked: who can know it? I the Lord search the heart, I try the reins, even to give every man according to his ways, and according to the fruit of his doings" (Jeremiah 17:9-10). Jesus adds: "Those things which proceed out of the mouth come forth from the heart; and they defile the man. For out of the heart proceed evil thoughts, murders, adulteries, fornications, thefts, false witness, blasphemies: These are the things which defile a man" (Matthew 15:18-20).

Solomon's fifth observation regarding transgressors was that the Lord *records their scorn:* "A scorner loveth not one that reproveth him: neither will he go unto the wise" (Proverbs 15:12). It is impossible to tell a scorner anything. He is too full of conceit.

Pharaoh was a scorner. He had been brought up to believe that he was God, the incarnation of Ra. No will but his mattered. When Moses requested that the Hebrew slaves in Goshen be permitted to go into the wilderness to worship their God, pharaoh instantly replied, "Who is the Lord, that I should obey his voice to let Israel go? I know not the Lord, neither will I let Israel go" (Exodus 5:2). Although pharaoh had been educated in all the wisdom of the Egyptians, he had not learned who God is. The Holy Spirit says this pharaoh's father "knew not Joseph" (Exodus 1:8); the son knew neither Joseph, nor Moses, nor Aaron, nor God.

Moses was about to teach pharaoh a lesson that would be recorded and read from then until the end of time. But Moses and Aaron looked more like shepherds than ambassadors, and Egyptians considered shepherds an abomination. Had Moses and Aaron been accredited messengers from Assyria or Babylon, or commanders of a mighty army, their reception might have been different. But God's way was different from pharaoh's. Their own names and titles were not impressive, but Moses and Aaron came with a name that was above every name: Elohim-Jehovah. Before this name every knee should bow, but the name meant nothing to pharaoh yet.

Then came the reproof of this scorner. Moses performed miracle after miracle. Pharaoh saw miracles of judgment and miracles of mercy, but they made no difference to him. Blood and boils, frogs and flies, lice and locusts, disease and darkness—nothing made any difference. Even when his own magicians admitted defeat, and even when his own counselors said, "Knowest thou not yet that Egypt is destroyed?" (Exodus 10:7) pharaoh was not moved. "Neither will he go unto the wise," Solomon said of the scorner. Pharaoh hardened his heart time and time again until at last God hardened it for him, and the man who would not repent could not repent. God ended up preparing a bed for him and his army at the bottom of the Red Sea. Woe to the scorner.

4. The Question of Temperaments (15:13-15)

In this passage Solomon showed us three kinds of temperaments: the sorrowful man, the seeking man, and the singing man. Proverbs 15:13 speaks of *the sorrowful man:* "A merry heart maketh a cheerful countenance: but by sorrow of the heart the spirit is broken." Mere amusement and entertainment are shallow and unsatisfactory because comedy brings a laugh only to the lips. Real emotions lie much deeper. What happens in the heart paints the face with a scowl, a smile, or a sneer.

Two extremes of emotion are mentioned in one verse in the Biblical narrative of Haman (Esther 5:9). Haman came from bad stock. He was an Agagite, which according to Josephus means he was descended from Agag, king of Amalek. The Amalekites were hereditary foes of Israel. Being an able scoundrel, Haman advanced to the highest post in the Persian empire under Ahasuerus, the Xerxes of Herodotus and Plutarch. Haman was the chief counselor and favorite of this wicked and powerful king. Haman's villainy was exceeded only by that of his royal master and the two of them plotted the extermination of all the Jews in the empire. Haman was motivated by a malicious antisemitism and a personal grudge against one Jew in particular: Mordecai, who pridefully refused to bow and scrape before an Agagite.

When Mordecai persuaded Esther to speak to her husband about the plot against the Jews, she decided on a strategy: she would invite Ahasuerus and Haman to two banquets.

Haman came away from the first banquet walking on air. "Then went Haman forth that day joyful and with a glad heart" (Esther 5:9). He was all smiles. All was right with the world! We can see him on his way out of the palace scattering largess to the poor, exchanging a cheery word with the guard, and laughing boisterously at some joke told him by one of his cronies. He was riding high.

"But when Haman saw Mordecai in the king's gate, that he stood not up, nor moved for him, he was full of indignation against Mordecai" (Esther 5:9). Sorrow of heart took hold of Haman. When he got home, after he had described the honors and preferments bestowed on him in the palace, he said to his wife, "All this availeth me nothing, so long as I see Mordecai the Jew sitting at the king's gate" (5:13). Because of Mordecai, Haman could not enjoy his power, his position, or his promotion.

Haman walked around the house with a long face, dispirited and disgruntled, until his wife suggested that he prepare a gallows fifty cubits (about a hundred feet) high for Mordecai. The thought of hanging Mordecai on a gallows as high as a twelve story building assuaged Haman's bitter spirit. A wicked smile replaced his scowl. We can picture him going out to inspect the gallows that evening with a cheerful countenance. We can imagine the jokes Haman shared with the court engineer and the workmen as they put the finishing touches on that spectacular instrument of death. And we can visualize Haman enjoying his supper that night—not knowing it would be his last. He had a cheerful countenance, but he would have been better off without it. He would have been better off if his spirit had been broken by heartfelt sorrow over his sins.

Then Proverbs 15:14 speaks of *the seeking man:* "The heart of him that hath understanding seeketh knowledge: but the mouth of fools feedeth on foolishness."

Mary of Bethany sought knowledge at Jesus' feet. It was not only love that brought her there; it was also logic. She had long accepted the fact that Jesus of Nazareth was all that He claimed to be: God manifest in flesh. So her great goal in life was to learn more and more about Him. She grasped one fact that seemed to elude His other followers: He was going to die. He was going to die the cruelest of deaths. He was going to be crucified. The disciples argued with Him about this fact, but Mary accepted it.

Mary knew what she had to do. She took her savings (nearly the equivalent of a year's wages for a working man), bought the most costly nard, and carefully concealed it. Mary was saving the spice for

His burial. Then her dear brother Lazarus died and needed embalming. She must have been torn between her love for Jesus and her love for her brother. But although she loved her brother dearly, she loved Jesus more. So she kept that costly ointment for *His* burial. It was a good thing she did. A few days later Jesus raised Lazarus from the dead. What a waste it would have been if she had used the nard to embalm him!

Then suddenly the resurrection of Lazarus brought the truth to life in her soul. She had been seeking knowledge and now it came in a flash. Jesus often said that He wasn't going to remain in His tomb even as long as Lazarus lay in his! Jesus was going to rise—on the third day. No spices would be needed for His body because God had promised that it would not "see corruption" (Psalm 16:10). In a magnificent act of reasoning faith, Mary brought out that flask of rare unguent the next time Jesus was in their home and she poured the nard on His feet.

Jesus was delighted but Judas was furious. What an incredible waste of priceless ointment and what a waste of money! The money could have been donated to the cause and put into the bag for him to dispense. His calculating mind quickly arrived at the market price of the ointment. His grasping heart thought too of another piece of property he could have bought for himself with that money. He spoke his mind like a fool. Jesus leaped to Mary's defense. "Against the day of my burying hath she kept this," He said (John 12:7) and silenced the mouth of a fool.

Proverbs 15:15 speaks of *the singing man:* "All the days of the afflicted are evil: but he that is of a merry heart hath a continual feast." Mark told us two stories that illustrate this proverb. He artistically laid them side by side, for in both stories a period of twelve years was significant.

The woman with an issue of blood had suffered for twelve years with her malady. The twelve years of misery had seemed interminable. She would have agreed that "all the days of the afflicted are evil." Her debilitating and defiling illness rendered her unclean. It put her beyond the pale of her people, excommunicated her, and denied her the consolation of religion.

Out of sheer desperation she went from one doctor to another, always hoping someone could cure her. Mark was almost rude in describing the incompetence of the doctors. He wrote that she "had suffered many things of many physicians, and had spent all that she had, and was nothing bettered, but rather grew worse" (Mark 5:26). Then she heard of Jesus. Bankrupt, broken, and bitter, she approached the Great Physician, the One who never lost a case or charged a fee. She "touched his garment....And straightway the fountain of her blood was dried up" (5:27-29).

About the time this woman had contracted her affliction, a bright beam of sunshine had burst into the home of Jairus. A little girl was born to him. He held her in his arms and marveled at the miracle. Bright eyes full of mystery stared up into his. A tiny fist, complete with miniature pink fingernails, held onto one of his fingers. When he thought he detected a smile, he went into rapture.

Then she took her first step and uttered her first recognizable word. And so the years passed until she was twelve. He taught her to read. She brought life and laughter into the old synagogue where he worked. She demanded picnics at the beach and boat rides on the lake. She delighted in the arrival of the fishermen with their catch at the Capernaum wharf. She probably knew Peter and she was captivated by Jesus from the start.

But now she was dying. The doctors had done for Jairus's daughter what they had done for the woman with an issue of blood. They had given up on her case. For twelve marvelous years Jairus's merry heart had given him a continual feast, but now the messenger said, "Thy daughter is dead" (Mark 5:35), and Jairus sank into utter despair.

Then Jesus came and worked His first resurrection miracle. Jairus, who had been in danger of making a god out of his child, worshiped henceforth at the feet of Jesus. Thus the sunshine in his home was multiplied by the factor of eternity.

I like to think that Jairus found the woman who had suffered for twelve years, apologized to her for his impatience, invited her home to supper, and made her an honorary aunt of his little girl! What new songs these two "merry hearts" would have sung together about Jesus and His love!

5. The Question of Trouble (15:16-23)

a. Trouble Caused by Ambition (15:16-17)

Solomon believed it is *better to have little* than to have trouble: "Better is little with the fear of the Lord than great treasure and trouble therewith" (Proverbs 15:16). I wonder if we agree with Solomon. If we were given the choice, would we choose to live in the home of Bob Cratchit or the home of Ebenezer Scrooge?

The ghosts in Dickens' story *A Christmas Carol* take us to visit Bob Cratchit's home more than once and always at Christmas. Dickens was quite right. Christmas is the best time of the year, even though

Scrooge detested it and begrudged giving his poor clerk a paid holiday.

First the ghost of Christmas Present took Scrooge to Cratchit's home. On the threshold of the poor man's house the ghost paused to bless it. (He did not pause to bless Scrooge's house.) Scrooge had to observe Mrs. Cratchit making the best of her twice-turned gown by adding a few cheap ribbons to it. He had to see the Cratchit children rejoicing in the good fortune of having a happy home. He had to see young Master Peter Cratchit enjoying his new status as a man in one of his father's shirtcollars. He had to see the two smaller Cratchits come home all excited because outside they had smelled their goose cooking at the baker's. He had to see Martha arrive late from work and play a trick on her father by hiding when the family heard him coming up the street. Then Scrooge had to watch Bob himself walk in with crippled Tiny Tim on his shoulder.

The ghost forced Scrooge to watch the Cratchits celebrate their merry Christmas, making the most of their meager means and even toasting the old miser himself (over the objections of Mrs. Cratchit) as "the founder of the feast." Scrooge watched them and listened to them until even his frosty heart felt the first touch of thaw.

Later the sinister ghost of Christmas Yet to Come took Scrooge back to Bob Cratchit's house. Tiny Tim was dead. There was an empty seat at the table and the sacramental crutch in the corner by the fireplace. There was a hush over the household now. Careworn Mrs. Cratchit was still busy with her needlework although her eyes were beginning to fail. Bob came home and broke down. "My little, little child!" he cried. "My little child!" He confessed he had visited the graveyard on the way home. "I promised him that I would walk there on a Sunday," he explained. But Bob pulled himself together, put on a brave front, and the house was again bathed in love, care, fond memories, and hopeful expectations. At last Bob Cratchit burst out, "I am very happy, I am very happy!" The spirit caught Scrooge away as Bob's family crowded around to hug, kiss, and bless their dear father.

Before giving us these glimpses of Bob Cratchit's home, Dickens takes us to Scrooge's house:

> Scrooge took his melancholy dinner in his usual melancholy tavern; and having read all the newspapers, and beguiled the rest of the evening with his banker's book, went home to bed. He lived in chambers which had once belonged to his deceased partner. They were a gloomy suite of rooms, in a lowering pile of building up a yard, where it had so little business to be, that

one could scarcely help fancying it must have run there when it was a young house, playing at hide-and-seek with other houses, and have forgotten the way out again. It was old enough now, and dreary enough; for nobody lived in it but Scrooge, the other rooms being all let out as offices. The yard was so dark that even Scrooge, who knew its every stone, was fain to grope with his hands.

Scrooge was startled by the door knocker, which suddenly seemed to take the shape of his long-dead partner, Jacob Marley. Nevertheless Scrooge went in and banged the door behind him in defiance. Dickens wrote:

> The sound resounded through the house like thunder. . . . Scrooge was not a man to be frightened by echoes. He fastened the door, and walked across the hall, and up the stairs . . . trimming his candle as he went.

He locked himself into his room and sat down before the fire to eat his gruel. Dickens continued:

> It was a very low fire indeed; nothing on such a bitter night. He was obliged to sit close to it, and brood over it, before he could extract the least sensation of warmth from such a handful of fuel. The fireplace was an old one, built by some Dutch merchant long ago, and paved all round with quaint Dutch tiles, designed to illustrate the Scriptures.

Scrooge was still uneasy about the door knocker. He seemed to see the face of dead Jacob Marley everywhere. "Humbug!" he said as he walked across the room. Then the haunting began.

A little later in the story we are taken back to the old miser's house. We see the old man dead on his bed and harpies stripping corpse and room alike.

Would we rather visit the home of poor Bob Cratchit, where there was love and laughter and the fear of the Lord? Or would we rather visit the haunted house of a man who possessed great treasure but who was terrified that he might spend a penny more of it than absolute need required? Surely it is better to have little than to have all Scrooge's meanness along with all his millions.

Solomon also believed it is *better to have love* than to have trouble: "Better is a dinner of herbs where love is, than a stalled ox and hatred therewith" (Proverbs 15:17).

Baroness Orczy, famous for *The Scarlet Pimpernel,* wrote other good tales as well. One of them is about Rome in the days of Caligula, the half-mad caesar who terrorized slaves and senators alike. In *Unto Caesar* Orczy's hero, Taurus Antinor, was the stern, incorruptible, and courageous prefect of Rome. A wealthy member of the patriciate and second only to the caesar in power, Antinor had a seat in the senate, a houseful of slaves, and the love of the people of Rome.

Antinor attended two feasts, both of which are described with great artistic skill. The first feast was held in the luxurious mansion of Caius Nepos. He was the praetorian prefect, all-powerful in the absence of the caesar and well-liked by the army. During the feast a group of powerful senators planned to discuss the assassination of Caligula. The conspirators felt it necessary to include Taurus Antinor in the conspiracy, but how to win him over was the problem. He would not be bought and the caesar, however despicable, had his oath. There was certainly no love among the conspirators, each of whom hoped to use the others as steppingstones to the throne. Solomon's "stalled ox and hatred therewith" does not even begin to describe the scene. Orczy wrote:

> Most of these men were assembled this night beneath the gilded roof of Caius Nepos' house. He had gathered all his friends round him, had feasted them with good viands and costly wines, with roasted peacocks from Gaul and mullets come straight from the sea; he had amused them with oriental dancers and Egyptian acrobats, and when they had eaten and drunk their fill he bade them good night and sent them home, laden with gifts. But his intimates remained behind; pretending to leave with the others, they lingered on in the atrium, chatting of indifferent topics amongst themselves, until all had gone whose presence would not be wanted in the conclave that was to take place.
>
> There were now some forty of them in number, rich patricians all of them, their ages ranging from that of young Escanes who was just twenty years old to that of Marcus Ancyrus, the elder, who had turned sixty. Their combined wealth mayhap would have purchased every inhabited house in the entire civilized world or every slave who was ever put up in the market. Marcus Ancyrus, they say, could have pulled down every temple in the Forum and rebuilt it at his own cost, and Philippus Decius who was there had recently spent the

sum of fifty million sesterces upon the building and equipment of his new villa at Herculaneum.

Young Hartensius Martius was there, too, he who was said to own more slaves than anyone else in Rome, and Augustus Philario of the household of Caesar, who had once declared that he would give one hundred thousand aurei for a secret poison that would defy detection.

"Why is not Taurus Antinor here this evening?" asked Marcus Ancyrus when this little group of privileged guests once more turned back toward the triclinium.

"I think that he will be here anon," replied the host. "I have sent him word that I desired speech with him on business of the State and that I craved the honour of his company."

They all assembled at the head of the now deserted tables. The few slaves who had remained at the bidding of their master had re-draped the couches and re-set the crystal goblets of wine and the gold dishes with fresh fruit. The long narrow hall looked strangely mournful now that the noisy guests had departed, and the sweet-scented oil in the lamps had begun to burn low.

The table, laden with empty jars, with broken goblets, and remnants of fruits and cakes, looked uninviting and even weird in its aspect of departed cheer. The couches beneath their tumbled draperies of richly dyed silk looked bedraggled and forlorn, whilst the stains of wine upon the fine white cloths looked like widening streams of blood. Under the shadows of elaborate carvings in the marble of the walls ghost-like shadows flickered and danced as the smoke from the oil lamp wound its spiral curves upwards to the gilded ceiling above. And in great vases, priceless murra roses and lilies and white tuberoses, the spoils of costly glasshouses, were slowly drooping in the heavy atmosphere. The whole room, despite its rich hangings and gilded pillars, wore a curious air of desolation and of gloom; mayhap Caius Nepos himself was conscious of this, for as he followed his guests from out the atrium he gave three loud claps with his hands, and a troupe of young girls came in carrying bunches of fresh flowers and some newly filled lamps.

These they placed at the head of the table, there, where the couches surrounding it were draped with crimson silk, and soft downy cushions, well shaken up, once more called to rest and good cheer.

"I pray you all take your places," said the host pleasantly, "and let us resume our supper."

He gave a sign to a swarthy-looking slave who, clad all in white, was presiding at a gorgeous buffet carved of solid citrus-wood which, despite the fact that supper had just been served to two hundred guests, was once more groaning under the weight of mammoth dishes filled with the most complicated products of culinary art.

The author described the jealousy, the petty spite, the suspicions, the lust for power, and the ambitions of the guests at that feast. The sudden arrival of Taurus Antinor, looking every inch the ruler these men were seeking, was greeted with silence. He was shown to a seat next to a man who detested and feared him. Indeed they were all afraid of him, wrapped as he was in his high sense of duty and loyalty. They cautiously tried to test the limits of his integrity, only to learn that he was not for sale.

When he was pressed by the anxious conspirators, now doubly aware that they needed this man, he gave them his final reply: "Render unto Caesar the things which are Caesar's, and unto God the things that are God's."

Antinor left that feast and went to another. He was accompanied by his personal slave and a newly freed slave girl for whom he wanted to find a suitable home. Antinor turned his back on the imperial palaces, skirted the majestic temple of Magna Mater, and plunged down a precipitous hill. He left the great circus behind him and continued on toward the labyrinths of the poor. Stopping at last before a square mud-walled box with a narrow ill-fitting door of unplaned wood, he knocked and went inside. Antinor, it turns out, was a Christian and had come to visit the humble home of a brother in Christ.

Once inside, Antinor recounted again how he had first met Jesus in far-off Galilee. He opened his heart to his brothers and sisters in Christ. He told them of his secret uncertainties, hopes, longings, and fears. The host spread a humble table. The mighty prefect of Rome, the humble believer and his mother who lived in that cottage, a newly freed slave girl, and the prefect's slave all gathered around. Orczy wrote:

> Then the five of them sat down and quietly partook of supper, sitting side by side, the disciple from Judea and his mother, the two slaves and the Prefect of Rome. The Christians

sat beside the pagans, the mighty lord beside his slave and they broke bread and drank wine, all in memory of Him.

Well said, Solomon! "Better is a dinner of herbs where love is, than a stalled ox and hatred therewith."

b. Trouble Caused by Animosity (15:18)

"A wrathful man stirreth up strife: but he that is slow to anger appeaseth strife." This proverb reminds us of Caiaphas and Gamaliel, two of the most influential men in the Jewish world of Jesus' day.

Joseph Caiaphas was appointed high priest in Jerusalem in A.D. 18 by Valerius Gratus, the immediate predecessor of Pontius Pilate and the Roman procurator of Judea. Caiaphas and Annas, his father-in-law, were high priests when John the Baptist began to proclaim the imminent coming of Christ. The two priests were a pair of scoundrels. Annas had been deposed from the pontificate by the time of Christ, but he continued to preside over the Sanhedrin. The place where Caiaphas had his house is called "the hill of evil counsel." There Annas, Caiaphas, and the others met to discuss their plans for getting rid of Jesus.

Caiaphas, like his father-in-law, was a Sadducee, a religious liberal who did not believe in demons, angels, resurrection, or the supernatural. This clever, unscrupulous, and wicked man orchestrated the judicial murder of Christ. We can well imagine how Caiaphas must have felt when it became all too evident that the Lord had risen from the dead. He could not deny the resurrection. The best he could do was bribe the guards who had fled in terror from the tomb and persuade them to spread the rumor that the disciples had stolen the body.

Caiaphas was in a quandary. His pet beliefs had been exploded by the recent resurrection of Lazarus and the even more notable resurrection of Christ. However he dared not admit his errors and crimes. All he could do was to try to stamp out the rapidly spreading new faction in Jerusalem that boldly and publicly proclaimed Jesus as Lord and Christ, resurrected from the dead and ascended on high.

"A wrathful man stirreth up strife" and that is exactly what Caiaphas did. He launched a program of intimidation and persecution aimed initially at the apostles and ultimately at the Jewish church at home and abroad. As far as he was concerned, this new movement had to be stopped at all costs. He wasted no time. When

Peter and John healed the lame man at the temple gate and boldly "taught the people, and preached through Jesus the resurrection from the dead," Caiaphas had the two disciples arrested and brought before him and his supporters. Caiaphas and his men made threats, but Peter bluntly told Caiaphas that he intended to obey God, not him (Acts 4:1-22).

Next Caiaphas and the entire Sadducean sect had the apostles arrested and incarcerated in the city jail, but God simply opened the prison and set them free. The apostles went back to the temple to preach again and a frustrated Caiaphas had them arrested again and brought before the council. Caiaphas thought he could browbeat Peter. "Behold," the priest raved, "ye have filled Jerusalem with your doctrine, and intend to bring this man's blood upon us" (Acts 5:28). (Not so! They had already brought it on themselves.) But Caiaphas was no match for a Peter full of the Holy Ghost and power. He and the other apostles were unimpressed by the robes and regalia of the high priest and by the combined wealth, power, and influence of the Sanhedrin. Peter replied:

> We ought to obey God rather than men. The God of our fathers raised up Jesus, whom ye slew and hanged on a tree. Him hath God exalted with his right hand to be a Prince and a Saviour, for to give repentance to Israel, and forgiveness of sins. And we are his witnesses of these things; and so is also the Holy Ghost (Acts 5:29-32).

Enraged and cut to the heart, Caiaphas and his colleagues conspired to silence the apostles by killing them.

At this point the voice of an appeaser was heard. To counteract the wrath of Caiaphas, Gamaliel spoke. He was the grandson of the celebrated Rabbi Hillel, one of the most famous Jewish religious philosophers. A member of the Sanhedrin and a famous doctor of the law in his own right, Gamaliel was held in the highest regard by the Jewish people. He told Caiaphas to put the apostles outside while he addressed the Sanhedrin.

It was quite obvious to Gamaliel that the hot passions of the Sadducees had to be cooled. The majority of the common people sided with the apostles and nobody could reasonably deny that Peter and John had performed a notable miracle in healing the lame man. People were already suspicious about the illegal trial of Jesus of Nazareth and it would be the height of folly to massacre the leaders of this extremely popular movement. Gamaliel advised caution and cited two recent cases of self-proclaimed messiahs

coming to a bad end. This new movement was obviously different
and it made sense to allow a cooling-off period. "Let them alone,"
he said in effect. "If this thing is of men, it will come to nothing. If
it is of God, you cannot overthrow it. Indeed you will only end up
fighting God."

For the time being the confrontation was avoided. The revenge-
ful Caiaphas applied balm to his wounded ego by having the
apostles beaten. Then after more threats he let them go and they
shouted praises to God for having been "counted worthy to suffer
shame for his name" (Acts 5:41). Gamaliel, who was slow to anger,
had poured oil on troubled waters and had appeased strife—at least
for a little while.

c. Trouble Caused by Apathy (15:19)

"The way of the slothful man is as an hedge of thorns: but the way
of the righteous is made plain." The lazy man's path through life is
always blocked with problems and obstacles. He is continually
running into trouble, much of it of his own making. He never gets
anywhere, mostly because he doesn't want to get anywhere.

The Lord Jesus told us all about the slothful servant in Matthew
25:14-30. We learn from His parable that a person may neglect his
duty out of downright laziness or out of resentment and envy. The
servant in the Lord's parable carried a grudge against his employer
right from the start. "I knew thee that thou art an hard man," he said.
The other servants offered no such criticism. They were delighted
with their employer's trust and the opportunity he had given them.
Perhaps even before he thought of taking a trip, the master had
detected a flaw in the slothful servant's character. Perhaps the
master had had to reprimand him for wasting time, money, and
opportunity. Still the master gave him another chance.

The slothful servant looked at his talent and scowled. Actually a
talent was the equivalent of thousands of dollars in today's money.
Indeed the talent represented a considerable degree of trust and
expectation on the part of the master. However, this servant looked
at his talent with a jaundiced eye. He knew how much more the
master had entrusted to the other servants and went away muttering
beneath his breath that he was just as good as they were.

His resentment clouded his judgment and fortified his instinc-
tive laziness. He took the money home, dug a hole, buried the talent
in the ground, and whiled away his time. We can imagine that at first
he talked a lot about what he would do with all this money. He made
grandiose plans, all wholly impractical, and one by one abandoned

them. Time went on and he became worried that he might make a really bad investment and lose his master's money. Obsessed with this fear, he dillydallied some more. His indecision and inaction hedged his way with thorns.

Then news came that the master was on his way back and the slothful servant panicked. It was too late now to do anything with the talent. All he could do was try to think of an excuse for having done nothing. His excuses were brushed aside as insulting, inadequate, and self-incriminating and he paid a high price for his slothfulness when the time of reckoning came.

The slothful servant didn't know what to do, but the way of righteous Noah was made plain. The Lord said to Noah, "Thee have I seen righteous before me in this generation" (Genesis 7:1). And what a generation it was—full of pride, utterly pornographic, marked by vileness and violence, clever enough but godless, and getting worse and worse. Much like our own, Noah's generation abandoned all knowledge of God and every standard of decency and then added to its sins by delving into occult mysteries and the deep things of Satan.

It was not enough for the godly remnant to maintain a policy of passive resistance to the sins of the age. God needed a preacher of righteousness and Noah was the man who qualified for the job (2 Peter 2:5). Noah's way was made plain. He was to build an ark and preach to a lost world. To Noah's generation was given a period of one hundred twenty years during which the Holy Spirit witnessed to the lost. The Lord Jesus tells us that the Spirit of God speaks to the unsaved about sin, righteousness, and judgment to come (John 16:8). He witnesses to the *nature* of sin, to the *need* for righteousness, and to the *nearness* of judgment. That, in essence, was what Noah preached to his generation.

Noah's altar calls and pleas were all ignored. He did not win a single convert outside his own family. But he was not much concerned about results. He left them with God. His conscience was clear. He had preached righteousness. When the storms of judgment howled around the ark he could look at his loved ones and be thankful that God had made his way plain.

d. Trouble Caused by Antipathy (15:20)

"A wise son maketh a glad father: but a foolish man despiseth his mother."

D. L. Moody, the great evangelist of a past generation, knew how to preach to a person's heart and conscience. He drew out of his own experience an enormous fund of true-to-life stories that he used with great power. Here are three that illustrate Proverbs 15:20:

> A friend told me of a poor man who had sent his son to school in the city. One day the father was hauling some wood into the city, perhaps to pay his boy's bills. The young man was walking down the street with two of his school friends, all dressed in the very height of fashion. His father saw him, and was so glad that he left his wood, and went to the sidewalk to speak to him. But the boy was ashamed of his father, who had on his old working clothes, and spurned him, and said: "I don't know you."

"Will such a young man ever amount to anything?" D. L. Moody demanded. "Never!" he exclaimed. Then he continued:

> There was a very promising young man in my Sunday School in Chicago. His father was a confirmed drunkard, and his mother took in washing to educate her four children. This was her eldest son, and I thought that he was going to redeem the whole family. But one day a thing happened that made him go down in my estimation.
> The boy was in high school, and was a very bright scholar. One day he stood with his mother at the cottage door—it was a poor house, but she could not pay for their schooling and feed and clothe her children and hire a very good house, too, out of her earnings. When they were talking a young man from the high school came up the street, and this boy walked away from his mother. Next day the young man said, "Who was that I saw you talking to yesterday?"
> "Oh, that was my washerwoman."
> That was a good many years ago. I have kept my eye on him. He has gone down, down, down, and now he is just a miserable wreck. Of course, he would go down! Ashamed of his mother who loved him and toiled for him, and bore so much hardship for him! I cannot tell you the contempt I had for that one act.

Moody continued:

> Some years ago I heard of a poor woman who sent her boy to school and college. When he was to graduate, he wrote his mother to come, but she sent back word that she could not because her best skirt had already been darned more than

once. She was so shabby that she was afraid he would be ashamed of her. He wrote back that he didn't care how she was dressed, and urged so strongly that she went. He met her at the station, and took her to a good place to stay. The day came for his graduation, and he walked down the broad aisle with that poor mother dressed very shabbily, and put her into one of the best seats in the house. To her great surprise he was the valedictorian of the class, and he carried everything before him. He won a prize, and when it was given to him, he stepped down before the whole audience and kissed his mother, and said: "Here, mother, here is the prize! It's yours. I would not have won it if it had not been for you." Thank God for such a man!

The Bible places enormous importance on parenthood. A child's parents stand in the place of God during the earliest and most formative years of his life. (That is true regardless of whether or not the parents realize it. Some parents do not live up to their responsibility—Nero, for example, had a tigress for a mother—but their failure does not alter the high honor vested in their office. God will hold them accountable and the final issues must be left in His hands. Somehow, God gets His work done in the world in spite of human failure.) Children are to honor their parents, for in honoring their parents they honor God. Children who despise their parents dishonor God—and He has His own ways of dealing with those foolish sons and daughters.

e. Trouble Caused by Absurdity (15:21)

"Folly is joy to him that is destitute of wisdom: but a man of understanding walketh uprightly." The first part of this proverb has its counterpart in the man who makes a joke out of everything and who makes fun of the misfortunes or foibles of others. He mocks people and things he does not understand and tries to elevate himself at someone else's expense. Nothing is sacred to him. In the extreme he is a practical joker who likes to engineer situations that put other people at a disadvantage so he can laugh at them. Much of his behavior is childish.

Herod Antipas, who murdered John the Baptist and mocked Jesus, is an example of those who are destitute of wisdom. Jesus called this Herod a fox (Luke 13:31-32). The son of Herod the Great by his Samaritan wife Malthace, Antipas was half Idumaean and half Samaritan. Certainly he was no Jew. He was educated at Rome with his half brother Philip. Antipas became tetrarch of Galilee and Perea. His wife was a daughter of the Nabataean Arabs whose capital was Petra. He divorced her in order to marry Herodias, the New Testament Jezebel. He stole Herodias from his brother Philip and she became Antipas's evil genius, driving him on from one sin to another. She prompted him, for instance, to murder John the Baptist because he had publicly denounced their unlawful marriage.

His conscience smitten, Antipas attributed the many marvelous miracles that Jesus performed all over his kingdom to John the Baptist, risen from the dead. Yet Antipas had a growing desire to see Jesus of Nazareth for himself; he wanted to see this "magician" perform a miracle just for him.

Since he was in Jerusalem when the Sanhedrin plot against Jesus was coming to a climax, Pilate deferred the case to Antipas. He was flattered and excited. Perhaps he would see a miracle (Luke 23:7-12).

But Jesus ignored him. Furious, Herod Antipas responded with a practical joke. "Herod with his men of war set him at nought [treated Him with contempt], and mocked him, and arrayed him in a gorgeous robe, and sent him again to Pilate" (Luke 23:11). As Solomon said, "Folly is joy to him that is destitute of wisdom." Herod had plenty of craft and cunning, but no wisdom. He was one of the biggest buffoons in history.

Joseph of Arimathaea was also in Jerusalem at the time of Jesus' trial. Joseph, a wealthy member of the Sanhedrin, exemplifies the second part of Proverbs 15:21: "A man of understanding walketh uprightly." For some time he had been excavating a rock tomb for himself in Jerusalem. It was nearly completed when Caiaphas and his crowd railroaded through the Sanhedrin a series of criminal decisions regarding Jesus. The protests of men like Joseph and Nicodemus were simply brushed aside. The Sanhedrin decided that someone was to be paid to betray Jesus. That part was easy because one of His disciples was for sale. Then He was to be found guilty of a capital offense, and Pilate was to be manipulated into passing the final sentence so any stigma would attach to him. Their plan guaranteed that Jesus would be sentenced to a particularly shameful and horrible death. Finally His dead body was to be dumped in a common grave or, better still, disposed of in the fires of Gehenna. Joseph was horrified.

Joseph of Arimathaea was like some of the men who supported David: "The children of Issachar...were men that had understanding of the times, to know what Israel ought to do" (1 Chronicles 12:32). Joseph determined to rescue the body of Jesus from desecration. He and his friend Nicodemus put their heads together and came up with a plan. Nicodemus would provide the costly spices and Joseph would provide a brand-new sepulcher. Together they would foil at least part of Caiaphas' plot to discredit Jesus, whom both men had come to love. At least these two men, of all seventy-one members of the Sanhedrin, had understanding and walked uprightly. As old Simeon had predicted to Mary and another Joseph many years earlier, the thoughts of many hearts were revealed by Jesus (Luke 2:35).

f. Trouble Caused by Adversity (15:22-23)

Solomon looked at *the cause* of adversity: "Without counsel purposes are disappointed: but in the multitude of counsellors they are established" (Proverbs 15:22). It is foolhardy to act without knowing all the facts. It is sensible to get a second opinion. It is sensible to consider that opinion even when it differs materially from our own. It is sensible to evaluate other points of view and to weigh all the evidence. Then, even if we do make a wrong decision, we will make an honest mistake.

How did Paul decide to go back to Jerusalem after his third missionary journey? Although debate continues as to whether or not he made the right decision, he had plenty of good reasons for going back.

One reason was that he loved the Jewish people and longed to be as great a blessing in Jerusalem as he had been in Antioch, Corinth, and Ephesus. He longed to wean the Jerusalem church from its narrowness, bigotry, and legalism and was hopeful that the story of his successes in Gentile lands might broaden the hearts and horizons of Jewish believers. He had wrung some grudging, half-hearted concessions from them, but many still misunderstood him and remained deeply suspicious of him. They were all too willing to accept the lies circulated by those Jews of the diaspora who rejected his message and resented his churches. *Perhaps,* he may have thought, *if I take a considerable contingent of Gentile converts to Jerusalem and a large cash donation from the Gentile churches, their hearts will soften.*

Paul also had plenty of good reasons for *not* going to Jerusalem. His primary ministry was to the Gentiles; God had told him so at his conversion (Acts 9:15). While he was praying in the temple he was instructed: "Make haste, and get thee quickly out of Jerusalem: for they will not receive thy testimony concerning me." Paul argued, but the insistent voice continued: "Depart: for I will send thee far hence unto the Gentiles" (22:17-21). When he first visited Jerusalem after his conversion, the church was suspicious of him. Even after the church accepted him, the Jerusalem Jews planned to murder him (26:21).

Yet we find Paul drawn back to Jerusalem as a needle is drawn by a magnet. (He always seemed to overestimate the importance of the Jerusalem church. It belonged to the past and had no future. The future belonged in the West, not the East.) He counted the cost of returning to Jerusalem and at Miletus spoke frankly to the elders of the Ephesian church:

> Behold, I go bound in the spirit unto Jerusalem, not knowing the things that shall befall me there: Save that the Holy Ghost witnesseth in every city, saying that bonds and afflictions abide me. But none of these things move me, neither count I my life dear unto myself (Acts 20:22-24).

At Caesarea, while Paul was staying with Philip the evangelist, a prophet named Agabus added his warning. He bound himself with Paul's belt and said, "Thus saith the Holy Ghost, So shall the Jews at Jerusalem bind the man that owneth this girdle, and shall deliver him into the hands of the Gentiles" (Acts 21:11). All present tried to dissuade Paul but he was adamant. "What mean ye to weep and to break mine heart?" he said, "for I am ready not to be bound only, but also to die at Jerusalem for the name of the Lord Jesus" (21:13). When they saw he was not to be persuaded, they gave up.

In Jerusalem Paul ran into legalism of the worst kind and James, the Lord's brother, championed it. Surely Paul should have refused to go along with James' demand (Acts 21:17-26), for it led to his arrest and imprisonment. We do not read that James so much as lifted a finger on Paul's behalf when he was in custody. Nor do we read that the church thanked him for the donation he brought. The fact of the matter was that Paul was not wanted in Jerusalem, and never had been.

Paul's purposes were disappointed. In retrospect it seems that he should have listened to counsel. Who can tell what would have happened if he had listened to his multitude of counselors? True, we have his prison Epistles, but who's to say that Paul wouldn't have written them anyway? And if he had not gone to Jerusalem, he could have evangelized Spain, France, Germany, and Britain and changed world history even more than he did.

Solomon looked next at *the cure* for adversity: "A man hath joy by the answer of his mouth: and a word spoken in due season, how

good is it!" (Proverbs 15:23) There are few satisfactions in life
greater than the satisfaction derived from saying the right thing at
the right time in the right way.

Winston Churchill was very clever at saying the right thing.
Someone asked him a question in the House of Commons about
German plans to invade Britain. Churchill, with the royal navy in
mind, responded, "I do not say they cannot come. I only say they
cannot come by sea." After the Battle of Britain, which destroyed so
many enemy planes that Germany could not come by air either,
Churchill eulogized the pilots: "Never before in the field of human
conflict have so many owed so much to so few."

Shortly after Dunkirk when Britain's future looked grim, the
BBC aired a lecture by Quentin Reynolds, an American newsman.
He spoke words "in due season" and made an instant hit. In his
lecture he pretended to be speaking directly to the German
dictator. Reynolds addressed Hitler by his real name: Mr.
Shickelgruber. The British people were delighted. There was
something so incongruous and comic about that name.

Some other words "spoken in due season" were connected with
a cartoon that portrayed an irate passenger standing at an airline
ticket counter. Apparently a flight had been canceled and a long
line of people were waiting for the next available agent. One
pompous businessman was particularly annoyed by the inconvenience because he was used to the streamlined services of his
secretary. "Young man," he demanded when he finally arrived
within speaking distance of an agent, "do you know who I am?" The
harassed agent turned to a colleague. "Fred," he said, "do you think
you can help this passenger? He's in serious trouble. He doesn't
know who he is!"

This proverb also reminds me of a story about Dan Crawford, a
missionary home on furlough from Africa. At a church gathering
he had sat patiently on the platform while he awaited his time to
speak. The program seemed interminable. There were songs,
announcements, special numbers, and responsive readings. Finally the chairman introduced the distinguished speaker. "And
now," he said, concluding a flowery introduction, "Mr. Crawford
will give us his address." The crusty missionary came to the pulpit,
looked over the audience, cast a jaundiced eye at the clock, and
said, "My address is Number 35 Bellevue Gardens, London E.C.1."
Then he sat down. One suspects he took sardonic satisfaction in
teaching the program committee a lesson in common sense and
proportion. There is nothing like a word fitly spoken.

6. The Question of Triumph (15:24-25)

Proverbs 15:24 declares *the triumph of the wise:* "The way of life is above [upward] to the wise, that he may depart from hell beneath." As we travel through life we are going in one direction or the other.

Darwin would have us believe that our feet are set surely on the upward way, that man is progressing by slow but sure degrees from protoplasm to paradise. The Bible contradicts that theory; so does human history with its endless wars, woes, privations, passions, and persecutions. Darwin would tell us that all this suffering is due to the law of the jungle—the survival of the fittest—and mankind will come out all right in the end. This teaching is cold comfort at best and an outright lie in fact.

Man was created perfect. He was made in the image and likeness of God and endowed with a spiritual capacity denied to all animals. Man was made to be inhabited by God, and so he was for a while. Then came the fall, which left man's spirit empty of the Holy Spirit. Man became wholly corrupted and cursed, and his body became prey to disease, death, and decay. His mind, created for the infinities, became greatly retarded. His emotions, while remaining capable of noble feelings, became prone to malice, anger, bitterness, hostility, spite, and revenge. His will became susceptible to enthrallment by terrible vices, rage, lust, and error. His conscience became weakened to the extent that he can persuade himself that right is wrong and wrong is right.

Everything about man advertises his former greatness. His mind is brilliant. His deepest longings and yearnings are for something bigger and better, even though by his own efforts he cannot raise himself up higher than he already is. There are lingering traces of nobility in even the worst of people. Yet apart from the grace of God, man is morally, spiritually, and eternally bankrupt.

Moreover civilization is going downhill. The Bible says concerning the last days that "evil men and seducers shall wax worse and worse" (2 Timothy 3:13). And so they are. Man claims to be wise but he is a fool. He says he can see but he is totally blind. He boasts of his power but he demonstrates his weakness. He is sure he has life but he is spiritually dead. Man needs a Savior, One who can set him on the upward way to life and save him from the Hell beneath. Jesus came to meet that need—"to seek and to save that which was lost" (Luke 19:10).

There is a Heaven and there is a Hell. Jesus spoke about both. He spoke more about Hell than He did about Heaven.[3] The most complete record of the sayings of Jesus is found in Matthew's Gospel. There, for every verse in which He mentioned the abode of the redeemed, there are three verses in which He referred to Hell. In the four Gospels the Lord spoke about the destiny of the damned nearly twice as often as He spoke about the destiny of the redeemed.

The incarnate Son of the living God knew what He was talking about. Let us make no mistake about that. Because He knew the horrors of Hell and the bliss of Heaven, He came to earth, became a man, went to the cross, died as an atonement for sin, and purchased salvation at infinite cost.

Now we can come to Him, accept Him as Savior, be washed in His blood, be baptized and indwelt by His Spirit, have our names written in the Lamb's book of life, be born into the family of God, and start on the heavenly way. Once we are saved the upward way becomes a greater reality all the time. As hymn writer Johnson Oatman Jr. put it:

> I'm pressing on the upward way,
> New heights I'm gaining ev'ry day—
> Still praying as I'm onward bound,
> "Lord, plant my feet on higher ground."
>
> Lord, lift me up and let me stand
> By faith on heaven's tableland;
> A higher plane than I have found—
> Lord, plant my feet on higher ground.

The way to Hell is a downward way. Solomon, in spite of all his sensuality and all the limitations imposed upon him by his dispensation, had enough sense to understand that reality.

Proverbs 15:25 declares *the triumph of the widow:* "The Lord will destroy the house of the proud: but he will establish the border of the widow." The word translated "border" here means "landmark." The land laws of Israel were designed to keep poverty at a minimum and property in the family. No wastrel could permanently bargain away the patrimony of his family, for the title to landed property belonged to the family. In effect, property could only be leased to an outsider. In the year of jubilee the land reverted to the original family. Actually all the land belonged to God and the landmarks, the boundary posts, were set by divine decree. To tamper with a landmark was considered to be a sin against God Himself. To move the landmark of the widow was the worst property crime one could commit.

God is especially mindful of the widow and the orphan, the helpless and the poor. Widows in Israel fared better than widows in surrounding pagan societies of Solomon's time (and better than widows in pagan lands today—under applied Hinduism, for instance). God champions the cause of the widow and included laws for her protection in His Book. God looks with great disfavor on proud and ambitious people who do not care if they hurt others in their scramble to get rich—who set aside His laws and trample on others who get in their way.

Father Chiniquy observed some cases of heartless oppression of widows and other poor people while he was still a Roman Catholic priest in French Canada. One incident occurred in Varennes, where he was giving a series of sermons. He wrote:

> The second day, at tea time, after preaching and hearing confessions for the whole afternoon, I was coming from the church with the curate, when, half-way to the parsonage, we were met by a poor man, who looked more like one coming out of the grave than a living man; he was covered with rags, and his pale and trembling lips indicated that he was reduced to the last degree of human misery. Taking off his hat, through respect for us, he said to Rev. Primeau, with a trembling voice: "You know, Rev. M. le Curé, that my poor wife died, and was buried ten days ago, but I was too poor to have a funeral service sung the day she was buried, and I fear she is in purgatory. For almost every night I see her, in my dreams, wrapped up in burning flames. She cries to me for help, and asks me to have a high mass sung for the rest of her soul. I come to ask you to be so kind as to sing that high mass for her."
>
> "Of course," answered the curate, "your wife is in the flames of purgatory, and suffers there the most unspeakable tortures which can be relieved only by the offering of the holy sacrifice of mass. Give me five dollars and I will sing that mass to-morrow morning."
>
> "You know very well, Rev. M. le Cure," answered the poor man, in a most supplicating tone, "that...I am too poor to give you five dollars!"
>
> "If you cannot pay, you cannot have any mass sung. You know it is the rule. It is not in my power to change it."
>
> These words were said by the curate with a high and unfeeling tone, which was in absolute contrast with the solemnity and distress of the poor sick man. They made a very painful impression upon me, for I felt for him. I knew the curate was well off, at the head of one of the richest parishes of Canada; that he had several thousand dollars in the bank. I hoped, at first, that he

would kindly grant the petition presented to him, without speaking of the pay, but I was disappointed. My first thought after hearing his harsh rebuke, was to put my hand in my pocket and take one of the several five-dollar gold pieces I had, and give it to the poor man, that he might be relieved from his terrible anxiety about his wife. It came also to my mind to say to him, "I will sing your high mass for nothing to-morrow." But alas! I must confess, to my shame, I was too cowardly to do that noble deed.

When I was feeling ashamed of my own cowardice, and still more indignant against myself than against the curate, he said to the disconcerted man: "That woman is your wife; not mine. It is your business, and not mine, to see how to get her out of purgatory." Turning to me, he said in a most amicable way: "Please, sir, come to tea." We hardly started, when the poor man, raising his voice, said, in a most touching way: "I cannot leave my poor wife in the flames of purgatory; if you cannot sing a high mass, will you please say five low masses to rescue her soul from those burning flames?"

The priest turned towards him and said: "Yes, I can say five masses to take the soul of your wife out of purgatory, but give me five shillings; for you know the price of a low mass is one shilling."

The poor man answered: "I can no more give one dollar than I can give five. I have not a cent...."

"Well! well," answered the curate, "when I passed this morning, before your house, I saw two beautiful sucking pigs. Give me one of them, and I will say you five masses."

The poor man said: "These small pigs were given me by a charitable neighbour, that I might raise them to feed my poor children next winter. They will surely starve to death if I give my pigs away."

I could not listen any longer to that strange dialogue; every word of which fell upon my soul as a shower of burning coals. I was beside myself with shame and disgust....

Before saying my mass the next morning, I went to confess my criminal cowardice, and I repaired my cowardice by giving five dollars to that poor man....

After the sermon, the curate took me by the hand to his dining-room, where he gave me, in spite of myself, the place of honour....The first dish was a sucking-pig....

... with painful anxiety, [I] looked at the curate and said: "Will you allow me to put you a question about this dish?"

"Oh, yes; ask me not only one, but two questions, and I will be happy to answer you," answered he.

"Is this the sucking-pig of the poor man of yesterday?" I asked. With a convulsive fit of laughter, he replied. "Yes; it is just it. If we cannot take away the soul of the poor woman out of the flames of purgatory, we will, at all events, eat a fine sucking-pig!"

The other thirteen priests filled the room with laughter, to show their appreciation of their host's wit. However, their laughter was not of long duration. With a feeling of shame and uncontrollable indignation, I pushed away my plate with such force, that it crossed the table and nearly fell on the floor; saying, with a sentiment of disgust which no pen can describe: "I would rather starve to death than eat of that execrable dish; I see in it the tears of the poor man; I see the blood of his starving children; it is the price of a soul. No! no, gentlemen; do not touch it. You know Mr. Curate, how 30,000 priests and monks were slaughtered in France in the bloody days of 1792. It was for such iniquities as this that God Almighty visited the Church of France. The same future awaits us here in Canada."[4]

Who can measure the wrath of God when He witnesses such scenes of oppression and wickedness? His wrath is equaled only by His patience as in grace He stays His hand. We know that the day of full reckoning is coming for Rome (Revelation 17:12-18) and for the whole world (Revelation 18).

7. The Question of Trespassing (15:26-28)

Solomon made some observations about *vile thoughts:* "The thoughts of the wicked are an abomination to the Lord: but the words of the pure are pleasant words" (Proverbs 15:26). Our thoughts determine what we say and do.

We often forget that God can read our thoughts as easily as we can read a book. We know, from Matthew 9:4 and 12:25 for instance, that Jesus knew people's thoughts. We can hide nothing from Him. An astute person can sometimes figure out what another person is thinking by observing a twitch of the lips, a raised eyebrow, a frown, or a shrug of the shoulders. "Body language" gives away some of our thoughts. But God does not have to rely on such outward signs. The cover of a book may tell us much; its contents tell us more. God does not have to rely on the cover picture. He goes directly to the invisible and inaudible words of the mind—to the thoughts themselves before they are clothed in words and deeds.

God holds us accountable for our thoughts. If that accountability is disconcerting to us, think how distressing it must be to Him to see what we dwell on in the deepest, most secret recesses of our souls.

On the day of judgment God will only have to say to us what Abraham said to the rich man in Hades: "Son, remember" (Luke 16:25). And back will come terrifying remembrances of all our evil thoughts—thoughts so vile that we were thankful no one knew about them, thoughts so vindictive that they must have been sparked by hellfire, thoughts so vain that they rivaled Lucifer's.

One day when Robert Burns, Scotland's beloved bard, was plowing, his plowshare went crashing into a mouse's nest. As he put it, the "wee, sleekit, cow'rin', tim'rous beastie" started away panic-stricken. Burns compared its plight with his:

> Still thou art blessed compar'd wi' me!
> The present only toucheth thee:
> But oh! I backward cast my e'e
>   On prospects drear!
> An' forward tho' I canna see,
>   I guess and fear!

As we contemplate the thoughts of the wicked, we are reminded of the story of Achan (Joshua 6:16-19; 7:1-26). Jericho had fallen and the spoils were to be God's firstfruit offering. There was not a soldier in the army who did not know that. The decree had been proclaimed on the parade ground to regiment after regiment, company after company. The order had been nailed up in all the barracks and posted on each company office door. And because of the discipline and morals of Joshua's army, only one soldier ignored that well-publicized command.

Jericho was rich in spoils because it was on an important caravan route, and the plentiful plunder was all placed on the altar for God—all except one warm Babylonian garment, a wedge of gold, and two hundred silver coins. The sight of those spoils turned Achan's brain and that was his undoing. It would have been better for Achan if he had plucked out his eyes before he saw those treasures and allowed them to take possession of his thoughts.

Thomas a Kempis described the process of temptation. First, he said, there is the bare thought of the sin. Then the imagination paints a picture and hangs it on the screen of the mind. Then that picture exudes a strange sweetness that falls drop by drop into the heart. That subtle sweetness destroys the moral faculty and wins the consent of the whole soul, and the sin is committed.

Once Achan allowed that goodly garment, that gleaming glob of gold, and those glittering silver shekels to begin their merry dance on the canvas of his imagination, he was as good as lost. His thought life ruined him and carried him headlong toward judgment. All through the day as Achan mopped up remaining pockets of resistance, marked houses for revenue inspection, and responded to commands of his superior officers, he thought about those spoils. He thought until his desire reached fever pitch. He even worried that his treasures would be confiscated before he could bury them.

And all day long God was reading his thoughts and proving his mind and pricking his conscience. But by the end of the day Achan had completely rationalized his behavior. Achan's thoughts were an abomination to God. God saw Achan when he first noticed the spoils. God saw the seed sown in his mind; He saw the seed germinate into a thought; He saw the thought fertilized and cultivated. God watched the thought grow into a mighty bramble bush that entangled every part of Achan's mind; He saw the thought become the deed.

Achan buried his treasures as deep as his thoughts, but God exposed him and sentenced him to death. Likewise, our abominable thoughts call for judgment.

In contrast to the thoughts of the wicked, the words of the pure are pleasant. How much more satisfying it is to listen to pure words than to listen to foul words belched up from the hearts of the vile.

Solomon didn't tell us *how* to be pure—Someone greater than Solomon was needed to tell us that. "Who can bring a clean thing out of an unclean?" asked Job. He instantly answered his own question: "Not one" (Job 14:4). But Jesus said, "I can." When a leper said, "Lord, if thou wilt, thou canst make me clean," Jesus instantly responded, "I will; be thou clean" (Matthew 8:2-3). The healing of that leper was His first miracle after saying, "Blessed are the pure in heart" (Matthew 5:8). Only Jesus can give us the pure heart that produces pleasant words.

Solomon also made some observations about *vain treasures:* "He that is greedy of gain troubleth his own house; but he that hateth gifts shall live" (Proverbs 15:27). All too often people give to get. The gift in view in this proverb is a bribe. In many countries little gets done without the discreet greasing of a palm. Bribery and corruption are common ways of doing business and ensuring that the decision of the bench will be favorable.

Some years ago I saw a cartoon depicting bribery and corruption in an American court. The judge told the prosecuting attorney and the defense attorney to approach the bench. "I have received a bribe from the defendant for $15,000," he said, "and I have also received a bribe from the plaintiff for $15,000. Now you can proceed with the case, both sides knowing that the bench is now quite impartial!"

Samuel could not be bribed. He was the last of the judges and the first of the prophets. When Samuel first met Saul, the seer said, "Ye shall eat with me to day, and to morrow I will...tell thee all that is in thine heart" (1 Samuel 9:19). In that short time Samuel would be able to measure Saul, inside and out. Samuel could see quite clearly into the hearts of his fellow men and he could see just as clearly into the heart of God. When the time came for Samuel to resign from his office of judge he could say:

> I am old and grayheaded; and, behold, my sons are with you: and I have walked before you from my childhood unto this day. Behold, here I am: witness against me before the Lord, and before his anointed: whose ox have I taken? or whose ass have I taken? or whom have I defrauded? whom have I oppressed? or of whose hand have I received any bribe to blind mine eyes therewith? and I will restore it you. And they said, Thou hast not defrauded us, nor oppressed us, neither hast thou taken ought of any man's hand. And he said unto them, The Lord is witness against you, and his anointed is witness this day, that ye have not found ought in my hand. And they answered, He is witness (1 Samuel 12:2-5).

Samuel died only two years before King Saul did. Consequently he was active in one capacity or another for thirty-eight years after Saul's anointing. He was about eighty-six when he anointed David. Like Eli before him, Samuel lived to be about ninety-eight years old.

Samuel was known all that time for his stainless integrity. His sons did not share their illustrious father's reputation. The Holy Spirit says: "And it came to pass, when Samuel was old, that he made his sons judges over Israel. Now the name of his firstborn was Joel; and the name of his second, Abiah: they were judges in Beer-sheba. And his sons walked not in his ways, but turned aside after lucre, and took bribes, and perverted judgment" (1 Samuel 8:1-3). It is strange how blind godly men can be to the sins of their sons. Even the seer was blind.

But the people were not blind to the sins of Joel and Abiah. "All the elders of Israel gathered themselves together, and came to Samuel unto Ramah, And said unto him, Behold, thou art old, and thy sons walk not in thy ways: now make us a king to judge us like all the nations" (1 Samuel 8:4-5). Because of one blind spot in his extraordinary vision, Samuel was in effect set aside as judge, though he still flourished as a prophet. His sons were banished from active service and Saul, who for all his faults and failures does not seem to have been a mercenary judge, took their place. It was all very sad. Samuel's sons illustrate Proverbs 15:27 in that they troubled their own house: they forced their godly father into premature retirement by their greed for gain.

Solomon also made some observations about *venomous talk:* "The heart of the righteous studieth to answer: but the mouth of the wicked poureth out evil things" (Proverbs 15:28). Second thoughts, while not always conclusive, are certainly worthwhile as a rule. It is wise to study a situation before responding to it. Many factors that influence a first reaction may be eliminated by second thoughts.

In English history the classic example of this proverb is the case of Thomas Cranmer, the first Protestant archbishop of Canterbury. He was favored for a while by Henry VIII because he supported the king's divorce from Catherine of Aragon, the daughter of Ferdinand and Isabella of Spain. But after Henry died and Catholic Mary came to the throne, Cranmer was thrown into prison. Mary's hatred of Cranmer was particularly venomous. Besides being an evangelical, he had assisted in her father's divorce proceedings, married her father to Anne Boleyn, and crowned Anne queen—all unpardonable crimes in Mary's bigoted mind. The historian described Cranmer's fate and his noble second thoughts:

> Cranmer was still in prison [when his colleagues Ridley and Latimer were burned at the stake]. Having acted so prominent a part under two monarchs, Henry and Edward, and in both Church and State, he must be made to drink the bitterest dregs of humiliation.... He was visited by the most accomplished of the Romish party, and treated with courtesy. They professed a sincere desire to prolong his life for future service, and hinted that he might have a quiet sphere in the country. His gentle spirit, his age, his failing courage, caused him to give way, and he fell into a disgraceful dissimulation by the arts of his seducers, and signed the submission required of him. The Catholics gloated over the humiliation of their victim, and hoped thereby to inflict a deadly wound on the Reformation.
>
> But Mary and Cardinal Pole had no thought of pardoning him. Instructions were secretly sent down to Oxford to prepare for his execution. On the morning of the 21st of March, 1556, the venerable archbishop, meanly habited, was led in solemn procession to St. Mary's Church. Meanwhile grace had wrought

deeply in the heart of Cranmer. He was truly penitent, his soul was restored, and fully prepared to make a bold confession of his faith. He was placed on a raised platform in front of the pulpit; Dr. Cole preached a sermon, as usual on such occasions. He that was late archbishop, metropolitan and primate of England, and the king's privy councillor, being now in a bare and ragged gown, and ill-favouredly clothed, with an old and square cap, exposed to the contempt of all men, did admonish men, not only of his own calamity, but also of their state and fortune. More than twenty several times the tears did gush out abundantly, dropping down marvellously from his fatherly face.

When the sermon was ended, Dr. Cole asked Cranmer to clear himself of all suspicion of heresy by making a public confession. Cranmer rose up and addressed the vast concourse. To the horror of the authorities, he declared his abhorrence of the Romish doctrines and expressed his steadfast adherence to the Protestant faith. Then he said:

> And now I come to the great thing that is troubling my conscience, more than anything that I ever did or said in my whole life. And forasmuch as my hand offended, writing contrary to my heart, my hand shall therefore first be punished; for, when I come to the fire, it shall be first burned.

The historian continued:

> Hardly had Cranmer uttered these words when the priests, filled with fury at hearing a confession contrary to what they expected, dragged him tumultuously to the stake. It was already set up on the spot where Latimer and Ridley had suffered. As soon as the flames approached him he held his right hand in the hottest part of the fire and exclaimed, "That unworthy right hand!" He kept his hand there until it was consumed and he repeatedly exclaimed, "That unworthy right hand!" His constancy amazed his persecutors. He stood in the midst of the flames as unmoving as the stake to which he was bound. His last words were first uttered by the noblest of all martyrs: "Lord Jesus, receive my spirit" (Acts 7:59).[5]

8. The Question of Truth (15:29-33)

This passage takes us into the daily round of a believer's activities and into the various meetings and gatherings of God's people. We are taken first to *the prayer meeting:* "The Lord is far from the wicked: but he heareth the prayer of the righteous" (Proverbs 15:29). A prayer meeting is about the last gathering a wicked man wants to attend. He cannot think of anything he would like to do less. He will willingly go to the tavern, the show, and the ballgame. You will easily find him at his business, his favorite golf course, or his vacation site. He will gladly attend college and university functions or visit museums and art galleries. You will often find him in his living room, shouting himself hoarse in front of his television screen as he watches an exciting sports event. But if you invite him to a prayer meeting, he will respond incredulously, "You've got to be kidding!"

The proverb states that God is far from the wicked. This is much more serious than the wicked being far from God. When John Wesley went to Georgia to preach the gospel to the American Indians, he was far from the kingdom of God. He wrote in his journal, "I have learned what I least of all suspected, that I who went to America to convert the Indians was never myself converted to God!"

God was pursuing him however. On May 24, 1738, Wesley opened his Bible in a haphazard way and read, "Thou art not far from the kingdom of God" (Mark 12:34). That night, he said, "I went very unwilling to a society in Aldersgate Street, where one was reading Luther's preface to the Epistle to the Romans." That night he was saved. He was far from the kingdom of God when he arrived in Georgia; he was "not far from the kingdom of God" when he opened his Bible that Wednesday morning; he was in the kingdom of God by 8:45 that night!

But what about the wicked man who has no thought of God? God will pursue him just as He pursued Hagar, Jacob, Ahasuerus, Saul of Tarsus, and many others down the long trail of His grace. However, if a person persists in running away and crosses that mysterious boundary line between God's mercy and His wrath, then God will be far from that person for all eternity.

The proverb also states that God hears the prayer of the righteous. Righteous people can come into His presence at any time, day or night. They can stay as long as they like and talk to Him about whatever they like. They can talk to Him about His Word, His Son, His Holy Spirit, His people, His divine plans, and His purposes. Righteous people can talk to Him about their sins and shortcomings, hopes and fears, ambitions and disappointments, family and friends, finances and future. What a blessing! God never sends anyone away empty. As the song writer put it:

Thou art coming to a King;
Large petitions with thee bring;
For His grace and power are such,
None can ever ask too much.[6]

Next we are taken to *the testimony meeting:* "The light of the eyes rejoiceth the heart: and a good report maketh the bones fat" (Proverbs 15:30). We parallel this proverb when we say someone is "a sight for sore eyes."

When Epaphroditus turned up in Rome, he brought joy to Paul's heart. Paul was in prison. He had exchanged the jail at Philippi for a prison in Rome. His Roman citizenship had thus far protected him from extreme harshness in prison, but his funds had about run out when Epaphroditus showed up full of good news and carrying a heavy purse. Paul expressed his appreciation to the saints at Philippi: "I know now how to live when things are difficult and I know how to live when things are prosperous....Now I have everything I want—in fact I am rich....[Your] generosity is like a lovely fragrance, a sacrifice that pleases the very heart of God" (Philippians 4:12,18, J. B. Phillips).

It was not so much the gift from the Philippians that pleased Paul, but their testimony. Their gift was the tangible token of their love for him. Every penny told him of their growth in grace and of their tender loving care. When Epaphroditus shared the news from Philippi, Paul must have felt like he was in a testimony meeting. We can be sure that testimony meeting lasted far into the night and on into the next day and the day after that. Paul would have wanted to know about everybody and everything. He would have asked: "How's Lydia? How's the jailer? His wife? His children? How's that poor little slave girl I freed from that evil spirit? Did Lydia buy her and set her free?" Paul would have brought his prayer book up-to-date and added new names to it.

Then the testimony meeting probably became a prayer meeting. We might envy the soldier who was chained to Paul! Doubtless that meeting soon swept the soldier into its embrace. Paul would have introduced him to Epaphroditus, and Epaphroditus and Paul would have laid siege to that man's pagan soul until he was won to Christ.

Next we are taken to *the gospel meeting:* "The ear that heareth the reproof of life abideth among the wise" (Proverbs 15:31). Some reproof is literally a matter of life or death and we ignore it at our peril. The gospel begins with reproof. Much modern evangelism is shallow and deceptive because it overlooks this fact. Many people today preach a social gospel of good works to be done, or a prosperity gospel of good things to be received.

Paul preached neither the social gospel nor the prosperity gospel. He began with the bad news before he proclaimed the good news. The bad news is that "all have sinned, and come short of the glory of God" (Romans 3:23). The bad news is that "the wrath of God is revealed from heaven" against all ungodly and unrighteous men (Romans 1:18). Jesus said, "They that are whole need not a physician; but they that are sick" (Luke 5:31). He said, "I came not to call the righteous, but sinners to repentance" (Luke 5:32). The first work of the Holy Spirit is to "reprove the world of sin" (John 16:8). The man who will not listen to the bad news, who will not agree that it describes him perfectly, is not ready for the good news that "Christ Jesus came into the world to save sinners" (1 Timothy 1:15).

When we open each of the four Gospels in turn, we discover that before we can hear from Jesus we must first hear from John the Baptist. John preached repentance; Jesus preached regeneration. The formula is "No John, no Jesus." The Herod who murdered John mocked at Jesus. There was no repentance, so there was no regeneration. Jesus did not speak a word to Herod because it would have done no good. Herod did not have an ear that would hear reproof, so he did not have a heart that was capable of receiving regeneration.

In the gospel meeting, when we tell people how to be saved, we must get back to the Bible's message. When Paul wrote the Epistle to the Romans ("the gospel according to Paul") he dealt first with the question of *sin* and then dealt with the question of *salvation*. His opening chapters take us into court to see the whole human race arraigned and found guilty. First the heathen are found guilty, then the hypocrites, then the Hebrews, then all humanity. All of us are guilty—without exception, without excuse, and without escape. God's Holy Spirit points unerringly to our vile thoughts, our venomous tongues, and our violent tempers. Then, and only then, does He introduce God's full, free, and final salvation.[7]

Next we are taken to *the ministry meeting:* "He that refuseth instruction despiseth his own soul: but he that heareth reproof getteth understanding" (Proverbs 15:32). The ministry meeting is convened especially to teach the whole counsel of God. There we hear a word of reproof, a word of exhortation, or a word of instruction.

This proverb reminds us of Paul's words to Timothy: "All scripture is given by inspiration of God, and is profitable for doctrine, for reproof, for correction, for instruction in righteousness: That the man of God may be perfect, throughly furnished [equipped] unto all good works" (2 Timothy 3:16). We can group all of Paul's church Epistles around this verse.

Three of these Epistles are pivotal and deal with *doctrine:* Romans deals with Christ's cross; Ephesians deals with Christ's church; Thessalonians deals with Christ's coming.

Corinthians and Galatians come after Romans. Corinthians deals with *reproof* and failure to live up to the moral teaching of Romans. Galatians deals with *correction* and failure to live up to the doctrinal teaching of Romans.

Philippians and Colossians come after Ephesians. Philippians deals with *reproof* and failure to live up to the moral teaching of Ephesians. Colossians deals with *correction* and failure to live up to the doctrinal teaching of Ephesians.

No church epistles follow up Thessalonians because once the Lord comes, there will be no more need for reproof and correction. There will be no more moral or doctrinal departure from the truth. We can group Paul's church Epistles as follows:

ROMANS: THE MYSTERY OF CHRIST'S CROSS
    Corinthians: Reproof (Moral Departure)
    Galatians: Correction (Doctrinal Departure)

EPHESIANS: THE MYSTERY OF CHRIST'S CHURCH
    Philippians: Reproof (Moral Departure)
    Colossians: Correction (Doctrinal Departure)

THESSALONIANS: THE MYSTERY OF CHRIST'S COMING

The Bible-teaching ministry of the church should revolve around the major themes of these church Epistles. It is almost impossible to overemphasize the importance of "the apostles' doctrine" (Acts 2:42). Unwillingness to heed sound doctrine opens a Pandora's box of error in Christendom.

Finally we are taken to *the worship meeting:* "The fear of the Lord is the instruction of wisdom; and before honour is humility" (Proverbs 15:33). Worship comes before service. Before worship comes humility, and before humility comes a healthy fear of the Lord. When we see Him as He is, we see ourselves as we are. When we see ourselves as we are, we see Him as He is. When we see Him as He is and ourselves as we are, He shows us what He intends us to be. When we see what He intends us to be, He shows us what He intends us to do.

This progression is illustrated in Isaiah's call (Isaiah 6:1-13). Isaiah received his call "in the year that king Uzziah died." That death made a profound impression on young Isaiah because King Uzziah had been one of the truly good and great kings of Judah.

However Uzziah had not learned that "before honour is humility." At the apex of his power he questioned the wise provision of the Mosaic law that permanently separated "church" and "state." He could not understand why he should have to share power with the priests. *I'm as good as any high priest,* he thought. *Why shouldn't I combine the offices of priest and king?* So he went into the temple, seized a censer, and barged his way into the holy place. He was hotly pursued by the indignant high priest, but there really was no need for the high priest to have been so disturbed; God is well able to protect His own laws. Uzziah was immediately smitten with leprosy and he remained a leper until the day of his death.

Now Uzziah was dead and for the first time Isaiah contemplated a vacant throne in Judah. Then he lifted up his eyes and saw a throne in Heaven that was never vacant! He saw One sitting there bathed in terrifying holiness. And suddenly Isaiah saw himself. He realized he was as much a leper as Uzziah. He covered his lips, like a leper. He voiced the leper's cry: "Unclean!" He said, "*Woe* is me! for I am...unclean" (Isaiah 6:5, italics added).

God has made provision for those who are unclean. A seraph laid a live coal from the altar on the prophet's lips and proclaimed the good news: "*Lo,* this hath touched thy lips; and thine iniquity is taken away, and thy sin purged" (Isaiah 6:7, italics added).

This scene captures the essence of all true worship in both the Old and New Testaments. Worship is that activity of soul which occupies us with the person, passion, and position of the Lord Jesus Christ. In worship we are absorbed in thoughts of Him—we are taken up with the glories of His being and all the wonders of His finished work. Worship distills in our souls a fresh appreciation of Calvary—a fresh understanding of who suffered there and what He did.

Three words leap out from Isaiah 6:1-13: *woe, lo,* and finally *go.* Having seen God as He is and having seen himself as he was, the prophet was ready to be commissioned. He heard the voice of God say, "Whom shall I send, and who will *go* for us?" (6:8, italics added). Isaiah's response was immediate: "Here am I; send me." Thus worship was translated into service. The young worshiper commenced a mighty ministry that made him the foremost seer and statesman of his day and ranked him among the greatest prophets of all time.

CHAPTER 20

Proverbs 16:1-33

Section 2: The Life of the Godly and the Ungodly Compared
  (16:1–19:5)

  I. The Right Focus in Life (16:1-33)
      A. The Lord and the Heart of Man (16:1-9)
         1. Man's Words (16:1)
         2. Man's Waywardness (16:2)
         3. Man's Works (16:3)
         4. Man's Wickedness (16:4)
         5. Man's Willfulness (16:5)
         6. Man's Well-being (16:6)
         7. Man's Walk (16:7)
         8. Man's Wealth (16:8)
         9. Man's Ways (16:9)
      B. The Lord and the Head of State (16:10-15)
         1. The King and His Pronouncements (16:10-11)
            a. How Judgment Is Decreed (16:10)
            b. How Justice Is Decided (16:11)
         2. The King and His Power (16:12-13)
            a. Personal Righteousness (16:12)
            b. Propagated Righteousness (16:13)
         3. The King and His People (16:14-15)
            a. His Fury Displayed (16:14)
            b. His Favor Desired (16:15)
      C. The Lord and the Happiness of All (16:16-20)
         1. Happiness and Gold (16:16)
         2. Happiness and Guilt (16:17)
         3. Happiness and Glory (16:18-19)
            a. The Haughty Spirit (16:18)
            b. The Humble Spirit (16:19)

The majority of the proverbs in the first section of Part Two present contrasts, signaled by the use of the word *but*. The majority of the proverbs in the second section of Part Two present comparisons.

Solomon began the second section by encouraging us in 16:1-33 to get the right focus in life. We see the Lord repeatedly in these proverbs. We see Him looking into the heart of man, looking at the head of state, looking out for the happiness of all, and looking along the highways of life.

Continuing to pursue his wide-ranging spheres of interest, Solomon moved quickly from one subject to another. His method of teaching was not so much to aim at one particular bull's-eye but to fire buckshot, hoping to hit a vital spot in somebody's life.

I. THE RIGHT FOCUS IN LIFE (16:1-33)

A. The Lord and the Heart of Man (16:1-9)

Here Solomon looked at nine aspects of our lives. He looked first at *man's words:* "The preparations of the heart in man, and the answer of the tongue, is from the Lord" (Proverbs 16:1). The word translated "preparations" means "arrangements or plans." The proverb can be paraphrased, "To man pertain the plans of his heart; but from Jehovah comes the final decree or the last word." God always has the final say. The book of Revelation tells us that God will have the last say about His church, Israel, and the nations.

God will have the last say about His church, for as Samuel J. Stone wrote:

> Tho' with a scornful wonder
> Men see her sore opprest,
> By schisms rent asunder,
> By heresies distressed,
>
> . . . .
> 'Mid toil and tribulation,
> And tumult of her war,
> She waits the consummation
> Of peace for evermore.[1]

The true church is the apple of His eye. Two "churches" are set before us in the book of Revelation: the true church and Christendom. The church itself, as seen by God, is "a glorious church, not having spot, or wrinkle, or any such thing" (Ephesians 5:27). As C. S. Lewis said, it is "rooted in eternity, spread out through all time and space and terrible as an army with banners." That church is to be raptured before the end-time judgments begin.[2] Thus God is going to have the last word about the church.

The apostate church, or Christendom, with its false creeds and cults, will be reabsorbed into Rome. The Vatican, in a final desperate effort to regain power, will make a deal with the antichrist. The Vatican, depicted as a scarlet woman riding a scarlet beast (Revelation 17), evidently forgets that someone who rides a tiger must never get off and must never lose her grip. Once the antichrist has extorted the final measure of usefulness out of apostate Christendom, he will turn it over to the secular power for dismemberment and dissolution. Thus God is going to have the last word about Christendom.

God will have the last say about Israel too. That Christ-rejecting nation will be handed over to the antichrist for judgment. The Jewish people will sign a treaty with the antichrist and under his banner rebuild their temple. Soon after the completion of the temple and the reinstitution of its sacrificial system, the antichrist will seize the temple and use it as the platform for his blasphemous defiance of God. He will put his image in that temple and proclaim himself to be God.

Then the antichrist will inaugurate a global slaughter of the Jews. He will hunt them down to earth's remotest bounds. Only a small remnant of Jews will escape this holocaust. These will be converted instantly at the final return of Christ and will go into the millennial kingdom as the viceroys and ambassadors of the King. Jesus will sit on the throne of His father David and Jerusalem will become the capital of a new world empire. God's Son will rule over all the earth in peace, power, and prosperity for a thousand years.

God will also have the last say about the Gentile nations. He will abandon them to their own follies after the rapture of the church. Wicked and foolish men will reduce the world to total chaos (Revelation 6) and will believe that the antichrist is the true messiah. The antichrist will unite Europe by reviving the Roman empire. He will bring the western hemisphere to heel, engineer the final demise of a revived antisemitic Russia (Ezekiel 38–39), and prevail upon the remaining nations of the world to submit to his universal sway (Revelation 13). People will be forced to receive his mark or suffer hideous persecution. Many will be saved in spite of him, thanks to the ministry of the two witnesses (Revelation 11) and their converts (the 144,000 witnesses in Revelation 7).

The horrors of the antichrist's reign will soon outweigh its benefits. The eastern half of his empire will break away. The kings of the East will mobilize against him, cross the Euphrates, invade Israel, and deploy in the plains of Esdraelon. The antichrist will mobilize the West and the stage will be set for the battle of Armageddon.

At this point the Lord will interrupt the proceedings by His return to earth. The antichrist and the false prophet will be consigned to the lake of fire and the devil will be incarcerated in the abyss for a thousand years. The survivors of the Gentile nations will be summoned to Jerusalem, to the valley of Jehoshaphat, where the Lord will choose some to enter the kingdom and consign the rest to a lost eternity. Thus the Lord will have the last say about the Gentile nations.

At the end of the millennial reign, Satan will be released for one last fling. The unregenerate masses who have lived under Christ's iron rule (Psalm 2) will see Satan as an emancipator. They will flock to his standard and he will lead them in the world's last rebellion. They will mobilize and march, determined to take Jerusalem and depose the Lord and His people. The Lord will remove His people to another dimension of space and time and then detonate the universe. He will set up His great white throne on the shores of eternity and the wicked dead will be arraigned and damned. After this He will create a new heaven and a new earth. Never again will sin be allowed to rear its head. We can thank God that He will have the last word!

Solomon looked next at *man's waywardness:* "All the ways of a man are clean in his own eyes; but the Lord weigheth the spirits" (Proverbs 16:2). The world says, "Just let your conscience be your guide," but conscience—unmonitored by the Word of God, and unconvicted by the Spirit of God—is a poor guide indeed. It can too easily be deadened, silenced, and seared.

Look at the book of Judges for illustrations of this proverb. The pages are black with apostasy. From Othniel to Samuel, the period of the judges was four and a half centuries long (Acts 13:20). The Hebrews spent no less than 111 of those years in captivity to various pagan overlords because of God's active displeasure with His people. The Mesopotamians, Moabites, Ammonites, Amalekites, Canaanites, Midianites, and Philistines all took turns in oppressing the Israelites. Even one of their own people, the son of one of their most famous judges, tried to become their dictator. His name was Abimelech and he is contemptuously referred to as "the bramble," in contrast to the fig, the olive, and the vine (Judges 9).

Time and time again God sent deliverers—Othniel, Ehud, Shamgar, Deborah, Barak, Gideon, Tola, Jair, Jephthah, Ibzan, Elon, Abdon, and Samson. Each one came and went. Each one, to a greater or lesser degree, sought to bring the Israelites back to God, but the word *failure* can be written over the whole book of Judges. At last under old Eli even the sacred ark—the most important piece of furniture in the tabernacle, the very throne of God among His earthly people—was captured by their enemies and paraded through the cities of the Philistines. The word *Ichabod* ("the glory is departed") was coined to express the dismay some Israelites felt at this final disaster.

Israel's decline began with compromise. Even Judah, the toughest of the tribes, failed to complete the conquest of Canaan. We read: "The Lord was with Judah; and he drave out the inhabitants of the mountain; but he could not drive out the inhabitants of the valley" (Judges 1:19). Benjamin, Manasseh, Ephraim, Zebulun, Asher, and Naphtali all failed. All this failure occurred in the days of Joshua himself (Judges 2:6-8). An angel told Israel of God's judgment:

> I made you to go up out of Egypt, and have brought you unto the land which I sware unto your fathers; and I said, I will never break my covenant with you. And ye shall make no league with the inhabitants of this land; ye shall throw down their altars: but ye have not obeyed my voice: why have ye done this? Wherefore I also said, I will not drive them out from before you; but they shall be as thorns in your sides, and their gods shall be a snare unto you (Judges 2:1-3).

During the lifetime of Joshua and his generation, Israel toed the line, but

> there arose another generation after them, which knew not the Lord, nor yet the works which he had done for Israel. And the children of Israel did evil in the sight of the Lord, and served Baalim...and followed other gods, of the gods of the people that were round about them, and bowed themselves unto them, and provoked the Lord to anger (Judges 2:10-12).

The compromise went even deeper; the Israelites intermarried with the pagans (Judges 3:6). The waywardness of Israel throughout the entire period is summed up in the last five chapters of the book of Judges. Those chapters paint a picture of moral depravity, spiritual wickedness, religious apostasy, and political confusion. Judges 21:25 gives the final summary of the entire era: "In those days there was no king in Israel: every man did that which was right in his own eyes." It is impossible to imagine what the condition of society would have been if they had done what was wrong in their own eyes!

Solomon said that no matter how depraved he is, "all the ways of a man are clean in his own eyes." In our own day, people practice the utter vileness of sodomy and society calls it "an alternate lifestyle." Some of those who practice this perversion have so deluded themselves that they think they qualify for ordination as clergy and imagine that they can serve God while participating in a lifestyle He expressly calls an abomination (Leviticus 18:22,26).

Solomon looked next at *man's works:* "Commit thy works unto the Lord, and thy thoughts shall be established" (Proverbs 16:3). The word translated "thoughts" here is translated "preparations" in 16:1

and means "plans." We are instructed by the wise man to submit our plans to the Lord; otherwise the best-laid plans can go astray. Too often we make plans, plunge into a course of action, and as an afterthought ask God to bless what we are doing. We belatedly find out He is not in our plans at all. However, when we consult God from the beginning, He establishes our thoughts—that is, He leads us in the way He has planned. His way is always best.

Paul's missionary journeys reveal a high degree of careful planning combined with a keen awareness of the guidance of the Holy Spirit.[3] On his second missionary journey Paul and his new colleague Silas headed north from Antioch and on to Galatia, where he and Barnabas had visited before. Back among his beloved Galatians, Paul added young Timothy to the missionary team. Timothy had been enthusiastically recommended by the elders of his church.

Having crossed from Galactic Lycaonia into Galactic Phrygia ("Phrygia and the region of Galatia" as Luke called it in Acts 16:6), Paul and his team were eagerly looking for the Lord's leading concerning where they should go next. It seems that Paul wanted to cross the regional frontier into Asia, but they were forbidden by the Holy Spirit to preach the gospel in that province. Paul had his eye on the Maeander valley and the strategic city of Ephesus, but the Holy Spirit gave him plenty of warning that it was not His will for the team to go there at that time. Paul must have wondered about this guidance. After all, Ephesus was by far the most important city in the area and it was Paul's policy to evangelize the big cities and leave the evangelization of surrounding areas to the churches he founded in the big cities.

If the province of Asia is closed, Paul thought, *perhaps we should go further north.* The highly civilized area of Bithynia in northwest Asia Minor beckoned, as did the Greek cities of Nicomedia and Nicaea. However, somewhere along the route, Paul received a mysterious intimation from the Holy Spirit that he was not to go to Bithynia either (Acts 16:7).

So instead of continuing northward, Paul headed westward until at last he reached Troas. Troas was a Roman colony, an important seaport, and an obvious port of call for vessels from Macedonia. Troas was not far from ancient Troy, a city famous in Greek history and legend. Troas was truly a place to dream dreams and there Paul received his famous vision of the man from Macedonia (Acts 16:9). The light dawned: God was calling him to preach the gospel in Europe!

During Paul's third missionary journey, the Holy Spirit directed him to Ephesus, the city he had wanted to evangelize on his second missionary journey. The Holy Spirit had permitted Paul to visit there on his way home at the end of his second missionary journey. At that time he had made friendly contact with the Jewish community in the city. Paul had left his helpers, Priscilla and Aquila, in Ephesus to prepare the ground for a later visit. Far from hindering Paul's original plan, the Holy Spirit improved it.

Ephesus was the most important commercial city of Asia Minor and extraordinarily wicked. By the time Paul was allowed to go there, however, the city was ringed with churches from Corinth to Lystra. Paul concentrated on Ephesus for at least two years and three months and planted one of the most important of all his churches.

Next Solomon looked at *man's wickedness:* "The Lord hath made all things for himself: yea, even the wicked for the day of evil" (Proverbs 16:4).

It took Habakkuk some time to realize the truth of this proverb. He was a prophet with a problem. From his watchtower he could see the terrible moral wickedness and senseless religious apostasy of the land of Judah. The prophet Jeremiah was sobbing his heart out over it; Habakkuk shut himself up to puzzle his mind over it.

Truly the country was deep in wickedness. The terrible, prolonged, and disastrous reign of Manasseh had established such a pattern of lust and lawlessness that not even King Josiah's noblest efforts could reverse the trend. Now the Babylonians in their world conquest had their eye on Judah and Egypt. Habakkuk had no doubt whatsoever that they were coming. Judah was so ripe for judgment that only deportation could root out the dreadful idolatries practiced everywhere.

Habakkuk knew that his own people were bad, but he also knew that the Babylonians were a thousand times worse. Judah needed to be punished but how could God use a worse nation as His instrument for punishing Judah? That was Habakkuk's problem. How he resolved that problem is the subject of his book.

Habakkuk could have saved himself a lot of perplexity if he had paid closer heed to Solomon's insight: "The Lord hath made... even the wicked for the day of evil." God prepares His instruments, uses them, and then breaks them. Jeremiah, who understood that sequence, pointedly directed some of his prophecies against Babylon. The captivity itself, he clearly foresaw, would last for only seventy years and then Babylon would fall. God was still on the throne.

In His moral government of this planet, God often uses wicked men. He does not for one moment condone their wickedness;

rather, He overrules it. When the communists came to power in China, for example, they inaugurated their control of the country with a holocaust. They massacred some fifteen million of their own people. When they were finished they had removed prostitutes, homosexuals, drug addicts, and the like from society and cleaned up the country. They believed that what they did, drastic and dreadful though it was, was necessary for the health of society.

Of course the terrible excesses of the Chinese communists cannot be denied. In addition to eliminating the criminal element, they liquidated or brainwashed all who opposed them. The communists cleansed their society of all threats to their culture—including the Christian community. God did not condone the excesses of the Chinese communists, but He does uphold the right of a nation's government to execute those whose lifestyles are a genuine menace to society. In the case of China God used wicked people to rid society of wicked people. When a nation's normal methods for curbing crime and corruption fail, other methods sometimes need to be used.

Remember that in Israel's early history, God commanded the extermination of the Canaanites. Joshua's failure to execute this decree led to all the moral and spiritual decadence of Israel during the five hundred years that followed.

Next Solomon looked at *man's willfulness:* "Every one that is proud in heart is an abomination to the Lord: though hand join in hand, he shall not be unpunished" (Proverbs 16:5). This proverb presents a picture of two people going arm in arm to carry out some evil enterprise.

There can be no doubt that King Ahab was proud, presumptuous, and perverse. The Holy Spirit's opening comment on this Israelite king is that he was more wicked than any king before him (1 Kings 16:30)—and some of his predecessors were very evil. Then the Holy Spirit adds: "And it came to pass, as if it had been a light thing for him to walk in the sins of Jeroboam the son of Nebat, that he took to wife Jezebel the daughter of Ethbaal king of the Zidonians, and went and served Baal, and worshipped him" (16:31). Proud Ahab was an abomination to the Lord, and so was his wife. God had to raise up the prophet Elijah to deal with the national religious apostasy and moral depravity that characterized their reign.

Yet Ahab was the king whose friendship godly King Jehoshaphat of Judah sought to cultivate. The two joined hand in hand. One suspects that they both had dreams of reuniting the two kingdoms and restoring the golden imperial days of David and Solomon. To this end, the pair planned a matrimonial alliance between Athaliah (the daughter of Ahab and Jezebel) and Jehoram (the son of Jehoshaphat) (2 Chronicles 21:1,6). Later history records how disastrous that alliance turned out to be for Judah. That diabolical woman Athaliah almost succeeded in wiping out the Judean royal family and the Messianic line.

Jehoshaphat went arm in arm with Ahab again, this time to battle against Syria. The expedition almost cost him his life (2 Chronicles 18:29-31). God sent Jehu to admonish Jehoshaphat. "Shouldest thou help the ungodly, and love them that hate the Lord?" Jehu demanded. He added, "Therefore is wrath upon thee from before the Lord" (19:2).

Jehoshaphat failed to learn not to fellowship with unbelievers. Later on he went arm in arm with Ahaziah, son of Ahab, into another disastrous enterprise:

> After this did Jehoshaphat king of Judah join himself with Ahaziah king of Israel, who did very wickedly: And he joined himself with him to make ships to go to Tarshish: and they made the ships in Ezion-gaber. Then Eliezer the son of Dodavah of Mareshah prophesied against Jehoshaphat, saying, Because thou hast joined thyself with Ahaziah, the Lord hath broken thy works. And the ships were broken, that they were not able to go to Tarshish (2 Chronicles 20:35-37).

The unequal yoke, if not actively punished, is invariably unblessed.

Next Solomon looked at *man's well-being:* "By mercy and truth iniquity is purged: and by the fear of the Lord men depart from evil" (Proverbs 16:6). Because God has our well-being at heart, He extends both mercy and truth to us. In the order of our experience, truth comes first and mercy follows. Truth reveals our sin; mercy removes our sin.

Truth and mercy were depicted in the tabernacle in the Old Testament. In the ritual connected with the tabernacle, provision was made for man to approach God. At one end of the tabernacle stood the sinner in his guilt, shame, and need. At the other end sat God enthroned between the cherubim in the blazing brightness of the shekinah glory cloud. God is a consuming fire and has eyes too pure to behold iniquity. Between that sinful man and that holy God were blood on the brazen altar and water in the brazen laver. Thus both truth and mercy were displayed. Truth revealed what God was like and what man was like. Mercy found a way to bring a lost, guilty individual to God.

As the sinner, even though he was a priest, approached God, he arrived first at the brazen altar. There he was confronted with the fact that he needed a radical cleansing from sin. His sin was of so deep a dye that nothing but shed blood could make him clean. A whole catalog of different kinds of sacrifices was set before him to teach him the horror of his sin and the dreadful cost of his cleansing.

As soon as the cleansed sinner passed the brazen altar, he arrived at the brazen laver. There he learned that just those few steps defiled him. He needed a recurrent cleansing from sin. He needed the washing of water (by the Word, as Paul added). The brazen laver was made of mirrors so when he came to it, he saw his reflection and realized his need for cleansing. The water in the laver enabled him to remove his uncleanness.

In the order of experience, truth comes first because we have to see ourselves as God sees us: hopelessly corrupted, compromised, and culpable because of our sin. Then we have to learn that we need mercy. Only God can provide that which removes sin—the blood and the Book.

In the logical order of the universe, however, Proverbs 16:6 is quite right. Mercy comes first. The Lamb was slain from before the foundation of the world. Otherwise the moment God discovered sin in us, His holiness would have blazed out and consumed us. When our eyes are first opened to our need and we tremble before revealed truth, we discover that God has already made full provision for the removal of our sin and guilt.

The fear of the Lord makes men depart from iniquity. There can be no stronger motivation. All sound evangelistic preaching begins with instruction in God's holiness, God's law, and the certainty of judgment to come. After the preacher lays that foundation he can proclaim the glorious news that God offers full and free salvation to all who come to Christ. The first work of the Holy Spirit in a human heart is to convict. Conversion and consecration follow, but conviction comes first.

Next Solomon looked at *man's walk:* "When a man's ways please the Lord, he maketh even his enemies to be at peace with him" (Proverbs 16:7).

Jim Vaus proved the truth of this proverb. His remarkable testimony is recorded in his book *Why I Quit Syndicated Crime.* I heard him tell the thrilling story years ago at a conference at Prairie Bible Institute in Three Hills, Alberta.

Jim was raised as a preacher's son, he married a sincere Christian girl, and they attended a warm and friendly church at first. Jim's spiritual interest was all on the surface, however, and soon he drifted from the church.

An electronics wizard in the days when that science was in its infancy, Jim began installing illegal wiretaps for a gangster named Mickey Cohen. Through him, Jim met a criminal named Andy, his big contact with syndicated crime. Andy asked, "Ya make lots of swell listenin' gadgets for Mickey, why doncha make a gadget so we can beat da Continental Wire Service by a minute and a half?" If Andy's scheme worked, the bookies who used Continental would get the result of a given horse race a minute and a half after Andy did. In that minute and a half the gangsters could place their bets and clean up on the bookies. Vaus was interested because he could see big money coming his way, so he arranged a meeting with Andy to close the deal.

The next day was Sunday. Out of boredom and a sense of duty, Jim took his wife to the big tent where Billy Graham was conducting one of his early crusades. That night Jim met Christ. His conversion made the newspaper headlines: "Wire-tapper Vaus Hits Sawdust Trail."

Soundly saved, Jim realized he could not close his deal with Andy, and that spelled trouble. He could hear Andy's cold voice threatening, "No one quits on Andy, see?" Jim could almost feel the St. Louis mob breathing down his neck in distant California. So he opened his wife's Bible. He needed some assurance from God before he made the fateful phone call that could result in a shower of bullets and a coffin. He found what he wanted in Proverbs 16:7: "When a man's ways please the Lord, he maketh even his enemies to be at peace with him." Jim dared to believe Solomon's words.

Jim placed the call. "Andy, I've changed my mind," he said.

Andy and Jim argued back and forth until Andy threatened, "Either ya come to St. Louis or us guys is comin' to see youse, see? Better change ya mind!"

A few days later Jim watched a big black sedan turn into his driveway. Instinctively he knew who it was. "This is it, Lord," he said. Several men piled out of the car. In the lead was Andy with *thug* written all over him. He stared at Vaus with black beady eyes and his three gunmen fanned out to make sure their victim couldn't escape. Here's how Jim described what followed:

> I was trapped, but trapped on the promise of God. I blurted out, "Andy, you must have read the story of my change in the paper. What do you think?"
>
> "I'll tell ya what I think," he answered in a low, menacing

tone. "I think dat guy Graham give ya a couple of grand for standin' up and sayin' ya got religion. Now ya got your dough, let's get goin'. We got a job to do, see?"

Sure, that was what Andy would think! His only reason for doing anything was money. I'd been that way once and knew how he reasoned. But I must make him understand I had changed. I began to talk, telling Andy what had happened to me.

The men looked at me as if I were telling one of the Arabian Nights tales. They must understand! I prayed harder and talked faster. For fully forty-five minutes I talked about the Lord, until Andy's look of unbelief became one of awe. He was convinced that one man had really "got religion."

He was so convinced that he began thinking about his own relationship to God. I know he was. His eyes were downcast, and his bulldozer expression was gone. There sprang up within me a desire to have all my gambling friends make the gamble of their life on Jesus Christ. I urged, "Andy, why don't you come and hear about this yourself? Why don't you come to the meeting tonight?"

He tapped his foot nervously on the brick walk. "I would, but I'm afraid."

"Afraid of what?"

He looked up and stared right at me. "Afraid I might get what you've got!"

"That wouldn't be too bad, would it?"

"Maybe not, but I don't think I could live up to it."

Yes, that took something, but encouraged by the way God had helped me, I said, "God will help you. He..."

"Nope, it's not for me. I got business to attend to. So long, Jim." There was a note of sadness in his voice, but he turned away and beckoned to his friends. They got into the sedan and drove out the driveway.

I felt like pinching myself but I didn't need to. I knew I was still alive, all right. I murmured, "Thank you, Lord," and went into the house.[4]

Solomon looked next at *man's wealth:* "Better is a little with righteousness than great revenues without right" (Proverbs 16:8).

Alexander Whyte said there was a soft spot in Zacchaeus's heart. He was as eager as any schoolboy to see Jesus and just like a schoolboy he ran ahead and climbed into a tree so he could see the prophet pass by and perhaps perform a miracle. Through that chink in Zacchaeus's armor, God was able to insert the dart of conviction and accomplish the conversion of that tightfisted, greedy, and grasping sinner.

Zacchaeus came from an outcast and outlaw segment of society. He was a tax collector, a bully, and a thief. In those days the Roman government farmed out the job of collecting taxes to independent collectors. The government required a certain revenue, but paid little heed to the means used to extract it from the people as long as that amount was paid into the imperial coffers on time. Nor did the government care what percentage the tax collector added to the assessment to cover his fee. He was entitled to whatever he could get. As a class, tax collectors were despised as traitors and detested and dreaded because of their greed and power.

It had been years since anyone who had any regard for his reputation had crossed the threshold of Zacchaeus's home or even said a kind word to him on the street. He had made himself rich collecting taxes but in spite of all his riches, Zacchaeus was a lonely man. So when Jesus stopped beneath that sycamore tree and invited Himself to Zacchaeus's house, the man was beside himself with surprise and delight. The Lord was not a bit concerned about the verbal abuse that followed Him and Zacchaeus all the way to the rich man's house. As a result, all Zacchaeus's defenses were down, his heart melted, and he was converted in his own home.

As proof of his conversion, Zacchaeus promised to beggar himself, to strip himself of all his ill-gotten gains. He pledged to give half of all he possessed to the poor and 400 percent compensation to every person he had robbed in the pursuit of his profession (Luke 19:8). The Mosaic law demanded 120 percent restitution (Leviticus 6:1-5), but Zacchaeus was no longer under law; he was under grace. And grace demands much more, just as it gives much more (see Romans 5).

By the time Zacchaeus liquidated his assets and paid what he had promised to the citizens of Jericho, he probably had to take his place among the poor. With his palatial house sold, his furniture sold, his bank accounts closed, and his purse empty, he would sit down to his meager supper and nod wisely as he recalled Solomon's words: "Better is a little with righteousness than great revenues without right."

Most likely the change in Zacchaeus gave every family in Jericho a fresh appreciation of saving grace. They thanked God for Jesus, for His coming to Jericho on His way to Golgotha, and for His astonishing visit to Zacchaeus's home.

Finally Solomon looked at *man's ways:* "A man's heart deviseth his way: but the Lord directeth his steps" (Proverbs 16:9).

The classic Old Testament example of this proverb is the story of Jonah. God told Jonah to go to the great city of Nineveh and stalk its streets proclaiming a message of impending doom. Jonah made up his mind at once to run away from God. He disobeyed not so much because he was afraid, although there was plenty to fear. The people of Nineveh were known to flay their enemies alive, or impale them on sharpened wooden spikes and leave them there to scream away their last pain-tormented days. Yet Jonah was not so much afraid as he was astonished at the prophecy of Nineveh's downfall.

The certain overthrow of Nineveh in forty days' time was the best news he had ever heard! He was prophet enough to know that although all seemed well with Israel, outward appearances were deceptive. Powerful Jeroboam II was on the throne, but the country was ripe for judgment. (In fact Jeroboam II was the last king to sit on the throne of Israel with any semblance of divine authority.) Jonah had enough spiritual insight to figure out that God would likely use Nineveh, capital city of the terrible Assyrian empire, to punish Israel.

Jonah consulted his own heart, measured his stock of courage, and devised his own way. He would board a boat headed for Tarshish, a city located at the utmost boundary of the known world of his day. It would take God more than forty days to catch up with him. If he were shipwrecked and he drowned at sea, so much the better. Then he could never go to Nineveh and prevent God's judgment from falling on that city—and perhaps his beloved Israel would be spared the horrors of a war with Assyria.

So Jonah's heart devised his way—but God directed his steps. God simply summoned the stormy wind and then "a whale" (the Old Testament version of Jaws) to pursue and punish Jonah. By the time God was through with Jonah, he was more than ready to do what he was told. God has His own way of getting His own way—which is just as well, for His way is always right.

B. The Lord and the Head of State (16:10-15)

1. The King and His Pronouncements (16:10-11)

Having changed his focus, Solomon told us *how judgment is decreed:* "A divine sentence is in the lips of the king: his mouth transgresseth not in judgment" (Proverbs 16:10). He was, of course, stating the ideal. Perhaps Solomon was thinking of the godlike sentence he pronounced when two harlots claimed the same baby. Or perhaps Solomon was giving his version of the Pauline dictum: "The powers that be are ordained of God" (Romans 13:1). Or perhaps Solomon was being cynical when he implied that the king is always right. Solomon was capable of a considerable amount of cynicism, as is evident in the book of Ecclesiastes.

Whatever Solomon had in mind, the proverb serves to remind us that human government is as much a divine ordinance as marriage. God instituted marriage in Genesis 2:18-25. According to Genesis 9:5-6 He vested "the power of the sword" (Romans 13:1-4) in Noah after the flood. That is, He instituted capital punishment for the crime of murder. Since the right to take human life is the highest of all governmental functions, it necessarily includes all lesser governmental functions, such as taking away a man's liberty for certain offenses. The whole concept of this kind of governmental function was later expanded in the 613 commandments of the Mosaic law.

God is on the side of law and order and constituted authority. When Paul upheld "the powers that be" in his day, God's people were under the yoke of the Roman imperial power. Nero, one of the worst of all human tyrants, was on the throne of the caesars.

There are proper ways to redress perceived wrongs in a country's government. England for instance never had a worse king than John. He was arrogant, treacherous, lustful, unscrupulous, given to towering rages, vindictive, and murderous. He had a genius for losing wars and offending people. He picked on the most important people and offended them on the most harmful occasions. He was hated by the common people, excommunicated by the pope, and detested by the barons.

At length Stephen Langton, the archbishop of Canterbury, spearheaded a move to curb the power of the ruler. He unearthed a copy of a forgotten charter signed by Henry I in the early stages of his illustrious reign. The document was yellow with age and badly tattered and torn, but it contained the first written safeguard of English liberties. One all-important clause read: "And I enjoin on my barons to act in the same way toward the sons and daughters and wives of their dependents." The clause was a written acknowledgment, signed by an absolute monarch, that common men as well as the nobility had rights. That charter became the foundation of one of the most famous documents in history, the Magna Carta, which in turn became the foundation of all our modern liberties. This "great charter" contained seventy pregnant clauses.

Spurred on by Langton, the barons of England united to force

King John, for whom they had nothing but hatred and contempt, to meet them at Runnymede, a meadow on the south bank of the Thames, not far from Windsor castle. At Runnymede on Monday, June 15, 1215, the barons forced the king to sign the Magna Carta. The document, however distasteful to the evil and wily King John, became a sworn covenant between ruler and people.

Clause 43 stated, "No freeman shall be taken, nor imprisoned...but by the lawful judgment of his peers, or by the laws of the land." Clause 15 affirmed the parliamentary principle that had been slowly but surely developed by the Anglo-Saxons.[5] The Magna Carta dealt widely and frankly with the rights of common men and opened the way for all subsequent parliamentary reforms. The rights of man now take the place of the often-abused "divine right of kings" of which Solomon wrote.

Solomon told us next *how justice is decided:* "A just weight and balance are the Lord's: all the weights of the bag are his work" (Proverbs 16:11). This proverb states an extraordinary view of the sanctity of business and commerce. Who would have thought that God Himself claims to have instituted such a mundane activity? God approves of the business side of life. It has His blessing.

Solomon of course was quite conversant with the Mosaic law. It decreed: "Just balances, just weights, a just ephah, and a just hin, shall ye have: I am the Lord your God, which brought you out of the land of Egypt" (Leviticus 19:36). In other words, God is not on the side of all business; He is on the side of fair and honest business. Those who cheat in their business activities sin not only against their fellow men, but also against God. God's scales weigh actions and He always keeps them in balance.

Jacob discovered that God often puts one cheat in the same set of scales with another cheat to keep His scales in balance. *Jacob* means "supplanter" or "one who takes you by the heel" or "one who twists your arm," as we would say today in colloquial English (Genesis 25:24-26). Jacob evidently decided that if he was going to be called a cheat, he might just as well be one. Early in his life he cheated his twin brother Esau out of his birthright and his blessing.

Before long Jacob and his Uncle Laban were locked in a twenty-year struggle, each doing his best to cheat and outwit the other. Laban was cut from the same piece of cloth as Jacob. The only difference between the two men was that Laban was older and more experienced. He proceeded to cheat Jacob with the same unscrupulous thoroughness with which Jacob had cheated his own father and brother.

God is usually not in a hurry to redress wrongs, but when He does get out His scales He balances them perfectly. For instance, on Jacob's wedding night Laban callously palmed off Leah on Jacob, who thought the bride he was receiving was Rachel. Laban's methods were underhanded, despicable, and mean. He was not bothered by the fact that he was trampling on the tenderest, most sacred feelings of Jacob's heart. But seven years earlier Jacob had treated his blind old dad just as callously. Jacob had palmed himself off on Isaac, who thought he was bestowing his blessing on Esau. Jacob's methods had been underhanded, despicable, and mean too. He had not been bothered by the fact that he was trampling on the tenderest, most sacred feelings of Isaac's heart. So ounce for ounce, God weighed out to Jacob exactly what he had measured out to others. We can see the scales balancing again when we remember that what Jacob did to Esau in the matter of the birthright parallels what Laban did to Jacob in the matter of his wages.[6]

Of course God balanced the scales for Laban too. His cheating cost him his daughters and his grandchildren. His determined effort to take them away from Jacob was forestalled by an angel who put the fear of God into him. Moreover God saw to it that Jacob amply repaid Esau in hard cash (even though the bartered birthright had never really belonged to Esau in the first place).

Often the crook and con man seem to get away with lying, cheating, and thievery because we cannot always see God meting out justice. But God balances the scales sooner or later, whether or not we see Him redressing wrongs.

2. The King and His Power (16:12-13)

Solomon noted that the power of a king is related to his *personal righteousness:* "It is an abomination to kings to commit wickedness: for the throne is established by righteousness" (Proverbs 16:12).

Perhaps Solomon belatedly realized his folly in succumbing to the nagging of his wives and allowing them to set up shrines in Jerusalem to their pagan gods. When he gave in to them he exhibited blatant unrighteousness. Because of this sin the prophet told Solomon that he would lose ten of the twelve tribes.

The subsequent history of the divided kingdom offers additional evidence of the truth of this proverb. The northern kingdom and the southern kingdom each had twenty kings. The rulers of the northern kingdom were uniformly bad. The northern kingdom lasted 253 years (975-722). The southern kingdom had a number of good kings, and a few remarkably good kings. As a result the southern kingdom lasted 378 years (975-597), 125 years longer than the northern kingdom.

The good kings ruled in righteousness and thus were able to delay the disruptive power of wickedness in the southern kingdom. Asa, Jehoshaphat, Jotham, Uzziah, Hezekiah, and Josiah were all good kings. Hezekiah and Josiah were remarkable in their stand for righteousness. Several of the Judean kings were unstable—good for a while and bad for a while. Not until Manasseh ascended the throne did wickedness become firmly installed in the southern kingdom. Then not even Josiah's vigorous reforms could stay the tide, and the last four Judean kings were uniformly bad.

The first mention of kings in the Bible is in Genesis 14, where ten are named. The first nine are mentioned at the beginning of the chapter and they are at war. Five of the nine ruled over the filthy cities of the plain where sodomy was an accepted lifestyle. These five kings were overthrown by an invading coalition of four kings from the East. At the end of the chapter a tenth king is introduced: Melchizedek. A king-priest, a king of righteousness, and a prince of peace, Melchizedek is a studied type of Christ, the King who will come at the last to establish His throne by righteousness for a thousand years.

Solomon added a thought about *propagated righteousness:* "Righteous lips are the delight of kings; and they love him that speaketh right" (Proverbs 16:13). Kings are often surrounded by sycophants, hypocrites, and self-servers. A man of integrity who will boldly tell a king the truth without fear or seeking favor is like a breath of fresh air to the ruler.

Such a man was Benjamin Disraeli—a shrewd, far-sighted politician and statesman. One of the most colorful and romantic of all British prime ministers, he helped make Britain great. Disraeli descended from a family of Jews who had been expelled from Spain during the reign of Ferdinand and Isabella. Benjamin's father, a scholar, left the synagogue and had his family baptized in the Church of England. The move was prudent, to say the least, and made a political career possible for his son.

Early in his career, Disraeli was discounted by his peers not only because of his Jewish background but also because of his extravagant dress, foppish manner, and affected style of speech. But in the House of Commons, even before he became famous, Disraeli made it evident that he knew what he was talking about. His friends listened to him with satisfaction and his enemies with apprehension—he won the post of prime minister on one occasion by calling his opponents "a row of extinct volcanoes"! When as an old man he moved to the House of Lords, he was greatly missed in the House of Commons. One politician remarked, "It's like playing chess without the queen, a miserable struggle of pawns." The compliment was well-meant, although it was not flattering to Disraeli's genius. He could have turned all his pawns into queens.

Disraeli came to power when Britain and France were bitter rivals, both reaching for an empire in the Far East. The key to such an empire was the Suez Canal, the gateway to India. The canal had been built by a Frenchman and was owned by the khedive of Egypt. In November 1875 word reached Lord Derby, Disraeli's foreign secretary, that the khedive wanted to sell his Suez Canal shares for four million pounds, a considerable sum in those days. Disraeli realized at once that he had to secure those shares before the French did. There was no time to be lost, but Parliament was not in session and such a vast sum could not be obtained from the treasury without a budget appropriation.

Disraeli did not hesitate. He summoned his secretary, Montague Corry, and sent him to borrow the money from Rothschild. The banker was having his lunch but received the prime minister's envoy at his table. Corry came straight to the point: "Mr. Disraeli needs four million pounds tomorrow morning."

The banker raised the obvious question: "What is his security?"

"The British government, sir."

"He shall have it," said Rothschild.

By this master stroke, Disraeli proved himself to be one who spoke right and acted right. When lesser men would have dithered, Disraeli acted. The time came when his farsightedness paid off and his prudence was widely acknowledged.

Disraeli was greatly admired by Queen Victoria, who loved to listen to him and who appreciated all that his foreign policy had done to make England great. Even his political rival Gladstone acknowledged Disraeli's genius. When Disraeli died, Gladstone proposed that the great statesman be buried in Westminster Abbey. However he was buried, as he had wished, in a small country graveyard beside the church at Hughenden. In the church Queen Victoria raised a monument which reads:

> To the dear and Honoured Memory of
> Benjamin, Earl of Beaconsfield, This
> Memorial is Erected by His Grateful
> Sovereign and Friend Victoria R.I.
> *"Kings Love Him That Speaketh Right."*
> Proverbs xvi.13.

3. The King and His People (16:14-15)

In these proverbs about the king we see *his fury displayed:* "The wrath of a king is as messengers of death: but a wise man will pacify it" (Proverbs 16:14).

The citizens of Calais, France, realized the truth of this proverb when they experienced the wrath of Edward III, one of England's great Plantagenet kings. Edward was eager to prove himself on the field of battle and the arena he chose was the old one: France. There he proceeded to win a string of victories that have long resounded in history. At Crécy, for instance, the English yeomen with their longbows cut the armored knights of France to ribbons and heralded the end of an epoch. The day of the knight was over.

The French seaport of Calais had long been a thorn in England's side. Calais was a hotbed of piracy and sent out ships to prey on English commerce. Edward determined to take the city and teach its citizens a lesson they would never forget. Calais resisted the siege stubbornly but Edward frightened off the French king and built a town of wooden huts around the doomed city. He even opened a market so that his soldiers could buy food and clothing from England.

Meanwhile Edward fumed and raged that the siege was taking so long and costing so much. He made up his mind to punish the people of Calais and hand the city over to sack and butchery. When his counselors urged him to compromise, Edward agreed but insisted that six of the most notable men in Calais come out in their shirts and bare feet and with ropes around their necks. They were to bring him the keys of the town and castle. Edward was determined to hang these men although he would treat the rest of the people with mercy.

The six venerable men came out and threw themselves on Edward's mercy. However the king's face was red with rage and he summoned the headsman to begin the executions. Then a dramatic incident occurred that will be told as long as English history endures. Queen Philippa, Edward's lovely Dutch wife who was about to be confined with a tenth child, knelt before Edward and pleaded for mercy. The king looked at his queen and took his time to make up his mind. His heart was really set on teaching Calais its lesson and once he raised his hand as if to signal the headsman to get on with his task. In the end, however, he reluctantly gave in to the queen. As Solomon said, "The wrath of a king is as messengers of death: but a wise man will pacify it."

Observing the king with his people we see *his favor desired:* "In the light of the king's countenance is life; and his favour is as a cloud of the latter rain" (Proverbs 16:15). The word translated "cloud" here means "a heavy cloud." In Palestine a heavy cloud was a valuable, dependable cloud that brought rain just before harvest. It was a cloud full of promise.

Daniel lived most of his life under the prosperous cloud of a king's favor. The prophet came into favor when Nebuchadnezzar had his famous dream. The king knew instinctively that it was not an ordinary dream, but a dream of destiny. But he did not know how he could be sure of its interpretation. He did not trust the court magicians, psychics, and astrologers because they would tell him anything. So he decided on a simple but clever test. He summoned the soothsayers and told them he had had a startling, vivid dream but he had forgotten what it was. If they could tell him what the dream was, he could trust their explanation of what the dream meant. When they protested he added a rider: If they couldn't tell him what the dream was, he would conclude they were quacks and execute them and all the other wise men in Babylon for their pretensions.

They were unable to comply with the king's unreasonable demand and their doom was sealed. Daniel, who had been promoted to their ranks, was in jeopardy. For some reason he did not learn about the king's demand until the executioners showed up at his door. Daniel sent the king a hasty message that he would tell the king both the dream and its interpretation the next day. A stay of execution was ordered and Daniel and his three friends had a prayer meeting. Then, calmly enough under the circumstances, Daniel went to bed. That night the Lord gave him the same dream He had given to Nebuchadnezzar.

The king's eyes must have opened wider and wider the next morning when Daniel told him his dream. Daniel described the image with its head of gold, its breast and arms of silver, its belly and thighs of brass, its legs of iron, its feet of iron and clay. He described the stone cut without hands that broke the feet of the image. He described the total dissolution of the image and how the wind blew it away. He described how the stone became a great mountain that filled the whole earth.

The king no doubt stared at this polished and princely young Jew who so accurately described what was known to him alone. "Son," we can hear him say, "what does the dream mean?" Daniel, having already told the king that "there is a God in heaven that revealeth secrets" (Daniel 2:28), proceeded to reveal the meaning of the dream. The dream was about world empire, now entrusted by God

to the Gentiles. The empire had begun with Nebuchadnezzar, and
Daniel told the king how it all would end.

From then on, Nebuchadnezzar was Daniel's friend. The young
Jewish prince was promoted and his friends were promoted. Ahead
of him lay honor, power, wealth, a long and godly life, and other
blessings men hold dear. Even when changes in the administration
led to Daniel's retirement, his fame lingered on. In the closing
moments of the Babylonian empire Daniel was summoned back on
stage. He remained there in the early days of the Persian empire
and was honored and consulted by its rulers too.

C. The Lord and the Happiness of All (16:16-20)

1. Happiness and Gold (16:16)

"How much better," Solomon wrote, "is it to get wisdom than
gold! and to get understanding rather to be chosen than silver!"

Consider again the example of King John, the worst king ever to
sit on the throne of England. It did not take Isabella, John's queen,
long to discover one of his most prominent and persistent traits:
parsimony. He was mean and miserly. He loved money and hated
to spend it, even for the coronation of the young bride with whom
he was so completely infatuated. Certainly John was more interested in getting gold than he was in getting wisdom.

He grew worse as the years went by. The closing scene of his
inglorious reign finds him at the Wash, a wide indentation on the
eastern coast of England. His kingdom was in turmoil. The French
had landed an expeditionary force and the barons could not decide whether to join the French or support their own detested king.
John had hired a gang of cutthroat mercenaries to fight the barons.

Tormented by gout, suspicious of everyone, John marched on.
His progress was slow because he could not bear to let the wagons
in the baggage train out of his sight. A few suspected, but only John
knew that those wagons contained his gold, his precious jewels, and
all the priceless royal regalia which were supposed to be kept in the
vaults at Winchester castle. These treasures had been accumulated
by a lifetime of imposing taxes on his suffering countrymen. In fact
the taxation was driving them to rebellion. There was also money
defrauded from a brother's legacies and gold extracted by pulling
teeth from helpless Jews. Except for the money he had grudgingly
doled out to his mercenaries, every coin he started out with was in
those wagons.

The tide was out as John's forces started across the sands of the

Wash. He summoned the wagons to follow. Before long, like pharaoh's chariots of old, the wheels were plowing deep furrows in the sand and eventually they ground to a halt. But the river that emptied into the Wash did not stop, and neither did the onrushing tide. The king watched helplessly as the swirling waters engulfed his screaming horses and drivers—the horses kicking madly at their traces and the drivers calling vainly for help. The crown, the scepter, and the nation's wealth were inundated and swept out to sea—forever lost. A day later John was dead. Much good his wealth did him. Wisdom would have served him better. The lesson is for us all.

2. Happiness and Guilt (16:17)

"The highway of the upright is to depart from evil: he that keepeth his way preserveth his soul." This proverb tells us that the rule of the road on the King's highway is simple: "Depart from evil." All that is required of us is to discern evil and to depart from evil. It is easy to see if we are on the wrong road and it is simple to change to the right road. The highway home is so well marked that only by sheer stubbornness and willfulness can we get lost.

If along life's highway we come to a place of questionable amusement, all that is required of us is to depart from it. If we come to a house of ill repute, we know we must depart from it. If we come to a place of business where promotion can be rapid if we abandon morality and ethics, the rule is the same: Depart from it. If we come to a tavern or a street corner where the wrong crowd gathers, we are told to depart from it. If we come to a college or seminary where the professors use their podiums to destroy the faith of the students, ridicule Scripture, and proclaim godless philosophies of life, we must depart from it. "The highway of the upright is to depart from evil."

The right road begins at Calvary. It is a strait and narrow way, often lonely and sometimes dangerous, but it leads home. Those who have entered the right road by the way of the cross must remember the rule of the road, for even they are in peril of wandering off down some beckoning path to the subsequent sorrow of their souls. Christian and Hopeful experienced such sorrow. Bunyan described what happened:

> Now, I beheld in my dream, that they had not journeyed far, but the river and the way for a time parted; at which they were not a little sorry; yet they durst not go out of the way. Now the

way from the river was rough, and their feet tender, by reason of their travels; "so the souls of the pilgrims were much discouraged because of the way." (Num. xxi. 4.) Wherefore, still as they went on, they wished for a better way. Now, a little before them, there was on the left hand of the road a meadow, and a stile to go over into it; and that meadow is called By-path Meadow. Then said Christian to his fellow, If this meadow lieth along by our wayside, let us go over into it. Then he went to the stile to see, and behold, a path lay along by the way, on the other side of the fence. It is according to my wish, said Christian. Here is the easiest going; come, good Hopeful, and let us go over.

HOPE. But how if this path should lead us out of the way?

CHR. That is not like, said the other. Look, doth it not go along by the wayside? So Hopeful, being persuaded by this fellow, went after him over the stile. When they were gone over, and were got into the path, they found it very easy for their feet; and withal, they, looking before them, espied a man walking as they did, and his name was Vain-confidence; so they called after him, and asked him whither that way led. He said, To the Celestial Gate. Look, said Christian, did not I tell you so? By this you may see we are right. So they followed, and he went before them. But, behold, the night came on, and it grew very dark; so that they that were behind lost the sight of him that went before.

He, therefore, that went before (Vain-confidence by name), not seeing the way before him, fell into a deep pit (Isa. ix. 16), which was on purpose there made, by the Prince of those grounds, to catch vain-glorious fools withal, and was dashed in pieces with his fall....

Neither could they, with all the skill they had, get again to the stile that night. Wherefore, at last, lighting under a little shelter, they sat down there until day-break; but, being weary, they fell asleep. Now there was, not far from the place where they lay, a castle called Doubting Castle, the owner whereof was Giant Despair; and it was in his grounds they now were sleeping; wherefore he, getting up in the morning early, and walking up and down in his fields, caught Christian and Hopeful asleep in his grounds. Then, with a grim and surly voice, he bid them awake; and asked them whence they were, and what they did in his grounds. They told him they were pilgrims, and that they had lost their way. Then said the Giant, You have this night trespassed on me, by trampling in, and lying on my grounds, and therefore you must go along with me. So they were forced to go, because he was stronger than they. They also had but little to say, for they knew themselves in a fault. The Giant, therefore, drove them before him, and put them into his castle, into a very dark dungeon, nasty and stinking to the spirits of these two men. (Psalm lxxxviii. 18.) Here, then, they lay from Wednesday morning till Saturday night, without one bit of bread, or drop of drink, or light, or any to ask how they did; they were, therefore, here in evil case, and were far from friends and acquaintance. Now in this place Christian had double sorrow, because it was through his unadvised counsel that they were brought into this distress.

As Bunyan reminded us, it is far easier, even for a Christian, to leave the right road than to remain on it. In the end Christian and Hopeful escaped from Doubting Castle and from the cruel beatings inflicted on them by Giant Despair. Their means of escape was a key called Promise. God's promises are "yea and amen" in Christ (2 Corinthians 1:20; Romans 15:8) and will keep us on the King's highway. Our duty is to "depart from evil."

3. Happiness and Glory (16:18-19)

The haughty spirit is not conducive to happiness. Proverbs 16:18 says, "Pride goeth before destruction, and an haughty spirit before a fall."

One illustration of this proverb is the case of Alexander the Great. Educated by Aristotle, Alexander was regent of Macedonia at sixteen, a victorious general at eighteen, king at twenty, and dead at thirty-three. During his brief life he conquered, in terms of classical geography, the whole world. Relentlessly pursuing his goal to humble Persia, Alexander chased Darius III from one stronghold to another.

First Alexander curbed the Greek city-states and brought them into line. Then he crossed the Hellespont and entered Asia Minor. His first major victory at the Granicus river opened western Asia Minor to conquest. City after city fell. The battle of Issus demoralized the Persian king, who tried in vain to come to terms with his implacable young foe. Down into Palestine the conqueror marched. Sidon opened its gates. Tyre was besieged and sacked with a savagery that displayed Alexander's growing impatience and imperiousness. Gaza gave in and the Nile delta lay before him. Egypt welcomed him with open arms as a deliverer. He was crowned as pharaoh on November 14, 332 B.C., and was made a god. Success went to his head and he built the famous city of Alexandria.

In the meantime he had his eye on the city of Babylon. Darius, who hoped against hope for a compromise, sent one offer after another but Alexander turned them all down. The final offer was so generous that Parmenio, one of Alexander's advisers, said, "If I were Alexander I should accept it." Alexander replied, "If I were Parmenio, so should I." The critical battle of Gaugamela was fought and Babylon fell readily into Alexander's hands.

But Babylon was not Persepolis and it was Persia that Alexander was after—Persia and Darius himself. Alexander entered Persepolis on January 31, 330 B.C., and the Persian holy city yielded an enormous amount of treasure to add to his coffers. Having pillaged the famous city, Alexander decided at a drunken orgy to burn down Xerxes' palace. Before long the entire city was in flames.

And so it went on in city after city. Outrage after outrage was committed. Persia fell. India fell. Alexander became increasingly oriental, his pride growing with each success. Elaborate feasts and drinking parties became regular features even of camp life.

Alexander died when he was still young, still undefeated, still yearning for more worlds to conquer. His death was a result of a drinking bout, but some say he was poisoned. They claim that Aristotle prepared the drug and one of the conqueror's cupbearers gave it to him. When generals and friends gathered at the deathbed, one of them asked, "Who is to get the kingdom?" Alexander cynically replied, "The strongest!" His last words were both prophetic and pathetic. He said, "I foresee a great funeral contest over me." No sooner did he move on than rebellion flared up in his rear. His empire was rapidly carved up.[7]

What had Alexander accomplished with all his pride and power? He left a twenty-thousand-mile trail of slaughter and rapine. His wife Roxana and their son were murdered by Cassander, and Alexander's line became extinct. All his efforts amounted to nothing. "Pride goeth before destruction, and an haughty spirit before a fall."

Solomon compared the haughty spirit with *the humble spirit:* "Better it is to be of an humble spirit with the lowly, than to divide the spoil with the proud" (Proverbs 16:19).

We can compare one of the greatest and most influential men of the twentieth century with a humble believer. The world still rings with Winston Churchill's speeches. On May 13, 1940, when the fury of Nazi aggression was turned on the British people, he spoke to his countrymen:

I have nothing to offer but blood, toil, tears and sweat....You ask, what is our policy? I will say it is to wage war, by sea, land and air, with all our might and with all the strength that God can give us; to wage war against a monstrous tyranny, never surpassed in the dark, lamentable catalogue of human crime.

France was collapsing. The British would soon be driven from the continent. Hitler's air force would bomb British cities into heaps of rubble. Germany's U-boats and pocket battleships would send 3,000 ships and 30,000 seamen to a watery grave, at a cost of 780 U-boats sunk in exchange. Rommel's tanks would all but chase the British army out of North Africa and come within striking distance of Palestine. Churchill was God's man for such an hour. With his indomitable spirit, courage, vision, conviction, drive, and speeches he rallied the British people in the hour of their greatest need.

Churchill was born to wealth and influence. His paternal grandfather was the duke of Marlborough. He spent his childhood in the magnificent Blenheim palace and was educated at Harrow, one of Britain's most prestigious schools. After serving in the British army in India and the Sudan, Churchill became a journalist and orator. During World War I he served in the admiralty. After the war he moved in and out of politics and made himself vastly unpopular by warning Britain and the world that Germany was a menace and its rearmament would be disastrous for mankind.

After World War II Churchill watched as the Russians overran Eastern Europe and launched the cold war. He coined the phrase *iron curtain* to describe the impenetrable ideological wall the Russians built across Europe and behind which historic nations were kept captive. Alarmed at the Soviets' enormous success, Churchill searched for a man who could tell him what the Bible has to say about prophecy and current events.

His attention was directed to Harold St. John—a former missionary, a first-class Bible student, a humble believer, a Christian gentleman, and a beloved member of a little-known and often-despised religious group known as Plymouth Brethren. Churchill scheduled a half-hour appointment with Mr. St. John, but it was extended to an all-day session as Sir Winston listened spellbound. In all his long, illustrious, varied, and colorful career he had never heard such an exposition of the prophetic Scriptures. When the momentous day was over and Mr. St. John was taking his leave, Churchill thanked his guest and added: "Mr. St. John, I would give half the world for your knowledge of the Bible." The Bible teacher replied, "Sir, I gave *all* the world for my knowledge of the Bible."

Sir Winston Churchill received his share of honors. He knew what it meant "to divide the spoil with the proud." But weighed in the balances of eternity, that quiet believer, who was "of an humble spirit with the lowly," was by far the greater man.

4. Happiness and Goodness (16:20)

In his concluding comment on happiness, Solomon said, "He that handleth a matter wisely shall find good: and whoso trusteth in the Lord, happy is he."

Daniel handled the problems of captivity wisely. We can imagine how the teenager Daniel must have felt when his beloved homeland was invaded by the Babylonians. He knew they would win. He had heard Jeremiah too often to have any doubts about that. Win they did, and he found himself, along with most of the Judean nobility, being marched off to Babylon. Ahead of him lay captivity, the slave market, and possibly a cruel death.

At the end of the long weary march was one of the most magnificent cities of antiquity. Babylon, which contained one of the seven wonders of the world, stood fifteen miles square. Its outer fortifications were 350 feet high, 700 feet wide at the bottom, and 300 feet wide at the top. Chariots could race six abreast around the top of this enormous wall. The inner wall was 250 feet high. A standing army patrolled this wall day and night. The city was laid out in squares, with 25 streets running north and south, east and west. In the center stood 150 pillars 88 feet high and 19 feet in diameter; these pillars supported the temple of Bel and his colossal image. The Euphrates river ran through the city from north to south. In this city were the awesome grand palace of Nebuchadnezzar and the fabulous hanging gardens. At the entrance to Babylon was the Ishtar gate through which royal processions marched on festive occasions.

The whole scene was one of splendor and magnificence. Little did young Daniel realize that he was destined virtually to rule this awesome city because his ways pleased the Lord.

Daniel was surprised when he and some other members of the Judean royal family were taken to fashionable quarters instead of being sold into slavery. They were told that they would be taught the Babylonian language and groomed for administrative posts.

Another surprise greeted them when they entered their dining room and saw the loaded table. The king had sent provisions from the royal kitchens. It was his command that his captives be treated as his guests and be fed as well as he was, so that they might be fair and flourishing when he summoned them into his presence.

Asking no questions for conscience's sake, Daniel's colleagues seated themselves at the banquet table and began to eat. Daniel, however, quietly passed up all the rich food. The food had been offered to idols and the meat contained blood. The Mosaic law prohibited Jews from eating such food.

We can imagine how his companions, alarmed that his scruples and stubbornness might imperil all of them, urged him not to be such a fool. "This is Babylon, not Jerusalem. We are slaves, not free. Nebuchadnezzar will be insulted. Don't you know, Daniel, that the Babylonian king keeps a fiery furnace and a den of lions for those who offend him? He will make a clean sweep and consign us all to the flames if you persist in this nonsense. The food is good. Try some of the shrimp salad and that honey-baked ham. Don't make an issue of mere ritual law. It isn't as though we are being asked to break some moral law."

Daniel remained completely unmoved by their rationalizations. He decided to handle the matter wisely and be strictly loyal to the Word of God. Whatever the others did, he knew he could not be happy if he compromised. He had a clear word from God on the issue at stake. The highest wisdom—the wisdom of the written Word of God—ruled on the subject and that settled it for Daniel. The essence of all wisdom is to do what God says.

Solomon said, "He that handleth a matter wisely shall find good: and whoso trusteth in the Lord, happy is he." Daniel found good and he was happy. He honored God and God honored him.

D. The Lord and the Highways of Life (16:21-33)

1. The Sensible Path (16:21-24)

a. How to Excel in Learning (16:21)

"The wise in heart shall be called prudent: and the sweetness of the lips increaseth learning." True wisdom cannot be hidden. When it is revealed, people are usually ready to acknowledge it. Moreover when wisdom is presented in a winsome way, people will generally listen, accept instruction, and increase their knowledge.

With just such sweet reasonableness, Jesus spoke to the two disciples on the road to Emmaus. Their hearts were heavy because their beloved Master had been crucified and buried. They gave no credence to the story of the women who said He was alive again and they had seen Him. The hopes of the two travelers lay in Joseph of Arimathaea's tomb along with the dead body of Jesus.

Then the Stranger joined them, drew them out, and opened the Scriptures to them. Their hearts began to burn within them. Surely, they thought, *never man spake like this man—except Jesus, and He is dead.* How often they must have peered at the Stranger as He expounded Genesis 22, Psalm 22, Psalm 69, Isaiah 53, and many other familiar portions of Scripture. But they were still too blinded by unbelief to see who was speaking "as one having authority, and not as the scribes" (Matthew 7:29).

Here was One who was wise in heart and prudent. He was building a case for Calvary. "Oh fools," He said, "and slow of heart to believe all that the prophets have spoken: Ought not Christ to have suffered these things, and to enter into his glory?" (Luke 24:25-26) He paraded Joseph, Moses, and David before two disciples. He piled up verse after verse from Moses and all the prophets. The sweetness of His lips increased their learning. His arguments were unanswerable. Everything made so much sense the way He explained it. No wonder when they reached their garden gate and the Stranger bade them a courteous good night, they begged Him to come in, have supper, and stay the night.

b. How to Excel in Living (16:22)

"Understanding is a wellspring of life unto him that hath it: but the instruction of fools is folly."

When I was a small boy I contracted diphtheria and missed more than a month of school. It took me a long time to make up the missing links in the learning chain, especially in arithmetic. I blundered through the rest of the school term with no understanding.

It was critically important to catch up. In those days the English education system required a student to pass a state examination before entering high school, and one of the key subjects in the exam was arithmetic. I was handicapped. The subject had become a nightmare and my mother's well-meaning efforts to supplement my education only added frustration.

Finally my parents decided that I needed special coaching in the area of my deficiency. Accordingly they arranged for a teacher to give me extra lessons during my summer vacation. I was to sacrifice half a day, five days a week, for three or four weeks, to attend special classes instead of roaming the countryside with my friends.

The teacher was a master of his art. Under his patient tutoring the light dawned. At last I understood! How simple it all seemed when he provided the missing links. The new understanding became a wellspring of life. Now I could face the all-important exam with confidence.

What a fool I would have been if I had resented my parents' efforts to fill the gap in my education. Suppose I had resented sacrificing part of the summer vacation. Suppose I had sulked and tuned out the teacher. I would have been like the student Solomon had in mind when he wrote, "The instruction of fools is folly." Doubtless Solomon was thinking of his own son, a young fool who had no understanding of things that mattered and despised all forms of instruction.

c. How to Excel in Leading (16:23-24)

In order to excel, one must be careful about *speaking with honesty.* Solomon said, "The heart of the wise teacheth his mouth, and addeth learning to his lips" (Proverbs 16:23). In other words, the wise man weighs the facts of a case and thinks before he speaks. He does not blurt out the first words that come to his mind, regardless of whether they are right or wrong. He has more honesty and sense than that.

We can compare Peter's words before and after Pentecost. Before Pentecost he was always blurting out whatever came into his head. Even his great doctrinal confession was more or less blurted out, although it accurately verbalized what Peter had come to believe: "Thou art the Christ, the Son of the living God" (Matthew 16:16). The instant commendation that followed was heady wine for the fledgling apostle, for a few minutes later he blurted out a suggestion and insinuation from Satan himself (Matthew 16:22-23). He was just as impulsive after the resurrection. Peter got tired of waiting for something to happen and suddenly he announced to a group of the disciples: "I go a fishing" (John 21:3). At once the six other disciples leaped to their feet (John 21:2). Their response was a tacit admission that they too were going back into business.

But at Pentecost when Peter was baptized, filled, and anointed by the Spirit, his heart was wise and his mouth was inspired. His courage was kindled, his eyes flashed with fire, and powerful words came pouring out of his mouth. A live coal from the altar touched his lips as it had Isaiah's of old. Holy Spirit conviction gave fuel and flame to Peter's words. Filled with an honesty and courage he had never known before, he charged the most powerful men in the land with murder. A glance at the structure and scope of Peter's

impromptu sermon at Pentecost shows his new grasp of the Scriptures, the situation, salvation, and the sovereignty of God. Here is
the outline of the actual message recorded in Acts 2.[8]

I. The Word of Explanation (2:14-21)
    A. Peter Rejected Their Supposition (2:14-15)
    B. Peter Recited Their Scriptures (2:16-21)
        1. The Fulfillment of Prophecy (2:16)
        2. The Facts of Prophecy (2:17-21)
            Having to do with:
            a. The Spirit of God: A Present Advent (2:17-18)
            b. The Severity of God: A Postponed Apocalypse
                (2:19-20)
            c. The Salvation of God: A Permanent Assurance
                (2:21)
II. The Word of Exposition (2:22-40)
    A. Condemnation (2:22-24)
        1. Jesus Was a Recognizable Messiah (2:22)
        2. Jesus Was a Rejected Messiah (2:23)
            a. God's Sovereign Government Explained (2:23a)
            b. Man's Solemn Guilt Explained (2:23b)
        3. Jesus Was a Resurrected Messiah (2:24)
    B. Confirmation (2:25-36)
        1. What David Accurately Foresaw (2:25-28)
            a. The Timeless Deity of Christ (2:25-26a)
            b. The Triumphant Death of Christ (2:26b-28)
                (1) David's Faith (2:26b)
                (2) David's Facts (2:27)
                (3) David's Feelings (2:28)
        2. What David Actually Foretold (2:29-36)
            a. The Incorrect Interpretation of David's Words
                (2:29)
            b. The Incontrovertible Interpretation of David's
                Words (2:30-36)
                (1) The Force of His Prophecy (2:30-31)
                    (a) The Messiah Would Be David's Son (2:30a)
                    (b) The Messiah Would Be David's Sovereign
                        (2:30b-31)
                (2) The Fulfillment of His Prophecy (2:32-36)
                    (a) The Present Witnesses (2:32)
                    (b) The Promised Wonder (2:33)
                    (c) The Prophetic Word (2:34-35)
                    (d) The Pungent Warning (2:36)

C. Consolation (2:37-40)
  1. The Agony of Conviction Experienced (2:37)
  2. The Answer of Conversion Explained (2:38-40)
    a. A Conscious Repudiation of the Guilt of the
       Hebrew Nation (2:38a-b)
       (1) Separation—By Personal Acknowledgment of
           Jesus (2:38a)
       (2) Salvation—By Personal Acceptance of Jesus
           (2:38b)
    b. A Consequent Reception of the Gift of the Holy
       Spirit (2:38c-40)
       (1) The Promise (2:38c-39)
       (2) The Plea (2:40)

This message burned in comprehensive detail in Peter's heart and poured in an orderly torrent from his lips. The Spirit of wisdom (Ephesians 1:17) possessed Peter's heart and mouth and enabled him to speak with a wisdom beyond his own natural intelligence.

The person who aspires to excel must also recognize the value of *speaking with honey.* Solomon wrote, "Pleasant words are as an honeycomb, sweet to the soul, and health to the bones" (Proverbs 16:24).

Abigail knew how to speak "pleasant words." Beautiful, intelligent, and spiritual, she was married to a boor and a beast of a man. Her husband, successful enough in business, was a drunken bully around the house. We do not need a great deal of wisdom to know what kind of life she lived with this man.

Then David came. He was the Lord's anointed and the embodiment of ideal manhood: handsome, brave, gifted, kind, thoughtful, spiritual, and a man after God's own heart (1 Samuel 13:14). But Nabal treated him in the same boorish way he treated everyone else. When David's messengers brought word of the insulting words Nabal had spoken about him, David's wrath kindled.

Then Abigail came. She flung herself at David's feet, pointed to the tribute she had brought, and enthroned David in her heart as lord. Fourteen times she referred to him as "my lord" in an eloquent and impassioned outburst of pleasant words (1 Samuel 25:24-31). Her words were a balm to David's soul. They were "sweet to the soul, and health to the bones." He acknowledged the effect of Abigail's words when he said: "Blessed be the Lord God of Israel, which sent thee this day to meet me: And blessed be thy advice, and blessed be thou, which hast kept me this day from coming to shed blood, and from avenging myself with mine own hand" (25:32-33).

2. The Selfish Path (16:25-26)

Considering the selfish highway of life, Solomon warned against going *where appearances beckon:* "There is a way that seemeth right unto a man; but the end thereof are the ways of death" (Proverbs 16:25). This verse is the same as Proverbs 14:12, but the thought is worth repeating.

The case of Cardinal John Henry Newman illustrates this proverb. He was born in London and raised an evangelical. A brilliant man, Newman graduated from Trinity College, Oxford, was elected fellow of Oriel College, became curate of St. Clement's Church, Oxford, and then became vicar of St. Mary's, the university church. He was considered the ablest and most influential preacher of Oxford and the greatest genius of his time. He became a leader of the Anglo-Catholic movement, a force within the Protestant church of England in favor of moving the church back into the arms of Rome.

In October 1845, halfway through his life, he decided to seek reconciliation with Rome, which he called "the one and only fold of the Redeemer." He shut himself up to vigils and fastings, living in utter isolation, then took the plunge. Nearly 250 clergy of the Church of England followed him into apostasy. In 1847 he was ordained a priest of Rome. He was given a doctorate and eventually was made a cardinal. Newman, who had authored the well-known hymn, "Lead, Kindly Light," abandoned the "kindly light" in favor of "the encircling gloom." He took the "way that seemeth right unto a man; but the end thereof are the ways of death."

About the same time Father Chiniquy—who had spent fifty years in the Church of Rome, half of them as a priest—saw the kindly light and left the Roman church. He brought more than six thousand French Canadian Catholics with him to the United States. What a contrast! Chiniquy brought thousands into "the light of the knowledge of the glory of God" (2 Corinthians 4:6), and Newman led thousands into the darkness and bondage of Rome.

When Newman was an old man, he made a secret pilgrimage to the modest cottage at Littlemore where he had made his wretched choice. Then he walked over to the church. The curate spotted Newman, "an old man, very poorly dressed, in an old gray coat with the collar turned up, leaning over the gate in floods of tears." Moreover the curate recognized him and asked if he could be of any help. "Oh, no, no," Newman replied. "Oh, no, no!" When the curate insisted, he received the same reply: "Oh, no, no, oh, no, no!" Having chosen "the ways of death," he was beyond all human help.

In the next proverb Solomon pointed to the road *where appetites beckon:* "He that laboureth laboureth for himself; for his mouth craveth it of him" (Proverbs 16:26). It is in our own self-interest to work, even if we just earn enough to buy something to eat.

In the Bible the work ethic is never demeaned; it is demanded. Even in the garden of Eden before the fall, God gave Adam work to do. The Biblical work ethic is that if a man refuses to work, he should be left to starve (2 Thessalonians 3:10). In Old Testament days, Israel had a social security system, but it was solidly based on work. Society was not obliged to provide free handouts for the indigent, but it was required to make sure work was available.

Economists of the past failed to realize that most people would much rather work than beg. The economists did not see "labor" as a body of individual men and women with needs and rights. Rather they viewed "labor" as a statistic, an abstraction, a commodity that the capitalist could use according to the law of supply and demand. The Bible never condones that perspective.

C. S. Lewis commented on such economics in *That Hideous Strength,* the third volume of his space trilogy. Mark Studdock was being drawn into the clutches of NICE, the fledgling new world order—a conglomerate of government, science, and the occult—that was engulfing Britain and the world. Mark was taken to a job by a man named Cosser, a fussy little bureaucrat with a sociology degree. NICE had plans to divert a local river, which in turn meant wiping out a picturesque little village called Cure Hardy. Mark did not much like the idea of destroying a beauty spot, but Cosser had no such compunction. "If it's a beauty spot, you can bet it's unsanitary," was his comment. He spoke disparagingly of renters and agricultural laborers, frowned on by NICE for being a "recalcitrant element in a planned community," and "always backward."

As they walked about the village Mark could not help noticing how interesting was the face of the "backward laborer"—much more interesting than the face of his fussy colleague. Mark's training in sociology, however, helped him overcome such thoughts and feelings. Statistics about agricultural laborers were what mattered to him. The numbers were the substance, the reality. The man who dug ditches or guided the plow or milked the cows did not matter. People were only shadows. Mark's training taught him to suspect such words as *man, woman, boy,* or *girl.* He envisioned *vocational groups, classes, elements in society,* and *populations.*

The Bible is never so foolish. It never sneers at people. They may be poor, they may be lazy, they may be sick, or they may even be wicked, but they are people with hopes, fears, needs, and potentials. The least and the worst are of such infinite worth that God loves them, Christ died for them, and the Holy Spirit seeks them out one by one to speak to them. Each one is a special individual, known and loved by God.

A working man may not have much ambition, he may not like what he does, and he may not be very good at it, but at least he works. God expects everyone to work unless he or she is incapacitated and unable to work. In keeping with this work ethic, rabbis were expected to support themselves by secular employment. Even scions of influential families were taught a trade. And Paul, who evidently was from a well-to-do family, learned tentmaking—a trade he plied from time to time even when evangelizing a great city such as Corinth.

3. The Sinful Path (16:27-30)

a. Beware of the Dangerous Sinner (16:27)

"An ungodly man diggeth up evil: and in his lips there is as a burning fire." This is the principle behind all blackmail. Get something on someone; then make him pay. It is bad enough to have a guilty secret. It is worse when someone else knows the secret, and it is insufferable when the person who knows uses that knowledge as a weapon. However it is far worse to be the blackmailer, for the Holy Spirit labels him "an ungodly man."

We can sympathize with Joe Sellon, the village constable in Dorothy Sayers' mystery, *Busman's Honeymoon.* The investigation of the murder of the wretched Mr. Noakes revealed that the constable had been at the scene of the crime at what appeared to be the crucial time and he had had angry words with the victim. So the whole story had to come out. Although the constable had not murdered Noakes, he certainly had a motive. Noakes had been blackmailing Sellon for five shillings a week for two years, a considerable drain on the unfortunate policeman's weekly pay. He had a sickly wife, a child, and another on the way, and on the night of the murder he had come to tell his blackmailer he couldn't pay that week's tribute. Noakes in turn had threatened to expose the constable, even though poor Joe Sellon's offense was trifling compared with the sin of blackmail. Truly, some sinners are dangerous.

b. Beware of the Deceitful Sinner (16:28)

"A froward man soweth strife: and a whisperer separateth chief friends."

Ziba is an example of a deceitful sinner. As a servant of King Saul, Ziba had seemingly used his position to improve his own lot. He became the father of a large family and acquired slaves of his own. When David adopted Mephibosheth (Jonathan's son) and gave him a place of honor at his table, he ordered Ziba and his entire household to work for Mephibosheth and to cultivate his fields. (See 2 Samuel 9:9-12.)

That assignment did not sit well with Ziba, who had his own ambitions. He bided his time, nursing his resentments until Absalom's rebellion erupted. Then Ziba abandoned the helpless Mephibosheth, who was crippled and unable to fend for himself. Ziba loaded a couple of asses with provisions for the king and hastened to David to tell him an absurd story about Mephibosheth and to assure David of his own loyalty. "Mephibosheth," Ziba said in effect, "is delighted at the course events are taking. He is confident that as a result of this crisis he will be seated on the throne of his grandfather Saul." (See 2 Samuel 16:1-4.) "A froward man soweth strife: and a whisperer separateth chief friends," said Solomon, possibly with this incident in mind.

Ziba's "news" meant more trouble and complications for David. He acted hastily. Without investigating Ziba's story, he arbitrarily transferred the title of Mephibosheth's estate to Ziba. From that day on the king harbored suspicions of Mephibosheth, the grateful son of David's chief friend Jonathan.

After Absalom died, Mephibosheth went to meet David. Mephibosheth must have looked pathetic, for he had deliberately neglected his personal appearance as a token of his grief for what had happened to his king. David, in his eyes, was a veritable angel of God. Mephibosheth explained to the king that Ziba had double-crossed him. (See 2 Samuel 19:24-28.)

David was now on the horns of a dilemma. Having just seen Ziba in the company of the despicable scoundrel Shimei (2 Samuel 19:16-17), the king was doubtless having second thoughts about his hasty decision regarding Mephibosheth's estate. However David could not afford to offend the Benjamite faction to which both Ziba and Shimei belonged, so the king treated Mephibosheth shabbily. "Thou and Ziba divide the land," David snapped (19:29). Mephibosheth at once put David to shame. "Let him take all," he said, "forasmuch as my lord the king is come again in peace unto his own house" (19:30).

This is one of the few shabby incidents in the life of David. We expect better things of him but in this time of continuing national crisis he had to tread warily with Ziba, who was supported by a thousand men of Benjamin and sharp-tongued Shimei as well. Ziba did great damage to the beautiful relationship between David and Mephibosheth. And by bringing out the worst in David, Ziba also did great damage to an almost perfect type of Christ and proved Solomon's proverb to be true.

c. Beware of the Destructive Sinner (16:29-30)

Beware of *his pleas,* wrote Solomon: "A violent man enticeth his neighbour, and leadeth him into the way that is not good" (Proverbs 16:29).

Consider again the case of kings Ahab of Israel and Jehoshaphat of Judah. Although Ahab was a violent man married to an even more violent woman, Jehoshaphat apparently became infatuated with them during his first state visit to their court. Jezebel, a raw pagan and Zidonian princess, was untroubled by the religious scruples that restrained a man like Jehoshaphat. She dressed to her advantage and had a pagan's skill in using cosmetics to enhance her looks. Her religion broke down all prohibitions and inhibitions and she was a daring and dangerous woman.

Jehoshaphat felt her fascination and could see that Ahab was completely under her thumb. Jehoshaphat must have felt like a country bumpkin in their court. So he offered little resistance when Ahab suggested a joint Judeo-Ephraimitic expedition to retake Ramoth-gilead from the Syrians. Step by step Jehoshaphat was lured into a dangerous and undesirable situation by his violent neighbor.

Then came the oddest suggestion of all: Jehoshaphat was asked to dress himself in Ahab's royal robes and pose as the leader of the expedition. Ahab would put on ordinary armor and go into battle in the guise of a common soldier. There was every reason to refuse such a masquerade, but perhaps the mocking, scornful eye of Jezebel robbed Jehoshaphat of even the most ordinary common sense. Too late he discovered that the Syrian king had issued orders for Ahab to be killed at all costs.

Enticed into another man's battle and wearing that other man's clothes, the Judean king barely escaped with his life (1 Kings 22:1-38; 2 Chronicles 18:1-34). Shaken and sorry, he returned to Judah. There the prophet Jehu soundly rebuked him for having fraternized with and succumbed to the pleas of such a wicked, deceitful, and violent man as Ahab.

Solomon said we are to beware of the destructive sinner's pleas and *his plots:* "He shutteth his eyes to devise froward things: moving his lips he bringeth evil to pass" (Proverbs 16:30). The godly man shuts his eyes to blot out distractions when he prays; he moves his lips to present his petitions before the throne of grace. The ungodly man shuts his eyes when he plots. He closes his eyes to concentrate on some diabolical scheme he wants to hatch. Then when the plan is all worked out in his mind, he calls his henchmen, gives them detailed instructions, and orders them into action. The wickedness that proceeds from such deliberate, premeditated thought is usually far worse than that which arises from a sudden fit of temper or a hasty word.

Wickedness proceeded from the communists' plots, so Marx, Engels, and Lenin illustrate Proverbs 16:30. For most of the years that Lenin worked in the Kremlin a bronze statue of an ape stood on his desk. The ape, which was about ten inches high, squatted on a heap of books and gazed with an expression of bewilderment and dismay at an oversize human skull. The skull gazed back at the ape. The ape was thoroughly bestial, with a small head, massive shoulders, and long dangling arms. The human skull, with gaping mouth and empty eye sockets, was even less attractive.

Lenin liked the statue. On the wall of his room, across from the statue, was a large photograph of his other idol, the apostate Jew Karl Marx. Karl Marx was the heir and successor of Charles Darwin, who believed that man descended from the ape. Well might that ape gaze quizzically at that human skull. No ape ever conceived the cold-blooded, calculated wickedness born in Marx's brilliant brain and translated into a system of tyranny by Lenin and his heirs. No ape ever conceived the God-hate and wickedness devised by the communists. Neither did any ape ever conceive the rampage of the capitalists whose reckless drive for wealth left the debris from which Marx and Engels drew much of their inspiration. Only fallen man can plan and deliberately execute wickedness.

4. The Successful Path (16:31-33)

Turning his attention away from the sinful path, Solomon pointed first to *the path of mature virtue:* "The hoary head is a crown of glory, if it be found in the way of righteousness" (Proverbs 16:31).

Not just any hoary head is a crown of glory. For instance, David warned Solomon against venerable and distinguished Joab, whose hoary head covered a life of wickedness. "Let not his hoar head go down to the grave in peace," David said (1 Kings 2:6).

In contrast to Joab, in old age Joseph was "found in the way of righteousness." He was 110 years old and ready to die, having ruled an empire and lived in pomp and power for some eighty years. All that Egypt had to offer was his. He could have commissioned a tomb to be built for himself in one of the great burial grounds of Egypt. The whole land had been beneath his feet. He had been lord of the land when as pharaoh's grand vizier all knees were made to bow before him. He had served Egypt's king, studied its religion, seen its riches, and scorned its pleasures. Through all his sojourn—from Potiphar's house to the prison to the palace—Joseph had remained true to the God of Abraham, Isaac, and Jacob.

Now Joseph was about to die. His hoary head was a crown of glory because he had walked in the way of righteousness. His last word and final act summarized his sterling faith in God. "God will surely visit you," he said, "and ye shall carry up my bones from hence" (Genesis 50:25). He warned his brothers not to put him in a tomb in Egypt. His heart was set on burial in Canaan, where he had lived by faith ever since his teens when the slave traders had carried him off to Egypt. The Holy Spirit mentioned this crowning demonstration of Joseph's faith in Hebrews 11:22.

Solomon next pointed to *the path of moral victory:* "He that is slow to anger is better than the mighty; and he that ruleth his spirit than he that taketh a city" (Proverbs 16:32). The comparison in this proverb reminds us of Joab and David. Joab could easily be provoked; David was slow to anger.

Joab knew how to take a city. Indeed he earned his rank of commander-in-chief of David's armed forces by taking the Jebusite fortress. At the time of the exodus the Jebusites were one of the mountain tribes of Canaan (Numbers 13:29; Joshua 11:3). They dwelled at Jebus (Jerusalem). Their king was slain by Joshua (Joshua 10:23-26) and their territory was assigned by lot to Benjamin. The Jebusites however were a tough crowd and difficult to conquer. The warriors of Judah took the chief city of the Jebusites and set it on fire (Joshua 15:8; Judges 1:8), but the actual citadel remained intact and in Jebusite hands. King Saul, a Benjamite with a vested interest in subduing the Jebusite fortress, made no attempt to do so. David however was determined to take it.

Mocking at David's troops, the Jebusites boasted that they could hold the fortress with their blind and lame. David passed on the challenge to his men by offering the job of commander-in-chief to the one who could capture the fort. Joab accepted the challenge and led a group of men up a rock-hewn passage or shaft through which the Jebusites drew their water supply from the upper Gihon. (See 2 Samuel 5:6-9; 1 Chronicles 11:5-8.) Joab knew how to take a city.

David, on the other hand, knew how to rule his spirit. He schooled his tongue to give soft answers that turn away wrath. He learned self-control in the countryside, in the court, and in the cave.

He learned self-control in the countryside when as a shepherd boy he had to face a lion and a bear. He demonstrated self-control at Elah when his brothers sneered at him and told him to go home, even though they knew he was the Lord's anointed. He showed self-control when he faced Goliath alone. David learned to rule his spirit in the court when Saul eyed him maliciously and murderously. The self-control David learned in the cave enabled him to sidestep many a snare in the years he fled from Saul as an outlaw with a price on his head. David showed self-control twice in his treatment of Saul when the king was in his power. David learned his lesson afresh during the Absalom rebellion and showed his self-control anew when foulmouthed Shimei cursed him to his face.

David was greater, far greater, than the man who could take a city. It is more of an accomplishment to write a Twenty-third Psalm than to take a thousand Jerusalems.

Finally Solomon wrote of *the path of mystic vision:* "The lot is cast into the lap; but the whole disposing thereof [its every decision] is of the Lord" (Proverbs 16:33). This proverb refers to the pocket of the ephod in which the urim and thummim were kept. These were the two stones by which the Lord gave true judgment and guidance in Old Testament times (Exodus 28:30). The two stones, carried in a pocket in the high priest's vestment, were probably precious stones. The stone drawn out would give the judicial decision. *Urim* and *thummim,* meaning "light" and "perfection," are examples of metonymy and actually refer to "that which was brought to light" and "moral perfection (namely the innocence of an accused party)."

We see the Lord sovereignly overruling the way the land was divided among the tribes and families of Israel. He controlled the division by lot. The high priest Eleazar, who had the urim and thummim, had to be present for the lot to reveal God's will and give Jehovah's decision regarding the division of Canaan (Numbers 26:55; 34:17; Joshua 17:4).

After King Saul in a fit of murderous rage slew Ahimelech the priest and the entire priestly colony at Nob, Abiathar escaped and fled to David (1 Samuel 22:20). Abiathar "came down with an ephod in his hand" (23:6). Presumably he brought the urim and thummim with him, for soon afterward David inquired of the Lord as though he had access to the sacred stones. He wanted to know if he should venture to Keilah where a Philistine army was besieging the city and if the Lord would deliver the Philistines into his hands. The Lord told him to go. David won a resounding victory at Keilah and was warmly received by its citizens.

Saul heard about that victory and thought he had David trapped in Keilah. However David summoned Abiathar, told him to bring the ephod, and posed two questions: Will Saul come down to Keilah? Will the men of Keilah betray me? The specific answer was yes to both questions. David sensibly left Keilah and headed again for the hills.

After the Babylonian captivity no judgment could be given unless the high priest was present with his urim and thummim, which gave the Lord's verdict of guilty or innocent, or the Lord's answer of yes or no (Ezra 2:63; Nehemiah 7:65).

In New Testament times we do not need to cast lots. We have a completed Bible and an indwelling Holy Spirit and do not need the mechanical guiding aids that were necessary in the kindergarten stages of God's dealings with His people.

CHAPTER 21

Proverbs 17:1-28

The comparison of the life of the godly and the life of the ungodly continues. We have seen the right focus in life—the emphasis is on the Lord. Now we will see the right features in life: contentment and character.

II. THE RIGHT FEATURES IN LIFE (17:1–19:5)

A. How to Build Contentment (17:1-28)

1. Peace (17:1)

Said Solomon: "Better is a dry morsel, and quietness therewith, than an house full of sacrifices with strife." The word rendered "sacrifices" is *zebach*, which can be translated "slain beasts." Nowadays we would paraphrase "an house full of sacrifices" as "a freezer full of meat." We instinctively feel that Solomon was right. Peace and quietness in the home is better than all kinds of material possessions in a house where every mealtime is spoiled by constant wrangling. Solomon knew what he was talking about. He had a houseful of wrangling women.

I once addressed a weekly devotional service conducted for five hundred women students at Moody Bible Institute. When the service was over and the students were dismissed to their classes, I watched all those young women leave the auditorium with the usual babel of voices that accompanies the breakup of any such gathering. I thought to myself, *Wow! And Solomon had twice as many to keep happy!*

We can well believe that his palace was a pandemonium of jealousy, rivalry, squabbling, and petty spite. Of all the fools who ever lived, Solomon—in his personal life—must have been one of the greatest.

His *Song of Solomon* is about the only girl he couldn't have. She turned him down cold. Having met her in the countryside, he arranged for her to be brought to his pavilion and kept for a while as a virtual prisoner. Solomon tried every approach he could think of to persuade her to marry him, but she had more sense than to consent. Moreover she was engaged to another man. She compared her beloved shepherd's simplicity and sincerity with Solomon's pride, power, and pomp, and had no trouble deciding which offer to accept. She loved her shepherd and would rather sit with him under an apple tree than feast in Solomon's banqueting house and share his sensual favors with hundreds of other women.

When offering the Shulamite his oft-held hand in marriage, Solomon boasted with singular blindness, "There are threescore queens, and fourscore concubines, and virgins without number." Then he added in effect, "You can be first" (Song of Solomon 6:8-9). She turned him down, but that only made her more desirable and him more determined. It was an uneven contest from the start. The Shulamite held all the moral and spiritual resources. The account of how she resisted the lustful king's advances is one of the great stories of the Old Testament.[1]

Solomon must have written about the Shulamite with tears in his eyes and great sorrow in his soul. She had taught him a terrible lesson. He had traded love for lust. Now he had a palace full of women—good, bad, and indifferent—and an empty heart. He had an enormous and expanding harem and the haunting memory of one pure and godly woman who could have brought heaven into his home. He gladly would have traded his plenty for her poverty, but the gates of that particular paradise were closed to him forever.

2. Promotion (17:2)

"A wise servant shall have rule over a son that causeth shame, and shall have part of the inheritance among the brethren." Solomon had to face this reality in his own house.

He had a wise servant named Jeroboam, an Ephraimite. His mother had been widowed before the boy was born. However, he was destined for success in life and was made stronger, more competitive, more diligent, and more eager to get on in the world as a result of overcoming early handicaps. Solomon spotted him as he worked on one of the building enterprises underway in Jerusalem. The king saw that Jeroboam was an energetic, capable young man and put him in charge of all the heavy work assigned to the house of Joseph (1 Kings 11:27-28).

Attentive to business and wise beyond his years, Jeroboam forged ahead. We can be sure the king had more than an occasional twinge of regret as he watched Jeroboam's progress, for Solomon's heir was a son that caused him shame. We cannot help wondering if Solomon at times wished that Jeroboam were his son, not Rehoboam. We can at least be sure that Solomon often wished that Rehoboam had half the wisdom, zeal, and talent of the widow's son.

In the end Rehoboam lost out to Jeroboam, who took ten of the twelve tribes away from him. Jeroboam received not only part of the inheritance, but the lion's share, in spite of Solomon's efforts to prevent such an outcome.

3. Punishment (17:3-5)

As the smith turns up the heat to rid precious metals of their dross and increase their value, so *the Lord* brings trials and testings into our lives to get rid of our dross: "The fining pot is for silver, and the furnace for gold: but the Lord trieth the hearts" (Proverbs 17:3).

The Lord meted out punishment on a grand scale to rid the ancient Israelites of their dross. From the time they made the golden calf in the wilderness, the Hebrews showed a marked propensity toward idolatry. An entire generation had been raised in the land of Egypt, where they had been surrounded by people who prayed to images of birds, dogs, cats, and even beetles. The swift and certain judgment that followed the making of the golden calf was intended to teach the Israelites the seriousness of the sin of idolatry, which had been expressly forbidden in the second commandment.

In Canaan the Israelites became even more idolatrous, running after the vile idols of the accursed inhabitants of the land. Solomon in his old age put the imprimatur of his approval on idolatrous practices, and nothing but God's refining fire could get rid of this dross. First He allowed the Assyrians to deport ten of the tribes and ravage the two that remained. The Israelites still did not learn their lesson, so He allowed the Babylonians to impose a seventy-year captivity on the people. The Israelites were deported to Babylon, the home of idolatry. There the accursed practice was burned out of the Hebrew soul. The remnant that returned to the promised land certainly committed other sins, but they forswore idolatry.

Strange to say, in a coming day at least part of the nation of Israel will return to idolatry. Israel will fall into the hands of the antichrist, who will put his image in the rebuilt temple and command that it be universally worshiped. Many Jews and Gentiles will be so terrified of the antichrist's horrendous threats that they will comply. This final lapse will be burned out of the nation of Israel in the fires of the great tribulation.

The next proverb draws our attention to *the liar,* who is always punished sooner or later for his untruth: "A wicked doer giveth heed to false lips; and a liar giveth ear to a naughty tongue" (Proverbs 17:4). A liar is always ready to believe a lie. Sometimes a liar even believes his own lies.

The history of Mormonism illustrates this proverb. Joseph Smith, the founder of Mormonism, was born in Sharon, Vermont, on December 23, 1805. His father spent much of his time digging for buried treasure, hoping to unearth Captain Kidd's legendary hoard. In 1820 God the Father and God the Son are supposed to have appeared to Joseph to tell him that he had been chosen to usher in a new dispensation. Soon afterward, however, Joseph was back with his father, digging anew for Captain Kidd's loot.

In 1823 Joseph supposedly had a visit from an angel he called Moroni—although later he said the heavenly messenger was Nephi. The confusion regarding the angel's name seemed to make little difference. Once a lie takes root, it boldly affirms its dogmas regardless of inconsistencies.

In 1827 the would-be prophet claimed to have received some golden plates on which *The Book of Mormon* was written. He supposedly found these plates in the hill named Cumorah near Palmyra, New York. The book was written in "reformed Egyptian"—a nonexistent language. Thanks to the thoughtful provision of a magic egg-shaped stone, he was able to translate the hieroglyphics into King James English. He dictated the book to Oliver Cowdery, an itinerant schoolteacher who never actually saw the plates. On May 15, 1829, Peter, James, and John sent John the Baptist from Heaven to confer the Aaronic priesthood on Joseph and Oliver—at least that is what the dubious pair declared. In 1830 *The Book of Mormon* was published and copyrighted. The same year Joseph and his brother Hyrum, along with Oliver Cowdery and a couple of others, founded the Church of Jesus Christ of Latter-Day Saints.

Before long the Mormons, as they were called, commonly practiced polygamy. Between 1831 and 1844 Joseph Smith issued 135 "revelations," including one on polygamy.[2] Smith not only urged the Mormons to practice polygamy; he said that the penalty for abstaining was eternal damnation. In 1842 *The Nauvoo Expositor* exposed the practice. Subsequently its offices were wrecked and the Smith brothers were incarcerated in Carthage, Illinois. While they waited in jail to be tried for their part in this reprisal, they were murdered by a crowd of some two hundred angry citizens.

The beginnings of Mormonism were unsavory and its subsequent history was not much better. Brigham Young took over leadership of the cult and established Mormonism as a bona fide religion. A zealous polygamist, he was also a violent and ruthless leader. Although it is based on lies and deceptions, Mormonism has grown to be a powerful religious system of vast wealth and great power. Its doctrinal aberrations include the teaching that the Lord Jesus was a polygamist and the belief that faithful Mormons can eventually become gods themselves.[3] They are an outstanding example of the truth of Proverbs 17:4.

Proverbs 17:5 draws our attention to *the laugh:* "Whoso mocketh the poor reproacheth his Maker: and he that is glad at calamities shall not be unpunished." The classic Biblical example of this proverb is Edom. Israel and Edom, the nations descended from Esau and Jacob, were neighbors and bitter enemies. The hostility between the two nations began when the Edomites refused to allow the Israelites to pass through their territory on their march to Canaan. Later Saul, David, and other Hebrew kings warred with Edom.

When the Babylonians invaded Judah and captured Jerusalem, the Edomites rejoiced (Psalm 137:7). They rubbed their hands with glee. They even seized fleeing Jews and handed them over to the Babylonians. When the Jews' captivity in Babylon rendered their land destitute and vulnerable, the Edomites seized it as far as Hebron. Various Old Testament prophets, particularly Obadiah, foretold the doom of Edom because the Edomites rejoiced over the calamities of Judah (Obadiah 10-16).

The Edomites occupied a rugged mountainous region near the southern part of the Dead Sea. They were a tough race and thought their stronghold of Petra (Mount Seir) with its jutting crags and narrow passages was invulnerable. But God is not intimidated by mountain passes, however precipitous they may be. After all, He made them! The Edomites, who were glad at Israel's calamities, tasted the bitterness of defeat.

4. Priorities (17:6-9)

a. The Priorities of Fathers (17:6)

"Children's children are the crown of old men; and the glory of children are their fathers." Here Solomon gave us a picture of a stable family. We see an aging grandfather delighting in his children's children and a son glorying in his father. Such a picture is becoming increasingly rare in western society.

It is no accident that God performed the first wedding as recorded in Genesis 2 and that the remainder of Genesis is firmly family-oriented. It traces the fortunes of Adam's children, particularly the remarkable father-son-grandson-greatgrandson line running down the centuries from Seth to Noah. That stable and solid family line preserved all that was good and godly in the world. All that was evil stemmed from the line of Cain. In Cainite society there was a growing breakdown of the family. Women became increasingly prominent, polygamy was an accepted lifestyle, and traditional family values were no longer cherished.

After the flood, Genesis concentrates on Abraham and his family. We read of Abraham's close ties to his father—ties that only death could break. We read of Abraham as a son, an uncle, a father, and a grandfather. Genesis traces his line as one generation succeeded another. Abraham died and was buried by his sons Isaac and Ishmael (25:9). Then Isaac was "gathered unto his people, being old and full of days." He was buried by his sons Jacob and Esau (35:29). After bringing Ephraim and Manasseh into the direct patriarchal line, Jacob died surrounded by his sons (49:1-33).

Genesis, the foundational book of the Bible, is all about the family: births, marriages, deaths, fathers, sons, and grandchildren. Our culture has lost sight of the importance of the family. We have "no-fault" divorce, common-law liaisons, broken homes, children unsupervised while both parents work, careless fathers, scattered families, old people left to the "tender mercies" of a welfare state, and a society degenerating into chaos. Many people have long since forgotten and pushed aside Proverbs 17:6.

b. The Priorities of Fools (17:7-8)

Turning our attention to fools, Solomon wrote of *their foolish words:* "Excellent speech becometh not a fool: much less do lying lips a prince" (Proverbs 17:7). We don't expect much wisdom to come out of the mouth of a fool. If he happens to say something significant, he is probably parroting something someone else said. In a few minutes the effect will be spoiled by what he says next.

Although the illustration is not exactly parallel, consider what happened at Ascot in *My Fair Lady*.[4] The story revolves around Professor Higgins, an irascible teacher of phonetics, and his efforts to turn Eliza Doolittle into a lady. He and his friend Pickering encountered Eliza selling flowers and making her pitch in a raw, cutting, cockney accent. The challenge to the gentlemen was to eradicate her fearful cockney dialect and replace it with a cultured Oxford accent and the poise, deportment, and manners of polite society.

After Eliza had thoroughly mastered the phonetics as well as the airs and graces of England's polished upper crust, the two men decided to introduce their protégé into the life of high society at Ascot, the famous annual horse race frequented by the aristocracy. Eliza arrived, escorted by Pickering and dressed to perfection. Higgins introduced her to his mother and some of her snobbish upper-class friends. Eliza carried herself with poise and dignity. Her "How do you do? How kind of you to let me come" was an excellent start. Professor Higgins congratulated himself.

A young man in immaculate attire was smitten by Eliza's good looks and charm. He told her about the first race and expressed his regret that she had missed it. Unprepared for this comment, Eliza replied in polished, flawless style, "The rain in Spain stays mainly in the plain." The number of blank stares increased when she added, "But in Hertford, Hereford and Hampshire hurricanes hardly ever happen." Her diction was absolutely flawless but her response was wholly foolish in content.

Higgins' mother tried to save the situation by blurting out something about inclement weather and the flu epidemic. In beautiful accents Eliza remarked, "My aunt died of influenza, so they said. But it's my belief they done the old woman in." Eyebrows were raised, but unaware that she had said anything wrong and rejoicing in being the center of attention, Eliza continued in a perfect Oxford accent, "And what become of her new straw hat that should have come to me?" She looked around her with a sophisticated air, her glance sweeping her paralyzed audience. "Somebody pinched it. And what I say is, them that pinched it, done her in."

As Higgins and Pickering were hurrying her away, another race was about to be run. A horse named Dover took Eliza's fancy. Surrounded by high and cultured society, the elegant and gorgeously attired Eliza urged on her favorite: "Come on, come on, Dover! Come on, come on, Dover!" When at the climax Dover

lagged behind, she reverted to her old self. Quite engrossed in the
race and quite oblivious to her elegant surroundings, she uttered
a vulgar gutter expression in coarse and ear-assailing broad cockney.

What poor Eliza Doolittle did, the fool does. He may acquire a
measure of outward polish and he may have a measure of innate wit
and personal charm, but what he truly is will be exposed the
moment he steps beyond the area where he has been schooled.
Both a born fool and a lying prince eventually betray themselves.

Eliza recovered after the professor taught her to think like a lady
as well as talk like one. There is hope for a fool and a lying prince
too if they each experience a complete change of heart.

Solomon next wrote of fools and *their false wealth:* "A gift is as a
precious stone in the eyes of him that hath it: whithersoever it
turneth, it prospereth" (Proverbs 17:8). The word translated
"prospereth" can also be rendered "sparkles." Here we have a
picture of a man who has just received a bribe. He thinks he has a
treasure and he is gloating over his ill-gotten gain. What he doesn't
know is that the flashing diamond he is turning this way and that in
order to admire its beauty is a worthless fake. Neither does he know
that the living God is watching him. As a jeweler displays a diamond
against a piece of black velvet, so God views that sparkling bribe
against the blackness of the culprit's heart.

Indulgences sold by the Roman church are nothing but religious
bribes. For so much silver that church will exempt its patrons from
punishment for so much sin. The invention of purgatory made it
possible for an unconscionable religious system to fleece its gullible
public wholesale. Catholicism postulates that purgatory (which is
foreign to Scripture) is an in-between stage between Heaven and
Hell. Souls can be assigned to this place of fire and punishment
until they accumulate enough merit to get out of purgatory and
into Heaven. Since they have difficulty acquiring merit after they
are dead, their loved ones can pay priests to say masses for the souls
of the dead to ease them on their way. Or even better for the system,
people can pay in advance. An indulgent papacy will sell merit on
the pay-as-you-go system. The faithful can also earn indulgences by
going to Rome on a pilgrimage, for instance. Catholics used to be
able to buy indulgences for cold cash.

The sale of indulgences finally ignited the fires of the Reformation in the sixteenth century. Leo the Tenth, the third son of
Lorenzo de Medici, donned the regalia of the papacy in 1513. He
needed a lot of money because, among other reasons, Michelangelo
had just given him the finished design for St. Peter's. A papal

jubilee could be an enormously successful moneymaker, but it wasn't time for another one yet and Leo needed money now.

Leo the Tenth, who came from an illustrious family, had a reputation for learning and a considerable fund of talent, polish, and flair. He was an immoral man and his court was pleasure loving and careless of religious duties. But Leo was an improvement over some of his predecessors (the dissolute Alexander VI and the wild warrior pope Julius II, who plunged much of Europe into war). All Leo wanted was money. Historian Andrew Miller wrote:

> To meet the various and heavy expenses of the extravagant Leo, the cry for money became louder and louder. "Money! money!" was the cry. "It was money," says one, "not charity, that covered a multitude of sins." Necessity suggested that the price of indulgences should be lowered, and that clever salesmen should be employed to push the trade all over Europe. The plan was adopted; but God overruled the shameless traffic for the accomplishment of the Reformation, and for the overthrow of the despotism of Rome. Germany, it was agreed, should be the first and especially favoured place with the sale of indulgences, as the geographical position of the country might have prevented many of the faithful from reaping the advantages of the Jubilee in Rome.

The original idea of indulgences seems to have been nothing more than a shortening of a penance in exchange for the payment of a fine. The practice is common in our courts of law where judges can say, "Fined five thousand dollars or six months in prison." Miller said:

> In like manner the poor deluded Papist supposes that the indulgence which he buys is placed to his credit in the statute-book of Heaven, which balances the account against him for lies, slanders, robberies, murders, and wickedness of all kinds; or, as some have compared it, to a letter of credit on Heaven, signed by the Pope, in consideration of value received. Of course, if the delinquent's sins are great and many, he must pay heavily for his indulgences.

The Vatican's super salesman was John Tetzel, who arrived, at length, at Wittenberg. Here is a sample of his salesmanship as he hawked his fraudulent wares from town to town: "Indulgences are the most precious and the most noble of God's gifts. Come, and I will give you letters, all properly sealed, by which even the sins that you intend to commit are pardoned. I would not change my privileges for those of St. Peter in Heaven, for I have saved more souls by my indulgences than the apostle by his sermons. There is no sin so great that an indulgence cannot remit. But, more than this, indulgences avail not only for the living but for the dead. Priest! noble! merchant! wife! youth! maiden! do you not hear your parents and your other friends who are dead, and who cry from the bottom of the abyss. We are suffering horrible torments! A trifling alms would deliver us; you can give it, and you will not! Oh, stupid and brutish people, who do not understand the grace so richly offered! Why, the very instant your money rattles at the bottom of the chest, the soul escapes from Purgatory, and flies liberated to Heaven. The Lord our God no longer reigns, He has resigned all power to the Pope."

The wild harangue of the coarse bellowing monk being over, the terrified and superstitious crowd hastened to purchase the pardon of their sins and the deliverance of their friends from the fires of Purgatory. From the royal family down to those who lived on alms, all found money to buy forgiveness. Money poured in plentifully; the Papal chest overflowed; but alas! alas! the moral effects were fearful. The easy terms on which men could obtain the Pope's license for every species of wickedness opened the way to the grossest immorality, and insubjection to all authority. Even Tetzel himself was convicted of adultery and infamous conduct at Innsbruck, and sentenced by the Emperor Maximilian to be put into a sack and thrown into the river; but the Elector Frederick of Saxony interfered, and obtained his pardon. The unblushing Dominican proceeded on his way as the representative of his holiness the Pope, just as if nothing had happened.[5]

This was bribery and corruption of the most blatant kind. The ecstatic pope rubbed his hands and gloated, and the golden hoard gleamed and glittered all the way to the bank. He was quite heedless of Solomon's exposure of his sin.

c. The Priorities of Friends (17:9)

"He that covereth a transgression seeketh love; but he that repeateth a matter separateth very [true] friends." Mark Twain gave us the classic example of this proverb.

Tom Sawyer, angling for the affection of Becky Thatcher,

persuaded Becky to become his girlfriend. Then inadvertently he let slip the damning information that he had been down this path before with Amy Lawrence. A tiff followed and then a period of estrangement. After the incident in which Tom and his pals attended their own funeral and achieved notoriety, Becky tried to get back in Tom's good graces but Tom, determined to get even, flirted openly with Amy Lawrence. Becky sought revenge by flirting with Alfred Temple. Finally it dawned on Alfred he was being used. Feeling humiliated and angry, he poured ink over Tom's spelling book. Becky, glancing through the window, saw him do it and debated with herself whether she should reveal what she saw or let things take their course.

About this time Becky herself landed in trouble. Mr. Dobbins, the schoolmaster, kept a mysterious book locked in his desk. Like everyone else, Becky was wildly curious about that book. One day the master inadvertently left the key to his desk in the lock. Becky was the only one in the classroom at the time and she thought this was her chance to peek at that book. She was turning its pages when Tom Sawyer entered the room. As she snatched at the book to close it, she had the hard luck to tear its colored frontispiece. About midafternoon the master opened the desk. Mark Twain wrote:

> Dobbins fingered his book absently for a while, then took it out and settled himself in his chair to read! Tom shot a glance at Becky. He had seen a hunted and helpless rabbit look as she did, with a gun leveled at its head. Instantly he forgot his quarrel with her. Quick—something must be done! done in a flash, too! But the very imminence of the emergency paralyzed his invention. Good!—He had an inspiration! He would run and snatch the book, spring through the door and fly. But his resolution shook for one little instant, and the chance was lost—the master opened the volume. If Tom only had the wasted opportunity back again! Too late. There was no help for Becky now, he said. The next moment the master faced the school. Every eye sank under his gaze. There was that in it which smote even the innocent with fear. There was silence while one might count ten, the master was gathering his wrath. Then he spoke:
>
> "Who tore this book?"
>
> There was not a sound. One could have heard a pin drop. The stillness continued; the master searched face after face for signs of guilt.
>
> "Benjamin Rogers, did you tear this book?"

A denial. Another pause.

"Joseph Harper, did you?"

Another denial. Tom's uneasiness grew more and more intense under the slow torture of these proceedings. The master scanned the ranks of boys—considered awhile, then turned to the girls:

"Amy Lawrence?"

A shake of the head.

"Gracie Miller?"

The same sign.

"Susan Harper, did you do this?"

Another negative. The next girl was Becky Thatcher. Tom was trembling from head to foot with excitement and a sense of the hopelessness of the situation.

"Rebecca Thatcher [Tom glanced at her face—it was white with terror] did you tear—no, look me in the face [her hands rose in appeal]—did you tear this book?"

A thought shot like lightning through Tom's brain. He sprang to his feet and shouted—*"I done it!"*

The school stared in perplexity at this incredible folly. Tom stood a moment, to gather his dismembered faculties; and when he stepped forward to go to his punishment the surprise, the gratitude, the adoration that shone upon him out of poor Becky's eyes seemed pay enough for a hundred floggings. Inspired by the splendor of his own act, he took without an outcry the most merciless flaying that even Mr. Dobbins had ever administered; and also received with indifference the added cruelty of a command to remain two hours after school should be dismissed—for he knew who would wait for him outside till his captivity was done, and not count the tedious time as loss, either.

Tom went to bed that night planning vengeance against Alfred Temple; for with shame and repentance Becky had told him all, not forgetting her own treachery; but even the longing for vengeance had to give way, soon, to pleasanter musings, and he fell asleep at last, with Becky's latest words lingering dreamily in his ear—

"Tom, how *could* you be so noble!"

5. Prudence (17:10)

"A reproof," wrote Solomon, "entereth more into a wise man than an hundred stripes into a fool." A wise man will get the point at once. "A word to the wise is sufficient," as we say. A wise man learns from his mistakes, accepts a word of admonition, bows to authority, and takes appropriate action. Not so a fool. Even if he is beaten black and blue, he'll go right back to his folly.

This proverb explains the essential difference between Abraham and Lot. Both had been down to Egypt. Abraham took the lead and set the pace but Lot was hard at his heels. In Egypt Abraham was out of the will of God and soon he was in deep trouble. His beloved Sarah was taken into pharaoh's palace to be groomed for the royal harem. Pharaoh, believing Abraham was her brother, showered him with presents. Abraham was beside himself with anxiety and self-recrimination. Lot rubbed his hands over the increase in their wealth. Then God stepped in. Abraham and Sarah were sent out of Egypt, covered with ignominy and shame. Abraham had learned a lesson.

Shortly afterward he and Lot parted because of squabbling by their herdsmen over the limited pastureland. Abraham gave Lot first choice and Lot chose the well-watered cities of the Jordan valley and the lush pastureland of the plain because it looked "like the land of Egypt" (Genesis 13:10). To Abraham that seemed like a good reason for *not* going there.

Then came the invasion, Lot's capture by the Mesopotamians, and his subsequent rescue by Abraham (Genesis 14). Again Lot had a choice. Would he stay with Abraham and cultivate the spiritual fellowship that Abraham had found at the table of Melchizedek, God's king-priest and the classic Old Testament type of Christ? Or would he go back with the vile king of Sodom to the filthy city, there to be promoted to a seat in the gate? One would expect Lot to choose Abraham, but Lot had not learned his lesson. A fool will not learn even if he is given a hundred stripes. Lot remained a fool to the very end. The last time we see him in the book of Genesis, he is drunk and disgraced on the blasted hills of the Dead Sea.

6. Principles (17:11-21)

a. The Question of Undermining Fundamentals (17:11-16)

Regarding *the unruly man* Solomon wrote: "An evil man seeketh only rebellion: therefore a cruel messenger shall be sent against him" (Proverbs 17:11).

The classic Biblical example of the unruly man is Absalom (2 Samuel 13–18). Although David tried to whitewash Absalom, Absalom was an evil man. Although David made excuses for Absalom and bitterly blamed himself for Absalom's behavior, Absalom was evil. Only an evil man could have done what Absalom did.

No doubt Absalom vocally justified the murder of his half brother Amnon. Amnon had violated Absalom's sister Tamar in a particularly sordid and inexcusable way. David refused to punish Amnon, so Absalom simply took the law into his own hands. After all, the law required the death penalty for such a crime.

No doubt Absalom also justified himself for setting fire to Joab's fields. How else could Absalom get the ear of the second most powerful man in the kingdom? With Joab blocking all the doors to David, how else could Absalom get through to David with a plea for pardon and an end to his exile?

No doubt Absalom justified his rebellion against David. After all, Absalom had been only half forgiven. He felt that he had lost his influence with his father. How else could he ever hope to be king?

No doubt Absalom justified the horrendous public crime he committed against David's secondary wives. Absalom assigned the blame to Ahithophel.

In spite of all his excuses and rationalizations, Absalom was evil and sought rebellion. Indeed Solomon might have had the Absalom rebellion in mind when he added Proverbs 17:11 to his collection.

David sent "a cruel messenger," but not until after he made a last-ditch attempt to get through to his son. David sent his dear friend Hushai to try to put some sense into the young rebel's head, but at no point in the subsequent discussions did Absalom show any sign of remorse, repentance, or willingness to lay down the arms of rebellion.

In the end David had no recourse but to send Joab against Absalom. Although David strictly warned his army that Absalom was to be handled with compassion, the king must have known in his heart of hearts that Absalom's death warrant had been signed the moment the desperate cause was entrusted to Joab, for Joab was "a cruel messenger." And sure enough, when Absalom became entangled in a tree and some of David's men, mindful of the king's command, spared him, Joab came along, coldbloodedly murdered Absalom, and thought the deed well done.

Regarding *the unthinking man* Solomon wrote: "Let a bear robbed of her whelps meet a man, rather than a fool in his folly" (Proverbs 17:12). An angry bear is a terrible animal to meet in the wilds of the Yukon or anywhere else!

Years ago when my wife and I lived in northern British Columbia, we used to entertain an annual visitor in our home. His name was Charles Bowen and he was a Christian gentleman of the highest character. We always looked forward to his visits because he was a delightful guest. He had great wisdom and a fund of stories from his pioneer missionary days in the Yukon.

One day when he was traveling north along the Alaska Highway, he came to a lonely wayside cabin. It was his policy to stop at all such isolated outposts to give a gospel witness and leave some literature. So he stopped his car and went up to the door. He introduced himself to the woman of the house and explained why he had called. She looked him up and down. "You're a minister?" she demanded.

"Yes, ma'am," he said.

"How come you wear a gun?"

Taken by surprise, he answered, "Everyone wears a gun when traveling through these wilds. What if I met a bear?"

She was not convinced. "Thought you said you trusted God. Can't He take care of bears?"

Charles Bowen went back to his car and worked through his dilemma before the Lord. Then he tossed the gun into a ditch and resolved never to wear one again. Not long afterward he was put to the test. He went for a walk and when he reached the crest of a hill, he came almost face to face with a grizzly bear, the most dangerous animal in the Canadian wilderness. The bear was about thirty feet away and as Charles loomed into its view, it instinctively reared up to a height of seven or eight feet.

What was the preacher to do? If he ran away the bear could overtake him in a flash. To stay where he was could be just as dangerous. His old army training came to mind as he lifted his heart in silent urgent prayer. Often the element of surprise had proven decisive in battle. *Do what the enemy least expects,* he thought. Acting on the idea immediately, he took off his hat, flourished it in his hand, gave a loud yell, and charged the bear! To his infinite relief it turned and fled.

A bear can be mastered, but a fool in his folly cannot. He is a menace to himself and everyone who has anything to do with him. The best strategy is to keep out of his way.

Regarding *the ungrateful man* Solomon wrote: "Whoso rewardeth evil for good, evil shall not depart from his house" (Proverbs 17:13). Perhaps Solomon had David in mind.

David had a coterie of warriors who were popularly known in the kingdom as his "mighty men." One of these was Uriah, a Hittite convert to David. No more loyal soldier ever held rank in anyone's army. Uriah was probably introduced to David by Ahithophel, David's cleverest counselor. Uriah was married to Ahithophel's granddaughter Bathsheba.

It was a bad day for David when his roving eye fell on Bathsheba. He was smitten at once and arranged a meeting. One thing led to another until the infatuated king succeeded in seducing her. Before long Bathsheba sent the alarming news that she was pregnant. David knew a national scandal was in the making.

He resorted to a low trick wholly unworthy of him. He had Joab send Uriah to the palace with tidings of the battle. David of course hoped that Uriah would take advantage of being so close to home and go see his wife. Then it would be difficult for Uriah to bring a paternity suit against David. But Uriah was so loyal to David and his comrades in arms on the battlefield that he refused to go home. David got Uriah drunk but even then he would not go home. David had rewarded good with evil and there was worse to follow.

Basking in extraordinary tokens of David's favor and quite unsuspecting of any foul play, Uriah returned to the front. He carried with him a note from David to Joab. The innocent-looking letter was Uriah's death warrant. The sealed orders were for Joab to put Uriah at an exposed place in the battle so that he would be killed. As soon as David received word of Uriah's death, the king sent for Bathsheba. He married her in the early stages of her pregnancy so that nobody would be able to prove the child wasn't legitimately conceived.

David thought he had gotten away with his sin. He had rendered evil for good, but who could prove it? Joab perhaps, but Joab was too sophisticated and ambitious a scoundrel to betray the king. Joab now had David in his power and knew how to use his hold over the king. Betraying David was not part of Joab's plan.

But "evil shall not depart from his house," Solomon warned. He grew up in the house of a man who rewarded evil for good. Indeed Bathsheba was his mother. Solomon knew that the son born to Bathsheba and David as a result of their illicit union died. Then Tamar, one of David's daughters, was violated and shamed. Absalom, David's son, murdered Amnon, another son. Then Absalom raised the flag of rebellion, publicly shamed David's concubines, and died an ignominious death at the hands of Joab. Adonijah, another of David's sons, tried to steal the throne in defiance of both God and David. The whole story is recorded in the Bible to warn us not to reward good with evil.

Regarding *the unstable man* Solomon wrote: "The beginning of strife is as when one letteth out water: therefore leave off contention, before it be meddled with" (Proverbs 17:14). A small leak in the bank of a reservoir, if not quickly mended, will grow larger and larger until it threatens the whole dam and spreads ruin and destruction everywhere. Likewise great feuds arise from insignifi-cant causes that could easily be controlled if dealt with promptly. Contention needs to be nipped in the bud.

Proverbs 17:14 is Solomon's version of the Lord's beatitude: "Blessed are the peacemakers" (Matthew 5:9). The Lord practiced what He preached. He stopped contention among His disciples.

While He was on His way to Jerusalem for the last time, He told the disciples what lay ahead: death by crucifixion and a change in the dispensations. They could not or would not understand. Then Salome, the mother of James and John, made a request. "Grant," she said, "that these my two sons may sit, the one on thy right hand, and the other on the left, in thy kingdom" (Matthew 20:21). In one sense the request was noble. It would be great if every mom and dad cherished an ambition for their children to attain positions of eminence and power in the coming millennial kingdom of Christ. Her request, however, was a mistake. The Lord corrected her error—and her sons'—at once. "To sit on my right hand, and on my left, is not mine to give," He said (20:23). The reason is clear. While God gives unmerited salvation, He never gives unmerited rewards. Rewards have to be earned.

In spite of the Lord's courteous rebuff, the ambitions of James and John made the other disciples angry. Matthew recalled the situation only too well: "When the ten heard it, they were moved with indignation against the two brethren" (20:24). Unchecked, this leak in the dike could have grown into a feud of ten against two, just as the Old Testament Hebrew monarchy was divided into two rival kingdoms. Such a breach could have wrecked the church before it was born.

The Lord nipped the strife in the bud. He was a peacemaker. He said in effect that the coveted positions are open to all. The way to achieve lasting fame in the coming kingdom is simple: "Whosoever will be great among you, let him be your minister; And whosoever will be chief among you, let him be your servant: Even as the Son of man came not to be ministered unto, but to minister, and to give his life a ransom for many" (Matthew 20:26-28). The Lord's words stopped the leak in the dike, for at that stage none of the disciples was prepared to meet those conditions.

Regarding *the unfair man* Solomon wrote: "He that justifieth the wicked, and he that condemneth the just, even they both are abomination to the Lord" (Proverbs 17:15). This proverb describes a marked feature of the moral relativism and humanism of our day. Traditional morality based on absolutes has been replaced by a morality based on relative values. Absolute morality says, "Thou shalt not kill." Relative morality says, "It may be quite all right to kill in certain circumstances."

Many people today justify the wholesale slaughter of babies in the womb on the grounds that a pregnant woman ought to have power over her own body and ought to have the right to choose whether or not she should have an abortion. These people say that it is nobody's business but her own; the unborn baby has no rights. The same type of thinking justifies euthanasia—the murder of the old, the hopelessly ill, and the malformed. The Nazis used the same warped value system to justify the mass extermination of Jews, Slavs, gypsies, and other "undesirable" elements in society.

Absolute morality says, "Thou shalt not commit adultery," and forbids every kind of sexual deviation. Relative morality sweeps all absolutes aside and condones premarital sex, extramarital sex, incest, child pornography, sodomy, and even bestiality. Relative morality is really no morality at all. The endless trail of broken homes, discarded children, disease-ridden victims, and warped minds seems to leave the proponents of relative morality unmoved.

Secular humanists believe that the real enemy of society is the Judeo-Christian ethic, which plainly states the difference between right and wrong, truth and error, good and bad, and moral and immoral. Secular humanists are the living incarnation of Proverbs 17:15. They justify the wicked and condemn the just. Their philosophy is an abomination to the Lord.

Regarding *the unteachable man* Solomon wrote: "Wherefore is there a price in the hand of a fool to get wisdom, seeing he hath no heart to it?" (Proverbs 17:16) In other words, it is a waste of good money to hire a tutor to educate a fool since he has already decided he doesn't want to learn. Rehoboam was a first-class fool so Solomon had plenty of opportunities to form his opinions on the subject of the unteachable man.

Today we say, "You can lead a horse to water, but you can't make him drink." Of course you can add salt to the horse's feed and make him thirsty and then he'll drink, but you cannot do that to a fool. He has already made up his mind. He doesn't like the teacher, or he doesn't like the subject, or he would rather be out fishing, or he cannot see any reason for going to school. He has no heart for learning so you might as well leave him alone.

Although Huckleberry Finn was not exactly a fool, he will serve as an illustration of someone who does not want to go to school. Huckleberry, the neglected son of the village ne'er-do-well, somehow scraped a precarious living together for himself. His dress, speech, petty thievery, illiteracy, and carefree ways made him the horror of the mothers and the idol of the boys of the village. But when Huckleberry and his friend Tom Sawyer found buried treasure, Huckleberry was adopted by the Widow Douglas, one of the leaders of village society. Wrote Mark Twain:

> Huck Finn's wealth and the fact that he was now under the Widow Douglas's protection introduced him into society—no, dragged him into it, hurled him into it—and his sufferings were almost more than he could bear. The widow's servants kept him clean and neat, combed and brushed, and they bedded him nightly in unsympathetic sheets that had not one little spot or stain which he could press to his heart and know for a friend. He had to eat with knife and fork; he had to use napkin, cup, and plate; he had to learn his book, he had to go to church; he had to talk so properly that speech was become insipid in his mouth; whithersoever he turned, the bars and shackles of civilization shut him in and bound him hand and foot.
>
> He bravely bore his miseries three weeks, and then one day turned up missing. For forty-eight hours the widow hunted for him everywhere in great distress. The public were profoundly concerned; they searched high and low, they dragged the river for his body. Early the third morning Tom Sawyer went poking among some old empty hogsheads down behind the abandoned slaughterhouse, and in one of them he found the refugee. Huck had slept there; he had just breakfasted upon some stolen odds and ends of food, and was lying off, now, in comfort, with his pipe. He was unkempt, uncombed, and clad in the same old ruin of rags that had made him picturesque in the days when he was free and happy. Tom routed him out, told him the trouble he had been causing, and urged him to go home. Huck's face lost its tranquil content, and took a melancholy cast. He said:
>
> "Don't talk about it, Tom. I've tried it, and it don't work; it don't work, Tom. It ain't for me; I ain't used to it. The widder's good to me, and friendly; but I can't stand them ways. She makes me git up just at the same time every morning; she makes me wash, they comb me all to thunder; she won't let me sleep in the woodshed; I got to wear them blamed clothes that just smothers me, Tom; they don't seem to let any air git through 'em, somehow; and they're so rotten nice that I can't set down, nor lay down, nor roll around anywher's; I hain't slid on a cellar door for—well, it 'pears to be years; I got to go to

church and sweat and sweat—I hate them ornery sermons! I can't ketch a fly in there, I can't chaw. I got to wear shoes all Sunday. The widder eats by a bell; she goes to bed by a bell; she gits up by a bell—everything's so awful reg'lar a body can't stand it."

"Well, everybody does that way, Huck."

"Tom, it don't make no difference. I ain't everybody, and I can't *stand* it. It's awful to be tied up so. And grub comes too easy—I don't take no interest in vittles, that way. I got to ask to go a-fishing; I got to ask to go in a-swimming—dern'd if I hain't got to ask to do everything. Well, I'd got to talk so nice it wasn't no comfort—I'd got to go up in the attic and rip out awhile, every day, to git a taste in my mouth, or I'd 'a' died, Tom. The widder wouldn't let me smoke; she wouldn't let me yell, she wouldn't let me gape, nor stretch, nor scratch, before folks— [Then with a spasm of special irritation and injury]—And, dad fetch it, she prayed all the time! I never *see* such a woman! I *had* to shove, Tom—I just had to. And besides, that school's going to open, and I'd 'a' had to go to it—well, I wouldn't stand *that*, Tom. Looky here, Tom, being rich ain't what it's cracked up to be. It's just worry and worry, and sweat and sweat, and a-wishing you was dead all the time. Now these clothes suits me, and this bar'l suits me, and I ain't ever going to shake 'em any more."

Huckleberry Finn had no intention of learning how to behave in polite society; he had no intention of going to school and learning how to conform. Whether or not he was a fool depends on one's point of view. The nonconformist Mark Twain probably would have sided with Huckleberry. But in any case it was a waste of money to try to educate him, at least conventionally. It is a thousand times more wasteful to try to educate a fool.

b. The Question of Understanding Friendship (17:17-18)

Proverbs 17:17 tells us *how to develop a friendship:* "A friend loveth at all times, and a brother is born for adversity."

When the prodigal son headed for the far country with money in his pocket, a gleam in his eye, and a spring in his step, he had plenty of friends—as long as he was a big spender. He soon discovered them to be fair-weather friends. They vanished when his money ran out and they couldn't be found when he needed a loan. A real friend remains true no matter what.

Solomon said, "A brother is born for adversity," and we say, "Blood is thicker than water." Joseph's brothers discovered that this proverb held true even though they were mean to him. They hated Joseph because of his special place of honor in the family, so clearly indicated by his coat of many colors. They hated him for his dreams, his goodness that insulated him from their own evil ways, and his transparent honesty that prevented him from telling his father anything but the truth. They could not speak peaceably to him, the Holy Spirit says (Genesis 37:4).

As long as Joseph's mother was alive, his brothers probably did not dare show more than petty spite. But not long after Rachel's death their malice and ill will came to a head. They seized Joseph in a lonely pasture far from home, flung him into a pit, plotted his murder, sold him into slavery, and concocted a story to account for his disappearance. It must have seemed to Joseph that these brothers of his were born to create adversity.

Time passed. Joseph was raised to the right hand of the pharaoh and as grand vizier of Egypt wielded enormous wealth and power. When the foretold years of plenty came, Joseph heavily taxed the farmers and stockpiled huge reserves of grain. During the years of famine Joseph sold the grain at record prices and greatly increased the power of the throne. As the famine spread throughout the entire region, foreigners arrived, eager to buy grain from the bulging Egyptian granaries. Among the foreigners were his brothers.

The light dawned in Joseph's soul. He understood the mystery of God's ways. He understood why it had been necessary for him to suffer and be raised up to power and glory in the kingdom. He had been born for adversity. He explained this insight to his brothers after they had been humbled and chastened. "Ye *sold* me hither," he said, "for God did *send* me before you to preserve life....God sent me before you to preserve you a posterity....it was not you that sent me hither, but God: and he hath made me...a ruler throughout all the land of Egypt" (Genesis 45:5-8, italics added).

After Jacob died, the brothers' fear of Joseph resurfaced. They thought that Joseph had shown them kindness and postponed his vengeance until the death of Jacob. They expected him to act the way they would have acted. But Joseph said:

> Fear not: for am I in the place of God? But as for you, ye thought evil against me; but God meant it unto good, to bring to pass, as it is this day, to save much people alive. Now therefore fear ye not: I will nourish you, and your little ones.

And he comforted them, and spake kindly unto them (Genesis 50:19-21).

Joseph was a brother born for adversity. Of course the whole story and the proverb it illustrates can be lifted to much higher ground in that they remind us of Jesus, the friend who loves at all times. Jesus is the brother born for adversity. Thanks to Adam's sin we were born into great adversity. But Jesus was born to bear our sins to Calvary, where He dealt once and for all with the powers intent on destroying us.

Proverbs 17:18 tells us *how to destroy a friendship:* "A man void of understanding striketh hands, and becometh surety in the presence of his friend."

One interpretation of this proverb can be stated as follows: To strike a bargain on behalf of a friend is the quickest way to destroy a friendship. When money comes between friends, problems often follow. It is rarely a good idea to loan money to a friend, to borrow money from a friend, or to ask a friend to provide security for a loan or guarantee a loan. It is not usually a good idea to sell a car to a friend. If something goes wrong with the transaction or some misunderstanding arises, the friendship will be strained.

Another interpretation is that Proverbs 17:18 refers to a transaction ratified publicly by a handshake (common in the East) in the presence of a friend in order to impress the friend. A pledge made in this fashion is hard to annul without acute embarrassment.

Such a pledge reminds me of the faith-promise plan of a church in a remote Canadian town. Years ago I was instrumental in starting this church. A number of people were saved, including one precious family that always seemed to be in debt. No matter how much the father of the family earned, he never had enough money. He owed money all over town and no amount of exhortation seemed to help him live within his means.

Our fledgling church was invited to participate in a joint missionary conference. A well-known preacher, a "missionary statesman," spoke and encouraged the congregation to raise money for the support of missionaries. The preacher explained the faith-promise plan: we should not just pledge what we could afford but what we could trust the Lord to give us over and above what we could afford. Money that was pledged at the conference could be paid all at once or over a period of a year.

There was a great deal of hoopla about the fund-raising. A large thermometer was set up in the auditorium and as people made pledges, a red ribbon was raised. The ushers scurried about collecting pledges and gave them to the preacher who called out the amount of each pledge. He kept the big pledges in a separate pile and announced them when interest seemed to flag. "Don't consider your pledge as final," he said. "You can use another envelope and pledge more if you feel so led." This method of fund-raising was all very exciting, and carnal.

I was the accountant stationed at the back of the platform with an adding machine to keep track of the pledges. I was astonished to see a large pledge come in from the new convert who owed money all over town. He was the kind of man who would be stimulated by all the emotional excitement in the meeting. Void of understanding, he was striking hands and becoming surety in the presence of his friends. I laid his pledge aside and did not include it in the total because I felt he needed to be counseled before the pledge became binding. It could always be added to the total later. Before long he made another pledge and then another. I laid them aside too and wondered how many other pledges ought to be annulled as well.

That meeting cured me of the faith-promise plan. I later remembered Paul's admonition: "For if there be first a willing mind, it is accepted according to that a man hath, and not according to that he hath not." J. B. Phillips rendered the verse this way: "The important thing is to be willing to give as much as we can—that is what God accepts, and no one is asked to give what he has not got" (2 Corinthians 8:12).

After the show was over I was left with the thankless task of trying to collect the pledges. Needless to say, the amount I collected fell far short of the amount people pledged. The losers were the missionaries—and also those whose tender consciences were plagued by their subsequent inability to meet the amounts they had so optimistically and emotionally promised.

As soon as possible I went to my friend whose pledges I had laid aside. "Well, William," I said, "how are things going?" I talked to him (not for the first time) about his need to live within his means, get out of debt, and pay the tradesmen around town to whom his name was a byword and his testimony worthless. Then I brought up the subject of his pledges at the missionary conference. "Do you really have faith enough to get all that money, William? What about you, Mary?" I said, turning to his wife. "Do you think you can take on these pledges? Don't you think the Lord would be more honored if you tried to get out of debt before taking on this extra load?" I told them about George Muller and his orphanages and how he had promised the Lord never knowingly to accept a contribution from someone who was in debt. He always returned such a donation.

Finally I produced the pledges. "Now then, William," I said, "here they are. I didn't count them, so you don't owe them. I am going to leave them with you. Talk it over. Pray about it. If you still think it's the Lord's will to go through with them, let me know and I'll add them to the total." He never sent them back. He frankly told me that he had been carried away by the excitement. When he went home after the missionary conference, he wished that he had not been such a fool.

c. The Question of Underlying Follies (17:19-21)

In Proverbs 17:19 we see a picture of *a man and his motives:* "He loveth transgression that loveth strife: and he that exalteth his gate seeketh destruction." The last clause refers to someone who flaunts his wealth.

In the East doors were generally low-pitched and unadorned. A rich man who made a display of his gate was inviting robbery and destruction. The sacred historian told us what happened in Jerusalem at the time of the Babylonian invasion:

> In the fifth month, on the seventh day of the month, which is the nineteenth year of king Nebuchadnezzar king of Babylon, came Nebuzaradan, captain of the guard, a servant of the king of Babylon, unto Jerusalem. [The captain of the guard was actually the chief of the royal executioners.] And he burnt the house of the Lord, and the king's house, and all the houses of Jerusalem, and every great man's house burnt he with fire (2 Kings 25:8-9).

If the rich man also takes delight in strife and wickedness, the situation is aggravated. He probably made his money by strife and in the process also made plenty of enemies who would be delighted at his downfall.

In *The Black Rose* Thomas B. Costain told of just such a situation. His heroes, Walter of Gurnie and Tristram Griffen, set forth to seek their fortune in the fabulous land of Cathay. On the way they befriended Maryam, half sister of a notorious Greek merchant, Anthemas of Antioch. The beautiful young woman was being sent as part of a caravan of beauties to Kublai Khan, the Mongolian chief.

Walter and Tristram became indebted to the grasping Greek who provided them with passage to the East and the bare necessities for their journey with the caravan.

In the course of the journey, Walter and Maryam fell in love but were separated. Walter found himself in the employ of the Mongolian warlord Bayan in the Chinese city of Kinsai. Walter was befriended by Chang Wu, leader of the peace faction in Kinsai. Chang Wu thought that making peace with the Mongolian was the city's only chance. One of Walter's assignments was to deliver a message to Sung Yung, a notable citizen of Kinsai and leader of the war faction.

"Sung Yung," snarled Chang Wu, "is a wolf who devours the bodies of those of his own pack who fall in the chase." Sung Yung had made a fortune from the war by supplying shoddy merchandise to the Chinese army. Worse than that, he had convinced the government that its troops could be paid with worthless paper money.

As Walter made his way through the city, he noticed the doors of the houses. Some had a willow branch nailed up, signifying a desire for peace. Others had a dagger, indicating a desire for war.

Then Walter learned that his beloved Maryam was in the same city. She was in the hands of Sung Yung, who intended to send her back to her brother who wished to wreak vengeance on her for running away from the harem caravan. Chang Wu explained to Walter the only way to rescue her from the clutches of Sung Yung: if Walter were to marry Maryam, Sung Yung would lose his hold over her. So they devised a plan to visit Sung Yung's warehouse where Maryam was imprisoned and get a Nestorian priest to perform the wedding ceremony in secret. Chang Wu would provide a gang of toughs to protect the couple while the ceremony was being performed.

In time Walter, Chang Wu, and the gang arrived in the market square where Sung Yung had his silk warehouse. His building, the most imposing in the square, had a high-tiered roof that towered above the rest. And over his flamboyant, resplendent door hung a golden representation of a mulberry moth.

The secret wedding was performed without discovery or interruption. When it was over, however, armed servants of Sung Yung appeared, followed by their enraged master. The confrontation that followed proved to be the spark needed to explode the gunpowder of popular resentment against the silk merchant. The people detested him for sponsoring the paper money that had ruined the nation's economy and soon a major riot erupted. Rioters tore down the golden mulberry moth and broke it to pieces. They threw the silk merchant to the ground, stamped on his head, and buried him under a great heap of gravel. They looted his warehouse and scattered his merchandise far and wide. Sung Yung had exalted his gate and he paid for it.

In Proverbs 17:20 we see a picture of *a talker and his tongue:* "He that hath a froward heart findeth no good: and he that hath a perverse tongue falleth into mischief." Some people always see the worst in everyone and put the worst interpretation on everything. They are not merely pessimistic; they cannot see the good side of anyone. If a good word is said about someone, they say something negative about the person.

Some years ago Dr. Eric Berne, formerly a consultant in psychiatry to the surgeon general of the United States Army and later a lecturer at the University of California medical school, wrote an immensely popular book entitled *Games People Play.* The games to which he referred are psychological games. They consist of a series of complementary and ulterior transactions that progress to a known and predictable outcome. Sometimes these games involve people who are unaware that they are players. After describing the psychological dynamics of these games, Berne gave numerous examples. One game that has always intrigued me is "Why Don't You—Yes But." Dr. Berne said it is the game most commonly played in a group situation.

The game goes something like this. Mrs. Woggins announces to the friends she has invited over for morning coffee that her husband is an enthusiastic do-it-yourself carpenter who botches every job he undertakes.

Mrs. Bigsniff says, "Perhaps he needs a good set of carpenter's tools."

Mrs. Woggins replies, "Yes, but he hasn't any idea how to use them."

Mrs. Pushmore says, "Why doesn't he take some lessons in carpentry?"

Mrs. Woggins responds, "Yes, but he simply cannot afford the time."

Mrs. Flapjaw suggests, "Why doesn't he get a carpenter to help him?"

Mrs. Woggins says, "Yes, but he can't afford that."

Mrs. Grinmore says, "Why doesn't he just forget it and hire a contractor?"

Mrs. Woggins replies, "Yes, but he wants to do it himself."

Mrs. Winker says, "Why don't you just let him do his own thing?"

Mrs. Woggins says, "Yes, but you should see what he does. The thing would collapse the first time it was used."

Usually the suggestions peter out, and a frustrated silence follows—which means that having successfully batted every idea all over the living room, Mrs. Woggins has won. Every suggestion has been rejected. What Mrs. Woggins was after, of course, was to build herself up while putting down her husband and her well-meaning neighbors. The same game is played by those who even more maliciously say backbiting words about everybody. Solomon knew about the game, although he didn't call it by its modern name.

In Proverbs 17:21 we see a picture of *a fool and his father:* "He that begetteth a fool doeth it to his sorrow: and the father of a fool hath no joy." Solomon uttered these words bitterly, with one eye on Rehoboam. The king feared that what he had built would be torn down by his son.

We can all remember our childhoods when with great patience and industry we built up towers of blocks. The higher each tower grew, the more careful we had to be. Our hands trembled as they added another block to the precarious pile. Then along came a younger brother who with one gleeful swipe knocked the tower down. It takes skill to build. Any fool can knock things down.

Solomon had the skill to build. Alexander Whyte wrote about Solomon's abilities and advantages:

> If ever anyone was once enlightened, and had tasted the heavenly gift, and was made a partaker of the Holy Ghost, and had tasted the good Word of God, and the powers of the world to come it was Solomon....Solomon was born of a father and a mother, the knowledge of which was enough to sanctify and dedicate both him and them from his mother's womb. If ever it was said over any child's birth, Where sin abounded grace did much more abound, it was surely over the birth, and the birth-gifts and graces of Solomon...And then, with a tutor and governor like Nathan...and then his father's deathbed...all ending in Solomon sitting down on the throne of Israel amid such a blaze of glory. Solomon would have been made of stone not to have been moved to make those vows, and promises, and choices of wisdom and truth and righteousness, which we read so beautifully that he did make at the beginning of his reign in Jerusalem.

Solomon sat down in splendor and rose up in zeal to accomplish great things. He mastered the Mosaic law, learned each of its 613 commandments, and understood the letter and spirit of every single one. He reviewed every legal decision. The executive and the judiciary functions of the nation were in safe hands with him. He took to the law as a duck takes to water. His insights, impartiality, and energy were known at home and abroad.

Solomon was a tireless builder. The great achievement of his reign was the temple. It stood on mount Moriah all agleam with gold, cedar, and rich tapestries. He also built a palace and he had plans to make Jerusalem the most magnificent city on earth. Caesar Augustus boasted that he "found Rome brick and left it marble." Solomon could have boasted much the same about Jerusalem. His great talent for organization enabled him to be involved in multiple projects employing thousands of men and exhausting even his fabulous treasury.

Solomon was filled with curiosity about other lands and peoples, and he even went down to Egypt to find his queen. That pharaoh's daughter should sit on the throne of David might have shocked the conservative element in Israel. To others Solomon's choice of a queen probably indicated his broadmindedness. Soon his court was the center of an internationalism never before known in Israel. Ambassadors from distant lands visited him, as did the queen of Sheba. Solomon cemented matrimonial alliances with kingdom after kingdom as his interests and influence grew. He launched fleets of ships to scour the seas and sent great caravans across the trade routes of the world.

Solomon's intellectual accomplishments added to his glory. As a student of psychology he was intrigued by human nature and human behavior. He was also a diligent student of natural history and was eager to learn about plants, animals, insects, and birds.

So Solomon built with his blocks until he reached heights of tolerance and accommodation of ideas that made his kingdom tremble even at his touch. And then Rehoboam entered the picture. Solomon knew only too well what to expect from his son. One touch from Rehoboam would cause the kingdom to come tumbling down. "He that begetteth a fool doeth it to his sorrow: and the father of a fool hath no joy."

7. Problems (17:22-26)

a. Facing Gloom (17:22)

Addressing the problem of gloom, Solomon told us *how it is overcome:* "A merry heart doeth good like a medicine." He also told us *how it can overwhelm:* "But a broken spirit drieth the bones."

There's nothing as effective as a good laugh for chasing away hypochondria. Many sicknesses are psychosomatic, brought on by emotional disorders, worry, anger, hatred, self-pity, or guilt. One researcher named stress as the single most important cause of human illness. A car doesn't stop running because it is fifteen or twenty years old. It stops because stress has worn out one of its parts. People living under constant physical or emotional stress eventually succumb to illness and death.

Dr. Hans Seyle, former director of the University of Montreal's Institute of Experimental Medicine and Surgery, discovered that when rats are subjected to cold, fatigue, frustration, noise, and other stressful conditions, they develop physical symptoms. Their blood pressure soars, their vital adrenal glands become grossly enlarged, their thymus and lymphatic glands shrink, and they develop peptic ulcers.

Whether a rat is subjected to extreme fatigue or a wife is subjected to an angry tongue-lashing by her husband, the result is the same: blood pressure and blood sugar increase, stomach acid increases, and arteries tighten. As soon as tension subsides, bodily functions return to normal. If an emotional tug of war continues, however, it will result in exhaustion, serious disease, and death.

Research has shown that in animals emotional stress causes fats to be drawn from the body, dumped into the blood, and deposited along artery walls. The lethal results are atherosclerosis and coronary-artery disease.[6]

According to Dr. Seyle, hatred, frustration, and anxiety are the worst stresses. If you forcefully restrain a normally active rat, deadly frustration results. If you put a mouse and a cat in adjoining cages, the mouse will die of anxiety.

Telling someone who is always frustrated to stop worrying is not helpful. However, it may be helpful to point out that his worrying is harming him. The person who is frustrated is harming himself; he is not harming the one who is causing the frustration. The person who hates is harming himself; he is not harming the one he hates. People who cause negative reactions usually go on their merry way oblivious of the damage they have done.

While stress can cause harm, there is an antidote. Solomon was right—a good laugh can break tension. I am reminded of the tension in the air when I have to preach to a new audience. Whether the congregation numbers a dozen or five thousand makes no difference. I stand before the people and look at them, and the tension mounts as I wonder about their ages, interests, backgrounds, levels of education, places in society, and spiritual needs.

They look at me and size me up. The first face-off is critical. I always try to break the tension by beginning with an uproariously funny story.

In some situations, however, laughter is not the remedy. We know from Solomon's proverb that gloom can overwhelm. A gaunt, sad-faced man entered the office of Dr. James Hamilton in Manchester, England, and said that he was tired of life. He said he could not find happiness anywhere and he was bored to death. Indeed he hinted at suicide. The doctor diagnosed his illness as severe melancholia, brought on by overwork. He prescribed some fun and laughter. "Go to the circus," the doctor said. "It happens to be in town. See Grimaldi the clown. He's the funniest man alive."

"Doctor," said the patient, "I *am* Grimaldi!"

b. False Gifts (17:23)

"A wicked man taketh a gift out of the bosom to pervert the ways of judgment." God thinks that judges who accept bribes and distort justice are wicked. The word translated "wicked" here is *rasha,* which means "lawless." In other words, judges who accept bribes are lawless.

In 1973 Charles R. Ashman published a book with an intriguing title: *The Finest Judges Money Can Buy.* He began the book by stating, "American justice is choking on judicial pollution."[7] Ashman wrote the book to prove that bribery and corruption in American courts are no longer occasional and exceptional occurrences, but part of a decided pattern. Everywhere he looked he saw evidence of conflicts of interest, chronic bribery, abuse of office, nepotism, sexual perversions, and payoffs. He claimed that all the bribes paid or offered in a single year could eliminate much of the poverty that breeds crime. Ashman's book describes more than seventy classic examples of judicial pollution. He even said that American judges have accepted payoffs and yielded to pressure from organized crime.

The chapter titles in his book make challenging reading in themselves. In the chapter entitled "Black-Robed Mafia" Ashman exposed eight judges who were guilty of leading double lives—sitting on the bench while being personally involved in crime. In "The High Cost of Justice" he cited ten greedy judges who were found guilty of barefaced bribery. In "Bargains" he named sixteen judges and magistrates who were guilty of petty robbery. In "The Sensuous Judge" he named half a dozen justices who were guilty of various forms of sexual impropriety and misbehavior. In "Court

Jesters" he cited seven judges who were guilty of clowning on the bench, being drunk on the job, resorting to temper tantrums, using strong-arm tactics, lying to the bar association, capriciously dismissing cases, ordering arbitrary trial delays, and exhibiting various forms of bizarre behavior. In "The Corrupters" he cited ten judges who were guilty of playing politics with their positions. In "Current Bench Warmers" he cited nine judges who were unwilling or unable to perform their duties properly. In "The Chicago Three" he gave examples of corruption and inefficiency on the bench. In "Article I, Section III" (this chapter title is a reference to clauses in the United States Constitution providing for impeachment of judges of the Supreme Court) Ashman said it is virtually impossible to impeach Supreme Court justices.

Ashman's whole book is depressing reading. Commenting on the fact that "there are over 7,000 American judges serving today on federal and state trial and appellate courts," he said, "There is one common denominator for all—an overabundance of incompetent, or corrupt or, at least, easily influenced judges."[8] Of course there are good, honest judges too, but Ashman's book is a sad commentary on the United States of America, a country that prides itself on its system of justice and fair play. We can only imagine conditions in countries where bribery is a way of life. Thankfully there is One who sits on high, who hears and sees all, who is incorruptible, and who judges the judges.

c. Foolish Goals (17:24)

"Wisdom is before him that hath understanding; but the eyes of a fool are in the ends of the earth." For the child of God, wisdom is as near as the Word of God and the Spirit of God. The Bible says, "If any of you lack wisdom, let him ask of God" (James 1:5). A fool looks everywhere else to find answers. Foolishness is evident today in the rejection of the Bible and the craving for false cults, spiritism, the occult, and oriental religion.

The floodgate to oriental religion was opened in the 1960s when flower power, rock and roll, the hippy culture, drugs, and Hinduism combined to offer a new age of enlightenment to jaded Western minds. About this time an obscure Hindu mendicant, A. C. Bhaktivedanta Swami Prabhupada, began a religious movement in America. Arriving in New York in 1965 with seven dollars in rupees, a phone number, and a few battered cooking utensils, he started a cult in a storefront. By the time he died in Vrindaban, India, in 1977, his International Society for Krishna Consciousness had more than two hundred temples and farms in sixty countries, tens of thousands of followers and tens of millions of dollars. In the United States alone the movement had fifty-seven temples and farms, more than five thousand devotees, and thousands of uninitiated followers.

The basic idea behind the movement is reincarnation. "Worship" consists of endlessly chanting the name *Hare Krishna*. The devotees chant and beg for alms. Many early followers were drug-tranced hippies, others were heirs to fortunes, and some were doctors. They shaved their heads, put on robes, pestered people on the street and in airports, and opened vegetarian cafes and health-food stores. The movement degenerated into a number of competing cults that have been accused of murder, abuse of women and children, drug dealing, and swindles worthy of the Mafia. People interested in the whole unsavory story should read the book *Monkey on a Stick* by John Hubner and Linsey Gruson. In places the book is crude, but so is the cult.

The fool rejects the wisdom of the Bible. Off he goes to the ends of the earth to join some immoral, soul-destroying, mind-enslaving, Christ-denying, image-worshiping Hindu cult.

d. Family Grief (17:25)

"A foolish son is a grief to his father, and bitterness to her that bare him."

Reuben was a foolish son. The grief he caused was aggravated by the fact that he was Jacob's firstborn and seemed at first to show great promise. In his parting blessing Jacob said, "Reuben, thou art my firstborn, my might, and the beginning of my strength, the excellency of dignity, and the excellency of power" (Genesis 49:3). But Reuben was all sham and show, a personable fool.

Reuben's first recorded display of folly occurred when his brothers plotted to get rid of Joseph (Genesis 37). Instead of categorically opposing his brothers, Reuben merely opposed killing Joseph and suggested putting him into a pit. Reuben hoped for an opportunity to set Joseph free when the brothers turned their backs. The suggestion was foolish. Reuben should have boldly warned his brothers that they would have to deal with him before he would allow them to lay a finger on their young brother. Reuben should have known that they would simply wait until his back was turned and then get rid of Joseph. It was foolish for Reuben to leave Joseph unattended in the pit for a single moment.

Reuben was surprised and horrified when he found the pit empty and Joseph gone, sold as a slave to a passing caravan. But it is obvious that he went along with the plot to deceive Jacob with Joseph's bloodstained cloak. Presumably Reuben accepted his share of the loot as well. "Here you are, Reuben," we can hear Judah say. "Here are your two silver pieces. You're in this as much as we are, you know. Don't you try to betray us or we'll get you too. We'll tell Father that you suggested putting him in the pit and that you sold him when we were off watering the flocks."

Reuben was a fool from start to finish in the way he handled this whole wretched business, but he already had another crime on his conscience. After Jacob's beloved Rachel died, Reuben committed a dastardly and extremely foolish act (Genesis 35:22). He committed adultery and incest with Bilhah, Rachel's maid and Jacob's third wife, the one to whom Jacob would naturally turn for consolation in his bereavement. Evidently Jacob knew about this act of wickedness. It was another grief to be added to his overwhelming sorrow. And the fact that it was Reuben who committed the crime was, as Shakespeare would have said, "the most unkindest cut of all."

From then on, Jacob never trusted Reuben. Years later when famine was raging and the children of Israel found it necessary to go to Egypt to buy grain, a delicate situation arose and Jacob's distrust surfaced. The governor who sold grain to the brothers demanded that they return to Egypt and bring Benjamin with them. To ensure their return the Egyptian lord kept Simeon as a hostage. Jacob was horrified and alarmed when he heard this news. Joseph was dead, Simeon was a hostage, and now young Benjamin was to be taken as well. At this point Reuben offered his own sons to be held as hostages by Jacob until Benjamin was returned to him. "My son shall not go down with *you*," was Jacob's prompt reply (Genesis 42:38, italics added). He wouldn't have trusted his dog to Reuben!

Jacob's grief and anger over Reuben's folly spilled out at last when he prophetically assigned his sons their future roles. He turned on Reuben and we can hear the wrath, grief, and indignation in Jacob's voice as he said: "Unstable as water, thou shalt not excel; because thou wentest up to thy father's bed; then defiledst thou it: he went up to my couch" (Genesis 49:4). Yes indeed, "a foolish son is a grief to his father."

e. Fatal Guilt (17:26)

"To punish the just is not good, nor to strike princes for equity." The word translated "punish" here refers to punishment by fire. The word translated "princes" refers primarily to people of high character. Solomon was denouncing the practice of punishing an innocent man and injuring a man of noble character. History records many such abuses of the judicial and governmental process.

Consider the case of John Hooper (1495-1555). While he was a monk in a Cistercian monastery he studied the works of Zwingli, the Swiss reformer, and the writings of Johann Bullinger, Zwingli's successor. These works convinced Hooper of the errors of Rome and turned him into a zealous advocate of the Reformation. When he opposed the infamous Six Articles enacted by Henry VIII, Hooper was severely persecuted. In 1537 he fled to Switzerland, where he married. After the death of Henry VIII Hooper returned to England in 1547 and was warmly welcomed by young Edward VI. Hooper became chaplain to the earl of Warwick and then bishop of Gloucester in 1550. He greatly aided the Reformation in England.[9]

Then Mary became queen. She was determined to put an end to the Protestant faith. Cardinal Pole arrived from Italy with full powers from the pope to receive the kingdom of England back into the arms of Rome. In 1555, called "the year of burning and blood," fires were kindled all across England to burn "heretics" at the stake. John Hooper was among those who perished. Historian Andrew Miller wrote:

> Hooper, late Bishop of Gloucester, was burnt alive in front of his own Cathedral. It was a market day, and a crowd of not less than seven thousand had assembled to witness the last moments of one so greatly beloved. His enemies, fearing the power of his eloquence, forbade him to speak, and threatened if he did to cut out his tongue. But it is said that the meekness, the more than usual serenity of his countenance, and the courage with which he endured his prolonged and awful sufferings bore nobler testimony to his cause than any words he could have uttered. He was much in prayer, and probably the greater part of the seven thousand were in tears.

Another historian wrote:

> To say nothing of his piety and the cause for which he suffered, he was a noble specimen of the true English character; a man of transparent honesty, of dauntless courage, of unshaken constancy, and of warm affections and a loving heart.

Hooper's last words were, "Lord Jesus, receive my spirit." Within a few days after Hooper's death, Saunders was burnt at Coventry;

Dr. Taylor at Hadleigh in Suffolk; Ferrar, bishop of St. David's, at Carmarthen, Wales. All these were clergymen. Andrew Miller wrote:

> Fires were thus kindled in all parts of England in order to strike a wider terror into the hearts of the people, and deter them by these terrible examples from siding with the Reformers. But they had just the opposite effect. Men could easily contrast the mild treatment of the Papists under the reign of Edward, and the cruelties practiced on innocent men under the reign of Mary. Barbarous as the nation then was, and educationally Catholic, it was shocked beyond measure with the severities of the court of Mary; especially when the council issued an order to the sheriffs of the different counties to exact a promise from the martyrs to make no speeches at the stake—otherwise to cut out their tongues. Thus were kindred and friends deprived of the last and sacred words of the dying. Even the most rigid Papists pretended to be ashamed of these savage proceedings when they saw their effect upon the nation.[10]

8. Pronouncements (17:27-28)

In Proverbs 17:27 Solomon advised us *how to show wisdom:* "He that hath knowledge spareth his words: and a man of understanding is of an excellent spirit." The supreme illustration of a man who showed wisdom is the Lord Jesus, who at the time of His trials controlled His tongue and resolutely refused to say one word more than was necessary.

First the Lord was brought before infamous Annas, former high priest and father-in-law of Caiaphas (John 18:12-14; 19-23). Jesus simply referred Annas to His public teaching and asked him to justify the behavior of the officer who hit Him in the face.

Next the Lord appeared before Caiaphas, the incumbent high priest (Luke 22:63-65; John 18:24). At that trial Jesus ignored the taunts of those who blindfolded Him and struck Him. He also ignored the false witnesses Caiaphas hired. Jesus refused to say whether or not He was the Christ, but when put under oath He testified to being the Son of God.

Brought before Pilate the first time (Luke 23:1-5; John 18:28-38), Jesus acknowledged that He was indeed a king but declared that His kingdom was not of this world. He ignored Pilate's insincere question, "What is truth?"

When Jesus appeared before Herod (Luke 23:6-12), He said nothing at all and silently ignored the mockery to which Herod subjected Him.

Back before Pilate (Luke 23:13-25; John 18:39–19:16) Jesus said very little. He endured the scourging and brutal horseplay of the soldiers in silence. When Pilate, alarmed by the complaint of the priests that Jesus claimed to be the Son of God, asked Him where He came from, Jesus ignored him. When Pilate in frustration boasted that he had the power either to release Jesus or send Him to the cross, the Lord quietly said, "Thou couldest have no power at all against me, except it were given thee from above."

We read with amazement of the matchless self-control of the Lord Jesus in the face of the most abominable lies, the most outrageous miscarriage of justice, the most spiteful acts of malice, and the cruelest abuse. He who had all knowledge spared His words. He who had the most perfect understanding displayed an excellent spirit. He actually loved those poor lost men—Annas, Caiaphas, Herod, Pilate, the false witnesses, and the callous Roman soldiers. Indeed He was on His way to Calvary to die for them—in accordance with a plan worked out in a past eternity. The plan was fully known to Him, understood by Him, and approved by Him. Being silent as a sheep before its shearers was all part of the prearranged and perfect plan (Isaiah 53:7).

In Proverbs 17:28 Solomon advised us *how to seem wise:* "Even a fool, when he holdeth his peace, is counted wise: and he that shutteth his lips is esteemed a man of understanding."

That is what Job said centuries earlier. The bottom had fallen out of his life. In one horrendous day he was stripped of all his material possessions. One seemingly capricious disaster after another swept away his oxen, asses, sheep, and camels. Far worse, a tornado killed all ten of his beloved children. Shortly afterward he contracted a mysterious, painful, and incurable malady that made his every movement sheer misery. Finally his wife turned against him. None of these misfortunes made any sense to this essentially righteous man.

Then Job's three friends came to rub salt in his wounds with pious platitudes and half-baked theories. They all assumed that Job had a terrible secret sin in his life; otherwise these disasters would not have happened. His friends were ignorant of the real explanation for his sufferings.

All three friends had hard words for Job, words he returned in kind. Zophar bluntly told Job that he was a wicked man; that no matter where he hid, his sin would find him out; and that his case was hopeless. Job knew that he was not the kind of sinner his friends said he was and that Zophar was too smart for his own good. "No doubt but ye are the people," said Job sarcastically, "and wisdom shall die with you" (Job 12:2). Then he turned fiercely on Zophar, his worst critic: "O that ye would altogether hold your peace! and it should be your wisdom" (13:5). In other words Job was saying, "If you would just keep your mouth shut someone might make a mistake and think you are wise!"

In the eighteenth century, English readers devoured the successive editions of *The Spectator*, a lively periodical aimed at improving both the morals and the wit of its readers. It adopted a fictional format featuring the "Spectator Club" and its members, one of whom was Sir Roger de Coverley, a country gentleman. Sir Roger de Coverley did not exactly hold his tongue to show his wisdom. Whenever he was faced with a problem beyond his capacity to solve, he would reply, "There's much to be said on both sides." He might as well have remained silent.

CHAPTER 22

Proverbs 18:1–19:5

B. How to Build Character (18:1–19:5)
  1. The Separated Man (18:1)
  2. The Selfish Man (18:2)
  3. The Sinful Man (18:3)
  4. The Speaking Man (18:4-8)
      a. The Man of Deep Words (18:4)
      b. The Man of Deceitful Words (18:5)
      c. The Man of Destructive Words (18:6-8)
          (1) The Words of the Muddled Man (18:6-7)
              (a) His Words and His Body (18:6)
              (b) His Words and His Being (18:7)
          (2) The Words of the Meddlesome Man (18:8)
  5. The Slothful Man (18:9)
  6. The Safe Man (18:10-12)
      a. The Hiding Place (18:10-11)
          (1) The Right Hiding Place (18:10)
          (2) The Wrong Hiding Place (18:11)
      b. The Humble Place (18:12)
  7. The Silly Man (18:13)
  8. The Stricken Man (18:14)
  9. The Seeking Man (18:15)
  10. The Successful Man (18:16)
  11. The Striving Man (18:17-19)
      a. The Loud Boaster (18:17)
      b. The Lifted Barrier (18:18)
      c. The Lost Brother (18:19)
  12. The Satisfied Man (18:20-24)
      a. Taming the Tongue (18:20-21)
      b. Winning a Wife (18:22)

c. Minding the Mouth (18:23)
d. Finding a Friend (18:24)
13. The Stupid Man (19:1-3)
   a. His Foolish Words (19:1)
   b. His Foolish Walk (19:2)
   c. His Foolish Ways (19:3)
14. The Superficial Man (19:4)
15. The Scurrilous Man (19:5)

The main theme of Proverbs 18:1–19:5 is character building in the individual. Although there is little or no doctrine as such in the book of Proverbs, its maxims and morals arise from a proper Biblical view of God and man, for belief and behavior are married— for better or for worse, for richer or for poorer, for time and for eternity. The sin question is never far from the surface of these proverbs.

B. How to Build Character (18:1–19:5)

1. The Separated Man (18:1)

"Through desire a man, having separated himself, seeketh and intermeddleth with all wisdom." This difficult verse has been translated in a variety of ways. Solomon's idea seems to be that the man who desires to improve himself separates himself from worldly entanglements so that he can involve himself with wisdom. There is a price to be paid for knowledge and wisdom.

From his youth a close relative of mine was determined to become a doctor. To that end he dedicated seven years of his life. During that time he and I were both living in western Canada. I was working for a bank; he was putting himself through medical school. One summer when he was working for a pulp mill in a remote town (doing a thankless, mind-numbing job because it paid fairly well) he came to Vancouver to spend a weekend with me. We were both poor as church mice. He had that "lean and hungry look" of which Shakespeare spoke. His clothes were threadbare. He was saving every penny to make it through another semester. I said, "Why don't you settle for less? Why not become a druggist? They make a good living." He answered fiercely, "I don't want to be a druggist, I want to be a doctor."

He scrimped and saved; he sweat and he studied. He worked as a waiter on the Canadian National Railway. He toiled for seven long years until he graduated from medical school. Then he served his internship and after that he spent another three years developing a specialty in pathology. He gave years of his life preparing to be a doctor, and half a lifetime later he is known and respected around the world as an authority on the pathology of the human liver. My relative separated himself, denied himself, and paid the price of acquiring knowledge, understanding, and wisdom in one small branch of medicine.

There is a price to be paid for success in any field—medicine, mathematics, meteorology, physics, philosophy, economics, ecology, gymnastics, geology, biology, or the Bible. The only place where *success* comes before *work* is the dictionary.

2. The Selfish Man (18:2)

"A fool hath no delight in understanding, but that his heart may discover itself." The word translated "discover" here means "vent." All the fool wants to do is sound off and have his own way. He doesn't care that what he says or does may harm others. He wants to be allowed to vent his anger and blurt out his opinions. The Bible has its quota of such people. The breed is as old as Cain. Shimei and Nabal belonged to the clan.

The trait described in Proverbs 18:2 is bad enough in ordinary people; it is much worse when it is characteristic of kings or people in powerful positions. For example Henry VIII was a strong-willed, untamable man who was always determined to have his own way. Although he is credited with bringing the Reformation to England, he was a most erratic individual and always ruled by his personal thoughts, passions, and will.

He came to the throne when he was about eighteen years old. A handsome, popular man abounding in animal spirits, his marriage and coronation were followed by a round of pleasure that all but bankrupted the treasury.

Henry VIII remained a Roman Catholic at heart to the end. He had a taste for scholarship and plied his pen in upholding the pope. For writing a book on the seven Romish sacraments in answer to Luther's "Babylonish Captivity," Henry VIII received the title "defender of the faith" from the pope. This title is still claimed by the crown and stamped on all English coins.

Conflict with the pope began when Henry's roving eye fell on Anne Boleyn. The pope dragged his feet about granting him a divorce from Catherine of Aragon, so Henry took matters into his own hands. He dumped Cardinal Wolsey and set out to abolish the pope's power in England. One of Henry's astute moves was to break the hold the 645 monasteries had on the country. Their combined wealth was valued at one-fifth of the kingdom. Henry seized them, turned the monks and nuns out to shift for themselves, distributed the land to his favorites, melted the lead off the roofs of the abbeys to enrich his own coffers, and left the great buildings to the ravages of weather and time. He declared himself to be the head of the church in England, divorced Catherine, and married Anne. Even so, Henry remained enslaved by Romish dogma and signed the infamous Six Articles, which condemned to death anyone who opposed half a dozen major Catholic doctrines.

Henry's temper became increasingly violent. He used all kinds of devices to get rid of those who stood in his way. Latimer was thrown into prison and hundreds more soon followed. When Henry tired of Anne Boleyn, he trumped up a charge against her and ordered her execution. Almost as soon as Anne's head fell to the ax, he married Jane Seymour, one of Queen Anne's maids who had excited his passions. No one was safe. "If a man was an honest Papist," said Miller the historian, "he denied the king's supremacy; if he was an honest Protestant he denied the dogma of the Mass." Either way he incurred the king's wrath.

In spite of all this turmoil, Tyndale's translation of the Bible was dedicated in England in 1535 and, probably through the influence of Cranmer, Henry ordered its free distribution. A copy in Latin and English was provided for every parish in the realm. Each copy was to be chained to a pillar or desk in the choir of the church so that anyone might read it.

Meanwhile the bloody-minded king sent thousands to their deaths. One historian set the number at no less than seventy-two thousand.[1] Henry VIII was a man whom Solomon would have called a fool; Henry had no understanding beyond wanting his own way.

3. The Sinful Man (18:3)

"When the wicked cometh, then cometh also contempt, and with ignominy reproach." The word translated "wicked" here indicates a lawless person. The word translated "ignominy" refers to disgrace and outward shame.

The history of the papacy is filled with ignominy: war, persecu‐ tion, and scandal. Proof of this statement comes from Malachi Martin, a former Jesuit and still a dedicated Catholic. His book

Decline and Fall of The Catholic Church has the following revealing chapter headings:

RAGS TO RICHES
 Pontian Who Waited for Jesus
 The First Rich Father
 The Curse of Constantine
THE NEW ANTHROPOLOGY
 Staking the Great Claim
 Gregory the Great and His Empire of the Spirit
 Enter the Snake
 Leo III: Renewing Old Ties
 The Christian Heartland
RIPENESS AND DECAY
 The Nymph Who Made Popes
 The Mark of Cain
 Lord of the World
 How They Invented Conclave
 The Pope Who Wouldn't Trust
 Popes in Babylon
 Pick a Pope, Any Pope
 Leo X: Hail and Farewell!
 The Last Chance
DECLINE AND FALL
 Going…Going…
 A Brainwashing and a Last Hurrah
 The Last Pope-King
 The Last Great Roman
 Decline and Fall
 Waiting at the Crossroads[2]

Martin recorded one papal scandal after another. Twice defrocked for improper conduct, Boniface VI (896) lasted a scant two weeks. He was replaced by Stephen VII (896-897), who was known to be insane and given to wild orgies of rage. He even had the rotting corpse of a previous pope (Formosus, 891-896) exhumed and brought to the Lateran palace to be tried for capital crimes.

Sergius III (904-911) took the promiscuous Marozia as his mistress when she was just fifteen years old. Their son became John XI (931-936). This evil woman was the mother of one pope (whom she bore to another pope), the aunt of a third pope, and the grandmother of a fourth pope. With the help of her equally unscrupulous mother Theodora, Marozia used her influence to create nine popes in eight years. Two of the nine were strangled. John XII (955-963), Marozia's grandson, became pope at age fifteen. He surrounded himself with boys and girls his own age and gave himself over to gambling, hunting, and womanizing with harlots.

John XIX (1024-1033) died under suspicious circumstances. His twelve-year-old son was elevated to the papacy as Benedict IX (1033-1044). A mere boy giving the papal blessing, ordering excommunications, consecrating bishops, and pontificating dogmas must have been quite a spectacle. The young pope participated in the most debased forms of sodomy and had a taste for murder, witchcraft, and Satanism. Benedict sold the papacy to John Gratian, who became Gregory VI (1045-1046). The price was the income derived from the English church for as long as Benedict lived. This tribute was called "Peter's pence." Benedict remained in the Lateran palace, which he turned into a brothel. He used the palace as a handy vantage point from which to murder Clement II (1046-1047) and Damascus II (1048).

All these scandals occurred long before the infamous career of the Borgia pope, Alexander VI (1492-1503). His gross carnality and worldliness contributed to the development of the Protestant Reformation.

Remember that these and many other profligate and murderous popes were called "Holy Father" by the faithful. The wicked came and, as Solomon put it, brought with them contempt, ignominy, and reproach. No wonder the historian Lecky said that the annals of the church were the annals of Hell.

4. The Speaking Man (18:4-8)

a. The Man of Deep Words (18:4)

"The words of a man's mouth are as deep waters, and the wellspring of wisdom as a flowing brook [or gushing torrent]." Our words come from deep down in our thoughts. Our thoughts come from the mysterious depths of our being where we are what we are.

Our thoughts, and hence our words, are a mysterious blend of memory and character. We each have a vast computerized store of information and experiences. Our memories are full of what we have read and seen and heard and felt. We also have a store of character traits, which may include lusts, longings, hopes, fears, and ambitions. From these underground wells of memory and character come our thoughts and our words.

Sometimes words come pouring out like a torrent and great

masterpieces of oratory leave their mark, for better or for worse, upon mankind. Words poured out like white-hot lava from the mouth of Adolf Hitler. Although little of what he said was spontaneous and most of what he said was calculated, he did have a great reservoir of hate on which to draw. He was a cynical student of the power of the spoken word and discovered that pounding repetition was the most effective propaganda. In *Mein Kampf* he wrote:

> The receptivity of the great masses is extremely limited, their intelligence is small, their forgetfulness enormous. Therefore all effective propaganda should be limited to a very few points and they should be used like slogans. The masses will ultimately remember only the simplest ideas repeated a thousand times over.

Hitler said, "People can be manipulated best when they are frightened." So in his speeches he pictured Germany's degradation at the hands of the World War I victors, Germany in the grip of the Jews, Germany held captive by international finance. He would work himself up into a frenzy and carry his emotionally hypnotized audience with him.

When the Olympic games were held in Germany, Hitler turned the event into a personal propaganda triumph, exploiting to the full such events as Party Day at Nuremberg. He drove through the city in splendor. After processions and parades he took to the podium and trumpeted the glories of the Nordic race. With fist clenched and face contorted, he screamed and bellowed into the microphone. At the end of the speech sixty thousand people roared and cheered. Hitler's words were the gushing torrent of which Solomon spoke. They moved people just as an overflowing tidal wave carries everything in its path.

b. The Man of Deceitful Words (18:5)

"It is not good to accept the person of the wicked, to overthrow the righteous in judgment." The word translated "to accept" here means "to show partiality." The word translated "to overthrow" means "to turn aside" and refers to perversion of justice. Those who would subvert justice may use deceitful words to try to persuade us to do wrong, but we are to resist their spurious arguments.

Deceitful words caused suffering for John Huss of Bohemia. One of the leaders of the Reformation in Europe, he was greatly influenced by Wycliffe. Huss became father confessor to Queen Sophia and was a bold and eloquent preacher who fearlessly opposed the abuses of Rome. Gregory XII issued decrees against Huss, but Huss's position at court protected him. He was summoned to appear before a tribunal of the Vatican and when he refused to come he was excommunicated. However he continued to preach all over the country.

Then Emperor Sigismund convened the Council of Constance. He asked his brother, King Wenceslaus, to send Huss to Constance and promised him safe-conduct. Under the cover of that guarantee Huss went to Constance. Upon entering the city he was seized and brought before Pope John XXIII. A long list of charges was filed against Huss and he was called on to retract his doctrines. He refused and was thrown into prison in spite of the emperor's promise of safe-conduct. To keep Sigismund quiet the council passed a decree that no faith need be kept with a heretic.

Loud complaints were sent to the emperor. When he arrived at Constance he threatened to break down the prison where Huss was incarcerated. The Vatican brought pressure to bear, including arguments from canon law. Civil powers, it argued, had no right to protect heretics. Bowing to the wicked and their deceitful words, the cowardly and faithless emperor caved in. He abandoned John Huss to the merciless priests of Rome. On June 5, 1415, Huss was brought to trial in chains.

The emperor said to the council: "You have heard the charges against Huss; some confessed by himself, some proved by trustworthy witnesses. If he does not forswear all his errors he must be burned." John Huss said, "I was warned not to trust his safe-conduct." So Huss was publicly defrocked, his soul was committed "to the infernal demons," his books were burned, and he was burned at the stake. The emperor stands indicted and shamed by the verdict of history, by the books that are kept by the living God, and by this proverb.

c. The Man of Destructive Words (18:6-8)

(1) The Words of the Muddled Man (18:6-7)

Solomon, thinking of the results of the words of the muddled man, wrote about *his words and his body:* "A fool's lips enter into contention, and his mouth calleth for strokes" (Proverbs 18:6). This verse means that the man of destructive words is held accountable for what he says and is punished accordingly.

A good illustration of this proverb is found in *Mutiny on the Bounty* by Charles Nordhoff and James N. Hall. The authors did a considerable amount of research and although their book is cast in the form of a novel, it nevertheless conforms closely to fact. The captain of the *Bounty* was Lieutenant William Bligh, a competent seaman but a tartar and tyrant at sea. His petty persecutions of both officers and men during the long voyage to Tahiti eventually resulted in open mutiny.

One of the mutineers, Thomas Ellison, was hardly more than a boy. He seemed to think the mutiny was a lark. He flourished a bayonet under Captain Bligh's nose and asked Fletcher Christian, the leader of the mutineers, to let him guard the captain. While the mutineers prepared the launch in which Bligh and most of his loyal seamen were to be turned adrift, Ellison clowned before the captain and threw insults in his face. The other mutineers cheered Ellison on. The narrator commented, "It was a bitter experience for Bligh to be baited thus by the least of his seamen."

Ellison's words came home to roost when he and several other mutineers were captured and brought to England to face a court martial. At the trial the master of the *Bounty*, John Fryer, was reluctant to testify against Ellison but was obliged to say that he saw him among the mutineers. Mr. Cole, the boatswain, was even more reluctant but the court probed: "Did you hear the prisoner, Ellison, make any remarks?" The boatswain was forced to reply, "I heard him call Captain Bligh an old villain." Thomas Hayward, one of the midshipmen, seemed to enjoy implicating as many of the mutineers as he could. He was generally malicious and particularly hard on Ellison. In the end Ellison was found guilty of mutiny and hanged. He was punished as much for his thoughtless words as for his foolish acts. Our words have a way of catching up with us.

Solomon continued to think of the results of the words of the muddled man and wrote about *his words and his being:* "A fool's mouth is his destruction, and his lips are the snare of his soul" (Proverbs 18:7).

This proverb aptly describes the philosopher Friedrich Nietzsche. He was born in 1844, the oldest son of a country clergyman in Saxony. Both his parents came from a long line of Protestant pastors, so he was raised in a God-fearing home and in the Protestant tradition. Yet he has been labeled the most blasphemous intellectual of the nineteenth century and some people have expressed their belief that he was demon-possessed.

As a young man he believed he had solved the problem of evil in the world. Blaspheming against the Holy Spirit, Nietzsche redefined the trinity as God the Father, God the Son, and God the devil.

This was only the first step in his revolt against everything he was taught at home.

Nietzsche was convinced that all religions were harmful. He kept pounding into the ears of anyone who would listen that "God is dead." He insisted on the absolute abolition of all morality. He glorified war and the superman. He believed himself to be a prophet. He called Christianity "the one great curse, the one enormous and innermost perversion, the one great instinct for revenge, for which no means are too venomous, too underhand, too underground, and too petty...the one immoral blemish of mankind." He gloried in power. He longed for a race of men who would be tough in body and mind, egotistical, and pitiless. His philosophy lay at the root of Nazism.

Nietzsche's words were his destruction. The violence of his words warred against the timidity of his soul. (He actually asked a friend to propose for him because he was afraid to do it himself. Naturally the woman turned him down.) At last he went stark, raving mad. He threatened to shoot the kaiser. He called himself "the Crucified." He saw a cab horse being whipped and threw his arms around its neck and kissed it. The collapse was absolute and he died insane.

(2) The Words of the Meddlesome Man (18:8)

"The words of a talebearer are as wounds, and they go down into the innermost parts of the belly." The classic Biblical example of this proverb is Doeg the Edomite.

Doeg, one of King Saul's cronies, was in charge of all the king's cattle and thus controlled a significant part of the king's personal wealth. We do not know how Doeg, a member of an alien and hostile race, managed to secure so important a post. We do know that he was a scoundrel of the deepest dye.

Doeg was at the tabernacle in the priestly city of Nob when David came by, fleeing from Saul's court. Perhaps Doeg was at Nob because he had made a vow of some kind. Perhaps he was in a stage of uncleanness. Some scholars have suggested that he may have shown signs of leprosy that required priestly surveillance (Leviticus 14:1-4,11,21). He may have been seeking sanctuary for some crime, as Adonijah did (1 Kings 1:50). Whatever Doeg's reason was for being at Nob, he took note of David and his activities and saw that David obtained food and Goliath's sword from Ahimelech the priest. Ahimelech, who did not know that David was fleeing from Saul, was certainly nervous at David's presence and anxious to get rid of him.

Doeg scurried off to tell Saul what had happened. He knew of

Saul's insane jealousy of David and saw a golden opportunity to curry favor with the king. The king, in turn, summoned Ahimelech and all the priests, demanded an explanation, and accused Ahimelech of treasonable liaison with an enemy of the throne. Dissatisfied with Ahimelech's explanation, Saul ordered his guards to murder the priests of Nob. When the guards refused to lay a finger on the priests, Saul ordered Doeg to kill them. Doeg complied. Not content with slaying eighty-five men, this wicked man massacred the women and children of Nob to prove his zeal, and even killed the cattle (1 Samuel 22:7-23). Such is the soul of the talebearer when fully exposed to view.

5. The Slothful Man (18:9)

"He also that is slothful in his work is brother to him that is a great waster." The words translated "a great waster" can be rendered "an absolute destroyer." God sees a family likeness in the person who wastes his employer's time and the person who, for instance, blows up a building. One brother is destructive of the work process; the other is destructive of the work product. Both are wasters. The one is as bad as the other.

We see everywhere in creation that God hates waste. When a tree falls, insects invade the fallen giant, burrow and bore into the wood, and turn it into fiber that degenerates into particles, which in turn become fertilizer. When a lion stalks an antelope and pulls it down, the lion devours its meal; then the jackal comes to eat; then the sky is quartered by vultures that descend upon the carcass; finally the ants clean up what is left. There is no waste.

The only miracle of the Lord Jesus that is recorded in all four Gospels is the feeding of the five thousand. The loaves and fishes from a little lad's lunch multiplied prodigiously in the Lord's hands. There was bread enough and to spare. A year's wages could hardly have provided a more bountiful feast. When everyone was finished eating, the Lord sent the disciples up and down the rows to gather the leftovers, which filled twelve baskets. The Lord's attention to leftovers was intended to teach the lesson of economy.

The Lord did not want people to get the idea that it would always be that easy to secure a meal. He was not a dealer in magic. All His miracles were performed with a purpose in mind. Indeed the Lord was very sparing in His use of miracles. There are only about thirty-six recorded in the Gospels—an average of less than three a month during His three and a half years of public ministry.

"Waste not, want not" is our companion English proverb to

Proverbs 18:9. It is evident from even a cursory reading of Proverbs that God endorses the work ethic. He sees something reprehensible in the behavior of a man who wastes his employer's time out of sheer laziness. The modern labor-union tactic of featherbedding has no place in the value system of the Bible. The wasteful practice of built-in obsolescence is equally condemned.

6. The Safe Man (18:10-12)

a. The Hiding Place (18:10-11)

Solomon pointed us first to *the right hiding place:* "The name of the Lord is a strong tower: the righteous runneth into it, and is safe" (Proverbs 18:10).

The name of the Lord is the subject of extensive Old and New Testament revelation. We first meet God as *Elohim,* the God who *creates. Elohim* is one of His primary names. It occurs some 2,700 times in the Old Testament and 32 times in Genesis 1, the great creation chapter. What a name! What a strong tower! *Elohim* is contracted to *El* some 250 times. *El* means "God the Almighty," the God who brought Israel out of Egypt (Numbers 23:22). God is also *Eloah* (first mentioned in Deuteronomy 32:15,17); in contrast to idols, *Eloah* is the living God who is to be worshiped.

We meet God most frequently as *Jehovah,* the God who *covenants* (usually this name is translated as LORD, in capitals, in the King James version). *Jehovah* is said to occur approximately 11,600 times in the Old Testament. The name combines the three tenses of the verb "to be." As *Jehovah,* God reveals Himself as the One who was and is and is to be.

Ten compound titles for God are based on the name *Jehovah.* He is *Jehovah Jireh,* "the Lord who provides"; *Jehovah Ropheka,* "the Lord who leads"; *Jehovah Nissi,* "the Lord our banner"; *Jehovah Mekkaddishkem,* "the Lord who sanctifies"; *Jehovah Shalom,* "the Lord our peace"; *Jehovah Sabbaoth,* "the Lord of hosts"; *Jehovah Tsidkenu,* "the Lord our righteousness"; *Jehovah Shammah,* "the Lord who is there"; *Jehovah Elyon,* "the Lord most high"; and *Jehovah Roi,* "the Lord who is our shepherd." Seven of these compound titles are referred to in the matchless twenty-third Psalm. What more could we need than is provided in these names?

The title *Jah,* which occurs 49 times, was first used by Moses when he celebrated Israel's triumph over pharaoh at the Red Sea. In the celebration Moses sang the first song in Scripture (Exodus 15:2). *Jah* signifies that God is the eternal One who inhabits eternity.

Adonai is the name of the God who *controls*. It conveys the idea of His absolute lordship and occurs in Scripture about 300 times. Almost always appearing in the plural and possessive form, *Adonai* is the God of ownership or mastery, the One who claims the unrestricted obedience of all.

No wonder Solomon indicated that the name of the Lord is a strong tower! The strongest towers built by men can be taken by siege or overthrown by storm. All along the Welsh border a visitor to my native land can see the ruins of great castles and strong towers built by men. The name of the Lord is a much better stronghold than any devised by man.

In northern Somerset, England, there is a rocky gorge known as Burrington Combe. Thereabouts sheep and cattle roam the moors, and small villages cling to valleys that look out toward the Severn. One of these villages is Blagdon, where Augustus Toplady lived and ministered as the curate. While he was walking down toward the Combe one day, a violent thunderstorm sent him hurrying for shelter. In all the great gorge cut between towering cliffs, there seemed to be no hiding place. Then he saw a cleft in the rocky limestone near the gorge. He hurried toward it and found he could just stand upright within its shelter. He took refuge there as the rain came down in torrents and the thunder pealed. Even as he stood there, these words welled up in his soul:

> Rock of Ages, cleft for me,
> Let me hide myself in Thee;
> Let the water and the blood,
> From Thy riven side which flowed,
> Be of sin the double cure,
> Cleanse me from its guilt and pow'r.

The church seized upon the hymn. Gladstone, prime minister of England, was so impressed by it that he translated it into elegant Latin. Every July thousands of people come from near and far to stand outside the cleft in the rock and sing Toplady's words. "Rock," after all, is one of those many and varied titles of God in the Old Testament (Deuteronomy 32:4,31) and another New Testament name for Christ (1 Corinthians 10:4).

Having pointed to the right hiding place, Solomon warned about *the wrong hiding place:* "The rich man's wealth is his strong city, and as an high wall in his own conceit" (Proverbs 18:11). This verse is obviously deliberately contrasted with the preceding one.

Three rich men appear in the record of the preaching ministry

of Jesus: the rich young ruler; the rich man who planned to build
bigger and better barns; and the rich man in Hell. I am inclined to
believe that they are one and the same person, seen by the omniscient Lord at three stages of life. If these men are not the same
person, they certainly embody three stages of the same principle.

Let's assume that these men were one person who made three
mistakes. We see his *first* mistake in Mark 10:17-22. When he came
to Christ he was full of enthusiasm, honest and sincere (or so he
thought), and eager to give himself to Christ. Jesus loved him. Jesus
loved his eagerness, his optimism, and his offer of fulltime service.
However he had a flaw. He was rich, and that was a major obstacle
because riches are deceptive. They bind people to this world and
give them an artificial sense of power and well-being. Seeing the
hold that wealth already had on the young man, Jesus challenged
him to give it up in exchange for a cross. Now the man's soul was laid
bare. Would he choose his money or the Master? The struggle was
short though sharp—and money won. The rich man's wealth was
his strong city. The bottom line was that he preferred to trust in his
wealth.

We see the man's *final* mistake in Luke 12:16-21. He plunged into
business to blot out of his mind the haunting face of Jesus. When he
heard about the cross and the terrible death of Christ, he probably
congratulated himself on his narrow escape. He heard rumors of
the resurrection but discounted them. He heard about the church
but wrote it off as some kind of new religious cult. He was consumed
with more important things. He was expanding his business, buying
new fields and farms, hiring new hands, and making more money.
He was doing extremely well. He had never seen such crops. He sat
up in bed one night and said to himself, *I'll have to build bigger and
better barns. I am far richer than I have ever been. I can afford an early
retirement. I can start making plans to enjoy myself. I can build a winter
palace in Jericho and a summer estate in Lebanon. Maybe I'll travel. I would
like to see some far country and get some fun out of life. Maybe I'll turn my
business over to my stewards. My "five-talent man" can be trusted to carry
on.* Little did the rich man know that he would die before morning.

We see the man's *fatal* mistake in Luke 16:19-31. He woke up in
a lost eternity. What use was his money now? He had left it all
behind. He was without God, without Christ, and without hope. His
strong castle had been made of sand. Lazarus, who had begged at
his gate for an occasional crust of bread, had made the wiser choice
and was ten thousand times better off. He was in Abraham's bosom.
The former beggar was rich and happy and eternally blessed. The
rich man longed for a drop of water, a moment's relief, and the

salvation of his lost brothers, who were already squabbling over his estate.

b. The Humble Place (18:12)

"Before destruction the heart of man is haughty; and before honour is humility." This proverb is illustrated in the story of David and Goliath.

The Holy Spirit tells us that Goliath was "a champion" (1 Samuel 17:4). The Hebrew word translated "champion" is *ish-habbenayim* and literally means "the man between the two hosts" or "the duelist."[3] Arrayed from head to foot in imposing armor, the great giant from Gath swaggered before the whole army of Israel. When the Hebrews had trouble finding a man to fight Goliath, his blasphemies and bravado increased. As Solomon said, "Before destruction the heart of man is haughty." Then David came.

> And when the Philistine looked about, and saw David, he disdained him: for he was but a youth, and ruddy, and of a fair countenance. And the Philistine said unto David, Am I a dog, that thou comest to me with staves? And the Philistine cursed David by his gods. And the Philistine said to David, Come to me, and I will give thy flesh unto the fowls of the air, and to the beasts of the field (1 Samuel 17:42-44).

David was only about sixteen or seventeen years of age, but he was already a seasoned veteran in his own right. He had killed a lion and a bear. But better still, David knew God. More than likely he had already written the matchless twenty-third Psalm.

David was astonished that nobody in the Hebrew army was willing to take on Goliath. Saul was a giant himself. Jonathan was twice the man his father was. Eliab, Abinadab, and Shammah—David's brothers—were in the camp. Abner, the commander-in-chief of the army, was there. *Doesn't anyone have enough faith in God to fight this Philistine?* David wondered. *Goliath has defied God and is as good as dead already.*

In all humility David offered to fight Goliath. David was nobody; the battle was the Lord's. David knew the Lord to be his shepherd. There was nothing to fear, even in the valley of the shadow of death. The Lord would be with him. The Lord would not be intimidated by the Philistine giant, however great and tall. Armed with his simple trust in God, David ventured into the valley. To Goliath's taunts he had but one answer: God!

Then said David to the Philistine, Thou comest to me with a
sword, and with a spear, and with a shield: but I come to thee
in the name of the Lord of hosts, the God of the armies of
Israel, whom thou hast defied. This day will the Lord deliver
thee into mine hand; and I will smite thee, and take thine head
from thee; and I will give the carcases of the host of the
Philistines this day unto the fowls of the air, and to the wild
beasts of the earth; that all the earth may know that there is a
God in Israel. And all this assembly shall know that the Lord
saveth not with sword and spear: for the battle is the Lord's,
and he will give you into our hands (1 Samuel 17:45-47).

"Before honour is humility." David was humble and honor came
soon enough. He slew the Philistine and within a short time David's
name was a household word in Israel and everyone had learned a
new slogan: "Saul hath slain his thousands, and David his ten
thousands" (1 Samuel 18:7).

7. The Silly Man (18:13)

"He that answereth a matter before he heareth it, it is folly and
shame unto him." This proverb is illustrated by the Philippian
magistrates.

Paul and Silas arrived in Philippi, preached with remarkable
power, and planted an infant church in this first European city to
receive the gospel. Paul, however, was disturbed by the unwelcome
attentions of a slave girl. This poor girl was possessed by an evil spirit
that gave her extrasensory powers. Through her the demon kept on
bearing witness that Paul was God's servant, but the last thing Paul
wanted was the testimony of a demon. Finally he cast out the demon
and restored the girl to normality. Her masters had made a great
deal of money by exploiting this demented girl's psychic powers, so
they were enraged by the exorcism and dragged the two missionaries before the authorities.

Philippi was a Roman colony and the magistrates were Romans.
They bore the same title *(praetor)* as the magistrates in Rome. The
magistrates in Philippi listened to the prosecution: "These men,
being Jews, do exceedingly trouble our city, And teach customs, which
are not lawful for us to receive, neither to observe, being Romans"
(Acts 16:20-21). The prosecution had the backing of the mob, for
antisemitism was never far from the surface in the Roman empire.

The magistrates did not call for the defense to testify. They made
up their minds at once. "He that answereth a matter before he

heareth it, it is folly and shame unto him," said Solomon. He was right, for there was another very important side to this story, as these foolish magistrates would soon find out. They took one look at the missionaries—obviously Jews, seemingly poor, disheveled from having been roughed up by the mob—and made up their minds. We can hear the magistrates saying, "Scourge them! Then secure them. Case dismissed!"

Beaten and imprisoned, their feet locked in the stocks, Paul and Silas sang! Then came the astonishing midnight miracle, followed by the conversion of the jailer. "Let those men go" was the word from the magistrates the next morning (Acts 16:35).

We can almost hear Paul's response: "Go? Not on your life! We have been subjected to a gross miscarriage of justice. Friend jailer, go to those magistrates and pass along this bit of news. Tell them that they have beaten us openly, uncondemned, and that we are *Romans*. Let them digest that. Then tell them we are not going to leave. We have no intention of being pushed unceremoniously out by the back door. No indeed! Tell them to come here and lead us out with every mark of the respect due our rank."

We can well believe that the magistrates were alarmed. Roman citizenship was rare. Those who had it were specially protected from abuses of the law. No Roman citizen could be scourged or put to death without an appeal to the governor. If the magistrates had given Paul a fair trial, they would have heard that chilling word *Romans*. If Paul and Silas demanded their rights, these magistrates would be in hot water, for Roman rules were of prime importance in colony cities such as Philippi. With their tails between their legs, the magistrates came, full of apologies and polite requests. They begged the missionaries to leave and not to press charges against them.

8. The Stricken Man (18:14)

"The spirit of a man will sustain his infirmity; but a wounded spirit who can bear?"

Years ago an English lady married an English man and the couple migrated to Canada. They settled in a railroad town in the Northwest, built a cottage, and established a new life. Presently two children were born to them and life followed a predictable course. The man worked on the railroad; the woman busied herself with her children and the everyday concerns of life in a small village.

Then tragedy struck. The woman contracted tuberculosis and, as was common in those days, was sent to a sanitarium. Her two girls were packed off to live with an aunt. The husband carried out his duties in loneliness and sorrow. From time to time he visited his girls and his wife. The wife became fretful, but hoped for a cure.

Time passed. The family was briefly reunited when the mother's health improved, but the separation had left scars. New stresses and strains appeared in the marriage and before long, sickness reasserted itself. The mother was sent back to the sanitarium, this time for good. Her spirit, however, was strong. She had remarkable determination. *I will get better!* she thought. *I will, I will, I will!*

Her husband remained at home. His work and friends were there, and he hoped maybe one day he could reunite his family there. The house however was so empty and the cold Canadian winters were so long. He did his work, he chopped and carried wood for the insatiable winter fires, he made his own meals, and he endured the loneliness.

Then the other woman came to town. She was clever, kind, and lots of fun. She visited the bereaved man's house and showed him little kindnesses. One thing led to another and before long the man was hopelessly entangled. He went to see his wife and suggested a divorce.

"Divorce?" she said. "Never!" She made up her mind that she would never divorce him. She would never let that other woman take her place. It was bad enough to have been so scandalously betrayed. But never, so long as the sick lady lived, would she let the other woman become her husband's wife. The wife was determined to outlive her husband so that the other woman could never marry her Bill.

Her husband was still young and healthy. By all the odds, he could have expected to outlive his consumptive wife, whose lungs were half eaten away. But her spirit was fierce, determined, and strong. She willed to outlive her husband. And she did!

The husband was a heavy smoker, breathing in death by the carton. He came to some kind of terms with his conscience and the other woman moved into his home. They lived together happily enough, conveniently forgetting the wife in the sanitarium. They even invited the man's children home for the holidays.

Years went by and the legitimate wife became the wonder of the wards. Doctors came to study her case. Other patients came to the sanitarium, succumbed to the disease, and died. The disease remained active in the wife, but she didn't die. "The spirit of a man will sustain his infirmity," said Solomon. So will the spirit of a woman. Her children grew up and married, and the strange stalemate continued. The guilty pair hoped for the wife's death so they could legitimize their liaison, but the wife lived on, fighting off death by sheer determination, willpower, and spirit.

Then Death came calling. But he didn't come to the sanitarium; he came to a Vancouver hospital where the husband lay, his smoke-blackened lungs full of cancer. My wife and I went to his funeral.

In the sanitarium the wife heard the news. Her husband was dead and the other woman could never marry him. It was a triumph of sorts. Then overwhelmed by her loss, the dispirited wife gave up the struggle. She felt there was no reason to live. Within six months she died and we attended her funeral. "A wounded spirit who can bear?" She had been in that sanitarium for an incredible twenty-five years, sustained by her spirit. But when the man she had loved died, even her indomitable spirit gave up.

9. The Seeking Man (18:15)

"The heart of the prudent getteth knowledge; and the ear of the wise seeketh knowledge." Man has an insatiable thirst for knowledge, a thirst Adam and Eve indulged in the garden of Eden to the ruin and eternal loss of the race.

God created us to be curious about the universe. He has left it up to us to find out all we can about its origin, nature, and history by the process of *reasoning*. But we can derive certain knowledge only by the process of *revelation*. Truths about God, the ultimate origin of the universe, the future destiny of the race, the great secrets of eternity, the mystery of iniquity, the true nature and character of extrasensory beings, and another person's true character and innermost thoughts—all these kinds of knowledge can be acquired only as they are revealed to us.

Some of the knowledge we derive in the process of reasoning is filthy, foul, and forbidden, and we would do well not to contaminate our minds with it. But vast fields of beneficial knowledge are open to us to explore and experience. The world's libraries bear evidence of man's yearning to know more and more.

It has been said that nobody has ever used more than 2 percent of his total mental capacity—not even Shakespeare, Beethoven, or Einstein. What would have resulted from the full employment of man's genius if the fall had not ruined the race? That remains to be seen by the redeemed in the ages to come. Doubtless Adam would have moved from ruling the garden to ruling the globe and ended up ruling the galaxy. When we get our resurrection bodies and are restored to our full potential, we will know what would have happened.

But even in his fallen state, man is a genius. One of the characteristics of the endtime is a tremendous increase in knowledge, as foretold by Daniel 12:4. Such an increase is a prominent feature of our own age. Our electron microscopes can magnify 20 million times and can photograph a particle that has a diameter of about 4 billionths of an inch. Our computers can do 80 million calculations a second (6.9 trillion a day!) and doubtless these statistics are already out of date.

Incidentally, a great effort is required even to begin to understand what is meant by a mere billion. The following examples may help us grasp the concept. A stack of a billion dollar bills would be 125 miles high (a pitifully short stack in terms of space mathematics). An airplane propeller spinning at a rate of 2,400 revolutions per minute without stopping day or night for a whole year would turn less than a billion times. The world's population is about 5.5 billion (July 1993). Our gross national product is calculated in trillions.

Sir Arthur Eddington, in his book *The Philosophy of Physical Science*, made the statement: "I believe there are 15,747,724,136,275,002, 577,605,653,961,181,555,468,044,717,914,527,116,709,366,231, 425,076,185,631,031,296 protons in the universe, and the same number of electrons." To give a more manageable figure, the earth weighs 6,585,600,000,000,000,000,000,000 tons. Biologists estimate that the human brain contains approximately 1 trillion cells—a mind-boggling number that we have calculated by using only 2 percent of them.

Still man yearns to know more and more about the things that can be *researched*. Surely those who know the Lord should show the same drive and determination to know Him better and to know more and more about the things He has *revealed*.

10. The Successful Man (18:16)

"A man's gift maketh room for him, and bringeth him before great men." Everyone has a gift he can discover, develop, and display.

Benjamin Franklin was a man of many gifts. One of America's heroes, he was the first man to show Europeans that his country was developing its own culture. When he traveled to Paris at the height of his fame, the French hailed him as a scientist, philosopher, educator, author, and statesman. Yet he left school at age ten and went to work making candles and soap. The fifteenth of the seventeen children of a poor candlemaker, Franklin became the first self-made American. He taught himself Latin, French, Italian, and Spanish. He found employment as a printer, went into business for himself, and started a newspaper and then a magazine. He had made a fortune by the age of forty-two. He then retired from business and devoted forty years to the service of his country, twenty-five of them in England and France.

Franklin has been acclaimed along with Newton for being one of the most important scientists of the modern age. His book on electricity was translated into several languages and was hailed in Europe. He was the first to identify positive and negative electricity. He invented the Franklin stove, which contains a hot-air radiator still in use. At age seventy-eight he invented bifocal spectacles. He was the first person to study hydrodynamics. He charted the gulf stream and discovered that storms rotate even as they move forward. In Paris he witnessed the first ascent of a balloon carrying people and at once saw its potential. When a skeptic asked what use an air balloon could be, Franklin asked, "What good is a newborn baby?"

In 1743 he founded the American Philosophical Society, the first scientific association in this country. He was elected to be a Fellow of the Royal Society, one of the most prestigious scientific societies in the world, and he was given honorary degrees by Oxford and Edinburgh Universities. Franklin founded the first professional police force, the first volunteer fire company, and the school that became the University of Pennsylvania.

He was a successful author who could write in elegant English style. His *Poor Richard's Almanack* brought him a reputation for wit and wisdom. He founded the first free library. Many of his sayings have become the common currency of our language: "Early to bed, early to rise, makes a man healthy, wealthy and wise"; "Nothing is inevitable but death and taxes"; "Half a truth is often a great lie."

Politically he did everything he could to prevent England from passing the Stamp Act, which precipitated the American Revolution. Franklin was a delegate to the convention that drafted the Constitution of the United States.

Truly, his gifts made room for him and brought him before great men. If he had lived in Solomon's day the wise king would have loved him. When at age eighty-two Franklin retired from public life, he received a letter that said, "So long as I retain my memory, you will be thought of with respect, veneration and affection by your sincere friend, George Washington." When Franklin died at age eighty-four he was the most famous private citizen and the best-loved public figure in the world. The entire French government went into mourning for three days and all America lamented his passing.[4]

11. The Striving Man (18:17-19)

Proverbs 18:17 presents *the loud boaster:* "He that is first in his own cause seemeth just; but his neighbour cometh and searcheth him." A man can usually make a good case for himself—until someone comes along with the other side of the story and casts a different light on the matter.

Consider the classic New Testament illustration of the Pharisee. He belonged to a strict fundamentalist Jewish sect that apparently started before the Maccabean war as a protest against the Hellenizing that threatened distinctive Jewish survival. As a group the Pharisees opposed the villainous persecutions of Antiochus Epiphanes (175-164 B.C.). They were devoted to the Mosaic law and championed what they called "the oral law." They believed in the immortality of the soul, the supernatural, resurrection, and a future life. By the time of Christ, however, the Pharisees had degenerated into an ultralegalist party dedicated to deadening and truth-eroding traditions.

The religion of the Pharisees was largely a matter of externals. They greatly burdened the people with endless rules and regulations that they appended to the law. The Pharisees became active enemies of Christ and, as recorded in the Gospels, took a leading role in opposing Him.

In Luke 18:11-12 we overhear one of the sect praying: "The Pharisee stood and prayed thus with himself, God, I thank thee, that I am not as other men are, extortioners, unjust, adulterers, or even as this publican. I fast twice in the week, I give tithes of all that I possess." According to him, he was a paragon of virtue. As Solomon put it, he was "first in his own cause."

"But his neighbour cometh and searcheth him," Solomon added. The Pharisee was exposed by the despised publican, who "standing afar off, would not lift up so much as his eyes unto heaven, but smote upon his breast, saying, God be merciful to me a sinner" (Luke 18:13). The Pharisee was also exposed by the Lord Jesus, who said with a fine touch of sarcasm that he "prayed thus with himself." Jesus added that the publican was the one who went home justified.

The Pharisee and his kind were denounced by John the Baptist as a "generation of vipers" (Matthew 3:7). The Lord pronounced eight scathing and terrible woes upon them (Matthew 23) in His last lengthy public utterance before preparing Himself for Calvary. The Pharisees do not appear to us to be the fine fellows they put themselves up to be.

Proverbs 18:18 presents *the lifted barrier:* "The lot causeth contentions to cease, and parteth between the mighty." This verse suggests a picture of two people at odds. Their disagreement has erected a barrier between them. To settle their difference they will cast lots. Nowadays we toss a coin to see if it comes down heads or tails. In Old Testament times the high priest used the urim and the thummim to settle difficulties.

Between Calvary and Pentecost the early disciples faced a difficult problem. Jesus had chosen twelve disciples, obviously intending them to have some relationship to the twelve Old Testament tribes, but Judas defected. When he turned traitor and committed suicide, he left a gap in their number. A replacement had to be chosen because Jesus had said, "Ye which have followed me, in the regeneration [the making of all things new] when the Son of man shall sit in the throne of his glory, ye also shall sit upon twelve thrones, judging the twelve tribes of Israel" (Matthew 19:28). There had to be twelve.

The disciples debated the question of who should replace Judas, spelled out certain criteria, and reduced the number of possible candidates to two. Then the selection process bogged down because both finalists had equal qualifications. So the disciples cut this Gordian knot by casting lots and their contentions ceased.

Actually it is highly debatable whether the disciples should have taken any action. Some people say this casting of lots was the last act of the old dispensation and a perfectly legitimate proceeding. Others say that the disciples should have waited until after Pentecost and let the Holy Spirit decide. Still others argue further that He *did* decide. Matthias, the man the disciples chose (Acts 1:21-26), is never heard of again. He plunged back into the obscurity from whence he came. Then the Holy Spirit indicated *His* choice for the vacancy and added the apostle Paul to the number. It will be interesting to see whose name is written into the twelfth foundation stone of the celestial city (Revelation 21:14). Still, the lot put an end to even latent contention in the upper room, so it served a useful purpose.

Proverbs 18:19 presents *the lost brother:* "A brother offended is harder to be won than a strong city: and their contentions are like the bars of a castle."

In Sir Henry Rider Haggard's *King Solomon's Mines,* Allan Quatermain first met Sir Henry Curtis aboard a coastal steamer heading for Natal. The famous African hunter struck up an acquaintance with the English baronet and his friend Captain Good. Curtis explained to Quatermain that he was in Africa to look for his brother Neville.

"He was," went on Sir Henry, "my only and younger brother, and till five years ago I do not suppose that we were ever a month away from each other. But just about five years ago a misfortune befell us, as sometimes does happen in families. We had quarrelled bitterly, and I behaved very unjustly to my brother in my anger." Here Captain Good nodded his head vigorously to himself. The ship gave a big roll just then, so that the looking-glass, which was fixed opposite us to starboard, was for a moment nearly over our heads, and as I was sitting with my hands in my pockets and staring upward, I could see him nodding like anything.

"As I daresay you know," went on Sir Henry, "if a man dies intestate, and has no property but land—real property it is called in England—it all descends to his eldest son. It so happened that just at the time when we quarrelled our father died intestate. He had put off making his will until it was too late. The result was that my brother, who had not been brought up to any profession, was left without a penny. Of course it would have been my duty to provide for him, but at the time the quarrel between us was so bitter that I did not—to my shame I say it (and he sighed deeply)—offer to do anything. It was not that I grudged him anything, but I waited for him to make advances, and he made none. I am sorry to trouble you with all this, Mr. Quatermain, but I must, to make things clear; eh, Good?"

"Quite so, quite so," said the captain....

"Well," went on Sir Henry, "my brother had a few hundred pounds to his account at the time, and without saying anything to me he drew out this paltry sum, and, having adopted the name of Neville, started off for South Africa in the wild hope of making a fortune. This I heard afterwards. Some three years passed, and I heard nothing of my brother, though I wrote several times. Doubtless the letters never reached him. But as time went on I grew more and more troubled about him. I found out, Mr. Quatermain, that blood is thicker than water."

Sir Henry Curtis had discovered the pride of a brother offended. He would discover too that winning his brother back would be a long and costly business. An agent in Africa was unable to find the brother and Curtis continued:

"Well, Mr. Quatermain, as time went on I became more and more anxious to find out if my brother was alive or dead, and, if alive to get him home again....So, to cut a long story short, I made up my mind to come out and look for him myself, and Captain Good was so kind as to come with me."

After a long, adventuresome search they found the brother. He had suffered great hardships trying to cross the vast desert that led to Kukuanaland, where King Solomon's diamond mines were rumored to be. Finally he reached an oasis, only to meet with a terrible accident that totally incapacitated him. There he had been forced to stay, hoping against hope that someone would turn up. When the older brother turned up, the younger brother was so relieved to see him that the old quarrel was forgotten altogether.

This particular "brother offended" was ready for reconciliation. That of course is not always the case. Nor are offenders always that willing to right wrongs. The Bible, a down-to-earth book, tells numerous stories of brothers who were "harder to be won than a strong city." We think of Cain and Abel, Isaac and Ishmael (from whom has come the age-long feud between Jews and Arabs), Jacob and Esau, and Amnon and Absalom.

We also think of the long and tragic history of the church. It is sad enough when a local church splits over doctrinal deviations. It is a greater tragedy when Christian brethren squabble over trivialities. Too soon people take sides and bitter hostilities are generated—sometimes over the color of the carpet or whether one cup or individual cups should be used in communion services. Such contention is enough to make even the angels weep. Before the church began, the Lord set up the machinery for reconciling brethren (Matthew 18:15-22). We would do well to enthrone these rules in our hearts. If we neglect them we will experience the tragic truth of Solomon's words.

12. The Satisfied Man (18:20-24)

If we are to live satisfied lives, we need to tame the tongue, win a wife, mind the mouth, and find a friend.

Proverbs 18:20 talks about *taming the tongue:* "A man's belly shall be satisfied with the fruit of his mouth; and with the increase of his lips shall he be filled." In other words, we have to live with the consequences of what we say. The word "belly" is a figure of speech for the man himself. Sometimes we have to live with bitter, upsetting consequences, and sometimes we have to live with blessed, happy consequences. When a man swallows something, he has to accept the consequences; similarly when a man says something, consequences follow. It is as important to pay attention to what comes out of the mouth as to pay attention to what goes into the mouth.

Consider the words of Rebekah. When she went to the well one day, she had an experience that changed her life. A stranger, obviously a person of considerable consequence judging by his camels and their accouterments, asked her for a drink. She courteously responded to his request and, going far beyond the ordinary demands of courtesy, offered to water his camels. Little did she know that the stranger was Abraham's servant, that he was seeking a bride for his master's son, that she had just passed a test, and that her life would never be the same again. She must have stared in wonder when the stranger gave her some expensive jewelry.

Her brother Laban took one look at the costly presents and rushed out to meet the stranger. He explained his errand and we can be sure he did not minimize the wealth and power of Abraham or fail to extol the character and prospects of Isaac. When her brother and mother asked, "Wilt thou go with this man?" Rebekah's answer was ready. "I will go," she said (Genesis 24:58). We can be sure she was satisfied with the fruit of her mouth.

Years passed. Twin boys were born to Rebekah. Of the two, her heart went out to Jacob. Esau was Isaac's favorite. When Isaac was old, he plotted with Esau to give him the blessing that rightfully belonged to Jacob (Genesis 25:20-23). Rebekah overheard Isaac and Esau and concocted a plan to forestall them. She said to Jacob, "Now therefore, my son, obey my voice." Brushing aside Jacob's obvious excuses she continued, "Upon me be thy curse, my son: only obey my voice" (27:8,13). Jacob obeyed his mother and used deception to obtain the blessing. The results were disastrous. Esau swore he would kill Jacob and Rachel had to persuade Isaac to send Jacob away. She suggested he visit her brother Laban in Padanaram. "Tarry with him a few days," she said, "until thy brother's fury turn away...then I will send, and fetch thee from thence" (27:44-45). Jacob was gone for twenty years and Rebekah never saw him again. The fruit of her lips was bitter this time.

"Death and life are in the power of the tongue: and they that love it shall eat the fruit thereof," said Solomon (Proverbs 18:21). The pen is mightier than the sword and so is the tongue.

Shakespeare acknowledged the power of the tongue in his great masterpiece *Julius Caesar*. After the assassination of Caesar, Mark Antony asked for permission to speak at the funeral. Brutus agreed. Cassius, a much more down-to-earth man than Brutus, tried to persuade Brutus that it was dangerous to let Antony speak. Cassius said:

Brutus, a word with you.—
You know not what you do: Do not consent
That Antony speak in his funeral.
Know you how much the people may be mov'd
By that which he will utter?

But Brutus was not to be dissuaded and Antony was given the permission he sought. A short while later, standing by Caesar's corpse, Antony vowed vengeance. He spoke to Caesar's remains:

O, pardon me, thou bleeding piece of earth,
That I am meek and gentle with these butchers!
Thou art the ruins of the noblest man
That ever lived in the tide of times.
Woe to the hands that shed this costly blood!
Over thy wounds now do I prophesy,
Which like dumb mouths do ope their ruby lips
To beg the voice and utterance of my tongue:
A curse shall light upon the limbs of men;
Domestic fury and fierce civil strife
Shall cumber all the parts of Italy.

Antony promised that before long he would "cry 'Havoc!' and let slip the dogs of war." When the time came for Antony to speak to the people of Rome, he kept harping on a single note, saying that Brutus and all the conspirators were honorable men. Antony played upon the people's intellects:

Friends, Romans, countrymen, lend me your ears;
I come to bury Caesar, not to praise him.
The evil that men do lives after them,
The good is oft interred with their bones;
So let it be with Caesar. The noble Brutus
Hath told you Caesar was ambitious;
If it were so, it was a grievous fault,
And grievously hath Caesar answer'd it.
Here, under leave of Brutus and the rest,—
For Brutus is an honourable man,
So are they all, all honourable men,—
Come I to speak in Caesar's funeral.
He was my friend, faithful and just to me;
But Brutus says he was ambitious,
And Brutus is an honourable man.

He hath brought many captives home to Rome,
Whose ransom did the general coffers fill;
Did this in Caesar seem ambitious?
When that the poor have cried, Caesar hath wept;
Ambition should be made of sterner stuff.
Yet Brutus says he was ambitious,
And Brutus is an honourable man.
You all did see that on the Lupercal
I thrice presented him a kingly crown,
Which he did thrice refuse. Was this ambition?
Yet Brutus says, he was ambitious,
And, sure, he is an honourable man.

Then Antony hinted at Caesar's will. He told the people of Rome that they were Caesar's heirs. He gathered the people around the corpse. He subtly reminded them of Caesar's victories. He accused the conspirators of cutting short an illustrious career. As Antony had played upon the people's minds, now he played upon their emotions:

If you have tears, prepare to shed them now.
You all do know this mantle; I remember
The first time ever Caesar put it on.
'T was on a summer's evening, in his tent,
That day he overcame the Nervii.
Look! in this place ran Cassius' dagger through;
See what a rent the envious Casca made;
Through this the well-beloved Brutus stabb'd;
And as he pluck'd his cursed steel away,
Mark how the blood of Caesar follow'd it,
As rushing out of doors, to be resolv'd
If Brutus so unkindly knock'd or no;
For Brutus, as you know, was Caesar's angel.—
Judge, O you gods, how dearly Caesar lov'd him!—
This was the most unkindest cut of all;
For, when the noble Caesar saw him stab,
Ingratitude, more strong than traitors' arms,
Quite vanquish'd him. Then burst his mighty heart.

Finally the clever orator played upon the people's wills. He appealed for action. He demanded redress. He stirred them up to go to war.

I am no orator, as Brutus is;
But, as you know me all, a plain blunt man,
That love my friend; and that they know full well
That gave me public leave to speak of him.
For I have neither wit, nor words, nor worth,
Action, nor utterance, nor the power of speech,
To stir men's blood; I only speak right on;
I tell you that which you yourselves do know.
Show you sweet Caesar's wounds, poor poor dumb mouths,
And bid them speak for me. But, were I Brutus,
And Brutus Antony, there were an Antony
Would ruffle up your spirits, and put a tongue
In every wound of Caesar that should move
The stones of Rome to rise and mutiny.

As a final prod, Antony read the will in which Caesar had made the ordinary people of Rome his beneficiaries. Yes, you were right, Solomon. "Death and life are in the power of the tongue."

Proverbs 18:22 talks about the need for *winning a wife:* "Whoso findeth a wife findeth a good thing, and obtaineth favour of the Lord."

Marriage was God's idea. Having created the world and all its wonders, and having put Adam (the crown of His creation) in the garden, God said that everything was very good (Genesis 1:31), and He rested. Then God saw Adam lordly, but lonely and He said, "It is not good" (Genesis 2:18). "It is not good that the man should be alone; I will make him an help meet for him."

One by one the various animals came to Adam to be named. It was obvious to Adam that each one had its mate and that he alone had no companion of his own kind. He became aware of a need. Then God put him to sleep. He went to sleep in the will of God and when he awoke, there was Eve: the perfect helpmeet, the woman God had created just for him! God married them and paradise was perfected. Marriage was His idea. It still is.

Finding a wife is not the same as finding a woman. Solomon had no trouble finding women. His position and power, his good looks and personal charm, and his wit and wisdom made him attractive to women. He collected a thousand women one way or another, but it is doubtful that he ever found a wife among them (Ecclesiastes 7:27-28). He did genuinely lose his heart to one woman and, from all we know about her, she could have been the perfect wife for whom he longed. However by the time he met her, he had already been married sixty times and was living with another eighty women (Song of Solomon 6:8), so she turned him down cold. What a fascinating, Christ-exalting, pride-abasing, devil-exposing story it is.[5]

The brides of the Bible make an interesting study. Seven of them taken together give us a picture of marriage and a picture of the church. Marriage, of course, is supposed to mirror the relationship of Christ and His church (Ephesians 5:22-33).

In Eve we see the *formation* of the church. She was a member of Adam's body, complete and one in him just as he was complete and one in her.

In Rebekah we see the *faith* of the church. She was united to the one who had been to mount Moriah and now stood on the resurrection side of death. We see her journeying to Isaac; she is led step by step by the one sent from his father.

Rachel's story sets before us the *foes* of the church. She gave her heart to her beloved, but she had to wait. She had to face greed and envy in others. She had to sow in tears before she could reap in joy.

In Asenath we see the *future* of the church. She was made to sit with Joseph in high places. She was joined to him who had a name above every name. Before him every knee was made to bow.

Ruth depicts the *footsteps* of the church. She walked from Moab— the land under the curse of God—to Boaz, the kinsman-redeemer who loved her and bought her and made her his very own.

Michal mirrors the *failures* of the church. Although she was married to David, she married another and lived a life of ease when she should have been sharing the rejection of the Lord's anointed.

In contrast to Michal, Abigail depicts the *fervor* of the church. In her life we see Christ given His rightful place as Lord. Fourteen times in eight short verses she referred to David as lord (1 Samuel 25:24-31). By the death of Nabal she was set free from the law of her husband to be married to another, even to him who was the Lord's anointed.

There is nothing accidental in the forming of this composite picture of the church. The types of the Old Testament, when properly understood, are as accurate as mathematics.

Proverbs 18:23 talks about the need for *minding the mouth:* "The poor useth intreaties; but the rich answereth roughly." God takes note of their conversations. Some people understand this verse to mean that the rich man does wrong and also uses abusive language, whereas the poor man begs humbly, asking pardon as though he were the guilty one. Rich men are often bullies. Wealth tends to have a hardening effect on the human personality.

Remember how poor Bob Cratchit had to beg for his Christmas

holiday. Scrooge spent the day before Christmas quarreling—with his nephew, with the men who asked for a charitable donation, with a poor caroler, and with his wretched clerk. Dickens told the tale as follows:

> The fog and darkness thickened so, that people ran about with flaring links, proffering their services to go before horses in carriages, and conduct them on their way. The ancient tower of a church, whose gruff old bell was always peeping slily down at Scrooge out of a Gothic window in the wall, became invisible, and struck the hours and quarters in the clouds, with tremulous vibrations afterwards, as if its teeth were chattering in its frozen head up there. The cold became intense....
>
> Foggier yet, and colder! Piercing, searching, biting cold. If the good St. Dunstan had but nipped the Evil Spirit's nose with a touch of such weather as that, instead of using his familiar weapons, then indeed he would have roared to lusty purpose. The owner of one scant young nose, gnawed and mumbled by the hungry cold as bones are gnawed by dogs, stooped down at Scrooge's keyhole to regale him with a Christmas carol; but, at the first sound of
>
> > God bless you, merry gentlemen,
> > May nothing you dismay!
>
> Scrooge seized the ruler with such energy of action that the singer fled in terror, leaving the keyhole to the fog, and even more congenial frost.
>
> At length the hour of shutting up the countinghouse arrived. With an ill-will Scrooge dismounted from his stool, and tacitly admitted the fact to the expectant clerk in the tank, who instantly snuffed his candle out, and put on his hat.
>
> "You'll want all day to-morrow, I suppose?" said Scrooge.
>
> "If quite convenient, sir."
>
> "It's not convenient," said Scrooge, "and it's not fair. If I was to stop half-a-crown for it, you'd think yourself ill used, I'll be bound?"
>
> The clerk smiled faintly.
>
> "And yet," said Scrooge, "you don't think *me* ill used when I pay a day's wages for no work."
>
> The clerk observed that it was only once a year.
>
> "A poor excuse for picking a man's pocket every twenty-fifth of December!" said Scrooge, buttoning his greatcoat to the

chin. "But I suppose you must have the whole day. Be here all the earlier next morning."

The clerk promised that he would; and Scrooge walked out with a growl. The office was closed in a twinkling, and the clerk, with the long ends of his white comforter dangling below his waist (for he boasted no greatcoat), went down a slide on Cornhill, and the end of a lane of boys, twenty times, in honour of its being Christmas Eve, and then ran home to Camden Town as hard as he could pelt, to play at blindman's-buff.

Jesus spoke the truth when He declared that it was easier for a camel to go through the eye of a needle than for a rich man to enter the kingdom of Heaven (Matthew 19:24). In the case of Scrooge it took a haunted house and four ghosts to bring him to his senses.

Proverbs 18:24 talks about the need for *finding a friend:* "A man that hath friends must show himself friendly: and there is a friend that sticketh closer than a brother." Scholars argue about this verse, especially the first clause. Rotherham rendered it, "A man having many friends shall come to ruin." One translator suggested, "There are friends who only bring you loss." Another rendered the text, "The man of many friends [that is, a man who is a friend of all the world] will prove himself a bad friend."

We may as well let the verse stand as it is in the King James version because it is certainly true that those who desire to have friends must show themselves to be friendly. Someone said of a friend of mine— a gregarious, outgoing type who is always ready with a cheery word and a hearty handshake—that he never meets a stranger. He treats everyone as a long-lost friend. I've never met anyone who didn't like him. On the other hand, we all know shy, reclusive people and surly, suspicious people who complain bitterly that they have no friends. They too remind us of Ebenezer Scrooge. Dickens wrote:

> Nobody ever stopped him in the street to say, with gladsome looks, "My dear Scrooge, how are you? When will you come to see me?" No beggars implored him to bestow a trifle, no children asked him what it was o'clock, no man or woman ever once in all his life inquired the way to such and such a place, of Scrooge. Even the blind men's dogs appeared to know him; and, when they saw him coming on, would tug their owners into doorways and up courts; and then would wag their tails as though they said, "No eye at all is better than an evil eye, dark master!"
> But what did Scrooge care? It was the very thing he liked. To

edge his way along the crowded paths of life, warning all human sympathy to keep its distance.

But that was before his conversion. At the end of the story we meet a different Scrooge. As Dickens put it:

> He became as good a friend, as good a master, and as good a man as the good old City knew, or any other good old city, town, or borough in the good old world. Some people laughed to see the alteration in him, but he let them laugh, and little heeded them; for he was wise enough to know that nothing ever happened on this globe, for good, at which some people did not have their fill of laughter in the outset; and knowing that such as these would be blind anyway, he thought it quite as well that they should wrinkle up their eyes in grins as have the malady in less attractive forms. His own heart laughed, and that was quite enough for him.

Of course no haunting spirits can really effect the change that was wrought in Scrooge. Conversion is the work of the Holy Spirit. His great work is to introduce us to the Friend "that sticketh closer than a brother." To know Christ is to have a friend indeed. When we know Him, we sing almost instinctively:

> What a Friend we have in Jesus,
> All our sins and griefs to bear!
> What a privilege to carry
> Everything to God in prayer!
>   (Joseph M. Scriver)

13. The Stupid Man (19:1-3)

Turning his attention to the stupid man, Solomon wrote about *his foolish words:* "Better is the poor that walketh in his integrity, than he that is perverse in his lips, and is a fool" (Proverbs 19:1). This proverb is illustrated by characters in *A Tale of Two Cities* by Charles Dickens.

Mr. Stryver, a lawyer, was a big bully full of his own importance. He made up his mind to marry beautiful Lucy Manette and announced his intentions to Sydney Carton, his employee who had long since lost his heart to good, gracious Lucy. Dickens wrote:

> "Now you know all about it, Syd," said Mr. Stryver. "I don't care about fortune: she is a charming creature, and I have

made up my mind to please myself: on the whole, I think I can afford to please myself. She will have in me a man already pretty well off, and a rapidly rising man, and a man of some distinction: it is a piece of good fortune for her, but she is worthy of good fortune. Are you astonished?"

Sydney Carton, though certainly astonished, declined to say so. Mr. Stryver continued, expounding his own views on marriage.

"Yes, Sydney, I have had enough of this style of life, with no other as a change from it; I feel that it is a pleasant thing for a man to have a home when he feels inclined to go to it (when he doesn't, he can stay away), and I feel that Miss Manette will tell well in any station, and will always do me credit. So I have made up my mind. And now, Sydney, old boy, I want to say a word to *you* about *your* prospects. You are in a bad way, you know; you really are in a bad way. You don't know the value of money, you live hard, you'll knock up one of these days, and be ill and poor; you really ought to think about a nurse."

The prosperous patronage with which he said it made him look twice as big as he was, and four times as offensive.

"Now let me recommend you," pursued Stryver, "to look it in the face. I have looked it in the face, in my different way; look it in the face, you, in your different way. Marry. Provide somebody to take care of you. Never mind your having no enjoyment of women's society, nor understanding of it, nor tact for it. Find out somebody. Find out some respectable woman with a little property—somebody in the landlady way, or lodging-letting way—and marry her, against a rainy day. That's the kind of thing for *you*. Now think of it, Sydney."

"I'll think of it," said Sydney.

On his way to the Manettes' residence Mr. Stryver stopped in at Tellson's bank to inform Mr. Lorry of his intentions. Mr. Lorry was a close friend of the Manettes.

"I am going," said Mr. Stryver, leaning his arms confidently on the desk: whereupon, although it was a large double one, there appeared to be not half desk enough for him: "I am going to make an offer of myself in marriage to your agreeable little friend, Miss Manette, Mr. Lorry."

"Oh dear me!" cried Mr. Lorry, rubbing his chin, and looking at his visitor dubiously.

This reception of his news made the pompous lawyer very angry. He demanded an explanation.

> "What on earth is your meaning, Mr. Lorry?" demanded Stryver, perceptibly crestfallen.
>
> "Well! I—were you going there now?" asked Mr. Lorry.
>
> "Straight!" said Stryver, with a plump of his fist on the desk.
>
> "Then I think I wouldn't, if I was you."
>
> "Why?" said Stryver. "Now, I'll put you in a corner," forensically shaking a forefinger at him. "You are a man of business and bound to have a reason. State your reason. Why wouldn't you go?"
>
> "Because," said Mr. Lorry, "I wouldn't go on such an object without having some cause to believe that I should succeed."...
>
> Mr. Stryver sucked the end of a ruler for a little while, and then stood hitting a tune out of his teeth with it, which probably gave him the toothache. He broke the awkward silence by saying:
>
> "This is something new to me, Mr. Lorry. You deliberately advise me not to go up to Soho and offer myself—myself, Stryver, of the King's Bench bar?"
>
> "Do you ask me for my advice, Mr. Stryver?"
>
> "Yes, I do."
>
> "Very good. Then I gave it, and you have repeated it correctly."
>
> "And all I can say of it is," laughed Stryver with a vexed laugh, "that this—ha, ha!—beats everything past, present, and to come."

Mr. Stryver was perverse in his lips and a fool. He was not so foolish, however, as to risk a rejection. He accepted Mr. Lorry's suggestion that he first be allowed to sound out the young woman. Later Mr. Lorry confirmed to Mr. Stryver that his advances would be most unwelcome. Mr. Stryver continued to be perverse in his lips. He declared:

> "Having supposed that there was sense where there is no sense, and a laudable ambition where there is not a laudable ambition, I am well out of my mistake, and no harm is done. Young women have committed similar follies often before, and have repented them in poverty and obscurity often before. In an unselfish aspect, I am sorry that the thing is dropped, because

it would have been a bad thing for me in a worldly point of view; in a selfish aspect, I am glad that the thing has dropped, because it would have been a bad thing for me in a worldly point of view—it is hardly necessary to say I could have gained nothing by it. There is no harm at all done. I have not proposed to the young lady, and, between ourselves, I am by no means certain, on reflection, that I ever should have committed myself to that extent. Mr. Lorry, you cannot control the mincing vanities and giddinesses of empty-headed girls; you must not expect to do it, or you will always be disappointed. Now, pray say no more about it."

In contrast to Mr. Stryver, Sydney Carton was one of those described by Solomon as "the poor that walketh in his integrity." Carton truly loved Lucy. He loved her enough to watch her marry someone else without feeling jealousy. He loved her enough to take the place of his rival—her husband—on the guillotine.

Solomon thought some more about the stupid man and wrote about *his foolish walk:* "Also, that the soul be without knowledge, it is not good; and he that hasteth with his feet sinneth" (Proverbs 19:2). Ignorance is dangerous.

Joshua realized he made a mistake when he acted hastily in ignorance. Jericho had fallen. After first humbling Israel, Ai had also fallen. A coalition of frightened cities was forming to muster united action against the conquering Hebrews. Then the people of Gibeon, one of the next cities slated for conquest by the Israelites, resorted to deception. They arranged for some of their people to visit Joshua to look for terms. They dressed their ambassadors in old clothes and worn-out shoes. They put old sacks on their mules and sent torn wineskins and moldy bread with them. The ambassadors said to Joshua:

> We be come from a far country....we have heard the fame of [your God]....This our bread we took hot for our provision out of our houses on the day we came forth to go unto you; but now, behold, it is dry, and it is mouldy: And these bottles of wine, which we filled, were new; and behold, they be rent: and these our garments and our shoes are become old by reason of the very long journey (Joshua 9:6,9,12-13).

The ambassadors from Gibeon begged Joshua to sign a treaty with them and he acted hastily in ignorance. The Hebrews looked at the evidence "and asked not counsel at the mouth of the Lord.

And Joshua made peace with them" (Joshua 9:14-15). Three days later he discovered his mistake, but by then it was too late.

Sifting the facts more carefully and calling to mind a verse of Scripture could have prevented the mistake, but Joshua acted without doing either. Joshua should have recalled Exodus 23:32 or Deuteronomy 7:2. God had emphatically declared:

> Thou shalt make no covenant with them, nor with their gods.... And when the Lord thy God shall deliver them before thee; thou shalt smite them, and utterly destroy them; thou shalt make no covenant with them, nor shew mercy unto them.

Joshua's ignorance was blameworthy. He had God's Word in his hand and God's warning in his heart:

> This book of the law shall not depart out of thy mouth; but thou shalt meditate therein day and night, that thou mayest observe to do according to all that is written therein: for then thou shalt make thy way prosperous, and then thou shalt have good success (Joshua 1:8).

Truly most of our ignorance is culpable and most of our hasty actions are sinful.

Solomon next wrote about the stupid man and *his foolish ways:* "The foolishness of man perverteth his way: and his heart fretteth against the Lord" (Proverbs 19:3). It is astonishing how many people blame God when they face the consequences of their foolish and sinful behavior.

The unrepentant thief fretted against the Lord. We know very little about him. We can presume that both of the thieves who were crucified next to Jesus had been colleagues of Barabbas. Probably the pair of them had been ringleaders in the robber band. It is likely that Barabbas and his band had adopted their outlaw lifestyle to rebel against Rome, since nearly all the Jews were rebellious in their innermost hearts. This pair had descended to thievery and robbery and we can imagine that in reaction to the constant hounding by the Roman garrison they had also been guilty of killing people during an insurrection.

Alexander Whyte wrote:

> The evangelist Luke had perfect understanding of all things from the very first. And no doubt he knew all about the early history of Barabbas and his band....But it would have been out

of place in Luke to have gone into this man's whole past life at the moment when he is fixing all our eyes on the crucifixion of our Lord....There was not a Sabbath synagogue, nor a passover journey, nor a carpenter's shop, nor a taxgatherer's booth, nor a robber's cave in all Israel where the name, and the teaching, and the mighty works of Jesus of Nazareth were not constantly discussed and debated and divided on. And Barabbas and his band must have had many a deliberation in their banishment about Jesus of Nazareth.

Barabbas and the two thieves were captured, condemned, and sentenced to death, but Barabbas miraculously escaped crucifixion. Jesus of Nazareth was to be nailed to his cross. The other two must have cursed their bad luck and envied Barabbas his good fortune. It did not make their death any easier, we can be sure, to know that the instigator of all their wild and wicked ways had escaped the due reward of his deeds. No doubt they cursed God for the injustice and unfairness of their situation.

Amid the jeers and mockery of the crowds, the terrible procession arrived at Calvary. Alexander Whyte commented:

> And all the way, as already in the high priest's palace, and in the Praetorium, and now at Golgotha, all hell was let loose as never before or since. And Satan entered into the two thieves, and into this thief also. And no wonder that they both cursed and blasphemed and raved and gnashed their teeth and spat upon their crucifiers, as all crucified men always did, so insupportable to absolute insanity was the awful torture of crucifixion. And all the time God was laying on His Son the iniquity of us all, and all the time He was dumb, and opened not His mouth.

The thieves mocked Jesus (Mark 15:32; Matthew 27:44). "Save thyself and us," one of them screamed (Luke 23:39). They cursed, they blasphemed, and they reviled the Son of the living God. Sometime earlier in the day the Lord had said, "Father, forgive them; for they know not what they do" (Luke 23:34) The words of Jesus had evidently reached one thief's heart but only hardened the other's. The same sun that softens the wax hardens the clay. Terrible oaths and blasphemies continued to pour from the mouth of the foolish thief. The floodtide of hatred against men and bitterness against God rushed on until even his dying fellow convict could not stand to hear any more. "Dost not thou fear God?" he said (Luke 23:40). As far as we know, the unrepentant malefactor went

into a lost eternity cursing. Doubtless he is cursing and blaspheming
still.

14. The Superficial Man (19:4)

"Wealth maketh many friends; but the poor is separated from his
neighbour." This truth is illustrated in the Lord's story of the
prodigal son. As long as he had money in his pocket and a liberal
hand to spend it, he had plenty of friends. When his funds gave out
his friends got out, leaving him bankrupt and alone in the far
country where famine, starvation, and beggary stared him in the
face.

In Sir Henry Rider Haggard's story, *The People of the Mist,* young
Leonard Outram discovered the truth of this proverb. The son of a
wealthy landowner, Leonard was engaged to be married to the
daughter of the local clergyman, a worldly and well-to-do parson
with an eye to his own advantage. But thanks to the prodigal and
profligate ways and subsequent disgrace and suicide of Leonard's
father, young Outram was left penniless. The estate and the manor,
which had been in the family for six centuries, was sold by auction.
Most of the property was sold to a wealthy Jew.

Leonard overheard a neighboring squire's wife and daughter
discussing the auction. Leonard knew them well. In fact the young
lady had been one of his favorite partners at county balls.

> "How cheap the things went, Ida! Fancy buying that old oak
> sideboard for ten pounds, and with all those Outram
> quarterings on it, too! It is as good as an historical document,
> and I am sure that it must be worth at least fifty. I shall sell ours
> and put it in the dining room. I have coveted that sideboard for
> years."
>
> The daughter sighed and answered with some asperity.
>
> "I am so sorry for the Outrams that I should not care about
> the sideboard if you had got it for twopence. What an awful
> smash! Just think of the old place being bought by a Jew! Tom
> and Leonard are utterly ruined, they say, not a sixpence left.
> I declare I nearly cried when I saw that man selling Leonard's
> guns."
>
> "Very sad indeed," answered the mother absently; "but if he
> is a Jew, what does it matter? He has a title, and they say that he
> is enormously rich. I expect there will be plenty going on at
> Outram soon. By the way, my dear Ida, I do wish you would
> cure yourself of the habit of calling young men by their

Christian names—not that it matters about these two, for we shall never see any more of them."

Worse was to follow. Leonard went to the parsonage, where he had always been a welcome visitor. He was ushered into the presence of the clergyman, who was gloating over the bargain price he had paid for one of the Outram heirlooms. He turned a cold eye on Leonard, who was soon to discover how greatly his fortune had changed now that he was no longer rich. The prospective father-in-law had no use for a poor suitor. He asked Leonard what he could do for him, if he could help him in any way.

> "Yes, Mr. Beach," he said earnestly, "you can help me very much. You know the cruel position in which my brother and I are placed through no fault of our own: our old home is sold, our fortunes have gone utterly, and our honorable name is tarnished. At the present moment I have nothing left in the world except the sum of two hundred pounds which I had saved for a purpose of my own out of my allowance. I have no profession and cannot even take my degree, because I am unable to afford the expense of remaining at college."
> "Black, I just say, very black," murmured Mr. Beach, rubbing his chin. "But under those circumstances what can I do to help you? You must trust in Providence, my boy; it never fails the deserving."
> "This," answered Leonard nervously, "you can show your confidence in me by allowing my engagement to Jane to be proclaimed." Here Mr. Beach waved his hand once more as though to repel some invisible foe.

The clergyman adamantly refused to consider for a moment Leonard's request that he be given time to make good. Mr. Beach suggested to Leonard that it would be best if he left. The young man burst out:

> "I will go as you bid me, but before I go I will tell you the truth. You wish to use Jane's beauty to catch this Jew with. Of her happiness you think nothing, provided only you can secure his money. She is not a strong character, and it is quite possible that you will succeed in your plot, but I tell you it will not prosper. You, who owe everything to our family, now when trouble has overtaken us, turn upon me and rob me of the only good that was left to me."

The sad tale is only a story, but it is all too true to life. Ida's mother and Jane's father were fair-weather friends. There are many of them around.

15. The Scurrilous Man (19:5)

"A false witness shall not be unpunished, and he that speaketh lies shall not escape." Sooner or later lies come home to roost.

From somewhere in my files comes the following poem by Edwin Markham. It purports to be the testimony of one of the Roman soldiers who guarded the sealed tomb of Christ and afterward accepted a bribe from the Sanhedrin to bear false witness concerning what actually happened on resurrection morning. This poem of singular pathos and power illustrates Solomon's proverb well:

> I was a Roman soldier in my prime;
> Now age is on me and the yoke of time.
> I saw your Risen Christ, for I am he
> Who reached the hyssop to him on the tree;
> And I am one of two who watched beside
> The sepulcher of him we crucified.
>
> All that last night I watched with sleepless eyes;
> Great stars arose and crept across the skies.
> The world was all too still for moral rest,
> For pitiless thoughts were busy in the breast.
> The night was long, so long, it seemed at last
> I had grown old and a long life had passed.
> Far off, the hills of Moab, touched with light,
> Were swimming in the hollow of the night.
> I saw Jerusalem all wrapped in cloud,
> Stretched like a dead thing folded in a shroud.
>
> Once in the pauses of our whispered talk
> I heard a something on the garden walk.
> Perhaps it was a crisp leaf lightly stirred—
> Perhaps the dream-note of a waking bird.
> Then suddenly an angel burning white
> Came down with earthquake in the breaking light,
> And rolled the great stone from the sepulcher,
> Mixing the morning with a scent of myrrh.
> And lo, the dead had risen with the day:
> The Man of Mystery had gone his way!

Years have I wandered, carrying my shame;
Now let the tooth of time eat out my name.
For we who all the wonder might have told,
Kept silence, for our mouths were stopt with gold.

NOTES

Chapter 1

1. The other five Hebrew words for "wisdom" used in the book of Proverbs are *bînah, lēb, 'ārmāh, sākāl,* and *sekel. Bînah* ("discernment, discrimination") is rendered "understanding" twelve times, "wisdom" once (23:4), and "knowledge" once (2:3). *Lēb* ("heart") is translated "wisdom" four times (10:21; 11:12; 15:21; 19:8). *'Ārmāh* ("shrewdness") is translated "wisdom" only once (8:5). Elsewhere it is rendered "subtilty." It is also rendered "prudence" (8:12). *Sākāl* ("prudence, common sense") is translated "wisdom" only once (1:3). *Sekel* is "insight." It is also translated "wisdom" (12:8; 23:9) and "understanding" (3:4; 13:15; 16:22).
2. From Mark Twain, "Christian Science" (New York: Harper, 1907).
3. Henry Rider Haggard, *Ayesha* (London: McDonald, 1956) 49-50.

Chapter 2

1. *Time,* May 9, 1988.
2. See John Bunyan's *Pilgrim's Progress.*

Chapter 3

1. Stephen Knight, *The Brotherhood* (London: Granada, Panther Books, 1983) 236.
2. R. E. D. Clark, *Darwin: Before and After* (Grand Rapids: Grand Rapids International Publications, copyright by Paternoster Press 1958).
3. Ibid.
4. Wilbur M. Smith, *World Crisis and the Prophetic Scriptures* (Chicago: Moody Press, 1951) 278.
5. Merrill F. Unger, *Archaeology and the Old Testament* (Grand Rapids: Zondervan, 1954) 115.

Chapter 4

1. A. E. Wilder Smith, "The Pink Professor," *The Paradox of Pain* (Wheaton, IL: Harold Shaw, 1971) 32.

Chapter 5

1. Alexander Whyte, *Bible Characters* (Grand Rapids: Zondervan, 1967) 297.

Chapter 6

1. See John Phillips, *Exploring the Psalms,* 2 vols. (Neptune, NJ: Loizeaux, 1988).
2. From "O for a Thousand Tongues" by Charles Wesley.

Chapter 7

1. *Time,* August 2, 1982.

Chapter 8

1. *Rūsh* occurs in Proverbs 6:11; 10:4,15; 13:7,8,18,23; 14:20; 17:5; 18:23; 19:1,7,22; 22:2,7; 24:34; 28:3,6,19,27; 29:13; 30:8; 31:7.
2. *Dal* occurs in Proverbs 10:15; 14:31; 19:4,17; 22:9,16,22; 28:3,8,11,15; 29:7,14.
3. *Heser* occurs in Proverbs 11:24; 21:17; 28:22.
4. *'Āni* occurs in Proverbs 14:21.
5. *'Ebyōn* occurs in Proverbs 14:31.
6. *Yārash* occurs in Proverbs 20:13; 23:21; 30:9.

Chapter 10

1. See John Phillips, *Exploring the Song of Solomon* (Neptune, NJ: Loizeaux, 1984).
2. *Time,* July 9, 1979.

Chapter 11

1. See John Phillips, *Exploring Genesis* (Neptune, NJ: Loizeaux, 1980).
2. "Come!" cried Tetzel, the Dominican monk as he went up and down the towns of Germany, "Come, and I will give you letters all properly sealed, by which even the sins you intend to commit may be pardoned. But more! Indulgences avail not only for the living but the dead. Priest! Noble! Merchant! Wife! Youth! Maiden! Do you not hear your parents and your friends who cry from the bottom of the abyss? Why, the very instant your money rattles at the bottom of this chest, the soul escapes from Purgatory, and flies liberated to Heaven. The Lord God no longer reigns. He has resigned all power to the Pope."
3. We know more about such diseases today. Herpes, "the new leprosy," is not really new. The Roman emperor Tiberius tried to stamp it out in vain. The so-called sexual revolution of the 1960s unleashed the disease wholesale. It infected entire college dormitories. It rode the

tidal waves of multiplying divorce and widespread promiscuity. It comes in seventy varieties, but the ones most dreaded are herpes simplex types 1 and 2. The first kind produces cold sores around the mouth, triggers various eye ailments, and can lead to blindness. The second type is more closely identified with sex, for it produces tiny painful blisters which, when they burst, release millions of infectious virus particles. The sores may go away but the virus lodges in nerves near the lower spinal cord where they remain for the life of the infected person. Herpes, however, is by no means the worst venereal disease.

Gonorrhea may produce no immediate symptoms, but it is infectious at all stages. Its complications include pelvic inflammatory disease, sterility, arthritis, and blindness. It can cause eye infection in newborn babies.

Syphilis at first produces painless pimples, then rashes, sores, swollen joints, and flu-like symptoms. It remains infectious up to a year or more after exposure and is always infectious for a fetus or a newborn baby. Its complications include brain damage, insanity, paralysis, heart disease, and death. It can cause damage to a fetus or newborn baby's skin, bones, eyes, liver, and teeth.

These are only a few of the possible rewards of non-chastity. There are eighteen sexually transmitted diseases, all of them loathsome. The latest horror is AIDS. It is fatal. It can be transmitted by an infected blood transfusion, but it is chiefly transmitted sexually or by drug users sharing infected needles. It can generally be avoided by abstinence. It is particularly cruel that children can be born already infected with an illness from which their parents could have saved them. In Africa alone it is estimated that nearly a quarter of a million children carry the virus and will die before they are two years old. In giving blunt advice to the general public a former United States surgeon general said, among other things: "Do not have sex with prostitutes. Infected male and female prostitutes...may infect clients." The virus is found in several body fluids and doctors are becoming increasingly concerned about their own safety. Surgeons especially, and nurses who are exposed to the blood of patients with AIDS, are becoming leery. Some think even the mist of blood in some surgical procedures could be infectious. It is a known fact (reported by the Center for Disease Control in Atlanta) that health-care workers have indeed contracted AIDS directly from their patients. Some doctors have begun turning away AIDS patients. The rationale offered is blunt and to the point: The person would have died anyway. The risk to the medical community, to the doctor's own loved ones, and to future patients whom a practitioner with AIDS may himself infect is such that a doctor is simply not justified in taking AIDS patients. Said one investigator summing up a growing trend among doctors, "Once they hear the patient has HIV (the AIDS virus) they can't wait to put down the phone."

Chapter 12

1. See Robert Jastrow, *God and the Astronomers* (New York: Norton, n.d.).
2. Ibid.
3. Cirrus, cirrostratus, and cirrocumulus clouds form at the higher levels. They are ice clouds, and they appear to have a fibrous or feathery texture. The *cirrus* clouds are detached clouds with delicate white filaments. *Cirrocumulus* is a thin layer of cloud devoid of shading and made up of small particles that look like grains or ripples, usually quite regularly arranged. *Cirrostratus* clouds are transparent whitish clouds. They look like a veil of fibrous or smooth material and may cover most of the sky.

   Two types of clouds dominate the middle region. *Altocumulus* generally looks like a sheet of small rounded masses, often merged together—commonly called a "mackerel sky." This type of cloud usually heralds the coming of rain. *Altostratus* is a gray sheet of cloud of more or less uniform appearance.

   At the low levels, three types of cloud occur. *Nimbostratus* is a gray cloud layer that is actually precipitating (from the Latin *nimbus,* meaning "rain"). *Stratocumulus* has rounded masses. *Stratus* is a ubiquitous gray cloud layer with a uniform base. If it precipitates a moisture, it becomes *nimbostratus.*

   Cutting across the height categories are two other types of cloud. *Cumulus* clouds are the familiar heaped-up clouds that look like cauliflower. They have sharp outlines and more or less flat bases. When the sun shines on them, the upper cumulus regions appear brilliantly white. *Cumulonimbus* clouds have a distinctive anvil shape.
4. What is called "creation science" is popular today in some circles, along with the "young earth" theory. According to advocates of this theory, the world only appears to be old and much of its history is flood-related.
5. C. S. Lewis, *Screwtape Letters* (New York: Macmillan, 1961) 17.

Chapter 13

1. From "Happiness Is the Lord" by Ira F. Stanphill, *Folk Hymnal,* comp. Norman Johnson and John W. Peterson (Singspiration: Grand Rapids, 1970).

Chapter 14

1. Charles Chiniquy, *Fifty Years in the Church of Rome* (London: Protestant Truth Society, 1885) 469.
2. Jay E. Adams, *Competent to Counsel* (Grand Rapids: Baker, 1970) 16.
3. Peter Z. Malkin and Harry Stein, *Eichmann in My Hands* (New York: Warner, 1990) 47.
4. See John Phillips, *Exploring the Future* (Neptune, NJ: Loizeaux, 1992).

Chapter 16

1. Attributed to C. G. Hall, *The Macmillan Book of Proverbs, Maxims, and Famous Phrases,* comp. Burton Stevenson (New York: Macmillan, 1948) 1048.
2. *Time,* May 9, 1988.
3. Jack London, *The Call of the Wild* (New York: Macmillan, 1963) 73-84.
4. Wilbur M. Smith, *Chats from a Minister's Library* (Boston: Wilde, 1951) 59.
5. Simon Greenleaf, *The Testimony of the Evangelists* (Grand Rapids: Baker, 1965).
6. See Byron C. Nelson, *After Its Kind* (Minneapolis: Augsburg, 1952) 133.
7. Ibid., 126-134.
8. C. S. Lewis, *The Great Divorce* (New York: Macmillan, 1946) 124.
9. Ibid., 126.
10. Machiavelli, *Discourse* II:13.
11. See F. J. C. Hearnshaw, *Dawn,* September 16, 1935.
12. James Stalker, *The Life of St. Paul* (Grand Rapids: Zondervan, n.d.) 73.
13. This deluded woman wrote: "There is no death" (*Private Directions for Metaphysical Healing*); "Death is the illusion" (*Science and Health,* 428); "Matter and death are mortal illusions" (*Science and Health,* 289); "Any material evidence of death is false" (*Science and Health,* 584).

Chapter 17

1. In Dickens' day there were twelve pennies in a shilling and twenty shillings in a pound. Mr. Micawber's warning was simple: overspend your income by one shilling, and be unhappily in debt. Save just six pennies and be solvent and happy.
2. *Decision,* July 1961.
3. "Casinos Wager on Families for the Future," *USA Today,* August 31, 1994.
4. Andrew Miller, *Short Papers on Church History* (Fincastle, VA: Scripture Truth, n.d.).
5. F. W. Boreham, *Casket of Cameos,* 21-32.
6. Alexander Whyte, *Bible Characters: Adam to Achan* (Edinburgh: Oliphant Anderson and Ferrier, 1898) 80-81.
7. See "Why Negroes Riot," *Reader's Digest* (November 1965) 67-72. This article was digested from *The Making of the President—1964* by Theodore H. White (New York: Atheneum, 1965).
8. Richard Llewellyn, *How Green Was My Valley* (New York: Macmillan, 1940) 188.
9. Ibid., 225-226.
10. Ibid., 240.

Chapter 18

1. See John Phillips, *Exploring the Psalms* I:327-329.

2. See "The Awesome Problem of Nuclear Wastes," *Reader's Digest*, August 1974. This article was digested from an article in the April 1974 issue of *Smithsonian*.
3. *Time*, February 18, 1991.
4. Wilbur M. Smith, *Therefore Stand* (Natick, MA: Wilde, 1945) 215.
5. Ibid., 228.
6. Ibid., 229.
7. Ibid., 235.
8. Ibid., 236.
9. Ibid., 241.
10. Herbert Asbury, *A Methodist Saint*, 27.
11. Antony D. H. Coxe, *Haunted Britain*, 179-180.
12. See John Phillips, *Exploring the Psalms* I:705.

Chapter 19

1. *Time*, July 13, 1987, p. 55.
2. *Time*, April 13, 1987, p. 72.
3. Jesus spoke about such things as Heaven, eternal life, Abraham's bosom, and so on in Matthew 5:12; 6:20; 7:14; 13:33; 19:16-17,21; 25:46; Mark 10:21,30; Luke 6:23; 10:20; 12:33; 16:22,25; 18:22; John 3:13; 4:14,36; 5:24,39; 6:27,44,47,54; 10:28; 12:25; 14:2-3; 17:2-3. He spoke about Hell, judgment, destruction, outer darkness, and so on in Matthew 5:22,29-30; 7:13; 8:12; 10:15,28; 11:22-24; 12:36,41-42; 13:40,42,50; 16:18; 18:8-9; 22:13; 23:15,33; 25:30,41,46; Mark 3:29; 9:43,45,47; 12:40; Luke 10:14-15; 11:31-32; 12:5; 16:23-26,28; 20:47; John 5:22,24,27,29-30; 9:39; 12:31; 16:8,11; 17:12.
4. Charles Chiniquy, *Fifty Years in the Church of Rome*, 267-270.
5. Andrew Miller, *Short Papers on Church History*.
6. From "Come, My Soul, Thy Suit Prepare" by John Newton.
7. See John Phillips, *Exploring Romans*, (Neptune, NJ: Loizeaux, 1969).

Chapter 20

1. From "The Church's One Foundation" by Samuel J. Stone.
2. See John Phillips, *Exploring the Future*.
3. See John Phillips, *Exploring Acts* (Neptune, NJ: Loizeaux, 1991).
4. Jim Vaus, *Why I Quit Syndicated Crime* (Wheaton, IL: Van Kampen, 1951) 83.
5. Thomas B. Costain, *The Conquering Family* (Garden City, NY: Doubleday, 1962) 311-322.
6. See John Phillips, *Exploring Genesis*.
7. Peter Green, *Alexander the Great* (New York: Praeger, 1970) 259.
8. For a complete exposition see John Phillips, *Exploring Acts*.

Chapter 21

1. See John Phillips, *Exploring the Song of Solomon*.

2. Joseph Smith, *Doctrine and Covenants of the Church of The Latter Day Saints* (1835) section 132.
3. As for the *Book of Mormon*, it appears to have been plagiarized from an unpublished novel written before 1816 by Solomon Spalding, a retired minister.
4. Alan Jay Lerner and Frederick Loewe, *My Fair Lady* (New York: Coward-McCann, 1956) act 1, scene 7.
5. Andrew Miller, *Short Papers on Church History.*
6. See *Today's Health* (July 1970) American Medical Association.
7. Charles R. Ashman, *The Finest Judges Money Can Buy* (Los Angeles: Nash, 1973) 3.
8. Ibid., 173.
9. Elgin Moyer, *Wycliffe Biographical Dictionary of the Church* (Chicago: Moody Press, 1982) 194.
10. Andrew Miller, *Short Papers on Church History.*

Chapter 22

1. *Wylie's History of Protestantism* III:401.
2. Malachi Martin, *Decline and Fall of the Catholic Church* (Bantam).
3. This corresponds to the subscription that appears as part of Psalm 8 in which David rejoices in the Lord over his victory over Goliath. See John Phillips, *Exploring the Psalms.*
4. *Great Lives, Great Deeds* (Pleasantville, NY: Reader's Digest Association, 1964) 147-156.
5. See John Phillips, *Exploring the Song of Solomon.*